VERTICAL URBAN FACTORY

Vertical Urban Factory

Author
Nina Rappaport

Published by
Actar Publishers
New York, 2015

Graphic Design
MGMT. design

Copy Editor
Ann Holcomb

Distributed by
Actar D Inc.

New York
355 Lexington Avenue, 8th Floor
New York, NY 10017
T +1 212 966 2207
F +1 212 966 2214
salesnewyork@actar-d.com

Barcelona
Roca i Batlle 2
08023 Barcelona
T +34 933 282 183
salesbarcelona@actar-d.com
eurosales@actar-d.com

Printed and bound in China

ISBN 978-1-940291-63-5
Library of Congress Control Number: 2015937102
A CIP catalogue record for this book is available from the Library of Congress,
Washington D.C., USA.

Front cover: Leaving the factory under the glass enclosed conveyors,
Van Nelle factory, ca. 1960. Courtesy Collectie Gemeentearchief Rotterdam.

Back cover: USM Modular Furniture robotic production line,
Munsingen, Switzerland, 2014. Courtesy of USM Modular Furniture.

VERTICAL URBAN FACTORY

BY NINA RAPPAPORT

CONTENTS

INTRODUCTION

What has happened in the working environment in fifteen decades of industrial revolution is by now only deducible, for its history had been written by the industrial employer classes. And architects are the last people likely to be able to tell us anything about it or to do anything about it at all.[1]
— Alberto Abriani

THE TWENTIETH CENTURY Czech philosopher Vilém Flusser describes mankind as a maker of things, *homo faber* rather than *homo sapiens*. Distinguishing man the maker from man the intellect, he asserted, "Production center or 'factory' is the characteristic of humans, what was once called man's 'reason for existence' — by their factories you will know them."[2] He suggests that one can gain greater insight into historical events by looking at workshops, because that is where great revolutions occurred, not in the isolated monasteries where art was produced. We may learn more from looking at factories, he adds, because that is where the common man labored. "Those wanting to find out about our past should dig in the ruins of factories. Those wanting to find out about the present day should study present-day factories. And those wanting to speculate on the future should ask questions about the factories of the future."[3] My project, *Vertical Urban Factory*, aims to investigate such questions of the future of factories.

Vertical Urban Factory, first conceived as an exhibition in 2011, culminates with this book and encourages continued exploration. In each iteration of the project I am probing the factory in terms of its architecture, its technologies, its sociopolitical culture, and the urbanism it creates. Manifest as places of production, factories are influenced by changing technologies and, in turn, impact the nature of work and the conditions for workers. While recognizing a change in both the definition of industry and its global space, my study intends to spark discussion stemming from the demise of urban manufacturing, and to provoke the integration of industries back into cities with equity.

Considering contemporary definitions of industry — post bubble and beyond oil economics — there are opportunities for the factory to establish a new paradigm, with nascent potential in design challenges similar to those of the early Modern era, when architects, urbanists, and engineers responded to the novel technologies of their time. Today we can ask — with a flexible, new economy, as well as cleaner, smaller-scaled production processes made possible by advanced, real-time manufacturing techniques — what ways can urban manufacturing reenvision, both ecologically and economically, the factory in newly sustainable cities?

The factory, however, is not solely one specific operational structure; rather, it is also shaped by a coalescence of all economic and logistical happenings. Referencing sociologist Henri Lefebvre's perspective on the components of spatial practice, as well as historian Fernand Braudel's explanations of industrial change, we see that the orientation towards rational systems of production *shapes* societies, architecture, and cities, in an urban industrial landscape.[4] These spatial and physical arrangements of production are in turn impacted by economic shifts and socio-political organization — whether in relation to a single structure, industrial zone, company town, or globalized free-trade zones. While trade has been global for hundreds of years, the supply chain has broadened, leaving factories to compress processes and people, and resulting in the negotiation of temporal, material, and spatial flows through a far-reaching interchange.

Paradoxes have emerged in this new industrial urbanism: places of innovation become subsumed by the capitalist drive and, with all roads leading to the company's bottom line, push the social and environmental consequences to a secondary consideration. The new economy has recast spatial systems, where globalized infrastructure has often resulted in inferior production quality and abusive labor conditions, seen most alarmingly in countries such as China and Bangladesh. Little has changed in the factories themselves, except in the small-scale, technology-driven companies where the worker supplies the intellectual capital and is often authored as the "maker" with capital rather than the worker. Apart from this new paradigm, which is not yet a standard, the global and mass-produced factory continues to exist and exploits workers in the same way that it did at the turn of the nineteenth century. If a new model for transparency reveals a company's organizational structure and its production processes that could counteract this long standing method of exploitation, socially-minded companies and not-for-profit organizations could start factories and collaborative workspaces which provide equitable opportunities.[5]

Spaces of production first captured my attention while I was researching Garden Cities and communities of nineteenth-century utopian visionaries such as Ebenezer Howard who envisioned the integration of industry and worker housing in new planned communities, such as Welwyn Garden City, England, and Sunnyside Gardens in Queens, New York. I also became fascinated with the huge volumes of goods in endless arrays, with how they were made, who made them along the supply chain, and how that action of making and the space where things are made was incorporated — or not — into cities. Writing for architecture journals, I explored both Modernist and contemporary factories and their production processes as well as the potential for a factory to be a place oriented around the worker. Engineers, who designed factories, were not afforded the same recognition and respect as architects of the day. At the same time, the role of the engineer as designer of Modernist factories impacted an entire period of architecture. It was this awareness of the marginalization of factory typology that intensified my focus. The question I continue to ask is — apart from the philosophical and spatial investigations of Karl Marx and Friedrich Engels, or Antonio Negri, Kevin Hetherington and Reyner Banham — why have so few factories garnered attention, in terms of their situation in the corporate and technological hegemony?

That the topic of the factory in architecture and society is historically secondary in the academic community inspired me to teach seminars on the subject. I believe this is an important historical narrative that encourages young architects to learn how factories are designed through means of production processes and economics of labor, so that they might better understand how the process and technological shifts are constantly redefined. To engage design issues through architecture, I co-taught an architectural studio in 2008 with Michael Tower that we called Vertical Urban Factory, which focused on factories and their urbanism. Thus, I elaborated on the theme of the project with the eponymous traveling exhibition to engage in public discourse through related series of panel discussions, tours, and lectures, which prompted meetings with city officials and innovators provoking ideas for the future vertical urban factory and how urban space could accommodate them anew.

Where did the factory typology have its start? As it transitioned from a place where things were made outside the home, it evolved into a highly specific building type. As inventors required workspaces outfitted with sometimes dangerous machinery, the manufactory came into being. The manufactory's trajectory throughout the eighteenth and nineteenth century was a catalyst for engineers, architects, and inventors as it traversed a more nonlinear history. By the end of the nineteenth century the factory became ubiquitous and at certain points served not only as a place of making, but also as a community and social center where human relations developed. Such relationships were often hierarchically conceived as control mechanisms. As a new building type, the factory provided architects and engineers with freedom to explore the spatial, structural, and organizational systems often led by machines and processes.

Early vertical urban factories, while perhaps not considered environmentally clean or safe for today's standards, were supportive of the urban context and its economics. In the nineteenth century, factories rose in multi-stories to harness natural resources in mechanistic spaces and fostered experimentation in vertical conveyance systems such as chutes, spiral conveyors, and lifts. In the twentieth century, with elevator capacities increasing and factories rising higher, companies saved on land costs, and the new vertical factories became a dominant typology in cities. However, Modernist architects never addressed appropriate urban integration of the new building typologies. In the postwar period, with the desire for cheaper space and prefabricated shed buildings, and influenced by wartime production, factories shifted to the urban peripheries and were eventually zoned out of cities.

Two main types of vertical factories dominate the urban landscape: integrated and layered. To clarify, the standard concept of the vertically integrated factory relates to factory management in which a company produces everything it needs, controlling its own supply chain. In the physical typology of the vertical factory, the *integrated* factory is similar, but differs in that it turns the organizational system into a spatial one as workers run the production from top to bottom, or vice versa. The other vertical urban factory type is the layered, which, rather than being a complete building, is a portion of a building with a series of separate stacked floors occupied by one or more companies sharing common services. This is the more prevalent urban factory today. Both types, integrated and layered, are described throughout the book.

In terms of urbanism, this book explores the symbiotic relationship between cities and factories. The city is home to labor, resources, and consumers, activating a chain of production, consumption, and reproduction. The factory served as a conduit for these cycles, with workers and owners in proximity to innovation and creativity. In past decades, before the dematerialization of space, the field of economic geography had a strong relevance to the factory site. It was a time when things were closely tied to resources. We would identify resources native to a region — e.g. coal, water, ore, minerals — understanding how they were formed and processed to become a product that contributed to an economy. But over time the focus on the spatial understanding of these resources, tied to land use, lost the general public's attention. As the supply chain elongated, and trade barriers melted, production became hidden from view, disappearing inside the global and ubiquitous factory that taps into resources more globally.

Yet, the definition of urban industry and the value ascribed to it have also changed, causing manufacturers to invent new ways of navigating urban space for operations in order to survive. As described in the forthcoming chapters, manufacturing spaces comprise the city. They impact city planning and design through land use and zoning regulations. This impact was keenly felt in Western cities when the factory left due to the rise of unions, class segregation, land costs, and perhaps most importantly, the proliferation of global production. Ascendant trends in accountability, sustainability, and workers' rights, as well as a stabilization of the manufacturing industry, provide new prospects for designers to engage with the issues posed in this book.

How can the idea of urban manufacturing become more ethical while it employs the lesser skilled and the 99 percent in the most densely populated areas of the world? If indeed 75 percent of the population will be living in cities by 2050, then 75 percent of our goods could be produced by those same people within the ecology of local economies and shared resources. This is a model antithetical to our competitive, protectionist cultural patterns of Western over-consumption. Together, with an increased awareness of labor abuses, such as at Foxconn or in Dhaka, today's consumer interest in product authenticity, the growing locavore movement which supports local food and clothing production, as well as the rise of sustainable lifestyles with decreased carbon footprints, might in effect reverse former manufacturing trends. How can we learn from the mistakes and initiatives, both successful and failed, of the modern era with regard to new technologies and the city? Why can't factories be in cities? Why not build them tall? How might we return to innovative design integrated with sustainability? While some might say the idea of a vertical and urban factory is limiting, for me it has become a broader metaphor for an ideology of making places for working people in cities.

This project has expanded from that of its original architectural focus to encompass economic and technological urban impacts. The book is organized into three sections: Modern, Contemporary, and Future. A timeline designed by Sarah Gephart serves as an overall framework showing the relationships between technology, architecture, and industry. These topics are the chapters that form each of the two main sections — Modern and Contemporary — with studies of specific factories. The final chapter, "Factory Futures," presents my provocation for the potentials contained herein. Diagrams throughout the book show the production flow within the buildings and the processing methods.

The Modern part of the book discusses the early Modernist period in architecture of the twentieth century. The story begins with a brief discussion of the first industrial revolution to show the influential production technology at that point in time. While much of the discussion is not, per se, a new discovery, my narrative parallels those of historians and sociologists such as Fernand Braudel, Karl Marx, Leonardo Benevolo, Spiro Kostof, Lindy Biggs, and Reyner Banham whose scholarship on manufacturing precedes mine. The material in this book intends to intertwine the architecture of these places of production, the urbanism that they create, as well as how people work within them.

The first chapter, "Production, Man, and Machine," explains the trajectory, not always linear, from piecework to rational mass assembly line production and wartime efficiency. The next chapter, "The Factory City," focuses on the factory's role in the city and the "company town" as a utopian ideal that resulted in a dystopic reality permeating industry even today, particularly in China. The surprising lack of interest by Modernist designers in the integration of labor and manufacturing in the city, or in analyzing the factory's impact on urban space, opens the door for additional research. The third chapter, "Modern Factory Architecture," emphasizes the origins of production spaces and the way that Modern architects embraced the factory aesthetic. This chapter includes individual examples organized into three themes — "The Art of the Engineer," "Factory as an Architect's Domain," and "Mechanistic Factory." Ultimately, in terms of design, the Modern factory proves to be significant in its own right, providing lessons and opportunities relevant today.

The Contemporary section of the book follows a parallel organization, but begins with a discussion of economic geography. In the chapter, "Consumption, Man, and Machine," the book continues with the analysis of new technologies of mass customization and electronic neo-cottage industries. The next chapter on "Industrial Urbanism" focuses on globalized production spaces, especially in East Asia, and the idea of glocalization — manufacturing that is localized — as new production spaces resume use in Western cities. It also sheds light on labor inequality and emphasizes workplace democracy as a goal. In the "Contemporary Factory Architecture" chapter, I shed light on three directions in which the architecture of spaces of production is moving in terms of consumer culture and new economics — the Spectacle, the Flexible, and the Sustainable — and describe specific projects in detail. While many concepts about the present condition of the economics and organization of manufacturing and urbanism have been addressed by Saskia Sassen, Jane Jacobs, Manuel Castells, David Harvey, Naomi Klein, Keller Easterling, and Andrew Ross, among others, I hope to provide a hybrid perspective on the architectural conditions of production in the city, urban spaces for making, and the relationships between technology, labor, and space.

The last chapter, "Factory Futures," focuses not on the far future, but what is next, tomorrow. Illustrated with concept sketches and proposals, some of these models, actually emerged in real-world examples over the course of my own investigations, such as the concept of the hybrid and small urban factory. This is the "What If?" section, in which these concepts aggregate to make a place for the newly defined factory in the city, with equity. A major thrust of the project is that of providing a comfortable, protected, and even inspiring space for workers rather than a paternalistic one. Whether this becomes a policy issue and a directive of urban governments, or whether it is a direction that manufacturers and smaller innovators engage with independently, the issue has become a new global imperative.

Throughout this project paradoxes emerge between the benevolent factory owner and the harsh reality of the workers, between the lack of ability to do anything about the spaces of manufacturing on the part of the architects and engineers, and interest in design that is not just marketing. The model in which the worker is hidden in the factory and segregated from other classes remains inequitable. The paternalistic factory of the Modernist era is no different from that of China today in its control of the labor force. Do the ideas of democratic capitalism have no resolve except to make "redemption factories" that paternalistic owners build to assuage their guilt of worker abuse, mirroring the nineteenth century panopticon? How can the factory utilize its potential to instead improve the environment in a new urban ecology of exchange of resources and materials, while at the same time supporting and advancing the workers' life?

And, although the ideas of transparency might offer a solution for the urban factory, transparency is deceptive as it is absorbed into a spectacle and a company's rhetoric. One struggle throughout the project is the seductive aura for the design of interesting spaces of production and technology without an understanding of the concept of working conditions. I acknowledge this tension, and pose it here as something for society to reconcile, given that today architects do know the extent of factory conditions within the generic structures of globalization.

I hope that this book, as it engages the social and economic issues of the built environment of the factory, provokes a reconsideration of industrial urbanism, and provides architects and urban designers with a place from which to move beyond these social and spatial paradoxes as they are inspired by the factory designs featured here and the stories of their place in cities. This book can be read in its entirety or by section. One can focus on technological history, architecture, or urbanism. But, taken together, I hope I construct a cohesion of issues and convey a new focus. For those who are not in the field of design, I hope that in reading this book you can be more informed about where and how the things you consume are produced and what that means for us as *homo faber* as well as *homo sapiens*.

THE FACTORY IN CONTEXT

Technology, culture, social issues, and economics influence architectural design and manufacturing production. This timeline presents a broader context for the vertical urban factory by relating innovations in industrial buildings with technology, management techniques, and culture through three industrial revolutions.

- ⛏ Industrial Buildings
- ⚙ Technology
- ◉ Cultural Events
- 👥 Management Strategy

⚙ BARREL

Invented over 2,000 years ago, the barrel is an early shipping container and a standard measure for bulk goods.

⛏ MANUFACTURE DES GOBELINS, PARIS

The factory is first a dyeworks in the 15th century, and then is organized by Louis XIV as the royal textile and tapestry company. Jean-Camille Formigé designs the current building in 1913. The company continues to manufacture textiles.

⚙ COTTAGE INDUSTRIES

Work conducted in the home primarily paid as piece work.

⚙ 1700–1800 | THE STEAM ENGINE

Steam-powered machinery in mills allows factories to be located anywhere, and are a force behind the Industrial Revolution.

⚙ 1730–1763 | SUGAR HOUSES, NEW YORK CITY

A system of copper "syrup pipes" carries boiled sugar up and down. The conveyance of heat is regulated by chimneys and vents with iron doors on each floor.

⚙ 1733 | FLY SHUTTLE FOR WEAVING

John Kay patents this shuttle to allow weavers to make textiles quickly and at wider lengths without the need of an assistant.

⚙ 1739 | DIGESTING DUCK (FIRST ROBOT)

Jacques de Vaucanson creates an early automated robot for grain processing. It appears to eat kernels of grain and then defecate.

◄◄ 1700   1710   1720   1730   1740

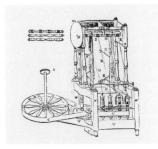

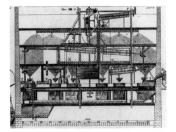

⚙ 1764 | **THE SPINNING JENNY**

James Hargreaves invents this multi-spool spinning wheel to reduce work needed to make thread, thereby increasing production.

🏭 1768 | **COALBROOKDALE FURNACE, ENGLAND**

The factory produces the first cast-iron rails for railways. The furnace is established in 1709 for cast-iron production.

🏭 1771 | **RICHARD ARKWRIGHT, CROMFORD MILL, ENGLAND**

A mill complex contains the first water-powered cotton spinning mill.

🏭 1775–1779 | **SALINE ROYALE ARC-ET-SENANS, FRANCE**

Architect Claude Nicolas Ledoux designs the royal saltworks based on ideals of the Enlightenment.

◉ 1776 | **ADAM SMITH, *THE WEALTH OF NATIONS***

Adam Smith publishes a definitive early theory of economic production.

🏭 1783 | **AUTOMATIC FLOUR MILL, OLIVER EVANS**

Plate IX from Oliver Evans' *The Young Mill-Wright's and Miller's Guide:* elevation of mill showing automated mill machinery. The first self-powered vertical assembly line is invented with this automatic flour mill. Raw materials flow in one end and down and out the other. Oliver Evans develops patents for this and many other machines.

🏭 1791 | **PANOPTICON**

This semi-circular structure designed by Jeremy Bentham was used for prisons and other institutions which needed a singular perspective for watchmen.

👥 1791 | **PATERSON, NJ**

The city of Paterson, founded by Alexander Hamilton and designed by Pierre L'Enfant, harnesses the energy from the Passaic Falls to support dozens of mills.

⚙ 1793 | **SIGNAL TELEGRAPH, CLAUDE CHAPPE**

🏭 1793 | **SLATER MILL, PAWTUCKET, RI**

The first cotton mill in America.

⚙ 1794 | **THE COTTON GIN, ELI WHITNEY**

It revolutionized the cotton industry but also contributed to the rise of slavery because the industrialization required more workers.

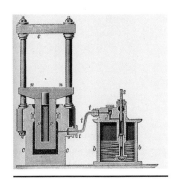

⚙ 1795 | **HYDRAULIC PRESS, JOSEPH BRAMAH**

A new press generates compressive force using a hydraulic cylinder.

⚙ 1798 | **MUSKET MANUFACTURING, ELI WHITNEY**

Whitney invents a musket that can be manufactured with interchangeable parts.

1799

1750   1760   1770   1780   1790

1800s | FALL RIVER, MA

A series of vertical stone mills contribute to the boomtown in Massachusetts.

1801 | JACQUARD LOOM

French inventor Joseph Marie Jacquard devises a mechanical loom controlled by punched cards to simplify textile manufacturing with complex patterns.

1809 | ELECTRIC LIGHT

Humphrey Davy invents the first electric light – an arc lamp – which improves lighting in factories.

1810 | PRINTING PRESS

Frederich Koenig, with the help of Andreas Bauer, creates a high-speed printing press in Germany.

1810 | KRUPP STEEL, ESSEN, GERMANY

A significant steel foundry expands to manufacture weapons in WW II and then merges with Thyssen AG in 1999.

1817 | 8-HOUR WORKDAY

During the Industrial Revolution, factories had 10- to 16-hour workdays, six days a week. In 1810, Robert Owen campaigned for a 10-hour day and by 1817 establishes the slogan "Eight hours labour, eight hours recreation, eight hours rest."

1820 | LOWELL, MASSACHUSETTS

The company town, based around textile mills employing mostly female workers, is the largest textile center in America at the time.

1820 | INCANDESCENT LAMP, WARREN DE LA RUE

These early lights increase productivity both in the home and the factory.

1824 | PORTLAND CEMENT

Englishman Joseph Aspdin patents Portland cement used in the production of concrete, which helps make longer floor spans and taller buildings.

1800

1800   1805   1810   1815   1820

⚙ 1830s | STEAMPOWERED RAILROADS

Steampowered railroads begin long-distance distribution

⚙ 1830s | SLAUGHTERHOUSE MECHANIZATION

Midwest slaughterhouses undergo their first factory mechanization.

⚙ 1830 | ELEVATORS USED IN FACTORIES

⚙ 1831 | DYNAMO, MICHAEL FARADAY

Faraday invents a generator capable of delivering electrical power at the industrial scale.

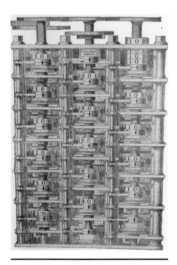

⚙ 1832 | EARLY PUNCH CARDS

Charles Babbage, an English mathematician and inventor, conceptualizes the first programmable computer. One of his later inventions, the Analytical Engine, is programmed with punched cards.

⚙ 1834 | TYPEWRITER

⚙ 1838 | ELECTROMAGNETIC TELEGRAPH, SAMUEL MORSE

⚙ 1839 | HOT VULCANIZATION OF RUBBER BY GOODYEAR

Heating rubber and sulfur together creates a rubber product used in tires and balls.

⚙ 1840s | FOURNEYRON TURBINES

Frenchman Benoît Fourneyron designed turbines for industrial production.

⚙ 1840–1870 | CAST IRON BUILDINGS

Cast iron is cheap, easily produced, and can be formed into endless shapes. A dense concentration of cast-iron facades from this period can still be seen on the historic commercial buildings in SoHo and TriBeCa, New York City.

⚙ 1842 | GRAIN ELEVATOR

The grain elevator, a tower containing a bucket elevator, which scoops up, elevates, and then uses gravity to deposit grain in a silo, is an early mode of vertical mechanization.

⚙ 1845 | SCIENTIFIC AMERICAN

Rufus M. Porter, an inventor and publisher, founds the magazine as a four-page weekly newspaper.

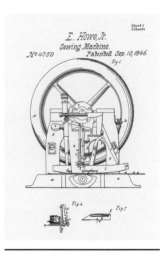

⚙ 1846 | SEWING MACHINE

American Elias Howe patents the lock-stitch sewing machine, which improves the efficiency and production of fabric and clothing.

⚙ 1846 | PNEUMATIC TIRE

Robert William Thomson invents a tire of India rubber filled with air.

1849

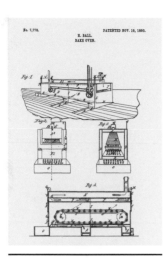

1850

⚙ 1850 | CONVEYOR BELT OVEN

The continuous belt allows for bread to bake as it moves in an automated process.

⚙ 1850 | FIRST KEY BOARD CALCULATING MACHINE, D. D. PARMALE

🏭 1851 | THE CRYSTAL PALACE, LONDON

Designed by Joseph Paxton, architect, this temporary cast-iron and glass structure in Hyde Park, London housed the Great Exhibition of 1851. It is revolutionary for its use of glass and prefabricated elements, minimal use of material, strength, and construction speed.

⚙ 1852 | AIRSHIP

Henry Giffard builds the first steam-powered airship.

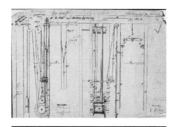

⚙ 1852–53 | ELEVATOR SAFETY BRAKES, OTIS ELEVATOR

Elisha Otis patents elevator safety brakes. While Otis didn't invent the elevator, his brake system makes skyscrapers a reality.

⚙ 1853 | MASS PRODUCTION OF WATCHES

Dennison, Howard, and Curtis use system of interchangeable parts for watch production.

⚙ 1855 | BESSEMER STEEL PROCESS PATENTED

Henry Bessemer develops the first inexpensive process for the mass production of steel from molten pig iron, increasing the dimensions of the product and the speed of manufacturing.

⚙ 1856 | LOUIS PASTEUR

Pasteur invents pasturization.

⚙ 1857 | OFFSET LITHOGRAPHIC PRINTING PRESS

The rotary offset lithographic printing press, invented in England, allows for the mass production of text and graphics.

⚙ 1858 | INTERNAL COMBUSTION ENGINE

Jean J. Lenoir, Belgian engineer develops the internal combustion engine.

🏭 1859 | JEAN BAPTISTE GODIN'S FOUNDRY AND FAMILISTERE, GUISE, FRANCE

A utopian industrial community is founded with attention to the worker.

⚙ 1859 | BIRTH OF PETROLEUM OIL

1850   1855

1868 | NAVAL SHIPYARD IN PHILADELPHIA OPENS

League Island operated as the Navy Yard until 1996.

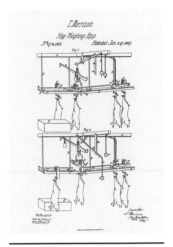

1860s | RISE OF CHICAGO AS MEAT PACKING CENTER

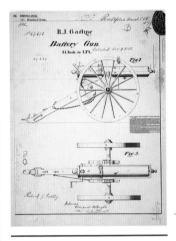

1861 | GATLING GUN

Richard J. Gatling designs a continuously firing gun, to be cranked by a soldier, that would reduce the size of armies.

1864 | SARGENT FACTORIES, NEW HAVEN, CT

Begun in 1810, the Sargent Manufacturing Company grows to be one of the largest hardware manufacturing companies in the U.S.

1865 | PLYWOOD PATENTED

A combination of three or more layers of wood is a flexible and cheap material for the construction and design industries.

1867 | *DAS KAPITAL*, KARL MARX AND FRIEDRICH ENGELS

Marx and Engels write an extensive treatise on political economy and a critical analysis of capitalism and its effect on society.

1869 | AUTOMATIC HOG WEIGHING APPARATUS

This machine, used in Cincinnati slaughterhouses, is a precursor to Ford's mechanized assembly lines.

1869

1860

1865

1870

⚙ 1870s | **CARNEGIE STEEL, PITTSBURGH, PA**

Andrew Carnegie opens his first blast furnace to begin what becomes the largest and most profitable industrial enterprise in the world.

⚙ 1870s | **REINFORCED CONCRETE, FRANCE**

François Hennébique, engineer, develops concrete with reinforcement bars ("rebars"), grids, plates, or fibers to strengthen concrete in tension.

🏭 1872 | **MENIER CHOCOLATE FACTORY, NOISIEL, FRANCE**

Jules Saulnier, architect, designs this factory with the first use of steel frame on the exterior of a building. It also harnesses water power with turbines.

🏭 1873–1875 | **TRIBUNE BUILDING, NEW YORK CITY**

Architect Richard Morris Hunt designs these high-rise headquarters and printing facility as part of a cluster of newspaper buildings downtown.

⚙ 1875 | **STANDARD TIME**

Standard time is set, for the first time, by the railroad industry.

⚙ 1876 | **ELECTRIC TELEPHONE, ALEXANDER GRAHAM BELL**

⚙ 1876 | **BICYCLE MANUFACTURING**

Pope Manufacturing founded in 1876 began making bicycles in Hartford, Connecticut in 1878.

⚙ 1877 | **PHONOGRAPH, THOMAS EDISON**

⚙ 1878 | **EADWEARD J. MUYBRIDGE**

Motion is captured with photography.

⚙ 1879 | **ELECTRIC LIGHTING IMPROVED, THOMAS EDISON**

Safe incandescent lighting and light bulbs are developed, and Thomas Edison starts his Edison Illuminating Company.

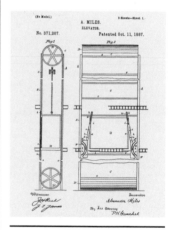

⚙ 1880 | **ELECTRIC ELEVATOR**

The first electric elevator is built by Werner von Siemens in 1880.

⚙ 1880 | **PULLMAN**

Train magnate Pullman started a company town outside of Chicago as a paternalistic community.

◀◀

1870   1875

1880s | MOVING IMAGES

Étienne-Jules Marey experiments with animated images leading to cinematography.

1882 | FIRST LABOR DAY PARADE, NEW YORK

First observed on September 5, 1882 by the Central Labor Union of New York, Labor Day becomes a federal holiday in 1894 following the deaths of workers during the Pullman Strike in Chicago.

1882 | REFRIGERATOR STORAGE, GUSTAVUS SWIFT, CHICAGO, IL

1882 | ELECTRIC LIGHTING IN LONDON

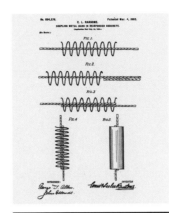

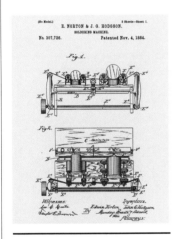

1883 | CAN MAKING (ASSEMBLY LINE)

The practice of canning food, invented to supply Napoleon's army, rapidly increases production with early assembly processing done by hand.

1884 | RANSOME CONCRETE REINFORCING SYSTEM

Ernest L. Ransome, structural engineer, develops a concrete reinforcing system still used today, which contributes to fireproofing and strengthening buildings.

1884 | PATERNOSTER

J. E. Hall invents a passenger elevator for two people that has a chain of open compartments that move slowly in a continuous loop up and down inside a building.

1884 | STEAM TURBINE

Charles Parsons develops a steam turbine to operate an electric generator.

1886 | TESLA ELECTRIC LIGHTING

Nikola Tesla starts his lighting company after having worked for Thomas Edison.

1886 | HAYMARKET AFFAIR

The growth of American industry in the 1880s paralleled the emergence of unions. In Chicago, a riot that begins as a rally supporting striking workers ends with a bomb blast and gunfire, killing police officers and civilians.

1886 | AMERICAN FEDERATION OF LABOR

AFL founded from the Knights of Labor union for primarily craft workers. It merged with Congress of Industrial Organization (CIO) in 1955.

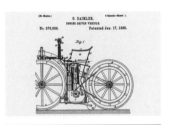

1888 | FOUR-WHEELED MOTOR VEHICLE

1889 | EIFFEL TOWER, PARIS

Named for its designer, engineer Gustave Eiffel, the open-lattice wrought-iron tower is built for the 1889 World's Fair and is one of the first structures to contain passenger elevators.

1889 | GALERIE DES MACHINES PARIS EXPOSITION

The Galerie, spanning 111 meters, with 20 giant three-hinged arches, is the largest wide-spanned iron-framed structure of its time.

1889–1890 | WORLD BUILDING, NEW YORK CITY

George B. Post designs the New York World Building to house offices and a printing plant for Joseph Pulitzer's *World* newspaper.

1889

1890

1890s | PHILADELPHIA: WORKSHOP OF THE WORLD

In its heydey, the city fosters a host of manufacturers including textile mills, paper factories, and the Midvale Steel Company where F.W. Taylor conducts his efficiency studies.

1890 | PORT SUNLIGHT, ENGLAND

A factory town on the Wirral Peninsula, Merseyside, England is built by William Hesketh Lever for the employees of the Lever soap factory.

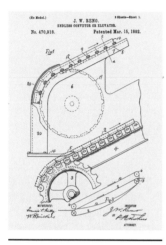

1892 | FIRST ESCALATOR

Jesse W. Reno's new novelty ride at Coney Island, a moving stairway on a conveyor belt constructed at a 25-degree angle, becomes known as the escalator.

1893 | CADBURY, BOURNVILLE, ENGLAND

A factory town on the south side of Birmingham, England is built to house workers for the Cadbury factory.

1894 | PULLMAN STRIKE

A conflict takes place between labor unions and railroads when 3,000 employees of the Pullman Palace Car Company in Illinois begin a wildcat strike in response to reductions in wages.

1897-1898 | PACIFIC COAST BORAX COMPANY, BAYONNE, NJ

Engineer Ernest Ransome creates an early example of load-bearing external walls and an internal structural frame of reinforced concrete for a factory building.

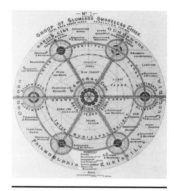

1898 | GARDEN CITY

Ebenezer Howard writes *Garden Cities of To-morrow*, in which he lays the groundwork for a utopian city where man lives harmoniously with nature. This leads to the development of Letchworth and Welwyn Garden Cities in England.

1900s | OFFSET LITHOGRAPHIC PRINTING PRESS

In 1904, Ira Rubel discovers how to make sharper and clearer prints by using rubber rollers. Offset printing becomes the most commonly used technique for high-volume text reproduction.

1901–1917 | *UNE CITÉ INDUSTRIELLE*, TONY GARNIER

Garnier publishes *Une Cité Industrielle*, describing a utopia that combines industrial and mixed uses in buildings made of concrete.

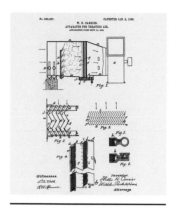

1902 | ELECTRIC AIR CONDITIONING

In Brooklyn, Willis Haviland Carrier invents the first modern air-conditioning unit for the Sackett-Wilhelms Company to improve manufacturing process control in the printing plant.

1902 | KAHN BAR CONCRETE REINFORCING SYSTEM

Moritz Kahn, brother of Albert Kahn, develops a system of reinforcing concrete with oblique reinforcing bars.

1903 | FLIGHT

Orville Wright flies first airplane with an engine at Kitty Hawk.

1903–1905 | UNITED SHOE MACHINERY CO., BEVERLY, MA

Ernest Ransome, engineer, designs the "daylight" factory with his newly developed concrete reinforcing system. It is visited by European architects and manufacturers.

🏭 1903 | **STEIFF FACTORY, FIRST CURTAIN WALL, GEIGEN, GERMANY**

Ernst Steiff, an engineer, designs the first glass curtain wall for his wife's toy factory using greenhouse technologies.

🏭 1903 | **PACKARD MOTOR COMPANY DETROIT, MI**

Albert Kahn designs the first reinforced concrete factory building for the auto industry.

🏭 1905 | **PIERCE ARROW MOTOR BUFFALO, NY**

Albert Kahn designs Pierce Arrow Motor's factory as a long low-rise building.

🏭 1906 | **BUSH TERMINAL, NEW YORK**

Large-scale industry complex on Brooklyn's waterfront begins construction.

◎ 1906 | *THE JUNGLE*, **UPTON SINCLAIR**

Author and journalist Upton Sinclair writes *The Jungle* to highlight the plight of the working class and to show the corruption of the American meat-packing industry.

🏭 1906–1925 | **MULTI-BAY SHED ROOF**

Also known as "sawtooth roofs," glass projects from the roof, facing north, to diffuse light and is commonly used in factories.

⚙ 1907 | **AUTOMATIC BOTTLE MACHINE**

Michael J. Owens invents a machine to manufacture glass bottles, speeding up the manufacturing process and revolutionizing the glass industry.

⚙ 1907 | **STEEL WINDOWS**

Crittall Windows Ltd., English manufacturer of steel-frame windows, begins the Detroit Steel Product Co., the first steel window factory in the U.S.

🏭 1907–1909 | **YENIDZE BUILDING, DRESDEN, GERMANY**

Martin Hammitzsch designs this tobacco factory with Islamic motifs for an iconic image.

⚙ 1908 | **FIRST ROLLER CONVEYOR PATENT**

The roller conveyor allows for the belt to move continuously in a line process.

🏭 1908–1909 | **AEG FACTORY, TURBINE HALL, BERLIN, GERMANY**

Architect Peter Behrens designs this factory, which has repeating three-pin arch steel frames and a pedimented facade, portraying an image of monumentality.

👥 1909 | **GARMENT WORKERS STRIKE**

Two years prior to the Shirtwaist Factory fire, the New York Shirtwaist Strike of 1909 is a labor strike primarily involving Jewish women working in New York's garment factories.

🏭 1909–1911 | **CHEMICAL FACTORY, LUBAN, POLAND**

Architect Hans Poelzig designs a factory expressive in form, and follows principles of the Werkbund.

1909

1900   1905

1910 | FORD PLANT, HIGHLAND PARK, MI

Architect Albert Kahn designs the largest American factory at the time and the first to use a full assembly line.

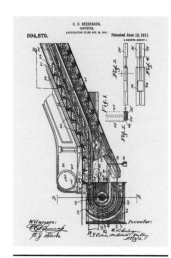

1911 | MODERN ESCALATOR

Charles Seeberger with the Otis Elevator Company produces the first commercial escalator in 1899 at the Otis factory in Yonkers, New York.

1913 | "INDUSTRIEBAU" *JAHRBUCH DES DEUTSCHES WERKBUNDES*, WALTER GROPIUS

Gropius writes an essay about industrial architecture, using American examples.

1913–1926 | FIAT LINGOTTO FACTORY, TURIN, ITALY

Engineer Giacomo Matte-Trucco designs this factory to support the vertical process through its concrete construction and rooftop track.

1911 | LARKIN WAREHOUSE, BUFFALO, NY

Lockwood, Greene and Co. engineers design this concrete-frame building with vertical supports and floor slabs exposed to view.

1911 | *PRINCIPLES OF SCIENTIFIC MANAGEMENT*, FREDERICK W. TAYLOR

Taylor publishes his ideas on improving industrial efficiency through what he calls "Scientific Management" with enforced standardization of methods for faster and more efficient work.

MARCH 25, 1911 | TRIANGLE SHIRTWAIST FACTORY FIRE

One of the largest industrial disasters in New York, the fire kills 146 garment workers, who are trapped on the upper stories behind locked exit doors. The fire leads to improved factory safety standards.

1913 | FAGUS WORKS, AN DER LEINE, GERMANY

The factory designed by architects Walter Gropius and Hannes Meyer is one of the first large structures to use steel frame and glass facades.

1913 | POWERED MOVING ASSEMBLY LINE

Henry Ford combines previous ideas of assembly, making the first moving line at his Highland Park plant in Michigan.

1914 | FORD FIVE DOLLAR DAY PROGRAM

Henry Ford offers his workers five dollars a day, which is an exorbitant amount at the time, as incentive to be efficient workers and consumers of his automobiles.

1915 | FRANK AND LILLIAN GILBRETH TIME AND MOTION STUDIES

The Gilbreths conduct studies focusing on how a task is performed. They use light and photography to find out how to eliminate unnecessary steps and increase productivity. Their book: *Fatigue Study: The Elimination of Humanity's Greatest Unnecessary Waste; a First Step in Motion Study* was published in 1916.

1910

1915

1910

1915 | GROWTH OF DETROIT AS AUTOMOTIVE MANUFACTURING CENTER

1917 | RIVER ROUGE, DEARBORN, MI

Architect Albert Kahn designs Ford's large-scale integrated manufacturing plant outside Detroit.

1919 | FIRST POWERED AND FREE CONVEYORS

Jervis B. Webb invents a multi-rail conveyor system that allows for overhead or inverted movement of goods.

1920 | HAT FACTORY, LUCKENWALDE

Erich Mendelsohn designs this dye works building in Germany, with a form that expresses the ventilation system.

1920s | GARMENT CENTER NEW YORK CITY

The Garment Center develops as the center for clothing manufacturing and design in the U.S., occupying full blocks of 30th to 40th Streets on the west side of Manhattan.

1921 | *R.U.R. ROSSUM'S UNIVERSAL ROBOT*

Karel Čapek writes a science fiction play that premieres in 1921 and notably introduces the term *robot*.

1922 | "DAYLIGHT" BUILDING, BRIDGEPORT, PA

Ballinger & Co. design the first industrial building to boast all-glass walls, which allow for ample day lighting.

1923 | *VERS UNE ARCHITEC-TURE*, LE CORBUSIER

Le Corbusier writes a collection of essays which profoundly advocates for the concept of Modern architecture influenced by industry.

1923–1939 | BAT'A, ZLIN, CZECHOSLOVAKIA

Architects Jan Kotera, František Lydie Gahura, Miroslav Lorenc, and Vladimír Karfík, design a factory city planned by Bat'a shoe company. It exemplifies Modern construction technologies and design.

1925 | BAUHAUS SCHOOL DESSAU, GERMANY

The Bauhaus school (1919–33), founded by Walter Gropius, embraces the idea of creating a "total" work of art, combining crafts, the fine arts, and architecture. Their new Modern building is built in Dessau in 1925.

1926 | *AMERIKA*, ERICH MENDELSOHN

Architect Erich Mendelsohn publishes a book of photographs he took of American cityscapes in the 1920s.

1926 | *THE MODERN FUNCTIONAL BUILDING*, ADOLF BEHNE

1927–1929 | VAN NELLE FACTORY, ROTTERDAM, NETHERLANDS

Architects Brinkman and Van der Vlugt, with Mart Stam, design a factory that is innovative for its glass facade, open floors, and comfortable working conditions.

1928 | OVERHEAD CONVEYOR

Jervis B. Webb improves his overhead conveyor system with new track and connection systems for fluid processing.

1929 | THE GREAT STOCK MARKET CRASH

1929–1935 | AUSTRIA TABAK, LINZ, AUSTRIA

Architect Peter Behrens expands the Linz tobacco factory, which is Austria's first major steel-frame structure.

1929–1945 | DYMAXION HOUSE

Buckminster Fuller designs the Dymaxion House, a prototype composed of factory-manufactured parts assembled on site.

1929

1930

◉ 1930s | CHARLES SHEELER PHOTOGRAPHS

Artist Charles Sheeler is commissioned by Ford to photograph Ford's River Rouge Plant, west of Detroit.

🏭 1930–1932 | BOOTS "WETS" FACTORY, NOTTINGHAM, ENGLAND

Sir Owen Williams, engineer, designs a vertical factory using gravity flow and conveyors for pharmacutical processing. Its reinforced concrete columns support large slabs and a glass curtain-wall allows natural light inside.

🏭 1930–1933 | TOPPILA PULP MILL, OULU, FINLAND

Alvar Aalto, architect, designs a mill and housing for factory workers.

🏭 1931 | STARRETT-LEHIGH BUILDING, NEW YORK CITY

Cory & Cory, architects, design a building that allows freight cars on trains to be moved into freight elevators that access the upper floors of the building. It is a significant example of Modern industrial architecture in New York.

🏭 1931 | BAKERY, KNODYNSKAYA STREET, MOSCOW

G.P. Marsakov, engineer, invents an automated bread production system with a circular assembly line. Eight other bakeries are built with the same methods.

◉ 1932 | *INDUSTRY* MURAL DIEGO RIVERA

Rivera paints 27 panels depicting the Ford Motor Company factory, now housed in the Detroit Institute of the Arts.

🏭 1934 | SAINSBURY'S, LONDON

Engineer Sir Owen Williams designs a vertical urban factory that uses concrete innovatively.

👥 1934 | FOREIGN-TRADE ZONES ACT

The act is created to encourage foreign commerce in the U.S., where merchandise can be held in a zone without being subject to customs duties, lowering the costs of U.S.-based operations engaged in international trade.

🏭 1935 | OLIVETTI, IVREA, ITALY

Factory begins construction of first phase by Luigi Figini and Gino Pollini in Ivrea, Italy which continued to for 50 years.

◉ 1936 | *MODERN TIMES*, CHARLIE CHAPLIN

The American film is a satire on the effect of modern industrialization on factory workers during the Great Depression.

🏭 1937 | DODGE HALF-TON TRUCK PLANT, WARREN, MI

Albert Kahn's solution for a cheap, single-story industrial building employs minimal use of materials, simple details, large surfaces, and prefabricated elements.

👥 1938 | RENAULT FACTORY OCCUPATION, PARIS

Economic setbacks for Renault lead to cuts in wages and hours. Worker strikes, union movement, and factory occupations require government intervention. New labor laws include a 40-hour work week, social security benefits, and paid holidays.

👥 1938 | FAIR LABOR STANDARDS ACT

The act establishes a national minimum wage, guarantees "time-and-a-half" for overtime in certain jobs, and prohibits most employment of minors in "oppressive child labor" in the U.S.

◀◀

1930   1935

1938 | FEDERAL MINIMUM WAGE

Established as a part of the Fair Labor Standards Act, minimum wage is set at $0.25 per hour in the U.S.

1940s | FLUORESCENT LIGHTING

Fluorescents allow factories to be less dependent on natural light, translating into longer workdays and larger, deeper floor plates. General Electric shows the fluorescent lightbulb at the 1939 World's Fair.

1940 | VICTORY SASH WINDOWS

Albert Kahn develops wooden windows to save much-needed metal for the war effort.

1941 | PREFABRICATED HOUSES

Walter Gropius and Konrad Wachsmann design prefabricated houses for the General Panel Corporation with wood-framed walls and ceiling units that can be adjusted without structurally changing the building.

1941–1943 | WILLOW RUN BOMBER FACTORY, YPSILANTI, MI

The Ford Motor Company constructs the Willow Run factory during WW II to manufacture B-24 military aircrafts. Albert Kahn designs it as the world's largest enclosed "room."

1942 | ROSIE THE RIVETER

A cultural and feminist icon representing the American women who replaced male workers in factories during World War II.

1945 | TATA MOTORS, INDIA

1946–1951 | USINE CLAUDE & DUVAL, SAINT-DIÉ, FRANCE

Le Corbusier designs the concrete frame factory, exemplifying his "modular" system.

1946 | FIRST NUMERICALLY CONTROLLED MACHINE

John T. Parsons develops numerically controlled machines automated by programmed commands, as opposed to manually-driven hand wheels or levers.

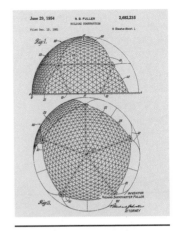

1947 | GEODESIC DOME

Buckminster Fuller builds his first geodesic dome.

1948 | COMPUTER ENIAC, THE FIRST DIGITAL COMPUTER, PHILADELPHIA, PA

1948 | *MECHANIZATION TAKES COMMAND*, SIGFRIED GIEDION

Giedion writes an influential history of society from the perspective of technology and mechanization.

1948 | MARSHALL PLAN

The financial aid plan was to help Europe recover post WW II and was in place for four years.

1948 | POLAROID

Edwin Land invents the Polaroid Land camera.

1949

1940   1945

1951 | BRYNMAWR RUBBER FACTORY, BRYNMAWR, WALES

Designed by the Architect's Co-op, the main production floor is spanned by nine huge concrete shell domes with punctuated circular skylights, and the outer sections are roofed with concrete barrel vaulted shells.

1952 | VERTICAL COTTON MILL

Architect Buckminster Fuller works on a project with students from North Carolina State University for a pioneering vertical factory.

1952 | COMPUTER NUMERICALLY CONTROLLED (CNC) MILLING

Massachusetts Institute of Technology's development of the CNC milling machine allows complex cuts with much higher accuracy than by hand.

1953 | GATTI WOOL FACTORY, ROME

Pier Luigi Nervi, engineer, invents a ferro-cemento system, which is intended to reduce the cost of form work and develop mass-production methods for complex floor constructions.

1953–1957 | FLOAT GLASS PROCESSING

Sir Alastair Pilkington and Kenneth Bickerstaff of the Pilkington Brothers develop the first successful commercial application for manufacturing glass, which involves forming a continuous ribbon of glass using a molten tin bath, for larger sheets of glass.

1954 | INDUSTRIAL ROBOT

George Devol invents the first digital and programmable robot called the Unimate. He sells it to General Motors in 1960 where the robot is used to lift pieces of hot metal from die casting machines.

1955–1957 | OLIVETTI FACTORIES, BUENOS AIRES

Marco Zanuso designs innovative factories that integrate systems and structure.

1956 | GM TECHNICAL CENTER, WARREN, MI

Architect Eero Saarinen designs the "Tech Center," GM's engineering center. The curtain wall system, held in place with gaskets, represents the company's use of new materials and technologies.

1956 | REDPATH SUGAR FACTORY, TORONTO

Redpath Sugar builds factory on the waterfront of Toronto.

1956 | CLEAN AIR ACT

1959 | BACARDI RUM FACTORY, CARRETERA, MEXICO

Félix Candela, engineer, designs thin-concrete shell domes to span 24 meters. The factory symbolizes Mexico's rapid industrialization of the postwar years. Candela's firm completes over 800 factories and warehouses in the 1950s and 1960s.

⚙ 1960s | ANDON BOARDS

Andon boards communicate status along the assembly line and are first used by Toyota to increase quality control.

🏭 1960–1964 | CARTIERA BURGO, MANTUA, ITALY

Pier Luigi Nervi, engineer, designs the paper mill with a cable-supported structure suspended from two reinforced concrete trestles.

🏭 1960s–PRESENT | HONG KONG

The city begins large-scale development of high-rise factories in the city center.

⚙ 1961 | FIRST MAN IN SPACE

Russian cosmonaut Yuri Gagarin is the first person to completely orbit around the earth, influencing President John F. Kennedy's decision to mobilize funding for the U.S. space program.

🏭 1961 | SDS ELECTRONICS, EL SEGUNDO, CA

The flexible "shed" structure provides separate spaces for research, production, warehousing, and administration, with movable internal partitions.

🏭 1964–1966 | CUMMINS ENGINE DARLINGTON, ENGLAND

Kevin Roche John Dinkeloo and Associates design the factory with a freely divisible inner space and a simple long-span structure of Cor-Ten steel.

🏭 1965–1967 | VOLKSWAGEN FACTORY, PUEBLO, MEXICO

The largest VW factory complex outside of Germany.

🏭 1965 | JORBA LABORATORY MADRID, SPAIN

Architect Miguel Fisac designs an innovative concrete construction stacked in spiraling layers.

👥 1965 | MAQUILADORAS

Manufacturing facilities arise on the borders of Mexico, where materials are imported and finished products exported, both without duties.

🏭 1967 | RELIANCE CONTROLS LTD., ENGLAND

Team 4 (Norman and Wendy Foster, Richard Rogers, Su Brumwell, Georgie Cheesman) designs the factory as a versatile enclosure that allows for linear expansion. It uses industrial components, such as sandwich-construction cladding panels faced with either corrugated steel or industrial glazing systems.

⚙ 1967 | SHIPPING CONTAINER STANDARDIZATION

Standard sizes evolve out of a series of compromises among international shipping, railroad and trucking companies to make compatible systems.

🏭 1967–1970 | OLIVETTI, HARRISBURG, PA

Louis I. Kahn designs a flexible organizational system with structural engineer August Komendant, using 72 prestressed locking concrete units.

⚙ 1969 | BAR CODE SCANNER

Product data can be read as optical machine-readable representations of data, making information on a product independent from the product size.

1969

1970

👥 1970 | OCCUPATIONAL SAFETY AND HEALTH ADMINISTRATION (OSHA)

OSHA is an agency of the U.S. Department of Labor, which prevents work-related injuries, illnesses, and occupational fatality by issuing and enforcing standards for workplace safety.

👥 1970s | BENETTON RETAIL TO FACTORY FEEDBACK LOOPS

Italian clothier Benetton substitutes information for inventory, making manufacturing decisions based on purchases and sales data with a direct feedback loop from the customer to the maker.

👥 1970s | JUST-IN-TIME PRODUCTION METHODS

The Just-In-Time (JIT) inventory strategy, also called the Toyota Production System, strives to improve return on investment by reducing in-process inventory.

⚙ 1970s | COMPUTER-AIDED MANUFACTURING

Computer-Aided Manufacturing (CAM) facilitates faster production processes and creates components and tooling with more precise dimensions and material consistency.

🏭 1971–1975 | WILLIS FABER AND DUMAS, IPSWICH, ENGLAND

One of the first "high-tech" buildings is designed by Foster & Partners. The center space is constructed from a grid of concrete pillars supporting cantilevered concrete slab floors.

👥 1972 | GENERAL MOTORS STRIKE

GM sets up a factory in Lordstown, Ohio, in hopes that a rural workforce will be more docile than an urban one. Instead, brutal line speed and dictatorial management culminate in protests by workers for three weeks.

⚙ 1973 | FIRST USE OF CELL PHONE

◉ 1973 | *SMALL IS BEAUTIFUL*, E.F. SCHUMACHER

Economist E. F. Schumacher publishes a collection of essays that critique Western economics and focus on appropriate technologies.

⚙ 1974 | NANOTECHNOLOGY CONCEPT INTRODUCED

Norio Taniguchi, scientist, introduces ways to study the molecular scale.

🏭 1974 | TONI MOLKEREI, ZURICH, SWITZERLAND

A. E. Bosshard and H. Widmer, architects, design the largest dairy processing enterprise in Europe, which operated until 2005.

⚙ LATE 1970s | BUILDING INFORMATION MODELING (BIM)

The process of organizing building data on linked computer platforms.

⚙ 1977 | APPLE II

First personal computer produced by Apple.

🏭 1979 | USM FACTORY MUNSINGEN, SWITZERLAND

Fritz Haller designs the USM factory as a modular steel system of 14.4 meters to enable extensions to the building.

👥 1980 | SHENZHEN SPECIAL ECONOMIC ZONE

Shenzhen is designated the first Special Economic Zone (SEZ) in China in 1980, with liberal economic laws allowing the city to grow to over 10 million people.

◉ 1980 | *THE THIRD WAVE*

Alvin Toffler writes book depicting the new prosumer.

⚙ 1980s | SILICON VALLEY

A hub for high-tech innovation develops south of San Francisco.

👥 1980s | OUTSOURCING

Subcontracting across national boundaries effectively disperses manufacturing practices away from traditional centers of production.

👥 1980s | INDUSTRIAL SYMBIOSIS, DENMARK

Kalundborg Industrial Park exemplifies early Industrial Symbiosis—a system of material exchanges in an ecological industrial development.

⚙ 1982 | DELOREAN CARS

A stainless-steel luxury car company went bankrupt after only eight years in business.

🏭 1982 | PA TECHNOLOGIES, PRINCETON, NJ

Richard Rogers, architect, designs this flexible building for efficient manufacturing, construction and maintenance, which is achieved through movable partitions within a column-free interior, under a cable-stayed roof.

⚙ 1984 | TAIWAN WORKING CONDITION

Harsh long hours found in home-base factory workers.

👥 1985 | 35-HOUR WORKWEEK, GERMANY

🏭 1986–PRESENT | HÔTELS INDUSTRIELS, PARIS

City-supported development of incubators of new industries.

🏭 1986–1987 | RICOLA WAREHOUSE, LAUFEN, SWITZERLAND

Ricola commissions architects Herzog & de Meuron. The company establishes a design program for their facilities.

◉ 1986–1991 | *RIVETHEAD, TALES FROM THE ASSEMBLY LINE, BEN HAMPER*

Author Ben Hamper exposes life working on the assembly line at a GM plant in Flint, Michigan.

🏭 1988 | IGUS FACTORY, COLOGNE, GERMANY

Nicholas Grimshaw and Partners, architects, design the factory with a flexible and movable system that so the company can readjust their use of space.

🏭 1988 | MANUFACTURING IN NEW YORK STUDY, JOHN LOOMIS

Wins a Progressive Architecture Award for study on integrating industrial buildings in New York.

👥 1989 | REUNIFICATION OF GERMANY

Berlin Wall comes down and Germany is reunified.

🏭 1989 | REDESIGNING THE URBAN FACTORY, BERLIN INDUSTRIAL CULTURE PROJECT

Numerous architects are invited to investigate reindustrialization of Berlin.

⚙ 1989 | INDUSTRIAL ECOLOGY

Term used by Robert Frosch and Nicholas Gallopoulos to define material flow of industrial process.

🏭 1989–PRESENT | VITRA CAMPUS, WEIL AM RHEIN, GERMANY

With factories designed by Frank Gehry, Nicholas Grimshaw, Alvaro Siza, and Zaha Hadid, Vitra develops a campus in Weil am Rhein, Germany, encouraging interaction between employee, product, client, and visitor. It also establishes the firm's design image.

1989

1980   1985

1990

⚙ 1990s | **WWW / HTTP / HTML**

👥 1990s | **NIKE SWEATSHOP INVESTIGATIONS**

In May 1998 Nike pledges to follow U.S. OSHA standards to end child labor abuse, and to allow external monitoring of its facilities in Vietnam, Indonesia, and China.

👥 1990s | **INDUSTRY CLUSTERS**

Industry clusters increase company productivity by geographically concentrating interconnected businesses and suppliers.

🏭 1992 | **L'OREAL FACTORY AULNAY-SOUS-BOIS, FRANCE**

Valode & Pistre, architects, design a three-petaled flower-shaped factory in which L'Oreal pioneers new manufacturing methods with worker-controlled mini-assembly lines.

🏭 1992 | **GREENPOINT MANUFACTURING AND DESIGN CENTER**

A nonprofit manufacturing space started in New York City now has over 200,000 square meters in various buildings in Brooklyn.

⚙ 1993 | **LEADERSHIP IN ENERGY AND ENVIRONMENTAL DESIGN (LEED)**

Development on LEED begins; finishes in 1997. The first pilot program is released in 1998.

🏭 1993 | **WILKHAHN ASSEMBLY HALL, BAD MÜNDER, GERMANY**

Herzog & Partner's design sets new standards for environmentally responsible industrial architecture.

🏭 1993–1997 | **NEW YORK TIMES PRINTING PLANT, QUEENS, NY**

Polshek & Partners' design for the New York Times factory consolidates printing in a vertical automated facility.

👥 1994 | **NORTH AMERICAN FREE TRADE AGREEMENT (NAFTA)**

NAFTA is an agreement between the governments of Canada, Mexico, and the U.S. to create a trade bloc.

🏭 1996 | **CHRYSLER ASSEMBLY PLANT, TUSCALOOSA COUNTY, AL**

Albert Kahn Associates design this new plant as one of the largest in the country at the time.

👥 1997 | **KYOTO PROTOCOL**

A protocol to the UN Framework Convention on Climate Change establishes an environmental treaty between global industrialized nations.

🏭 1997 | **VEENMAN PRINTING PLANT, EDE, NETHERLANDS**

Neutelings Riedijk Architects design the plant with a central open-air courtyard to unite two programs of printing and administration. The envelope forms a graphic identity for the company.

🏭 1999 | **VALDEMINGOMEZ, MADRID, SPAIN**

Abalos & Herreros design a vertical recycling plant that can itself also be recycled.

👥 2000 | **35-HOUR WORKWEEK, FRANCE**

🏭 2000s | **GREENING OF RIVER ROUGE FORD MOTOR COMPANY**

William McDonough & Partners, architects, master plan the greening of the facility.

🏭 2000 | **AMERICAN APPAREL LOS ANGELES, CA**

The company reuses existing industrial buildings with a commitment to producing in L.A.

◉ 2000 | *EMPIRE*

Antonio Negri and Michael Hardt publish the groundbreaking book, *Empire.*

⚙ **2000s | OPEN SOURCE MANUFACTURING**

A system of manufacturing that is cost- and/or license-free and accessible to the public.

⚙ **2000s | PDAs USED IN FACTORIES**

Small handheld devices are used to make the worker more mobile and flexible in a plant.

🏭 **2001 | VW GLÄSERNE MANUFAKTUR, DRESDEN, GERMANY**

Henn Architects designs the first major new vertical factories in a reunified Germany, and make manufacturing processes visible to the public.

🏭 **2001–2004 | TRUMPF FACTORY, GRUSCH, SWITZERLAND**

Barkow Leibinger Architects stack labs and production spaces in a concrete frame system.

👥 **2002 | SOCKS CITY, DATANG, CHINA**

Nearly 75 percent of the international market's sock supply is produced here, earning it the nickname "Socks City."

◉ **2002 | *GLOBALIZATION AND ITS DISCONTENTS*, JOSEPH E. STIGLITZ**

🏭 **2003 | FERRARI RESEARCH CENTER, MARANELLO, ITALY**

Massimiliano Fuksas' design brings the natural environment into a highly tech-nological center to create a comfortable working environment.

👥 **2003 | REGIONAL GREENHOUSE GAS INITIATIVE**

A Northeastern and Mid-Alantic U.S. initiative reduces greenhouse gas emis-sions through cap and trade.

🏭 **2004 | INOTERA FACTORY, TAIPEI**

tecARCHITECTURE designs largest computer chip factory to date.

◉ **2005 | *THE WORLD IS FLAT*, THOMAS L. FRIEDMAN**

Journalist Thomas L. Friedman writes book focusing on globalization.

👥 **2005 | 35-HOUR WORKWEEK ABOLISHED IN FRANCE**

🏭 **2005 | VACHERON CONSTANTIN FACTORY, GENEVA, SWITZERLAND**

Bernard Tschumi Architects design the sprawling factory and tower administration building in an iconic complex that represents the precision of watchmaking.

🏭 **2005 | BMW FACTORY, LEIPZIG, GERMANY**

Zaha Hadid Architects design central spine of BMW Factory.

2005

1998

2002

2006 | HIGH-TECH ASSEMBLY

Workers in a high-tech assembly line of photodiodes, handle the receiving end of a signal coming across an optical fiber.

2007 | WAL-MART STRIKES, MANILA, PHILLIPINES

In Wal-Mart's subcontracted factories, Philippine workers hold illegal strikes.

R-O-B-About.com

2007–2008 | R-O-B, MOBILE FABRICATION UNIT

A robot that can be used on building sites with Computer-Aided Design and Manufacturing

2008–2015 | DUBAI INDUSTRIAL CITY

Expected to be completed by 2015, this industrial zone covers 500 hectares, with factories and housing for workers.

2008 | BUILDING 500 AND 502, BIZKAIA INDUSTRIAL PARK, BILBAO, SPAIN

Coll-Barreu Architects design clean, high-tech, and flexible manufacturing buildings.

2009 | PAJU BOOK CITY

Paju Book City planned in South Korea as a cluster of book- and media-related trades with architects designing numerous buildings, including Stan Allen (pictured here).

2009 | LAFAYETTE 148, SHANTOU, CHINA

Architects Mehrdad Hadighi and Tsz Yan Ng, design a factory with innovative concrete.

2009 | HACKERSPACES

Hackerspaces, in large machine shops or small studios, gather people with common interests in computers and the digital arts to collaborate on products.

2009 | JEPPE, JOHANNESBURG

Residents reuse former office buildings for small-scale industries.

2009 | IPEKYOL TEXTILE FACTORY, TURKEY

Emre Arolat Architects use green factory design to focus on employee comfort. The project is short-listed for an Aga Kahn Award for Architecture.

2010 | FOXCONN SUICIDES

Worker injustice influences suicides at the Chinese electronics factory complex Foxconn.

2006

2010 | THE GREENING OF THE BROOKLYN NAVY YARD

Designed by various architects, the comprehensive redevelopment of the site focuses on greening existing and new buildings for industrial use.

2012 | AMERICAN INDUSTRY CENTER, SAN FRANCISCO

This giant industrial complex in San Francisco is home to mixed uses for industrial and commercial spaces.

2013 | NOERD BUILDING, ZURICH

Freitag leases space in a new flexible factory building in Oerlikon, Zurich.

2011 | LOCAL BREWERIES

Breweries see a comeback in cities around the world such as Steam Whistle, in Toronto.

2013 | RANA PLAZA

Factory buildings collapse in Dhaka, Bangladesh and workers' conditions are reevaluated by multinationals.

2014 | WASTE-TO-HEAT TRANSFER PLANT

BIG Architects design a mixed use infrastructural project in Amager, Denmark.

2011 | SMALL-SCALE 3-D PRINTERS

Companies like MakerBot develop small 3-D printers for personal and industrial use.

2014 | HYBRID FACTORIES

Normal builds a hybrid factory-showroom designed by HWKN Architects in the Chelsea district, New York.

2014

THE MODERN FACTORY

▶ Giacomo Matté-Trucco,
innovative concrete spiral
ramp system, Lingotto, Italy,
1926–1930

PRODUCTION ECONOMY

THE MODERN FACTORY as an architectural, social, and spatial typology is physically and conceptually significant in cultural history.[1] Though it is not formally recognized as a specific building type, I identify the vertical urban factory as a place of innovation that both impacted the city, and was influenced by the city, through controversial and conflicting social issues, which has great relevance today. The vertical urban factory ubiquitously developed with the rise of capital and new manufacturing methods during the Modern machine age at the end of the nineteenth century and beginning of the twentieth. The capitalist's desire for an efficient factory catalyzed continuous investigations into new methods for spatial organization, worker management, and deployment of operational strategies.

In the factory, architects and engineers were keen to innovate with new materials, experimental construction methods, and building technology systems such as elevators, as well as manufacturing technologies such as conveyors. New professional collaborations with industrial engineers motivated architects to formulate diverse spatial arrangements through which the building's function followed manufacturing flow. Modernism's maxim, "form follows function" was almost tailor-made for a synergy with the formal and function developments of the factory typology, as the factory exemplified Modernism itself.

As many before me have written on the history of the development of factories and the emergence and varieties of production techniques in manufacturing,[2] I emphasize here significant points of innovation in terms of the architecture of the factory, and the technologies that lie at the core of industrialization, and the capitalist hegemony of the Modern era as it impacts society. While the Modern factory of the early twentieth century was a place of architectural and urban innovation led by engineers, architects, and inventors, it also became subsumed by the capitalist who neglected substantial social and environmental consequences in a paradox that is clear to us now.

During the rise of capitalism, merchants and industrial inventors participated in the factory system at every scale. As early as the seventeenth century they obtained economic power and social status via investments and commodities that resulted in abusive environments for workers. When industrialists attempted to be benevolent to their workers, the progressive social reforms they enacted gave them greater dominance over their workers' public and private space and time. In fact, even the progressive factory owner, influenced by utopian thought, strove to make improvements in workers' day-to-day lives which ultimately were not as equitable as imagined: by definition the capitalist's goal was profit — and the factory-as-machine, because of its increased efficiency, was the capitalist's utopic environment.

The factory, in its unique social and physical form, became an often-negative societal model, and an isolated environment conforming to its own systems of organization. Philosopher Michel Foucault (1926–1984) noted, but did not emphasize, the factory as a *heterotopia* — isolated from the city and society, yet a mirror of it.[3] A corollary to spaces of production, the factory had its own tenets of design dictated by production methods; the factory and its organization were often spatially sequestered. As a space of both abuse and freedom, it impinged upon and altered society as a whole. The factory fits perfectly within Foucault's discussion of heterotopias as institutions of control, crisis, and deviance — prisons, schools, hospitals, gardens, and cemeteries — that were distinct from, but still part of, society. A heterotopia has its own physical space while still being a part of society; it is parallel in organization and function in its mirrored spaces, yet is distinguished by otherness and separation from society. Foucault suggests that a heterotopia "has the power of juxtaposing in a single real place different spaces and locations that are incompatible with each other."[4] Heterotopias are linked to time in terms of opening hours and events, such as with libraries and museums or even county fairs, and often one needs special permission to cross the border between simultaneous space-times. Foucault considered the ship "heterotopia *par excellence*" with brothels and colonies as additional strong examples.[5] The factory can be compared to the ship: it is a compressed space, it carries with it a social organization, and it has some of its own rules of conduct for safety, but is still part of society. It is organized and captained by a leader who tells his crew what to do and how to make it run. Foucault doesn't dwell on the factory as his main typology, even though it exemplifies characteristics that define his heterotopia.[6] Yet, the factory relates to the social order within the industrial spatial order. It is a condenser of behavior, society, and process in a hierarchy or a new reformist order, which can result in either spaces of abuse or spaces of freedom, depending on the enlightened attitude of the factory owner. Thus the idea of *heterotopia* aids the understanding of the factory as both a place that reflects and influences societal issues.

During the second industrial revolution Karl Marx (1818–1883) defined "labor power" as the workers' capacity, including time and energy, to make a product for which they receive a wage, so that their labor adds to the commodity's value. For Marx, the proletariat was "the class of modern wage-labourers who, having no means of production of their own, are reduced to selling their labour-power in order to live."[7] Labor-power is converted into monetary value for the industrialist, increasing at a greater rate as more workers (and thus more labor-hours) multiply the industrial output — and by virtue of low wages and an abundant supply of labor, labor-power provides an ever greater yield for the industrialist to claim as profit and surplus. Workers, who are part of the term *labor* as a category, along with the capital invested in machines, were considered commodity investments and bestowed additional value to products in the economic theory of capitalism. As Marx noted, people produce their own material life and the tools needed to produce this life. He believed that people had an inherent drive to work, and that they gained satisfaction from producing the products themselves — which would be theirs in a socialist organization of the production process.

What I present in this section is not simply a discussion of how manufacturing buildings were designed, or how they were integrated in the urban environment. I endeavor to formulate a proportioned measure of discussion between the production process, and the space in which that processing takes place — from the individual Modernist factory to urban industrial networks — and to consider how vertical urban factories and the organization of factories at a broader scale impacted modern cities, and the social diversity, vitality, and hybridity of those cities which we now so highly value.

Included in this discussion are three sections: the first encompassing the new technologies of production; the second, the factory in the urban context; and the third, the development of the vertical urban factory as a Modern architectural typology and its significance as an exemplar of the Modern era. *Modern,* in terms of social and cultural transformation, can be defined as the period spanning from the "first" industrial revolution of the eighteenth century, run by water and steam power and cottage industries; to the nineteenth century's development of the American System of Manufactures; and to the "second" industrial revolution of the early twentieth century, energized with electricity and mass production. On one hand, the idea of the "modern," in the sense of industrial progress, predates Modernism as a period of architecture and urban design, and thus also modernity, which is intrinsically associated with the early twentieth century. Modernity is a discursive attempt to come to terms with what it means to be modern, as discussed by Marshall Berman (1940–2013).[8] Within this Modern period the vertical and urban factory is a place of architectural transformation and of essential employment, but also of often discomforting and contradictory discourse.

▶ Clark's Spool Thread Factory, *Scientific American,* May 10, 1879

CLARK'S SPOOL THREAD FACTORY.—(See page 289.)

PRODUCTION, MAN, AND MACHINE

My dear Miss Glory, the Robots are not people. Mechanically they are more perfect than we are; they have an enormously developed intelligence, but they have no soul.[1]
–Harry Domin, R.U.R.

IN THE 1923 PLAY *R.U.R. (Rossum's Universal Robots)* by Karel Čapek (1890–1938), robots outsmart their creators, initiate an uprising, and take over a world that has become primarily inhabited by robots, based on the premise that humans are no longer necessary for work and therefore stop reproducing. It is in this play that Čapek invents the word *robot,* which in the Czech language means *worker*: "Young Rossum invented a worker with the minimum amount of requirements. He had to simplify him. He rejected everything that did not contribute directly to the progress of work — everything that makes man more expensive. In fact he *rejected man* and made the *robot*."[2]

As a metaphor for society, *R.U.R.*'s robots were not to have feelings, although one engineer altered them to do so, so that they realized their inferiority. The robots organize uprisings to protect their rights and to claim their intrinsic power in making products. As *R.U.R.* demonstrates, the relationship between worker and company impacts society as a whole, because if those in charge lose power, production ceases and the progress on which economies depend stagnates. *R.U.R.*'s factory-island enclave was ideal for capitalists who aspired towards maximum profit by employing robots without anyone looking on. Less than a decade after the mechanization of the continuous processing production line, the idea of the robot as described in *R.U.R.* was nearly indistinguishable from a human worker. The notion that humans would operate as machines increasingly specialized in their tasks became a palpable and harsh reality. Robot-workers who could perform like automatons, as seen in early experiments with wind-up toys, such as Jacques de Vaucanson's 1739 duck and flying machines, appealed to profit-seeking capitalists.

Between 1917 and 1920 German dramatist Georg Kaiser (1878–1945) wrote the futuristic and moralistic *Gas* trilogy — *Die Koralle* (1917, *The Coral*), *Gas I* (1918), *and Gas II* (1920) — about power, money, the machine, and utopia. However, the workers are competitive and greedy, and they become so dependent on the machines that their lives become tied to them. They produce gas, a dangerous but profitable enterprise. The tyranny of the machines dominates their life and, after an explosion on site, the son proposes to build a utopian community in its place. However, much to the son's surprise, the workers are not interested in this paradise with "domains for all of us in the midst of green promenades." Workers have no desire to be transformed into the "new man;" ethical socialism is doomed to failure, and technology rules. In a discussion with his engineer, the Billionaire exclaims, "Are you the slave of your calculations? Are you fettered to those girders, which you constructed? Have you delivered up your arms and legs, your blood and your senses to this frame, which you devised? Are you a diagram covered with a skin?"[3]

In the *Gas* trilogy, the workers who have physical hearts have no spiritual hearts, while in *R.U.R.* the robot has no heart, yet is secretively given one. The engineer who operates the factory in *Gas I* wants to continue gas production, and rather than return to the rural life, he asks, "Would you barter power for a blade of grass that sprouts at will?"[4] beckoning to the workers' desire to produce. At the end of the play, the government, through what resembles eminent domain, requires that the factory continue manufacturing gas for wartime use, shattering "the Billionaire's" utopian dreams.

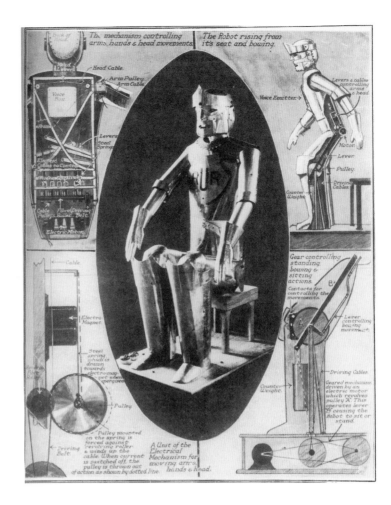

▲ An illustration of a robot from the first staging of Karel Čapek's play *R.U.R*, 1923

The attitude of early-twentieth-century industrialists took on this aspect of faith in technology. As technology changed, each iteration of a method or system became a driver for spatial and architectural design as well as an intellectual and physical cultural adaptation. In the 1930s, cultural critic Lewis Mumford (1885–1990) defined three historic transformations and overlapping phases in society's relationship with technology as the Eotechnic (1000 to 1700), Paleotechnic (1700 to 1900), and Neotechnic (1900 to 1930).[5] Mumford described the belief in the endless potential of the machine as one "whose power must be increased, whose prosperity is essential to all existence and whose operations however unnatural or compulsive cannot be challenged still less modified."[6] In essence, many considered machines as gods. Modern factory owners readily adopted the notion of improving manufacturing processes and profits by harnessing the workers as if they were part of the automated machinery.

FROM PIECEWORK TO MANUFACTORY

The evolution of this continuously running machine is seen in early experiments as part of what I call "vertical urban factories." Since the first industrial revolution of the eighteenth century, mechanized systems in the multistoried factory building (even those just three stories tall) strove for an automated, fluid organization. How

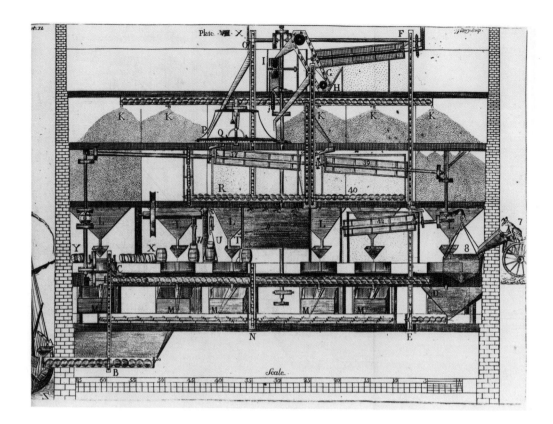

▲ Flour mill planned by Thomas Ellicott at Occoquan Virginia, using Oliver Evans' inventions, from his *Young Mill-wright and Miller's Guide*, 1795

▶ An engraving of soap works in London from Dodds, *Days at the Factory*, 1843

to form a space to house these machines became the major challenge. Inventors as early as Oliver Evans (1755–1819), a millwright from Delaware, who devised an Automatic Flour Mill for milling grain, utilized a contraption that limited manpower. His continuous process moved wheat downward through various hoppers and chutes, where it was ground in the bottom of the building, and then was hauled back to the upper floors again by bucket elevators for the final stages of drying, sorting, and barreling, culminating in finished grain products. Evans' bucket elevators were based on a chain pump system for carrying water that had been in use since Roman times. The bucket elevators rose vertically, employing an inclined screw conveyor called an Archimedes screw, which pulled water up through a spiral mechanism. Evans also used his invention, the hopper-boy, to spread the grain with a rake mechanism, gather, and transfer it. After processing, it was funneled to wood barrels, the standard mode of containerized transport for ships of the time. Evans' automated mill represents an early continuous process rather than the stop-and-go of most manufactories of the time. This process was improved in a new mill project in 1795, by a Virginia flour mill owner, Thomas Ellicott (1738–1799), who used the apparatus he and Evans described in *Young Mill-Wright and Millers Guide*, as so many did at the time.[7] Ellicott's mill relied on physical verticality, using not only the multiple stories to accommodate quantity, but also a process using gravity flow through height by harnessing pulleys and levers, as well as leather belts with steel slots, inspiring ideas for future moving conveyors. The simple but unified machinery, often with ad hoc technologies, could be combined in numerous ways, with incremental shifts towards a fluid production line, moving up and down on a condensed site.

Sigfried Giedion (1888–1968), a Swiss historian and architectural critic whose 1945 book *Mechanization Takes Command* recognized these "anonymous" inventions — those made by everyday tinkerers and inventors — and describes the significance of Evans' continuous flow production for the future of manufacturing:

> For Oliver Evans, hoisting and transportation have another meaning. They are but links within the continuous production process: from raw material to finished goods, the human hand shall be replaced by the machine. At a stroke, and without forerunner in this field, Oliver Evans achieved what was to become the pivot of later mechanization.[8]

That pivot of continuous flow, which saved even more time and cost in the manufacturing cycle, resulted in increased profits.

While the mechanized flow was one aspect of the production, how people worked within that system was another. In early-eighteenth-century factories, products were assembled with separate tasks apportioned to individual workers, as observed by economist Adam Smith (1723–1790). In striving for the continuous process, for example, mid-nineteenth-century factories were often not streamlined. Their processes involved moving heavy objects from place to place in a workshop, and the transfer of dangerous materials between containers, vats, and carts by hand. This cumbersome processing is especially evident in factories that produced natural or organic goods, such as soap and candles, or large items such as clock bells, described in minute detail in the handbook, *Days at the Factory* (1843).[9] At the Soap-Works in London, laborious manual work was required at each step of soap making: "coppers are filled with soap or materials for its formation, in various stages of progress" and then boiled; alkaline liquor was then pumped in, and the solution was then purified. The carbonate of lime from the purification of the alkalis was to be used for fertilizers, and the liquid soap was poured into large wood-framed containers three and a half meters high. After the soap solidified, its frame was removed and was cut into slabs by two workers drawing a wire through the block. These bars were carried to a standing machine, also fitted with wires, that cut them into rods and then bars, and they were "piled up in tiers, like bricks in a wall." However, this factory was disorganized, as the handbook's author observed: "the connecting doors, passages, and stories between one part of the factory and another are so tortuous and perplexing that we can not be properly topographic in our details."[10] Each area had a place for work, but processing was not laid out in a smooth sequence — these systems would come later.

Smith realized the importance of the effective division of labor in contributing to efficiency and economies of scale in manufacturing such as soap processing. In his lengthy description of the pin factory in his magnum opus, *The Wealth of Nations* (1776), he writes:

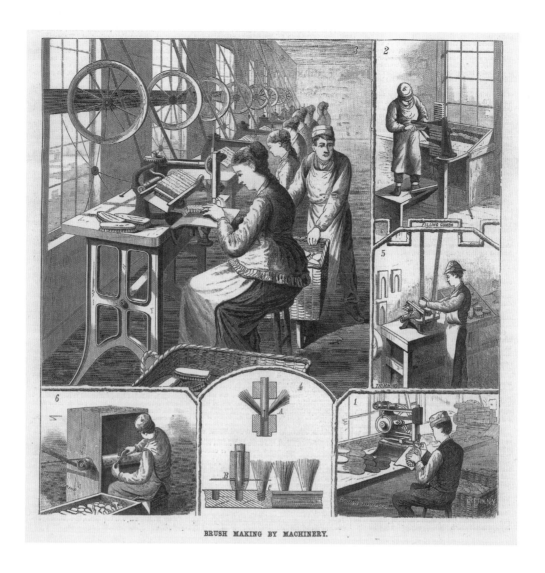

BRUSH MAKING BY MACHINERY.

▲ An illustration of a clean, well-lit brush factory, *Scientific American*, 1878
▶ interchangeable parts of a rifle improvement, cited in "Improvement in Magazine Firearms," patent from 1866

One man draws out the wire, another straights it, a third cuts it, a fourth points it, a fifth grinds it at the top for receiving the head; to make the head requires three distinct operations; to put it on is a peculiar business, to whiten the pin is another; it is even a trade by itself to put them into the paper; and the important business of making a pin is, in this manner, divided into about eighteen distinct operations, which, in some manufactories, are all performed by distinct hands, though in others the same man will sometimes perform two or three of them.[11]

He figured out that "ten persons, therefore, could make among them upwards of forty-eight thousand pins in a day….But if they had all wrought separately and independently, and without any of them having been educated to this peculiar business, they could certainly not each of them have made twenty, perhaps not one pin in a day."[12] He continued, "Each individual becomes more expert in his own peculiar branch, more work is done upon the whole, and the quantity of science is considerably increased by it."[13]

In fact, urban advocate Jane Jacobs (1916–2006) recognized that:

> Smith gave to the division of labor unwarranted credit for advances in economic life, a mistake still much with us. *Division of labor, in itself, creates nothing.* It is only a way of organizing work that has already been created. Even the first four labors of pin making did not exist until making metal carding combs was added to economic life. Division of labor is a device for achieving operating efficiency, nothing more.[14]

Each step that the worker took contributed to the holism of continuous production of a product, bit by bit. Jacobs also recognized that dividing work leads to new economies and methods tangential to the original product idea, and that, in building new work upon the old work, "division of labor becomes something infinitely more useful than Adam Smith suggested when he limited its function to the efficient rationalization of work." Jacobs emphasized that each of these divisions can lead to a new innovation not only in the production of the product in consideration but also in affiliated methods to produce things that relied on similar technologies. In other words, at each step of the way a new invention could emerge through the adaptation of the workers' techniques or the new tools employed. We see this with the improvement of the roller conveyor, or bicycle parts developing into carriages and then automobiles, as each new item led to another. Jacobs mentions how research conducted by the Soviet space program led to the invention of an artificial hand; elements of this invention came to be utilized throughout electronics manufacturing. One can also see this product development in the field of adhesives as new kinds of tapes, glues, adhesive fabrics, and even construction materials are developed through incremental innovations and competition between companies such as 3M and DuPont. Each invention contributes to the next; patents build upon patents, even with minute changes, and each method of making alters a process, with tweaks and adjustments creating new forms of labor for new forms of work, reorganizing the factory method.

FROM THE AMERICAN SYSTEM TO CONTINUOUS PROCESSING

Each stage towards the mechanization of production — from the organization of the workers to the innovations of engineers — coalesced into the continuously moving assembly line and mass production. Among the first efforts was the American System of Manufactures, a production process for assembling parts into uniform products by means of stamping and pressing metal and exchangeable connection parts at stationary workplaces. Small arms companies developed the process via competition from French arms makers in late-eighteenth-century New England at workshops such as Whitney Arms in New Haven, the Springfield Armory, and Remington Arms in Bridgeport. Numerous products, including Sargent hardware in New Haven; Waltham Watches in Waltham, Massachusetts; Singer sewing machines in Elizabethport, New Jersey; and Pope bicycles in Hartford,

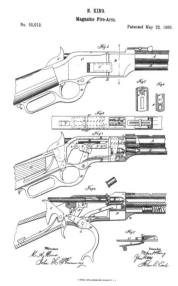

▲ Workers welding bicycle
frames in a bicycle factory,
1880
▶ T. Morrison, patent for a
hog-weighing conveyor, 1869
▶ Wristwatches used the
system of interchangeable
parts manufacturing

Connecticut, were assembled from interchangeable components that could be easily swapped out for repair or adjustment without reconfiguring the entire product.[16] Fabrication of multiple but similar parts was gradually adopted worldwide through the early twentieth century. After the establishment of interchangeable parts manufacturing, the speed of production held constant until the advent of the moving assembly line shattered the production plateau, drastically speeding up processing, with the worker intertwined between the process and machines themselves. Consumer goods with replaceable parts built of iron and then steel, such as sewing machines, bicycles, and stoves, led to the development of increasingly larger products, such as the mass-produced automobile.

Some new household amenities, such as Singer sewing machines, marked a period of transition in production processes. The sewing machines produced by Singer initially lacked interchangeable parts and required refined hand adjustments during their manufacture, prior to being mass produced.[17] For example, the close fit between shaft and bearings needed customization because each tool was not made specifically for each job. The solution blended two methods of production: the European, handcrafted, approach, and the American strategy of standardized parts. The spatial organization of Singer's factory in Elizabethport, the largest factory in the U.S. in 1873, lacked fluidity, and reflected a more sporadic and disorganized system of production. Singer had a department dedicated solely to the design and production of specialized machine tools, automatic screw machines, jigs, and gauges. Singer's production goals (8,000 sewing machines per week in 1883) were not always feasible, as absolute interchangeability was not yet possible; the inconsistency of the components used in manufacturing the machines slowed down an otherwise systematic production line.[18]

The developments surrounding the introduction of interchangeable parts, as well as new refinements in processes such as metal stamping, coalesced around the burgeoning industry of bicycle manufacturing. The early American bicycles manufactured by Albert Pope (1843–1909) in a corner of the Weed sewing machine company's factory in Hartford, Connecticut combined these new advances.[19] Both companies used components taken from armories, and drop-forging for metal work. Here, old methods begot new inventions; for example, ball-bearing manufacture used the grinding machines previously used for optical parts and needle making. An invention of major consequence for all industries, ball bearings were first invented for bicycles. Wheel hubs and rims were assembled with spokes, and the wheels had to be carefully trued, taking longer than desired. By mid-1881, Pope produced 1,200 safety bicycles (those with new breaks) per month and he maintained a patent that other manufacturers, many of them originally firearm manufacturers, had to license. Pope's bicycles had a chain, two sprockets for the drive and axle, a crank hanger for ball bearings, and more framing than the high-wheel bikes. The resultant weight increase created a challenge in production speed. Pope grew to manufacture bicycles and their components for other companies, increasing to 3,000 employees, and 60,000 bikes annually during the 1880s. In purchasing and consolidating various plants in the heart of cities for steel tubing and rubber tires, Pope established the Hartford Cycle Company in 1895 to produce a less expensive bicycle, exploiting new methods of machine tooling and inspections to ensure quality. In Detroit, bicycle companies switched to metal stamping rather than forging and machine work for parts such as crank-hangers, hubs, and sprockets. The manufacturing of interchangeable parts for bicycles, which was a hands-on assembly process, then influenced the burgeoning automobile industry, and has been revived recently as a new urban industry.

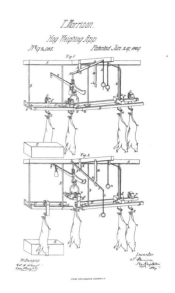

In 1870, manufacturers in the Midwestern United States began to combine the American system of interchangeable parts with the method of continuous processing to optimize the meatpacking industry's slaughterhouses.[20] The slaughterhouses in cities such as Cincinnati, Chicago, Toronto, and Shanghai used the verticality of their factories to exploit gravity flow in the operation of overhead pulleys that held the carcasses of slaughtered animals, such as hogs. This arrangement was described viscerally in Sinclair Lewis' (1885–1951) book *The Jungle*:

> There were groups of pigs being driven to the chutes, which were roadways about 4.5 meters wide, raised high above the pens. . . . Our friends were not poetical, and the sight suggested to them no metaphors of human destiny; they thought only of the wonderful efficiency of it all. The chutes into which the hogs went climbed high up — to the very top of the distant buildings. . .and their weight carried them back through all the processes necessary to make them into pork.[21]

The processing was also continuous, but unlike in a typical factory, was a process of disassembly, as opposed to assembly. The plants in Cincinnati used overhead rails with wheels that had chains to pull them or used an incline from which workers would deconstruct the carcass, performing a series of separate tasks as it moved past them. Giedion focused on the significance of the slaughterhouses' various overhead mechanisms, which often boasted improvements upon the rail systems on which they were based, resulting in an increased production speed. As plant managers became increasingly aware of the integration of the flow of materials with the spatial organization, designs evolved.

TIME MANAGEMENT AND MOTION EFFICIENCY (1912)

The Americans Frederick W. Taylor (1856–1915) and Frank (1868–1924) and Lillian (1878–1972) Gilbreth, a husband-and-wife team, each invented systems, which they later shared, for analyzing the worker's speed and efficiency, yielding improvements to the production process, and launching a new field of worker optimization. Their studies influenced not only the production line, but also architects and social thinkers of this early Modern age. Taylor and the Gilbreths were obsessed with speed, an essential aspect of modern life, with its new perception of time in relationship to production and society. Making things faster was a goal not only for the sake of production efficiency and profit, but also for the very idea of speed itself. Modernity was about speed made possible by electric engines, new machines, and power — both physical and social — that led to the "human motor": man as a machine, just as in *R.U.R.* man had literally become a robot.

The science of understanding and organizing human movement for fast manufacturing production became intertwined as a new profession of industrial engineers was established. The Gilbreths published efficiency studies in their 1916 book, *Fatigue Study: the elimination of humanity's greatest unnecessary waste*. Frank Gilbreth, who was first a bricklayer and then owned his own construction company, invented new types of scaffolding that raised the bricks to the workers' level, and a new method of lining up mortar joints with a trowel. The designs were published in great detail for companies to follow in his book, *Applied Motion Study,* of 1913. Although the Gilbreths' goal was to find the "one best way" to perform a task, they were also concerned with worker satisfaction and articulated a "happiness principle." They cornered the market by providing consulting services to companies to improve worker productivity through humane methods.

The Gilbreths' studies were based on observation and documentation through photography and film — new technologies that could enhance physical research and allow for applied use. Using a stereo camera they created 3-D photographs — *chronocyclographs* — that traced the paths of human motion in pulses of electric light, resulting in a kind of time-motion-writing. "Chronocyclographs detached human movement from its bearer or subject, and achieved its precise visualization in space and time."[22] They abstracted human motion, inventing a new way to measure human action towards improvement, but Taylor interpreted their methods in a dehumanizing way. The Gilbreths began their motion studies by attaching small lights to the arms and hands of a worker conducting a task, and then recorded his or her movements in long exposure photographs. The camera registered the movements as single lines of light. The photographs were then used to construct wire models of the paths of movement recorded for the "efficient" workers — whether it was filing papers, typing, or working on an assembly line. The models were used to train less-adept workers on the fastest

way to execute a job by replicating efficient movements. The Gilbreths made two
exposures, first photographing a transparent screen with a grid on it, and then
recording the worker's movements. They made hundreds of these photographic
studies, which were depicted as perforated lines of light encircling workers' limbs
with a sort of stopwatch or clock measuring the duration of a given activity, and
called each motion a "therblig" (Gilbreth spelled backwards with "th" transposed), which they would analyze for efficiency improvement.

Time-motion studies became a standard tool for industries seeking ways to
save time and labor costs; they represented a capital investment aimed at greater
profits. In developing methods to accelerate worker production and efficiency, and
to reduce fatigue and wasted time on the assembly line, the Gilbreths provided the
factory owner with more financial value in terms of the workforce and labor power.
Their philosophy evolved from a renewed social consciousness of human behavior,
and they treated the worker with humanity.

▲ Photograph of the light
tracking system for Time and
Motion Studies, by Frank and
Lillian Gilbreth, 1915

Other photographers were also experimenting with documenting motion,
including the Englishman Eadweard Muybridge (1830–1904), who, working in
Philadelphia, used multiple cameras with synchronized shutters and stop-motion
grids to record the motion of humans and animals. It was with this method that
Muybridge proved that horses in a gallop have all four hooves off the ground at
once. Prior to the Gilbreths, French photographer Étienne-Jules Marey (1830–1904)

invented a photographic gun capable of registering successive images on the same negative. He too was interested in human locomotion and animal movement, as well as the kinetic behavior of objects. His images appear as almost schematic representations of birds in flight, people running, jumping, and so on. As Giedion describes, "Marey called his procedure 'time photography' or 'cronophotographie;' its object is to render visible 'movements that the human eye cannot perceive.' "[23] The photographs and films of Muybridge, Marey, and the Gilbreths later became recognized as an art form, inspiring Italian Futurists such as artists F. T. Marinetti (1876–1944) and Giacomo Balla (1871–1958), who depicted movement in two-dimensional works on paper or canvas, or over time frozen as a sculpture. Marey's investigations into the dynamic laws of the body in motion created a new science of human labor power based on human energy. The amount of effort in understanding motion was harnessed into capital production beyond that of Marx's concept of labor power to that of Hermann von Helmholtz (1821–1894), who studied human motion and ways to exert minimal energy to combat fatigue. Helmholtz portrayed the worker's body as "a universal, degendered motor, whose specific and nonenergetic needs could be bracketed. Energy conservation became a social doctrine."[24] Sociologist Anson Rabinbach recognized that, "In national economy, as in the work of Marx, the body was the site where the natural force of labor power was converted into the energy to power the industrial dynamo. The working body was thus recast in the image of the Helmholtzian Cosmos, as the cosmos itself became an industrialized automata."[25]

The motion studies served Taylor's interest in reconfiguring the workplace to speed up operatives' tasks. He conducted his own worker behavior studies at the Midvale Steel Company in Philadelphia, using regimented systems for keeping time and regulating movement in the steel mill. He observed how workmen set the work-pace to gain control of production, but Taylor disapproved as to how the gang-boss, or foreman, should direct production organization. He then went on to reorganize Bethlehem Steel's task time and wage relationship to the work performed, a process he explained in his 1903 book, *Shop Management*, considered an essential guide for factory owners. Beginning in 1906, Taylor argued that labor problems including waste, low productivity, high turnover, soldiering (or slacking off), and the adversarial relationship between labor and management, arose from defective organization and improper work methods. Production, he contended, was governed by universal and natural laws that were independent of human judgment. The object of his new technique — later called task, or Scientific Management, published in his 1911 book, *The Principles of Scientific Management* — was to discover these laws and apply the "one best way" to conduct managerial functions such as hiring, promoting, setting compensation, training, and supervising production. Taylor had used motion studies as the Gilbreths did to record workers' speed and introduced the stopwatch to improve output. His focus combined speed and profit, turning to the organization's bottom-line and firm's profit structure.

Taylor believed in paying employees through the piece-rate system, which meant a worker was paid by the number of goods or parts completed, rather than by the amount of time it took to do the job. He would place a foreman in each department, instead of having one foreman for an entire factory, so as to supervise each worker's performance. While some philosophers at the time believed in man's general interest in productivity, and subscribed to the concept of a Protestant work ethic, as propagated in 1904 by Max Weber (1864–1920), Taylor had a cynical and antagonistic attitude towards the worker, saying, "the natural instinct and tendency of men is to take it easy, which may be called natural soldiering."[26] His tough-minded solution, which eventually did spur on union formation and workers striking for rights, was that work was science and could no longer be managed using rule of thumb techniques (intuitive working methods) — that a manager had to run every aspect of the production process with detailed breakdowns of each job, so that no one worker would possess knowledge that might put this worker in a position of power vis-à-vis management. He centralized planning and phased production, analyzing each operation with instructive supervision, and used payments to provide incentive to work.[27] Taylor organized fewer than thirty factories before 1917, but his methods gained popularity, and by the 1920s, thousands of factories, at the time mostly vertical ones, were organized by his methods. As Taylorism grew far and wide, Henri Fayol (1841–1925), a French engineer, used the approach as a base for streamlining manufacturing in wartime but was more focused on administrative management. For Fayol, manufacturing was made more efficient by forecasting and planning through worker surveys, reporting, and organizational charts that distinguished between the abilities of workers in a chain of command. His ideas contributed to the division of labor and early organizational management for variously scaled companies and their significance within industrial organizations whose basics continue to this day, and for many have been an issue of constant debate.

Taylor promoted time and motion studies, combining aspects of the Gilbreths' methods along with his own techniques, influencing the speed of production, relying on the worker's tasks, and piece rates. Henry Ford (1863–1947), who learned of Taylor's methods from his published books and articles, had been experimenting with a comparable systematic factory organization. Ford hired workmen according to his need for both semiskilled and unskilled work, just as Taylor would have specified, and had a clear division of labor; yet Ford did not come to learn of Taylor's Scientific Management until years later. New organizational management concepts were already being talked about in 1910 at Ford's Highland Park plant and at numerous other Detroit factories.[28] Ford's distinction lay in the automation of the factory with the moving assembly line. Rather than having each worker at individual stations to construct one Model T, Ford and his engineers instituted a mechanized conveyor on which the car parts moved past the workers who performed the same repetitive task such as adding a break, working on a magneto, or assembling a wheel.

MOVING ASSEMBLY LINES

Moving assembly lines originated in simple stages for convenience in earlier factories, such as canning facilities of the nineteenth century, which had contiguous platforms that could be used to push material from one worker to another at different stations. In 1890, the Pittsburgh Westinghouse Foundry employed a continuous chain of individual tables connected to wheels on tracks below, running in a loop.

The tables carried molds into which men would pour molten metal that was processed in the Bessemer oven and removed impurities, hardening it into steel. After the metal cooled, the molds would be broken open, and the sand used in the molds would then be fed into hoppers from conveyors in the floor. There was no need for "pushers and shovers" to move carts for each phase, which took time away from production.[29]

The roller conveyor of Westinghouse was brought to the attention of Ford engineers, along with the canning machine. At that time, Thomas Edison (1846–1941) in New Jersey was working on a magnetic method for processing low-grade iron ore using a simple belt conveyor to carry the ore from the mine to the processing plant in a continuous flow to make the process economical. Light canvas belts had been previously used for carrying grain, but never before something as heavy and bulky as ore. The following step was to make a belt with a tougher abrasion, to link to pulleys. Rubber was used as a surface to carry items up and down inclines without slipping and additional friction provided traction at high speeds. Other belts were made of wire so that the open mesh could allow parts of products to be heated or washed as they proceeded on the line.

Combining the foundry techniques and overhead methods, Charles Sorensen (1811–1968), Ford's chief engineer, unified the earlier ideas for movement at the workplace with that of the continuous assembly line in 1908, which was then implemented at Highland Park in 1913. In 1915 Jervis B. Webb, a Detroit–based conveyance manufacturer, invented the forged rivetless chain conveyor, a fluid system that Ford adopted at Highland Park. Webb had been working in coal mines, and the linked chain he developed there, similar to Edison's, inspired his redesign for a mechanized system for auto manufacturing. The overhead conveyors were first installed at Studebaker and then at Highland Park, and transformed the organization, layout, and speed of production at both plants.

By 1913, Henry Ford's Highland Park plant assembly line could produce a Model T every three minutes, establishing a new paradigm of efficiency for material production. By using similar parts and producing only one model, Ford had hit upon a method of achieving economies of scale, but it was not until 1926 that he first used the term "mass production." Writing of his systems in a *New York Times* article, Ford described it as, "the modern method by which great quantities of a single standardized commodity are manufactured. As commonly employed it is made to refer to the quantity produced, but its primary reference is to method."[30] For Ford, mass production, as it began to be defined, was all-encompassing as "a doctrine, a business philosophy, a large production output, and a technological system."[31]

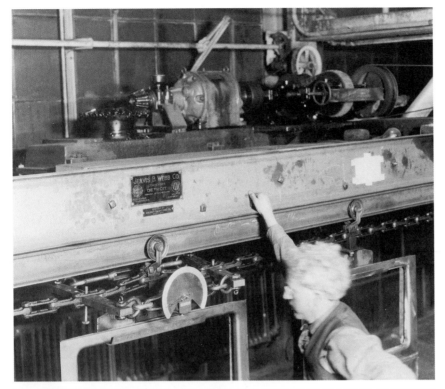

▲ Jervis B. Webb's overhead
conveyor, 1928
▲ 1,000 Ford Model T chassis awaiting production at
Highland Park factory, Detroit,
1911

Taylor's management analysis and efficiency systems combined with Ford's manufacturing methods, and in addition to new machinic devices, catalyzed a total reorganization of production, increasing the number of goods in the market multifold. Ford was filling a void with a new product, the car. But products quickly went the way of planned obsolescence as new companies produced similar goods and upped demand for ever newer goods. The cycle of consumption and production shifted the scale of capitalism in many regions at various stages, energizing a dynamic urban workplace. Production became as conspicuous as consumption; factories were ubiquitous. It represented capitalist hegemony in society.

MACHINE AND WORKER ALIENATION

The streamlined factory and the increase in production tempo also affected worker dissatisfaction and the alienation that Marx had identified as early as the 1880s.[32] Workers suffered physically in this system. Often they did not move their bodies save for their hands or arms, which worked in the same endless and tedious motions on the assembly line for twelve hours a day. The trance of production led to fatigue and eventually injury; eyes became tired and muscles strained under repetitive use. It was clear, even to those outside the factory system, that people served literally as the motors that made their consumable goods.[33] Charlie Chaplin cleverly depicted the workers' dilemma in his film *Modern Times* (1936), clarifying to the general public the specialization that Adam Smith described, wherein each workman would make one portion of an object that would later be assembled by others, or by machines, to make the whole. The film was a satire on the factory condition, but very real. Workers' alienation from each other and from the process of making a finished product itself proliferated with automated machinery.

As machines encroached upon the workplace and the workers had less control, French historian Marc Bloch (1886–1944) noted, "Wherever labour is dear, it must be supplemented by machines; this is the only way to compete with those countries where it is cheap. The English have been telling Europe this for a long time."[34] Mechanization began to be perceived as a threat to jobs. Historian Fernand Braudel described an uprising by silk workers in France who were angered at their replacement by Frenchman Joseph Marie Jacquard's (1752–1834) automated loom. In 1801, Jacquard developed perforated cards strung together whose hole patterns triggered which part of the loom lifted up the threads for the shuttle to pass through to change the patterns in the fabric. Textile workers resisted the change for fear of losing their jobs, and were called "Luddites" for their anti-technology stance, exemplifying the growing pains of industrialization. Jacquard's loom was actually a revision to Jacques de Vaucanson's (1709–1782) earlier loom, hidden at the Conservatoire des Arts et Métiers in Paris because it too was considered to be a threat to employment as technology was advancing faster than workers could reorganize.[35]

As factories continued to grow, the population of wage labor workers increased exponentially as a result of rising capitalism.[36] Ideals of collective action and organizational power united them as they banded together to achieve improved rights, wages, and reasonable hours. Because there was no unified wage rate across factories, within one factory wages could be paid by the hour, the day, or by the piece, and employees were frequently disgruntled. In America, this resulted in a doubling of union membership between 1916 and 1920.

▶ Joseph Marie Jacquard's loom punch-card system

> Industrial workers in America, like their counterparts in Europe, were at that very time vigorously and explicitly challenging management's pretensions and the value system which supported them. Those workers were keenly aware that the 'science of work,' as Harry Braverman said, was in reality a '*science of the management of others' work* under capitalist conditions,' that is, where 'labor power. . .is bought and sold.' [37]

Workers and researchers devised various methods for fighting the overtly hierarchical factory system through union membership and factory-based social welfare assistance. They battled the physical and psychological ramifications of repetitive, alienating work, attempting to reverse the *R.U.R.* robot-worker trend. In Europe many psychologists and sociologists (including Weber, who was instrumental in the Verein für Sozialpolitik, or Association for Social Policy) were skeptical of treating people as machines. In the United States, new social work organizations took on the conflicting issues afflicting the workers in the 1920s. The physiology of movement developed into the field of "Social Helmholtzianism" a name that indicated the intellectual acknowledgment of the fatigue and injury that resulted from working in industry.

Weber conducted numerous surveys of fifteen companies for the Verein, examining not only work environments, but also nutrition, culture, and physical and mental fatigue, in order to determine how these factors could impact work and regulation of productivity in relationship to the economy.[38] Much of this research shaped the *Verein*'s own social programs, which analyzed performance and depicted an entire sociological portrait of the worker for their own benefit and to enhance the company's profits. These social programs led to the initiation of reforms which improved the number of hours worked as well as overall employee well-being, for the first time making the connection between happiness at work and increase in productivity.

Other humanists "reacted more negatively, condemning Taylorism for abandoning the most cherished principle of science, its social neutrality."[39] This neutrality was essential. As Rabinbach notes, even "ergonomic scientists were divided over the research and its findings, reflecting a deep, unacknowledged ambiguity in their own industrial ideology."[40] Some, such as Georg Schlesinger (1874–1949), focused on "psychotechnics," which was critical of previous studies, to find a middle ground between the German interest in the worker's psychology and physiology, and Taylor's focus on worker productivity. This German version of the new management systems eventually contributed to enhancing wartime production efforts.[41]

While some industrialists continuously exploited workers, others formed welfare organizations increasingly sympathetic to workers' needs. These included the International Relations Association for the Study and Promotion of Satisfactory Human Relations and Conditions in Industry, later called the International Relations Institute (IRI). Founded in the 1920s with George Cadbury (1839–1922) of England, numerous prominent sociologists, and the humanitarian Russell Sage Foundation, the IRI analyzed both physiological and psychological aspects of people at work and sought to improve the workplace.

Lillian Gilbreth was active with this group and made a point of contrasting her work with that of Taylor, noting the issues of fatigue as well as the

speed of production in her *Fatigue Study* of 1916. Kees Van der Leeuw (1890–1973), the owner of the Van Nelle company, was also involved, presenting his 1920s project for his Modernist factory at meetings. The IRI also visually depicted worldwide issues of employment and economics, an antecedent of today's infographics, using economic philosopher Otto Neurath's (1882–1945) graphics of economic and employment statistics, and drawn by designer Gerd Arntz (1900–1988), a student of the Bauhaus.

Other American sociologists implemented worker studies firsthand, as in the now well-known observations of Western Electric's Hawthorne factory outside of Chicago. Beginning in 1924, sociologist Elton Mayo (1880–1949) inquired into workers' behavioral improvements with an altered environment. He devised tests for different situations and two subject groups, first changing lighting conditions by raising and lowering the light levels, then the air quality by opening and closing windows. The worker's speed and quality of production changed when the testers altered the environment in both positive and negative ways, leading the sociologists to realize that it was actually the *attention* the workers were receiving rather than the *condition* of the space that impacted their behavior. The researchers also observed that group behavior influenced performance and played a role in work incentives. In hindsight, many in the field concluded that the study was imprecise, and that workers' awareness of being tested had also influenced their performance. So the question remained, in the second industrial revolution, as to how labor conditions and the factory environment could be improved.

Although mechanization resulted in scores of disgruntled workers, the modernization of production offered positive improvements, in contrast to early nineteenth-century mills. These improvements were both technological and environmental, affecting machinery, safety, air quality, and lighting in new rationalized systems. Simultaneously, labor unions renewed a focus on workers' conditions, and helped them to stand up for their rights.

CRAFTSMEN VS. UNSKILLED WORKERS

The development of automated manufacturing broadened the divide between that of the traditional craftsman, or those skilled with tools in a specific trade, and the semiskilled and unskilled workers, who were just as replaceable and interchangeable as the machine parts. Historian David Montgomery highlighted the consequences of the systemic and machine-driven factory organization as the divorce between the technical and social systems of control, resulting in more acts of sabotage, protest, and slacking by workers; a chaotic working-class life often accompanied by unemployment; and finally, corporate power over everything from food prices to reduction of workers' personal spending power. The factory organization resulted in continual conflicts between craftsmen, operatives, and laborers.[42]

The strict organization of the workplace, the applied science of time and motion studies, and the streamlining of the production line resulted in greater limitations

▲ Cover of the *Voice of Labor* depicting the steel industry as a robot "pounding" its workers, 1919

on the craftsman's ability to perform his work and to oversee lesser-skilled workers. Perhaps it is a romantic myth that we believe the craftsman held a special place in the hierarchy of the workplace. The craftsman's power, which

> had rested on superior knowledge of their work relative to their employers was undermined, and the traditional dualism of craftsmen operating the machinery while laborers fetched and carried, was remodeled into a continuum of specialized machine tenders performing functions which required only minor variations in training and agility, and all of which were directly under the detailed supervision of a swarm of managerial officials.[43]

While craftsmen were more autonomous and had more direct control of their work — subcontracting out to others — operatives and management squashed their command of how things should be made as they themselves often made assembly decisions on site during the manufacturing process. Skilled workers had the upper hand, and could also sequence and schedule the work according to how long it took them to make something, especially in terms of machinists and those working with highly precise tools combining hand and machine work. As unskilled workers doing precise repetitive tasks rose in number and craftsmen began to diminish, so too did the craftsman's workplace position. While wrestling with the chronic menace of unemployment, skilled workers adapted to keep their jobs by learning new skills through factory training, and fought to enforce collective work rules through which they regulated workplace relationships. Skilled workers and craftsmen started to disappear because there was no more need for them — unskilled workers could just as easily tend machines, and semiskilled operatives could replace craftsmen.[44] This began the de-skilling of labor, leaving more power in the hands of the owners with dispersal of responsibilities among many, rather than know-how invested in the hands of a small class of craftsmen, who could gain power through their knowledge.

Labor division was not always part of manufacturing, as seen in the decades between 1870 and 1930. Labor historians David M. Gordon, Richard Edwards, and Michael Reich consider this to be a "homogenized" period when semiskilled operatives were united in common goals and labor was competitive in what was called the "drive system." Shop foremen increased their supervision quite drastically.[45] "Work that had been organized by relatively particularistic relations between supervisor and supervisee was transferred to the larger factories, where personal relationships were much more difficult to sustain and authority became more impersonal."[46] Worker discontent increased because the pace of work, lack of interest, and the rise of wages were unpredictable, however they could share their issues in the density of the urban industry, to make changes.

Factory management did not keep pace with evolving factory technologies. To save costs, following Taylor's model, employers set up incentive systems through piecework and payment per task, or item completed, rather than a set salary, even though the laborers all worked together in the same factory space.[47] This management style undermined the autonomy of the craftsmen, and the rules of trade unions. Besides leading to standardization of tasks, new systems of work influenced by Taylorism supplanted the earlier ad hoc method of making things. "Furthermore, during and following World War I, miners, metal workers, garment workers, railroad employees, and others simultaneously forced their employers to rescind various aspects of the new managerial practice, and demanded the immediate adoption of their own plans for the reorganization of work relations from below."[48] This led to the organization of unions and subsequent collective actions. The machinists' answer to Scientific Management was to demand a "truly scientific" reorganization of the whole society on a collective basis. As skilled workers influenced the production method on the assembly line, they infiltrated the capitalist hegemony of their employer and the industrial ethos, generally demanding increased rights.

Beginning in the 1920s, the division of labor became "segmented," in contrast to homogenization, as labor was separated into skilled, semiskilled, and unskilled categories. Around 1930, those skilled workers who were more independent became increasingly separated from the more subordinate operatives. Gordon, Edwards, and Reich argue that early on, these divisions led to a divided union movement, which dissipated worker control after World War II.

WARTIME SPEED

Looking back to the origins of the paradigm shift from skilled worker to machine operator through automation, one finds that it was the urgent demands of the military-industrial complex in World War II that catalyzed industrial production in the postwar period. War has historically galvanized industrial production. Consider the uniforms and canned food developed for the improved mobility of soldiers. In the late eighteenth century, during the Napoleonic Wars, Frenchman Nicolas Appert (1749–1841) devised a system for preserving food in glass jars through heat application so that armies could carry food to the battlefield that would not spoil over time. The method was perfected with the use of tin-coated iron cans in the early nineteenth century, which in turn launched the tin can industry. Cans became a standard method of packing, as barrels had been for other perishable goods. It wasn't until the mid-twentieth century, however, that the cans were mass-produced with speed. Men were not only carrying the industrial innovations, they were wearing them as well. Uniforms became standardized during the American Civil War; instead of being tailored to the individual, they were produced in large numbers based on average sizes that would accommodate soldiers' various sizes. This wartime system was then readily adopted by garment factories, which developed a series of average sizes for ready-made clothing, a method of sizing and selling clothing still in place today.

As Joel Davidson pointed out in his 1995 essay, "Building for War, Preparing for Peace," World War II represented an all-out effort on the part of American industry; citizens took responsibility for the war effort as well.[49] Davidson emphasizes how critical this movement was, as the U.S. was not prepared for war, and it subsequently changed industrial manufacturing forever. Military plants needed to be built from scratch or overhauled for new production lines, and more advanced factories were required due to the new emphasis on air power. The army was ill-equipped in specific ways; in practice maneuvers between 1939 and 1940, broomsticks were used to simulate rifles, and trucks used as stand-ins for tanks.[50] Materials were scarce and they had to protect supplies of certain materials to use in the war. A material goods board regulated the use of "Essential Materials," such as steel, rubber, aluminum and tungsten, all of which were needed for aircraft and weapon production. Another organization created by President Franklin D. Roosevelt (1882–1945), the War Production Board (WPB) of the Office of Production Management, supervised the increased production needs. This agency was created to address mistakes made in World War I, by establishing organized systems that combined public and private enterprise. The army's management of industry turned out to be infeasible, so businessmen were sought to run production lines and faster distribution chains. One officer wrote, "The average officer lives a life as remote from our day-to-day business struggle as a cloistered monk."[51] In other words, the military officers lacked the knowledge to run industrialized factories for wartime production. The army surveyed 30,000 industrial firms that supplied 70,000 products, such as tanks, arms, helmets, uniforms, cookware, haversacks, footwear, and tools — the production for these items was transformed from quotidian to wartime production. However, it was not until Pearl Harbor that President Roosevelt struck a bargain with industrialists, and a full-fledged manufacturing effort came into being. To organize a more efficient wartime production line in 1942, the WPB appointed Donald Nelson, former chairman and a businessman of Sears, Roebuck & Company, to coordinate the procurement work. Unlike individual companies retooling for wartime, the army manufactured their own products through direct contracts with companies such as DuPont and Remington in what was called Government-Owned Contractor-Operated facilities (GOCO).[52]

One of the first steps was to allocate funds and give manufacturers incentives to build factories. Factory owners could take tax write-offs by reducing their production of domestic goods, and switching to making wartime supplies — from producing automobiles to manufacturing tanks, for instance. Aircraft facilities increased their annual production more than threefold, from 13,000 to 50,000 airplanes. They used an adaptive technology that combined Ford's production methods with those of airplane manufacturers such as Douglas Aircraft in Long Beach, California, which was housed in a 43,000-square-meter space. By mid-1945, $4 billion had been invested in new plants and equipment, increasing production space to a total of fifty million square meters around the country. This was built primarily by the Defense Plant Corporation, which by 1945 had funded one thousand factories, totaling $7 billion. The Army Air Forces also sponsored 190 projects. As Davidson said, "the wars made us in a state of permanent preparedness."[53]

▲ Wartime advertisement featuring Albert Kahn's Willow Run Bomber Factory, Willow Run, Michigan, 1942

WARTIME LABOR

Labor issues intensified as well. So as not to overwork the limited personnel, factories employed more women, doubling the number in the workforce from 15 to thirty percent, totaling over eight million. The stories of Rosie the Riveters are well known, as women fought the war on the national front while men were in battle. Prior to the war, few women worked outside the home. As to workers' rights, the American Federation of Workers pledged that there should be no strikes or walk-outs, even though the high production levels would have made higher wages easy to obtain. Despite this pledge, there were 14,471 strikes, involving almost seven million workers. This number exceeded that of any other period in history, including those strikes held during the 1930s, when the Congress of Industrial Organizations (CIO) was formed.[54] The CIO (which later merged with the American Federation of Labor to become the AFL-CIO) pushed production as a national obligation and chanted in a radio advertisement — "Work, work, produce, produce." But workers realized that they had the upper hand — they were in demand. Accordingly, they fought for equity over such issues as discipline, work hazards, and control of the assembly-line tempo, as well as higher wages. Two forgotten, incredible statistics provide an odd twist to the wartime story: between 1940 and 1945, 88,000 workers were killed and over eleven million were injured as a result of industrial accidents, 11 times the total U.S. casualties from combat.[55] The CIO became more right-wing during the war, attempting labor management cooperation more than ever before. The members couldn't quit the union and had to continue paying dues, and thus became more dependent on the government for both contracts and jobs. Detroit led defense production, earning the city the nickname "The Arsenal of Democracy." However, towards the war's conclusion, two or three strikes per week were common in Detroit's factories, even though they were the center of production and jobs.

Nonetheless, as the military combined with industry to form the military-industrial complex, burgeoning new automation techniques and material experimentation advanced the scale and speed of wartime manufacturing. Factories such as Chrysler shifted from making cars to producing fuselages, and Ford's Willow Run automotive plant made B-24 Liberator bombers. At Willow Run, 1.5 million parts were assembled to make each plane, with one bomber produced every 63 minutes. Scovil Manufacturing in Waterbury, Connecticut made numerous items for the war effort, from clothing to equipment. Most factories operated 24 hours a day in an intensity of production that left its mark on the capitalist production machine to this day.

As technology historian David F. Nobel (1945–2010) emphasized, wartime automation underscored,

> control over the workforce, technical enthusiasm for fascinating new devices, an ideological faith in mechanization as the embodiment of progress, a genuine interest in producing more goods more cheaply, concern about meeting military objectives — [though] not everyone viewed the trend as a blessing. Automation, it appeared, generated a serious problem — a shortage of skilled workers.[56]

There was less of an apparent need for tool and die workers, for example, and machinists who were trained in mechanics and skilled with their hands. However, during World War II, factory owners needed thousands of such workers, and initiated training programs to satisfy the demand.

In this Modern age the juxtaposition of work organization and time management systems and the mechanization of the continuous assembly line did not fully usurp the essentiality of the human in the industrial process. Continuous flow in handling materials through the production process was simply the natural law as applied to industry, calling for the least amount of action necessary for a given task.[57] Manufacturers' use of machines threatened to supplant human workers, but the machines of the early twentieth century, not yet computerized, still relied on human judgment and ingenuity. Two capitalist interests operating together

— the efficiency of humans and the power of technology — regulated and determined the workers and their productivity.

Historians of technology, such as Umberto Eco in *The Picture History of Inventions* (1963), Giedion in *Mechanization Takes Command* (1948), and Mumford in *Techniques and Civilization* (1934),[58] were enamored with the machine and its future potential through technology as a way of understanding history. But after Mumford resolved this machine worship, he pronounced that, "If we wish to have any clear notion about the machine we must think about its psychological as well as practical origins and appraise its aesthetic and ethical results. For a century, we have isolated the technical triumphs of the machine; we have bowed before the handiwork of the inventor and scientist."[59] He saw technology's negative impact on humanity and how the routinized operation of machines resulted in human debasement. The power of the machine is especially poignant in terms of its impact both on man and on urban culture, considering the new cultural relationships being forged within the factory space, itself a heterotopia with its own defined rules of conduct — both social and technological. Manufacturing technologies guided the design of factories and determined the flow of production, thus impacting the factory layout not only in terms of its internal organization, but also in its external connections to the urban fabric.

▲ A woman working on a production line during World War II

FACTORY CITY

AMID RAPID URBAN GROWTH and the modern sanitization of cities, the physical place reserved for factories varied according to urban land use directives and the ebbs and flows of local economies. Urban design rarely incorporated manufacturing and was mostly ignored by the Modernists. Industrial areas were not designed; most often, land was simply set aside for clusters of factories, or cities with zoning ordinances relegated them to specific blocks with minimal urban integration, leaving the relationships between factory buildings and the urban fabric unconsidered by designers or planners. However, such disregard for the industrial development was an ironic phenomenon. From their inception, cities developed at sources of *energy power* — natural resources such as water, seams of coal and clay, and forests — and *labor power* — human labor, intellect, knowledge, invention, and consumption. Commerce was one ingredient that led to the establishment of cities, and cities became prosperous because factories were located there. Cities, by virtue of their location and their density, encouraged distribution of goods to the consumer. They contained organized systems of dispersal, such as trade routes, marine ports, shipping networks, and marketplaces, and were defined by informal or laissez-faire systems of bartering.

In the late eighteenth century, cities also became known for specialized industries, having developed robust markets for specific goods. For example, London was known for textiles; Hamburg for shipbuilding; Boston for grain exports; Chicago for machinery and meat processing; and Philadelphia was referred to as the "workshop of the world" for machinery. Trade activated and accelerated the pace of modern life in the late nineteenth century, increasing commerce and exchange with vital energy and urgency. Cities aggregated according to labor and resources, including new infrastructure. Although urban populations and factories seemed to be at odds with one another because of the factories' pollution (especially in the cases of coal and chemical plants) and their intensive infrastructure needs, people nevertheless moved to cities in large numbers because of the employment opportunities there. Industries relied on urban populations both for labor and consumers, contributing to a synergistic flow. Density reinforced the potential for industrialization and entrepreneurship. In the early twentieth century, however, factories became sequestered from daily urban life with the rise of new zoning regulations, leading to their separation from the life of the city in what I call "process removal" — that is, the process by which things were made was no longer a visible part of urban life as power and resources were dispersed and the cycle of urban symbiosis dissipated to what it has become today — industry's move to the hinterlands.

By default, industry often determines the physical arrangement of urban land, contributing to new spatial organizational systems. In the nineteenth century, land use planning was *laissez-faire*, echoing the capitalist approach, and factories could be located anywhere, although the owners favored sites that supplied sources of energy and ease of access to transportation. In the early twentieth century, the physical organization of factories within cities accommodated working and living, through rationalized Modernist city plans and zoning regulations. These allowed either industrial or residential use, but not both intermixed. The place of manufacturing did not become a considered part of urban planning until it was seen as a nuisance, and as such, was relegated to the edges, leaving fewer and fewer factories in the city.

▲ Men in gas masks at a power plant, c. 1920

The constant evaluation and improvement of working conditions had long been part of utopian philosophies wherein the factory was seen to be a potential place for change, reform, and equity — from the time of French social reformer Henri de Saint-Simon (1760–1825), and Charles Fourier (1772–1836). The utopic intention of many early-nineteenth-century factory owners paradoxically resulted in dystopia for the workers, who were treated poorly and whose lives were destabilized. The exception to this inevitability was when a progressive owner commandeered the social order of the factory itself. Some of this resulted in paternalism — of factory owners overseeing the workers' lives, as in the model community of Bournville, England;

cooperatives; or in profit sharing, as in Robert Owen's (1771–1858), New Harmony, Scotland. Other examples of the impact of paternalism, like with Pullman, near Chicago, led to the rise of exploitation and worker alienation. But even the more socially minded owners were not as equitable as they imagined themselves to be. Workers were viewed to be as much a capital investment as a piece of equipment or a commodity, in terms of Marx's definition of labor-power. The industrialist's utopia required constant productivity, with the goal of non-stop economic growth, and supported the Enlightenment's emphasis on progress, profits, and productive people. As Kevin Hetherington points out, "Factories as heterotopia created new freedoms as well as new forms of control, and it was only over a considerable period of time that this deferral between control and freedom was contained to the benefit of the capitalist."[1] Workers themselves were integrated into that production-consumption cycle. After the workday they became consumers and partook in the system of commodities, buying that which they produced, supporting the manufacturer.[2]

The industrialists' vision for a utopic factory in a production/demand cycle fell short of their aspirations as the reality of factory conditions was dystopic. Owners' profit motives were in direct opposition to worker objectives, and that inconsistency became inherent to the system that continues today. Marxist philosopher Henri Lefebvre (1901–1991) notes that,

> Utopia is to be considered experimentally by studying its implications and consequences on the ground. These can surprise. What are and what would be the most successful places? How can they be discovered? According to which criteria? What are the times and rhythm of daily life which are inscribed and prescribed in these 'successful' spaces favorable to happiness?[3]

In order to envision a future, architects, planners, and industrialists would create designs that exceeded what was feasible, in hopes that even a portion of their idea might be implemented. Planners and civic leaders, however, often ignored the factory's importance in urban design. Industrial entrepreneurs and skilled workers relied on the same urban principle — that cities required industry and that industry required employees. But how to orchestrate the location of factories in the urban environment remained unsolved. By the early twentieth century, zoning restrictions on land use directed economic growth and the realities of urban real estate and high taxes tended to direct factory locations away from the urban core.

▶ Depiction of the "rustic economy" of cottage industries in Denis Diderot, *Encyclopédie*, 1751–1772
▶ Gerd Arntz with Otto Neurath infographic showing change from home to factory work in late-nineteenth-century England, 1939

SCALE SHIFTS

As spaces of production expanded from small to large, a comparison between understanding space in society and the space of the factory was implicated in the growth and culture of cities. Vast spaces were no longer just those of castles, cathedrals, and train stations, but of industry. In 1911, historian Hubert Bourgin (1874–1955) defined four types of spaces for making things, focusing on the growth of production that contributed to urbanization.[4] These same categories were absorbed into historian Fernand Braudel's (1902–1985) understanding of the development of commerce and trade, its impact on society, and the issues of spatial scale shifts. The first type of spatial configuration for making things beyond that of cottage industry, or independent workshops or spaces in the home, was the cluster of small workshops where artisans employed special tools, and were less a part of a capitalist organization; a second type was a series of workshops connected by process but spatially dispersed, in which the director of the work organized all materials, processing methods, and wages "culminating in the appearance of the finished product and its marketing."[5] These were seen in the Middle Ages through to the first industrial revolution of the eighteenth century. The third category was the concentrated and supervised form of manufacturing, or the "manufactory," with operations together in one area, or under one roof, such as water-operated forges, breweries, and glassworks. This also encompassed textile manufactories with a new division of labor for what was beginning to be defined as mass production. Bourgin's fourth category included factories (*fabriques*), consisting of larger-scale complexes, with machinery and energy sources, utilizing mechanized processing methods, impacting economies of scale both in terms of goods and space needed for production. These stages of urban development for factories did not necessarily replace each other from decade to decade. Instead, the efforts were cumulative and overlapped, as German economist Werner Sombart (1863–1941) noted: "there certainly was no natural and logical transition from the manufactory to the factory," and technologies were not obsolete but grew by accretion, which was evident to Jane Jacobs decades later.[6]

The jump from the scale of the cottage industry to full-scale manufactories was catalyzed by resources in the urban environment and entrepreneurs, as well as by numerous inventions that influenced spatial organization systems. As Bourgin and Braudel described, garment piecework began in homes and small workshops, known as "cottage" industries (though not always in cottages or in rural areas) and later expanded as workers banded together to form guilds.[7] But these pieceworkers had no system through which to raise their wages or to change their work

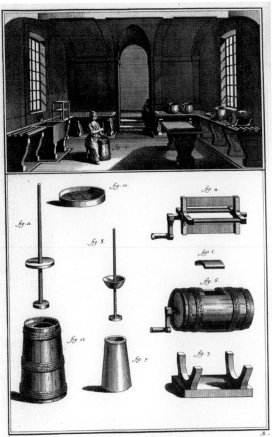

Economie Rustique.
Laiterie.

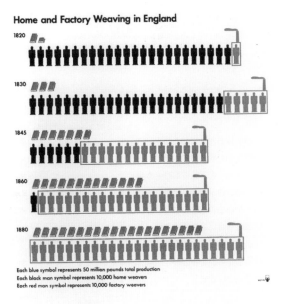

Home and Factory Weaving in England

Each blue symbol represents 50 million pounds total production
Each black man symbol represents 10,000 home weavers
Each red man symbol represents 10,000 factory weavers

conditions. On the other hand, as craftsmen or artisans they had a kind of independence, working at their own pace, with the time and liberty to complete other necessary work, such as household tasks and farming.

The small-scale cottage industries were revolutionized in European medieval cities to include more specific divisions of labor.[8] Residents of towns or villages began specializing in a specific trade. The idea of diversified specialists and skilled workers clustering together in one area or region naturally strengthened that economy. The agglomeration in economic geography relates *place* to the work produced. The skilled workers could share tools, information, and materials. For example, in the thirteenth century, silk weaving was focused in Lucca, Italy; linen in the mountains of fifteenth-century southern Germany; watchmaking in the Jura mountains of Switzerland; or woolen stockings made by fishermen's wives in the sixteenth century in Norfolk, England (in the off-season). Regions specialized in products according to natural resources available, trade networks, and the traditions of passing craftsmanship from one generation to the next.

A specific groundbreaking invention of the first industrial revolution was Englishman James Hargreaves' (1720–1788) spinning jenny that combined the ease of weaving with steam-powered mechanization. By the 1780s inventor Richard Arkwright organized weaver clusters near waterways in a new factory system outside the home.[9] The inclusion of the weavers in manufactories allowed for worker supervision and increased division of labor to specialty, resulting in greater output and higher quality products. Often they were grouped as guilds determined by skillsets, which provided high level work suitable for upper-class clients.

Another worker in early Medieval capitalism was the journeyman, who made goods (often with a guild master) and then traveled from place to place, delivering the products as he was also exposed to new skills. This option left fewer farm workers in the fields as the journeymen's mobility could react to the market demand for products.[10] As the economy grew in Europe in the late eighteenth century, waves of laborers moved from central locale to central locale depending on demand. As industries expanded in one place, the artisans moved to capture the demand for their skills. Textiles — a luxury good both for clothing and households — were at the forefront of the first industrial revolution, in which cities became the heart of the merchants' activity as they took over enterprises from the Medieval guild system. Until the larger manufactories and factories were established, Medieval Europe used what in German was called the *Verlagssystem,* or "putting out system," a handmade process. The merchant provided materials to the artisan, as well as an upfront payment that was then supplemented when the work was complete. Organized distribution of manufactured goods for sale in a network of marketplaces ultimately replaced the guild system.

ECONOMIC GEOGRAPHY AND CLUSTERED PRODUCTION

The strength inherent to clustered businesses was realized early on in this phase of capitalism, as Adam Smith observed; the formation of industrialized areas evolved from the specialization of work. He also acknowledged the specialization of locations between that of the towns that housed workers who made goods for farmers, and the rural production itself in relationship to regions that depended on

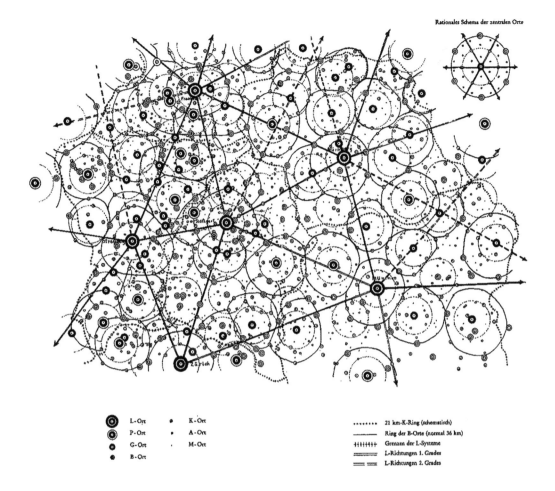

Rationales Schema der zentralen Orte

◉ L-Ort	● K-Ort	••••••••	21 km-K-Ring (schematisch)
◉ P-Ort	• A-Ort	——————	Ring der B-Orte (normal 36 km)
◉ G-Ort	· M-Ort	++++++++	Grenzen der L-Systeme
● B-Ort		═══════	L-Richtungen 1. Grades
		══ ══	L-Richtungen 2. Grades

each other for goods and services, thus enhancing production and even international trade, especially in areas of textiles and tools. Johann Heinrich von Thünen's (1783–1850) model of land use looked at trade-offs between land costs and transportation to the marketplace and the unplanned outcome of Smith's concept of the "invisible hand" that maximized income and rent.[11] He considered how agricultural growth occurred in concentric rings away from the marketplace, with each specialty filling a gap without a conscious planning effort, in a symbiotic relationship; each enterprise developed on an as-needed basis. But land value decreased further away from the urban core, thus often making more remote locations preferable for new companies, despite increased transportation-related costs. Von Thünen observed the loss of land's economic value away from central locations, but did not address why industries tended to concentrate in such locales.

▲ Illustration of Walter Christaller's Central Place Theory, 1933

In the 1890s, Alfred Marshall (1842–1924) completed another significant spatial-economic study, analyzing the rise of business clusters, regardless of industry. He determined that industrial enterprises, when grouped together, have the same economies of scale as the large monopolies by pulling together three variables — what he called his "magic trilogy." These were: *sharing* of like-skilled workers, or so-called labor market pooling; *matching* of specialized input and output with

localized technology externalities; and *learning,* or knowledge in a relationship that has economic and productive results.[12] Marshall noted that the clustering between companies was spontaneous, as in his citing of the concentration of cutlery industries in Sheffield, England. To him, "The mysteries of the trade become no myster[y]; but are as it were in the air, and children learn many of them unconsciously. . . . If one man starts a new idea, it is taken up by others and combined with suggestions of their own; and thus it becomes the source of further new ideas."[13]

This was the case with the auto industry, which used production techniques adapted from the bicycle and carriage industries. The raw materials supply chain, labor market pooling, and the ease of information exchange depended on the local market, but was rarely formalized by urban planners. Clustering later became a way of organizing urban industrial districts because it reduced costs for suppliers and manufacturers — shared knowledge and materials are most cost-effective, whether for a supplier of time cards or steel dyes for an industry, or a manufacturer looking for the best production methods. Business organizations also provide assistance to help at various stages of production development, beyond that of the basics of shared power and transit infrastructure. Marshall observed that clustered industries also become an economy of their own.

▲ Factory town of Premana, Italy
▶ Clusters of multistory factories in Eibar, Spain in the 1950s

Even more incongruous has been the minimal interdisciplinary discourse in visualizing the spatial economy, despite the research benefits seen in other fields. In the 1930s, German geographer Walter Christaller (1893–1969) developed a system called Central Place Theory, mapping cities and their regional marketplaces into hexagonal connected patterns to plot ways to reduce transportation distance along diagonals.[14] Following this work, August Lösch (1906–1945), in the 1940s, showed how combining the urban grid as a lattice of central places allowed for location of businesses in closer proximity to marketplaces in three directions — on the horizontal, vertical, and diagonal axes — thus emphasizing hexagonal groupings as nested sets in a hierarchy, indicating the most efficient business locations and also considering transportation.[15] Analyzing ways industries minimize expenses by locating close to energy resources and the consumer, economist Alfred Weber (1868–1958) recognized the continuous viability of cities as manufacturing centers. Theorists then merged concepts of the political economy, location, and growth with spatial arrangements and industrial development to form densely knit industrial districts.[16] Economists observed this phenomenon for decades, but never explained how and why the agglomeration occurs. This was because they didn't have the method to compare to the market structure — they were focused on the economics and growth of the companies rather than their spatial organization.

One architectural typology at a smaller, but dense, scale began in mountain valleys such as Premana, in Northern Italy, and Eibar, in Northern Spain, where metal workers (who to this day have small workshops) forge knives, scissors, sewing machines, bicycles, guns, and other metal goods in adjacent multistoried buildings near power sources. The factories were housed in the lower level with large casement windows, and the workers lived above. By settling among the mountains close to the power sources, the residents developed an expertise and industry around them without having to move to a larger city. They manufactured in place, where they and the materials were situated.

SPACES OF PRODUCTION

As the scale of places of making incrementally aggregated from smaller individualized workplaces in homes to manufactories, and then factories, supervision under one roof was made easier for the industrialists in the nineteenth century. For example, local brewers began in households and then expanded with larger and more centralized facilities as each home brewer distributed its beer through a wider network, then eventually consolidated into large-scale urban breweries. The drastic change from pieceworkers in smaller units to the lineworkers in factories also impacted land use, as manufacturers built expansive clusters of buildings around energy and transit sources. This growth in the late nineteenth century, especially after the 1897 recession, triggered a "second" industrial revolution of electrification, proliferation of steel, creation of communication and transportation networks, and as a result, a rise in larger-scale industries. These industries developed trade in world markets and, combined with increased production for export, influenced the development and expansion of factory building in cities. As cities became increasingly dense and as land became more valuable, urban factories were built taller to integrate equipment and infrastructure. Ports provided shipping access, railheads and yards made convenient loading and unloading, and trucking systems distributed goods from local to broader regions.

How these changes impacted space, and how space was produced as an organized entity, became a topic of French philosopher Henri Lefebvre, who emphasized that,

> We may therefore justifiably speak of a transitional period between the mode of production of things in space and the mode of production of space. The production of things was fostered by capitalism and controlled by the bourgeoisie and its political creation, the state. The production of space brought other conditions in its train, among them the withering-away of the private ownership of space, and, simultaneously, of the political state that dominates spaces.[17]

That the state is capitalist in nature must be taken as a given for the Western or "developed" world, even at the point of this second industrial revolution. While some countries were oriented towards socialism, it is the capitalist motive that created the factory system. In identifying this production of space, Lefebvre also focuses on the understanding of space as a marketable element of production. The factory — along with all of the non-physical elements of finance, operations, and logistics that go into the working space — results in a kind of hidden spatial organization that then has real value, and is a product itself: not simply is it the "production of things in the space," but it is itself a commodity. To see this, the spaces of production have to be revealed and understood in new ways.

The capitalists' production of space and the emergence of space as a commodity led to other consequences in terms of what was believed to be progress. "Progress" occurred hand in hand with pollution of the urban environment, flowing from production's catalytic momentum and a lack of understanding of consequences of human and environmental ecologies. As the "dark satanic mills"[18] spewing smoke from burning coal became burdensome to growing populations, industry negatively impacted health and well-being, despite declining death rates. Disease arose from overpopulated cities, a result of people living in close proximity to the factories, as well as inadequate sanitation systems.

On the other hand, as economist Eric Hobsbawm (1917–2012) noted, "The 'drama of *progress*,' is a metaphor. But for two kinds of people it was a literal reality. For millions of the poor, transported into a new world, often across frontiers and oceans, it meant a cataclysmic change of life. For the peoples of the world outside capitalism, who were not grasped and shaken by it, it meant the choice between a doomed resistance (in terms of their ancient traditions and ways) and a traumatic process of seizing the weapons of the west and turning them against the conquerors: of understanding and manipulating 'progress' themselves."[19] So the paradoxes were real: factories helped some, and were detrimental to the health of others. The need to sequester noise, nuisances, detritus, and pollution provided the impetus for modern city planning, however it also influenced the disinterest in mixed uses both of districts and individual buildings that today defines the multiplicity of the dynamic city.

Unlike the smaller dispersed factories of the earlier laissez-faire capitalism, large-scale nineteenth-century factories were often enclosed within walls, had a central entrance gate, and towers for surveillance to counter industrial espionage, watch worker productivity, and secure materials; as a result, they were basically cordoned off from the urban fabric. The vast spaces of the new walled factories, larger workforces, and new management tiers created and reinforced a hierarchy that was considered the road to "progress," with increased flexibility and efficiency. The separation of industrial sites also limited access to facilities from the general public.

The factories located outside of cities became a part of process removal, that is, removing all evidence of how and where something is made: the workers and what they do; the conditions of the workplace, the soot and coal, the refuse from products, the animal waste; the managers' directions and their organizational charts; the time clocks and cards; the lunch boxes and lockers; and the coming and going at the end of the day. Process removal eliminates from the view of the consumer both the difficulties and hardships of the commodity's production, and its distribution networks; rather, what arrives at the end of the line is all that is visible to the consumer. In the urban shops are the products, clean and tidy, organized and available to purchase. Sometimes the products had to be packaged on site, as with organic or perishable goods such as coffee or flour, but others were labeled in tins or burlap bags directly from the factory, without evidence of a production process. The removal of work allowed for increased sequestering or hiding of factories

▲ Women workers in the garment industry on strike in 1909 in New York City

spatially, thus concealing what goes on inside as well as distancing laborers from the rest of society — especially the upper classes.

But workers benefited from being in cities, as they could more frequently share common issues of the workplace in their dense proximity, contributing to their homogenization in terms of unity and strength. Especially powerful was the rise of worker solidarity after the well-known Triangle Shirtwaist Fire in New York in 1911, a result of the company owners' decision to lock the doors so that the women workers could not escape in the middle of a shift. When a fire broke out on the eighth floor (the factory occupied floors eight, nine, and ten), 149 trapped women were forced to leap to their deaths, or died in the fire. This incident changed workers' rights and building codes forever. Sympathy strikes in other garment-based industrial cities created a groundswell of support for the International Ladies' Garment Workers' Union (ILGWU) and the Amalgamated Clothing Workers of America. Other unions grew in stature and strength too, such as the Industrial Workers of the World (IWW, known as "Wobbies"). New labor-led agreements were put into place, establishing new workers' rights, contracts, and negotiating options. Regulations were designed to eliminate sweatshops and other unhealthy conditions and to establish fire safety procedures, but ultimately it was unions, protests, and organized strikes with their power through numbers that gave the workers a foothold in the capitalistic world. Similar patterns of resistance, followed by reform and experimentation, occur throughout the history of labor and manufacturing and in our current times, as we are now seeing in China.

The workers' organization and company management is part of the story of urban industrialization and directly relates to the factory as a space of production. As discussed earlier, manufacturing systems influenced factory layout and worker surveillance. The workplace became a space charged with regulation and determinism. Workplace safety, social reform in the factory, labor law, and equality are just some of the issues that have been unstable for labor. Workers, exploited in manufacturing booms, were often treated poorly and fought for better wages and work environments, citing their "rights," which they later obtained through collective action. Lefebvre noted the working class was "the only class capable of putting an end to a segregation aimed essentially against it. Only this class, as a class, can decisively contribute to the reconstitution of the center destroyed by segregation and redeployed in the menacing forms of 'centers of decision-making.' "[20] While reformers had good hearts, their efforts were diminished in light of the industrialists' need for progress and profit, and the result of this conflict was social and economic polarization.

THE PLACE OF THE FACTORY

From philosophers and theologians to industrialists and architects, numerous professions became interested in ameliorating the ailing city in the late nineteenth century. They hoped to improve the physical and social environment of the fractured urban landscape in what I identify in three modes of planning: utopian, pragmatic utopian, and technocratic. Two concepts are borrowed from categories

enumerated by architectural historian Leonardo Benevolo in his seminal book, the *Origins of Modern City Planning.* He described the utopian vision of factories in cities (often resulting in dystopias), and factories planned by technicians as a piecemeal response to urban problems without a comprehensive vision.[21] The need to find a place for the pollution and nuisance of industry, Benevolo believed, led to the formation of the urban planning profession. To these conceptual plans for the factory in the city, I am adding the idea of a "pragmatic utopia," stemming from the growth of company towns, which were founded on the idealism of the factory owner, yet following a profit motive, as Margaret Crawford discusses.[22] While the three directions for the configuration of industrial urbanism increasingly found a place for industry, they divided laborers from non-laborers and led to class exclusion compounded by divisive social issues.

UTOPIAN FACTORY CITY

The more humanistic industrialists who acted as utopian socialists, considered methods to transform the industrial dystopias of their time into a productive area where the means of organization, even with social considerations, met the industrial goals. French and British utopian and spiritual thinkers, such as Fourier, Jean-Baptiste André Godin (1817–1888), Robert Owen, and Henri de Saint-Simon influenced philosophers to start communities. For example, Jeremy Bentham (1748–1832) became a partner of Robert Owen, who developed spinning mills and a self-sufficient community in New Lanark, Scotland in 1799. Owen's early socialist ideas resulted in an ideal community with buildings (including dormitories and communal kitchens) and open spaces deployed to engender social harmony, to value labor, and to provide better wages, but which neglected "authority and individual freedom" because of the total organization of a worker's daily life through the spatial divisions of the town.[23] Owen began what he called the Institution for

▲ Ilustration of Robert Owen's New Lanark, Scotland, 1801

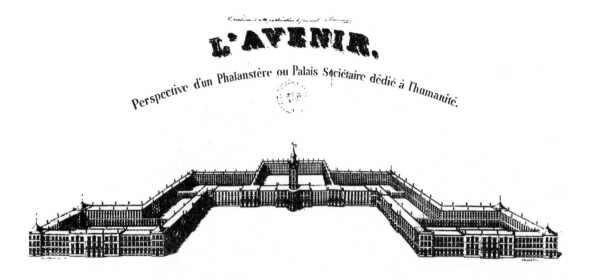

the Formation of Character. Here, "for the first time a philanthropic enterprise was taking the form of a permanent education organization and, with this as a starting point, was beginning to affect the lives of the entire community, complementing work in the factory with study and leisure, and allotting suitable accommodation, and time, to each activity."[24] New Lanark became a model community in which Owen practiced his principles of co-operation. Prior to state-led worker reform, he was attentive to labor issues and the formation of unions, and believed that agriculture and industry should be mixed, not separate (as it was starting to become), moving towards his development of a self-sufficient town. He set aside a specific amount of land and designed the layout with a town square in the shape of a parallelogram, and placed apartments and warehouses in buildings on the perimeter and institutional buildings in the center. In 1825, Owen moved to Indiana to start the community of New Harmony, but upon its failure he returned to England and became active in labor reform and promoting new ideas for industrial development, including shortening the workday.

French philosopher Henri de Saint-Simon focused on the theme of the proletariat overthrowing the ruling classes in his treatises and books, including *L'Industrie* (1817) and *L'Organisateur* (1819), which inspired Charles Fourier, who in turn inspired Marx. Fourier, originally a shopkeeper, published a treatise in 1808 that proposed harmonizing society by fostering reform through the transformation of the built environment.[25] He developed utopian socialist town plans in detail, imagining a kind of Garden City with streets laid out in concentric circles so that commercial and administrative spaces were focused in the center, and the industrial and agricultural zones beyond it, with specific building relationship rules. He outlined stages of civilization, which included a final collective goal where people would live in what he called "phalansteries." This universal building, institutional in character, would house 1,620 people and combined urban and rural features, including communal and educational facilities. It was intended to replace the city

▲ Charles Fourier, Phalansterie, engraving, 1850s

with its own civic life. It took on the appearance of a palace; one wing contained the industrial workshops and workers, and also included children, whose noisiness would be absorbed by the working machines' noise. Fourier's ideas failed to take physical root, except in their influence on open-minded American transcendentalists who founded the short-lived Brook Farm community in the 1840s in Roxbury, Connecticut, which had its own phalanstery, and a joint-stock company communal settlement that became the home of social reformer George Ripley (1802–1880) and writer Nathaniel Hawthorne (1804–1864).

The utopian thinkers believed that they could solve social problems through architecture, and could improve men simply by housing them in a phalanstery or a co-operative parallelogram. French industrialist Godin also organized his iron foundry around the idea of the phalanstery in his Familistére de Guise of 1859. He planned a common workplace, but independent living areas; a concept that later influenced Le Corbusier's Unité D'Habitation.[26] In 1880, Godin converted Guise into cooperatives, which the workers managed. Russian philosopher Peter Kropotkin (1882–1921) in his *Fields, Factories and Workshops* of 1898 focused on other prospects for self-sufficiency in rural life that were more anarchistic, combining industrial work and agricultural work through cooperatives and worker ownership instead of being organized in top-down bureaucracies. Other utopian socialists, such as anti-monarchist Étienne Cabet (1788–1856), also discussed the layouts of cities and a shop-based economy for another type of ideal community called Icaria that he described in his *Voyage-en-Icarie*, and created in 1849 in Nauvoo, Illinois. The settlers disliked Cabet's system, and the group split into different communities. None of these aforementioned social experiments succeeded, remaining as utopian ideals. However, the reality of the era's industrial situation (one of large-scale factories and capitalist hegemony) did not deter the experimental vision of these reformers, as they turned to more practical matters of wages and workday length.

Many of the social reformers strove to improve workers' welfare not only through physical improvements, but also by relating to how the day was regulated. Factories of the first industrial revolution had ten-to-sixteen-hour workdays, a six-day workweek, and little social engagement. In England, some industrialists realized the disadvantages of overwork. The Factory Acts, which began in 1802, affected a series of changes over the following decades by helping to limit the working day to ten hours per day for women and children employed in textile mills. New stipulations required factories to be ventilated, and children to be educated, supplied with clothing, and to sleep no more than two to a bed. Owen himself initiated a movement advocating for an eight-hour workday, better pay and housing, and recreation time — thus, the slogan, "Eight hours labour, eight hours recreation, eight hours rest." The reformers who pushed these laws recognized that it was nearly impossible to regulate the factory owners due to a lack of inspectors. By 1856, in England, all factories were required to follow the same ten-hour workday. The minimum age of a child worker continued to rise from the alarmingly young age of nine, reaching 12 years by 1901, and daily work hours were reduced to eight. The reform of time and space for the worker began to coalesce both in the utopian imagination and in social action, issues that inform the design and operation of factories to this day.

Cité Industrielle

Fourier also influenced the visionary scheme of
Tony Garnier (1869–1948) for his Cité Industrielle.
Garnier promoted a version of the ideal Modern
city, while incorporating industry. His plan was one
of the few that carved out a place for work with
any detail. After finishing his architectural studies at the École des Beaux-Arts in Paris, Garnier
designed the Cité Industrielle, a plan for a socialist
community that he published in 1917, noting that,
"Since most new towns built from now on will
focus on industry, this example is conceived as a
general model."[27] Basing his concepts on his hometown of Lyon, he separated the town's functions:
industry was located near the train station and
adjacent to the historic town center, with a commercial center and concrete housing on gridded
streets. Lyon was already an industrial hub — with
growing automotive industries as well as new technologies — and so Garnier included "workshops
for outfitting automobile bodies. . .vehicle testing
tracks and farmsteads for food production, silk-
worm production, spinning-mills etc."[28] He drew
detailed images of a metallurgic factory, mines, a
silk mill, a dam, and a hydroelectric power plant.

The Italian Futurists shared Garnier's enthu-
siasm for electricity. Marinetti, in his *Manifesto of
Geometrical and Mechanical Splendor,* in reference
to his compatriot Antonio Sant'Elia's (1888–1916)
drawings of an electric power plant, which was
comparable to Garnier's, exclaimed that, "There
is nothing in the world so beautiful as a great
generating station, humming with power, holding back the hydraulic pressures of a
mountain chain, storing the power for a wide landscape, integrated by control panels gleaming with switches and communicators."[29] Yet the factory and the machine
were separated from the city, as a spectacle to view. Garnier imagined separate
land uses and building functions providing hygienic improvements, drainage and
sewage, and ample space for roadways. His scheme also brought into play issues of
decentralization and regionalism in France, as discussed by philosopher Pierre-
Joseph Proudhon (1809–1865), "who emphasized the autonomy of industry and
agriculture from one another."[30] In this regionalist movement, the urban centers
encouraged local industries, so that "raw materials come from nearby mines, and
energy is drawn from the local stream." As a socialist but not an industrialist, he
also considered methods for sharing property obtained by the government, affecting key food industries such as bakeries and dairies. "He organized the industrial
character of his ideal city because he felt that industry satisfied a natural or basic

need to work." Garnier envisioned a professional industrial school that would "offer two specialized courses devoted to the study of the separate production phases and procedures," similar to that of Fourier's utopia.[31] With detailed drawings of his imagined Cité, Garnier was able to receive commissions in Lyon including abattoirs, a hospital, a stadium, schools, and a bourse. His visionary, expressive ideas paralleled Sant'Elia's manifesto: "We must invent and reconstruct the futurist city on the model of an immense, bustling shipyard, every part agile, mobile and dynamic; the futurist house must become a kind of gigantic machine."[32]

Utopian visions for improving the burgeoning industrial towns and cities were most dramatically expressed by artists and writers who could elaborate fictional futuristic societies. Edward Bellamy's (1850–1898) book, *Looking Backward 2000–1887* (1888), was a critical response to capitalism in a Marxist perspective. His vision nationalized companies with workers as shareholders and was influenced by Charles Fourier's philosophy. Thea Van Harbou (1888–1954), the German author of the 1919 novel *Metropolis* that Fritz Lang adapted to a film in 1927, depicted a dystopia that harshly juxtaposed the capitalist industrialist and the alienated worker: the worker operates machines in the subterranean worker city and is led to rioting by a robot created by the factory's scientist-engineer. "Death to the machines" they shout as they riot, breaking down the gates, and storming the factory. The factory owner's righteous intent to provide workers a place in society was ruptured and fragmented through dissatisfaction and unrest.

PRAGMATIC UTOPIAS

Utopian schemes are by definition unbuildable. Those workers' communities that were realized can instead be called "pragmatic utopias." Rather than pure utopian schemes, they have a layer of practicality and buildability: they are not just schemes of the imagination, but have social ambitions that could be met. Pragmatic utopias stem from a utopian vision in that they were beyond expectations of social norms, but their founders conceived of more realistic plans (both socially and physically) primarily because of the profit motive, in contrast to the experimental communities initiated around farsighted and benevolent ideologies. The first construction efforts, after the factory complexes themselves, would have been housing as owners realized the benefit of establishing local housing development for workers that their management could supervise, as a form of paternalism. These complexes would include social buildings and retail, where workers could use an internal payment token that was part of their salary. As Margaret Crawford observed, company towns proliferated, providing industrial organization that laid the groundwork for welfare reform and better working conditions.[33] But, as workers came to realize that they were living under a magnifying glass, they began to organize protests for specific rights.

As early as 1776, architect Claude Nicolas Ledoux (1736–1806) laid out the Royal Salt Works in Arc-et-Senans, France, designing what he believed was to be a temple and a theater for the workers in an Enlightenment–defined worker community. The Works was a series of masonry structures arrayed in a rounded arc with worker housing provided on one edge of the complex. Doric columns and rusticated pilasters elevated it to "high architecture." Often using Diderot's *Éncyclopedia*

for a model layout, Ledoux situated his work under the fold of a traditional industrial aèsthetic.[34] But, as architectural historian Anthony Vidler recognizes, "Ledoux
encountered the resistance not only of the economically minded, but also of
socially conventional patrons."[35] The semicircular arc-shaped plan has been likened
to the "Panopticon" defined by Bentham as a building form allowing for continuous
surveillance. But beyond that supervisional instrument, Ledoux's plans and designs
adopted a theatrical form. The workers, like actors, participated in the production
of goods that were dramatized in the play of production, with audience approval
similar to that of the consumer.[36] At an early moment in industrialization, Ledoux's
design emphasizes the spectacle of making things by patronizing the salt workers
and romanticizing their activity.

Both the theater and the Panopticon became metaphors for the organization of
manufacturing. In his discussion on discipline Foucault wrote,

> Bentham's Panopticon is the architectural figure of this composition:
> We know the principle on which it was based: at the periphery, an
> annular building; at the centre, a tower; this tower is pierced with wide
> windows that open onto the inner side of the ring; the periphery building
> is divided into cells, each of which extends the whole width of the
> building. . . . They are like so many cages, so many small theatres, in
> which each actor is alone, perfectly individualized and constantly visible.
> The panoptic mechanism arranges spatial unities that make it possible
> to see constantly and to recognize immediately.[37]

The form of the building, or town, regulated observation, keeping the workers
constantly on alert. Other communal typologies such as Sampson Kempthorne's
(1809–1873) mid-nineteenth-century paupers' workhouses, in England, were similar
to a panopticon in their all-visible form, organized by either hexagonal or cross-
shaped layouts. Kempthorne's walled work-fortress was composed of four-story
buildings radiating from the center, and the poor could freely come and go from the
workhouse; in exchange for labor, they were provided with food and shelter, not
unlike later labor camps, or prison factories.[38] Embedded within this panopticon
was a heterotopia in terms of the social institution and its separation from society.

But what pragmatically developed from the company town soon became a
false freedom with top-down ideals. In 1854, Aaron Dennison (1812–1895) built
a watch factory on the Charles River outside of Boston with large windows for
air circulation, for worker comfort and to keep the space dust-free. However, he
went bankrupt and the company which was restarted as Appleton Tracy & Co., in
1885 became the American Waltham Watch Company. Using the aforementioned
American System of Manufactures, 2,500 men and women performed 3,746
mechanical operations — from the making of a stem-winder to assembling the 150
separate pieces, boring a hole with a machine needle, polishing, or making refined
adjustments — to produce 360,000 watches per year.

Journalist and liberal thinker John Swinton (1829–1901), who had been an editor of *The New York Times* and *The New York Sun*, and who knew Peter Kropotkin,
Karl Marx, and Emma Goldman, felt that the Waltham Watch Company instilled

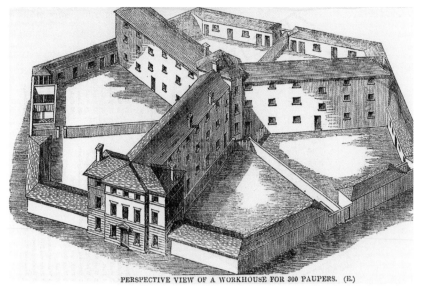

PERSPECTIVE VIEW OF A WORKHOUSE FOR 300 PAUPERS. (E.)

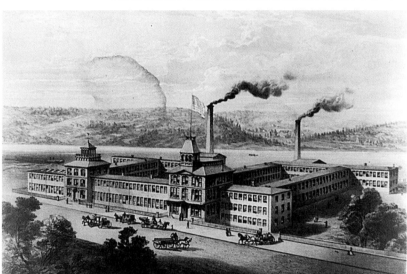

WORKS OF THE AMERICAN WATCH COMPANY,
WALTHAM, MASS.

hope for the future of the working class.[39] They had union organizing, generous health benefits, a mutual aid society and profit sharing, and a hospital; they also owned their own homes, contributing to what Swinton viewed as crucial elements for worker contentment.

In contrast, Lowell, Massachusetts started out in the 1820s as an idealistic working community with boarding houses for young women whose lives were regimented by the ringing of communal bells at the Merrimack Textile Corporation's mill. As author Lewis Mumford noted in terms of the organization of early monasteries, the early mechanization of our lives by the clock and bell signifies recognition of the division of time as "not merely a means of keeping track of hours, but of synchronizing the actions of men."[40] First based in Waltham, the Merrimack Textile Corporation was founded by Francis Lowell (1775–1817) along the Merrimack River

△ Drawing of a workhouse for 300 paupers, similar to Kempthorn, 1836
△ American Watch Company, Waltham, Massachusetts, early 1800s

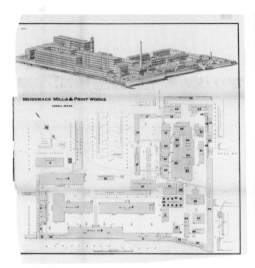

in 1823 and was organized by an engineer, Kirk Boott (1790–1837). While there was no organized town plan, the sequence of buildings followed the newly organized production process dictated by the large-scale spinning and power looms within a complex of multistoried brick buildings. "The spatial order of Lowell's mill settlements mirrored precisely the division of labor in the factory"[41] with each housing unit as a hierarchical expression of order by class, for executives, skilled workers, unskilled operatives, and day laborers. Other types of buildings included inns and commercial spaces. This textile society of working girls was another Foucauldian heterotopia — closed and removed from society with its own social and physical order, parallel to the everyday, and eventually resulting in negative consequences for women — a dystopia.

The paternalistically regulated dormitory living of the "factory girls," who came from the countryside and worked until they were of marrying age, has a parallel in today's Chinese factory girls, who migrate from the countryside and live in dormitories, also struggling to make ends meet. Women workers in Lowell stayed just four years on average; within that time, not only did they work to support their families but they also organized leisure activities, including lectures and concerts, and they founded a literary journal called the *Lowell Offering.* But the capitalists' utopian vision did not last. The women organized a strike in 1836 to demand schools and a shorter workday. When steam power became widely available, their water-based mills could no longer compete, so the owners cut wages and housing benefits and the company declined. As a result, working girls had to find their own housing, and the community became a badly managed, failing company town.

At the Pullman Palace Car Company, to ward off potential worker strikes, George Pullman (1831–1897) built his rail-car company town outside of Chicago and provided welfare and social services to dominate every aspect of workers' lives based on the precedent of company towns like Lowell. It became a heterotopia in its organization: goods and housing were part of the workers' compensation packages, but they could not spend money elsewhere; they were paid in vouchers, and rent was deducted from their paychecks. He also enforced a curfew and a ban

▲ Merrimack Mills and Print Works, Lowell, Massachusetts. New York: Barlow's Insurance Surveys, No. 5404. September 11, 1878 (date surveyed)
▲ "Lowell Girl," Lowell, Massachusetts, 1840
▶ Pullman company town, near Chicago, 1880
▶ Factory housing, Krupp, Germany, 1880s

on smoking and drinking. The town itself was perhaps one of the most consciously designed of any of the nineteenth century in general. The urban plan featured red brick Queen Anne-style public structures including an arcade, a market, a school, and a church in a gridded plan. Designed by architect Solon S. Beman (1853–1914) and landscape architect Nathan F. Barrett (1845–1919), who had worked with Pullman on his personal properties, Pullman, Illinois was praised as a model company town.[42] However, in 1893 the workers protested, fed up with the restrictions, and the general observation of their lives. They had been inspired by numerous strikes occurring around the country at this time. The American Railway Union, with a membership of 150,000, joined in, and together they boycotted Pullman by not switching the tracks for trains to pass. In 1894, 125,000 men went on strike for higher wages. Subsequently, the Chicago rail networks were shut down when an additional 260,000 railroad workers joined the strike. The Federal government, called upon to break the strike, sent troops, prompting violence and sympathy strikes across the country. The strike action was called off because of the American Federation of Labor's (AFL) policy of nonviolence. These types of struggles were complex instances of class warfare and seized the nation's attention. The workers' growing distress reinforced their solidarity and their increasing awareness of the injustice of company towns, foregrounding the dystopic aspects of their life, and their suppression.[43]

Many company owners would, at a minimum, build housing for their workers. This was true for the Sulzer's turbine factories in Winterthur, Switzerland, and the Steinway piano company in Astoria, New York. The separate workers' housing areas, however, divided the city spatially and socially, preventing workers from coming into contact with the upper classes. Some worker housing estates, like those of the Menier chocolate factory in Noisiel-sur-Marne, France — whose houses were exhibited at the Universal Exhibition in Paris in 1867 — were more like feudal towns, with the workers' houses domi-nated by the factory looming in the landscape just as previously farms were dominated by the castle. The accommodations built in the textile center Mulhouse, France by the Societé Mulhousienne Cité Ouvriéres were considered "model houses," with ample room and gardens for workers and as many as one thou-sand houses built over a thirty-year period beginning in 1859. Other notable nineteenth-century examples include housing for workers at the Bayer pharmaceu-tical plant in Leverkusen, Germany; for the miners employed by Le Creuset in France; for employees of Peugeot in Sochaux, France; and for workers at the steel giant Krupp, in Essen, Germany. By 1902, Krupp had become "A great city with its own streets, its own police force, fire department, and traffic laws. There are 150 kilometers of rail, 60 different fac-tory buildings, 8,500 machine tools, seven electrical stations, 140 kilometers of underground cable and

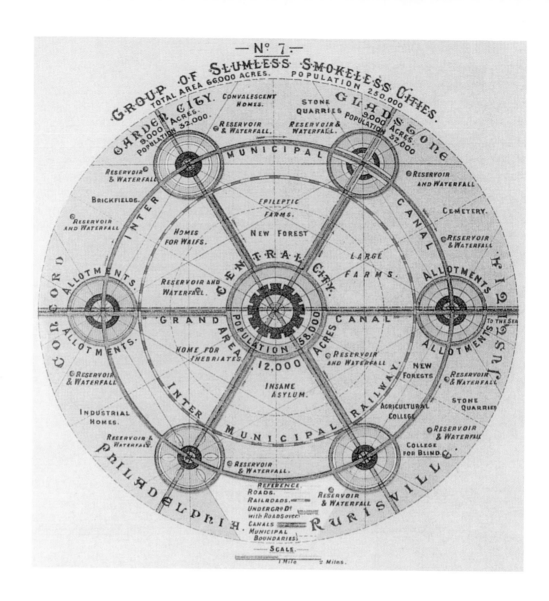

46 overhead."[44] Many of these arrangements were improvements to slum living in densely populated cities, but still segregated the working classes.

If a company on a dense urban site could not provide housing, it often incorporated amenities inside the factory, both as a paternalistic gesture, and as a way to keep the workers close at hand throughout the day. Stetson Hats in Philadelphia was one such company, the "largest and most complete felt hat factory in the world, solely fine soft and stiff felt hats. The plant covered about ten acres of floor space and employed 2,200 people."[45] Illustrated in Stetson's promotional booklet on the human element of their workplace, were the dining room, a meeting room capable of holding the entire staff, a barbershop, a reading room, a health clinic, and athletic grounds. Sinclair Lewis' description of the Chicago Harvester Trust factories showed how they even "were the sort of place to which philanthropists and reformers pointed with pride. It had some thought for its employees; its workshops

were big and roomy, it provided a restaurant where the
workmen could buy good food at cost, and it even had
a reading-room, and decent places where its girl hands
could rest."[46] Van Nelle included playing fields and
cafeterias, all with the workers' health in consideration.
In these factories the workers were provided for — they
had jobs, and amenities, but they were not free within
the confines of the workplace. Perhaps it was relative, but
they were nonetheless a part of a capitalist hegemony, to
which the spatial organization adapted.

Garden Cities

Another planning concept, to ameliorate the industrialized city, pragmatic in its organization and utopic in its
goals, was the Garden City, based on Fourier's philosophy.
British government clerk Ebenezer Howard (1850–1928)
described his concept in elaborate detail in the 1898
book *Garden Cities of To-morrow*, which he promoted to
industrialists and their architects. Scottish biologist-geog-
rapher Patrick Geddes (1854–1932) influenced Howard's
ideas in combining comprehensive physical planning
with economic and social improvements, new to the
time.[47] Howard envisioned a new town in the countryside
surrounded by a greenbelt of open land to be shared in
common. He proposed a central area for commerce and
living and set the factories away from the residential
neighborhoods. In the industrial sections of the Garden
City, Howard envisioned workers with "profit sharing and
no sweated labor" and placed industry on the perimeter
of the circular ring roads. In his plan, the "Smokeless
Slumless City," the wind blew factory smoke away from
the residential area, keeping it clean. The first communities, based on his ideas, were established by companies
who could purchase land and promote a specific design
concept, such as Port Sunlight for Lever and Bournville
for Cadbury in 1893. Quakers such as Cadbury, and Henry

G. N. R. Letchworth from the Air.

Isaac Rowntree (1839–1883), founded chocolate compa-
nies as an alternative to alcohol, chocolate being primarily a beverage when it was
first introduced. They provided philanthropic, albeit patronizing assistance, to their
workers. Barry Parker (1867–1947) and Raymond Unwin's (1863–1940) designs for
the Garden Cities at Letchworth (1903) and Welwyn (1920) in England were all
founded on improved quality of life and living in a presumed harmony with nature.

In Welwyn, for example, the factories to the east of the railroad included
Shredded Wheat and Dawneys steelworks and later Cresta Silks, as well as
companies that made, and still make, candies, corsets, books, false eyelashes,
and plastics. On the one hand, the factory's removal from the urban core relieved

congestion but, on the other, it placed the workers in isolation. The trend towards moving factories out of sight returned the proletariat worker to his or her past agricultural life similar to Kropotkin, but was based on an unwarranted romanticism. The factory in the city, however, could provide the worker with opportunities for advancement, and a more vital urban interactivity, with chance encounters, and community energy, which could turn to their social advantage.

TECHNOCRATIC PLANNING — PROCESS REMOVAL

As factories were removed from urban centers, urban planning became considered reactive rather than proactive. It was about the undesirable, rather than ideas for the future. Planning for manufacturing was a form of process removal, where making became hidden from the city residents and the ramifications of that trend are felt today. Planning was a surgical process in the urban context, removing the unwanted nuisances, including marginalized communities, rather then incorporating them in an inclusive way.

Marx's and Friedrich Engels' (1820–1895) oft-quoted visits to Manchester, England in 1845 from *The Condition of the Working Class in England* and Charles Dickens' (1812–1870) descriptions of London in his literary works all emphasize the overcrowding, darkness, foul air, and dampness of the living spaces of the working poor, which were adjacent to the spaces of production. Often as shantytowns, or substandard instant housing, cities grew beyond their walled edges to accommodate the growing poor at the periphery, similar to Kowloon Walled City in China. Manchester's population grew from 12,000 to 400,000 residents from 1760 to 1850. Or, as in Vienna, a buffer zone of new institutions divided rich from poor and led to the construction of the Ringstrasse. "For the city's planners the poor were a public danger, their potentially riotous concentrations to be broken up by avenues and boulevards which would drive the inhabitants of the crowded popular quarters they replaced into some unspecified, but presumably more sanitary and less perilous locations."[48] In other words, city planning was just as much about systematizing the behavior of the masses as it was about sanitation and hygiene. Cities were divided between the working class living in the speculative houses adjacent to the factories and the wealthy residing in new suburban homes. As the wealthy moved out of cities, urban residents became increasingly reformist, dreaming of new modes of living.

In contrast to the more theoretical utopian visions — legislation for new infrastructure systems such as sanitation, water, and parks — which were seen as necessities for healthy living, paved the way for other urban improvements such as roadways and ports, cutting through neighborhoods, and pushing aside the poor. The development of Baron Haussmann's (1809–1891) boulevards in Paris, or *grandes traveaux*, between 1850 and 1870, surgically removed slums and improved roadways and plumbing, as a panacea for the urban degradation that came with conditions of density.[49] Haussmann's methods, along with Napoleon III's (1808–1873) leadership, followed that of railroad engineers and bureaucrats who moved residents from one place to the next in order to demolish blighted neighborhoods and to dominate urban space. The boulevards, which later became much loved by the upper classes, were a spectacle of engineering and urban organization, but for the working classes, they were a source of upheaval. But the discontent of the dis-affected from what became called "eminent domain" was as much an antithesis of the new urban restructuring as what Paris officials were hoping to halt: the upris-ing of the working masses, as had occurred in 1848 during the June Days Uprising. Removed from public spaces, citizens could not gather in broad open roads, and thus were denied their right to the city. The restrictions increased pressure on the workers' needs, raising them to the boiling point of the Paris Commune and the overtaking of the bourgeoisie in the revolution of 1871.

Zones of Industry

Zoning, or the dividing up of land by specific uses, dictated where to place industry and undesired or noxious uses. Beginning in the early twentieth century, it was a way to also control land value and segregate populations, while couching these manipulations as simple issues of land use. In the examples of London, New York, Los Angeles, Chicago, and Dresden, the use of zoning to separate both industry and classes is evident. London, which was the center of focus from the first, and into the second, industrial revolution, declined in its industrial production through World War I, relying increasingly on imports to feed heavy industries. In 1900, forty percent of the jobs were in manufacturing, both in the center of the city and along its bustling docks. In the late nineteenth century, the London Building Acts limited industries that were "dangerous and noxious," or those with flammable substances, so that these buildings had to be fifteen meters from other buildings and twelve meters from public ways, thereby restricting where industry could go. The Factory and Workshops Act of 1907 not only regulated the workers' rights, but also the spaces available for the workers. In 1909, the Housing and Town Planning Act provided a legal basis for the planning of new districts and the clearing of slums, as well as new building standards. While industry was designated as sepa-rate B1 and B2 zones, planning permissions were required for use. The 1940 Barlow Commission gave factory owners incentives for the distribution of industry to areas of economic inequality, resulting in the 1945 Distribution of Industry Act, which helped promote economic growth outside the city following World War II.

In the United States, technocratic urban planning became the crux of system-ized land use regulation through zoning laws. The local laws controlled the divi-sion of land into areas by their use, permitted by national government. New York City was already dividing its different functions into zones according to the 1916 Zoning Resolution, becoming the first American city to establish a comprehensive zoning ordinance regulating land area and building heights. New York City's codes served as a model for "A Standard State Zoning Enabling Act," a 1922 federal law allowing each local area the power to regulate land use. For example, in California, land use laws prohibited Chinese laundries from being located next to residential areas because they were considered "undesirable" uses.[50]

The situation was similar in Los Angeles. In order to maintain the status quo of the middle classes in homogeneous residential developments, the City Council in 1908 used what was called "districting" to maintain property values and exclude trades or business from residential areas, which hampered industrial development. But residential areas could expand onto industrial areas, which

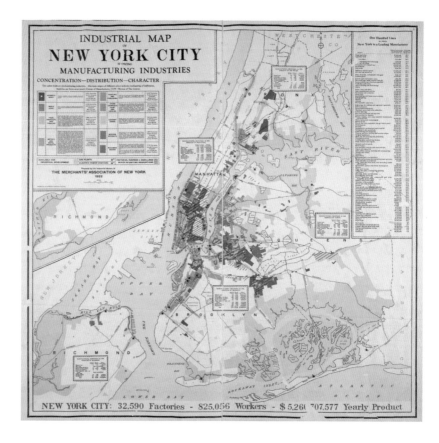

NEW YORK CITY: 32,590 Factories · 825,056 Workers · $5,260,707,577 Yearly Product

▲ Industrial location map of
New York City, showing wide
distribution of manufacturing,
1900–1916

pushed industry further out of the urban core and contributed to a patchwork of
industrial areas; even with an active rail and port, highways transformed transit
and thus industrial location. In Los Angeles, the guise of health and safety, as
well as protection of land value, was used to segregate uses before the adoption of
zoning there in 1921.

Many German city administrations established zoning regulations arising out
of nuisance laws, resulting in the marginalization of working-class populations.
As early as the late nineteenth century, new rules were adopted in cities such as
Leipzig and Dresden, where industrial areas were placed in separate sections of
the city. This type of zoning was invented to protect homeowners who wanted to
safeguard the value of their homes over the long term. The only reason for industry
to be desired in an area was for its taxable property value. Wealthy residents
considered the worker population undesirable and objected to workers coming and
going throughout their neighborhoods — workers were considered an unstable
population, in contrast to homeowners. Zoning situated the lower classes alongside
industry and counted the workers themselves as nuisances too. These unskilled
laborers and artisans were pushed to the edges of the city and co-opted to work
for the wealthy. As the wealthy realized the advantages to city living, they rallied
for the division of the city into economic zones. As Lefebvre recognized about
today's conditions, "the very existence of the working class negates and contests
the strategy of segregation directed against it. As it did a century ago, although
under new conditions, it unifies the interests of society as a whole (going beyond

the immediate and superficial), and especially the interests of those who *inhabit*."[51] He emphasized that the wealthy didn't inhabit a city in the same way as the poor because the wealthy had enough income to come and go as they pleased. These separate zones segregated places of work from places of meeting and intellectual activity, so that the working class, the intellectuals, and the middle class led separate lives; the poor were marginalized, with little opportunity to interact. The working class stayed with the working class — an arrangement purposefully designed by the bureaucrats who made land use policy, in order to limit the working class' potential and social welfare.

In addition, the issue of pollution as a rationale for sequestering industry was often unjustified. One common misconception was that foul air, or pollution, would stay in one zone above an individual factory, instead of moving throughout an area (although there are in fact stagnant places and often air inversions). Giving rise to such opinions as early as 1929, some, such as urban planner R. D. MacLauren, argued rightly that, as pollution is impossible to contain within a physical boundary, there should be methods, such as fees and other regulations, to control the noxious odors, airborne dust, and fumes of industrial pollution.[52] He pointed out that "the elimination of every form of waste was one of the objectives of scientific management and the idea that it was an advantage for one industry to be maintained as a public nuisance had no scientific basis in fact."[53] The issue constituted a battle between land use, property rights, aesthetics, and value. While the purpose of planning was to conserve and restore impaired land values, to supervise the use and occupation of land, to regulate the city's tenements, office buildings, circulation means, distribution of public spaces and private land, and to promote the productivity and efficiency of its market activities, planning also resulted in unequal segregation of all kinds.[54]

Planned Districts

As the factory expanded from its own boundaries and walls to that of the economic and material networks that supported manufacturing's needs, it became grounded in new infrastructure as well as financial assemblages, forming hubs in cities such as Montreal, Toronto, Detroit, Chicago, Berlin, and New York, among others. Patterns of development emerged and converged from the small-scale manufacturers along the waterfronts, to large open spaces where firms erected massive structures, as well as multistory lofts in downtown areas. As industries were encouraged to migrate to urban edges along rail and road networks, and away from central ports and harbors, the industrial landscape morphed into a swath of networked industries in clusters of similar and related types, agglomerating to optimize their use of resources. These trends were those cited by von Thünen's studies of economic geography. In Montreal, "The closely bunched set of suppliers, subcontractors, customers, and producers serviced in the city center provided advantages for firms seeking strong inter-firm linkages. Proximity to a large labor pool and transportation terminals contributed further to the cumulative attractions of the central districts."[55] Montreal's manufacturing districts in the late nineteenth century included over 1,300 firms along the traditional transit routes, and stretched from the St. Lawrence River and the Lachine Canal, closely resembling the industrial layout of other cities like Toronto or Boston. Clusters of factories that specialized in printing, baking, and the manufacture of machines, garments, and carriages, among others, supported each other.[56] Molson's brewery was sited on the eastern edge of the city, along the river to Sainte-Marie, with other firms, such as Canadian Rubber, comprising an industrial suburb. To the west, new factories developed along the canal, beginning in 1856 with those of Redpath Sugar, and over time, other factories such as metal and iron works. As with many cities, there was a variety of movement and a diversity of scale in the migration of firms to the urban edge, as existing loft spaces were filled with smaller industries as they are again today.[57]

Simultaneously, factories scaled up as their machines and production increased, and they consolidated enterprises. New multistory loft spaces of the 1920s provided light manufacturing space adjacent to Old Montreal's center in the Outer Core with the Jacobs, Blumenthal, Kellert, and Wilder Buildings on St. Catherine and Bleury Streets. Some of the buildings were rented to multiple companies, and others to single firms such as the Benson & Hedges tobacco company, in 1929. The National Breweries plant on St. Maurice Street grew to over 6,000 square meters while the port was still strong. It expanded its warehousing potentials, despite being driven by financial incentives to remain in the urban core. Companies such as Landau and Cormack Tobacco maintained a central plant location in a vertical urban factory in 1907 to stay close to the financial center, transit, and labor market. Each segment of processing was divided floor-by-floor, starting with the raw leaf on the top; separating, grading, blending on the third; cigarette making, inspecting, and packing on the second floor; and shipping and offices on the first.[58] After World War I, the multistory garment manufacturing buildings were built up to ten stories tall to save valuable land, while some, such as Northern Electric's eight-story plant, was as large as 46,500 square meters. Other firms continued to migrate en masse out of the center, to the north along the train route, eventually establishing a center for the paint industry. Shoe manufacturers relocated to the east and the west, becoming a hub for raw material facilities, thereby segregating each manufacturing specialty not only from one another, but from the residential areas as well.

In the Chicago meatpacking industry, many companies strove to consolidate their operations as they moved to the Union Stock Yard and Transit Co. in 1865, as vividly evoked in author Sinclair Lewis' *The Jungle*. Two hundred operations were housed in a network of multistoried loft buildings, which expanded to adjacent sites with a networked system of underground freight tunnels and stations for the movement of goods, so as not to interfere with the residents. As historian Robert Lewis describes, this 16-hectare area called Packingtown was situated at the edge of the city center on marshy land that was drained for development (cheaper than building in the central waterfront area) and included scattered areas used for slaughterhouses along various rail lines around the city. An opportunity to consolidate the businesses along with the railroads arose in the late 1860s. The businesses were reconfigured and reopened in 1865, with about half of the companies participating and others moving nearby. The new district encompassed 48 hectares of pens, 24 kilometers of rail, railway turntables, water tanks, wood yards, and 80 kilometers of sewers (leading to the Chicago River).[59] Engineer S. Scott Joy

(1860–1942) designed the standardized buildings in reinforced concrete. This infrastructural organization of urban land became a top-down spatial strategy, with power and rail lines going directly into the factory buildings, sequestering the messy slaughtering and packaging functions from the heart of the city.

Another Chicago manufacturing enclave purposefully developed by and for industry was the 121-hectare Central Manufacturing District (CMD). The U.S. Leather Company initially established the district in 1905 in a factory that was the first to be built as a real estate development, with financing from the industrial sector: that is, co-ownership by several railroads. By 1920 there were two hundred companies and fifteen thousand workers situated there, proving to the chair of the zoning commission that segregation of manufacturing from residential was warranted.[60] The district provided financial and infrastructural support to the companies within it and used the immediately adjacent railroads for their shipping services. This resulted in one hundred thousand carloads of freight per year by 1910. Growth continued, with 111 firms and 23,000 workers constituting the district by 1950.[61] Numerous multistory daylight factories, which allowed in light and air through large windows, also designed by Joy, were constructed and leased. A wall of buildings along 35th Street visibly separated the residential from the manufacturing district. It many ways, these kinds of speculative areas presaged the industrial parks of today.

A similar industrial district in Chicago, The Clearing, was built in 1927 along railroad tracks, though more sprawling than the CMD. What now we would call incubator or multi-tenanted buildings, were constructed so that companies could begin incrementally with short-term leases and expand as needed, without committing to large investments. Participating companies were able to network and to build upon adjacent manufacturers' skills and experience, and could further congregate in clubhouses provided by the development company. These segregated sites were still part of the city's infrastructure, and were networked with the urban business community.

▲ The Chicago Stockyards, 1924
▲ S. Scott Joy, The Clearing, Chicago, 1927

Between 1901 and 1910 there were over 800 loft buildings erected in Manhattan between eight to twenty stories tall used for many smaller manufacturers such as garment, printing, paper bags and boxes, flowers and feathers, textiles, woodwork, hats, and glove manufacturing. These were not purpose-built machines of the Modern factory, but were comparable to the flexible workshops and smaller businesses that relied on one another. In the early part of the century, surveys sponsored by the New York Regional Plan Association identified primarily food industries, such as processing plants, to remain in the city in order to be close to consumers and a more available labor pool.[62] After New York City's 1916 zoning regulations, industrial

▲ Ballinger & Co., Loose
Wiles Bakery, Degnan
Terminal, Long Island City,
New York, 1919

land areas excluded residential and higher-end uses, and, conversely, industrial
use was excluded from commercial and residential zones. But this separation had
already begun with speculative industrial development in various zones of the city,
from Brooklyn around the massive complexes of the Army Terminal and Sunset Park
Bush Terminal to Queens, with projects such as Degnon Terminal.

Long Island City's Hunters Point waterfront had grown into a major industrial
area specializing in paints, varnishes, printing, and box and pipe fabrication. These
numerous industries were accessible from Manhattan only by water transit until
the Queensboro Bridge opened in 1909. At that time, Degnon Realty and Terminal
Improvement Company built one of the region's first industrial parks on a 50-hect-
are site adjacent to the Long Island Railroad's Sunnyside Yards. Degnon was a
friend of Andrew Carnegie, and excavated the Steinway Street subway tunnel,
built bridges, and constructed the Brooklyn anchorage for the Williamsburg Bridge.
The company dredged Dutch Kills to promote access to various industries, and
erected a series of superblocks facing Skillman Avenue containing multistoried factory buildings which were leased by Packard Motors, Loose-Wiles Sunshine Biscuit
Co., White Motor Company, Adams Chewing Gum, and American Ever Ready.

On New York's Fifth Avenue, businessmen protested the garment industry's
central location because it prevented the relocation of upscale department stores,
which sought exclusive neighbors in order to encourage upper-class shoppers.
Irate at the tensions over land use, the garment industry leaders combined forces
to establish denser factory districts further north and west of Midtown, resulting
in the construction of a cluster of vertical factories, in what became known as the
Garment District, in the 1920s. Almost 2.5 square kilometers comprising 25 blocks
on the west side of Midtown, from 35th to 41st Streets between Sixth and Ninth

Avenues, was once home to the highest concentration of clothing manufacturers in the world. Constructed with astonishing speed in the early 1920s, the district was developed with high-rise loft buildings, typically 12 to 30 stories tall, which adapted the setbacks mandated by the city's 1916 zoning law. Generally, they were built speculatively as rental buildings that provided well-lit, open-plan workspaces on the upper floors, as well as showrooms on the floors above ground-floor shops.

Industrial uses also required a more robust infrastructural system that many of the adjacent residential owners didn't require, leading residents to protest taxes levied to pay for those more intensive sewers, roadways, and pipes. That planners supported the efforts of wealthy communities to segregate the city by economics, as well as by use, had deleterious effects. Homeowners didn't want undesirable and noxious land use next to their houses, as they thought values would decrease; "central city industrial property thus lost its own competitive advantage and started to evacuate the American City."[63] Without the land made available to them (due to zoning excluding industrial uses), no incentives to remain in the city, as well as rising taxes, many manufacturers decided to find new sites elsewhere — often with government support — and so the process removal of industries away from public view became a standard.

Industrialists who abandoned urban land ultimately decreased the values of adjacent properties. The Depression enhanced this dichotomy between cities, relying on industry versus other forms of development, deemphasizing the integrated urban manufacturing that was the source of economic growth through the early twentieth century, and emphasizing the renewed physical heterotopia of the districted factory enclave.

Labor and urban solidarity

Factories that remained in cities saw their workers establish a new social landscape, as life outside of the home and family was enabled by urban density and new work organization. Urban historian Sam Bass Warner describes of Philadelphia: "By the early decades of the twentieth century the process of industrialization had advanced so far that three-quarters of all manufacturing workers, and probably a majority of all other workers, labored in industrially organized work groups."[64] These work groups provided a structure and hierarchy both for worker efficiency and for the strengthening of worker associations and created a sort of protection within the groups.

Through World War I, companies consolidated into major monopolies. None of them wanted their workers to form unions, and labor groups were in trouble. There were numerous strikes brought on by agitators and mass meetings of laborers and political activists throughout this and subsequent decades. Whether it was Paterson or Passaic, Bridgeport or Philadelphia, Chicago, Detroit, Paris, or Turin, agitation traveled between cities like a virus infiltrating the systems. These protests "took place in downtown factory districts. Given the concentration of factories and working-class housing in the largest industrial cities, protests launched in one plant or neighborhood quickly spread."[65] If workers were dissatisfied, they could broadcast their dissent in the dense urban environment, giving support to the urban location of manufacturing. By 1930, Philadelphia "offered more social relationships

to its citizens than it had ever offered before."[66] Workers organized unions, and companies had to respond with new collective bargaining structures which, in turn, directed some of the unions' own initiatives.

Workers undertook the improvement of the workplace themselves, often through protest. A few examples of manufacturing spaces which became sites of protest (and which still reverberate today in the global factory) are Chevrolet and GM. In addition, union membership rose in the U.S. in the 1930s, finding power in numbers during the Great Depression. The rise of unions during the Modern era sparked movements worldwide to abolish child labor, establish a minimum wage, eliminate unpaid overtime, and increase workplace safety. Union membership increased in urban factories as waves of unrest spread from place to place by word of mouth or in impromptu protests, transforming production spaces to those of dissent.

Increase in production speed was the concern in Flint, Michigan. In 1934, in the camshaft department of the Chevrolet factory, workers attempted to regulate the speed of production so that it would be impossible for management to ask them to go faster and produce more. As they could communicate more easily across the space, they could come to each other's assistance, collaborate, or substitute for each other when work got tough and breaks were needed.

When Chevrolet started to transfer machinery and steel dies to factories outside Flint, workers took over the plant on December 30, 1936, and started the longest sit-down strike in history. Wives and community members brought workers food and supplies as they protested their overly regulated workplace. The strikers divided spaces for eating, sleeping, and hygienic needs, taking care of one another as they occupied the factory. The United Auto Workers (UAW) gained power, the negotiations made some progress, but a riot ultimately ensued. President Roosevelt intervened, and the owners came to a cooperative resolution with the unions. At the same time, other factories in Detroit, as well as hotels and stores, also held sit-down strikes in sympathy with the Chevrolet workers. The movement spread throughout the country and was seen as a powerful mode of gaining worker representation and better working conditions. The Congress of Industrial Organizations (CIO) worked with management to protect against strikes and "was able to channel the sitdown movement back into forms of organization far less challenging to the power of the corporate managers."[67]

These were contentious times in factory spaces. The sit-down strikes at GM were instigated by the speed-up in production. A worker was "not free, as perhaps he had been on some previous job, to set the pace of his work and to determine the manner in which it was to be performed."[68] Workers were not happy with the American Federation of Labor's negotiations with management, or with President Roosevelt taking sides with the owners. As a result, union memberships reduced from 20,000 to just 528. Nonetheless, they began to organize work stoppages or slow-downs to gain attention — the unions then had to support the sit-downs to prevent them from descending into chaos. Workers were successful with a 1936 strike, when Flint's UAW membership increased from 150 to 1,500 within two weeks.[69] The power of the union was seen in its ability to organize strikes, so striking, rather than collective bargaining, became the ongoing approach. With GM,

◀ Aerial photograph, Garment District, New York, 1930s
◀ Workers in the Garment District, New York, 1920s

the union requested "an annual wage to provide 'health, decency, and comfort,' elimination of speed-up, spreading work through shorter hours, seniority, and eight-hour workday, overtime pay, safety measures, and 'true collective bargaining.'"[70] Even at the risk of losing their jobs, the auto workers would often just stop the line and strike, independently of the union organization. The sit-down strikes were spatial; workers occupied a space that was not theirs but that they were physically commanding by remaining in place. Their actions of occupation signaled an operation of territorial ownership, even if it was temporary.

MODERNIST FACTORY CITY

TAYLORISM AND MODERN URBAN DESIGN

Diverse populations on all sides of the political spectrum were interested in Taylorism. Planners "believed that a more efficient organization of transportation and services would produce less fatigued workers and thus prevent the 'degradation and disintegration of human capital.'"[71] Architect Le Corbusier (1887–1965) envisioned the "revolution" of Fordism and Taylorism as an improvement to corporate capitalism, premised on efficiency and economy. As other advocates believed at the time, social justice was a result of technical rationalization, not of material or social equality. "Le Corbusier saw Taylorism as a means of breaking with prewar society, a key to social renewal. Ville Contemporaine and Plan Voisin, premised upon speed, efficiency, and economy, were architectural visions of the American industrial utopia made manifest."[72] Decades later, in 1940, the Vichy government's Raoul Dautry of the French Ministry of Armaments commissioned Le Corbusier to design a "green factory." Like the Garden City ideology of transforming "dark satanic mills" into "happy places that make work friendly,"[73] Le Corbusier's utopian concept would have reengineered the wartime factory for peacetime uses, extending out into a verdant landscape a horizontal factory housing a continuous production line that combined efficiency and a good life for the workers.

New zoning regulations, put into place to eliminate chaos, danger, haphazard construction, and laissez-faire urbanism, also developed from Modern ideas of rational functionality. Taylor's concepts of Scientific Management and Fordist standardization of production post-World War I further impacted cities and their new layouts. The organizational systems stemming from Taylor's ideas were implemented around the world in such a forceful way that some say that 1913 strikes in Paris were a result of worker discontent due to the strict "Taylorized" work methods. Taylor's methods of worker control were adopted by politicians and planners to make the city run like a machine.

In terms of city design, Taylor's thesis of segmenting each task in the workplace was transferable to that of separating each function of urban land use through comprehensive planning regulations. The ideas of efficiency of labor for increased productivity transferred to the potential for rational urban growth and planning and a city's efficiency. Architects also were interested in the machine and the factory and how that could be applied to a new aesthetic ideal. Architects grasped the machinic city — the need to make it "run" as a way to organize its innate chaos. Architectural historian Eric Mumford noted, "Over and over it is stated that modern architects must align themselves with this altogether new and complicated evolution, rising to the aspirations of their new epoch by adopting the identity of mechanization. They must become artist-diagnosticians and scientist-surgeons for the city's machine-body."[74]

The polemic of the city machine continued in the discussions of the organization of the new avant-garde with the architects who were members of the Congrés Internationale d'Architecture Moderne (CIAM) between 1929 and 1959. Rarely did they account for the specific location of factories in cities with the same vigor that they designed individual factory buildings. CIAM's manifesto from their first meetings focused on the four functions — dwelling, transportation, recreation, and work — but where was work actually, except perhaps in general diagrams of an urban zone? The machine was applied to architecture in terms of aesthetic or approach, more than the actual functional aspects of the industrial process. Industrialization of building construction was dominant, as architects including Le Corbusier found in Taylorism a method for standardization of parts. In Le Corbusier's 1914 Dom-ino system of concrete construction — an open floor plan consisting of concrete slabs supported by reinforced concrete columns — he saw the ideas of mass production and systemization of construction as an ideological issue and as a way to house people faster postwar. He felt that "Taylorism and new industrial methods were the only way the architect could continue to be relevant in a society threatened with potential destruction."[75]

However, industry as a land use was not discussed in detail and it was never a primary theme during the decades of CIAM meetings. It was tangential in terms of the recognition to set aside space — it was outlined but not filled in, leaving a void both intellectually and pragmatically. In detailed discussions at meetings and in publications, CIAM primarily focused on the dwelling unit or "living cell" and "the relations between living place, place of work, and place of recreation."[76] The idea of separating uses into distinct zones of the "Functional City" was wrapped into CIAM's polemic but the members did not consciously consider the place of industry and its interconnection to the whole of the city. Where was the machine in their urban machine? Modern communities — from Gropius' Torten in Dessau (1926), or Weissenhof Siedlung in Stuttgart (1927) to Ernst May's vast housing districts in Frankfurt (1926–32) — did not incorporate working spaces or industries as part of an urban fabric. Living and working in Modern urbanism became separate.

In contrast to Garnier's utopian Cité Industrielle, CIAM's urban planning concepts incorporated industry only on a case-by-case basis when, for example, major companies hired Modern architects to design pragmatic utopias such as Siemens' Siemensstadt, Olivetti's Ivrea, and Bat'a's Zlín. These planned communities, combining utopian dreams and the practicality of the profit-oriented business, ordered workers' lives and promised better living conditions but often were patronizing and limiting for the workers.

Grosseidlung Siemensstadt

North of the Spree River in Western Berlin, in Charlottenburg and Spandau, is an area that combines Siemens' large-scale industrial complex with the Modernist housing experiment. Over three decades it grew to encompass a large district named Siemensstadt. In contrast to Bat'a's Zlín and Olivetti's Ivrea, Siemensstadt was not touted as a utopian community, nor an expression of an ideology, but instead a pragmatic solution: a planned development integrated with the city that provided housing for thousands of Siemens' factory workers.

Founded by Werner von Siemens in the mid-nineteenth century as Siemens and Halske, today known as Siemens, the company was at the forefront of innovation in electrical technology and consumer products, along with AEG, the company's primary competitor. Siemens had numerous "firsts": telegraph lines, electrical conductors, fire alarms, dynamos, electrically powered trams, and telephone receivers. Beginning in 1887, the company constructed factories on open land beyond the city center, adding housing around this nucleus; by 1914, the area had come to be called Siemensstadt. The vast district contains an impressive collection of Modern industrial buildings, striking in their massive brick volumes and distinguished cubic forms, and incorporates Modern housing of the *Neues Bauen* ideology.

The two primary architects employed in Siemens' building department included Karl Janisch (1870–1946), who developed buildings from 1898 to 1914, and Hans Hertlin (1881–1963), who was responsible for the designs after 1915. Together, their work incrementally shaped the industrial district. Most of the early factories were oriented towards an interior *werkhof* (work courtyard) in a form similar to the urban blocks typical of Berlin's commercial districts. Subsequent factory buildings had penthouse roofs with narrow dimensions and clerestories that allowed light and air to penetrate the space, thus improving working conditions.

In 1898, Janisch, with engineer Carl Dihlmann, designed the first building whose function was the manufacture of cables and electric motors. Called Kabelwerk Westend, it was located on the west bank of a canal off the Spree River. The U-shaped, four-story brick building encircled a courtyard with smaller workshops. Janisch also designed the seven-story Wernerwerk I plant (1903–12), which housed the telecommunications and measuring technology production, on a full block with 12 interior courtyards arranged in an impressive gridded scheme. The courtyards followed an orthogonal layout, which derived from the nascent production line organization. In 1905, Janisch also designed the Kleinbauwerk, a six-story structure that enclosed four interior courtyards for smaller appliance production, in which narrow windows alternating with brick piers articulated the brick facade. Other office and research buildings filled in the district in a manner similar to AEG's complex in Wedding, Berlin.

Between 1914 and 1929, Hertlin took on the company's design responsibilities. His 11-story Wernerwerk II represented Europe's first high-rise factory building. The concrete slab block structure on a 176-by-76-meter podium base had additional towers housing support services that also reinforced the building against strong winds. Within its seven courtyards, workers produced low- and high-voltage measuring equipment. A water storage tower, Siemensturm, became an iconic identifier

of the district. As Siemens became a global company, it increasingly harnessed architectural design in developing its image through today.

Over the years, Siemens had built worker housing adjacent to the factory, on the undeveloped park-like landscape. As part of the 1909 Gross-Berlin Plan, urban planner Hermann Jansen (1865–1945) designed north-south-oriented streets for the development of single-family houses encompassing this area. At the time, 60,000 workers commuted to Siemens from the city center via tram, causing major congestion problems for the factory as workers swarmed the factory entrances. To ease the bottleneck and to facilitate worker access, the company built its own elevated train spur, called the Siemensbahn. Development halted during World War I through Weimar Germany's Social Democratic government public housing agenda to provide clean and healthy living. This expanded the possibility for reconfiguring and improving Berlin's tenement-type dwellings. The city's chief planner, Martin Wagner (1885–1957), recruited Modern architects to design housing projects for middle and working-class tradesmen and their families. These developments were part of the *Neues Bauen*, or "New Building" and the Modern movement, and in Berlin was spearheaded by the architectural collective called "The Ring." Other Modern housing developments were already underway, such as Le Corbusier's and Hans Scharoun's projects of the Weissenhof Siedlung in Stuttgart (1927), Ernst May's Romerstadt in Frankfurt (1927–29), and Bruno Taut and Martin Wagner's Britz in Berlin (1926).

▲ Aerial view of
Siemensstadt Berlin, c. 1930

On 14 hectares, adjacent to the Siemens factory, Wagner began the development — in semi-collaboration with the Siemens-owned building corporation (so owners didn't need mortgages) — of a large-scale housing estate called Grossiedlung Siemensstadt. The initial concept was for thousands of apartments to be reserved for Siemens' workers.[77] Construction began on the first 1,260 units

in 1928 and the entire project was completed in 1934. There is conflicting evidence as to whether or not Siemens provided funding for the projects; on the one hand, the company appeared unsupportive of the Modernist aesthetic for housing design, on the other, its factories were indeed Modern and their workers needed accommodations.[78] The situation was akin to public-private partnerships today in which a company exchanges job creation for city-sponsored infrastructure for the common benefit.

Wagner awarded Hans Scharoun (1893–1972) the role of primary planner in a competition to design parallel ribbons of four-to six-story housing blocks (higher than the housing code at the time) following Jansen's earlier north-south street layouts. Leberecht Migge (1881–1935), the landscape architect, designed the area's gardens with public and semi-public pathways. An on-site heating plant made Grossiedlung Siemensstadt one of the first centrally heated housing estates. The project, which developed into a city within a city, included parks and playgrounds, a swimming pool, laundry rooms, and local shops.

Wagner asked the architects Hugo Häring (1882–1958), Walter Gropius (1885–1969), Otto Bartning (1883–1959), Fred Forbát (1897–1972), and Paul R. Henning to design different block units according to their individual interpretations of Modernist principles. Gropius designed his with recessed balconies for shade; Häring's were organic with exposed brick to soften the facades; Forbát designed the eastern block contrasting a vertical stair tower with a ribbon window that accentuated the play of shadow and light. Bartning's project, situated along curved railroad tracks, featured brick walls separating back-to-back balconies. In a plan that we take for granted today, kitchens and living rooms were combined. Scharoun designed a grouping of three five-story buildings and an interior garden courtyard to conceal the railroad tracks. His heavy sculptural forms quickly earned the moniker of the "naval tanker." The public did not appreciate the project, which architecture critic Adolf Behne (1885–1948) defended as achieving a balance between the monumental and the practical.[79] In addition, the concentration of Siemens' fifteen thousand workers living there was seen not only as a threat to the new corporate establishment but was compared to socialist Russia.[80] The housing development was an experiment in low-cost, mass-produced construction, exemplifying the social aspirations of the Modern movement.

▲ A streetscape in Grosse-Siedlung, Siemensstadt, Berlin, 1930
▲ Model of the Grosse-Siedlung, Siemensstadt, Berlin, 1930

After Siemensstadt was bombed during World War II, Siemens was forced
to move its manufacturing out of the city, especially as its factories had
been conscripted to produce weapons for the Nazis, who used the prisoners
in labor camps as workers. Despite the bombing and relocation, Siemensstadt
housing was restored in two phases and was recognized by UNESCO as a World
Heritage Site in 2008.

Bat'a

Inspired by British Garden Cities in which sections for living and working, as well
as recreation space, were separated, Moravian shoe manufacturer Tomáš Bat'a
(1876–1935) established the company town of Zlín in southeastern Czechoslovakia.
Zlín was conceived as a pragmatic utopia, but Bat'a treated its citizens as elements
in the production process. One worker wrote: "the Young Men are the shoes...
everything is mechanized here (even culture is manufactured here as if on an
assembly line)," and falls into the factory paradox.[81]

▲ Bat'a industrial district with
railroad, Zlín, Czechoslovakia,
1923–32
▲ A Bat'a factory, Zlín, 1932

Bat'a had inherited a shoe empire in Zlín, established by his father in 1894. The
business launched with stitched, woolen shoes that were cut and shaped in the factory then sent out to homeworkers in cottage industries to assemble. Realizing the
need to upgrade both the product and the factory, Bat'a began producing canvas
shoes and altered the traditional brick factory buildings by adding steam-powered
machines in 1900. He then expanded the plant through two additions in 1906 and
1918. The company supplied shoes to the Czech army in World War I, increasing
the number of employees to 400 and enlarging the facilities to include a tannery,

electric power plant, farms, brickworks, a forest, and a sawmill in a vertically integrated manufacturing process. Bat'a absorbed cottage shoe industries around Czechoslovakia and expanded abroad as he systematically cut shoe prices and built his consumer base. Simultaneously, he streamlined his manufacturing process in the Taylorized system, increasing his production from 1,750,000 pairs of shoes in 1922 to 15,200,000 in 1927. By 1928, he controlled 55 percent of Czechoslovakia's shoe export.[82]

From 1923 to 1932, Bat'a, as the town's mayor, engaged in an unprecedented town planning effort. He incorporated Modern design, new mass production construction technologies, and Garden City planning, and even borrowed ideas from Le Corbusier's design for the Cité Voisin. Bat'a hired the foremost Czech architects of the day, many of whom studied at the Prague Art Academy. These included planner Jan Kotěra (1871–1923); his student, urban designer František Lydie Gahura (1891–1958); the engineer Arnošt Sehnal: and architects Miroslav Lorenc (1896–1943), J. Voženílek, M. Drofa, and Vladimír Karfík (1901–1996). Karfík is perhaps the most well known, as he had worked not only with Le Corbusier but with Frank Lloyd Wright (1867–1959) on Taliesin West and East. Karfík designed many of the central buildings, including the office tower, Building No 21. Gahura was in charge of the residential and town center and, after winning a design competition in 1940, standardized the modular system and designed Zlín's Labour Square. Voženílek became the lead architect after the shoe company was nationalized in 1945.

Many nationalists and socialists were opposed to Bat'a and his original ideas for modernizing the city, primarily because Bat'a's ideas threatened to destroy the city's historic center, including its Renaissance town hall.[83] In contrast to Bat'a's gridded city, architects such as Lorenc were inclined towards designing in the more animated Modernism of German architect Hans Poelzig (1869–1936), designer of the Luban Chemical Factory (1911–1912). Nonetheless, Bat'a commissioned the design of an entire town for 50,000 people, including factories, offices, schools, worker housing, residential neighborhoods, a hospital, a hotel, public buildings, a department store, and a cinema — all following a 6.15-by-6.15-meter concrete frame module. The modular concrete framework with large steel casement windows and brick or steel infill was developed with the builder Arnošt Sehnal. The town expanded through the valley with workers accommodated in individual brick houses, dormitories, and apartment buildings, while executives had larger houses. These structures were load-bearing brick buildings, while the vertical factories and institutional buildings' concrete frames were filled with brick and/or glass. Similar to Le Corbusier's Dom-ino system, Zlín was built quickly and efficiently. The new uniform buildings were a test of standardized construction; fifty-two factory buildings opened in 1933, the epitome of modern efficiency and mass production.

With the establishment of health and social welfare departments at Zlín, Bat'a's efforts to design a utopian industrial city was evident not only in the physical organization of the plan but its social aspect as well. Bat'a had gained experience before creating his own factories: he worked for a few months at a Lynn, Massachusetts shoe factory in 1906 to better understand the American workflow, then in 1913 visited Ford's factories where he noticed insufficient attention to workers' issues. Bat'a also started a school wherein workers could learn trades at night. In 1939, his half

▲ Valdimir Karfík, Bat'a office building No. 21, Zlín, Czechoslovakia, 1936–38

brother Jan Bat'a established a Bauhaus-derived School of Arts that taught industrial design and art related to the design of company graphics and machinery. In the exhibitions held at the School, the sculptor Vincenc Makovský (1900–1966) juxtaposed factory machines such as awls with artworks and he redesigned the standard fabric scissor for use with various strength materials in a more ergonomic form, focusing new attention on the worker's comfort and productivity. In contrast to many top-down companies, Bat'a extended profit sharing to his employees but also penalized the worker if a quota was not met. The idea of employee participation was also part of Henri Fayol's concepts in industrial labor psychology, as discussed earlier. As Eric Jenkins noted, "This can be lauded as an innovative attempt to implement performance-based merit compensation. Alternatively, it perhaps reveals how the Bat'a Company's social benevolence was strained when it did not align neatly with corporate profitability."[84]

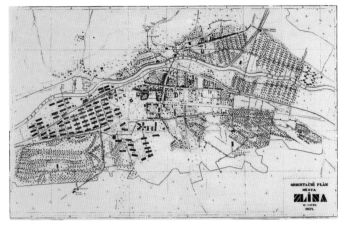

The entire town was based on production and achievement — even open spaces, theaters and leisure activities were monitored so that the workers filled their time.[85] According to the company code "Work is communal — living is individual," thus work and life were kept strictly separate. But the worker regulations seem to be in contradiction with Bat'a's ideas of Autonomous Workshops, which were independently established cottage industries: one workshop made shoe soles while another made uppers, for instance.[86] Through these independent workshops employees could receive profits and they had a stake in the overall outcome. Because workers purchased products from each other, and they needed a perfected piece with which to finish the shoes, quality control was built in. Carl Zeiss ran similar workshops in his factories in Germany in the 1920s.

▲ Zlin plan,1939
▲ Workers in Zlín at a Bat'a-sponsored parade, Czechoslovakia, 1930

In 1917, five thousand workers made two million pairs of shoes annually; by the early 1930s, production was up to thirty-six million. As the company continued to expand by opening up new factories and thus new towns, the country's infrastructural systems and roadways simultaneously developed. By 1931, Bat'a had developed numerous industries tangential to shoe manufacturing, including automotive and bicycle tires, shoe polish, publishing, flooring, socks, toys, and stockings. During the Depression, his canvas shoe with leather soles (not unlike sneakers) became a hit. As the corporation expanded to become a joint-stock company with over 175 million crowns in assets in 1931, Tomáš Bat'a's power increased; he even proposed moving the regional government center to Zlín. At that time Bat'a epitomized the global company and produced and sold shoes in 37 countries through 666 shops, even opening up factories in Baltimore, Maryland and India. Modern urbanization and manufacturing were implicated in the new mass-produced technologies; increased economies of scale enabled standardized systems for living and working.

Bat'a, who thoroughly embraced new and innovative technologies, learned to fly, but he met his end through new technology, as he died in a plane accident in 1932. Jan took on the company and continued with incremental and continuous expansion, first with a housing competition in 1935 on whose jury Le Corbusier participated, and through which model colonies were built. In 1938, Jan Bat'a hired Karfík to design a 17-story office building (the tallest in Czechoslovakia at the time). In a unique elevator he included an office with phone lines from which Jan could survey the workers in a panopticon. Ironically, this dynamic was reversed when Tomáš Bat'a's glass-clad memorial allowed workers to "survey" both his coffin and a replica of the Junker F-13 in which he crashed.

Bat'a's employees — part of a closely knit yet isolated community — were removed from nationally prominent issues, including worker solidarity and human rights. Marxist critics denounced the company's double standards that provided for housing and schools, but demanded rigorous hours and exercised extreme paternalism. The situation was described in the book *Der Unbekannte Diktator Tomáš Bat'a (The Unknown Dictator Tomáš Bat'a)*. "They saw 'Batism'— the totality of the Bat'a system and its principles — as nothing other than a particularly sophisticated form of capitalist exploitation."[87] The way Bat'a stressed the hiring of younger workers echoes abuses seen today in factories of China, India, and Bangladesh: at first, only unmarried women and young people were hired and no unions were allowed. One can see how Karel Čapek was inspired by the situation to write his play *R.U.R.*, depicting a robotic, rebellious society. The residents, there to fulfill a vision of the founder, and without their own independent pursuits (which were seen as despotic and arbitrary), were caught in a paradoxical situation in the dream for a productive society. As Jean-Louis Cohen observes, it "was a secure and ordered industrial universe which fulfilled in one single body the functionalist dream of a Modern city at the same time productive, healthy and obedient."[88]

During World War II, Jan immigrated first to the United States and then to Brazil — he had to escape attention because he sympathized with the Nazis. Tomáš Jr., his son, who self-exiled to Canada, became head of the Bat'a empire. What remained in Zlín was nationalized in 1945 and then, in 1948, the Communist government eliminated the corporation's control, parceling off the company into many divisions. Zlín was also bombed by the Allies and then liberated by the Red Army. The city's name was changed to Gottwaldov until Tomáš Jr. returned in 1989 and changed it back to Zlín. Today Bat'a operates forty production centers in twenty-six countries, with numerous Bat'a towns in India, England, and Africa.

Olivetti

The vision of the company town as the pragmatic utopia became as close to a reality as any, in a section of Ivrea in northern Italy for an industrial community organized by Camillo Olivetti (1868–1943). Olivetti had established an electrical

measuring instrument company there, moving into a traditional red brick factory
building. He later moved to Milan to try his business acumen, but in 1908 moved
back to Ivrea, restarting the company with manufacturing machinery purchased
on a 1903 trip to the United States. By 1955, the company town had grown to over
eleven thousand people. Olivetti's primary innovations were adding machines,
typing machines (including the first portable typewriter — the Olivetti M-1 model
— that was displayed at the Turin Universal Exhibition in 1911), and the first
Italian computers. He also produced machine tools using technology that was later
adopted for the production of gun and airplane parts during World Wars I and II.

Olivetti embraced Modern design as a way to attract consumers, keeping the
typewriters and office machines simple, streamlined, and colorful. At this time the
fields of graphic and industrial design were in their infancy, and Olivetti capitalized
on the ambition of Modern designers by hiring them to design his products. The
company came to stand for quality and innovative design, similar to the Modern

▲ Luigi Figini and Gino
Pollini, Olivetti factory, first
expansion Via Jervis, Ivrea,
Italy, 1939

industrial production companies who hired architects to design furniture and
tableware. Typewriters simultaneously became an essential tool, accessory, and
a piece of furniture within the office landscape. In engineering them, industrial
designers understood the need to balance function and form. Graphic designers
created eye-catching, avant-garde logos and advertisements. This design *gestalt*
was recognized in the 1952 Museum of Modern Art exhibition, *Olivetti: Design in
Industry,* which also foregrounded the idea of corporate responsibility in the arts as
well as attention to the worker.

After Camillo died in 1943, his son Adriano took the company's helm. He had
already traveled to the United States with engineer Domenico Burzio, visiting 105
factories and learning about Scientific Management as so many other European
industrialists had done before him. By combining American innovation with a
socialist attitude towards working environments Adriano sought to create an "intellectual workers' community."[89] He calibrated a lower-than-standard speed for the
automated conveyors so that workers could spend more time with each step on the
production line and required supervisors to not only observe workers, but to more
holistically engage in research tasks and to contribute to production improvement.

Adriano Olivetti applied the same aesthetic principles to the factory environment that he did to his products and marketing materials. He hired architects Luigi
Figini (1903–1984) and Gino Pollini (1903–1991) "to design a factory that would be
suitable for human beings as well as machines, appearing hospitable and colorful,
both in its facade and its interior."[90] Both men were involved in the Movimento
Italiano per l'Architettura Razionale, a Milan-based avant-garde architecture
group. Their work — along with that of Giuseppe Terragni (1904–1943) and Cesare
Cattaneo (1912–1943) — was exhibited at the 1933 Milan Architecture Triennale.

Figini and Pollini's factory design featured a series of additions to the traditional two-story brick building designed by Camillo Olivetti himself on Via Jervis
in Ivrea in 1908. Between 1934 and 1936, the architects designed and completed a
100-meter-long building, which also included a common room capable of holding meetings for all two thousand employees. Originally designed to have a large

curtain wall, the building was constructed as two
stories with multi-paned steel ribbon windows. Two
subsequent additions — the Officine I.C.O. (Società
Ingegneria C. Olivetti & Co., 1937–1939) with a glass
facade, and a separate building, the Nuova I.C.O.
(1956–1957) — increased the company's manufacturing capabilities. In their streamlined functional
form, all three structures embodied Olivetti's goals
and recast the ideals of Modern factory design in the
mid-twentieth century.

As with many factory designs, the close involvement of the production engineer made it difficult
to attribute the design of the project to a single
individual. Such collaborations between architect
and engineer, however, were what made the Olivetti
factory progressive. The two-story concrete addition
constructed between 1937 and 1939 continued along
the initial development on Via Jervis, connecting the
main building via interior ramps. Another story and
four new bays were added between 1939 and 1940 so
that a new workers' entrance with a concrete portico
could be centrally incorporated in the longer facade
length. Each addition utilized the same structural
grid of four by 13 meters. The smaller workshops at
the rear were accessed through a volume glazed with
large, steel, multi-paned windows to house a cantilevered staircase. The windows were set off-center, in a
formal abstracted composition.[91]

Figini and Pollini's most innovative element was
the 1939–1940 four-story, 400-meter-long glass facade. Mushroom concrete piers
supporting the upper floors were set back from the facade to allow for an uninterrupted glazed wall. The double-glazed facade had an air circulation space that
also contained the vertical blinds, similar to the glazing of Le Corbusier's Cité de
Refuge, in Paris (1929–1933). The windows were secured with brackets along a
curtain wall eighty centimeters beyond the structural grid. The uniformity of the
facade expressed the potential flexibility of the interior production spaces without
separated bays or facade divisions. At night, when the entire building was illuminated, the interior was revealed. On the other facade, facing Via Monte Navale,
Annibale Fiocchi of the technical office recommended the addition of concrete
brise-soleil shading devices to protect the interior from direct sunlight. From this
facade an overhead pedestrian bridge with concrete trusses formed a walkway
between the buildings.

▲ Worker inspecting typewrit-
ers in Olivetti factory, Ivrea,
Italy, 1950s
▲ Workers assembling
Lettera 22 typewriters Olivetti,
Ivrea, Italy, 1950s

In 1956, the expansion of typewriter and calculating machine production areas
became necessary due to the increased specialization of the manufacturing of basic
parts. The parts were then assembled as separate units, each in a similar manner.
This didn't require unique buildings for each model of the machines but rather

workshop divisions within the building itself. Figini and Pollini designed a new building, called Nuova Ico with G. Boschetti that again expanded the complex. The 20,000-square-meter factory constructed on the perimeter of the city block has two rows of poured concrete column-beams and columns supporting its structure. A one-story internal courtyard covered with twenty 12-by-12-meter-square sky-lights allows for diffused light in the central space. Eduardo Vittoria (1923–2009) designed the integrated roof and lighting system as a unique design element. The services such as bathrooms and lockers were concentrated at one side in two triangular independent volumes, keeping the manufacturing spaces open.

The spatial organization followed the production sequence from presses and mechanical production on the lower central covered courtyard to machine assembly of the electric calculators on the two upper floors — consecutive models such as the Divisumma 24, Tetractys, Elettrosumma 22, and Multisumma 22. Overhead conveyors as well as individual workstations linked by roller conveyors made for a fluid and flexible space. Two lateral passages were reserved for truck transit and material delivery. Elevator towers clad in bright yellow majolica tiles made by well-known ceramicists Pozzi and Sparanise, and windows with different mullion depths, create a punctuated rhythm — in a strong contrast to the singularity of the company's earlier transparent factories. Olivetti's concept of the "factory as a measure of man" was here expressed through what he hoped to be a humanistic space that also functioned efficiently.

From the development of the production line came the design of a pragmatic utopia in Ivrea that sought to provide a better life for workers and services for families. These included various types of housing, a nursery school for workers' children, a swimming pool and gardens, community service buildings, a canteen, hospitals, a cultural center, a library, a cinema, schools, and off-site holiday camps on the coast. Welfare services were organized such that employee representatives engaged directly with the workers to develop the amenities rather than through a top-down paternalistic relationship as at Ford. Working and living was adjacent and even intertwined, something rarely seen in current urban design and industry.

After designing his company town, Olivetti developed a regional plan with architect Enrico Peressutti (1908–1976). This plan linked city and factory, endorsing a socialist philosophy of community in a democracy that he emboldened in a political party called Movimento Comunità (Community Movement) founded in Turin in 1948. The concept was for self-sufficient communities that exercised a meta-political action, in a social forum that included land use and urban planning as well as worker advocacy.[92] The organization supported Adriano Olivetti as mayor of Ivrea; a parallel situation can be seen in Tomáš Baťa's running of Zlín. The Community Movement spread to smaller industrial towns in the region, spawning community centers, cultural activities, and publications. They even translated writings by American architectural critics such as Lewis Mumford and George Kidder Smith (1913–1997), and CIAM's Athens Charter.

Convinced of the power of design to improve quality of life, Olivetti hired numerous architects to design additions to the town. Today, we might call this interest in the worker's well being social responsibility, with Olivetti — as with Baťa, Van Nelle, and Ford — the profit motive was combined with ambitions of worker happiness. After Olivetti's death in 1960, his son Roberto continued as a patron of architecture and art and commissioned Olivetti factories throughout the world: Louis I. Kahn in Pennsylvania (the Olivetti-Underwood factory, 1966); Marco Zanuso in Buenos Aires (1954) and in Guarulhos (near São Paulo, 1957–1959); James Stirling in England (1973); and unrealized plans by Le Corbusier in Rho (near Milan, 1963). The company's shops were designed by architects such as Carlo Scarpa in Venice in (1957) and BBPR (Lodovico Barbiano di Belgiojoso, Enrico Peressutti, and Ernesto Rogers) in New York (1954). Merging humanism with Modern design, Olivetti created an industrial community as a *gesamtkunstwerk* that served as an inspiration to the few progressive factory owners of his time. Many believe that this community was indeed the best of its kind, exemplifying the pragmatic utopia.

DISPERSAL

LINEAR FACTORY CITY

One urban form inspired by industrial locations' influence on urban expansion was *La Ciudad Lineal* (Linear City) a concept devised by the Spanish engineer-planner Arturo Soria y Mata (1844–1920) in 1882 for Madrid. Cities for centuries developed along roads and rivers in a linear manner. His idea would lay out factories in a line, incorporating tram and phone cable infrastructure in parallel with residences and gardens, placing work and home in proximity.[93] Rather than the concentric circle plan of the Garden City, the Linear City maintained a more heterogeneous

◀ Workers leaving the Nuova Ico factory, Olivetti, Via Jervis, Ivrea, Italy, 1950s
◀ Adriano Olivetti, *La Fabbrica e la Comunità*, Edizioni di Comunità, 1940s

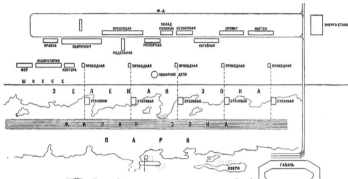

▲ Arturo Soria y Mata, La
Ciudad Lineal (project), 1892
▲ Nikolai Milyutin, Linear
City plan for Sotsgorod,
Russia,1930

development, with each program —
housing, industry, and government —
parallel to each other along a dominant
spine. Soria proposed a city along train
routes from Spain to Russia, expanding from either side. Soria designed
plans for areas of Madrid and built a
small portion, which still exists along
a former tramway.[94] These concepts
of the Linear City already occurred
naturally; it was common that industrialists moved out of cities along new
train routes in places such as Toronto,
Philadelphia, and even Moscow. Henry
Ford began to move his companies
out of cities such as Detroit for larger
blank-slate spaces, building his River
Rouge Plant in 1917 along Detroit's train
and transit routes. Ford also proposed
ideas for a series of industrial towns
along a 75-kilometer strip powered
from new electric dams, decentralizing
industry in a linear mode. The line
of the city echoes the assembly line
— as a line it signifies movement, allowing for the city's expansion and endless
production. Just as the Modern architect embraced the industrial aesthetics, the
industrialist, like Ford, demonstrated an interest in spatial planning in Taylorist
streamlining of cities.

In Moscow we see the idea reappear with the work of planner Nikolai Milyutin
(1898–1941) of the Communist Academy and then as counter to the Moscow First
Five-Year Plan that maintained heavy — up to 53 percent — industrial production
in the city. In the plan, smaller industries were not as regulated and ended up with
only ten percent of the productive economy. These smaller industries were more
freely organized, even with less investment and fewer resources. A competition for
the steel town of Magnitogorsk in the Urals, in 1929, included designs by Milyutin
and constructivist Ivan Leonidov (1902–1959) for a linear city of 150,000 people.
German architect Ernst May's (1886–1970) scheme was selected, but lacking the
power and influence to change the course of the development, housing was built
separate from industry altogether because of pollution.

Milyutin specifically imagined the linear city as an industrial city along the
Volga River in Stalingrad in his scheme for a 35-kilometer-long Tractor City, with
each function running parallel along a transit line.[95] Stalingrad fulfilled this plan
more than other cities of the time. Influenced by this Russian plan, Le Corbusier
designed the Radiant City, his version of a linear industrial city as a spine off of
which would stem superblock housing developments. In the mid-1930s he was
asked to explore planning ideas for the valley of Zlín in Czechoslovakia for Bat'a's

industrial city. His scheme called for a linear flow following the valley terrain, but was not ultimately selected.

It is also important to note that as part of Joseph Stalin's (1878–1953) five-year plan for socialist industrialization, Pittsburgh and Bethlehem, Pennsylvania were models for his towns, as was the industrial architecture as propagated by Albert Kahn (1869–1942). Ford's mass production methods and Taylor's Scientific Management were closely followed as early as Lenin's drive for industrialization in 1917 and the Revolution.[96] From 1929 to 1932 Kahn and a team of thirty architects technicians, and local engineers led by his brother, Moritz, designed 520 factories for heavy industries such as steel, auto, chemical, and tractor plants in cities including Moscow, Cheliabinsk, and Stalingrad. Both Ford and Amtorg Trading Corporation, a Soviet import and export organization established by Armond Hammer that was thought to spy on American companies, had a major presence in Russia. But Kahn was not interested in the Russian avant-garde or new ideas there. He was more concerned with the pragmatic organization of the factory space. His first factory was the $40 million Cheliabinsk tractor plant, relating to the new collectivization of agriculture and its recent mechanization. Kahn's Russian office also began a training program in Moscow to enhance the speed of building production. The adoption of Kahn's methods became straightforward and essential, shunning the theoretical. The linear city as organic urban growth could mirror production methods, but, as it dispersed, it contributed to deurbanizing the factory.

WARTIME

Decentralization also occurred for safety and secrecy of factories during World War II. The secrecy of both the product and method of production was paramount to success. As reported in a World War II–related publication, *National Security Factors in Industrial Location,* "Industry, through location or relocation, can achieve a reasonable degree of security if faced with the reality of the risks of attack."[97] Thus, the manufacturing areas around shipyards and ports during the war were abandoned as manufacturers were advised to move inland for security. The planners argued that dispersion of industry "will go a long way toward combating a potential enemy's effort to cripple our industrial capacity by any mode of attack, conventional or otherwise."[98] And planners encouraged moving industries to areas of 50,000 people or less, to maintain a 4.8 kilometer radius around a plant for safety. This dispersed industry required larger expanses of land than previously needed, for a new kind of industrial buffer zone.

For the sake of decentralizing manufacturing, industrialists such as Henry J. Kaiser (1882–1967), for example, moved his shipbuilding plants inland to Fontana, California from Los Angeles, which then required shipping of materials and steel offloaded from ships to trucks on highways to the inland settlements. Turning Fontana into Kaisertown, the major steel producer on the West Coast developed following the ideals of agriculturalist A.B. Miller, whose agricultural community was organized in a paternalist fashion. As Mike Davis points out in *City of Quartz,* Kaiser organized a "postwar contract between labor and management,"[99] developing health plans, unions, and housing for his workers. As another effort at decentralizing industry, he also built a regional plant for Alcoa

▲ Oakridge, Tennessee, home of the Manhattan Project, 1940s

outside of Vancouver, Washington to capitalize on hydroelectric power from the Bonneville Dam. In order to encourage workers to move out of the city, government agencies developed housing in parallel to the factory, which resulted in the McLoughlin Heights community, and has since been incorporated into the city. Other methods of decentralization encouraged aviation plants farther afield, like the Douglas Aircraft Company, working jointly with the federal housing offices to create an "air industry city" funded by the Federal Housing Authority in 1944. New partnerships were initiated between industrialists, housing authorities, and town planners, who saw these developments as a way to grow the populations of their municipal regions — even as some wartime industries declined. Similarly, the better-known Levittown, developed near Grumann Aviation's plants in Long Island, also contributed to the idea of living and working in a suburban community — as jobs moved, so could the population.

Urban planners supported suburbanization of industry by promoting a new mode of community planning, such as that of Clarence Stein (1882–1975), who designed numerous garden cities with Henry Wright (1879–1936), including Sunnyside Gardens in Queens in 1926; Radburn, New Jersey in 1929; and then Greenbelt, Maryland in 1935. Stein found wartime industrial dispersal — as encouraged by the War Production Board — to be a way to promote his greenbelt planning and new towns by reminding the planning commissions that, "The costs of building new communities is less than that of rebuilding old and obsolete cities. The total cost of carrying on industry and business in the United States would be greatly decreased by a more scientific distribution . . . of goods and people."[100] He thus advocated for the move away from cities and encouraged companies to locate to new communities which could accommodate the numerous defense workers.

The dispersal also suited the scale and volume of the new factory construction. Companies needed vast amounts of space to quickly build the large-scale machinery and fighter planes required for the war effort. This land was unavailable in the already dense cities, but urban edges and greenfields could accommodate the buildings. The ease of construction on empty land was preferable to the industrialists of the time just as today it is often easier to build on open land than to struggle to fit within a preexisting condition.

Often, for the sake of national security, the manufacture of weaponry was scattered amongst a series of plants, instead of being contained under a single roof that was an easy target. Each plant produced separate components that would then be assembled in another remote facility. This was touted as the best and most efficient manufacturing practice to ensure wartime safety. The smaller assembly lines would protect against industrial espionage since production was completed in bits and pieces.

Companies used camouflage to hide factories that they considered high-risk bomb targets. They either painted camouflage directly on the structures or erected mesh nets, painted with suburban landscape scenes, over them. Depth being difficult to perceive from the air, the factory blended in with the surrounding landscape. For the Douglas airplane plant in Santa Monica, California in 1943, complete street scenes were painted.[101] In Long Beach the acres of flat-roof factories were painted to look like streets that connected with the city grid. In addition, blackout factories were constructed, such as the Douglas C-47 and B-17 Boeing plants; these were windowless and thus did not emanate light. By these means the factories were made invisible to the enemy from the air, ensuring wartime safety.

An alternative to hiding weapons manufacturing was to produce arms underground; this was done in the quarries in France north of Paris. There were ideas for inflatable factories and a collapsible factory in England that would retract, forecasting the avant-garde forms of the 1960s. During World War II, V-1 bomber factories in the Hartz Mountains of Germany were installed in former mining tunnels. These used air vents rising above the surface in such a way that they were completely hidden, both from the enemy and from any public scrutiny of their abusive working environments.[102] This continued in Germany through 1944 with unbuilt concepts designed by Eberhard Kuen for Messerschmitt, the aircraft company. Camouflaging industry inspired and resulted in a non-landscape, a superficial place without identity.

Dispersal was also a priority in the UK during World War II, which influenced industry locations for their future. The British government established the Barlow Commission in 1940, to focus on distributing industry to areas of economic inequality and repression. Out of this came the Distribution of Industry Act in 1945, which suggested an effort towards balanced regional growth; the act was intended to provide jobs, to tame congestion in cities, and to maintain safe industries outside of metropolitan areas. The government dictated where and what kind of industry could be developed (similar to U.S. zoning policies and directions for economic development), in an effort to attract industries, but this policy led to controversies about planned economies in Great Britain, with many saying this top-down organization was socialist.[103] In five years, almost one thousand industrial areas were built; half were government-funded and provided thousands of jobs to areas outside of London where previously there had been little growth. It was the first time that decentralization was encouraged as policy, even though politicians acknowledged the advantages to urban industry. Wartime destruction of inner-city London and suburban growth contributed to workers having to move out to be near the anticipated factories. The result was the development of satellite towns reducing London's and other cities' densities. This trend, dubiously presented as a planning strategy, ruined the green expanses of the countryside. Nevertheless, government agencies enticed industries to these satellite towns and regions, result-ing in thirteen million square meters of light industrial and manufacturing space constructed by 1970.[104] These were linked to ports and potential trade centers on the southeast coast, focused on Ipswich and the Milton Keynes area in the west and spreading development away from the urban cores. While much of the develop-ment became tied to local government issues, industrial enclaves grew as regional cities expanded throughout Great Britain.

The drastic separation of living and working and urban decentralization continued long after the war had ended, causing numerous problems for which we continue to feel the ramifications in the detrimental effects of environmental waste. Issues of economics, land use, and separation of uses contributed to urban uniformity. As architectural historian Spiro Kostof (1936–1991) noted:

> Our conventions of delimiting urban problems through what amounts to regulatory quarantine have, in the final reckoning, denied us the expe-rience of interdependence as a larger community. In a society driven by discrepancies in wealth, race and privilege, that experience may not be comfortable. It is, however, prerequisite to any hope for a lasting resolu-tion of our differences. In the case of cities, to divide is not to conquer.[105]

The spatial segregation of the Modern city resulted in social segregation, and the divisions it left in cities were irreparable. At the same time, industry still influenced urban development and the potentials for the modern city. The uto-pian, pragmatic, and architect-led visions for rational Modern cities subsumed the factory's importance in urban planning and design. However, industries continued to require dense populations and entrepreneurs to thrive, and cities relied on industries for food, goods, and jobs, all in close proximity. But land use regulations tended to direct the location of industry elsewhere.

▶ Lockheed Martin, wartime camouflage in Burbank, Los Angeles, 1941 (top and bottom)

MODERN FACTORY ARCHITECTURE

IN THE EARLY TWENTIETH CENTURY, the factory exemplified modernity and modernization, both as a system of new mass production, and as a building typology, inspiring Modern architects in their development of an avant-garde design aesthetic. As a building type that fluctuated between that of "building" and that of "Architecture" (with a capital A) the factory evolved according to the needs of burgeoning industries in the late nineteenth century, from a wrapper or envelope housing machinery to that of an integrated machine itself, and arranged to better facilitate the flows of production inside. Spatially, the typology I have identified as the "vertical urban factory" embodied the industrial ideals of manufacturers in cities, requiring innovative engineering that was dependent upon and integrated with the networks of natural, human, and infrastructural resources of the urban environment. As architecture became a dominant mode of expressing power for upper-class industrialists, they gradually hired architects to build not only production spaces, but symbols or lasting images for their companies. Modern architects, for their part, embraced the factory as a place for experimentation and its relationship to the city itself was not integrated, but rather internalized and removed. As much as their designs were spatially and technologically innovative, engineers and architects could not predict, nor address, the unjust social issues that would arise in factories.

In tracing the urban factory it is first essential to recognize the significance of multistoried early-nineteenth-century factories or "works." These structures, well-suited for the successful operation of power machinery at a river's edge and in dense cities, rose upwards for the expediency and economy of the manufacturer. Since the size of a plot of land in the city could determine the size of the factory, it was often cheaper to build up rather than out.

The massive, vernacular urban buildings held a heroic aspect for many, including German architect Karl Friedrich Schinkel (1781–1841), who was the Prussian Counselor for Public Works. While on a trip to England in 1826 with Christian Peter Wilhelm Friedrich Beuth (1781–1853), a trade commissioner, they visited the new factories rather than the more formal country houses typical of an architect's design. Schinkel sketched and wrote about the multistoried vernacular brick structures dramatically situated on Manchester's waterfront; for him, they embodied strength in their solid massing and large volumes with repetitive window apertures.

At the same time, he romanticized them for their visual and physical qualities and not really for what went on behind the imposing walls, which Frederick Engels would have described in a very different way, in terms of the working conditions of the poor. Schinkel mused, "They built seven to eight floors, as long as the Berlin

Palace and as deep, to be absolutely secure against fire, there is one canal on one side and in the interior. The life of the city runs along these massive houses, the streets crossing in a passage of communication."[1]

It was not until later that the factory became infused with complex meaning — symbolizing progress, modernism, and industrialization — that architects began to pay attention to the typology as more than a signifier and it became a source of inspiration; then the responsibility of design still fell chiefly on the engineer. The load-bearing brick buildings were standardized in construction method to house the large-scale textile and cotton production machinery.

TECHNICAL FUNDAMENTALS

New methods of production were invigorated simultaneous to innovations in building materials and technologies in the late nineteenth century, and much scholarship has been completed on the subject. Architects embraced reinforced concrete, structural steel, and large sheets of glass as an opportunity to support mass production methods and to develop a new design aesthetic. Manufacturers began to realize the need for workspaces filled with light and air, as well as uninterrupted and flexible space. Working conditions were taken into consideration by the designers with new ergonomic design. These functional requirements inspired new factory designs that were rational, economical (and thus efficient for the industrialist), and superseded aesthetics. Yet, as fascinated as architects were with the factory as a new vernacular, engineers, rather than architects, were equipped to address the factory's spatial organization and management systems, including the layout for equipment, processing flow, methods of manufacturing such as gravity-flow systems, and later automated assembly lines — increasing productivity and, economies of scale, and thus, inventive construction techniques.

▲ Sugar Houses, Liberty
Street, New York, 1730–1963

Often the designs for early mills and works, were copied directly from handbooks written by industrialists, so that the mills in Lowell and Waltham, Massachusetts had similarly built masonry brick structures with densely spaced wood columns for the support of multiple floors. Sometimes the factory designs were determined by the machine inventors who also sold plans to the owner in order to properly house the equipment, but were not asked to design the spaces. Millwrights, such as Oliver Evans, as discussed previously, set up operations with a textile machinery designer to coordinate the shafting to the water wheels. Sometimes an owner would supervise the construction themselves, such as Harvey Firestone (1868–1938), of the tire company, who used a string to study the material flow and production sequence for his factory in the 1870s.[2]

Factories were thus arranged with efficiency at the forefront of the industrialists' requirements. It was not until the early twentieth century that a profession developed to combine the skills of the management experts, mechanical engineers, and production managers — that of the industrial engineer, who "sought profits through factory efficiency instead of the traditional business pursuits of sales and was concerned with managing every element of production."[3] The industrial engineer was hired to expedite production processes — often following Taylor's Scientific Management methods — and to address safety, hygiene, and worker comfort, which was believed would improve the worker's efficiency and thus profits. The engineers worked with plant layouts arranged in various letter shapes such as L, H, or E that would compact the distribution, keep power sources nearby, or create an internal courtyard for outdoor work, railroad spurs, and access to additional light. The raw materials would enter at one end, circulate through the production process and the final product would be packaged and ready for shipping at the other end in a sequential — but not always efficient — process. Sometimes, as factories grew, interior courtyards would be filled in haphazardly with smaller workshops and sheds.

▲ Karl Friedrich Schinkel, sketch of Manchester, England, 1826
▲ Typical urban factory, Chicago, 1921
▲ James Bogardus' drawing of cast iron construction, New York, 1856

To improve the flow, the Gilbreths used what they called a Route Model, following the idea of architectural models to better visualize a layout. The Butt factory in Providence, Rhode Island tried this out in 1912 by making a three-story scaled model of the factory interior, showing each floor and placing cardboard rectangles cut to scale to represent the area for the best arrangement of machinery. The model was much more flexible than a two-dimensional drawing. Then plant managers used strings of different colors to represent the routes of the different materials to find the shortest path of work through the building. They would then place colored tickets on the machinery to indicate which ones to move into place. These methods continued in the design of factories through the 1950s with increasingly complex physical models.

New loft building typologies developed for multiple tenants, such as in the cast iron buildings of what is now the SoHo district in New York City, or those afore-mentioned in Montreal and along the Hamburg waterfront. The loft structures had greater floor-to-ceiling heights for large machinery, increased light and air, and were generic and standardized in their dimensions according to column spacing and window types. Numerous inventions — from new forms of power distribution and electric lighting to materials handling equipment and elevators — allowed for, or required, factories to be built in multiple stories. The loft building typology was the result of high land values; by building upwards, a company could achieve more space at a cheaper cost than the value of the land. New elevators made this height worthwhile and profitable. They compressed the building to a smaller site and, within that new organization, the manufacturing process as well. Promotions for factory space leases noted that the distance from the center of one floor to that of the upper floor was a shorter distance than if one-story floors were laid side by side. The loft form of construction therefore saved human energy, as elevator transport was faster than horizontal pushing of hand trucks and carts.[4] Other constraints and requirements assisted in the resolution of urban factory and its pragmatic value.

▲ Gilbreth Route Model
in use at the Butt Factory,
Providence, Rhode Island,
1912

POWER

The height of a mill or loft was also advantageous for power distribution in the nineteenth century. A network of gears and shafts could harness energy from a water wheel along a river or canal — this system functioned best for textile mills.

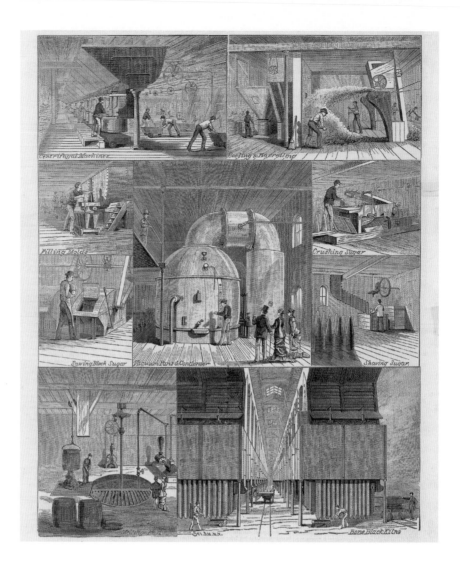

▲ Havemayer & Elder's
sugar refinery, Williamsburg,
New York, *Scientific
American*, 1879
▶ Clutter of belt drives at
Ford's Highland Park, 1911

The change in method of power generation from water wheels to steam-powered
drive shafts greatly impacted the need for the construction of vertical factories so
that power could reach the upper floors; power was transmitted through the vertical
shaft system via leather belts — later made of wrought iron — and bevel gears,
called millwork.[5] With steam power, shafts that ran the length of the building with
power take-off connections at each workstation resulted in a clutter of belts and
overhead line shafts in tight parallel rows. Each workstation was powered with a
belt drive and wide belts that ran from machines to the ceiling, blocked light and visibility across the floor. There was also little space for the workers to move, and safety
was an issue as the belts were exposed. To facilitate access to the power source, the
floors had lower ceiling heights and the space became more condensed. This density
and disorder necessitated the separation of operations by floor.

The forest of belts was gradually phased out in the early twentieth century
as individualized electric engines, or single-drive motors, were conjoined into
a more seamless unit, without the need for so many belts.[6] Sometimes a variety
of power generation was used simultaneously, from coal-fed steam to electricity.

Electricity had the greatest impact on factory space as it eliminated the line shafts and opened the interiors, allowing for more flexibility for the manufacturing process, increased light, and freedom of movement for workers.[7] Workers stood or sat behind the equipment, which was spaced apart more generously. There was increased visibility between workers and for supervisors to see them.

MATERIAL HANDLING

Material handling machinery in the late nineteenth century simplified and expedited the production process, first aiding workers' convenience moving goods and equipment, then becoming integrated with the building itself, turning the factory into an automated production machine. As with Oliver Evans' mill schemes, the vertical factories of this period used height as an opportunity to process goods by integrating vertical elements such as chutes and ramps into the building in order to move materials without using power. Gravity played a large part in conveyance for vertical urban factories, with the development of spiral conveyors that would streamline the movement of goods from floor to floor, or between mezzanines and first floors — a technology still in use today. The spiral form allowed for control over the speed of conveyance, depending on the spiral's curvature, which paced a product's passage.

Pushcart trolleys, hand trucks, cranes, and interior rails precluded workers from lifting by hand, relieving slowdowns. Mechanisms such as overhead conveyors, moving conveyors, interior floor lifts, and elevators aided between-floor operations. Traveling overhead, conveyors, such as those developed by engineer Jervis B. Webb, revolutionized shops as they could move across a vast space on a beam above or rails below, and hoist heavy objects up and across the multistoried spaces. Often, balconies were cantilevered and staggered in an interior court for loading and unloading materials to an internal rail via the use of a traveling crane. This was the case in the Brooklyn Army Terminal, in New York (1919), and in the Boots factory, in England (1932), among others.

For example, products in the food and beverage industry could be packaged on one floor and moved by crane down to a lower floor for storage or shipping. Double-runway spirals placed in parallel could deliver cases to the next steps on an assembly line; roller conveyors with wheels like roller skates could be used to follow curved belt lines, smoothly following the flow of a particular process. Chutes were used to connect disparate steps in a manufacturing process, which by necessity were often separated on different floors of a factory; they allowed goods to move down vertically through holes cut in the floor slab, or even out of factory windows and down adjacent courtyards or lightwells, exploiting both the building's height and the force of gravity to improve the workflow, long before electric machinery began to be implemented.

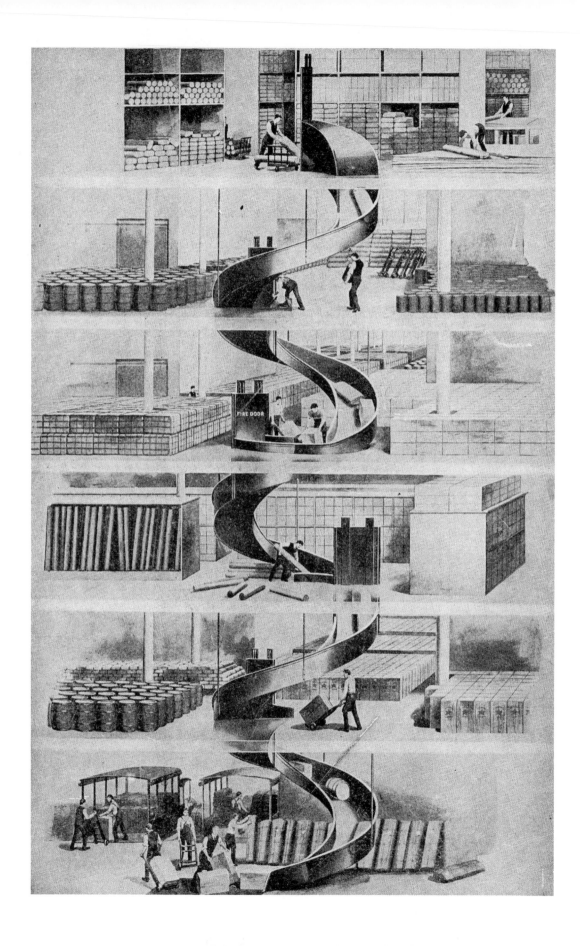

ELEVATORS

Elevators, first used in workshops and factories, directly contributed to the ability of factory owners to build tall structures. At first, elevators were simple platforms, cut out of the factory floors, operated by hand to hoist heavy objects; later they were powered by steam and hydraulics. The platforms then became enclosed and grew in dimension. Factories and warehouses typically had one elevator dedicated to freight and another for the workers. After Elisha Otis (1811–1861) invented the brake system for elevators in 1852, buildings could rise higher because a safety mechanism would snap to lock the carrier in place if the hoisting rope broke, allowing for safer passenger use. Later, elevators became an integral part of industrial buildings.

One of New York-based architects Cory & Cory's patents from 1929 explored the flow of trucks to enter elevators in restricted spaces. They invented a rotating platform system, similar to that of a rail car turntable, that rotated trucks into position, so that they could maneuver into elevators and deliver goods to upper floors. The elevator contours, or *slings*, allowed for trucks to pivot, gaining additional turning radius. Among their other patents was the design of an hourglass, or X-shape, pair of truck ramps, with ends that pivot along vertical guide rails. These innovative ramps were inscribed into the floor slab itself, with rounded edges, enabling trucks to safely move from one ramp to another. Other elevators were designed in rows along a semicircle of freight platforms, in which channels would line up the truck to the appropriate elevator. Cory & Cory's 1931 elevators at Starrett-Lehigh, in New York were designed to be more robust so as to accommodate the weight of a full truck or boxcar filled with raw materials or goods which would enter the building directly, facilitating distribution to each floor. Cory & Cory provided space for a truck to back out at a landing pit on each floor. To ensure these turnaround pits would fit within the floor slab spacing, they staggered the landings, such that they were sunken below the surrounding floor by several meters, on each floor. This also allowed for pairs of trucks to be processed at once, preventing a bottleneck at elevator entrances.

As noted in a handbook of the time, there were advantages to multistory factories, "the development of high-speed lifts, elevators, hoists, mechanical and gravity conveyors and chutes" made them popular. "Single story buildings naturally need a much greater site area than multi-story buildings, and are therefore most economical where land values are low and ground space plentiful." With multistory factories, "more compact planning is possible and the planning of pipe runs, ventilation, trunking, communications and services generally can be more economical and supervision and general communication and access easier."[8]

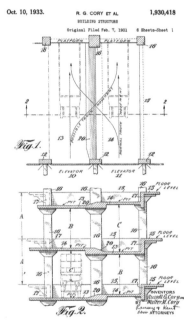

◀ Spiral chute in a vertical factory to move materials by gravity, 1917
▲ Steam-powered elevator, similar to the Otis concept, from the 1860s
▲ Cory & Cory elevator shaft patent, used at Starrett–Lehigh Building, New York, 1931

THE ART OF THE ENGINEER

The engineer's role as a designer, not only a structural innovator, is rarely recognized.[9] Early twentieth-century engineers including Jules Saulnier, Owen Williams, Ernest Ransome, Eugene Freyssinet, François Hennebique, and Robert Maillart, who experimented with reinforced concrete and long span steel, influenced the ways in which buildings could be designed. Their focus on the structure as informing the building shape was capitalized on in the design of factories, which were also seen by them as opportunities for experimentation that arose from new programmatic challenges and new materials such as steel, concrete, and glass inspired by greenhouse construction. Iron frameworks provided a practical solution for the 1872 Menier chocolate factory designed by architect Jules Saulnier (1817–1881). Coincidently, it was one of the first exposed iron-frame buildings in engineering history. Iron had formerly been used for interior structural supports and for increased fireproofing. When combined with brick masonry and terracotta cladding, the resultant innovative engineering solution to a well-apportioned design made for an integrated building.

Natural light transformed spaces of production and their organization. In the early vernacular mills of the eighteenth century, most window openings were small, and the heavy masonry walls cast shadows as a result; buildings' dimensions were narrow to admit as much daylight as possible. Workbenches were placed along the windows and larger equipment in the center aisles. The mills buildings' width followed the relatively short length of wooden joists until iron, and then later steel, was used, which expanded the column-to-column distances. As the

distribution of power through gears and shafts was eliminated, sunlight could then enter unobstructed through the windows, filtering deeper into the space. Sawtooth-shaped light monitors on the roofs also illuminated the upper floor. Even with densely spaced workstations, this structural form allowed light to penetrate the space. With the potential for larger windows via stronger structures, the factory loft type became most predominant in the nineteenth century. At the beginning of the twentieth century, as structural frames were made sturdier, complete facades could be built in steel and glass.

STEIFF

One significant example of a unique glass facade that presaged Modern curtain wall systems and was made possible from the new steel and greenhouse typologies was the Steiff factory of 1903. Here, Margarete Steiff (1847–1909) manufactured stuffed animals, dolls, and the Teddy bear (after Roosevelt) in Giengen an der Brenz, Germany. Production took place in her own house, which the company quickly outgrew, and she expanded into a new vertical factory that, though not urban, is noteworthy for its engineering and aesthetic innovations.

The factory was designed, not by architects, but by Margarete's husband Friedrich and her son Richard, who were builders. The family's primary concern was providing light for the workers. Their three-story steel rectangular structure was built on a concrete foundation, and constructed by local steel and glass fabricators who normally built greenhouses. Refined steel framework, with welded T-sections bolted to the columns, held sheets of glass in a unique double-skin system to regulate the building's climate. The building was supported by a structural steel frame sized 30-by-12-meters with six trussed columns on the shorter side, and I-section columns running along the longer side, where there was an additional X bracing system that provided lateral stiffness. The double windows allowed for access between the skins for maintenance and ventilation; the translucent layering of the facade also animated the building. A covered bridge connected the second building to the original structure.

Perhaps because this building type was more closely aligned with greenhouse construction and the vernacular, it was never published in architecture journals, and architectural historians have overlooked Steiff. This omission may be due to the product as well — toys — and because the factory was one of the few owned by a woman. Regardless, it did not garner the interest of the architectural elite, as did other factory building designs. Like the Crystal Palace, erected to house the Great Exhibition of 1851 in London, Steiff (and the vernacular, generally) meant to provide a functional system rather than a self-consciously Modern aesthetic. Pierre Francastel's observations about the Crystal Palace could also be applied to Steiff: "Rather than searching for forms that could be generated from the arrangement of large plates of glass, the architect remained faithful to the greenhouse model. He did not realize that the glass panel cleared the way for new types of volumetric systems."[10]

◀ Jules Saulnier, Menier Chocolate Co., Noisiel-sur-Marne, France, 1872
▲ Friedrich and Richard Steiff, Steiff Factory, Giengen an der Brenz, Germany, 1903
▲ Friedrich and Richard Steiff, Steiff Factory, south facade, Geingen an der Brenz, Germany, in 1991

But it was concrete that held the biggest breakthrough for Modern factories as engineer-entrepreneurs developed steel reinforcement, hence the name "ferro-concrete," that concealed its iron meshwork composition. The new ability for the material to work in both compression and tension allowed for major changes in factory designs, including: increased strength of concrete slab floors for heavier machinery and stability; longer spans between the spacing of structural columns; reduced vibrations and fire hazards; and larger openings for windows. These daylight factories — inspirational to Modern architects — had the added benefit of improving the workers' space.

Numerous engineers contributed to inventive concrete systems. One system was French engineer François Hennébique's (1842–1921) method for creating a singular concrete slab by using steel rods secured together with stirrups and binding rods to reinforce concrete in a T-shaped beam. Hennébique's patented tension bars countered diagonal shear to withstand the tension; thousands of structures in France used his reinforced system. American Ernest L. Ransome (1852–1917) developed a concrete reinforcing system called the Ransome Bar. It was a simplified system based on Ransome's addition to the 1903 Borax refinery in Bayonne, New Jersey, in which reinforcing bars were twisted to increase the bond to the concrete, making a unified concrete frame structure. His patented system could extend the floor slab beyond the column line of the facade to support brick walls and larger window openings and made possible horizontal ribbon windows. Reyner Banham (1922–1988) suggested that Le Corbusier's Dom-ino system reflects this system because of the way the slab is extended, in a kit-of-parts fabrication method, and the superimposition of floor upon floor, with the wall as a separate element.[11] Ransome's 1903 Beverly, Massachusetts United Shoe Machinery Company employed this system to limit vibration from the machines in concrete floor slabs and to make longer concrete girders for increased spans. The four-story building with large windows had a planar facade and greatly influenced Giacomo Matté-Trucco's (1869–1934) design for Fiat's Lingotto, Italy factory in 1923. Precast structural beams could be set in place and then the floor cast on top, in an early pre-fabricated system with infill brick walls.

In Europe, the engineer-builders Wayss and Freytag of Germany, French architect-engineers August Perret (1874–1954), and Eugène Freyssinet (1879–1962) designed concrete structures including factory buildings and warehouses, advancing concrete and its capabilities for construction in terms of speed, economy, and scale. Swiss engineer Robert Maillart (1872–1940) experimented with concrete construction for three-hinged arched mountain bridges, using minimal materials. Maillart invented a beamless floor slab in a two-way system that was lighter and thinner than the American mushroom-and-slab column system devised by Henry C. Turner (1871–1954) of Milwaukee. Maillart also experimented with the mushroom column at a box company warehouse in 1913 in Lancey, France, which had a beamless floor slab and round columns with corbels to hold a running crane.

An American company invested in Boots, the English pharmaceutical company, for a Modern factory design built between 1927–1933 in Beeston, Nottinghamshire. Designed by the engineer E. Owen Williams (1890–1969), the same engineer who would design the Sainsbury's factory two years later, Boots was modeled on the process set up by its parent company, the United Drug Company of America. Williams designed a factory that followed the production flow, rather than attempting to squeeze the process into a more generic space. Working with the company's production engineer, Henry Jessop, the original plan called for a 900-meter-long plant with two wings, one for the wet processing and the other for the dry. However, only the wet area was built in the 60,300-square-meter building.

Williams had worked for Julius Kahn's London branch of the Trussed Concrete Steel Company (Truscon Steel) and experimented with concrete. He recommended it for use at Boots. A flat concrete slab construction with octagonal concrete mushroom capitals supporting a shallow inverted pyramid shearhead was constructed a few years later. The natural structure of palm trees inspired his design, with columns spaced in bays 9.75-by-11 meters.[11] The plant would have two four-story halls, one for manufacturing and one for packing.

Using the full verticality of the building, the raw materials and supplies moved up and down throughout the space. The pharmaceutical mixtures were made on the ground floor and traveled upward for packaging via a conveyor in the central hall, to filling bottles or cases, and then on to packing, storage, and shipping. As in Ford's Highland Park, workers sent boxes from projecting third-floor balconies down chutes to the main floor for packing, thus utilizing the full flow of the building and its vertical dimension. The glazing and concrete construction has been compared to the Van Nelle factory, although among other differences Boots has offices contained within the main volume rather than a separate administration building.

The building received plenty of light and air through large steel casement Crittall windows, internal courtyards surrounded by working balconies, and skylights comprised of glass disks set within the concrete roof. The space had three bridges to connect the two main building units. The raw materials entered by train or truck into the central space, via a covered loading dock that was integrated into

▲ E. Owen Williams, Boots Pure Drug Company, Beeston, England, 1927–1933
▲ E. Owen Williams, interior hall showing gravity chutes and conveyor systems, Boots, Beeston, England, 1927–1933

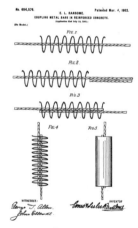

▲ United Shoe Machinery
Corporation, Beverly,
Massachusetts, 1903–1905
▲ Ransome, patent for rein-
forced concrete, 1884
▶ Pier Luigi Nervi, Burgo
Paper Mill, Mantua, Italy, 1962

the building (similar to the Starrett-Lehigh building) and were offloaded via a traveling crane mounted on corbels on the columns.

Although an engineer designed the building, the architectural press recognized the project's importance in terms of furthering Modernism and functionalist architecture, publishing the project in numerous places.[12] Williams considered the factory as a three-dimensional processing system, noting in a lecture that "I can picture the factory of the future as a great single span shell, housing a vast machine with its workers dotted about in no way that can be related to definite horizontal plans or floors."[13] The building's success furthered that of the company, validating the ideas of production efficiency made possible by the layout of the factory itself. The factory flow and the worker's efficiency increased enough to allow the management to reduce the workweek from 47.5 to 42.5 hours.

Concrete experimentation continued through the 1950s with more dynamic and expressionist forms by engineers such as the Italian Pier Luigi Nervi (1891–1979), Spaniards Eduardo Torroja (1899–1961) and Felix Candela (1910–1997), as well as Swiss engineer Heinz Isler (1926–2009). These engineers completed the design of more horizontal concrete factories that were expressive in their function while following the flow of the factory processing, often with the sole purpose of creating uninterrupted space that was then made possible by the new techniques for shell, structure construction. In particular, Candela's Bacardi Rum building in Mexico of 1960 featured three hyperbolic paraboloid groined vaults in a thin shell structure that spanned a series of production spaces and then could be easily expanded.

In a clear relationship between design engineer and project, Nervi's Burgo Paper Mill near Mantua, Italy in the early 1960s merges building with machine. Constructed by Beloit Italia of Pinerolo for paper making in a linear sequence, the 100-meter-long plant transformed wood pulp into newsprint and packaging paper

in large spools at the speed of 1,000 meters per minute. Just as Oliver Evans' flour
mill was one continuous process, this building allowed the machinery to follow
a fluid process to convert a raw material to a finished product. The building size
was not only determined by the size of the machinery, which would have occupied
a length of 250 meters, but also took into consideration the potential for future
expansion. Nervi designed a building that would have been double the size in parallel, and would share a central common space so that one of the vertical supports
would have to be eliminated. While this scheme didn't come to fruition, the idea
of production-as-expansion was paramount to the building of so many factories of
this optimistic period.

For Nervi, the length of the papermaking process suggested a bridge structure to house an open expanse of space, and he stacked two levels for optimum
production. Included on site were vats for pulp, refining, tanks, pumps, spooling
mechanisms and an overhead bridge crane. The roof is an uninterrupted structure of rectilinear steel beams, each weighing 700 tons, suspended by four double
trestle tie beams, in reinforced concrete, 47-meters high at a distance of 164 meters.
Between the base and the roof there is a continuous facade of steel and glass that
allows plenty of natural light into the space. The building combines the feats of
structural engineering with that of new geometries and concrete experimentation
in order for the production to work efficiently.

Engineers defined a new art of construction as they became designers in their
own right, whether or not they were collaborating with architects focusing on
technical potential or organizing the production flow. The following more detailed
examples of vertical urban factories incorporate the innovations by Modern engineers who designed factories such as the Packard Plant, Fiat Lingotto, Sainsbury's,
and the Moscow bakeries.

PACKARD PLANT

ALBERT KAHN, JULIUS KAHN, AND ERNEST WILBY, DETROIT, MICHIGAN, 1903–1906

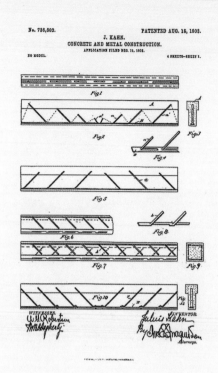

In the late nineteenth century, Detroit capitalized on its myriad skilled workers to establish the city as a center for manufacturing. The welded and molded interchangeable iron and steel parts workers used to assemble goods such as bicycles, carriages, stoves, and engines evolved into parts for automobiles. Many manufactories were housed along the Detroit River waterfront in vernacular multistoried brick buildings with small windows, wood floors, beams, and window sashes; as they grew, the factories often expanded incrementally across adjacent blocks. As dense manufacturing mixed with other uses in the city center, and grew along railroad lines to the north, Milwaukee Junction became an industrial transportation hub and numerous factories purchased sites along it for ease of transport. By the early twentieth century, multistoried concrete frame buildings rose block by block, with people bustling to work via tramlines along Woodward Avenue and other main thoroughfares.

At this time, over forty auto manufacturers made Detroit their home, harnessing the expertise of machinists and inventors such as Ford, Oldsmobile, Studebaker, Dodge, Packard, and Fisher, among many others who started automotive companies. During World War II, these industries coalesced into the identity of the city as the Great Arsenal of Democracy, and contributed to Detroit's thriving economy. Eventually the automotive companies consolidated into what came to be known as the Big Three: Ford, Chrysler, and General Motors (GM). In 1947, there were 3,772 manufacturing establishments and 338,373 manufacturing jobs in Detroit.

Albert Kahn (1869–1942) and his engineer-brother Julius (1874–1942), founded the Trussed Concrete Steel Company of Detroit, or Tuscon, and developed an innovative concrete reinforcing system called the Kahn bar, which used two steel bars on 45-degree angles to counter diagonal tension stresses.[14] This system was used in the Packard Plant Building No. 10 in Detroit.

Together the brothers designed and built what was known as Building 10 at the Packard Motor Car Plant on Grand Boulevard, which was also accessible by railroad. In 1903 they erected nine, multistoried traditional brick mill-style structures

around a courtyard with offices, assembly rooms, machine rooms, and storage. Building 10 embodied all the aspirations of the Modernist movement including the activity within – to manufacture the new mass-produced automobile.

As Detroit's first reinforced-concrete factory, it was built directly on the ground with the location of heavy machinery on that first floor and the lighter parts assembly above. Anticipating expansion the building was originally only two stories high but the roof was designed to hold extra load as a floor. This allowed it to grow by two additional stories a few years later. Building 10 "shifted the race to the fast track of the automotive industry. It also indicated Kahn's readiness to try what was an unusual path for an architect – putting aside the formalistic paraphernalia of the typical practice to try a less glamorous kind of design determined solely on practical grounds."[15] The building is Modern in construction, with beams supported on columns without girders to allow for larger fenestration and taller space. Although still designed with the traditional double-hung sash grouped in triplicate to give the impression

▲ Julius Kahn, Kahn system of reinforced concrete patent (Kahn bar), 1903

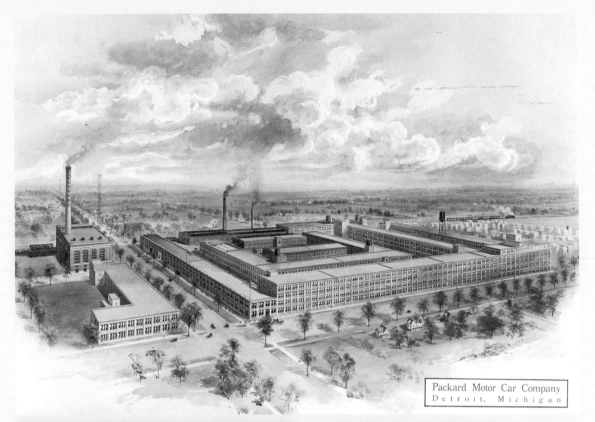

Packard Motor Car Company
Detroit, Michigan

▲ Julius and Albert Kahn, drawing of Packard
Motor Car Co., Detroit, Michigan, 1903
▲ Completed cars
▲ Interior administration office

FINISHED VEHICLES
IN PROCESS MATERIAL
RAW MATERIALS

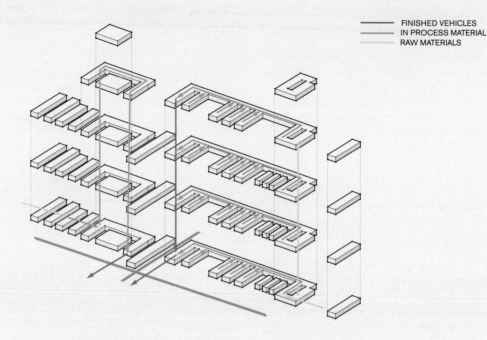

of a larger opening, the windows rose to the full ceiling height, thus increasing the natural light. This strategy, in turn, allowed the concrete structural grid to be expressed on the facade in what could be considered a vernacular modern. In the 18-by-100-meter building, columns widely spaced at ten-meter intervals opened up the interior for large-scale equipment and flexible space for manufacturing. The Kahn reinforcing bars resisted tension along the bottom of the beam or girder and then lay adjacent to each other along the span to resist shear in the concrete beams.

Although Building 10 had glazed tile and brick spandrels on its main facade, its chief characteristics were minimal detailing and tough structural expression – sharp edges and a flat facade and roof made for an economic building pared down to its structural bones. As Banham noted about the project, "It is the null-value condition, the zero-term of architecture, and hardly any other architect or builder with a professional conscience could have done it."[16] This simplicity of construction is where the engineering takes precedence over the architectural detailing, and became an influential Modern vertical factory trope.

Infrastructure connections were essential to the factory location: a railroad spur ran alongside the building and pedestrian bridges connected the different levels of the shops of the one-million-square-meter complex. The company employed six-thousand workers making up to 54,000 cars in 1928. After decades of neglect, the building is now being renovated into a mixed-use manufacturing building.

▲ Julius and Albert Kahn, Plant No. 10, Packard Motor Car Co., Detroit, Michigan, 1905

FIAT LINGOTTO

**GIACOMO MATTÈ-TRUCCO,
TURIN, ITALY, 1913–1923**

Italian industry in the early twentieth century was supported by a newly constructed network of transit and communications in the north, which became home to automotive and aircraft industries including Alfa-Romeo, Bianchi, Pirelli, and Olivetti. Giovanni Agnelli (1866–1945) founded the Fiat automobile company in 1899 with a group of investors, beginning its first large-scale production line in 1912 in Turin on the Corso Dante. The company's subsidiaries, located nearby, fed into its supply chain. Agnelli realized the potential for cheaper production and made a popular smaller car, the Tipo Zero, from 1912 to 1915. In World War I, due to pressing demand for vehicular transport, a new plant was needed to produce 25,000 engines, trucks, ambulances, and aircraft per year. Fiat diversified to steel works, shipyards, aviation, and larger engineering complexity to corner the wartime market.

Like so many European industrialists, Agnelli toured American factories to see the design and the management style, including Albert Kahn's Highland Park, which was inspirational to him.[17] Upon returning to Italy, he hired structural engineer Giacomo Mattè-Trucco (1869–1934) to design the new Lingotto factory, which opened in 1923. Mattè-Trucco studied mechanical engineering in Turin and worked not only for Fiat but for the foundry Michele Ansaldi, which had been absorbed by Fiat in 1909. He became Fiat's mechanical director and ran the company's steel foundry, then worked on the development of diesel motors. Mattè-Trucco went on to study structural engineering and built naval dockyards, arsenals, silos, and the hydroelectric plant of Perosa on the Chisone River in 1928.

Ugo Gobbato (1888–1945) also joined the team as production engineer, along with engineers Francesco Cartasegna and Vittorio Bonadè Bottino (1889–1997). The new plant was designed as an integrated vertical factory, with the manufacturing organization based on continuous flow processing. Lingotto, unlike most vertical factories, had a unique distinction: its production was inverted, flowing from bottom to top. The process culminated in a dramatic kilometer-long, oval, banked rooftop test track that embodied the new cult of the automobile and was immediately embraced by Italy's Futurist

artists and architects. In fact, the Gruppo 7 salon of architects considered it one of the few industrial buildings in Italy that possessed architectural value. Futurist poet F. T. Marinetti called it the "prime invention of Futurist construction." Although Mattè-Trucco was never involved in the Rationalist movement, the Fiat building figured prominently in the first Esposizione dell'Architettura Razionale in Rome in 1928.

Lingotto was unprecedented in scale for a European factory, with 4.8 million square meters of manufacturing space accommodating six-thousand workers. The complex included a main production building, smaller buildings for pre-assembly, and a small office building with classical columns called the "Palazzina" (Little Palace). The five-story main plant was composed of two elongated wings running parallel for 536 meters. Two four-story workshops joined at the ends for material flow. At regular intervals, towers – three inside and one at each end – linked the parallel volumes to create interior courtyards for light and air. A square press-shop for handling sheet metal sat at the south end and a five-story building housing the assembly workshop was at

▲ **Giacomo Mattè-Trucco, helical concrete interior ramp, Fiat factory, Lingotto, Italy, 1926**

the north. The trains arrived in Turin via the goods yard alongside the factory (unlike many American urban factories, where they entered a courtyard) and cars were assembled moving upwards floor by floor, to the final production area. On the first floor the workers produced individual parts such as axles and transmissions and then the work was subdivided according to the process, then tested at each step, culminating in two assembly lines, one for the engineering and the other for the final car assembly.

Agnelli was inspired by Taylorism to enhance worker productivity and by Ford to implement manufacturing methods that would reduce the cost of his automobiles.[18] He made several visits to meet Henry Ford, which established a connection between the two families that continues even today. But he also used a system developed by French-born Charles Bedaux (1886–1944), who immigrated to the U.S. and pioneered methods similar to Taylor for his wage allocations. Wages were based on how much a person could produce within a specific time in a point system and, similar to the Gilbreths' studies, it allowed for worker rest time. Bedaux also believed that productivity could be improved if workers were satisfied on the job. He founded a consulting firm (still in existence), but the unions rejected his methods in the 1930s.[19]

By the time the Lingotto factory was completed, new movements organized by Communist Party-leader Antonio Gramsci (1891–1937), together with Palmiro Togliatti's socialist organization, L'Ordine Nuovo, protested Agnelli's new rationalization of production, advocating for increased pay and better working conditions. A revolt ensued, with workers in groups, or Councils occupying the factories in 1920. Agnelli attempted to foster cooperative management and established a "school of workers and technicians qualified for industrial change and work with 'rationalized' systems" but his efforts were rejected.[20] As many Italian industrialists, Agnelli supported the Facists to improve the economy, with much worker protest and dissatisfaction from the Communist party. With the Depression of 1929, Agnelli shifted the mass assembly line to piecework production, reducing production costs but also workers' pay.

In spite of the lack of consideration of the worker, the building itself was an exemplary Modern structure. In the factory construction Mattè-Trucco used the concrete structural system of French engineer François Hennebique, with G.A. Porcheddu, its Italian supplier. The module – six meters by six meters by five meters – was repeated to form a building that was 507 meters long by 80 meters wide by 27 meters high. Similar to the Kahn bar, Hennébique's patent combined the column with the floor slab. Square, concrete, thirty-five-centimeter-diameter columns with chamfered edges, spaced six

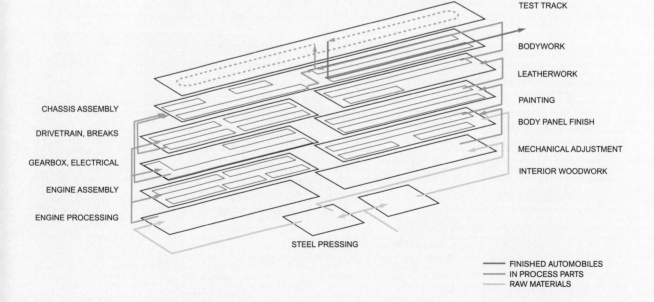

TEST TRACK

BODYWORK

LEATHERWORK

PAINTING

BODY PANEL FINISH

MECHANICAL ADJUSTMENT

INTERIOR WOODWORK

CHASSIS ASSEMBLY

DRIVETRAIN, BREAKS

GEARBOX, ELECTRICAL

ENGINE ASSEMBLY

ENGINE PROCESSING

STEEL PRESSING

―― FINISHED AUTOMOBILES
―― IN PROCESS PARTS
―― RAW MATERIALS

meters apart, were also similar to those used in Ransome's 1903 United Shoe factory in Beverly, Massachusetts. In fact, Banham found its design and detail more similar to Ransome's shoe factory than Kahn's Highland Park. The design of Lingotto – and its architectural features – constituted an immense change in the company's production from the smaller factory (or series of shops), to the large-scale all-under-one-roof building in a vertically integrated production process where all of the car parts came together in one factory. The windows were steel-frame Crittall multi-pane windows with central-tilt operating panels. Mattè-Trucco integrated the water pipes and electrical conduits through perforations in the concrete beams. In 1924 he added two spiral ramp towers – these allowed for the cars to reach the test track as well as for trolleys with supplies to be delivered between floors. The unique radiating concrete ribs of the spiral ramps

▲ Giacomo Mattè-Trucco, the crowning rooftop test track above the city, Fiat factory, Lingotto, Italy, 1926
◀ Architect Le Corbusier at the wheel, Fiat factory, Lingotto, Italy, 1934

iconic rooftop track was in the family of Chrysler in Buenos Aires and Imperia in Belgium.

Le Corbusier, along with Marinetti and the Futurists, considered Lingotto exemplary of Modernism both symbolically and ideologically. Corbusier visited the factory in 1925, at which time he noted that "windows in a grille-like pattern are too numerous to count. The top is like that of a taffrail of a ship, with decks, chimneys, courtyard and catwalks, surely one of industry's most impressive sights. . . . It is the Esprit Nouveau factory, useful in its precision and with the greatest clarity, elegance and economy."[22] Le Corbusier also featured the concrete structure in his manifesto, *Vers une Architecture* (*Towards a New Architecture*, 1923), as an iconic expression of industry. But as Banham points out, perhaps it is a "kind of testament to a lost future." Likewise, the Italian Marxist sociologist and political philosopher Antonio Negri said that with it "the period of industrial archaeology closes."[23] That Lingotto was perhaps the penultimate expression of an age that was to decline after World War II – consuming all the energy and innovation of optimistic and utopian capitalist ideals – was its paradox. Art and cultural critic Edoardo Persico (1900–1936) wrote about the Lingotto extensively, and Banham, citing Persico, writes that the track performs in a such a way that "the car and its speed are celebrated in a form that presides over the work of the factory below, not only in terms of utility, but also following a secret standard that governs the ends of things."[24]

In 1939 Fiat expanded production with a new factory in nearby Mirafiori designed by Vittorio Bonadè Bottino. In 1943, Lingotto was bombed but resisted destruction; the factory continued operations until 1982. The company enjoyed both an expansive domestic market and a strong postwar export market.

are a precursor to the structural concrete design work of Italian engineer Nervi. When drivers took the cars to the ovular rooftop track, they could only test at speeds up to sixty kilometers per hour, which, while exceeding normal road speeds of the time, was limited by the steep 27-degree curve embankments. As Banham said, the ramps "delivered the rolling vehicle into a cramped and awkward space under the shadow behind one of the banked turns that remain an essential part of the image of the building. From here the 'neo-nato' would emerge into Turin's smoggy sunshine on the roof, there to prove itself on the test track before finally returning to ground level in the parking yards between the plant and the Via Nizza."[21] The complex exemplified speed and progress, and was considered a crown in the Turin cityscape. Normally, testing tracks were spread out in fields adjacent to automotive plants, but Fiat's

▲ Fiat Lingotto under construction, 1923
▲ Interior courtyard, 1926
▲ Mario Palanti, Palacio Alcorta Chrysler, Buenos Aires, Argentina, 1927
▶ Steep bank of rooftop test track, Fiat factory, Lingotto, Italy, 1926

INFLUENCES

Fiat was inspired by the test tracks at other factories such as Belgium Imperia car factory in Nessonvaux. The low 1907 building provided a ramp from which the cars could drive up to the roof for testing. Others continued in the tradition as in Buenos Aires, Italian architect Mario Palanti designed what was called the "First Palace Speedway South America" in 1927. Capped with a test track/roadway, the building was a car and assembly facility for the Resta Brothers – representatives for Chrysler in Argentina. The country did not produce cars until this four-story factory was built, and then was later used by Plymouth, DeSoto, Dodge, and Imperia.

Known more simply as the Chrysler Building, the factory had four floors, which included a first-floor sales room and offices with assembly and parts manufacturing at the rear. On the second floor were workshops for retouching, finishing, and vehicle storage. The block-scaled building located on the edge of a residential area featured six bays on one facade with garage doors embellished with classical details, including a pediment over the main entrance. Behind the ornamental facade was a decidedly Modern reinforced concrete structure divided into five sections by vertically and horizontally inclined seams.

The cars would complete a high-speed road test on the 1,700-meter oval rooftop track with banked curves. A bridge provided pedestrian access from the rim of the track to the center for demonstrations, car and motorcycle races, and other events. The semi circular track was nested into the trapezoidal building as in a stadium. The main facade had sloped skylights to allow light into the showroom and assembly spaces. Unlike Fiat, the Chrysler Building had seating for three thousand spectators. The test track was originally divided into two parts: the upper level, where cars could reach speeds of 100 kilometers per hour on the brick pavement that was inclined, at some points, to greater than 45 degrees. To protect cars from going over the edge, there was a reinforced concrete parapet. The bottom section was for slower cars – test runs and amateurs. Adjacent to the racetrack was a restaurant with a colonnade from which the races could be observed. After the car company vacated the building, the National Government used it as an Army depot until 1994. The factory was redeveloped as housing, with the oval track repurposed as a central patio.

SAINSBURY'S

SIR OWEN WILLIAMS & PARTNERS,
LONDON, ENGLAND, 1931–1933

Engineer Sir Owen Williams (1890–1969) who had designed Boots' Wet Goods pharmaceutical factory went on to design numerous others including Sainsbury's in London. His work with concrete transformed modern construction technologies.[25]

Owen Williams saw concrete as a universal material representing the future that provided factories with obstruction-free spaces in the form of a "shell surrounding a process." Food processing and meatpacking are processes essential to urban life. Proximity to customers became all the more necessary as such food-related commerce moved from the home to large production facilities in the early days of mass production. As grocers became monopolies they often made their own prepared food, which was processed in cities to save on transport and refrigeration costs. One such company, Sainsbury's, founded in 1863, was for decades the largest grocery retailer in Great Britain. The company was best known for their own brand of cooked meats, sausages, pies, and prepared meals (which they invented). Scraps of discarded meat, dirty floors, and crowded conditions in early facilities instigated a project in 1930 for a new hygienic processing factory in London.

In the heart of the industrial city, Williams designed a six-story, 46,000-square-meter building on an irregularly shaped site along Rennie Street in Blackfriars. By using 25-centimeter-thick, flat-slab concrete floors supported on pyramidal mushroom columns that had a folded Cubist quality (1.5 meters in diameter for the basement and decreasing in diameter on the upper floors), Williams was able to design the structure with a regular, 13-by-11-meter grid and 4.5-meter floor-to-floor heights. The Sainsbury's factory was the first flat-slab concrete construction in London and the first structure in England built of poured-in-place concrete. Steel casement windows with translucent upper panes filled the structural framework with diffused light. The central section of the roof contained glass round lights set in concrete, as a skylight, and the interior had partitions in metal and glass. The factory was built in two phases: the main building and an annex. Seemingly, form followed function in every detail, including the hygienic,

easy-to-clean tile floors that were impervious to spills and food waste.

The ample light and cleanliness gave the sense of "going from a slum into Buckingham Palace," stated a former employee in 1937.[26] Designed to accommodate 700 workers during one shift, the factory could accommodate 2,100 workers per day over three shifts. Production was organized vertically. The basement held the curing cellar, storage, pigs' heads and brisket boning, the boiler room, and a paternoster elevator that ran on pulleys in a circular motion. The ground-floor loading bay spanned the full 26-meter width of the building. There, pig carcasses and raw goods were unloaded and moved to the upper floors by lifts, and final goods were sent

▲ Owen Williams, Sainsbury's factory, exterior view under construction, London, 1934–1936
▲ Working from overhead conveyors, 1936
▶ Women in company work uniforms stuffing sausage, 1936

down for packaging via lifts and gravity chutes. The fourth floor housed the meat kitchen, and the third floor was the Holy of Holies. It featured a seasoning room for storing garden-grown fresh herbs, as well as ovens and grinding machines. The second floor, with its mechanized overhead conveyance system, contained the butchering and sausage-making areas with chopping machines down the center of the floor; the meat parts went onto racks and were packed into flats and cut into sections for pies and sausages. The first floor housed the packaging, offices, and cooling areas for sausages and steak and kidney pies. The annex housed the dough and flour storage. Completing the processing loop, the ground floor received the return of parts, including the

fat and bones that went to the first-floor annex and tanks for the fat to settle. The annex also contained smokehouses and tanks for sausage cooking. The processing used the full verticality of the building, beginning at the bottom and looping down to the first floor again for waste.

Workers had a coatroom, washrooms, an area to hang aprons, and a tearoom. They were issued with a "clean wiper (laundered handcloth every day)," and there was an in-house clinic and nurse.[27] For safekeeping of company secrets, the recipes were locked up each night, then given out to the workers each morning. Sainsbury's occupied the factory until 2002.

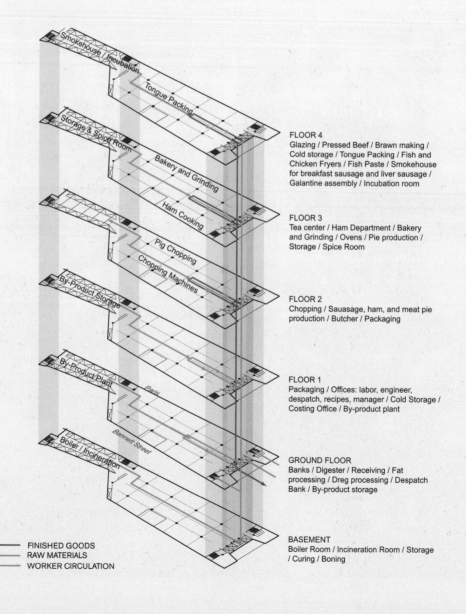

FLOOR 4
Glazing / Pressed Beef / Brawn making / Cold storage / Tongue Packing / Fish and Chicken Fryers / Fish Paste / Smokehouse for breakfast sausage and liver sausage / Galantine assembly / Incubation room

FLOOR 3
Tea center / Ham Department / Bakery and Grinding / Ovens / Pie production / Storage / Spice Room

FLOOR 2
Chopping / Sauasage, ham, and meat pie production / Butcher / Packaging

FLOOR 1
Packaging / Offices: labor, engineer, despatch, recipes, manager / Cold Storage / Costing Office / By-product plant

GROUND FLOOR
Banks / Digester / Receiving / Fat processing / Dreg processing / Despatch Bank / By-product storage

BASEMENT
Boiler Room / Incineration Room / Storage / Curing / Boning

—— FINISHED GOODS
—— RAW MATERIALS
- - - WORKER CIRCULATION

BAKERIES
G. P. MARSAKOV, MOSCOW, 1930s

Some of the most impressive engineered factories, both formally and functionally, are a series of
Russian Constructivist bakeries by the engineer
Georgy Petrovich Marsakov (1886–1961), one
of which is still in operation. An example of how
production was mechanized – which had previously been more of a cottage or even homemade
industry – is seen in the consolidation of bread
baking in Moscow in the late 1920s and early
1930s. Bread baking had begun to be more
mass produced in the early nineteenth century,
again for wartime, with kneading machines,
rollers, molds, and new ingredients which could
replicate the process in a consistent way each
time. Ovens, in particular, were designed in
tunnel shapes in order to support continuous
and larger scale production; patience was
required due to the unpredictability of the action
of leavening agents such as yeast and the time
involved. To speed up the baking process, substitutes such as baking powders from carbonic
acids were used; these also supported a more
controlled method and consistent quality in the
bread. As bakeries became mechanized, their
processes became more tightly controlled and
their scale ballooned.

In Moscow, bread baking became mechanized through government decree, which, in
turn, required new factories to be built with all
the rational systems of Modernist manufacturing technology and design. Due to a sudden
increase in population created by the influx of
peasants into cities for work – a result of collectivization and industrialization – bakers had to
increase their production. Government-funded
bakeries usurped the smaller private bakeries.
Bakeries were considered to be part of the
national infrastructure, along with transportation
and plumbing, and received capital investment
between 1924 and 1934. Twelve bakeries were
completed at this time in order to feed the burgeoning urban populace; they can be divided into
two organizational and structural types.[28]

One system, developed by the joint-stock
company Melstroy, was rectangular, with suspended cradles moving along a straight line and
allowing for a continuous process. But a more
complex and interesting system was by engineer
Georgy P. Marsakov, who revolutionized the
baking industry. He employed a circular conveyor

system that provided continuous automatic production of bread from the top of the factory down
to the loading docks in a vertical production
system similar to Oliver Evans' machine from the
eighteenth century.

For the round factories No. 5, or the V. P.
Zotov on Khodynkaia Street, and also for No. 9
Novodmitrovskaya, the flour arrived by train on
tracks adjacent to the factory so that it could be
directly delivered to the basement warehouse. It
was then conveyor-fed to the fourth floor where
the starter yeast was located and the dough
was mixed. From the fourth floor, the dough was
moved through three circular chutes to the third
floor, where the fermentation process occurred.
After the end of fermentation, dough fell through
slats into the second floor dough-cutting facility
where workers made them into loaves, then
moved them to the nearby round-ring furnaces via
a conveyor system. After baking, the loaves were
unloaded from the furnaces and lowered to the
first floor via inclined metal spiral chutes, ending
up on a circular, shelf-like suspended table from
which they were gathered to be packaged and
stored. From the internal loading areas the bread
was delivered to the city residents by trucks.
The factory had the capacity to bake 240 tons of

▲ **Georgy P. Marsakov, Bakery, Moscow, 1930s.
Photographs by Richard Pare, 2001**

bread per day. Marsakov designed infrastructural systems such as the pipes, furnace, machinery, and fittings, which he improved in subsequent iterations, such as the plants in Moscow and two plants in St. Petersburg.

Each factory is a variation of the same design concept: the series of primarily four-story brick buildings housed the factory in the cylindrical volume with offices in rectangular side buildings. Double-height, operable, narrow vertical wooden windows admitted light into the factory floors and the interior – including the columns and wall surfaces – was glazed, with white, easy-to-clean tiles. In the main mixing space, circular tables or

conveyors held the vats of dough as they moved through the production process. The structural ribs of the ceiling were exposed and fanned out to the building edge. Towers, placed at the edges of the bakery so as not to interfere with the processing, provided circulation for the workers. The stacking of the factories on multiple floors took advantage of the flow of vertical processing as well as the compact center city sites. Marsakov's round factories may have been influential precursors to Buckminster Fuller's Cotton Mill of 1952.

▲ **Georgy P. Marsakov, interior of Moscow Bakery, 1930s. Photograph by Richard Pare, 2001**

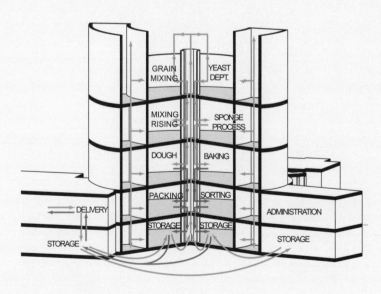

GRAIN MIXING   YEAST DEPT.

MIXING RISING   SPONGE PROCESS

DOUGH   BAKING

PACKING   SORTING

DELIVERY

ADMINISTRATION

STORAGE   STORAGE

STORAGE   STORAGE

—— BREAD
—— INGREDIENTS
—— WORKER

FACTORY AS AN ARCHITECT'S DOMAIN

Architects were often not placed in charge of factory design until a company desired to improve a worker's well-being or to align the company's interest in expressing a company image or brand, merging identity with what could be called the "spectacle." Sometimes architects were hired to design only the administration buildings and meeting places for the industrial clients and their customers (not laborers). Sometimes architects were included in a commission to decorate factory facades — perhaps just the parapets or entryways — just as Swiss engineer Robert Maillart was asked to embellish the structural bones of his 1903 bridges with carved stone motifs. Even Albert Kahn continued to decorate factory parapets while the heart of the manufacturing spaces were increasingly Modern. Ornamentation was frowned upon, as Gropius explained in 1913:

> For a long time factories were regarded as belonging to the unavoidable evils one had to bear and a bleak tumble-down establishment was thought to suffice. It was only with the general growth of property that something more began to be expected. The first steps were taken with improved lighting, heating and ventilation, though now and again an architect was called in somewhat belatedly to adorn the bare utility structure with what were invariably unsuitable trimmings, a procedure which unfortunately is still a favorite one today. This misguided approach simply conceals the unsolved difficulties from the outside, distorting the true character of the building by allowing it to masquerade in borrowed garments from an earlier period which have absolutely nothing in common with the sterner purposes of a factory.[29]

But as industrialists started to see the value in hiring an architect to design their buildings, architects also began to take advantage of their expanded role and value, as described in *The American Architect*:

> To plan an industrial building that will operate at maximum efficiency requires an intimate fore-knowledge by the design, of the process of manufacture contemplated in the finished structure. Intimate cooperation between the architect and those who will operate the plant is also essential in order that the practical knowledge possessed by them may be utilized to the best advantage.[30]

And, at this time, we see many more architects such as Peter Behrens (1868–1940), Gropius, and Erich Mendelsohn (1887–1953) receive commissions to design factories that inspired innovation and experimentation with materials and spatial organization.

THE VERNACULAR INFLUENCE ON THE EUROPEAN AVANT-GARDE

For these European avant-garde architects, America was a utopian domain, an

ideal to which they aspired.[31] They appreciated the vernacular and engineer-de-
signed structures such as those by R.J. Reidpath & Sons, or the Larkin Plant in
Buffalo, New York (1917), the aesthetic which they emulated in their own work.
The significance of these newly discovered structures — cylindrical grain silos and
exposed concrete grids — was made evident in their publication through architecture journals and trade magazines and inspired Le Corbusier and Mendelsohn to be
Modern. Banham wrote so lucidly in *A Concrete Atlantis* in the 1980s, after studying
Buffalo factories himself, that "the utopian view was not imaginary, improbable,
nor located in a distant future. The industrial buildings of North America were
distant from the younger European Modernists only in mileage and were not imaginary; they had concrete — literally concrete — presence here on earth."[32]

 Mendelsohn was fascinated with the factory as a Modern typology and the
expressive but primary forms of the American grain silos seen on his trip to
the United States in 1924.

> Mountainous silos, incredibly space-conscious, but creating space. A
> random confusion amidst the chaos of loading and unloading corn ships,
> of railways and bridges, crane monsters with live gestures, hordes of
> silo cells in concrete, stone and glazed brick. Then suddenly a silo with
> administrative buildings, closed horizontal fronts against the stupendous
> verticals of fifty to a hundred cylinders, and all this in the sharp evening
> light. I took photographs like mad. Everything else so far now seemed to
> have been shaped interim to my silo dreams.[33]

Mendelsohn's second project commission after the sculptural Einstein Tower in Potsdam, was for the Steinberg-Herrmann company's hat factory in 1921–1923 in Luckenwalde, Germany. Hans Poelzig's 1912 chemical factory in Lubon, Poland that was heavy and solid in form influenced Mendelsohn's project. The hat factory's central production hall was comprised of four 150-meter-long bays and five-meter spans with reinforced concrete arches that formed a zigzag profile on the exterior with their faceted angles. This could be a repeatable module if production increased. The open work halls were flooded with natural light via wooden skylights and triangular windows on the facades at the intersection of the roof and concrete frame, acting as a large-scale clerestory.

The layout followed the production flow from north to south, with the administration space around a central courtyard and manufacturing surrounding the larger courtyard to the south. The most dynamic structure was the dye works building with its 17-meter-high trapezoidal roof that resembled a hat, which contained the exhaust system, and became the factory's iconic element. It had double arched concrete structural supports in a five-meter-long span. A higher arch posed on top of this double-arch system created a layer of filters for the fumes. The roof had a Ruberoid cladding for the ventilation system, and large eave-like overhangs, similar to barn or train-shed construction of the time. A boiler house was more rectilinear and rational in its Modernist form with a simple concrete grid. The factory only operated until World War II when the Jewish owners were forced to close. However, as a building, the flexible and adaptable space for numerous kinds of production allowed the building's life to continue first as a munitions factory and then, postwar, a machine shop for the Soviet Army, and finally, through 1991, a ball-bearing factory.

◀ Lockwood, Greene and Co., Larkin Warehouse, Buffalo, New York, 1911
▲ Silos, Quaker Oats factory, Akron, Ohio, built 1932

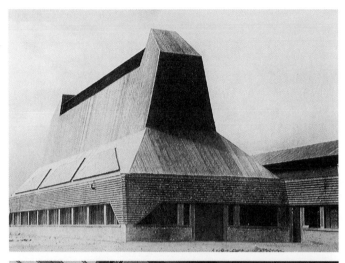

▲ Erich Mendelsohn,
Luckenwalde Hat Factory,
Luckenwalde, Germany, 1923
▲ Erich Mendelsohn, interior
Luckenwalde Hat Factory,
Luckenwalde, Germany, 1923

Mendelsohn also designed the Expressionist Red Flag Textile Factory in St. Petersburg in 1925, a large-scale scheme for 8,000 workers. He designed the dye shops, as a series of three volumes similar to the hat factory, with a functional purpose. The proposal was for two five-story blocks perpendicular to the street with large windows and a ten-story administrative building with work areas on the ground floor. The heating plant, situated at the triangular intersection of two streets, was the circular form seen in many of Mendelsohn's sketches. However, because of the many changes made by the company and their local architects, only part of the building was realized. The heating plant is the only still-extant part of the building by Mendelsohn. His work, featured in the Russian magazines, inspired artist El Lissitzky's 1930 design for the House of Heavy Industry, and also recalled the Lazur chemical factory in Stalingrad.[34] Mendelsohn's projects captured the industrial machine-like form, incorporating the design of factories as a coalescing of his aesthetics with a functional program. The Modern factory embodied the machine as the holism of the integrated industrial object. As Adolf Behne observed, "Thus all the particularities of the great manufacturing plants in steel framing, iron and reinforced concrete, which dart blindly back and forth out of the conventional jungle we have inherited, now appear integrated, understood."[35]

European architects embraced the radical simplicity, which was "true to form" in the concrete grid of the American factory, as the expressive vocabulary of Modernism. Gropius professed that, "America, the home of industry, possesses some original majestic constructions which far outstrip anything of a similar kind achieved in Germany."[36] The American vernacular factories were also discussed in lectures and described in manifestos by industrialists and architects who usurped these vernacular forms in ways both subtle and obvious to justify their own ideologies and to promote their Modernist polemics. The gridded and spherical primary forms — naked and solid — became uplifting as Modernist icons of the Machine Age with a new functional aesthetic. They became part of a new dogma, a self-referential ideology.

While the European architects continued to praise the new building type as a starting point for creative exploration, or the possibility of the factory organizational

system for the design of other typologies in a functional Modernism, the more pragmatic architects continued to fulfill the needs of a company. Russian architect Mosei Ginzburg (1892–1946) saw that the factory program as the "dynamics of the production process can easily be represented in a *graph of movement*. The division of the process into distinct phases makes it possible to describe its dynamics in terms of a static system of separate but interdependent production operations, each of which corresponds to a particular piece of equipment."[37] Historian Grant Hildebrand notes in reference to Albert Kahn's pragmatism, "[it] was an at least equally fertile approach in that it held great promise for real operational solutions, from which new formal patterns could be generated — patterns that had not been part of the original, conscious intent of the designer."[38] The repetition of forms and business-like approach of Kahn's was synthesized in the design of the factory.

European architects also were drawn to the functional aspects of the factory as a potential for the future. In their writings and projects they celebrated formal and functional simplicity, embracing the ideals for other building types, both in actual use and the symbol of progress to which they aspired. Ginzburg concluded,

▲ Erich Mendelsohn,
Red Banner Textile Factory,
St. Petersburg, Russia,
1925–1937

> Modern industrial plants condense within themselves, in an artistic sense, all the most characteristic and potential features of a new life. Everything capable of establishing the essential thrust of creative process is to be found here: a picture of modernity that is extremely lucid and differentiated from the past. . . . Can there be a picture that more clearly reflects the purposeful way of life of modernity?[39]

As a new typology, the factory was the synergistic link between physical function, engineering, and form to which the Modern architects aspired, embodying a suitable place of appropriation. The act of borrowing from or being inspired by history is a norm in architecture as we know from Renaissance architects who incorporated Roman and Greek details and proportions into their work, or Gropius, who believed that American engineers had retained some aboriginal "feel for larger, sparse, compact form fresh and intact and that their work was therefore comparable to that surviving from ancient Egypt."[40] Modern architects absorbed aspects of the engineered factories, justifying the formal aspects as aligned with their Modern aspirations and inspired by what could be considered "found objects" in the straightforward American industrial landscape. The point is well illustrated by Le Corbusier, who altered (or purposefully mislabeled) the photos of American silos which he received from Gropius to emphasize his own point about flatness and abstraction, "whiting out every one of its numerous pediments"[41] in order to make them additionally sparse.

The architect-tourist has always been a scavenger, seeking foreign objects that others might not know or notice to absorb into their new creations. Travel was an essential pre-professional rite of passage at the École des Beaux-Arts. In the late nineteenth century, architectural students traveled to Greece and Rome to study and sketch classical buildings; to America in the early twentieth century to see work of Frank Lloyd Wright that had been published in the *Wasmuth Portfolio* in 1910 and 1911; to world expositions; to Niagara Falls; and, later, to the awe-inspiring U.S. hydroelectric dams and automotive factories, like those represented in the Buffalo photographs by Gropius, then Le Corbusier and later, Banham.

These *flaneur*-architects were not alone in their fascination with industrial buildings. Their clients — industrial businessmen — also visited American factories for lessons on the efficient and productive workplace. When he began his Fagus Factory, industrialist Carl Benscheidt Sr. (1858–1947) went to the Beverly Shoe Works with his designer Walter Gropius; other company owners, including Kees van der Leeuw of Van Nelle, Giovanni Agnelli of Fiat, and Andrea Olivetti, also traveled to the U.S. and visited Ford's Highland Park. Le Corbusier visited Fiat at Lingotto in 1925 and pronounced it both a symbol and realization of Modernism. To him it was "certainly the most impressive spectacles of industry."[42] The American system of manufacturing and corporate organization, in turn, modeled production methods for European companies.

Fagus

German architect Walter Gropius had only seen the American factories in photographs — he had not yet traveled there. He thus had to borrow the patron of avant-garde art and architecture, Karl Osthaus' (1874–1921) images for a 1910 lecture at the Folkwang Museum in Hagen, Germany titled, "Monumental Art and Industrial Building." The images were later published in the *Jahrbuch des Deutschen Werkbundes* to illustrate his article.[43] To Gropius, America as "the Motherland of Industry possesses some majestic original constructions which far outstrip anything of a similar kind achieved in Germany."[44] In 1912, Gropius organized an exhibition of excellence in industrial building and Carl Benscheidt

Jr. wrote to the manufacturing association in New York for images.[45] Even by 1913 the journal issue titled *Die Kunst in Industrie* explored new territory by publishing photographs of industrial buildings such as Fagus and AEG's Turbine factory with Gropius' American factory essay.[46]

Walter Gropius found himself at an opportune moment in terms of factory design when Benscheidt Sr. hired him to design the Fagus (meaning "beech wood") shoe-last factory (lasts were wooden molds used to make and stretch leather); his design solutions served to improve the company image, as the factory complex in Alfeld an der Leine, Germany was a mélange of individual buildings. Benscheidt Sr. had hired Eduard Werner (1847–1923) to design a factory, which was precise in its layout but not innovative in its design. With investments from the United Shoe Machinery Company — whose Beverly, Massachusetts-based factory featured maximum light and minimal concrete — Benscheidt changed his design direction.

▲ **Walter Gropius, Fagus Factory, Alfeld an der Leine, Germany, 1911–1914**

In 1911, Gropius and Adolf Meyer (1881–1929) were commissioned to redesign only the facades of Fagus — especially those visible from the railroad — with Modern materials. They transformed the heavy masonry complex into transparent, light, steel and glass structures. This was in marked contrast to the concrete infill and steel seen in the AEG turbine factory that Gropius had worked on with German architect Peter Behrens. The three-story Fagus main office building had projecting casement windows separated into bays by tapered brick columns; a new truss-less south corner of the main building in steel and glass became an iconic architectural element. Through the glass, the staircase was visible and "the building seemed to defy the laws of gravity and the landings, too, seemed to be suspended in thin air."[47] The transparent corner was set off with a solid entrance in dark horizontal brickwork. Gropius and Meyer's design elaborated on their Model Factory project, on display in the 1914 *Werkbund* exhibition in Cologne. There they designed a circular staircase and round glass enclosure as the striking element. At Fagus, the architects designed all of the supporting buildings, including the power plant, sheds, and smaller production buildings.

While for a long time Fagus was considered the epitome of Modernism in the glazed corner, Benevolo noted (and Banham corroborated) that a "fleeting moment of transition is crystallized, and this may be the explanation of its particular attraction."[48] Banham continued that:

> Even if it now seems less "modern" than carefully chosen propaganda pictures have made it appear, and less American than some observers might suspect, it is still possible that the experience of design, and the encounters with the Benscheidts were both instrumental in turning the attention of Gropius to what was to become the revolutionary topic of the development of modern American industrial building.[49]

During the twenties, Le Corbusier picked up where Gropius left off, with essays first published in *L'Esprit Nouveau* and *Vers une Architecture*, addressing both European and American examples of factories. Le Corbusier actually borrowed Gropius' images, such as those of the silos in Buffalo, and used them to support his well-known manifesto: "Let us listen to the counsel of American engineers, but let us beware of the American architect."[50]

Critics were also drawn to the new functionality of the rational Modern factory. The Architectural historian, Behne, included images in his essays on factories designed by architects Albert Kahn, Peter Behrens, and Hans Poelzig of examples of the balance of function and form. In the article, "No Longer a House but a Shaped Space," he noted that, "Industrial commissions had already produced surprising solutions in America."[51] Behne states Gropius' acknowledgment that the "distinguishing feature of these American buildings (without exception the work of engineers, not architects) is their complete absence of compulsive ideas about form, their quite unprejudiced design, and their spatial realization of production and working processes."[52] Behne stressed this underlying expression of production that serves as an intersection between the architectural and production discourse as he also quoted Henry Ford, whose autobiography had just been published in German.[53]

The praise for engineering buildings in Hans Richter's (1882–1971) journal *G* (*Gestaltung*) indicates another acknowledgment of their significance. In issue two (out of six published), the *Wasmuth Ingenieurbauten,* a portfolio of architecture, was reviewed, featuring three large photographs of industrial buildings showing, "An example of clear and impressive organizational whole." *G* issue number three included Mies van der Rohe's article "Industrielles Bauen," about both the industrialization of construction and factory buildings themselves, illustrated with images of German train sheds, including an article on Matté-Trucco's Fiat factory in Turin, Italy.[54]

▶ Albert Kahn's Highland Park factory published in *Jahrbuch des Deutschen Werkbundes*, 1913

▶ Bunge y Born grain elevator in Buenos Aires, Argentina, published by Le Corbusier in *Vers une Architecture*, 1923

This aspiration towards an industrial aesthetic continued further as American art critic Sheldon Cheney (1886–1980) noted that European architects were looking to the "examples of direct thinking and creative handling of new materials in response to new needs." The engineers' work in "the molding of concrete and glass into industrial buildings, by their utter absence of ornament and elaboration, proclaimed sufficient solidity, trapping of light, and efficient shelter." Cheney continues, "Many a traveler from Europe has picked out these common structures for comment while overlooking our swankier banks and libraries."[55] The factory — as an icon of *progress* and a place of dynamic convergence between architecture and engineering — came to epitomize the Modern aesthetic.

AEG
PETER BEHRENS, BERLIN, 1904–1912

As the German coastal and river cities of Hamburg, Cologne, and Frankfurt emerged as manufacturing powerhouses during the first industrial revolution, Berlin, an inland city, developed as an intellectual center. The "New Prussia" built world-class universities and research centers there, giving Berlin the nickname "Athens by the Spree." Prior to World War I, industrialists benefited from this aggregation of scientific minds to develop new industries, such as machinery, chemical, and electrical companies, even though the natural resources of coal, iron ore, and hydropower lay far beyond the city's front door. A new factory typology developed that integrated working and living with the use of courtyard blocks that could enclose the workspace and shelter residents. For the new smaller industries and handworkers it was convenient for deliveries to be transferred from the streets to the workspace. Tenement-type dwellings, were frequently cramped and unsanitary, but the perimeter arrangements provided light and air from the inner courtyards which are still used today.

The rise of electrical power that launched a second industrial era in the late nineteenth century focused cities on displaying their wares. Berlin held a trade exposition in 1896 that showcased the city as an industrial center commensurate with Chicago or Philadelphia, which both held similar expos around the same time. During the Berlin fair, philosopher Georg Simmel lauded the "heterogeneous industrial products"[56] that signified the basis for the growth of Berlin's new economic and electrified energy, both literally and symbolically. Berlin's modernization took place through a streamlined rational planning process that spurred growth with new boulevards and government buildings; by 1905, it was the most densely populated city in Europe, with two million inhabitants. After World War I, despite wartime devastation, intellectual flight, and inflation, Berlin rose again as an intellectual capital of Europe.[57] Post-World War II, with much of the city in ruin, the Spree and Havel rivers flowing north to south through Berlin and canals flowing east to west were filled with boats carrying goods and supplies for rebuilding.

One of its major corporations, AEG (Allgemeine Elektricitäts-Gesellschaft or General Electric Company) began as a manufacturer of the American company Edison electric light systems under patents. It was developed from the 1880s to the 1900s over a vast expanse in northern Berlin, an area now called Wedding. With Siemens, AEG contributed to the city's moniker, "Elektropolis." Berlin shifted from being a center of intellectual capital to a center of industrial power, despite the locational disadvantages of being built inland and on sand. AEG produced small parts such as electrical cables, motors, bulbs, and lamps, as well as trains and massively scaled turbines and power stations. By inventing ways to monopolize the market, they controlled the development of electric power and its dependent machinery. At the time, the Werkbund collective of industrialists, economists, and artists, founded in 1907, initiated conceptual thinking around the possibilities for design for industry. One member of the collective, architect and designer Peter Behrens, became acquainted with AEG founding director Walther Rathenau, also a member of the Werkbund on the business side, who then influenced Paul Baurat of AEG's building programs to hire Behrens to design their new factories.

By combining interest in design and industrial objects, AEG launched the new field of industrial design. Behrens designed one of AEG's first commercial products – the arc lamp, designed to hang from the ceiling, from which it cast a wide arc of light. In this design "he saw his problem as the formulation of an aesthetic which accepted the blunt, prosaic power of the machine, of engineering, and of industry, but which also raised this power to an electric, economical poesy expressive of a suprapersonal and modern Kuntswollen" (or will to art or that of making an art form).[58] Behrens designed other appliances for the company and was "retained as an artist who could provide the signs of technical perfection through beauty of form, whether this involved a well-formed housing for the electrodes of an arc lamp, a well-formed factory building for a workforce which the AEG was proud to say operated almost militaristically, or an elegant letterhead for an intelligent and complex executive staff."[59]

As a result, Behrens was commissioned to design increasingly larger projects, such as exhibition installations and a pavilion for the 1908 German Shipbuilding Exhibition in Berlin. Behrens' architectural commissions began with alterations to AEG's Moabit complex of massive brick buildings (1904–1907) by Johann Kraaz.

Behrens added a clock tower and assembly halls around the company's large interior courtyard; a powerhouse on Huttenstrasse; and the now well-known Turbine Hall; Large Motor and Small Motor Factories; and additions to the former Train Factory buildings. Most of the factories were vertical and enclosed large open spaces.

Similar to Albert Kahn, Behrens saw the industrial buildings as a new typology with room to explore new ideas, independent of clients, the public, and the architectural profession's standards. "Behrens chose not to emphasize that 'functional directness' which was already mani-fest in many engineer-designed factories; he rather sought to incorporate such works within an established but evolving political and architectural tradition. Behrens sought to bring the factory under the rubric of the embassy, or the temple — not to bring the embassy under the rubric of the factory."[60]

TURBINE HALL

The most dominant or unusual of Behrens' buildings was his temple to industry, the Turbine Hall. Situated on a prominent corner, it expressed the overwhelming power of the machine and modern industry. Oskar Lasche (1868–1923), the company's in-house engineer, selected the production hall's site with requirements to accommodate large machines and products in a massive multistoried volume that included two

▲ Peter Behrens, AEG Turbine Hall, Berlin, Germany, machinists working on a turbine, 1908–1909

overhead traveling cranes and railroad tracks for train cars. Behrens, according to architectural historian Stanford Anderson, didn't have the skills for the design of such a mammoth and highly technical task; he thus collaborated

FINISHED PRODUCT
PARTS & ASSEMBLY
WORKERS

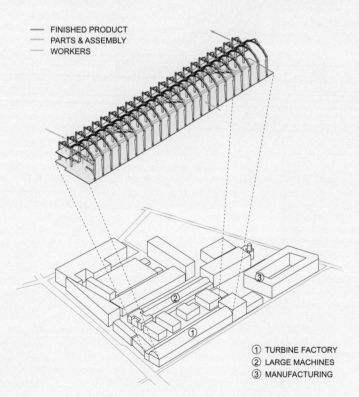

① TURBINE FACTORY
② LARGE MACHINES
③ MANUFACTURING

▲ Peter Behrens, Turbine Hall, AEG factory, Berlin, Germany, 1908–1909

with engineer Karl Bernhard on the structural system. Their joint effort resulted in the largest skeletal steel hall in Berlin, measuring 151,000 cubic meters within a 207-by-39.3-meter open volume. An adjacent two-story hall was also built for gantry cranes using the full height of the two buildings. There was also storage space below.

The Turbine Hall was both corporeal and expressive of a new tectonics in the material and structural techniques of skeletal steel construction. The building embodied the opposing ideas that Gottfried Semper (1803–1879) described, contrasting the stereotomy of the mechanical whole to the structures of the tectonic and the move from the tectonic to the spatial. The open volume housing the machinery was supported by asymmetrical three-hinged arch girders exposed on the exterior, rather than concealed, as was the norm. The central hinge lay at the apex of the 27-meter-high building. A continuous skylight comparable to a glass ceiling rose above the traveling crane track supporting asymmetrical arches along the length of the building, a more typical internal steel bracing contemporaneous to other factories. On the Berlichingenstrasse side of the building, 14 steel columns, each spaced 9.22 meters apart, tapered outward to support the 127-meter-long steel beam. Between the columns, full-height steel framed windows with both fixed and operable panes provided light to the workspace. The heavy weight thus appeared inverted, as the stanchions were raised on a base and connected with an exaggerated riveted steel hinge. The rivets were visible throughout the structure, demonstrating how the building parts were connected and emphasizing the functionality of a space created for the production of machines. The upper portion of the piers was also made more prominent as the planar windows slanted outwards, resulting in the protruding stanchions.

For the monumental main facade, Behrens created a self-conscious design that doubled as a built-in advertisement using a faceted gable-shaped pediment within which the company name was carved. Large, vertically oriented multi-paned steel-framed windows made for a transparent central section. However, an ambiguity resulted between the facade's corners, which were made of concrete over lath, rather than solid concrete, resulting in a false massiveness, dematerializing the structure. Some historians, including Reyner Banham, thought the pediment's

▲ **AEG Turbine Hall interior**

form echoed the traveling crane structure but there was too much symbolism in the pediment shape as honorific for that to be the sole reason for the design, notes Anderson.[61]

The contrast between physical mass and line was a dominant theme in Behrens' "Art and Technology" lecture of 1907. He claimed, "If it is said that the beauty of a pure iron construction lies in the line, I must repeat that the line is of no substance: architecture lies in corporeality. The practical purpose of large industrial buildings and our general need today for air and light call for large openings, but nevertheless there is no reason for the entire architecture to convey the impression of a thin, wiry scaffolding. . . . Architecture is the design of volumes, and its task is not to disclose but enclose space."[62] This rejection of thinness led to his use of concrete as infill to create a solid mass; the result, however, was more like a stuccoing of the surface. The essence of the Turbine Hall's corners became unstructured, not holding anything, in contrast to the interest in the "truth to the structure" of the time. "It brought about a confrontation between the artist's stereotomic preferences and the tectonic character of the ferro-vitreous wide-span frame. The resolution of

this conflict was facilitated by a shift in German architectural theory from emphasis on material form to emphasis on space."[63]

Perhaps some of this material theory was more authentic in the building's rear and side yards of glass and steel that Mies van der Rohe claimed as his design decades later.[64] Walter Gropius also worked with Behrens, noting that he "provided the aesthetic scaffolding for modern industrial architecture," which can be seen in Gropius' designs for the Fagus factory a few years later.[65]

AEG COURTYARD COMPLEX

While Behrens' Turbine Hall has historically represented the image of the new modernity, many overlook that he was also commissioned to design a series of buildings in the AEG's older courtyard off Voltastrasse. This factory complex was located within an urban enclave through which there was rail access to each building and access to exterior cranes. For the existing five-story brick Gothic Revival Old Factory, in

which railway equipment was produced, Behrens added a wing designed with a stripped medieval aesthetic. He designed a Small Motors Factory building (1910–1912) in an abstracted classical style; its Voltastrasse facade created a regular rhythm along the streetscape with a long, undulating series of rounded brick pillars with steel and glass windows. The High Voltage Factory (1909–10) had repetitive bays along its four-story brick mass, with corner towers and windows cascading up around the stair towers. Behrens designed two dramatic entrances capped by triangular pediments. The New

Railway Factory (1911–1912) united the courtyard's aesthetic by the use of flattened pillars. This cluster of buildings facing inwards formed a cohesive unit which lent substance to AEG through its scale and massing.

At the far end of the yard, the Assembly Plant for Large Machines (1911–1912) along Hussitenstrasse had a clear span of thirty meters with open trusswork in the interior. The span was supported by a triple-hinged girder, which Bernhard engineered in a similar method as his work in the Turbine Hall. However, this brick plant was more straightforward. It embodied the potential for structural directness in brick and glass, adhering to Modern ideals. AEG also commissioned Behrens to design workers' housing. In 1915, his plans for modest three-story apartments in Berlin's Hennigsdorf and two-story houses in the Obsershöneweide neighborhood were also realized.

Behrens aestheticized the factory, envisioning the technological utopia of the newly electric and dynamic city. "He sought to bring the factory under the rubric of farm – to restore to factory production and that sense of common purpose innate in agriculture, a feeling for which the newly urbanized semi-skilled labour of Berlin would supposedly still have a certain nostalgia."[66] The factory was incorporated within the emerging urban capitalist system both economically and socially while its design ushered the factory typology towards a new aesthetic.

▲ Entrance to interior courtyard
▲ Aerial view of the AEG factory site, Berlin, Germany, 2013

FORD PIQUETTE AVENUE PLANT
FIELD, HINCHMAN & GRYLLS, DETROIT, 1903

In 1903, Henry Ford's first efforts at automobile manufacturing was minimally housed in a one-story brick shed on Detroit's Mack Avenue. Later that year he built a larger-scale factory to support his invention of a lightweight motorized vehicle designed for the masses. The new factory was designed by Field, Hinchman & Smith, (which later became Smith, Hinchman & Grylls). These firms, along with Albert Kahn Associates, were the architects of choice for the booming automobile industries in the new American industrial age. Their design methods and experiments in concrete and steel, which were characterized by large expanses of casement windows, resulted in mass production of factory buildings as a typology that was reproduced worldwide.

The two-story 20,000-square-meter brick Ford factory was built on a one-hectare site on Piquette Avenue. This 122-meter-long by 17-meter-wide three-story brick building was constructed in the manner of an early mill structure, with wood floors and beams and supporting wood columns spaced on either side of a central aisle. The double-hung wooden-sash windows allowed plenty of natural light to penetrate into the second- and third-floor workshops. Owing to the wood structure, the building needed enhanced fire protection; this was supplied by firewalls with large metal doors, and a rooftop water tank that could distribute water to an integrated sprinkler system. For similar safety reasons, Ford construction engineer Edward Gray built a power plant adjacent to the factory rather than enclosed within the central space.

The factory's first floor contained administrative offices for clerks and bookkeepers as well as shipping and receiving, and testing areas. The second floor housed the now-famous "secret room" in which Ford and his engineers developed new car designs. Early on, Ford autos were assembled by workers at clustered stationary stands to which parts were delivered piece by piece. Ford Motor Company produced Models B, C, and F and, later, models K, N, R, and S. In 1907, the company consolidated engine production into a separate plant integrated into the site. In 1908, the first Model T was completed, and the other lines were discontinued. As Ford experimented with new systems that eventually evolved into the widespread practice of manufacturing interchangeable parts, his company's production and sales increased, resulting in the need for additional space. Ford moved his new production center to the Highland Park factory, designed by Albert Kahn in 1910. In 1911, Studebaker Corporation bought the Piquette Avenue building and added another Kahn-designed building in 1920.

HIGHLAND PARK PLANT
ALBERT KAHN ASSOCIATES, DETROIT, 1909–1917

By coordinating and streamlining his production technologies, Henry Ford transformed the automotive industry and contributed to the solidification of Detroit's primacy as a manufacturing center. To expand his production empire, Ford hired Albert Kahn who, working with associate Ernest Wilby, designed Highland Park, creating a new belt of urban industry just outside the city core. In the first building, or "Old Shop," completed in 1910, Kahn's large open floors for machinery and expansive windows for light and air elaborated even further upon the concept of the more vernacular daylight factory that many industrialists were building at the time – so much so that, with the installation of large Crittall steel-sash windows imported from England, the factory was nicknamed the "Crystal Palace."

The four-story, 42-meter-wide by 256-meter-long building used the Kahn bar reinforcing system (as did the Packard Plant's Building 10),

▲ Field, Hinchman & Smith, Ford Piquette Avenue Plant, Detroit, Michigan, 1903

allowing for columns to be spaced on a wide, 6-by-7.5-meter grid with integrated beams, joists, and slab. The vertical and horizontal supports were thus flush with the facade, exemplifying the new Modernist continuity of surface. The repetitive bay could continue endlessly, just like the production line – and be expanded if necessary – synchronizing the system of architectural and automotive production. Even though the building was Modern in idea and form, Kahn incorporated more glazed brick and terracotta ornamental details at the cornice. This ornamentation, the showpiece glass facade, the placement of the administration building at the street's edge, and the attachment of a large Ford sign to the five smoke stacks created an indelible presence for passersby on Woodward Avenue.

In many architectural histories, the other Kahn, Louis Kahn (1901–1974), is touted as inventing the idea of architecturally defining the service and served portions of buildings; this can be seen in his Richards Medical Research Laboratories at the University of Pennsylvania (1965). Albert Kahn, however, had achieved the same concentration of stairs and services at Highland Park decades earlier. The four corner and four central towers of Highland Park contained the stairs, elevators, and washrooms to allow for uninterrupted open spaces throughout the factory floor. They also punctuate the vast building by projecting

above the parapet line and additionally provide a visual break and relief from the block-long building. More importantly, they provide a lateral stiffening to the overall building, making for more open space. Clad in brick, the towers are more pronounced against the simplicity of the concrete grid of the production, or served spaces.

As discussed earlier, Ford emphasized efficient methods of mass production for the continuously moving assembly line. Adopting methods of labor division similar to Frederick Taylor's Scientific Management doctrine, and conveyance systems based on the meatpacking industries, Ford focused on worker speed, the rationalization of process, and increasing production. He accomplished the latter by assigning workers specific tasks along the moving conveyor belt. For example, instead of each worker assembling a complete magneto (a hand-cranked electrical generator), Ford separated the task among 29 workers, each completing one component. This division of labor increased the production of the flywheel magnetos from forty per worker to 1,188 per each nine-hour workday. This process evolved

▲ President Wilson visits the Ford Highland Park factory, designed by Albert Kahn, Detroit, Michigan, in 1916. The banner reads "Our hats off to the President who has kept us out of war."

▲ Test marriage of body to chassis using gravity ramp and pulleys at Ford Highland Park factory, 1911

▲ Gravity chutes move goods from top to bottom of the Ford Highland Park factory, ca. 1911

▲ Woman on assembly line at Ford Highland Park, ca.1911

from the interchangeable parts system where each piece, produced by smaller suppliers, was exactly the same, a technology co-opted by Ford production engineers Walter Flanders and Charles Sorenson who arranged production in sequence of assembly rather than by spatial area (as practiced previously).[67] It has been debated whether Ford actually followed Taylor or whether these ideas were part of a collective consciousness that developed from the need for rational production methods on the ground.[68]

Ford managed his workers far beyond the usual scope of a company head and certainly beyond that of the paternalistic utopian company towns. He was disinterested in his employees' well-being. He hired social workers through an actual Sociology Department to inspect the workers' habits in a manner similar to how engineers inspected his cars – in the first case he sought a well-oiled working class, in the second – optimal production. Workers were watched for deviant or rebellious behavior not only in the factory but at home, in an unspoken form of surveillance. Ford's assembly line, in fact, was the subject of ridicule in Charlie Chaplin's film, *Modern Times* (1936), and influenced the ideas presented in Karel Čapek's *R.U.R.* and Aldous Huxley's *Brave New World* (1932). One must also contextualize Ford's class and religious biases – his well-known anti-Semitism, for instance – which

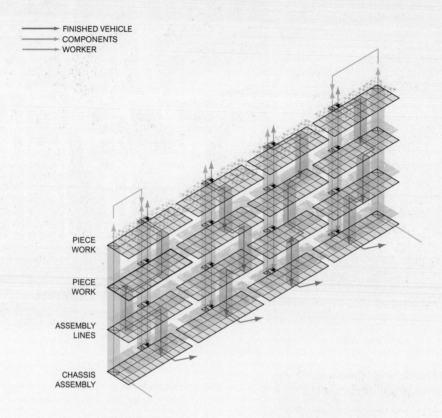

FINISHED VEHICLE
COMPONENTS
WORKER

PIECE
WORK

PIECE
WORK

ASSEMBLY
LINES

CHASSIS
ASSEMBLY

underlay his need to control his workers and their production; any improvement he made to the workspace was strictly to maintain worker loyalty. Despite Ford's famed "five dollars a day," which workers could use to buy their own Model Ts, his company had an employee turnover rate of 370 percent per year.[69]

To house the new assembly-line production process, the plant was expanded to adjacent vacant sites beginning in 1914 with the New Shop, a compound consisting of two reinforced concrete, 19-by-256-meter six-story buildings covering 180 acres, a new four-story building along John K Street, and machine shops. These structures were all linked by craneways through which trains could enter a central space protected by glass-covered roofs similar to those of numerous factories integrated with urban infrastructure. In the multistoried building, heavy materials were lifted to cantilevered platform-balconies by means of efficient, mechanized handling systems with which workers hoisted parts and materials up to the top floor; the work in process then descended to the various stages of the production process.[70] Gravity chutes and slides moved parts

and materials through the vertical stacking of the production process, eliminating movement normally conducted by floor workers called "pushers and shovers," but also compressing the factory floor space vertically. The moving conveyor belt eased and sped up the process of distributing parts to the lower floors. The overhead conveyor, invented by the Detroit-based firm Jervis B. Webb, was also introduced around this time; the innovation was prominently depicted in a 1932–1933 mural by Diego Rivera at the Detroit Institute of Arts titled, *Detroit Industry*, in a panel called "Making a Motor."[71] As a three-dimensional grid matrix, the processing at the new Highland Park factory flowed from floor-to-floor and end-to-end in a manner similar to Oliver Evans' concept for the automatic flourmill. The ability of management to control the speed of the assembly line in turn controlled the workers' movement.

By 1914, the factory's performance was integral to the production lines' efficacy as Ford reduced the production time for a Model T from 728 to 93 minutes. By the end of that year, the plant completed 248,307 Model Ts; by 1917, the number had nearly tripled. Thus, Ford quickly

outgrew Highland Park and began to build a plant at River Rouge south of Detroit. Designed again by Albert Kahn, the new plant was conceived as groupings of single-story factories. By 1920 at "The Rouge," one Ford rolled off the assembly line every minute; half of the world's automobiles were Model Ts. Even in these early days, Ford was restless and began to develop the Model A, which was based on a new system of mass production – representing Ford's focus on standardizing products.[72]

Kahn ran his office in an efficiency-management style, systematically mass-producing thousands of projects in the United States. In addition, during the Depression, his company designed 520 factories in Russia. Many details and construction methods of the concrete grid and large casement windows were repeated from building to building. Kahn often said, "Architecture is 90 percent business and 10 percent art." More businessman than intellectual, Kahn lay outside of the Modernist circles that made up the architectural avant-garde. In many ways, he was a natural, unassuming visionary – a product of the *zeitgeist*, but not a promoter of it. In lectures on Modernism, Kahn derided the aesthetic of the glass box, while being himself one of its inventors and provocateurs in the factory typology.[73]

While Ford with Kahn spearheaded the vertical urban factory, Ford was not too attached to its organization near the city, and, in building new plants south of Detroit he contributed to the demise of urban centrality for production processes. This continued during World War II in the Willow Run bomber plant, which spread out over acres of land. "[T]he company...embark[ed] on a policy of one-story buildings to the virtual exclusion of the multistory scheme."[74] Ford at that point felt such factory designs were more flexible and economical. However, the vertical factory continued in cities for some time.

▲ Albert Kahn, interior of craneway in New Shop, Ford Highland Park, 1913

STARRETT-LEHIGH BUILDING

**RUSSELL G. CORY AND WALTER M. CORY
WITH YASUO MATSUI, ASSOCIATE ARCHITECT,
NEW YORK, 1930–1931**

The recognition of the factory as a Modernist aesthetic inspired a more self-conscious design as design and commerce became intertwined. One of the first Modern buildings in the United States to receive any attention from New York's Museum of Modern Art in the 1932 *International Exhibition of Modern Architecture*, alongside works by Frank Lloyd Wright and Mies van der Rohe, was the massive brick-and-concrete Starrett-Lehigh Building. The vertical industrial building, with horizontal bands of concrete floor plates exposed on the facade, was developed and constructed by Starrett Investing Corp. & Eken Inc. and the Lehigh Valley Railroad Co. as manufacturing loft rentals. The multi-tenanted building dominated the Chelsea waterfront between 26th and 27th Streets and 11th and 12th Avenues in New York and was similar in its 610,000-square-meter volume to that of the Empire State Building, which also began construction in 1930 by the same builder.

One of the most difficult aspects of urban manufacturing was transport and delivery access. It was a standard in the early nineteenth century that the urban factory would have train tracks situated in its courtyard, run alongside the building, or be elevated, as in New York City's train spur. For Starrett-Lehigh, the builders integrated train and truck transit directly into the building. In partnership with the Lehigh Valley Railroad Co., the Starrett-Lehigh building was built directly over the railroad's working freight yard and adjacent to its carfloat pier, thus linking freight transport from New Jersey to Manhattan's West Side. The trains ran directly from New Jersey waterfront piers (having crossed the Hudson with a float barge to a ferry slip) into the building's ground floor. Similar to the Bush Terminal with its coordinated services in Sunset Park, Brooklyn, or the Brooklyn Army Terminal, where the railroad services were coordinated for goods transfer from one transit source to another with shipping and truck delivery, these complexes created fluid logistics systems.

Architects Cory & Cory, in association with Yasuo Matsui and engineers Purdy & Henderson, designed the building to have a "vertical urban

THE STARRETT LEHIGH BUILDING ADDS TO EFFICIENCY BY PROVIDING MORE LIGHT

Special cantilever construction allows all columns to be set back from the outside wall 8′ 9″. Outside walls are almost completely of glass. Only a narrow band of brick and steel at top and bottom. This allows light, which ordinary window construction would obstruct, to flood the building.

Compare the windows in the Starrett Lehigh Building (above) with those usually found in industrial buildings (below) and reflect how this would add to the efficiency of your employees.

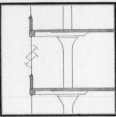

Modern offices made possible by the fine construction of the building, will enable all departments of a business to be housed under one roof. The small tenant in the Starrett Lehigh Building enjoys practically the same facilities that he would find in a one-story building erected for his exclusive use in the centre of the city with a railroad siding right at hand. Lobbies will have cafeteria, lunchroom, cigar and news stand, telegraph office, bootblack, etc.

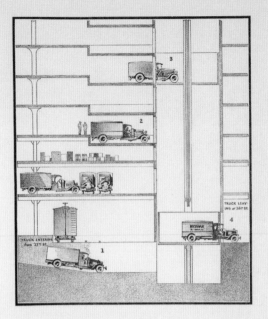

Trucks enter the building on a ramp from 27th Street which runs under the Lehigh tracks. (See No. 1 above.) They are loaded onto special truck elevators and carried to any floor of the building (No. 3), backed into truck pits and unloaded (No. 2). They leave the building at 26th Street (No. 4). This ingenious arrangement makes each floor the equivalent of a ground floor and gives each tenant the practical effect of a separate building. It also saves a vast amount of time and labor and prevents the theft or damage of goods unloaded on the sidewalk.

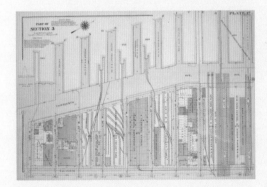

street." A train could drive into the building from West 27th Street and proceed to the elevators located in the central core, load or unload onto trucks and then exit onto 26th Street. The elevator system was similar to Russell Cory's New York Dock Trade Facilities Building of 1928 at Joralemon Street on the East River in Brooklyn. Here Cory developed patents for elevator systems in industrial buildings in which the utility core was combined in the same core as elevators that had the capacity to carry trucks. At Starrett-Lehigh, the elevators had additional concrete structure to carry the weight of trucks or train cars. This central core functioned as "a vertical industrial thoroughfare," providing all the services that would be expected on a horizontal industrial site by distributing them at each level, reducing infrastructural costs, taking advantage of economies of scale, and relieving streets of truck traffic.[75]

The foundation work necessitated innovative deep footings to get below the landfill at the river's edge and to reach bedrock, which was 13 meters below street level on the east side and 44 meters on the west. This required reducing the 13th Avenue wing to be only nine stories because they couldn't drill down deep enough to support a taller building at this side, but could support an 18-story 11th Avenue wing, and a 19-story central section with the elevator

◀ Cory & Cory, Starrett-Lehigh building with elevated train line in foreground, New York, 1932. Photograph by Berenice Abbott
▲ Pages from promotional brochure showing natural light and truck elevator logistics, Starrett-Lehigh building
▲ G.W. Bromley Map, 1920–1922, Plate 17, part of Section 3: bounded by (Hudson River Docks) 13th Avenue, W. 32nd Street, 11th Avenue and W. 23rd Street

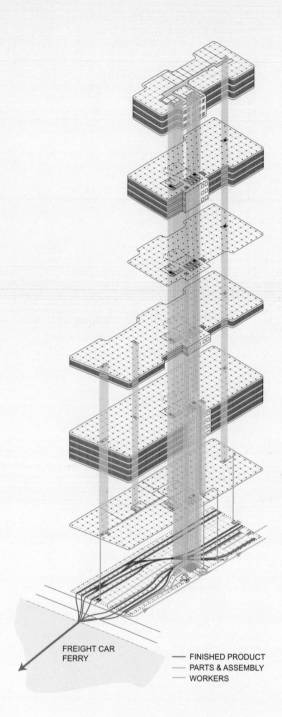

FREIGHT CAR
FERRY

—— FINISHED PRODUCT
—— PARTS & ASSEMBLY
—— WORKERS

massive concrete mushroom columns spaced six meters apart in the north-south direction and up to six meters in the east-west direction for the train track layout. The columns were set back from the perimeter wall which is picked up by the concrete slab cantilever, similar to the Van Nelle factory, allowing additional light to penetrate into the interior and the floor space to remain open. As critic Lewis Mumford noted, "Here a cantilevered front has been used, not as a cliché of modernism, but as a means of achieving a maximum amount of daylight and unbroken floor space for work requiring direct lighting. The aesthetic result is very happy indeed. The contrast between the long, continuous red-brick bands and the green-framed windows, with sapphire reflection or depths, is as sound a use of color as one can see about the city."[76] The building was the largest flat-slab reinforced concrete frame multistoried building in the United States when it was completed in 1931. Advertising 38,000 square meters on six floors housing 200 meters of linear production with four meter heights, the total building had 550,000 square meters of leasable space. After the demise of rail freight and the influx of truck-based transportation, trucks became the prime users of the lower-level circulation system and elevators, one of which still continues to operate today.

In 1930, Colonel William A. Starrett promoted the building in the leasing brochure: "When water and rail and automotive transportation can be joined up in a great terminal, where under the same roof, executives, sales, storage, assembly and distribution all can be carried on in a single terminal unit we will have defeated the major affliction of modern metropolitan life – traffic congestion."[77] The extraordinary capacity of this vertical circulation inspired the building's marketing slogan "Every floor a first floor."[78] Companies including printers, doll makers, clothing manufacturers, and die cutters leased space to have access to a floor with a vertical street that would connect "between the tenant and the services just as real and just as effective as in the horizontal street."[79] On the mezzanine floor, amenities such as a cafeteria, barbershop, and first aid clinic were included as services for the workers and industrialists in the building. This collaboration between investors, engineers, transit, and manufacturing specialists contributed to the development of a building type that uniquely provided hybrid services in the city.

penthouse projecting above the roofline. The resulting exaggerated ziggurat massing was structural and built according to New York City setback requirements.

Steel casement ribbon windows wrapped the building, emphasizing the horizontality of the concrete floor slabs. These were supported by

VAN NELLE FACTORY
BRINKMAN & VAN DER VLUGT, ROTTERDAM, 1926–1931

A seminal project of the *Nieuwe Bouwen* group of Dutch Modern architects, the Van Nelle company – a tobacco, tea, and coffee production facility with glass facades, dramatic bridge overpasses for conveyors, and smooth surfaces – exemplified the Modern aesthetic in a prime European port of Rotterdam. At the time, the city was already home to many multistoried, new factory waterfront developments up the Nieuwe Maas River at the town of Delfshaven. From there, the Dutch West Indian Company conducted their importing and exporting of goods and the Pilgrims set sail in 1620 for North America.

The engineering of waterways epitomized the Dutch manipulation of land. First, a dam and lock were built in the River Rotte, which spurred the development of the town. Deep harbors were dug in the sixteenth century, but access to the North Sea was limited as ships had to travel meandering routes. Engineer Pieter Caland proposed a canal, the Nieuw Waterweg, for shipping traffic in 1873. This new river opening joined the Rhine and the Meuse rivers to the North Sea, developing into the largest transit harbor to Germany and then Belgium with two thousand ships making passage in 1850 and five times as

many in 1910. The city's population increased in parallel from 86,000 to 425,000. Rotterdam's economic urban center beckoned industrialists such as the Van der Leeuw family, which was importing, tea, coffee, and tobacco. Another similar company, but one that was organized as a cooperative, was the coffee, tea, and grain collective HandelsKammer, or HaKa, a wholesaler established in 1914 for the working class. Haka's new building, designed by Herman Friedrich Mertens (1885–1960), was erected in 1931–1932. The narrow site both fronted the water and rail networks, and inspired cantilevering of the six floors of the concrete frame building, which had circular and ribbon windows resembling a ship at the port's docks.

Van Nelle's owners, Kees van der Leeuw and his brother Dick (1894–1936) were inspired by Theosophy, a mystical religious movement that gained popularity in the late nineteenth century. In 1923, Kees helped to build the Amsterdam-based headquarters of the Order of the Star in the East, an offshoot of the Theosophical Society's India branch. He was also extremely active as the Order's secretary, and determined that the Van Nelle factory's design, construction

▼ Johannes Brinkman and Leendert van der Vlugt, Van Nelle factory view from the main gate, Rotterdam, The Netherlands, 1926–1931

methods, and spatial planning should coalesce with Theosophist beliefs. Their orientation towards philanthropy, humanism, and light as a symbol of life, became the driving guidelines for the development of their new production space.

Kees Van der Leeuw had also researched successful American factories prior to constructing Van Nelle.[80] At first he was keen to test Taylorized efficiency models by consolidating the company's numerous factories, scattered around the city, into a focused organization under one roof. He looked to Ford's Highland Park for its vertical integration of processing from top to bottom, use of overhead conveyors, and gravity flow, but was concerned by the plant's lack of natural light, writing that: "Many halls are so wide that people in the middle have to work with artificial light all the time. And most of the time a sort of Moorlight (mercury tubular lamps) is used which produces a bluish tone. In some halls there are too many labourers, which deteriorates the quality of the air, something the Labor inspectorate in our country would not accept."[81]

Van der Leeuw also cared about the quality of the workspace. In a 1930 lecture titled "Beauty in Industry" delivered at a joint meeting of the Theosophists and the workplace efficiency organization, he said: "In each human being lingers a need for beauty. . . . Beauty in the factory is therefore not only an ideal pursuit but also in our own interest. . . . If the work is monotonous and hardly interesting, we ought to consider whether the environment could play a role in easing that monotony."[82] He also combined Modernist and industrial design approaches to provide cost advantages for items such as the curtain wall, and described in his lectures guidelines such as:

1. The outward appearance of a factory should be derived from the requirements of its contents.
2. In the design, the human element deserves at least as much attention as the mechanical.
3. Extra expense for finishing details that does not demonstrate an immediately identifiable advantage can still be justified.[83]

Van der Leeuw hired the architects Michiel Brinkman (1873–1925) and Leendert C. van der Vlugt (1894–1936), who had designed a steam-driven flour mill in 1913 with Mart Stam. The commission was to build the Van Nelle factory on new landfill plots – polders – along a canal next to the Overschie River in Rotterdam, a short distance from the city's bustling harbor. Land was purchased in 1910, but due to the outbreak of World War I, the project was not started until 1926. After Brinkman died suddenly, the project went to his son Johannes (1902–1949), who continued in partnership with Van der Vlugt. They designed retail stores, worker housing, and Modern houses for the company owners. They later joined with Jaap Bakema (1914–1981) designing other factories and warehouses along Rotterdam's waterways through the 1950s.

The Van Nelle complex included a series of separate but connected buildings of varying heights for the processing and packaging of coffee (six stories), tea (three stories), and tobacco (eight stories). Additionally, there were warehouses, offices, and worker amenities such as a soccer field and a library. Plans for expansion included a parallel addition with crossbar volumes connecting to the main factory spaces, but they were never implemented. Fire safety analysis determined that it was necessary to

▲ Leaving the factory under the glass-enclosed conveyors, Van Nelle factory, ca. 1960
▶ Transport cradles move tea from the factory to the warehouse and then through glass-enclosed conveyors, Van Nelle factory, ca. 1960

place the boiler house away from the main factory along the Schie River, not only for access to water in case of explosion, but for proximity to the delivery of coal. This decision made more open space available in the factory, which was used for additional workshops.

The Van Nelle factory's emphasis on transparency created a new model for manufacturing spaces by exemplifying a hygienic, light-filled, airy environment, one open to both internal and external views while at the same time being a result of Theosopist ideas reflected in architectural details such as the admittance of light and fresh air and the use of ergonomically sensitive furniture. The building glistened at night and reflected and refracted sunlight during the day. To improve working conditions, Van der Leeuw supplemented the factory lighting with Modernist Siemens & Haske spherical and conical hanging lamps and installed the best available heating systems. General Electric's Lamp Works in Nela Park in Cleveland in 1926 served as a lighting model for the factory, while the Bauhaus school (founded 1919) and the Fagus factory in Germany inspired the transparent facade.[84] Van der Leeuw incorporated portable screens to block drafts and installed American-made aluminum blinds that workers could control individually.

Van der Leeuw's notion of a happy workforce may have been naïve, but his paternalistic approach, which was more oriented to the worker, led to better conditions and an optimized work environment with light and air and common spaces. From the curved, glass and steel facade of the four-story administrative building that joined the factory via a glass-clad pedestrian bridge to the ample and airy office layouts, the project exemplified the Modern aesthetic.

The managing director's office was followed by a sequence of meeting rooms, drafting offices, sample rooms, the general administrative offices with a mezzanine, and then cafeteria. Other design strategies created a sense of floating volumes such as the use of *pilotis* to support the curved volume, and a semicircular glazed rooftop tearoom and viewing platform that cantilevered from the southeast stairwell of the factory. Four prominent glazed exterior stair towers – two for women and two for men – provided separate access to each work area and separate washrooms and locker rooms.

As a vertically organized factory, production flowed from the upper to the lower floors, with the raw goods delivered to the topmost floor as organized by the production engineers. Transport shafts and conveyors were aligned adjacent to the staircase volumes. The final products were transferred into the glazed dispatch buildings via overhead U-shaped platform conveyors circulating from the interior of the factory to the enclosed

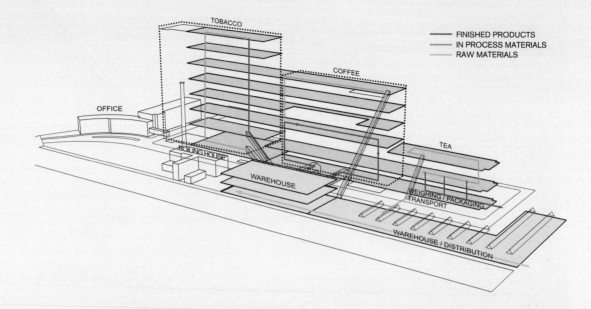

glass bridges traversing the site's internal street. Van Nelle hired the graphic designer Jac Jongert (1883–1942) to design the company's packaging and rooftop signage. His choice of a Modern sans serif typeface set an avant-garde tone for the company's identity and advertising and reflected new directions in Dutch design.

Innovative structural engineering allowed for new manufacturing configurations. The eight floors of the tobacco factory were designed to be flexible for machinery to be moved as needed, by means of a structural system that engineer Jan G. Wiebenga (1886–1974) developed. It constituted a minimal framework employing octagonal, reinforced concrete columns to support beamless poured-in-place concrete floor slabs. During a 1924 trip to the U.S., Wiebenga had conducted a great deal of research into the most efficient construction systems. Based on his findings, he reworked the Turner mushroom column to meet his own needs.[85] The first concrete pour was in October of 1926 for the tobacco factory floors; they cantilevered beyond the last row of columns in a 5.75-by-5.75-meter module containing two rows of five central columns. A narrow corridor along the interior of the wall was set aside for the running of conduits and heating. The tobacco factory's glass and steel facade was a groundbreaking curtain wall system. Erected from the interior, the full-height unit, combining glass, steel, and metal spandrels, was mounted to the building's concrete frame.[86] The vertical steel mullion system was supplied by a Dutch subcontractor

of the ever popular Crittall Windows of England with both fixed and operable glass panels sized 50 by 120 centimeters, forming a flush facade. The steel spandrels represented an early sandwich panel of thin insulating Torfoleum made of compressed peat moss, a new thermal insulation material, rather than traditional brick spandrels. But the panels did not respond well to the climate and have since been replaced.[87]

In the production process for cigarettes, the tobacco leaves were unloaded on the first floor, separated, and then moved to the seventh floor for fermentation. They traveled back down to the first floor to dry on conveyor belts and then were cut, after which workers wrapped and packaged the cigarettes on the third and fourth floors. Tobacco was separately processed on the fifth and sixth floors. Vertical systems for goods distribution were integrated into the building with elevators and chain conveyors, conveyor belts, rollways, and overhead conveyors. This kept the artificial stone floor free of carts until palettes and forklifts were used in the 1970s.

The building for tea processing was only three stories high so that workers could transfer tea leaves quickly through the bridges to the dispatch buildings, thereby maintaining the leaves' consistency. In a fluid movement system, the tea was placed on an elevator to the second floor and the empty boxes were fed down and out of the building through exterior slides. On the second floor the leaves were separated, cleaned, and blended, then poured down through openings in the floor to the first floor for tasting. The ground floor, as in the other buildings, contained the packaging and labeling.

The verticality of the six-story coffee factory was used to the fullest, including a two-story volume to house the roasting machines and stainless steel storage silos. This section was built between 1928 and 1930, with the ceiling heights from 3.5 meters to seven meters high to allow for the machinery, and factory 18.9 meters deep.[88] The module was a bit reduced from the rest of the factory, at 5-by-5.70 meters. North-facing roof monitor skylights illuminated the space where the coffee beans were sorted by color. Coffee was ground on the second floor and then transferred to the main floor for packaging.

Van Nelle had a sophisticated mechanical system. Like the Usine Claude & Duval, instead of running ducts along the ceiling, the concrete floor incorporated the building's electrical conduits and water pipes. The vertical piping was painted in bright colors to indicate their purpose in a color-coded system. Natural ventilation was used for cooling. To clean the windows, a metal rail was installed at the parapet from which to suspend a cleaner's scaffolding, integrating the mechanism as part of the Modernist, ship-like building's aesthetic. This feature was inspired by similar systems that Van der Leeuw had seen in factories in Cleveland, Ohio.

Many praised the complex, including Le Corbusier, who noted Van der Vlugt's "perfect form for the architect's mission, which is to bring happiness to people and he has chosen the factory to do so."[89] Photographers and cinematographers were intrigued by the conveyor bridges, overall transparency, reflective qualities, and light. However, others derided the working conditions and claimed that the design really didn't change the workers' treatment. With the advent of new machinery, the workers as operatives were doing mundane tasks combining machinic and handwork skills. Van Nelle was kind to workers, providing benefits and a pension fund even in the early twentieth century, but there was oppressive worker supervision. As a coffee worker commented decades later, "When the supervisor gave a sign, all the sorters went to the toilets at the same time (so as to keep the peace in the department. . .always everything at the same time). If there were any machinery defects the machinists could then set to work at that time."[90] The factory paradox prevailed with the improved

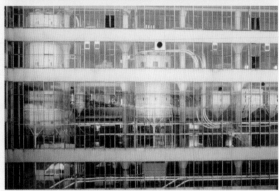

space and harsh work unreconciled. As Dutch artist R.N. Roland Holst (1868–1938) observed, "A factory such as this is perfect, but it sickens me nonetheless to see the work done there; work is reduced to the most deathly monotony and the highest intensity, a perfected system of exploitation, but one that is more or less mechanized and that has a strongly aesthetic character."[91] Van der Leeuw failed in his construction of a model society, as "when the building was finished the labourers did not become healthier, or more dedicated to their work. On the contrary, in the thirties, serious social problems among the personnel even got out of hand"[92]

But Van der Leeuw continued to be committed to the Modernist experiment and befriended Austrian architect Richard Neutra (1892–1970), funding his efforts with a $3,000 contribution to build a glass house in California that he named the VDL Research House.

▲ Aerial photograph from the east, Van Nelle factory, 1966
▲ Glass facade of coffee roasting building, Van Nelle factory, 1990s

USINE CLAUDE & DUVAL

LE CORBUSIER, SAINT-DIÉ-DES-VOSGES, FRANCE, 1946–1951

Le Corbusier emphasized the significance of industrial architecture – the vernacular, primary forms of American factories designed by engineers – in his polemical writings of the 1920s including *Vers une Architecture* (*Towards a New Architecture*) and *L'Esprit Nouveau*. He also had direct experience with factories. In 1917, he organized the brick factory, La Briqueterie d'Alfortville, with friend Max Dubois for the Société des Etudes Industrielles et Techniques just outside of Paris. In this project, Le Corbusier was fascinated with ideas of Taylorism, best management practices, and ways to develop new products. Even though the brick factory went bankrupt in 1921, the experience influenced him considerably; through it he learned principles of management, industry, finance, and commerce, and formed many important business contacts.[93] He also designed a project for the aforementioned Green Factory, which he imagined as integrated with the landscape. All of these concepts coalesced into the design for Usine Claude & Duval, a project that furthered many of Corbusier's architectonic

ideas while incorporating his knowledge of the functioning factory.

Following the destruction of the western French city of Saint-Dié-des-Vosges during World War II, industrialist Jean-Jacques Duval commissioned Le Corbusier to design a master plan for the town. Because Le Corbusier presented a Modern solution rather than rebuilding the past, the plan was rejected "by the bourgeois associations, large and small, by the workers' unions, by socialists and communists" who unanimously arrayed against the new proposal.[94] Nevertheless, Duval asked Le Corbusier to redesign his own millinery factory destroyed in the war using funds allotted for postwar reconstruction. It allowed him to "not only build a factory better organized than the old one, but renovate with the advantage of impeccable order of engineers, also with simple decoration (clear colors, music at work. . .that were elements of comfort) and that would be sensible through to the details,"[95] as noted by Paul Duval, the son of the owner.

With the Usine Claude & Duval, Le Corbusier initiated his primary design ideas of the postwar period and incorporated a system of proportions called the "Modulor" based on human measurements and the Golden Section. Le Corbusier also employed architectural devices of Modernist distinction including *pilotis,* the ribbon window, the roof garden, and the concrete *brise-soleil.*

After three project design concepts, the Duvals with Le Corbusier organized the factory production as a model so that the primary raw materials would be delivered by electric lift to the third floor and then descend level by level, for each operation until they left for distribution at the ground floor.[96] The solution allowed for the raising up of the floors on *pilotis* so that the ground floor was open for storage of the workers' bicycles. It also framed the entrance to the caretaker's house, and allowed coal for the heating to be delivered directly from the street to the coal bins underground.

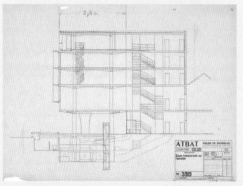

◀ Le Corbusier, design of city of Saint-Dié (project), France, 1945
◀ Le Corbusier, section of Claude & Duval factory, Saint-Dié, France, 1946–1951
▶ Le Corbusier, Claude & Duval factory
▶ Rooftop terrace of the factory

The factory is divided into two main zones – one for work preparation with fewer employees and the other for intense production with a high density of workers. The mezzanine floor was inserted between floors as a work area above the double-height main space where the more intense production took place. Large oak windows on the northwest side brought in natural light.

Le Corbusier describes three distinctive volumes in his *Oeuvre Complète*: the colonnade of the *pilotis,* the workshops, and the crowning top-floor office space with terrace.[97] These elements combine to create a Modulor system of rhythms in the lengths of 6.25, 5.92, and 3.66 meters that have a pattern similar to musical harmony and provide an organizational system for the building. The concrete *brise-soleil* on the southeast facade enlivens the concrete structural grid and protects the studios from direct sunlight – with its grill of vertical concrete support and horizontal wing-like forms, it shades the sun in summer months but allows light to penetrate in winter. Le Corbusier also used strong color

▲ Interior view from mezzanine down to workshop showing delivery systems
◀ Round metal staircase in the factory

accents to identify different mechanical functions: greens and yellows on interior conduits, red for fire stations, green for air circulation, yellow for electricity, and blue for water. The end walls he maintained in the local pink stone that remained in situ from the original Duval factory, which contrasted with the exposed concrete structure. He painted the ceilings different colors for increased light reflection.

The factory's vertical distribution facilitates the manufacturing process even today as the company continues production. From the tall, narrow storage room, elevators move materials to the top floor. Along the southeast facade, workers cut fabrics, which they place on carts to move up to the third floor on tracks. From there, gravity chutes guide goods progressively down the production chain – from fabric cutting, to decoration, to sewing, pressing, packaging, and shipping. On the second floor, the garment

workers press garments and send them down to the first floor to be packaged for delivery. The double-height workshop spaces have northern windows to receive diffused natural sunlight.

The administration offices on the top floor, with furniture designed by Le Corbusier, have a calm serenity that Duval felt "was already in the spirit of the future Ronchamp Chapel."[98] The offices open onto rooftop terraces – one on the south and the other on the north – with sculptural concrete planters, loggia, and colored tile details; their low walls hide the neighboring rooftops. Additional steel supports projecting from the roof allow for future vertical expansion. The project unfolded as a significant building not only for industrial architecture, but also in the trajectory of Modernism. The Usine Claude & Duval also incubated many of Le Corbusier's ideas for his later and larger 1952 Unité d'Habitation housing project in Marseilles.

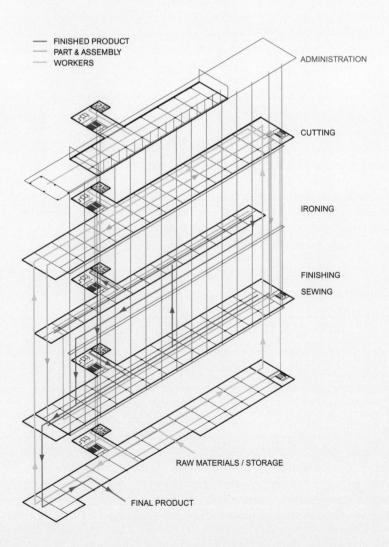

—— FINISHED PRODUCT
—— PART & ASSEMBLY
—— WORKERS

ADMINISTRATION

CUTTING

IRONING

FINISHING

SEWING

RAW MATERIALS / STORAGE

FINAL PRODUCT

JORBA LABORATORIES
MIGUEL FISAC, MADRID, 1965

Miguel Fisac (1913–2006) capitalized on the ability of architecture to communicate the progressive zeitgeist in his experiments with material and structure, which harnessed the optimism of Modernism, and responded in his design to the rise of corporate culture. Based in Madrid, he was a prominent Spanish architect in the second half of the twentieth century. His approach and formal interests were similar to Antonio Gaudí (1852–1926), in that Fisac experimented in material and structure and embraced an organic Modernist style. He worked at every scale, from furniture to urban planning. The latter resulted in the Urban Molecule, a system of organizing cities.

Moving beyond the rigid concrete grid of the early Modernist factories, Fisac's work was formally playful yet unabashed in its structural rigor. He imbued materials such as brick and concrete with a new tactility. Fisac molded, stacked, structured, and curved brick, a local material, and played freely with concrete – hollowing, reinforcing, and sculpting this initially liquid substance into a voluptuous solid. He exploited these material properties to create new roof systems as well as craftsmen-like wall panels and window details. For Madrid's IBM headquarters (1966), Fisac created vertical *brise-soleil* from curved concrete – as they wrapped the building they resembled butterfly wings opening and closing. In later works Fisac experimented with concrete panels in a softened flexible polyethylene lamina, which gave them the effect of geometrically decorated, pillow-like tiles.

The son of a chemist, Fisac was familiar with the program and spatial needs of pharmaceutical companies and had designed laboratories for the companies Alter (1960) and Made (1963), both in Madrid. For Alter he introduced a ribbed roof structure that turns a seemingly flat roof into a variegated volume, allowing light to penetrate between the beams. This solution went beyond utility and incorporated the fifth facade – the roof – as the company's new identity. For Jorba Laboratories, located along the main highway to the Madrid airport, he exploited the simplicity of structural concrete, forming a unique sculptural stacked and rotated volume.

Fisac's design approach to Jorba's sloped and compressed urban site included a six-story tower for visibility from the road. Within it he stacked the labs on the lower floors and administrative and research offices above, placing the more spacious workshops in an elongated three-story rectangular adjacent building. This lower building slid into the tower's first floor, maintaining the stepped ground plane. The configuration was similar to Fisac's 1960 Center for Hydrographic Studies, also in Madrid, which had a larger multistoried volume with offices that abuts a lower laboratory workshop building.

The form and structure of Jorba's tower was unique. Like a spinning top or "pagoda," as it was fondly nicknamed, the design displayed a rare dynamism for a static form. This unusual achievement was the result of a series of 16-meter-square floor slabs stacked and rotated 45 degrees off the previous, or upper, slab – with a floor sandwiched between each one. Built from top to bottom, these units were connected by hyperbolic paraboloids that were hung from the underside of the floor. Fisac described that, "It began to give me surfaces that we love in geometry: hyperbolic paraboloids that have the advantage of not resolving to curved molds, [so that we could] instead use straight planks that twist slowly. I arranged the hyperbolic paraboloid pieces to make them fit the geometry, and then what was left was quite eye-catching."[99]

At the point of load resistance, the stacking forms made an octagon, which was reinforced so that the cantilever could be reduced in weight in order to project out from the core. The central stairs were hung from the roof slab and then the elevator was installed within a steel structure with all four sides in glass, allowing views into the floors. The bands of windows also fluctuated, either projecting beyond the core or flush with it, creating variety for the workers and visual interest on the exterior. On the roof he placed a more decorative element, using vertical triangular slabs arranged in a crowned pinnacle onto which the company sign was mounted.

The tower was not the only place in which Fisac explored the plasticity of concrete. The roof of the lower volume continued the development of his thin, hollow, prestressed tubular beams. Continuing the research previously executed in the concrete work of his Hydrographic Institute – where staggered triangulated concrete slabs created openings – Fisac reinterpreted the standard ribbed concrete roof systems by using hollowed tubes with the assistance of

consulting engineer Vicente Piero. Fisac realized that "the pieces that I have obtained using this architectonic-static means have resulted in sections with forms very [much] like the bones of vertebrates. It's not that I wanted to make them like bones, it's just that they turned out that way. That makes you think that, naturally, some parallel exists. You could interpret it as proof that this is the right path, [as] it corresponds to concepts, which we see in Nature. My collaborators, in many cases, have called these pieces bones, in a pejorative sense, because setting up their production entails numerous difficulties."[100]

The distance between the exterior walls was 11 meters, which he realized he could span

▲ Miquel Fisac, tower of Jorba Laboratories, Madrid, Spain, 1965
▶ Jorba Laboratories under construction

RAW MATERIALS
PROCESSING
FINISHED GOODS

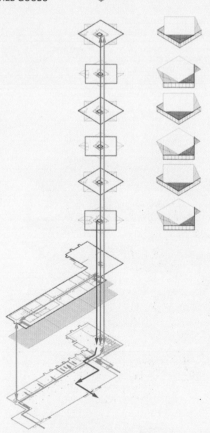

using prestressed concrete as he had previously in the design for the Asuncion College and Church, which had thin concrete slabs. Fisac noted how much he had to resolve the structural concept: "Beforehand, I did some tests at the Torroja Institute – we broke two or three beams, but it took a great deal of effort to break them."[101] The idea of structural bones can be taken literally but also results in an interesting ornament: when the tubes with their organic end cuts are juxtaposed in a line, they form a holistic undulating form.[102]

Fisac gave the concrete a variegated texture from the wood formwork impression. U-shaped metal extrusions formed structural columns that the builders welded to keep the vertical elements at a minimum and make room for open workspaces. Metal work was also used in extruded anodized aluminum window frames with plastic roller blinds nested within handrails on the main stairs. For the entrance marquee he employed a more standard structural triangulation in steel.

The plan of the building shows the process and functional siting that allowed for raw materials and packaging supplies to enter the buildings from the north side via trucks from the highway in an "uninterrupted route with simple movements, both vertical and horizontal, to their exit from the warehouses and the packaging zone."[103]

Fisac's work demonstrated architects' innovations within the typology of the vertical urban factory, although the horizontal shed had already begun to dominate the industrial landscape in the 1960s. The building complex was destroyed in 1999, causing a great outcry from the architectural community.

▲ **Jorba Laboratories showing the bone-like beams**
◀ **Jorba Laboratories under construction showing the concrete hyperbolic forms**

MECHANISTIC FACTORY

After the innovative explorations of Modern engineering and design, the architectural emergency posed by World War II shifted the direction of factory design. The postwar model was more mechanistic, both in terms of its operation and its mode of construction, wherein aesthetic concerns were of less importance. The war called upon architects and engineers to solve urgent building needs in the U.S., Great Britain, and European countries; what was produced, however, was stripped of aesthetic agendas and contributed to new design agendas. The innovations were not found in the formal design or in the self-consciously Modern attributes but elsewhere: in the speed of construction, the massive scale, the harnessing of new technology, and the development of new materials for supporting wartime objectives. The scarcity of the critical materials caused by the war — steel, aluminum, and tungsten, in particular — necessitated the use of alternatives such as glue-laminated wood, plastics, and fibers. Developing ingenious designs and practical solutions, designers learned to produce things quickly and with minimal materials. A well-known example of this was the 1942 design of leg splints in plywood by Charles (1907–1978) and Ray (1912–1988) Eames.

Questions can be asked as to how the propaganda used to endorse war impacted the architecture of manufacturing, as everything — from the product name to promotional methods and articles in architectural magazines such as *Architectural Record* with headlines such as "Industrial Buildings Back the Attack" — doubly endorsed the war.[104] The advertising found in architecture magazines also validated the war, featuring recommended products and providing guidance on how factories could contribute to the war effort, even at home. The ads emphasized the need to build in concrete and plywood, rather than the "critical" material of steel, and announced: "Build munitions factories, use plywood."[105]

Architects such as Albert Kahn and industrialists like Ford were already fully deployed in this effort, both in their offices and in their factories. Kahn, whose office had grown to over six hundred employees, was instrumental in developing new organizational systems for architectural production. He ran his office much like a factory production line, and designed over two hundred buildings relating to wartime use. Kahn stressed the importance of organization and good management, as well as the appropriate use of materials and need for standardization. He foresaw that a National Building Code would encourage the planning of buildings utilizing a minimum of materials. Building systems — air conditioning and filtration systems, materials of fluorescent lighting, and glass block, among others — were incorporated into industrial buildings, forever changing factory design. The reintroduction of one-story sheds emerged at this time, about which Kahn emphasized, "It is questionable whether the enormity of the building program for national defense is generally appreciated. Never in history has so staggering a program been undertaken. . . for manufacturing buildings there has been developed a certain type. . .generally accepted as best. . .the one-story structure of incombustible materials, with enormous uninterrupted floor spaces under one roof, with a minimum of columns."[106] The shed changed the dynamic of manufacturing in a way that was irreversible.

▶ Albert Kahn Associates, Willow Run factory, Ypsilanti, Michigan, 1941
▶ Albert Kahn Associates, Chrysler Tank Arsenal, Warren, Michigan, 1941

Kahn's feats of speed for large-scale construction were impressive. His Glenn Martin aircraft plant in Baltimore had the footings poured on February 1, 1937, and was completed 77 days later. It set a building and operations record as the largest one-story industrial building of the time. The Willow Run Bomber plant built in 1942 in Ypsilanti, Michigan, was expanded after Pearl Harbor to 1.2 million square meters, which covered approximately 65 acres. The single-story building — a semi-blackout plant — included a training school and testing field, and admitted no daylight to the production areas. The defense concerns overruled the earlier interests for factories to be well-lit. Blackout, like camouflage, was used to conceal the factories and to prevent their detection by bomber aircraft. The Willow Run factory also included schools and community facilities and served lunches for 80,000 workers.

The Chrysler Tank Arsenal was built outside of Detroit at the request of William Knudsen (1879–1948) of the Council of National Defense, Office of Production Management. In 1940, Kahn organized the general plant, which was assembled in the field, and the first armored tank was produced before the building was even finished. The building required maximum flexibility and large, open spaces, resulting in a single-story structure with a butterfly roof monitor that was 420 meters long by 160 meters wide; adjacent to the factory was a figure-eight test track. Ninety-five percent of the wall was glazed with 80,000 windowpanes. The receiving, manufacturing, and assembly areas were expressed by different structural framing organization. Raw materials entered from the north, and production proceeded to the south side of the building. By the war's end the facility housed the production of 25,000 tanks and had received numerous awards. By this time, Kahn had given up the kind of architectural embellishments and ornament that he had previously used, but to make the pragmatic, performative shed structure he retained the play of contrasting masses, patterns created by solids and voids, and innovative use of glass and steel.

Architects experimented with other new methods to create column-free manufacturing spaces, such as in the pneumatically controlled thin steel membrane circular factory designed by Herbert H. Stevens Jr. (1927–2013) for an airplane factory in 1942.[107] The factory, illustrated by Hugh Ferris (1889–1962), showed how a circular ring would be fastened to a concrete anchor ring which would then be raised and stretched into a dome shape into which air would be blown, continuously filling the voluminous, 35-meter-diameter, column-free building. It also used one-tenth the amount of steel in normal construction and other priority materials, as the strips of steel would be only 1.2 millimeter thick. The dome-shaped factory organized assembly differently from most — from the outside in — and then the finished airplane would move through a passage to the exit on the side. It would have been suitable for the 24-hour-a-day blackout requirements and would have been easy to camouflage.[108] As a mechanistic system, it would have been demountable and could have been deployed anywhere.

An intensity of invention transformed materials such as concrete and wood through experimentation and offered alternatives to steel construction. Giffels & Vallet Inc., L. Rossetti Architects built a precast concrete construction combining roof and crane bay support with a wood truss and wood roof and concrete walls. It saved steel and time. The concrete lintels and columns were slotted together and bolted in place. Other engineers, Roberts and Schaefer, developed thin-shell concrete roofs as mass-produced barrel-shells using reusable wooden forms; in this way, one module of the factory was built daily. The curve of the roof allowed it to withstand "bomb action" — an impossibility, but a marketable technology.[109]

New techniques for wood beam lamination, which both strengthened and preserved wood, were deployed such that laminated wood joists spanned factory spaces which were supported by laminated timber columns, rather than with steel. In South Weymouth, Massachusetts, a blimp hangar built for the Navy using timber in 1942 boasted the largest spans — 75 meters — for wood construction of the time. One hundred and sixty-six airships could be accommodated in the three-hectare facility. Due to limited labor and material resources, the factory skimped on materials and was built below construction code.

Other factory building systems invented during this period included new insulated wall panels which would simply clip on a facade to cover windows to conceal the light as required during a blackout. This spurred the invention of new ventilation for the sealed sheds with Freon for air conditioning and air filters. Since workers labored through the night there was a need for consistent artificial lighting. Regular lights used tungsten, a restricted war material, so instead glass or porcelain-enameled steel casings and fluorescent lights were arrayed across factory ceilings. Advertising in architectural journals promoted the architect's role in supporting the war and how architects' factory designs would win the war. Or, the power of their designs would lend to the war effort by using "seven inches of wood in pencil," conserving the often used copper, a critical material for machines. The conservation of critical materials in wartime as well as the need for speed in construction, presaged generic factory designs that resulted in the mundane but economical shed, wrapping the mechanism of production rather than responding to a specific production program or unique machinery. As part of the industrial machinery — the sheds emanated a non-architecture, supporting players to the rational and organized military industrial complex.

◀ Julius Kahn, advertisement for Truscon Steel company showing the standardized sheds they designed, 1915
◀ Advertisement for conserving copper during wartime, 1944

INTEGRATING MECHANISMS

One design reaction ensuing from the World War II factory was the innovative integration of mechanical systems with building structure as a new Modernist functional expression. This was exemplified in Marco Zanuso's (1916–2001) Olivetti factory in Buenos Aires, Argentina, of 1954. Zanuso was primarily an industrial designer, and this project launched his work in architecture. It allowed him to further explore the idea of a building as a product and the structure as service;

Zanuso's factory transformed the concept of the "machine for living" to the paradigm of a "machine for working," demonstrating his transitions between industrial design and architecture. From the small component to the larger complex building, he addressed tectonics at two scales. Buildings to him were enlarged machines which integrated the building-as-machine with the machines it housed, so that specific components became his points of design innovation.

For this Olivetti factory, expandability was a central design idea for what was originally planned as a 25,000-meter-square production hall. Zanuso designed an 18-by-12-meter module with a grand axis for interior distribution. The assembly room was L-shaped, with separate administrative offices and a technical zone, as well as a space for leisure housing a cafeteria, an infirmary, and locker rooms. Between these two zones was a place of social interaction, a microcosm that transitioned between consumption and production.

One innovative systems concept was the tubular hollow concrete girder that contained air conditioning and circulation. Four-pronged, lightweight concrete columns, spaced twelve meters apart, supported the hollow ovoid-shaped girders spaced eighteen meters apart, which in turn supported the canopy roof that cantilevered beyond the last row. Between the columns, glazed walls were set back from the roofline, and in its overhang created a much-needed shading device for the hot climate. The sheds opened to interior courtyards, separating the assembly space from the main hall.[110]

The concrete reinforcing system of spiral steel formed helical metal cages. Other columns were prefabricated and the hollow girders that included air exchange and technical cables formed an integrated and coordinated system between structure, physical plant, and tectonics. Zanuso considered the building as a living organism, with the life support elements distributed throughout the structure.

As Banham noted, "the need to be able to see the difference between the structure, which is supposed to be permanent, and the services, which are hoped to be transient, and to see that difference made expressive. The building is serviced, and manifestly seen to be serviced; the fact of servicing is seen to be within the architect's control, even if what is seen is not, in detail, entirely of the architect's design."[111] Later, a cigarette factory leased the space and could adapt it for their production line by shifting the partitions without changing the exterior. The building and others of Zanuso for Olivetti could be considered early concepts of high-tech architecture, where the pieces of the building are functional not only as systems of support but as the building's internal plant, electrical systems, and building organs. The Italian critic Luciano Crespi also recognized the linkage between a building as an industrial object in terms of the design process for highly functional objects.[112] While this building was one-story, its significance carried through to the ideas of postwar machinic factories that could rise vertically, employing a similar holistic ideology of efficiency. Buckminster Fuller's Vertical Cotton Mill, the Toni Dairy, and factories that process resources in more open-air environments, such as the Redpath Sugar refinery, all exemplify the mechanistic factory in various organizational and material approaches, described in detail here.

▶ Marco Zanuso, Olivetti, Buenos Aires, Argentina, 1954

VERTICAL COTTON MILL

**BUCKMINSTER FULLER AND STUDENTS
NORTH CAROLINA STATE COLLEGE,
(UNREALIZED), 1952**

Factory design during World War II became increasingly simple large sheds on suburban sites, expansive in scale but lacking in design concept. Postwar inventors such as architect-scientist Buckminster Fuller (1895–1983) instigated models for sustainable and integrated multistoried factories at a time when most were constructed as horizontal, monolithic boxes. Realizing the efficiency of vertically stacking manufacturing processes to save space and energy, Fuller investigated the potential for a vertical textile cotton mill. In concert with twenty graduate students from the architecture and textile schools of North Carolina State College of Design (NCSCD) at Raleigh, he conceived the "fountain factory," designed to integrate the flow of materials and processing from floor to floor. By recalling Oliver Evans' eighteenth-century gravity-guided manufacturing methods with integrated systems, Fuller created a provocative concept, which, although never built, is an inspiration for future vertical factory designs.

▲ Buckminster Fuller building Vertical Cotton Mill model with students TC Howard, Jim Fitzgibbon, and Duncan Stuart from North Carolina State College, 1952

Fuller had worked in textile factories in Sherbrooke, Quebec, where he learned about textile manufacturing and mill construction and worked in foundries to repair machine parts imported from Europe. Fuller, who frequently taught at Yale, Harvard, and the University of Pennsylvania where he designed and built projects with students, was introduced to faculty and students at North Carolina State College. In summer 1949, two NCSCD students, Jim Fitzgibbon and Duncan Stuart, met Fuller at Black Mountain College and invited him to give a series of lectures in North Carolina. He proposed a class that was ultimately carried out between the two departments of architecture and textile engineering.

Fuller was opposed to the excessive energy consumption of air-conditioned factories. He noted that when the factories moved from New England to North Carolina to avoid unions they built "one-story buildings and they just had concrete floors because the machinery had to be well held, it [was] very heavy and a lot of vibration."[113] Fuller instead sought to produce a fully automated factory with efficient cooling and flexible internal floors and walls that rose vertically.

He asked the students to formulate ideas for a new cotton mill using principles derived from his Dymaxion House and the geodesic dome – including the rounded forms and central pier. The father of one student, TC Howard, organized trips to cotton mills so that the textile and architecture students could see the cotton manufacturing process firsthand.[114] Fuller was inspired by the automation he saw in the process of doffing (separating cotton into threads), to develop a smoother process. He also envisioned the factory floor as more appropriate to the task and weight of specific equipment rather than the typical one-size-fits-all floors throughout a factory.

For the vertical cotton mill, Fuller conceived of a central mast core with six 45-centimeter-diameter spiral reinforced concrete columns set three meters apart in a hexagonal pattern, to carry a load of over three million pounds and braced by concrete rings at each floor, four meters apart. The mast would suspend a triangulated or tetrahedron open trusswork floor in a three-way space frame system. The mast would house all operating systems – elevator, utility lines, air ducts, and water supply – as well as pneumatic tubes through which raw cotton would be blown upwards after being cleaned and processed on the

ground floor. So, unlike a one-story factory where the processing winds its way through numerous sidestepping and zigzagging and in which workers need to use hand trucks to move parts and materials to each separate zone, carding machines would be located on the seventh floor and the cotton would descend, level by level, to the second floor where workers would use looms to weave it into muslin.[115]

The idea for the open truss as an isotropic geometry was unique to space frame structures, not only for the factory typology. The openness would allow the goods to transfer between floors at multiple points through the trusswork, as a sieve-like floor, not just through one conveyance

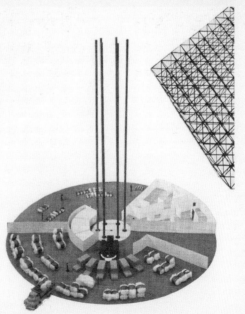

▲ **North Carolina State College students building the Vertical Cotton Mill dome, 1952**
▶ **Vertical Cotton Mill, drawing of interior floor, 1952**

system that would likely cause bottlenecks. Fuller harnessed gravity in a fluid process similar to the Claude & Duval or the Van Nelle factories, but in an even more exaggerated open network, as the seven layers of floors could be flexible. The machinery would be installed radially rather than in parallel rows and the product would descend from level to level, simplifying the process.

To explore the truss concept with more precision, the students built a full-scale mock-up, the first of its kind. TC Howard, who later joined Fuller's company, Synergetics, Inc., was the key welder and collaborator in the studio. The tetrahedron's sides were equilateral triangles that could support equally distributed stresses radiating out in concentric circles for equally weighted loads. The model was built using six-millimeter-round hot rolled rods welded together to be 15 centimeters in diameter with length-over-radius of 60 for each column, resulting in a 14-centimeter-deep truss. They built a 15-square-meter section to test loads of 300 pounds per square meter.[116] The truss was designed to carry a maximum load of 115,000 pounds in total and the machinery arrangement alone would control vibration without other dampers. The structure, with its light steel units, would make for fast construction and the

potential for enlarging the original as needed if the factory space had to grow.

Fuller conceived of catwalks above the factory floor with small vehicles for employee transport suspended as a monorail to provide quality control access. He also had ideas for monorails to be suspended from the frame for access to the machines. The shell of the building was known as a geodesic sphere. It had a double-layered plastic skin, which would facilitate return airflow, could function as insulation, and could expand with the factory's needs as in a plenum chamber to reduce pressure. The factory's upper level would contain a water tank and humidity control unit.

Many of Fuller's students, including TC Howard and Duncan Stuart, later established the Fuller Research Foundation in Raleigh to develop the geodesic dome. They also developed triacon grid mathematics and experimented with test loading working with Fuller on patents under the aegis of the companies Geodesics, Inc. and, later, Synergetics, Inc.

Although Fuller knew people in the industry, no one was interested in exploring new inventions for the cotton mill and it exists only in the periodicals of the time.

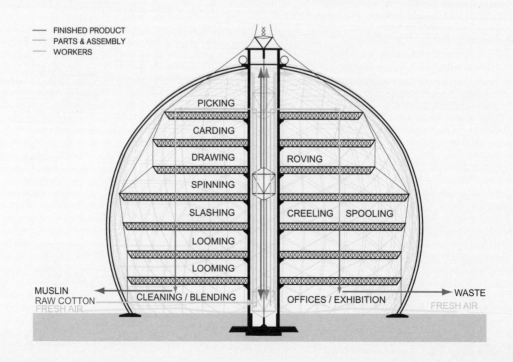

FINISHED PRODUCT
PARTS & ASSEMBLY
WORKERS

PICKING
CARDING
DRAWING   ROVING
SPINNING
SLASHING   CREELING   SPOOLING
LOOMING
LOOMING
MUSLIN   CLEANING / BLENDING   OFFICES / EXHIBITION   WASTE
RAW COTTON
FRESH AIR   FRESH AIR

REDPATH SUGAR FACTORY
TORONTO, 1950s

The manufacture of sugar began at a small scale but quickly became global, both culturally and economically. Now a major refining and processing industry, it commands large sites on urban waterfronts. Sugar was originally discovered in the seventh century in Persia as a product derived from sugar cane – a sweet spice similar in flavor to honey. It was Christopher Columbus who brought sugar cane plants with him from the East to harvest on the islands in the warm Caribbean climate. The extraction of sugar from sugar cane and sugar beets quickly became the grueling job of African slaves in the hot tropical climates of India, the Americas, and West Indies. The great demand for sugar led ultimately to the slave trade. Sugar plantations were one of the most exploitative work environments in the world, with living and working conditions so harsh that job-related death tolls were surpassed by few industries. Similar conditions continue to take the lives of cane cutters from Latin America to Africa today.

In New York, some of the first manufacturing buildings in the seventeenth century were the Sugar Houses in Lower Manhattan. These were multistoried brick and stone buildings used by merchant families for the storage of raw sugar from the West Indies. As the sugar industry grew, and processing could be conducted separately from the material extraction, companies developed refineries in large complexes of buildings. Together these functioned as a processing machine, the volumes reflecting and expressing the transformation of one material into a consumable product, in contrast to an interiorized undertaking.

One Modernist plant of interest is Redpath Sugar, located on the Toronto waterfront. Similar plants, such as Domino Sugar, located in Brooklyn, New York; Chicago, Illinois; and Baltimore, Maryland, developed simultaneously. Redpath is a continuously functioning company that nineteenth-century Scottish immigrant John Redpath (1796–1869), a construction company owner in Montreal, founded as the Canada Sugar Refining Co. His first plant was constructed on the Lachine Canal in 1854. With sugar imported from the British West Indies, he processed conical – or loaf – sugar, and then used the latest production techniques to manufacture granulated sugar packaged in bags and, later, cartons. The company also produced Paris Lumps (sugar cubes) and Golden Syrup. In the 1860s, with the help of new partners Peter Redpath and George Alexander Drummand, Redpath then built a six-story plant on the same site. In the early twentieth century, the company went through various ownership configurations. In 1930, Redpath merged with Dominion Sugar Co. Ltd., after which the Canadian government assumed control for twenty years. In the 1950s it became the Canada and Dominion Sugar Co. Ltd.

Responding to growing demand and anticipating future expansion, the company purchased a four-hectare tract of land on the Toronto waterfront to facilitate distribution to the Ontario market. Their completion of a concrete, steel-clad refinery coincided with the opening of the

▶ Redpath Sugar refinery, Toronto, Canada, 1957–1959
▶ Aerial photograph, Redpath Sugar refinery

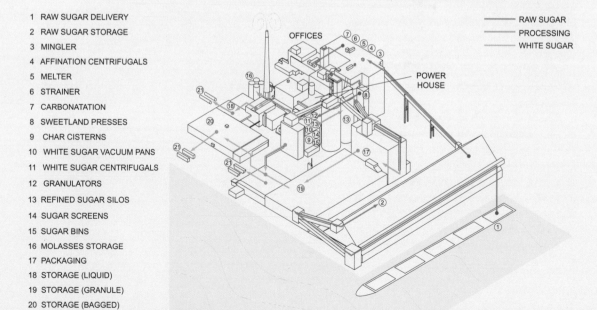

1 RAW SUGAR DELIVERY
2 RAW SUGAR STORAGE
3 MINGLER
4 AFFINATION CENTRIFUGALS
5 MELTER
6 STRAINER
7 CARBONATATION
8 SWEETLAND PRESSES
9 CHAR CISTERNS
10 WHITE SUGAR VACUUM PANS
11 WHITE SUGAR CENTRIFUGALS
12 GRANULATORS
13 REFINED SUGAR SILOS
14 SUGAR SCREENS
15 SUGAR BINS
16 MOLASSES STORAGE
17 PACKAGING
18 STORAGE (LIQUID)
19 STORAGE (GRANULE)
20 STORAGE (BAGGED)
21 DISTRIBUTION

OFFICES

POWER HOUSE

RAW SUGAR
PROCESSING
WHITE SUGAR

St. Lawrence Seaway, which provided water transit to the Great Lakes. The plant included a raw sugar shed, a steel-frame process building, a charhouse, two refined sugar silos for storage, a packaging building, the refined sugar warehouse, and the powerhouse – all linked via conveyors and bridges. The company offices, testing laboratories, and a museum are housed in a separate building.

The processing begins near the sugar plantations at mills, where the cane juice is extracted from cane stalks. The by-products of the cane are also used for fuel, construction materials, and paper products. This cane juice is delivered to the plant where it is filtered and boiled down, creating brown crystals of "raw sugar." This raw sugar is then exported to refineries.

At the Toronto plant, raw sugar is off-loaded from 25,000-ton ships with two mobile cranes traveling on rails along a 167-meter-long dock. The sugar is then scooped up and onto moving conveyors to be deposited into the 26-meter-high ridge of the raw sugar storage shed, which can hold 65,000 metric tons of sugar. The raw sugar is then dropped down through openings in the shed floor to moving conveyors in a below-ground tunnel and transferred to the refinery in an enclosed bridge that exploits the verticality of the plant. Conveyors move the sugar between the buildings in covered inclined bridges in a fluid production line.

The essential task is to clean the raw sugar of its impurities. This purification process is accomplished by filtering the raw sugar with chalk and then boiling it, which separates the pure sucrose crystals from molasses, plant residue, and other extraneous elements. To do this, the raw sugar is fed into a mixing trough called a Mingler, where it is blended with allination syrup (a mixture of hot water and molasses). This results in a thick, dark brown slurry, or magma. The magma is then boiled in a white vacuum pan, until crystals begin to re-form. This semi-crystalline substance, called white massecuite, is then dropped into a storage tank and spun to further separate and re-form the crystals. A large tumbler dryer completes the process. Workers sift crystals through mesh screens of various sizes, from fine to rough granularity, funneling the product into storage bins. Workers then move the sugar to the packaging hall where they use machines to package the sugar in various size bags, boxes, or bundles, or turned into a thinner liquid in large stainless steel tanks.

At Redpath, the entire manufacturing complex is integrated so that waste is transformed into spin-off products such as syrups or carbon for fertilizer. The manufactory is a closed-loop ecological system with the steam from the refining used for heating the complex.

This and other similar plants where raw materials are transformed in an alchemy of procedures, requires the factory to be a fluid machine, not only a machine housed in a container.

◀ Exterior covered chutes under construction, Redpath Sugar refinery, 1957
▲ Sugar refining tank, Redpath Sugar refinery, 1959

TONI DAIRY

A.E. BOSSHARD AND H. WIDMER,
ZURICH, SWITZERLAND, 1974

Urban manufacturing inspired fluid factory projects integrated with the city as vertical performative machines, which were housed in pragmatic wrappings. Founded in 1905, the company Toni-Molkerei produced butter, yogurt, cream, ice cream, and cheese in facilities across Switzerland. By the early 1970s, however, a shift towards automation and government restrictions on hiring foreign laborers reduced the availability and need for large numbers of workers, prompting Toni-Molkerei to consolidate manufacturing into one urban production space closer to their consumers. Today, food continues to be a vital urban commodity.

In 1974, Toni hired Zurich-based architect-engineers A.E. Bosshard and H. Widmer to design a Modernist rational and unified state-of-the-art factory with all departments housed under one roof on a vacant site in west Zurich. The site was accessible to highways and rail lines, and the zoning allowed for a 44-meter-tall building. Toni-Molkerei's slogan, "fresh from the farmer to the table," directed a design scheme focused on transportation infrastructure, resulting in an unprecedented three-story, 400-meter-long ramp connecting the city to the factory. In cities, trucks often clog traffic as they are making deliveries, block pedestrian movement on streets, and generate excessive exhaust as their engines idle. Here the architects integrated truck access with the three main production floors as well as with intermediate floors and the roof. As the trucks approached the building they could immediately leave the street and drive onto the three-story spiral ramp that was integrated into the building. They could be loaded and unloaded, and serviced below a concrete cantilevered canopy. The trucks would proceed to different floors for further goods transfers. Just as train tracks and then roadways could enter the Starrett-Lehigh

▲ A.E. Bosshard and H. Widmer, truck ramps integrated with the Toni Dairy, Zurich, Switzerland, 1974–1976
◄ Toni Dairy, view from city
▶ Truck logistics area on ground floor of Toni Dairy

building, or trucks could move up into the building, or trucks could move up into the building via the massive elevator, so could the Toni-Molkerei sequence the deliveries in a continuous logistics flow by means of ramps and thick floors.

The new factory was designed as a vertical machine capable of processing over one million gallons of milk per day. Raw goods flowed in one end and were moved via chutes and ramps up to each staging area, and then back to the loading area and distribution area at the other. The south side was an eight-story volume built around a system of stainless steel tanks for new powdered milk manufacturing. For this process they dried the milk in stainless steel tanks, and then completed the packaging. Refrigeration was contained on the third, fourth, and fifth floors. The dairy incorporated 10,000 meters of metal piping

and an internal communications network for 28 telephone lines and communication stations between the milk, the ice cream making, and the yogurt departments. The massive concrete foundation and thick concrete floors supported the weight of equipment and vehicles. At the north side of the site a three-story building with parking on the roof housed the workers' restaurant and an apartment for the CEO, which later housed the caretaker. As the largest dairy processor in Europe at the time of its opening, the new Toni-Molkerei received international press coverage, including a ceremony presided over by Prince Charles. However, the company fell into financial troubles and was sold to the Swiss dairy, Emmi, in 2005.

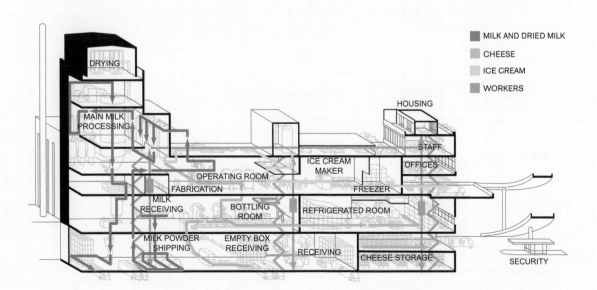

▲ Stainless steel milk tanks (top), and central plant
controls (bottom), Toni Dairy

CONCLUDING THOUGHTS

The first half of this book is focused on the rise of industrialization in the Western world which becomes instrumentalized in today's global factory. These examples of factories and their architecture reflects the production processes and Taylorized efficiency, contributing to a fundamental development of the vertical urban factory typology. In urban clusters and districts, the vertical urban factory followed the flows of economics and land use as well as technological changes, impacting space and people.

In combining the issues of modern manufacturing methods, labor, urbanism, and design, the multistoried factory embodies the Modernist city. It is a heterotopia as Foucault describes it, but one activated by the culture of the city and the workforce, bringing the factory to life. In the Modern era, the factory design problem — from the level of product to that of the architecture itself — was rooted in repetition, seen in the mass production of Ford's cars, the shoes of Zlin, and the typewriters of Olivetti. That infinite reproducibility of product was also echoed in the potential infinity of urban form as in the repetition of the Modernist productive city. The duplication of the Modern factory organized the city in a space of control and segregation.

If the factory is one piece of corporate capital, the value of it lies not only in its architecturalization, but in its use. How can we make a place of production that is urban and inventive, in terms of its tectonic and architectural value, without the rational production and profit motive of the corporation overwhelming the humanitarian requirements and issues? We can ask: has the factory improved over time, with the increase in information and a greater understanding of production and workers' needs? How do we develop a new space for making things if the profit motive is constant? Therein lies an inescapable give and take between the desire for profit, space, and equity.

Innovative factory design still rarely arises; most industrial solutions are utilitarian and architecturally undistinguished sheds for mass-produced products. Perhaps that is why an architect such as Albert Kahn succeeded in so many ways, as his repetitive but not totally generic spaces could adapt to the production methods. The more formal work of Fisac and Fuller or Van der Vlugt and Matté-Trucco were awe-inspiring — their clients' interest in design allowed for correspondingly increased experimentation.

This next section turns to how factories, their technologies, and urbanism, in serving the new economy — both from the mass-customized to the immaterial product — offers opportunities for new working conditions but cannot begin to address the inequitable issues engendered by the global factory and its disregard for a democratic and sustainable workplace.

THE CONTEMPORARY FACTORY

► Henn Architects, VW
Transparent Factory, Dresden,
Germany, 2001

THE CONSUMPTION ECONOMY

THE MODERN FACTORY often demonstrated its significance as a place of innovation in architecture and technology through the force and speed of automation, entrepreneurship, and technological synergies in cities. Concurrently it operated as a top-down organizational machine. In order to create environments to both house today's new economies and also support the people who work in the globalized production spaces, the urban factory offers opportunities to be reconsidered as a democratic and sustainable model. As manufacturing is reinserted into urban centers, former industrial cities are experiencing a resurgence of entrepreneurialism; new producers capitalize on available densities of knowledge and labor to counteract urban entropy and to contribute to a new cycle of rebirth. The interdependency of new technology and economies, in turn, influences the production process by affecting various labor forces and the spatial organization of manufacturing.

In this second half of *Vertical Urban Factory*, I describe the contemporary issues of how and where manufacturing has shifted technologically, urbanistically, and architecturally. Here the factory space, which from its conception was a building that housed manufacturing activity, is redefined more broadly as a *place for making things*. The Modern factory was a holistic environment, a complete space that housed the manufacturing process under one roof and, in many cases, throughout a group of adjacent buildings on one site, or layered in different floors within one structure. The organizational or management system was enhanced with architectural and production technologies within which manufacturing thrived amid capitalist hegemony. The factory however, began to be increasingly detached from the city at the time of World War II. Today the decentralization trend of factory locale can be seen to reverse, as factories move to inhabit vertical urban buildings filled with inventors clustered in districts, unfolding a new paradigm towards increased sustainability and urban integration at both the large and the small scales.

This section begins with a synoptic overview of the new economy; the technology of manufacturing; industrial urbanism, encompassing issues of globalization and workers' self-awareness; urban design for industry; and various functions and forms of factory architecture. The latter encompasses three primary themes that I have identified for the vertical urban factory typology: spectacle, sustainable, and flexible.

THE ECONOMIES OF THE CHANGING FACTORY

Acres of abandoned and ruined brick sawtooth-roofed factories sprawl across the Northeast Corridor of the United States, from Boston to Bridgeport, Newark, Philadelphia, and Baltimore, along the coastal transit routes. The same can been seen in the Rhein-Ruhr region in Germany and the mining areas in France. These relics of urban core divestment represent the postwar shift to new manufacturing methods; from the Fordist economies of scale in mass production, to the real-time machinic production and automization. The decay in developed countries' manufacturing regions is a physical manifestation of a fundamental shift in society towards the global and the virtual, that raises the questions: why, how, and what next?

Sociologist David Harvey uses the helpful term "flexible accumulation" to evaluate post-Fordist, post-industrial late capitalism.[1] This period can be called the third industrial revolution, or sometimes the next industrial revolution, in which microprocessors and other advances in information technology, digital computing, and new energy-efficient systems reorganize manufacturing through networked infrastructures at both the macro and micro scales.[2] The flexible accumulation of the economy encompasses the new economy of the 1980s' technology boom (a boom that was intrinsically informational, global, and networked) which, in turn, flows into the post-2008 recession of what economists call the next economy.[3] These current economic tendencies coincide with the necessity to redefine manufacturing to now embrace evolving industries.

Three stages of capitalism parallel those of the three industrial revolutions — the first, market capitalism of the eighteenth century; then the monopolies or imperialism of the nineteenth and early twentieth-centuries; and thirdly the multinational capitalism that Ernest Mandel in his 1974 book, *Late Capitalism*, called the postindustrial.[4] This postindustrial or high-tech culture as observed by Czech philosopher Vilém Flusser extends:

> Machines are tools that are built according to scientific theory when science is understood as meaning chiefly physics and chemistry, and robots can additionally bring neurophysiological and biological theory and hypotheses into play. To express this in terms of the simulation of hands and bodies: Tools are empirical, machines are mechanical, and robots are neurophysiological and biological.[5]

The postindustrial is still industrial it has just been redefined and broadened to include contemporary mechanisms that extend from human potential.

Homo faber is defined in this book's introduction as "man the maker" — it is humankind's first instinct to make and to reproduce. The small-scale appliances, or robots, Flusser described have "a far more abstract learning process" and indeed, since his writings, the individual directly making objects via computer technology in an intellectualization of the new workforce has been abstracted to the immaterial. The third industrial revolution is not only one of digital technology, but of economic reorganization exemplified by the new global free trade agreements from Mexico to China in the 1970s through the present. The expansive free trade zones were physical manifestations of transnational corporate production at multiple levels from financial organization, logistics, and labor, to the automated processes themselves. Adopting the metaphor of the "flat" world[6] — or the more pejorative politically infused label, imperialism — transnational corporations dominate world commerce, and knit together globalization in an interdependence of capital and production.[7]

As the new economy has subsumed the organization of material production, production spaces are being reconfigured, internally and urbanistically, for a renewed industrial urbanism. The industrial spaces of this economy, described in the following section, are simultaneously dispersed globally and decentralized, and more intensely rooted in urban places, both in what can be called new entrepreneurial spaces of light industries, as well as in large-scale factories which persist as heavy industries, though with increased digitization and often fewer workers. These spaces comprise a burgeoning generation of companies linked in digital space with a broader physical reach, which Saskia Sassen describes as communication networks between the globe's financial cities and larger spaces of digitally-linked mass production through open source computer software and hardware that allow cooperative, real-time task completion.[8] Centralized production in a command and control organization, which agglomerated in key cities in the 1980s, surprisingly demonstrated increased potential for a decentralized work force. New places of production invigorate a new economic web and signify a return from the global expanse to local places for object making; in turn these companies have the added benefit of being close to their consumer — of being made in place.

The need for low-cost labor, which companies deem as economically necessary for low-cost mass production, prompts companies to relocate offshore or to use subcontracted facilities, thus isolating and hiding factories in the process of globalization. This current of "process removal" goes beyond that of the early twentieth century, as factories are moved far away from the consumer, and the worker becomes invisible. By removing factories from the urban realm, factories become societies in and of themselves, societies that breed oppression and manipulation through their physical environments and the confinement of the people working within them. Many factories, or their organizational systems, are structured as a panopticon where injustice and inequality are perpetuated. With new opportunities posed by factory resuscitation and reformatting, cities and their citizens can revisit questions including: How can factories be reintegrated into cities? What kinds of factories can be designed that are sustainable and innovative? How does the changing economy influence the changing spatial practice of those involved in industrial urbanism, which itself has the potential to be a new practice of cross-specialization?

Fordism and mass production based on innovation, labor power, and then labor control, was organized in a paternalistic supply and demand system. Previously discussed in terms of the rise of the company town and continuous assembly-line processing of the Taylorist rational factory, the factory organization that alienated workers from what they produced never progressed toward the envisioned utopia, either economically or socially. The factory system, for the most part, was a heterotopic enclosure dramatically separated from civic society, an insular space that was invented and sustained by capitalism.

World War II rescued the U.S. economy by employing thousands of people, including women and minorities, by retooling existing factories, and by building new spaces of awesome dimensions. Wartime industry mobilized production, solidifying the relationships between companies and governments, universities and industries, architects and clients, all with a common goal toward safeguarding the world.[9] World War II increased the U.S. Gross National Product from $88 to $135 billion in 1941, increased industrial workers' salaries by almost a quarter, and U.S. industry comprised over fifty percent of world production. But production harnessed for wartime did not stabilize all economies: the destruction of Europe for example, took decades to repair.

World War II also changed the landscape of manufacturing in the U.S. to one of horizontal shed-like structures. While these sprawling structures are diametrically opposed to the vertical urban factory typology, they offer a necessary context — they arose in a landscape degraded by the blasting of coal mines and the belching furnaces of the steel mills and one that reflected the destruction of open spaces, as well as the establishment of expansive logistics networks in the broader industrial geography. The postwar reliance on the 65,000-kilometer U.S. highway network called the Interstate system — an idea born by Eisenhower in the 1930s but not implemented until the Highway Act of 1952 — provided opportunities for industrial expansion. Uninterrupted physical plants were necessary for the production of large aircraft, tank, and vehicle machinery. Once connected to a material supply chain and distribution system, the factory was flattened into a rectilinear pancake slab. A state of military emergency catalyzed an efficient method of production and rapid construction of simple-to-build factory buildings, which enclosed vast amounts of space for the masses of people employed and the scale of items produced.

▲ Hong Kong squatter district, 1950s

The volume of people employed (eight million — non-farm and non-military jobs — from 1940 to 1944),[10] the scale of the airplanes and tankers being made, as well as the palpable perceived danger of being attacked, required a more dispersed, flexible and therefore horizontal, secure, and camouflaged environment. When the war ended, some of this new technology was retooled for the everyday, but other industries then moved south and overseas where space and labor were cheaper.

The history of the rise and fall of economies in the twentieth century provides insight into our current industrial urbanism. The steady climb of corporate conglomeration into monopolies was imbalanced by two factors: the economic decline in Europe and assistance provided by the 1944 Bretton Woods conference of the forty-four Allied countries. Bretton Woods' outgrowth was the General Agreement on Tariffs and Trade (GATT), the International Monetary Fund, and later, the World Bank; these entities were intended to reconstruct the physical damage and the economies of the developed world and link currencies, first to the price of gold, and then to the dollar. The goal of continuous economic growth, deemed as a right, liberated postwar debilitated countries in order for them to cooperate in new trade agreements. Furthermore, free trade was formally organized, expanding upon the idea of Adam Smith's invisible hand, in which the ability of the free market allocates factors of production such as land, labor, capital, and enterprise along with goods and services.

As historians have observed, capitalist aspirations for profit contributed to labor unrest post-World War II, as manufacturing was boosted for consumer (rather than military) use, and social goals were disparate, no longer unified for producing war.[11] Mass production and management rose globally, and industrial production in the 1950s was no longer solely concentrated in the West or developed world, but expanded beyond even the early colonialist trade markets of Japan, China, and India whose economies were developing, or emerging, and still dependent on Western nations. Japan focused on privatizing industries, while Russia and China underwent state-organized industrialization, in contrast to the tenor of U.S. capitalism.

Skilled workers in free-market postwar Japan jump-started their economy with new goods such as bicycles and electronics for the global markets. But this came with comprehensive reorganization of their economic system, including a dispersal of corporate powers of the *Zaibatsu*, the Japanese conglomerates, in 1947, and the potential to organize labor unions. A recession was counteracted by the American purchase of military goods, including those made by Toyota, for the Korean War. When Hayato Ikeda became prime minister in 1960, his goal was to double national income, which he accomplished within seven years. Their surplus economy had a Gross Domestic Product (GDP) growth rate of 10.5 percent annually, in contrast to the U.S. at the time of 2.23 percent.[12]

Urban journalist Jane Jacobs credits the explosive growth of Tokyo due, in part, to import replacements or substitution (the manufacturing, versus importing, of things needed at home). Jacobs illustrated her point with the example of the bicycle, which was produced by skilled workers in Tokyo that adapted to new technologies close at hand rather than working in newly built large-scale factories of the *Zaibatsu*. In this way, they cornered the market.[13] With larger funds in savings, national organizations such as the Ministry of International Trade and Industry (MITI), which from 1949 to 2001 primarily focused on setting regulations concerning import- and export-infused industries with know-how.[14] Once the war ended, Japan could focus on growth. In the global economy in general, as early as the 1940s, economist Joseph Schumpeter (1883–1950) recognized the destruction of creativity in the marketplace in that, "The fundamental impulse that sets and

keeps the capitalist engine in motion comes from the new consumers, goods, the new methods of production or transportation, the new markets, the new forms of industrial organization that capitalist enterprise creates."[15] Schumpeter's "creative destruction" of new things that change the old ways parallels Jane Jacobs' observations of the way innovators build upon old products to make new enhancements and resultant positive growth.

China, along with Russian aid and their own Five-Year-Plan, invested in heavy industries that doubled their industrial production from 1953 to 1957. But it was the "Made in Hong Kong" boom in the 1960s that initiated a strong center of international manufacturing utilizing the combined skills of British colonialists and low-cost workers. Together, in the heart of the city, they made everything from garments to car parts to plastic flowers. A flood of new immigrants from China and Southeast Asia packed into the city, seeking jobs in these new industries. At the same time, Japan's exports rose and India and Latin America moved to import substitution, increasing the global marketplace. With new free markets and free trading zones and a not-so-sound dollar in the 1960s, manufacturing in the U.S. was about twenty-three percent of the GDP and comprised thirty percent of the jobs. The focus shifted from making machines to run the factories to the production of consumer goods. But the renewed factory system of large-scale manufacturing

▲ Workers in the Lafayette 148 garment factory, Mehrdad Hadighi and Tsz Yan Ng architects, Tianjin, China, 2010

in the 1960s U.S. led to an ineffective adaptation to worker needs, as companies focused on the consumer. Rigid corporate control and new computer management systems increased alienation in the workplace, the rise of unions resulting in labor disputes and strikes.[16] Workers shifted emphasis to their own welfare and satisfaction, while consumer feedback and preferences for specific goods influenced supply and demand — an incongruous simultaneous shift — as supply was more responsive to consumer feedback, which eventually could be directly assessed via online orders and produced just-in-time. As a result, both the labor conditions and mechanisms for spatial control were re-evaluated determining a flexible factory environment within which the worker is in flux, as also described by French philosopher, Jean-Paul de Gaudemar.

De Gaudemar discusses this factory flexibility as a factory of mobility and free movement in that, with the "autonomization" or the dispersal of the factory, in contrast to the "fortress" factory, the factory is destabilized, making the worker dispensable along with their space. The worker can be more autonomous because of new information technologies so that the "crisis of the factory is not the end of the factory, but rather the beginning of a social 'factorization' and a time when wage earners escape from spatial constraints and again transform their relation to time."[17] Workers' time becomes their own but it also means that they can work all the time and also work part-time without the required social and economic benefits of the full-time worker, as a pawn in the system. This contradiction could be seen as dissolving the structure of the factory and disaggregates the importance of the worker because work can be done at a distance by means of automation and digital technologies. However, autonomization implies a false freedom from work in that leisure time is also spent on the same machines (computers) as those used to perform work activities.

Within the idea of the flexible factory is that of the neo-cottage enabled by the shrinking scale of technologies and facilities. The worker can be mobile within networked systems, and robotics forming a new paradigm for urban production spaces. However, just as factory workers were tied to their massive machines, now they are tied to their electronic machines as a kind of prosthetic device, pushing buttons rather than doing heavy lifting. New seeds of inspiration can come from ideas of sustainability, bartering networks, hacker spaces, and niche manufacturing, and cities need to respond quickly to physically accommodate them in ever more flexible space.

In the U.S., the hard-hit economic instability of the 1973 recession, paired with the oil crisis, shattered the Fordist model of the formal economy of top-down systems of corporate management.[18] The Organization of Arab Petroleum Exporting Countries (OAPEC) oil embargo and the devaluation of the dollar contributed to inflation and stagnation, unemployment, factory shut-downs, and manufacturing losses, overwhelming the new world economic system. As the Cold War ended in 1989, Eastern European markets gradually opened up due to new infrastructure that increased free trade and exchange and released property ownership for privatization, including new agreements such as the formation of the European Union in 1993 with primarily western European countries, until further expansion in 2004. The new ASEAN Free Trade Area unified trade and eliminated restrictions

▲ Plastic toys in China from
The Real Toy Story exhibition
and installation. Photograph
by Michael Wolf

between Asian countries in a similar way beginning in 1992. What are called "super regions" (such as the Pearl River Delta, Yangtze River Delta, and Bohai Gulf Region), served as catalysts for other development in regional projects based on new infrastructural transportation network systems. China alone has the third largest trade volume after European and NAFTA areas. By 2015, the other nations in the group — Indonesia, Malaysia, the Philippines, Singapore, Thailand, Brunei, Burma (Myanmar), Cambodia, Laos, and Vietnam, along with China — formed the ASEAN Economic Community, opening up trade to China and to a market of 1.8 billion people with a potential economic activity of $2 trillion. These global trade organizations became more inclusive in response to a rapidly integrating global marketplace. With each global financial crisis, increased connections between countries in trade agreements remixed the economic potentials.[19]

While instrumental, Marx and Engels' 1848 analysis of material production and their prediction of late capitalism's growth and organization did not foresee that in the first and second industrial revolutions, the rise of textile industries and production of machinery to make goods would harness industrial growth at such an incomprehensible scale. This created a global reliance on new products and created a continuous cycle of consumption and production, then planned obsolescence. The Fordist methods of mass production, combined with the new mass consumption, triggered an economic theory that focused on the control of the free market. John Maynard Keynes (1883–1946) believed in free trade, and increased government spending rather than total reliance on the free market in order for consumer-led demand to trigger economic growth. As the capitalist economy began to fail in the 1970s, this unstable, ever-moving unbalanced economy became defined by "flexible accumulation." It is with this shift in the economy that my discussion of the contemporary factory begins.

FLEXIBLE ACCUMULATION

This investigation of factories in cities necessitates not only the aforementioned role of technology, but also the change in economics and its subsequent impact on the flow of goods and on the spatial organization of production. As late capitalism — a post-Fordist economic undercurrent — was faced with new and debilitating issues, economists found that flexible accumulation became embedded in the economy. Identified by Harvey as malleable new economic patterns, flexible accumulation spurred fractured industrial growth, which increased capital returns while reducing returns to labor. In the 1980s, new financial services grew, building an intensity of fiscal interaction organized through networked economies, mobile transnational banking, and industrial growth in emerging countries and their tax-free trade zones.[20] Flexible accumulation also enabled new manufacturing processes such as automation, Just-in-Time (JIT) production, consumer customization, on-demand goods, adaptive assembly, knowledge-based industries, and mass customization. The new economy depended on the adaptability of workers' skills to special tasks, and a company's ability to make small batches through flexible processes, computer-run machinery, or increasingly, customizable computer-integrated manufacturing. But manufacturers also have the capacity to make new products cheaply by way of outsourcing labor to low-cost workers, who they exploit to their own ends.

The new flexible economy also impacts how workers are hired and drives the perception of temporary workforces of "precarious workers" without insurance or labor rights. From Fordism to flexible management styles and workforces consisting largely of subcontractors, the shift to the new economy provides both freedom and instability. Flexible accumulation plays out in the day-to-day life of a worker in both schedule and number of work-hours and, consequently, the company owner's reduced commitment to the worker. Post-Fordist labor becomes flexible, mobile, and unstable as capital can move, invest, or divest as companies find new opportunities at a rate never before seen in previous industrial eras.[21] Workers have to be flexible enough to follow the flow of jobs. Mobility and flexibility are physical and philosophical imperatives aided by the shrinking of information technology's influence on the rising culture of nomadism, both outside and within the factory, and in terms of production itself. In the "new geometry of production," termed by sociologist Manuel Castells, the ubiquitous networks expand at all scales. [22]

Manufacturers in emerging economies organize factories similar to nineteenth-century sweatshops — a throwback to paternalistic patterns of production in the company towns, discussed earlier. Overconsumption contributes to social and environmental injustice and directly trickles down to the factory worker on the other end of the consumer product. Situations such as the spring 2013 factory fire in Bangladesh, where workers were trapped in a building fire reminiscent of the 1911 Triangle Shirtwaist Factory fire, along with countless other incidents of untenable factory conditions, wasteful expenditure of resources, and environmental degradation, bring to light the dated paradigm and call for a contemporary model shift. In response to top-down management and lack of worker justice, workers around the world have initiated self-ownership of factories and communal management, including Guatemalan cooperative factories, the Swedish *Bruk* system, or the Mondragon Cooperative Corporation of Spain. At the smaller scale, profit sharing or the ability to own company stock as part of pay can be a partial solution for worker control; at the larger scale, the welfare state assists the financing of labor justice issues that have arisen in the global factory as a political concern.

PRODUCTION SPACES

The changing economic structures and expansion of global exchange directly impact the standards for the physical space, land use regulations, and protocols of the real estate industry. Although rarely incorporated in the discipline of urban design, economic geography and location theory provide robust analyses on how and where business should best be located. In the case of industrial zoning and urbanism, the theories of business location have a central role. In terms of space as a social place, philosophers such as Henri Lefebvre have defined the method with which we operate and influence space in its broadest terms, as it impacts the understanding of industrial space today. From Lefebvre's perspective, actions such as the functional efficiency of Fordism and its rational production systems influence architecture, real estate, and the shape of cities. The organizational machinations of financing, development, administration, infrastructure, information, and transit are all components of designing a space and therefore comprise what Lefebvre terms a "spatial practice" of those whose work impacts the design of the physical environment.[23] Lefebvre identifies a "spatial practice" in terms of how architects, planners, and others address the making of, and reading of, urban and other spaces. He therefore expands the definition of space to that of spaces formed by the actions that occur in that space. The result becomes a space that is organized, developed, bought, and sold as a consumer good. In this framework, his concepts can be applied to contemporary factory spaces and the industrial landscape, both in physical and social terms. Space as a product has a monetary and social value beyond the design value that the architectural profession places on it. Space relates to financial markets, the real estate market, and the organization of the factory space (and its territory) by means of zoning regulations, resource sharing, transit coordination, infrastructure, and even tax incentives that entice factories to a specific region. This recalibrated production space of flexible accumulation is what forms the industry-scape in terms of the economic shift and the mechanized systems of production. In turn, flexible accumulation influences the urban industrial space and the design of factories across scales, in relation to a single structure, clusters of factories, urban industrial zones, or globalized free trade zones whether a individual factory or entire industrial zone.

In terms of the Modernist or Fordist factory spaces described earlier, Lefebvre notes, in contrast, that they were "discrete points: the place of extraction or origin

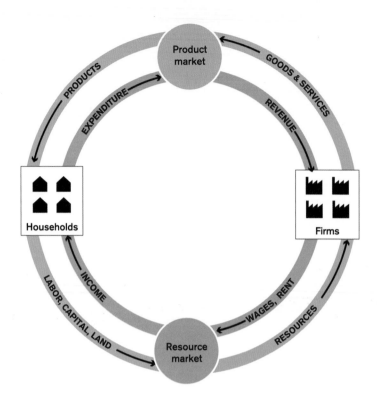

of raw materials, the place of production (factory), and the place of sale. Only the distribution networks of this system had a wider spatial dimension."[24] However, this has changed in the flexible industrial system, as factories are no longer a singular place or situated megastructure. Lefebvre recognizes the factory's expansion and placelessness, in that,

> the elements themselves are produced and reproduced, however, the relationship of productive activity to space is modified; it involved space now in another way, and this is as true for the initial stages of the process (for example, the management of water and water resources as it is for the final stages within urban space) and for all the steps in between.[25]

▲ The provision of goods and resources in a capitalist consumer system

These spaces don't have to be connected physically, but can be linked through digital logistics in the global sprawl of factories located at distant points. In many ways, Lefebvre's ideas are directly related to production, to the spaces which determine the production of things, and to this study of the vertical urban factory in terms of the architectural form. It is within these concepts that the potential to redefine the urban factory occurs.

Harvey expands upon Lefebvre's concept of spatial practices for post-Fordist industrial production, and offers succinct organizational categories: the use of land, flows of goods across the land, transportation, market uses, and networks. In these practices, industry appropriates space, locating control via zoning that regulates use, ownership, and what is produced on that property — on the other hand, the production of the space establishes the built systems and reinforces the infrastructure. In this new industrial landscape, expanded from the isolated factory, Lefebvre, notes that,

> commodity is not only the thing itself that has to be considered. . . The stores and warehouses where these things are kept, where they wait, the ships, trains and trucks that transport them — and hence the routes used — must also be taken into account. Furthermore, having considered all these objects individually, one still has not properly apprehended the material underpinning of the world of commodities. Nor do such notions as 'channel', derived from information theory, or 'repertoire' help us define such an ensemble of objects. The same goes for the idea of 'flows.' It has to be remembered that these objects constitute relatively determinate networks or chains of exchange within a space. The world of commodities would have no 'reality' without such moorings or points of insertion, or without their existing as an ensemble.[26]

The ensemble described is the full complexity of all that goes into making and selling a product and all the material and immaterial investments of a company, including the trade relations and agreements. Industrial labor had previously controlled many aspects of life, but Antonio Negri observes that,

> in the final decades of the twentieth century, industrial labor lost its hegemony and in its stead emerged 'immaterial labor,' that is, labor that creates immaterial products, such as knowledge information, communication, a relationship, or an emotional response.[27]

This immaterial labor is also what Buckminster Fuller called the "ephemeralization of work," as the computer programming guides the manufacturing process, requiring less physical work. But it is the physical making of objects — not virtual products of the digital realm — which is the focus here, following Flusser's concept of *homo faber*.

The worker who runs the machines is also the producer and has an increased role as a subject in the production process. In the developed world, flexible accumulation relates to new production methods that depend on the computer, logistics within the mesh of digital networks, and communication to increase company dispersal and the making of things. Since the 1950s, even though computers have run factories, companies required a physical space in which to produce the object though production is often subcontracted to disparate places rather than within one space, changing the concept of the monolithic factory.

Factories can be decentralized, dispersed, scattered, and expanded with control centers in one place and production in another. In the 1980s, clustered regions such as Silicon Valley, California; Route 128 through Boston; and the Indian cities Bangalore and Hyderabad, emerged as new knowledge production and computer programming centers, bastions of engineering and calculations, the output of digital communication and information economy. These regions developed in parallel to Saskia Sassen's definition of global cities of New York, London, Tokyo — places of command and control as major financial centers. Even if things are not made in those places, they provide the infrastructure and organizational systems for production.[28] In addition, the renewed interest in urban lifestyles in mature Western cities contributes to entrepreneurs' desire to start factories there. The shift to smaller-scale flexible factories returns some spatial forms of manufacturing to neo-cottage industries that manufacturing previously displaced, continuing the life of these factory buildings.

Service jobs that support industry's virtual systems, on the other hand, have a different relationship to the thing produced in terms of the result. Because of today's prolific production of "non-things," like financial instruments representing other things such as stocks and bonds, or "immaterial labor," a new hegemony of virtual production altered the factory and the way of working. Today labor and society have to "informationalize, become intelligent, become communicative, become affective."[29] The goods and their processes become part of this spatial network, just as Negri describes: "The hegemony of immaterial labor tends to transform the organization of production from the linear relationships of the assembly line to the innumerable and indeterminate relationships of distributed networks."[30] The work can be scattered in different kinds of physical spaces. People who make these "immaterial things" do not have the same physical contact with the object being made. For example, the making of computer software, while it is producing some*thing*, it is not made of matter, that thing is immaterial. The product is removed from the maker, who continues to be alienated, in Marx's terms, as they are displaced from the point of production to the point of consumption until the good is distributed in the electronic network.

However, in the third industrial revolution, the immaterial combined with physical production through computerization and rapid prototyping reinserts itself into productive culture and also changes the method of labor and organizational involvement. The worker becomes the author, not just the laborer. The physical labor of Do-It-Yourself (DIY) production in developed countries, and handwork in a new maker culture beyond arts and crafts, contrasts with the virtual, contributing to a new interest in things and production in general. This individualized innovation economy and more craft-based production has yet to be analyzed in terms of its impact on urban economies.[31] Those who are the new maker class can obtain capital through their investments, private funds, and new forms of financing including Kickstarter campaigns. They are usually highly educated, and are not part of the working class in the same way as their grandparents, but, rather, part of another level of economy of tech workers, computer programmers, or more oriented towards the arts. In an extreme example, Silicon Valley employees of Internet companies are committed to handcraft and the physical making of things as well as learning with digital tools — so much so that they send their kids to the Rudolph Steiner School in Palo Alto in order to learn handwork rather than only computer skills.[32] This generation feeds into the new educated maker culture, as innovators and entrepreneurs have the ability to raise capital to start companies. The making of things, of that which is tangible, infuses the worker with pride. This kind of worker then becomes desired in cities for economic development, and is not shunned the way many blue-collar workers have become.

In the global economic arena, with contributions made by information and computer technologies, flexible accumulation is absorbed in a loosening of trade restrictions identified as globalization. Some economists such as James Petras and Henry Veltmeyer refer to this as a revived imperialism through their focus on the power of the Northern developed countries over the Global South and Third World populations for atavistic ends.[33] Tax-free Export Processing Zones (EPZ's) spearheaded the ease of a globalized economy, with efficient, low-cost labor production. In Marx's terms, labor as a flexible component of capital investment fluctuates more easily than the more solid capital of land and machinery and can be adjusted with profit margins and a bottom line.[34] While globalization has relocated manufacturing to Mexico, China, the Philippines, Bangladesh, and Vietnam (among other countries) where cheap labor subcontractors are distanced from the corporations that hire them to make their products and EPZs offer incentives, today's interest in economies of localized production and reshoring and insourcing might reverse, or at least parallel, these manufacturing trends, bringing the factories back to the vacated Western cities.

As theories of space, industrial infrastructure, and places where things are made create a new understanding of the transformation of the urban landscape and that of the developing industrial world, these spaces are of two extremes — those that are in flux and fragmentary and those more massive and permanent, with capital infusion into that space of production. Flexible accumulation also inspires new mixed-use spaces for value-added real estate, in terms of the flexibility of building types.[35] Spatially, this flexibility — often seen in easily divided open industrial lofts — is then also required in factory buildings to become a closed-loop system with the company's on-demand and Just-in-Time (JIT) production methods for a complex industrial ecology.

Renewed potential for a decentralized workforce, the organizers of that workforce, and for places of production, invigorate not only a new economic web, but also local places where objects can be made in urban networks. This revised structure could serve as a model for the new vertical urban factory. Advancements in technologies shrink the scale of products and clean industrial ecologies create new potentials for a mobile worker within complexly networked systems as well as a new paradigm for future urban production spaces. While large-scale spaces are necessary for the mass production of cars, logistics centers, and shipping ports, the smaller scale has potential for spillover from the larger companies to new urban innovators. The spaces of urban production are thus pervasive, and can be placed everywhere. Flusser describes that mankind worked everywhere, taking his tools with him. Perhaps we have returned to that concept with our electronic prosthetic devices. How new technology, manufacturing organization, worker issues, and urban ecologies shape and are shaped by the design and place of the factory in the city will be discussed in the following chapters.

CONSUMPTION, MAN, AND MACHINE

FROM CALCULATING MACHINE TO PRODUCTION MACHINE

The goal of the fluid rational factory was to produce things efficiently via systematized production. By World War II, with the invention of calculating and computing machinery, the factory space contributed to continuous economic growth as a bastion of production, both in its physical scale and the quantity of goods being made, and crescendoed from the first, through the second, and now third industrial revolution. The third industrial revolution is characterized by computers and technology-connectedness and is defined in turn by the consequential production speed, flexible accumulation, facile money, and fast-paced connections between organizational systems of finance and banking. In this current explosion of electronically networked technology and instant communication, a major scale shift was triggered by the computer's miniaturization. As the room-size computers of the 1950s diminished to the size of minuscule silicon chips, so too did the spaces of production. At a territorial scale, an expansive network technology formed by the data freeway in the 1990s has become the Internet "superhighway," which feeds production distribution and allows it to be dispersed. At the scale of the individual factory, smaller-scale ubiquitous technology reconnects workers to the activity of making, but separates the skilled from the unskilled workers, as discussed earlier. At the scale of the factory building itself, immense spaces for production are needed for larger products, as well as smaller and individual workshops for assembly of aggregate parts. The spaces now accommodate a globally oriented, flexible production process that dominates the industrial landscape.

As I described in "Modern Factory," the shift of the worker's relationship to manufacturing through new technologies go hand in hand with a cultural zeitgeist. But, as people are retrained, change is incremental, not instantaneous, and it takes some distance to evaluate the effects historically.[1] Automation comes at a cost to the worker, as technology did in the first industrial revolution, but as the computerized factories are more highly customized than in the early twentieth century, the worker's role is precarious because of lack of stability for blue collar jobs. The worker is no longer a laborer in the sense of the working class, resembling an R.U.R. (Rossum's Universal Robot)or a Taylorist cog in an endless assembly line, but a highly trained operator such as a computer programmer. Production is no longer necessarily linear, nor is it repetitive. In the multifaceted stages of today's mass customization, low-skilled jobs are minimized and marginalized in comparison to the skilled positions requiring complex mathematical calculations and handwork. The skill set changed from craftsman to programmer and scientist. This is seen, for example, in textile factories where, rather than having workers stationed at individual sewing machines, large automated weaving machines are run by a few supervisors and skilled workers, reducing jobs for unskilled workers, who repeat increasingly menial tasks, such as mounting spools of cotton to the machine's frameworks.

More recently, with the desire to follow the ever-changing marketplace, companies have turned to a variety of production tactics that contrast with the standardized mass-production approach of Ford and Singer in the early twentieth century. New strategies focus on what is called Just-in-Time (JIT) production, a system developed by Toyota in the mid-twentieth century. This differs from the traditional mass production methods from which evolved "real time" production wherein things are made immediately by new technology such as 3-D printing machines. A paradigm shift in these changing production systems have impacted not solely the manufacturing processes, but every aspect of society, as the integration of factory spaces within cities and an emphasis on local production has generated today's entrepreneurial zeitgeist. A closer look at the development of

increased automation in the factory and the relation of the consumer to the process will reveal how the third industrial revolution impacts future factories.

AUTOMATION

Automation has a long history that began well before World War II — first incrementally, then infiltrating many levels of production from mass production to customization. This historic and contextual perspective is important to understanding the contemporary aspects of Computer Numerical Control (CNC) production machinery in urban manufacturing. The first computer had roots in small calculating machines such as the Difference Engine No. 1, invented in 1822 by English scientist Charles Babbage (1791–1871) that made numerical tables following the difference method. His 1840s Difference Engine No. 2 ran on steam power, and a later model, which is still used today, calculates without manual labor. The production of the engines alone required hundreds of repeatable similar manufactured

▲ Large-scale IBM 702 mainframe computers at the IBM headquarters, 1955. Photograph by Ezra Stoller/ Esto

▲ Ipekyol Textile Factory, Emre Arolat Architects, Ipekyol, Turkey, 2010

parts in metal to handle up to fifty digits stored in a gear wheel using the numbers zero to nine. The manufacturing technology needed for stamping and repetitive manufacturing was not up to the precision that his machinery required; the process was slow and expensive.[2] The Difference Engine No. 2 — also called the Analytical Engine — had 25,000 parts and weighed 15 tons!

Babbage realized the difficulty of production and, using metal parts, began in 1836 to investigate paper punch cards. Punch cards were used to direct player pianos, with metal pins that rotated through the perforations on the cards to direct the hitting of keys. They were also used for mechanical toys, or automata, such as the mechanical Digesting Duck invented by Jacques de Vaucanson in 1739. De Vaucanson then went on to use similar cards for more automated weaving machines, inspiring an improved loom by Joseph Marie Jacquard in 1801. The punched cards, strung together in a sequence, were folded and run through the loom to make the textile weaving patterns. The holes in the cards related to the pattern in the weave, either opened or closed by means of rods that allowed a hook to lift the thread so that the weft thread could cross through to weave the pattern or the type of thread. Thus, the loom punch cards stored a kind of map that operated the system and represented the tangible beginnings of numerical control.

For the Analytical Engine calculating machine, Babbage's operation cards were the instructions for adding, subtracting, and multiplying in codes that stored information and could be repeated. This Analytical Engine can be considered a precursor to early digital decimal machines that were be guided by the user and therefore, a forerunner to the computer. It had an ability to process, store information, and repeat tasks, inspiring the next generation of computing machines used in manufacturing.

By the early twentieth century, American mathematician Norbert Wiener (1894–1964) identified ways human behavior could be transposed to machine operations, which influence computers and manufacturing processes. Interaction was communicated within a single machine and changed dynamically through numerous iterative and responsive processes in computer programming. To balance out what Weiner saw as inevitable entropy, information could both feed into a system and have the computer system make a response with additional information that would then be fed back into the system again. The more open systems altered and adjusted according to new information, in a totality of what he called "cybernetics," coined in 1947. The machine in manufacturing processes could thus be more than just a tool receiving a command, could run the process independently by incorporating new commands (as with robotics) and reacting.

Early computing was enhanced by cybernetic methods, especially in wartime aeronautics industries, when microcomputers were introduced to the production process. During World War II, the computing machines operated at many levels, from calculating, to planning, to spying — in short: communicating. The impact of computers for manufacturing objects is what is of interest in the factory context, but also for the communicating between machines. One cryptologist, Alan Turing (1912–1954), took Babbage's achievements to another level. The "Turing Machine," a theoretical machine, read and wrote information beyond what a calculator could do. The Pilot ACE was a Turing-designed computer that used vacuum tubes, similar to early computer microprocessing chips. During World War II computers were used for calculations — both the Colossus in England for communications and code breaking, and the Electronic Numerical Integrator and Computer (ENIAC) for testing artillery performance. Like the early IBM machines, these were room-size machines. With the development of transistors and smaller elements, such as silicon chips, the scale of hardware was reduced while mathematicians perfected the software of algorithms to direct the tools of the machinery to make things.

One productive application was developed by the U.S. Air Force, in 1950 during the Korean War, improving the machining of airplane parts by using algorithms in computer programs for Computer-Aided Design (CAD) with Numerically Controlled (NC) and CNC machines. These microcomputer controls could program lathes or cutting tools to make products rather than assembling them from aggregate parts. The data message on the machine would be sent digitally on paper or plastic tape. It was modeled on the punched card concept of the early Babbage Engines, merged with ideas of feedback suggested by Wiener in computer numerical controls. The computer program guided the machine to cut wood, punch metal, or grind material, for example. Each element could be shifted or changed according to the script of the computer program. At first this was only possible in two dimensions because the computers weren't capable of storing the intensive data of three-dimensional objects. This has all changed.

The method to form finished product from algorithmic inputs to production machines was further expanded in the 1970s as the idea of repeatable parts could be integrated into production at a large scale. "The new generation of supercomputers, which can compute a billion bits of information in a second, is the reason why the B-2 bomber, with its rounded surfaces, was designed entirely by computer computations."[3] At first this was done with faceted sheets, which were combined into three-dimensional objects — for example, the stealth fighter aircraft manufactured at Lockheed's Skunk Works in 1975.[4] In 1977, the French company Dassault Systémes invented a computer software program to design objects, which then could then be built in the round from computer-rendered drawings. The program, called Computer-Aided Three-dimensional Interactive Application (CATIA), became the preferred method in industrial production. Boeing employed the program to both design the 737 aircraft in 3-D renderings so it takes on a solid appearance on the computer, and to orchestrate the production of each airplane in an aggregated simulated production that would advance the design.[5] The process was in contrast to unstable trial-and-error or rule-of-thumb approaches where one tested and made things continuously in advance of putting it on the production line. CATIA could repeat a path or direction or make a variety of outputs in the laser cutting of sheet metals, which were then identified, labeled, and later assembled.

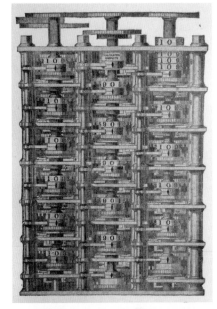

▲ Charles Babbage Difference Engine illustration, 1871
▲ Rows of transistors in an IBM computer, 1955. Photograph by Ezra Stoller /Esto

At first, to upgrade production equipment, computers were spliced onto older machines in a piecemeal way. Then, computing mechanizations were designed as part of the machinery; this occurred as shop equipment was replaced by digital machines in Computer Integrated Manufacturing (CIM).

CIM, which uses CNC machines, made it easier to set up a project and repeat it in a similar but computerized version of interchangeable parts manufacturing. A part can be either identical or have slight variations in mass-customized production. For example, for cutting same-shaped panels to make light fixtures, an automated laser-cutting machine would be fed information via a computer program to cut or punch out shapes from the metal sheet for later assembly. Elements could also be made of dissimilar parts in a mass customization iterative process in which the computer program directs different shapes or parts in a variation. In the digital fabrication process, the designer can change and tweak the product and customize the elements using new parameters. From mass production to mass customization, the original concepts of Babbage's Difference Engine instrumentalized this potential for constant variables of difference, based on a uniformity of parts with infinite adjustables for form, material, and scale.

CAD, which is the design and rendering step of the digital fabrication process in two or three dimensions, then merged with Computer Aided Manufacturing (CAM) which makes the path for the tool — be it a cutting or carving tool — for the machine that will shape the material to the design; sometimes the machine has its own ability to draw or cut as well. The programs are vector-based, using lines, points, and curves rather than pixels, and follow calculations; the three-dimensional programs include parametric logics. The CAD file is then transferred to the CAM files within the machine tools for output using a complementary computer language that embeds a "G-Code" into the software to direct the path that the tool will make in terms of length of lines, depth of surface, and the speed of its movement. Used for prototyping, to test an object, and for the final product, the CNC routers for carving materials can now be used for such tasks as modeling automobiles in an industry that had previously used clay. In industrial design during the 1980s, the three-dimensional mapping in CAD permitted rapid prototyping and parametric design with computer programs, such as Alias, to assist the design production of objects from the computer to the prototyping shop.

IMPACT OF ROBOTICS

▶ A Unimate robot in use at GM's Flint factory, Michigan, 1961

▶ A computer numerically-controlled (CNC) mill in use, 2010

Computer machinery, combined with an operating tool, gained new functionality in order to be moving machines. As early as 1921, robotic hands functioning as steel clamps on large-scale machinery could streamline the production process in automobile factories and limit human error and accidents. However, the precision of human action and interaction in the assembly process continued to take precedence. It was not until 1954 that the first robots were used in production to move heavy items in factories; they were developed by the company Unimation, headed by George Devol with engineer Joseph Engeberger. In 1961, the first production robot, which had a 4,000-pound arm called the Unimate, was installed on the assembly line at General Motors (GM) in Ewing, New Jersey. Taking over a process

too hot for people to withstand, robots picked up forged car parts, sequenced, stacked, then dipped them in a cooling bath. The arm was controlled via data stored on a magnetic drum that directed the joints and thus the movement of the arms. Robots were essential in automotive production for dangerous or diffi-cult-to-reach assemblies, such as spray painting, eliminating the need for workers to be exposed to noxious fumes. Robots also lifted heavy objects: the GM prototype had ten times the lifting capacity of a human. The development of the Tentacle Arm computer in 1968 demonstrated that robots could handle more than just heavy lifting. The Tentacle Arm could more precisely spot-weld in the depths of a machine, or in difficult-to-access angles, more effectively than a human.

The motion of these robots is eerily anthropomorphic. The movement, dexterity, and control of a robotic arm sways over the surface of an automobile in the factory paint booth like a human being. By 1969 at GM, most welding tasks began to be automated using the Unimation robots. As computer programming improved, so did the making of robots that could respond to increasingly complex commands; this led to improved articulation of robotic joints or the addition of multiple arms. The set-up of the robot itself was often much more complex than the actual task it was used to accomplish, but the use of microprocessing computer chips allowed the robots to be scaled down in size and to be streamlined so that they

▲ The control room at
DONG Energy, Kalundborg,
Denmark, 2012
▲ Engineer controlling CAD
machines in factory, 2013

can do smaller, more intricate operations. By adding vision capabilities, they can be programmed using CAD operations to move, select, and sort materials. Highly complex robots now operate with precision at extremely fast speeds in areas such as electronic component assembly.

While factories are scaled to fit objects they make, the computerization of output also allows for the product to be designed and created remotely over digital networks. The idea that a worker can push a button far from the factory floor to run continuous processing is especially valuable for the chemical industries as well as continuous-process industries such as foods, paper, and canning. In such remote manufacturing, workers are neither endangered nor forced to operate like machines themselves. This is true at energy chemical plants such as those operated by DuPont, as well as at oil refineries, among others.[6] Computer controls increase production efficacy, resulting in fluid supply chain management for larger economies of scale in the source of materials, production, and assembly of goods, and their distribution. The distant control of the factory, combined with the deployment of robotic devices that increasingly operated with the dexterity of a human being, indeed run the factory, even unattended by workers. Electronic systems can monitor the flow from one area of the factory to the other. At first, power plants and refineries used analog computers to keep track of performance. During the 1950s, many of these systems were set up in large control rooms that served as containers for giant machines.

In the 1970s, as factories transitioned to automation through computerization, the skill required of the workforce changed yet again. Instead of hand and craft work, factory workers had to train as computer programmers and engineers with knowledge of mathematics, while the unskilled became simply machine operators.

In many factories workers sat fixed at one station, running the production machines via computer, bored by the repetition, and ultimately alienated. They, in turn, became less productive yet had to handle more intensified levels of assembly (as compared to machinery of responsive action of the first or second industrial revolutions). A new class of workers emerged within the factory, one adept at the engineering and design of machines rather than skilled in manual work.

While both categories of workers continued to be essential to the production line, the factory's flexibility was enhanced by computer programming's ability to make fast changes. Programmers controlled the machines rather than workers and eliminated the unpredictability of human error. Many thought this would provide more humane working conditions, with increased free time and less physical labor, but instead work demands were not attached to place.

When factory automation and distribution networks replaced the worker with the monotonous rhythm of machines, cultural critics such as Lewis Mumford praised the new technology but derided its lack of humanism.[7] As early as the 1950s, Wiener, who developed cybernetic theory, grasped a clear understanding of the potential and harm of robotics: "Machines much more closely analogous to the human organism are well understood, and are now on the verge of being built. They will control entire industrial processes and will even make possible the factory substantially without employees." He later envisioned what eventually came to pass and foresaw the abandonment of the factory worker as part of the system of the factory process, as robotics would reduce the "economic value of the routine factory employee to a point at which he is not worth hiring at any price. If we combine our machine-potentials of a factory with the valuation of human beings on which our present factory system is based, we are in for an industrial revolution of unmitigated cruelty." Wiener further warned, "We can be humble and live a good life with the aid of the machines, or we can be arrogant and die."[8] At each stage in the advancement of computational systems, a level of work for diverse abilities then slides away, unable to be recaptured. It could be said that just as factory workers had previously been tied to their massive steam-run machines, now, as literal button pushers, they are subservient to their electronic machines.

But robots can also be an asset to a factory. The robot FRIDA, designed by the Swiss firm ABB works in tandem with people, using sensors to detect where a product is on the production line.[9] Robots can assist older workers in lifting heavy components, allowing for the delay of retirement. They are also considered to be labor-saving devices and are of critical importance during periods of labor shortages. But these new robotic technologies require increased investments, retooling of factories, and retraining of workers. The robot becomes part of the collaborative manufacturing effort, though the struggle for factory workers to maintain their jobs persists, and their labor power has been co-opted by machines. In addition, watch-like devices, made by Motorola, can now monitor the worker, keeping them tethered to production efficiency, recording even their bathroom breaks as the supervisor did in the past.

FROM JUST-IN-TIME TO REAL TIME

With the advent of increased automation, companies began to realize the limits of Ford's one-product, one-color philosophy. Mass production lines led inevitably to processing bottlenecks and overproduction. Stockpiled orders and extraneous materials also sat in the warehouses as wartime industries dialed down their production numbers for peacetime. Industrialists, including Alfred Sloan (1875–1966), the president of GM, invented new strategies for a renewed rational efficiency, catalyzing the engineering and production of new automobile models and the development of unprecedented marketing strategies; Toyota invented Just-in-time (JIT) production; and Volvo designed automated cellular systems. Twenty years later, United Colors of Benetton and Zara reorganized manufacturing for instantaneous customer feedback with their "fast fashion" concept— that of quickly changing design. These changes impacted the design of the factories and new commodity economies.

Sloan was regarded as one of the toughest managers within his firm. Focused on the consumer, he was concerned not only with his customers' desires but fine-tuning his own production and turned his manufacturing methods towards what we know today as "mass customization." In observing the varying personal tastes of his customers, Sloan came up with the notion of creating a variety of new models of cars from which they could choose. Following some of the early methods of interchangeable parts of the American System, he selected elements in the production process that could be easily changed while maintaining larger components like the construction of door panels and engines. The outcome of his new enterprise was a limited selection of cars with varying features scaled for affordability. Sloan even transformed automobile financing to accommodate the consumer for the first time, offering them loans through payment plans to the company rather than banks.

Indicative of Sloan's new interest in igniting consumer desire, in 1947 he commissioned architect Eero Saarinen (1890–1961) to design the GM Technical Center in Warren, Michigan. The Center was to feature a new type of space, what Sloan called a Styling Dome, that was neither factory nor office complex nor science center, but a combination of all three.[10] The integration of the various aspects of production from concept to final product presaged future Research & Development (R&D) centers and was a new innovation. This once novel approach to place R&D in close proximity to production in order to improve operations on the factory floor also contributed to early ideas of production flexibility, so that GM surpassed Ford in sales.

JUST-IN-TIME PRODUCTION

Another company that galvanized a shift away from Fordism was the Japanese Toyota Motor Company, founded in 1937 by Kiichiro Toyoda (1894–1952) as an outgrowth of Toyoda Automatic Loom Works. The loom company, which today continues as an automatic loom machine company, manufactured automated weaving looms that could continuously operate at high speeds, the most advanced

and productive of their time. They maintained their dominance in the industry until the 1930s when raw silk production declined. Toyoda, later called Toyota, was inspired to produce cars after the 1923 earthquake destroyed the railroad system and cars emerged as a more reliable transportation option. The automotive company's approach followed production engineer Taiichi Ohno (1912–1990) and industrial engineer Shigeo Shingo's (1909–1990) philosophy of taking on every innovation and doing more with less. They initiated what became known as JIT production, focusing on faster manufacturing oriented towards consumer demand, a new system of teamwork enhanced with automated technologies encouraging social interaction, employee responsibility, minimal stocks in warehouses, and creativity in the production line. Toyota's methods harnessed a kind of cybernetic interchange as defined by Norbert Wiener and developed from the new economy of flexible accumulation.[11] Toyota's JIT method implemented transformational streamlined production methods that were triggered by technical and organizational feedback loops.

▲ Eero Saarinen, The Sloan Styling Dome, GM Technical Center, Warren, Michigan, 1951–1955. Photograph by Ezra Stoller/Esto

One element in this system was the methodology of *Kaizen* (meaning to take apart and make good), which was seen as continuous improvement developed initially during World War II by W. Edwards Deming, an American statistician who studied with Walter Shewhart. Shewhart invented ideas for Total Quality Management (TQM), a way to inspect and refine a product. Deming, who had assisted manufacturers in the war, taught Japanese scientists quality control methods in the 1950s that involved input from a holistic team of manufacturers and managers. *Kaizen* principles were basic management techniques that focused a company on creating a standard, following it through, and repeating it, based on constant evaluation. Toyota embraced Deming's concepts in devising a system to adopt these innovations. It involved ways for workers to make decisions independently, to improve their work routine, to participate in arranging their production spaces, and to engage in a more collaborative process. Employing Quality Circles, organizational work teams that focus on review of production and cellular manufacturing rather than a continuous sequential line, the factory reduced set-up time and could produce smaller batches of goods. Cellular production, in groups rather than along a line, provided autonomous production in units. Toyota invented an electronic monitoring system that used overhead digital signboards, called Andon Boards, which were programmed to track the production process and gauge the product status.[11] The boards set up a feedback loop between the production line and the workers, providing numerical codes between such manufacturing concerns as scheduled production and actual timing, missing items, downtime, or the impact of robotic movement. With this mode of cybernetic interchange, employees could self-regulate, relieving production bottlenecks to maintain continuous assembly. Floor supervisors were not as necessary, providing the workers with more autonomy as well as responsibility. While the signaling boards might have initially produced anxiety and pressure for the workers, they also relieved those effects because, as workers looked to the board, they gained an element of control — for instance, they might anticipate that slight machine malfunctions would create problem areas and therefore slow production and proactively take ameliorative measures.

Whereas Modern factory production focused primarily on speed and efficiency, JIT production expanded upon Scientific Management by striving toward waste reduction at all levels and incorporating what is called Lean Manufacturing. JIT provided tighter controls on the assembly line and considered the labor and cost-to-task relationship along Statistical Process Control for inspection, inventory control, smaller batch production, and complex advance planning. It provides a more condensed processing system and an efficient organization. JIT is demand-focused, so that not more than is needed is produced. Rather than making large batches of the supplies to assemble a product in what is called "batch and queue," the process is in a "one-piece flow" so that many steps can be conducted simultaneously, with different parts being worked on simultaneously. Lean Manufacturing as applied to the automotive industries is often organized in modular or cellular units so that each unit on the factory floor can produce one product part. For example, a shaft can be made while the body is constructed, unlike the early days at at Ford, where the automobile was added to and incrementally shaped into a final product along the assembly line. These work cells, or job shops, divide the process when volume is lower, rather than a continuous, moving line that, when interrupted,

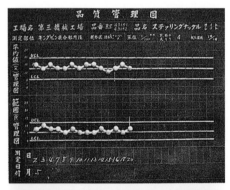

causes stoppages in the production flow. Both physically and metaphorically, production takes place no longer only in a "straight line"; the line can now zigzag or be composed of clustered groups in cellular production, allowing for a flexibility in the building layout and the potential for use of multiple floors. Workers are also less specialized, in contrast to the specific tasks that Adam Smith observed in the eighteenth century.

Other production strategies emerged from industrial engineers, a now full-fledged profession. Their names describe their essential processes: Continuous Flow Production, Stockless Production, and "Six Sigma" which employs statistical analysis to reduce defects in the production process. All of these, and others, have contributed to more efficient and rational production processes. The factory layout is thus impacted as flow follows production — for example, the use of U-shaped work cells for a more circular process, or star-shaped to feed into each area of production simultaneously. As a mass production process, cellular manufacturing relies on flexibility, which is vastly different from Ford's consistent flow. Unlike the latter's rather top-down organizational systems, cellular manufacturing is based on the organization of people into teams or work units in which shop floor workers not only take on, but increase their responsibility.

◄ Kaizan process diagram, Toyota factory, Japan
◄ A typical Andon board in use in a factory, 2008
▲ Industrial engineers reviewing factory plans in layout room, 1952

Toyota continued improving their production process, adding a system called *Kanban,* which in JIT maintains low inventory levels. It is a part of the logistics within the factory itself and was developed by Taiichi Ohno in 1953. *Kanban* is also the tracking method of the consumption level of a product's parts within the factory itself. To regulate the ins and outs, workers at first use a physical card or messages in what is called a "push/pull" system. The demand, or "push" system, signals to the worker the need for more supplies exactly when they are required for a product in demand. In the "pull" side, it "pulls" or stocks up from the demand in

the next phase of the production — as needed, rather than being scheduled even when not required — contributing to a demand-focused production process and less inventory.

The Toyota method also caused management hierarchies to blur so that workers had the ability to act more effectively in a collaborative process that influenced the factory designs. The emphasis on teamwork was physically expressed through the design of common entrances for both workers and managers, as well as shared break areas. R&D was placed near production teams, and workstations were situated adjacent to the production line, promoting white-and blue-collar worker interaction. Along with the growing postwar consumer society, JIT advanced Japanese industry multifold, and in part contributed to the downturn of America's competitiveness in the automotive industry worldwide.

Lean Manufacturing and JIT also found new places in ecological industrial practices combined with closed-loop processing systems. The ecological thinking is that of "cradle-to-cradle," wherein materials do not die or get discarded but are recycled, in contrast to "cradle-to-grave" processing where products end up in garbage dumps.[12] By focusing on eco-efficiencies, and not just on profits, many companies are undertaking a sustainable orientation rather than overly large production lines, and are closely overseeing supplier connections, particularly in the especially volatile industries of pharmaceuticals or electronics. The cradle-to-cradle method can

▲ Kalmar carriers at Volvo, Gothenburg, Sweden, 1973
▶ Hexagonal layout of factory, Gothenburg, Sweden, 1973
▶ Aerial view of the factory, Gothenburg, Sweden, 2013

begin in the initial design of a product, as an ingrained sustainable consciousness of a company. The sustainable technologies comprise part of the new Triple Bottom Line (TBL), which serves to measure companies' social, environmental, and financial profits.[13]

FROM LINEAR TO CELLULAR PRODUCTION

The impact of new computerized technologies on manufacturing processes, JIT production, and worker responsibility were all intensified as companies began to evaluate new worker organizational systems. Of interest are the 1973 Volvo factory and the 1990s Skoda plants that have changed the flow of production to that of a fluid system based on work patterns and task relationships. After numerous strikes at Volvo's factory in Kalmar, Sweden, management renewed focus on the workspace and organizational systems, following the union's wishes. As at Toyota, rather than following a step-by-step line of production, the assembly line was instead organized into work groups, or cells, which worked collaboratively. Pehr Gyllenhammar, Volvo's director at the time, reorganized workers into teams, increasing communication between them and management and providing greater quality control. He also supplied workers with ergonomic workstations, and changed out shifts for a variety of tasks throughout the day. The workers could continue to alter their work in the factory, pacing themselves in a more fluid rather than rigidly defined workday, relieving boredom and monotony.

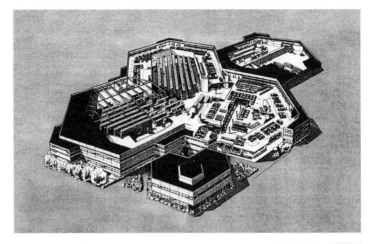

Contributing to the streamlined reorganization was the "Kalmar Carrier," a 5.5-meter-long battery-operated platform, or mobile workstation, that carried each car that was being assembled. The workers could access the cars from all six sides, including below. A radical change from the more one-sided conveyor assembly, working "in the round" with the Carrier became the standard in Volvo factories. The tires of the six-by-two-meter, aluminum-clad unit ran in tracks along the floor. The Carrier was battery-operated and either electromagnetically controlled or moved manually. The device made the car more ergonomic for the workers to handle because its height and angle could be adjusted.[14] The car was in process for five minutes at each workstation, with the production speed set at 15 cars per hour in 1974. The aluminum and steel Carrier moved according to a pace that the team agreed to, via computer controls. As in the Toyota system, quality control is embedded into the manufacturing process in 25 stages. The Carrier could also be docked to the side of the line at various points along the process.

The new manufacturing systems impacted the physical space of the Kalmar factory, which was designed by production engineer Togny Karlsson and architect Gehrad Goehl. The architectural historian Kenneth Frampton described the plan in Gothenburg as tri-partite hexagonal blocks forming a "butterfly" layout, rather than the more standardized rectangle.[15] The two-level factory featured an assembly area of two-and-a-half kilometers, with clustered workstations relating to the 25 steps of quality control organized in the hexagonal structures around a triangular central core. Supplies were delivered by forklifts to each work zone from an adjacent hexagonal tower. Assembly teams thus had workshop-like environments rather than a massive horizontal floor area, and the process was organic and spatially compact, far from linear, with nodal feeders carrying finished parts and goods to the main processing floor. The workers would complete a full car assembly rather than just work on one part consistently so that they could decide their own tasks, as long as the job would reach completion. Teamwork increased wages, quality control, and participatory management, benefiting the workers; however, the building design and amenities, coordinated by the socialist Swedish government for a still-capitalist enterprise, was only in place to appease the workers.

Commenting on the new organization of work, Frampton reinforces the tension in the issues of automation,

> which is at once the most advanced sector of modern industry and the epitome of its practice, confront[ing] the world of the commodity with a contradiction that it must somehow resolve: the same technical infrastructure that is capable of abolishing labor must at the same time preserve labor as a commodity — and indeed as the sole generator of commodities.[16]

However, while Frampton commends this new organization and technology and how Kalmar is a "faceted spatial loop — a sort of productive Möbius strip — wherein the unit passes freely from team to team," he also does not hesitate to point out that "a feeling of almost deliberate isolation, in the physical and psychological sense, pervades the entire structure and site."[17] The machinery and the production organization influenced the factory design, yet the work environment, for all the architectural efforts, remained a bland and bleak "non-place," forming this inherent paradox challenging the factory to incorporate social, economic, technological, and aesthetic perspectives of place.

TOWARDS MASS CUSTOMIZATION

Increased mass customization stepped beyond GM's product choice in a consumer-led market and flexibility for workers provided by Toyota's and Volvo's assembly method. Mass customization inspired economist Alvin Toffler to coin the term "prosumer" in 1980, indicating the potential for consumers to customize products according to their tastes and desires.[18] Toffler saw the individual as both producer and consumer, selecting things for one's own consumption rather than depending on companies setting the demand. The effects of the prosumer can be seen in the responsive retail space interaction, the design of products online, the "externalizing labor costs," and even DIY product assembly.[19] New mass-customized manufacturing in which the consumer is involved in controlling both the financing of the product, as investors, and the product design through selection of a variety of offers, was a long way from the traditional demand-supply circuit of a product that exists ready-made in the marketplace. Varying levels of customization — from a choice within design parameters, made-to-order products, flexible production, and modularizing some of the process — are involved in making product differentiations along with rapid mass production. "The more we shift toward advance manufacturer, and the more we de-massify and customize production, the stronger the customer's involve[ment] in the production process must necessarily grow," noted Toffler already, back in 1980.[20]

As manufacturing declined in the Western world and developing countries grew manufacturing sectors in the 1970s, taking advantage of cheaper labor and free trade, the new de-massified manufacturing in the West could occur in shorter production runs and smaller batches of niche production rather than the long runs of mass production such as the Model T. Many everyday products are needed by the masses, such as paper goods, textiles, food, and quotidian supplies, but those make up only a portion of the production sector; other products made up of customized interchangeable parts, formed a new paradigm. As Toffler observed, "We are revolutionizing the deep structure of production, sending currents of change through every layer of society."[21]

Customers are seen as part of the "new experience economy," in which they desire better quality and more precise goods that they are involved in selecting from a broader range of options and that provide a memorable experience.[22] This movement is both trendy and efficient. Internet and web-based orders have been able to speed up a direction that began in the 1980s using interactive information and the coordination of requests in e-commerce flowing between consumer and producer. Digital information that can direct the customization of the product back at the factory requires companies to be agile within their own product line. The company continues to design the base framework but provides customers with a broader selection available in terms of size, color, and material, like the Motorola phones now owned by Google.

Society has become the "society of the spectacle" — in Guy Debord's (1931–1994) terms, a harbinger to the fast-paced functional obsolescence of so many products.[23] In addition, new global financial systems have accelerated the market with computer-driven trade. Companies from Benetton to Zara, Nike and Uniqlo, among others, harnessed mass customization to also embrace consumer desires in a new paradigm that revolutionized the scale, dynamics, speed, and efficiency of productive consumption.

Fashion companies were some of the earliest to use the new consumer-led feedback technologies. The Italian company Benetton was groundbreaking in its transition from a manufacturer to a brand culture through advertising and product placement. Benetton's production methods exemplify a shift towards flexible factories where sweaters of one style can be knit in a neutral color gray and then dyed according to their clients' taste. On-demand production, rather than predicting the consumer market, responds to consumer preferences in real time, following JIT production and mass customization.

In the 1970s, Benetton grew rapidly, opening six thousand franchise stores around the world. In a feedback loop, the stores connected the consumers to the factory using Electronic Data Interchange mechanisms that notified the warehouse managers when to restock shelves as sales increased. Fiber-optic cable networks guided the manufacturing of 7,500 items per day. The information about the product, embedded with bar codes, was transmitted to the factory, where they increased the production of the most popular items or decreased others. Their advanced JIT production and fluid supply chain, from manufacturing to distribution, influenced the layout, design, and siting of their facilities. By the 1990s, the highly automated system provided information to the administrative offices for the controlled retail distribution.[24] At the scale of the corporate manufacturer, Benetton returned to the idea of networking local small manufacturers using a group of local cottage industries. As with Toyota, smaller industries, comprised of local producers similar to medieval guild systems, carried out piecework orders. In the 1980s, networks of companies in the Bologna region of Italy developed for Benetton. But Benetton has lost its edge in the global marketplace after being pushed aside by trendier and even faster fashion-oriented companies in the 1990s, and has since initiated a megastore model with fewer franchises. Since the early 2000s, they have also been producing in the global factory of Bangladesh, including in Rana Plaza, the factory building which collapsed in 2013.[25]

Another consumer-responsive company is the Spain-based Zara, which caters to consumers' desires and directs their preferences by producing smaller batches of clothes quickly alongside ever-changing fashion trends; the company designs 40,000 clothing items per year in 10,000 different styles.[26] Zara has vertically integrated production, meaning that all aspects of production are owned and managed by the company as a consolidated enterprise. The clothing is significantly less expensive than that of fashion houses and designer labels, and maintains better quality than a lower-end production. Similar to Benetton, the transfer of information between different sections of the company is speedy. The Spanish parent company Inditex (Industria de Diseño Textil) centralizes its designers in the production process in their facility in Coruña, Spain. They also own 18 factories there, as well as in Barcelona, forging local and immediate accountability. Starting with gray fabrics, they can decide on trends spontaneously. They subcontract out the stitching, to nearby workshops in Portugal and in northern Spain, rather than outsourcing to China. Unlike most apparel manufacturing in which each element of the garment is made in another place, the local production is rare. In Zara's central factory, designs are revised by marketing and production staff at worktables in close proximity to one another. Personnel can collaborate on fabrics, colors, and production methods simultaneously, not in hierarchical departments. They also run the product lines tightly without interruption, and they can adjust designs according to consumer preferences, sending messages via their handheld smart devices in the stores. The limitation on the numbers of products results in no waste, or

▶ Stoll automated textile looms, 2010. Photograph by Alaistar Philip Wiper

underselling, so they don't need to discount. The Zara method is a Quick Response (QR) method, deriving from Lean Manufacturing in food and textile industries that responds to market shifts between retail inventory and manufacturing supply chain, thus condensing the production time and fashion cycle. Every three weeks, new styles are shipped to the over 1,200 Zara stores worldwide; the short lead time and low inventory enhance desirability. The company uses new information technology systems, JIT manufacturing, which the company worked on with Toyota, and telecommunications that connect management, supply, production, and sales.

Designs can be completed in as short as two weeks, in contrast to the average fashion house, which needs at least a four-month lead.[27] Zara therefore purchases fabrics and completes designs when other companies are already well into the season, catering to potentially stale tastes. Nothing languishes on Zara's display racks, and fashion is a ploy for artificially accelerated consumerism — because of the fast design turnover, consumers visit the stores more often. The executive, José Maria Castellano has said: "Fashion stock is like food. It goes bad quickly."[28]

Uniqlo is another model of rapid production, even adopting the name "Fast Retailing" for a period in 1991.[29] The Japanese company first capitalized on the need for less expensive but fashionable basic clothing during the 1990s recession. They developed from Ogori Shoji, a men's clothing store that first opened in

CENTRALIZED

DISTRIBUTED NETWORK
Differentiated as aggregates

DECENTRALIZED

UNDIFFERENTIATED
DISTRIBUTED NETWORK

DISTRIBUTED NETWORK

NEW FORMATIONS
within Distributed Network

1949, and then expanded by the 1980s to a unisex store, keeping costs down by producing in seventy offshore contracted factories. Those factories are located in Shanghai and Shenzhen, China; Ho Chi Minh City, Vietnam; Dhaka, Bangladesh; and more recently Indonesia, as China is becoming too costly for production. Founded and owned by Tadashi Yanai, it is now the fourth largest retailer in the world, and focuses on branding and identity, along with the development of innovative materials and classic designs. They make each item in over fifty colors in a similar way as Benetton, but with cheaper production lines. The company exemplifies what author Naomi Klein calls "brand factories." They "hammer out what is of true value: the idea, the lifestyle, the attitude. Brand builders are the new primary producers in our so-called knowledge economy."[30] Uniqlo's online marketing, designs, and brand have greater presence than the merchandise they produce.

Production engineers, called the Takumi Team, supervise the dying, spinning, knitting, weaving, sewing, finishing, and shipping of the products around the East, working with the subcontracted factories, including the Chenfeng Group, a garment company in the Jiangsu Jintan Economic Development Zone near Shanghai that has 8,000 employees and produces over forty million clothing articles per year. Uniqlo also subcontracts to Pan Brothers in Solo, Indonesia, and its sister company Pancaprima Ekabrothers has 20,000 workers making over forty-two million pieces per year.[31] The concept of fast retailing capitalizes on a rapid version of JIT, non-excess, and automated manufacturing to turn a base material into an instant commodity.

SPATIAL IMPLICATIONS

In JIT production, interconnectivity via handheld devices and embedded codes combine the virtual and physical and contribute to yet another level of precision at every scale — from worker to worker, worker to robot, product to manufacturer, worker to the world, and finally, product to the world. The advent of "smart" handheld wireless installations impact worker activity and the organization of production spaces.[32] A virtual and invisible umbilical cord links production and sales, factories and stores in a controlled manufacturing ecology. Since the computer often directs the workflow, the factory in many ways adopts the internal workings of the computer itself. This is exemplified by Paul Baran's analysis for the Rand Corporation, which was at the forefront of organizational research in the 1960s where, rather than emphasizing a hierarchical system, he recommended distributed networks which extend branches of communication that can overlap, retract, or spread out into further expansive networks.[33]

The reduced scale of machine controls and the robotic factory also parallel the workflow of organizational systems.[34] Organizational sociologist Luther P. Gerlach classified social networks as having three attributes: segmentation, where each area works separately; polycentrism, where there is a central control of different nodes; and integration, where each area networks together, "where there are real-time adjustments for continually changing circumstances across potentially expanding fields of operation."[35] These real-time fluctuations parallel manufacturing networks for mass customization and new manufacturing methods as they constantly evolve with customers' new desires.

Production Simulation

The advent of digital software presents major spatial implications, as digital tools enable fine-tuning of the production space to greater levels of optimization than at any point in history. As part of the suite of digital tools manufacturers use to optimize their process, new production simulation software is an invaluable resource in ensuring that a factory can physically accommodate the rapid changes in production that may be necessitated by adopting a real-time adjustment regimen. Production computerization software illustrates the flows of material and goods along the layout of the factory, and can now provide spatial simulations and even three-dimensional animated renderings of the process in motion. Similar to the way engineers collaborated with architects in the early twentieth century to design factories, today software companies provide tools for architects and manufacturers to optimize factory layout systems. In some instances, factory flow is simulated in real time with physical models in facilities such as the Experimental Factory in Magdeburg, Germany designed by Berlin architects Sauerbruch Hutton (2001). This research organization creates miniaturized production lines for testing, and companies can use the space to set up roller conveyors to try out the turning radii of their products on the line, prior to the actual factory construction, or to retool their process.

In contrast, computer simulation programs use digital animation to resolve issues such as bottlenecks which enable architects, engineers, and manufacturers to organize virtual production lines that can be tested and retested. Once operational, any errors are digitally reported in real time, and the process can be instantly adjusted. In the factory itself, once constructed, rather than referring to a large-scale Andon board that is visible to all, each worker can negotiate production issues on the individualized small screen of their Personal Digital Assistant (PDA) or tablet. Teamwork continues in virtual communications, but with less face-to-face interaction, leaving workers to move freely as they achieve the production goals.

One such suite of factory design software is that produced by Autodesk. This program can combine the design software for factory layouts with the design of the production process itself, in order to assist industrial engineers in designing both the optimal production process, and the optimal factory layout to match. The software can conduct audits of production times, detect conflicts between machinery using three-dimensional modeling, and produce renderings and videos illustrating the interior of the factory. The virtual three-dimensional factory design programs only work when the designer and industrial designer manipulate all of the interlinked tools to develop strategies for each design problem in order to customize the production processes.

◄ Organizational models developed by the RAND Corporation, 1960s

Handhelds in Factories

PDAs and their computer enhancements increase the mobility of workers in production plants who can use remote controls to complete their tasks, then report to a head office elsewhere. This is seen also in the physical manifestation of the worker-to-supervisor relationship, and team-to-team communication. The complexity of the networked distributed system guides the computer modeling of automation accordingly, which includes quality control, the worker's skill level, and consumer response. High-powered handhelds can communicate between departments, and to and from robots on a factory floor for scheduling, maintenance, and inventory. PDAs can track repairs and work on machinery remotely, which can enhance the productivity of the mobile worker and increase flexibility of divisions of labor. Numerous computer hardware and software companies such as Cisco, SAP, Accenture, and Oracle have created systems that run programs for handheld PCs, as do logistics companies such as UPS and FedEx. UPS uses embedded codes that the company has developed itself for tracking a product and its movement around the world.

The German company SAP's software programs for production and supply chain management and information services allow employees to view work instructions on their handhelds in the factory, and with bar code scanners, check and control production processes through embedded chips, resulting in synchronized communication systems for real-time inventory, production control, and warehousing. Cisco Systems can track inventories of material in real time by connecting with mobile devices integrated with SAP's systems and wireless devices, becoming a mesh of wireless technology for production and dispatching of completed goods.

Intel designed network processors with Rockwell Automation, part of a line of high-performance tools that provide manufacturers with seamless information flow between the factory floor and the R&D offices, wherever they may be outsourced. The food and beverage industry has taken advantage of high-performance tools for quality control, organization of goods for shipping on palettes (or palletization), gauging consistency and sizing of the food item, temperature control, and robotic arm movement in loading and packing food products.

Another system from the European Commission and a consortium of groups through the Fraunhofer Institute in Germany is an Intelligent Networked Manufacturing System (INT-MANUS) that foresees further use of wireless and smart controls which will network people, machines, and robots for smart flexible customization, with sensors and cameras embedded in the equipment. In this process, computers are not reprogrammed with each change in a design, but new information is input to the system that then fluidly adapts the Smart Connected Control Platforms. Communication is also enhanced with mobile controls and headsets for workers to move freely. The program guides proactive maintenance, customized production, and error reporting.[36] In the most extreme scenario, the factory can run automatically, as does a power plant, or remotely by robotic control. The factory scene is like a puppeteer controlling, from a central hub, the actions of the workers with a virtual string attached to each movable element. This information flow allows instant decision-making that improves productivity, flexibility, and, ultimately, the goal of profitability. When various components of a product, such as a car motor, need to be changed — just as in interchangeable parts manufacturing of the nineteenth century — workers can direct computer-controlled robots to perform the job.

Internet of Things / Wireless Management

With new technologies constantly augmenting JIT manufacturers, Zara as well as Wal-Mart and Levi-Strauss, among others, switched in 2009 from the use of more standardized bar codes to "smart shelf" technology that was employed in the manufacturing of all kinds of products. These Auto-ID tracking systems used for locating items in shipping containers, palettes, and warehouses are embedded with Radio Frequency Identification (RFID) tags developed at the Massachusetts Institute of Technology's (MIT) Auto ID Center to track inventory, location, and manufacturing needs in real time.[37] The RFID tags precisely record information so that retailers do not have to physically monitor store shelves, and data is automatically transferred to the factory managers. Developed from bar codes (which have been in existence since the late 1950s) on which parallel black lines of varying thicknesses are coded, information about an item, such as price and customer, can be scanned at the cash register or in a factory at the point of production for information about a product's quantity, location, and demand.

In factories, RFID tags are particularly useful for tracking products, in addition to supporting quality control manufacturing. RFID tags are more advanced than bar codes and are paired with electronic reader machinery in a modem. Via electromagnetic radio waves, the electronic tag sends data to a transceiver interface. The tags reflect back to the reader and the information is transferred to a computer, or a handheld device. In 2012 the technology advanced to the point where the operator could work remotely, without the object in sight. An antenna on the transceiver picks up the necessary information from the tag and sends it to the microchip on the computer. At first, the codes could only be printed on paper labels that were attached to products; these were easily destroyed by exposure to water or harsh climatic conditions. Now, there are methods to print the codes embedded with information on the surface of objects made of various materials, including wood, metal, and plastic. This is particularly useful in situations where workers have little or no access to the dangerous product being made, such as in chemical plants, recycling facilities, and nuclear power stations.[38] The processing can also be monitored closely to determine the inventory or track parts for assembly so that the processing is in real time. Instead of the overhead Andon boards signaling the production issues, objects communicate with the workers directly through handheld devices.

As one-dimensional diagrams, RFIDs store minimal data on a minuscule surface and can be placed on other material surfaces, embedded in clothing, and eventually the skin itself. Science fiction writers and directors started predicting this phenomenon decades ago in movies featuring cyborgs, or cybernetic organisms, which are both human and machine, organic and electronic.[39] The RFIDs can perpetually hold information about a person or the product as part of what Kevin Ashton in 1999 called the "Internet of Things," a network of "things" that can talk to other "things" electronically in an in-between space of a kind of new electronic ether.[40]

Consumer Customization

The development of computerization and the "Internet of Things" directly affect consumer product choice. As early as the late 1990s, companies such as Levi's and Lands' End offered the consumer made-to-measure garments that could be ordered online. Japanese watch manufacturers, which focused on a wide variety of production, unlike the specialized luxury watches of Switzerland, capitalized on

mass customization. Starting in 1996, Citizen Watch developed a series of made-to-order watches called My Creation that featured special designs and logos and required shorter lead times than traditional watch and small batch production. Customers used computer software to design the watches, which they mailed back to the company with their personalized designs. Later, through the Internet, customers could return the data about their preferred case pattern, band, face, and hands electronically. Offering personalization through the interactive mass-customization process creates a new kind of added value for the company.[41]

Customization is seen in the Nike company's development of NIKEiD in 1999. Customers can shop for a new sneaker by arranging its virtual details on the screen — color, type, pattern, graphics, and materials. Even high-end fashion shops such as the Ferragamo shoe company encourage consumer interaction by allowing them to select from a limited palette of small details such as bows and heels, empowering the customer as "designer." The products that have interchangeable parts, or those with a primary design base, are the easiest for this type of customization. Other companies use this customization to focus on brand image and marketing as bespoke products for the informed consumer.

Another advanced technology, called Quick Response Codes (QR Codes), which contributed to the consumers' ease of direct product information, are now ubiquitous. Frequently seen alongside advertisements in magazines, they are composed of a black square of pixels to be decoded using the camera on cellular phones. By taking a picture of the code, the individual can link to specific websites in order to get more information. The information is embedded in the object as codes through which data can be housed and retrieved. The objects communicate with each other in a digital realm of other smart objects and interfaced systems.

Identification devices that use Global Positioning Systems (GPS) and geo-tagging to pinpoint the location of an object or person can be transmitted via satellite or Internet connections, then downloaded and plotted by coordinates on a map so that the location is trackable and recorded afterwards in real time. GPS also can assist in the factory for routing goods and assist the truck driver to find their destination. However, potentially negative and abusive uses of this technology abound. The worker can be tracked on the factory floor with large watch-like devices that even monitor bathroom breaks. Ubiquitous computing, and an "Internet of Things," compromise individual privacy. GPS allows the company to know where all of their products go, who buys them, and how they are consumed. This ever-increasing surveillance of consumer and worker behavior is, and will continue to be, used by companies in unpublicized ways.[42]

DEMOCRATIZING PRODUCTION

A next step towards autonomous and ubiquitous production is sharing of machinery and software. To reduce operating costs, people can design a product that is

then printed via computer software linked to shared hardware, which is leased or rented by the hour in a common workshop space. This also occurs at the company scale as the outsourcing of a specific task such as welding, or for a part to be manufactured in a better-equipped or more skilled shop. For individuals, it is possible to design a product that is then printed with 3-D printers in workshops the same way one goes to a copy shop for paper printouts. Shapeways, a subsidiary of Siemens that opened in Long Island City, New York in 2012, is one such new company that provides rapid-prototyping as a service. Individuals can send designs worked out in computer programs and upload them to the company's host computer, which is connected to the company's 3-D printers to output in metal, plastic, and wood. Shapeways also sells products via their website; since they are printed on demand, there is no overhead for the stock. While these kinds of machines for additive manufacturing, with layers of materials being added sequentially, might not take over

◄ Making lost gauges for a World War 2 Submarine at TechShop with Rich Pekelny, 2012
▲ Textile factory in Denmark, 2012
▲ Detail of the weaving apparatus, 2012

mass production, they have potential for making more than one thing in a shorter time span, using less energy and fewer materials as they are added to rather than carved, and take up less storage space. This method of production also makes it cheaper for start-up companies which experiment with small batch or individual product manufacturing to test future production.

This collective process of sharing machinery, space, and expertise is instrumental to the design of new urban manufacturing spaces. The machines are shared in new hacker spaces and collaborative workshops such as TechShop, which offers space and tools, including computers and high-tech machinery, in a multistory building in San Francisco, as well as in a former Ford space just outside of Detroit. GE Garage also established well-equipped pop-up spaces where designers and inventors can experiment with the new machinery. The manufacturing process has become democratized as people are manufacturing in smaller batches, firms are smaller but solvent, and the quality control is more immediate and manageable. "Fab labs" like these are cropping up all over — from schools and universities to community centers — and, while many are outgrowths of engineering groups, others are collaborative corporate efforts to share materials and tools in a more organized system for entrepreneurs, beyond the traditional corporate model.

Other products also benefit from this collaborative process that makes high-tech computerized machinery available to individual manufacturers who could not otherwise afford it. Stoll, a sophisticated German garment company that manufactures machinery to make knitwear, designs patterns for its own lines, and supplies machines to other companies, has spearheaded the customization of specific weaving patterns for fashion designers. In Stoll's Fashion Design and Technology Centers, including one in the Garment District in New York and another in Shanghai, a designer can rent the machine on-site and the production engineer helps to create a sample pattern for small batch production that then can be developed into a full product line. The company's pattern archive also includes knit sample swatches that designers can either work from or adapt for a current product. Stoll supplies CAD/CAM knitting machines programmed by engineers who follow the design specifications with different gauges that can accommodate different types of wools and yarns. Its website provides downloadable digital templates for knitwear patterns, which are then produced at the designer's own factory. The company goes even further and runs educational workshops and training sessions on topics ranging from the making of knitwear to operating machinery and establishing the quality control of knits in a factory setting. This combination of manufacturing, automated knitting machines, and design assistance is a new model for an urban manufacturing system that can multiply in cities, promoting production and skills. But it is also a step towards a horizontal agency in production. No longer is the consumer dependent on the corporation, but the corporation listens to the DIY movement and takes ownership of it by providing educational classes and tools.

Other computer software initiatives also contribute to the shared manufacturing, such as open-source information and crowdsourcing, as illustrated by the Local Motors car company in Wareham, Massachusetts. A product can be designed and tested prior to bringing it to market at the end of the chain in a "virtual micro-factory." Facilitated by a Creative Commons license, the open-source method of information sharing, hobbyists can improve a car design.[43] As technology author and manufacturer Chris Anderson describes, "One of the great advantages of building such a car today is that it plays into the global automotive manufacturing trends of the past three decades."[44] The factory production techniques can be harnessed by small companies, or even individuals who don't have to start a huge factory but can now share tools and information for smaller batches, making a unique prototype for testing before committing to a larger production run.

ELECTRONIC COTTAGE INDUSTRIES

The shrinking of machines influences production space and time, as the scale shift from large to small, and the potential dispersion of the factory as neo-cottages, becomes increasingly locally based. In the 1970s and early 1980s, economists Toffler (in *The Third Wave* and *Future Shock*[45]) and John Naisbitt (in *Megatrends*[46]) both forecast the computer's insertion into every home and its ubiquitous presence throughout contemporary life. They conjectured that this scenario would contribute to the demise of offices and result in the "electronic cottage," an idea that has come to pass even more than they imagined and resulted in telecommuting, flextime, and decentralization.[47] Toffler noted that the "new production system could literally shift millions of jobs out of the factories and offices into which the Second Wave swept them right back where they originated: the home."[48] He suggested that the idea of working at home had been a cultural condition and shaped the structure of family life for centuries until the formation of the manufactory, as discussed earlier. But he was primarily referring to immaterial production, to white-collar workers who did data entry and computer engineering and those who didn't have to handle physical goods. In 1975, Toffler saw many advantages to the shift to telecommuting. During the Oil Crisis, he estimated that 75 million barrels of gasoline could be saved if the 88 percent of the population who commute didn't, or used public transit, and that both pollution and unproductive time could be reduced. The new flexible hours enhanced by data processing and fax machines to connect to the office exploited "distance-independence" that is now full-blown. In the factory, the same is true, neo-cottage industries are evolving with workers in their own spaces producing goods.

Even in large-scale manufacturing processes, the smaller-scale additive manufacturing, or 3-D printing, as discussed earlier, has reduced the numbers of parts to make things as the output results in holistic objects. In a self-contained system, computer-programmed machines not only subtract materials but can add them, and are changing the way we make numerous products.

Rather than cutting and stamping materials as with the CNC routers and milling, the process includes additive layers of material such as plastic powders. With CAD modeling on the computer, as in earlier manufacturing technologies, the powder builds up an object layer by layer and then sends the forms to be cast and tested. The 3-D printers melt fine pieces of plastic to make or "print" the object. Micro-industries are developing with fewer workers using prototypes made via 3-D printing. Larger-scale mass-produced items can be made in factories with lower costs per volume, or created increasingly on-demand in micro-factories by those inventors of the new creative culture. This changes the economy of making a product as well, because the investment of capital is not as intensive upfront.

3-D printing is also used by large-scale manufacturers. One company, Filton of Bristol, England makes smaller components of airplanes using 3-D printing for prototype parts.[49] As it is an additive rather than subtractive process, only the essential material is used, and there is no waste. This process thus saves costs, energy, and materials, bit by bit. Will Sillar of Legerwood, England imagines the future "digital production plant" as no longer needing large amounts of capital tied up in tooling costs, work-in-process, and raw materials.[50] Instead, production machinery will be shared following JIT production methods to one in real time. It is cheaper, well-controlled, and tested but more heavily used for prototype components in larger factories such as Ford's Chicago plant, where the rapid prototyping developed brake rotor design testing for the Explorer SUV to ascertain which design would reduce the brake noise. Other companies are using 3-D printers to perfect prosthetic devices and parts of artificial hips in customized manufacturing. GE and Boeing both use the method for their aviation division for parts, but it is slow for large objects and they often need finer grade finishing post-production. On the other hand, the variety of parts that can be produced often are at a lower cost, even if changes are made at the last minute.

At the smallest scale, MakerBot is a company that produces 3-D printers, one called the Thing-O-Matic and another the Replicator 2, with which people can make objects just as with a computer desktop printer, at much lower cost than the industrial-sized machines. MakerBot, now a subsidiary of a larger 3-D print company, was founded in New York in 2009, and is based on open source collaborations. Chris Anderson exclaims, "MakerBot is not just a tool. It's also a plaything. It's a revolutionary act. It's a kinetic sculpture. It's a political statement. It's thrillingly cool."[51] The company is now public and has produced thousands of machines for anyone to make their own things in their own electronic cottage. Others such as Pirate3D and Cube have joined this market. These companies either design their own software or use more generalized software products. Inventors can send designs from computers or a PDA to their website and from there the designs can be produced.

Designers can choose their desired material among plastics and polymers, and, while unusual in other processes, liquid metal, which can be used to create freestanding structures. The liquid material solidifies into the desired shape from droplets, which are combined into complex structures that retain their shape or by using a polymer template that can be molded by hand.[52] It is a challenge, however, to combine materials or integrate within other 3-D printed components.[53]

Architects have been using 3-D printing for their models for years and testing building elements for mass customization, as have industrial designers. Now the fashion world has caught on to this technology's potential, including the team of Michael Schmidt and New York architect Francis Bitonti, who fabricated a dress using 3-D printing in 2012. The long nylon dress used the additive manufacturing process of selective laser sintering (SLS) to fuse particles of plastic powder together. Resembling a body-size fishnet stocking, the form was fitted to a model from a computer scan of the body and the dress fabric is a rigid plastic that was adapted to move by using smaller units in a webbing. A few years earlier, Continuum Fashion collaborated with Shapeways to 3-D print a bikini that was custom-fit as well. This flexible surface was made from thousands of circular plates connected by springs that followed the surface curvature using an algorithm.

With the possibilities afforded by 3-D printing, we can make things as we desire in real time instead of shopping in stores or even shopping online. Author Neal Stephenson predicted this desktop printing phenomenon in his 1995 book *The Diamond Age,* with his "Matter Compiler" (M.C.), a sort of computer printer "deke bin" from which objects such as mattresses, clothes, and other everyday needs just appeared. "Whenever Nell's clothes got too small for her, Harv would pitch them into the deke bin and then have the M.C. make new ones. Sometimes, if Tequila was going to take Nell someplace where they would see other moms with other daughters, she'd use the M.C. to make Nell a special dress with lace and ribbons."[54]

And soon things will even be able to self-assemble, as with the 4-D Project Cyborg, which programs matter of various scales in a cloud-based computing and web-based CAD shell. At a MIT Self-Assembly Lab, scientists are investigating ways for physical materials to program themselves to self-assemble without people physically working at all. CAD Nano is used to design 3-D shapes and uses DNA to self-assemble the structures from the nanoscale to the human scale. Programmable materials, such as piping, could expand and contract according to the needs of the system and then assemble themselves in 4-D systems. Flat sheets can fold into 3-D forms and are reconfigurable. Multiple materials are printed and then transformed as they simulate the behavior of objects. A program is embedded into the materials. The concept is useful to make things in extreme environments, including cold and dangerous places such as outer space.[55]

Science fiction writers such as Philip K. Dick, who envisioned self-assembly in his 1953 story, *Autofac,* wrote:

> The bits were in motion. Microscopic machinery, smaller than ants, smaller than pins, working energetically, purposefully — constructing something that looked like a tiny rectangle of steel. 'They're building,' O'Neill said, awed. He got up and prowled on. Off to the side, at the far edge of the gully, he came across a downed pellet far advanced on its construction. Apparently it had been released some time ago. This one had made great enough progress to be identified. Minute as it was, the structure was familiar. The machinery was building a miniature replica of the demolished factory.[56]

Perhaps the machine recognized the obsolescence of the factory in its own ability to directly print a product. As designers improve their ability to print unique objects, or like the average consumer as described by Dick, production capability

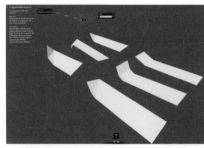

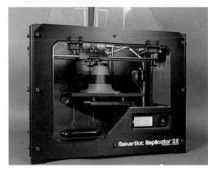

▲ **4-D Project Cyborg, 2014**
▲ **The MakerBot 3-D printer, 2014**

shifts the relationship directly between the consumer to the product, economics, and the spatial requirements for production.

In reflecting on the topic of material production, people continuously make things in the home. Bicycles, for example, can be built in a home. Parts can be ordered from around the world, bit by physical bit, and assembled in a neo-cottage industry. Other tinkerers and craftspeople such as bakers, dressmakers, knitters, and flower arrangers can also produce goods for broader distribution from their small, personal urban spaces as long as they are plugged into a supply and distribution chain — that is, if they distribute in the marketplace. Product and fashion designers continue to find that the physical aspects of production are essential to source their raw or semi-finished materials to be close to their consumers who still like to try on clothes, for example. In those design-to-production-related industries, the knowledge exchange, as well as the physical sense of touch and individual response to the color or feel of a fabric needs to be experienced in person.[57] Plus, there comes a moment of mutual trust when a buyer or supplier knows one another, so that exchanges thrive through personal loyalty in cities, where trade was original basis. The shift in scale of production of both the spaces and the equipment, and that of the relationship between the inventor and the manufacturer, or between designer and worker as being one and the same, form a new industrial organization not fully recognized or analyzed economically. A new urban manufacturing paradigm of digital production and customization has gained strength in spite of the continued focus on service industries and immaterial labor. With smaller batches, or personally designed items, autonomous production refocuses on cottage industry.

The new clean industrial technology, in contrast to the rusting heavy machinery of the past on its entropic trajectory, is light, ephemeral, and now nano-scaled. The sublime of the massive "machine in the garden" as described by Leo Marx, has evaporated into micromanufacturing and the barely visible.[58] But, in emerging economies, large-scale factories continue and are in demand for mass production of consumer goods. The contrasting systems between the two are as divergent as between new textile looms and handwork of the early nineteenth century.

Tasks and jobs that rely on the intelligence of computer programmers rather than manual skills and experience create a divide between skilled and unskilled workers. In Marx's terms, the capitalist system swept the worker into the new cycle of supply and demand, but the unreliability of immaterial production and new skills required pushed aside a former working class. In this age of automation and unstable economies, the worker's tasks have become, in Jean-Paul de Gaudemar's words, "uncertain, linked to the contingencies of production, to the contingencies of flux. As such, these tasks could only be regulated by an institutionalization of fluctuation."[59] The fluctuation is a result of the unstable new economy and the new high-tech class taking over jobs from the working class. But in shrinking employment for unskilled workers, who struggle to gain recognition and to earn decent wages, a new kind of work is emerging: that of *making* rather than *working*. The possibilities of making things in a smaller-scale workshop, although by automatic machines, as noted previously, harkens back to early cottage industries. A new autonomy of making transforms the idea of work in relationship to the working class to one that is not about labor, but has become an intellectual and creative pursuit. Does the direction towards the maker in digital fabrication, as in 3-D printing, and as an autonomous and individualized design-to-production process, provide the worker with a place?

In the extreme scenario today — not the one that respects labor and the working ethic or that of the provision of jobs for the unskilled — "the worker" has been pushed aside and out of sight, as part of process removal, outsourced to countries such as China and Bangladesh. This worker is a reminder of the often-times inhumane conditions of work; the worker that developed countries don't want to see because then they have to be incorporated into a welfare system. If a new idea of work is really now about making, where does work reside? Even the word, *maker*, versus *worker,* has a new connotation that removes the idea of work from the process. Is *maker* a euphemism for the worker; is to make something more acceptable? Or, has the notion of work changed so that there is no longer a working class? The maker is different from the worker, she has capital, uses the website Etsy; the worker does not, she is a wage laborer. Where is the place of the worker in the diverse and livable city that is upheld as the way of the future for so many urban thinkers?[60]

One can also ask how the shrinking scale of industrial machines affects cities, as the automated mobile industry technologies can impact the change of scale to smaller urban factories (as is discussed in the book's next section "Industrial Urbanism"). This scale-shift counteracts, in many ways, the globalization of industry, bringing it back to the local and regionally based manufacturers, as seen in the locavore food movement. With smaller-scale spaces that are flexible and dynamic, there is a potential for manufacturing to be reinserted into existing vertical urban factories. This can increase industrial urbanization, taking advantage of proximity and agglomerations of related industries — as districts around the world — or as constellations throughout a city, thereby reversing the trend of the mega-scale horizontal suburban factory that arose postwar.

Flusser foresaw the historical trajectories of manufacturing, noting that in the second industrial revolution humans were subordinate to the machine, but in the third industrial revolution he said that appliances (as prosthetic devices) are more versatile as we carry them with us. He predicted:

> [T]he factory of the future will be much more adaptable than those of today, and it will be sure to redefine the relationship between human being and tools. . . .[T]he factory of the future will cease to be a mad-house and will become a place in which the creative potential of *homo faber* will come into its own.[61]

In this third industrial revolution it is the combination of the new technologies and the making of things that maintains the future of the vertical urban factory.

INDUSTRIAL URBANISM

ECONOMIC GEOGRAPHY

Industry as a spatial organizational system of land use is a major force in the development of cities. Due to the need for proximity to power sources, entrepreneurs, labor, and transit routes, a region's economic stability relies not only on local commerce but also on exported goods that can bolster the economies of tightly knit intra-metropolitan regions of exchange. Industry's determinate location deserves renewed attention with a lens on the interrelations between space and economy. Urban industrial development contributed to the expansion of cities beyond their defined borders and dense environments. Today, local industries have the potential to contribute to a vital equilibrium in new urban clusters, as well as dispersed throughout cities as constellations of activity.

The factory buildings of previous eras and their interstitial spaces can be reoccupied today by new forms of manufacturing, for new types of industries. How has the change in urban industry from the individual site and city block to districts or zones, and then regions, impact the factory building's development? How does the adjustment to the new economy impact previously established as well as potential future industries, reorganized in the hinterlands? In this chapter I focus on the more recent developments in industrial urbanism, the location of the factory in the city, and industry's perceived strength or weakness. The potential for a new factory city — either clustered in agglomerated areas for sharing resources, decentralized in a field condition with resources everywhere, or virtually networked and scattered for a new kind of industrial interchange — inspires a new urban paradigm at different scales, pointing to industry in mixed-use communities.

When steam power was replaced by electricity, the need for proximity to sources of natural power diminished, extending the reach of production over vast territories and encouraging a new spatial organization. In the ever-changing industrial landscape post-World War II, the ease of new highway-based truck transit and standardized containerized shipping, which transitioned from more urban-based train hubs to dispersed distribution with highway-cities spread manufacturing globally.

In the third industrial revolution, employment became flexible and malleable, with an unprotected labor force. The space where things were made moved away from vertical factories in urban cores to marginalized manufacturing zones where there was cheaper land and labor in both emerging economies and more established societies. The economic, land use, and zoning structures persuaded manufacturers to redistribute to urban edges and beyond.

One of the major contributions to this urban exodus was the strength of unions which proved detrimental to many corporations and spurred the relocation of industries from the northern cities in the U.S. In the 1960s, many companies moved south where union organizing was not as strong and factories could thrive, thereby shifting the economic and social hierarchies throughout the country. But this gave less power to workers. The expansive U.S. highway system facilitated the new access and distribution. Higher-tech factories were also drawn to the Sunbelt because of more lenient tax laws as well as warmer climates. Military manufacturing moved even further south to more expansive sites at the Mexican border.[1] The resulting labor shifts combined with later free trade agreements incentivized manufacturers to move beyond their singular corporate identity to countries that offered even cheaper labor. Diminished standards of living and lower, or nonexistent, minimum wage requirements became defining factors of the new era of globalization and international trade.

More recently, in emerging economies, global corporations are seen as advantages to jumpstart local commerce. Countries accept these large multinationals with open arms, initiating free trade zones, with a new working class, often made up of a migratory agricultural community drawn to the cities, as happened in the

▲ *Red Containers Stacked*, Newark, New Jersey, 2001. Photograph by Victoria Sambunaris

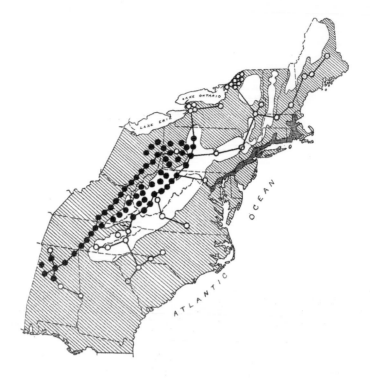

▲ Benton MacKaye's illus-
tration of the Appalachian
Trail as a commodity network,
1924

West over a century earlier. For the factory, this locational flexibility became essential, both economically and architecturally. Industries moved further from their markets to new incentivized tax-free zones where the global market could enter the newly defined cycle of consumption and production. These newly configured economies in countries such as China and India have embraced the idea of factory cities of former eras, and have built minimum dormitory accommodations for their low-paid workers.

As a ripple effect of offshore manufacturing landing in these emerging economies, urban planning offices in the developed countries interpreted the change in the industrial landscape as an indication to rezone urban land. Enticed by free-trade zones overseas, companies moved out, which effectively signaled a change to reduce the amount of industrial zoned urban land, and instead to convert it to other uses. Governments cut economic assistance to manufacturers, leaving few places for factories to grow within cities. The decrease in available space and concomitant decrease in jobs and skilled worker training, dramatically affected these former urban industrial economies and also contributed to the shrinking city. Both the departure of industry from cities and the decline of urban centers in general left land and former industrial buildings vacant. In places where real estate interests were still strong, the trend resulted in residential and commercial gentrification that could not be reverted to industrial use without a huge time lag, creating an imbalance between land use and economic potential.

With the new economy of flexible accumulation, and the expansion of a global economy and free trade, questions arise as to the spatial organization in former industrial cities where manufacturing was the prime economic force and urban generator. Additionally, the impact of new technologies and digital logistics played a part in industrial dispersal beyond cities, affording potential for new industrial networks. As the factory became segregated to spaces beyond cities in process removal, the place for urban manufacturing was negatively evaluated. Because of this decline, few urban designers focused their energies on the place and space of industry, both in the Modernist period and then again during the 1960s, at the height of industrial growth; the architectural avant-garde was more interested in cultural buildings, housing, and infrastructure than improving the spaces of manufacturing.

AGGLOMERATION

Empirical studies in the fields of location theory and economic geography have struggled to define how the location of businesses and industries can influence their success or failure. These spatio-temporal-economic disciplines, which also include transportation and distribution costs, began to infiltrate economics again more recently as a new field of investigation hitherto seen through the separate lenses of either economics or geography, but not both. Now this industrial ecosystem seems to be obvious in the discussion of space, land use, and land value in relationship to urban economics. While in traditional education commercial geography dominated history and social studies classes as a standard subject of study, and books about urban industries explained where and why products come from specific places, more recently, a gap in the study of land and economics led to a disconnect between place, production processes, and land value.

Some historically global thinkers such as Benton MacKaye (1879–1975), an originator of the idea for the Appalachian Trail in the 1920s, created an unusual compendium called "A World Atlas of Commodity Flow," that was presented in essay form across a few issues of *The Nation* magazine in 1927.[2] In it he described a vision of reorganizing the landscape and linking places and their economies. He understood the geographic connection between place and resources and their ecosystems. He proposed forming connections along the Appalachian Mountains by documenting all of the energy sources and other natural resources with the goal of connecting coal and hydroelectric power sources to a nature trail. Comparing industrial networks to nature, he believed that industry was part of a regional exchange. "For the intricate equipment of civilization is in itself a wilderness. He has unraveled the labyrinth of river and coast line but has spun the labyrinth of industry."[3] MacKaye believed that all resources were intertwined. His atlas of industrial geography was at the forefront of a larger shift in thinking about a complex network of resource management and production and its potential global reach.

As we learn from MacKaye, there is the potential for collaboration between the distinct fields of economics that focuses on profits and capital issues, land use planning on the value of land, and design on urban form, with each benefiting from the others' specialization. This would broaden a mutual reach for modeling and forecasting, which could be applied to that of returning manufacturing to cities today. Many factors influence a company's decision to locate in a specific place. It is often because it is the home base of the owner; it is the historical center of a trade and of a skilled workforce; or, it is dependent upon local resources and, perhaps, climate. There is much more flexibility with regard to the location of industry in today's global economy than in the past. In terms of the spatial distribution of factories in the urban landscape, formations that fall within the new "flexible agglomeration" combine the post-Fordist shift to a flexible economy with local networking of shared resources and materials in urban clusters.[4]

Issues of agglomeration, according to Alfred Marshall, have been further elaborated to understand urban industrial organization. These pertain to overlapping of expertise, separation of companies into discrete specializations, and spillover in learning processes. These urban traits and potentialities contrast with the self-contained and isolated factories in the hinterlands. Economist Walter Isard (1919–2010) shed further light on economic and spatial issues in land use and industry in what became the discipline of regional science. He saw a natural dispersal of industry independent from zoning regulations because of lower costs beyond center cities, emphasizing the importance of a conscious focus on location and spatial economics in order to enhance manufacturers' needs and those of job retention.

Clusters

Economists, urban geographers, and urban planners have opportunities to evaluate fundamentals of manufacturing location studies and that of clustering. Historically, specific types of industries in selected locations around the world dominated industrial clusters, as discussed earlier. Examples noted throughout this study include the garment and diamond industries in New York City; the auto industry in Detroit; the manufacture of shoes and textiles in Emilia-Romagna, Italy; watch-making in Switzerland, and factory cities formed around specific industries in China, among other countries.

One focus of numerous studies has been the shoe, fashion, and textile industries of northern Italian cities in the 1960s. The Emilia-Romagna region became known as the "Third Italy," and attracted poorer workers from the south. The area made a concerted effort in the 1970s and '80s to foster a vital network of small manufacturers, such as artisanal shoemakers and textile weavers, through economic, technological, and land use assistance. An exchange between manufacturers was close-knit because familial ties formed a trust and synergy between companies.

In the 1980s, when anthropologist Michael L. Blim researched the shoe industries of the Marche coastal region of Italy, he found that the numerous small factories and workshops and home workers that formed the backbone of the industrial areas relied on trust and strong interpersonal relationships for their productive economy.[5] But he also discovered that, despite this collective effort, these enterprises could not keep up with the changeover to computerization at the small scale. The area was home to both larger companies such as Benetton and Vespa, as well as smaller workshops specializing in fashion, textiles, furniture, musical instruments, and toolmaking. A flexible labor force of 2,500 workers was employed by 225 smaller industrial workshops, and another one thousand illegal workers contributed to the fastest growing economy of any nation comparable to postwar Japan. In an era of flexible accumulation, the element of trust between manufacturers in this region, and their "flexible specialization," supported the

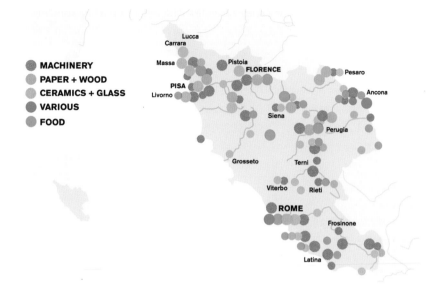

- MACHINERY
- PAPER + WOOD
- CERAMICS + GLASS
- VARIOUS
- FOOD

▲ Industrial production in
Italy's Marche region, 2012

area's ascendance by the 1980s.[6] Even though the small firms received no government assistance, including labor insurance, their industries excelled, and the region became a model in the "emergent neoliberal critique of advanced capitalist industrial decline."[7] This lasted through the 1990s, when the stability of the local small-scale producers was uncertain because they could not adapt to changing markets, as technology was too costly a capital investment. Their rise demonstrates the significance of clusters and relationships, but they could not compete with large multinational corporations. Today there is a small resurgence of industrial clusters in this region, primarily around food produce; shoemaking also continues, but at a smaller scale.

The clustered concentration of industry has inspired a model for new industrial zones in China, each of which has their own specialization after which they are even named, in places such as Socks City, Tie Town, and Sweaters Town in the Zhejiang province. Sectors are organized in a spatial concentration also following trade and land-use regulations. Each of these conditions poses a unique combination of resources and access in spaces set aside for industry, such as economic trade zones and districts zoned for industry. Similar to commercial spaces which congregate specialty shops, such as art galleries or antique shops for the consumer's ease, the groupings of factories are interdependent.

While physical clustering is useful to most industries, it isn't always beneficial to interdependent industries if all don't want to upgrade at the same pace; this can be seen in the steel industry's involvement with unions where they were often in conflict in the 1980s, and then failed drastically. Or, in centers of high-tech industries, one company's failure can pull others down with it when they are all dependent upon the same resources. This occurred in Minneapolis, where a huge decline of tech firms created a domino effect. Toyota's decline in the 1990s was felt across its region in Japan — called Toyota City — as smaller suppliers were impacted by reduced contracts. The same happened to small auto suppliers around Detroit when the auto industry weakened in the late 2000s, indicating the industry's general malaise as they were too closely tied to the Big Three.

As fields of spatial economics and general spatial analysis began to merge in the late twentieth century, some economists expanded their views of the relationship to land and industry, indicating that economic improvement results from proximity in *sharing*, *matching*, and *learning*. Paul Krugman emphasized that costs of trade in a region are more than just that of goods transit — that distribution of goods, the location of the factory, and resources can be combined to create economic models for industrial geography and spatial economics in which activities have multiple cores in much the same way that Christaller diagrammed Central Place Theory.[8] Land value analysis and economic geography, which determine the value of the location of an industry, is not as precisely modeled, or tested. Thus, Alfred Marshall's observation that proximity influences "something in the air" became a legitimate way for industries to organically choose locations and interact with each other.[9]

When other variables, such as free trade, cheap labor, and low-cost materials entered the manufacturing picture in the 1960s, the choice of firm location was broader, and the cheaper hinterland was seen to just as easily connect to the market as the city. However, although factories could adapt to suburban sprawl, and contributed to it, forming the new industrial landscape, manufacturers still had more advantages for trade and consumer proximity in cities. The networked information technology contributed to a nonlinear and unpredictable model for where industry would remain in advanced economies. The new industrial context that capitalizes on a virtual rather than a physical clustering or agglomeration of supply-chain logistics further deemphasized the need for physical clusters. To counteract this process removal, which displaced so much urban industry, governments established new clustered districts and export processing zones to encourage new industrial settlements. What many did not acknowledge was that within cities the change in industry to smaller scale and niche markets with new manufacturing techniques, as discussed earlier, enabled smaller manufacturers using JIT production to compete in the larger market and to reinhabit former industrial locations. This enabled digital networking for a broader community through virtual communications. While there are advantages of using the new resources for many product manufacturing and distribution networks, this infrastructure was not of prime consideration in economic geography models.

Similar to Marshall, urbanist Jane Jacobs recognized the location of industries in terms of how the skills of workers build and develop, first by chance; but then, as businesses capitalize on the region, they fine-tune the production, and invest in training highly skilled workers. In fact, relationships between industries (and their workforces) build upon one another at the metascale, impacting overall production methods, and the new products that are developed, introduced, and improved upon by other manufacturers. Jacobs calls this, "The process of adding new work to old," which multiplies divisions of labor, as one type of expertise can build on the older methods, and as entrepreneurs learn from old industries to build anew.[10] Industrial mix-and-share concepts determine why industries grow in a specific area through a mix of industries, a relationship between socioeconomics, and a region's assets.[11] But Jacobs also recognized that in a large city where there are more diverse products, clustering is not as necessary, nor does it always occur, because a city has a broad base both in terms of employees, potential product sales, and niche markets. In larger cities, companies innovate and are resourceful in the same way that city-dwellers are, with broad networks and intense competition for similar and quality goods available to the consumer. "When new work is added to older work, the addition often cuts ruthlessly across categories of work, no matter how one may analyze the categories."[12] The iterations of work methods disperses both the expertise and the jobs.

Manufacturing clusters often influence regional economic growth because of collaboration and the density of goods produced, creating a cross-pollination, both in exports and local sales. The clusters of industries are in direct contrast to the distances, both physical and social, between suppliers and producers when goods are outsourced overseas. Even though the decentralization of industry networked virtually doesn't require physical proximity to suppliers, production can be enhanced through shared skills and resources, increasing profits because of the expertise developed, the jobs provided, and the transparency of the supply chain.

New studies on urban agglomeration would help to develop a more complete understanding of the spatial and location-based issues of this phenomenon. The nodes of specialization, and skills that workers obtain in a single region, become spatial in terms of the economic production of a given area, as that area becomes associated with a particular trade, craft, or expertise, such as watchmaking in Switzerland. Many governments have been touting this form of industrial clustering as a regional economic solution, and an inventive cycle of industrial ecology could provide a future catalyst for a truly social symbiosis, beyond that of a purely economic model. With more research-based innovation, a new sustainability consciousness can be incorporated to further enhance urban manufacturing that has already developed in agglomerated clusters, as is discussed in the sustainable architecture section later in this book.

Urban Constellations
Economists focused primarily on the understanding of decentralization and its impact on the demise of cities in the 1960s and '70s, but didn't explore as closely the urban factors that first galvanized this movement to the hinterlands in both the U.S. and Europe. Numerous factory towns were developed pre-World War II in smaller towns ranging from those following Jeffersonian ideals to Garden Cities in England. Even Henry Ford developed a series of 19 villages with smaller factories along southern Michigan's rivers from 1918 to 1944, soon after he built his acclaimed Highland Park and the River Rouge complex, harkening back to the rural industrial villages.[13] But, as discussed earlier, World War II had the most dramatic and irreversible impact on the urban industrial landscape, spatially and architecturally, both by the factory's dispersal and its shift to horizontality for new logistic supply chains.

Industrial decentralization and the horizontal factory became a standardized kit-of-parts in the next phase of the generic factory in the 1950s and instrumental to the new logistics landscape. The ubiquitous shed-shaped factories formed a new industrial urbanism resulting from wartime efficiency, bringing with it a new infrastructure that supported development. The nationwide infrastructures of highways, both in Europe and the U.S., opened up new potentials for peacetime industrial development along the same service lines of transit and communications previously used in the war. The logistics and infrastructure of the new manufacturing systems also contributed to a fractured and sprawling degraded landscape. The efforts to return manufacturing to cities would have been too costly, so they remained on the urban outskirts, de-densifying cities and requiring workers to commute by automobile. Instead, the urbanism was within the factory organization itself in scale and density of workers.

Logistics and goods distribution for globalized manufacturing became its own specialization in the 1960s, as numerous companies became experts in delivery and supply, employing fleets of vehicles and trains. The shipping of goods coming from various ends of the earth then became a component of the manufacturing process supply chain involving the ordering, goods organization, and reconfiguration for distribution through the appropriate shipping system. Since the ultimate goal in an increasingly globalized economy was to reach the consumer, integrating the feedback loop between supply and demand with the creation of a combined factory/warehouse/retail outlet became the catch-all functioning vessel. Architecturally, this meant that the black-out shed factories were the perfect typology for a factory landscape of internalized mechanized production for manless storage and retrieval systems in high-bay warehouses.

Volvo, whose manufacturing technologies were described earlier, was also part of the exodus of factories out of cities and the decentralization of factory infrastructure throughout the Gothenburg-Stockholm corridor. Frampton notes in his 1976 article, *The Case of Volvo*, that, "the full benefits of this liberation still stand to be outweighed by the wanton neglect of the most basic resource of all, namely land."[14] This land, as in-between space beyond the city, was a lost opportunity for urban development. It "constitute[d] the wasted interstitial matter — the so called leftover space — of the modern urbanized region, that instead of being leftover should really serve as the cellular organic material that significantly articulates the various aspects of the human domain."[15] This space could instead have been preserved as greenfields rather than developed, and cities could have been densified with industrial growth. The move of factories away from cities, as noted earlier, also resulted in a form of social repression in a contradiction between the socialist Swedish society and the desire for control.

Urbanistically, what resulted was a network where the command centers of companies controlled a broader, decentralized economy, where physical distance no longer mattered as much, until the 1970s oil crisis and the increased prices encouraged a reevaluation. While shipping is one of the components of the economic equilibrium in determining location, its general low cost is supported by the new logistics supply chain. Some shipping companies also mend and repair products, or supply a missing part stocked in their warehouses, which are closer to major shipping hubs than the originating company.

The means of production and distribution removed from the city or physical marketplace that once was the town square results in another index of de-urbanizing manufacturing. As Manuel Castells studied in 1988, the "new industrial space"

is "characterized by the technological and organizational ability to separate the production process in different locations while reintegrating its unity through tele-communication linkages, and micro-electronics-based provision and flexibility in the fabrication of components."[16] This expanded the production space, making new kinds of spaces and manufacturing possible.

Additionally, the "space of flows" of information and transportation networks is a spatial form, "just as it could be 'the city' or 'the region' in the organization of the merchant society or of the industrial society."[17] Castells compares this infra-structure to the way that the railway defined economic regions in the nineteenth century and the nodes of concentrated economic transactions that these regions formed. As new nodes are not tied to cities, they become logistics centers of transit and exchange removed from managers or corporate hierarchies — places such as Chicago's Intermodel hub at Rochelle, Illinois, which Alan Berger would define as a horizontal "drosscape," in that it is a non-place wasteland that destroys precious greenfields and open space.[18] Other mega-scaled hubs like those in Alliance, Texas are supply and delivery points through the logistical chain of command. The ability to ship goods by truck also encouraged the development of intermodal hubs such as those in the southern U.S. that could service the Mexican *maquiladoras*, the border factories, described below. Containerization simultaneously dominated the

▲ *Loaded Coal Train Cars*, Norfolk, VA, 2011. Photograph by Alexander MacLean shipping industry in general as the most efficient way to switch from ship to train to truck.

As Keller Easterling observes, "Global trade involves not simply the control of virtual packets of information, but also the movement of enormous amounts of material between port installations and the logistical fields that form around them."[19] These new spaces contributed to the de-urbanization of manufacturing; the idea of densifying these logistics fields led to sprawl and developed natural spaces. However, the economic efficiency of industrial parks and intermodal hubs, and their concentration, also boost their effectiveness with shared resources.

One of the essential ingredients to this ever-moving global goods landscape is that of the standardization of the shipping container which, like the barrel before it, could move from train to ship to truck with the ease of a dimensional standard that would fit both a truck and train car. The corrugated steel shipping container designed by trucker Malcolm Purcell McLean in 1956, in set dimensions of 12-meter or 6-meter lengths by 2.5 meters high, could be lifted from ship to truck and train by crane.[20] The container became an international standard that lent itself to time- and energy-saving systems and a known quantity that became an accepted transport method globally; it also represented a fluid vehicle for truck transport, to and from anywhere. Frederick Taylor would have approved of the highly orchestrated engineering and connective infrastructures designed to move and maintain the fluidity of the mobile supply chain. The horizontal spreading of logistics, distribution, and communications is not that of the vertical and urban factory, but contributes to the dynamism of space. A formless space, but one shaped by invisible networks and interaction, it is kept in constant motion by the economy of global trade and consumer demand.

In industrial location theory, each country capitalizes on its land assets to encourage and stabilize production economies to create equilibriums and increase GNP. Sometimes economic growth is encouraged by governments, and at others it is more homegrown and bottom-up. In the postwar period, manufacturing location depended on many variables, from land prices to skilled worker availability to government loans or grants that encouraged development, and thus jobs. With the burgeoning potentials of the new consumer society, which has more disposable income, new investment strategies and economic incentives have expanded worldwide. As global trade exchanges broadened, new networks sprouted, both for obtaining raw materials and selling finished products. How the industries then relocate (to capitalize on the economics and logistics of a particular location) in this global paradigm has opened up an intense discourse on the impact of spaces of production on both the communities and employees, as well as on the fragile and increasingly limited environmental resources of the places they inhabit.

▶ **French student street protests in Paris, 1968**

WORKPLACE DEMOCRACY

As frustrations arose from the automation and dispersal of factories in the 1960s, as well as a shift in union management that favored corporations, low wages and long hours, issues that had been rampant in industry since the beginnings of large-scale manufacturing came to the fore. Workers protested in France, Italy, and the U.S. around many similar issues with a specific path to change. With factory worker strikes in France in the 1960s, and Italy and the U.S. in the 1970s, what began as a trickle of activity rose against capitalist control to a fervor of protest. In the 1970s, some agreements made between workers and companies were resolved in terms of time and money or the involvement of workers in management issues, and others had spatial ramifications in terms of factory organization. Alternative methods create what has been called by many the "democratic workplace," envisioned alternatives to the top-down system.[21] While I describe this in a synoptic way, as the topic is larger than that of this book, these issues shed some light on social and spatial relationships in the factory and deserve emphasis from a sociological perspective.

French political philosophers, such as the Situationists International led by those such as Guy Debord and left-wing communist thinkers, contributed to political upheaval in France, inspiring the well-known May 1968 student protests. A split occurred between the "new left" and the French Communist Party and the unions became institutionalized in a social democratic model. At Nanterre University in Paris, students demanded increased rights and greater involvement in their curriculum. The Nanterre campus closed and students continued their protests at the Sorbonne where riots ensued because of police brutality. Factory workers capitalized on the unrest, initiating a general strike. By the summer of 1968, eleven million workers were on strike and a nationwide wildcat strike occurred as the workers fought against union management practices, low wages, and long hours.

Workers protested at major factories during this time. As students joined in the first strikes at the aircraft factory of Nantes, with just a few hundred strikers, the unrest spread to the Renault factory, first in the suburbs and then the Bologne-Billancourt factory was occupied in Paris on May 16. The strikes caught on as other unjust conditions were revealed, such as Citroën's prison-like dormitories. Life there was harsh: workers paid for their own meals, lived in crowded rooms with little heat in winter, had no recreational reading materials or other forms of entertainment, were not allowed visits by either family or friends, and non-resident workers traveled for up to two hours per day to work.

When workers occupied factories, they demanded increased pay, unemployment compensation, and control of their workday beyond what the unions had demanded. At that time in France, one could choose which union to join as the unions were not organized by factory. Waldeck Rochet, the General Secretary of the French Communist Party commented, "It has been said that the student movement was the detonator of the great strike movement by workers, technicians, white-collar workers and civil-servants. Let us note that speaking of a 'detonator' is admitting that there had been an accumulation of tinder in the working class,"[22] which the communist party did not support.

The intellectuals and the workers found common ground in the general strike, spurring new negotiations. At the end of a series of protests the students increased their political focus, seeking to overturn De Gaulle who had fled France in late May. When workplaces resumed their activities almost two months later, amid continued discontent, the strikers won some increase in compensation, and reduction in hours (depending on the factory), and more beneficial labor contracts, which were crafted through an agreement called the Grenelle Protocol. Industries became fractured and internally focused.[23] Surprisingly, De Gaulle was reelected and little was achieved.

In Italy, as in France, the students and the intellectuals aligned with factory workers in their struggle for independence and in gaining a political voice. In Italy, this struggle was even more intense. Often, outside the organization of unions, which were more conservative, the workers strove for a way to fight capitalist hegemony and to harness a new autonomy, which gave them a choice to work, or not work, within the system. Poorer workers in the south migrated north to the industrial belt and there were not enough jobs for all, resulting in a major political issue. Antonio Gramsci's Marxist ideas from the 1930s, and Marxist philosophy in general, was adopted by Antonio Negri and other intellectuals of the 1960s. The women's movement gained strength as women were not included in decisions during the strikes so they started their own initiatives regarding work and homelife against the male-dominated culture, including a proposal for wages for housewives. Negri's focus on labor as part of *operaismo* (workerism) recognized the issues of estrangement from labor (in Marx's terms), or alienation, as workers became alienated from their jobs and society. His group, Potere Operaio (Workers' Power), was involved in the protests and struggles for worker empowerment in Italy, making a distinction between the 1960s of *operaismo* and in the 1970s, *autonomia* (autonomy) as a critic of the communist party.[24] Marxist estrangement to him also meant laborers' refusal to work; their decision to do so resulted from a heightened awareness that they had been removed from the process of decision-making and the control of production.[25] Workers felt alienated politically, contributing to general civic unrest which coincided with an increase in computerization of factory work, as discussed earlier. Beginning with the 1962 strikes at the Fiat factory in Turin and protests at chemical plants in Maghera, not even the unions came to workers' aid because of a new conservative bent.

Negri noted that, "we located the point at which the capitalist mechanism of production could be interrupted by means of a strike or "down-tools," which was a fundamental element in the productive life of the factory and of production in general."[26] The issue of control and the desire to work more independently — not aligned with the capitalist system of constant production — became a stronger goal for the Italian workers who actually started smaller factories in northern Italy as a result. The smaller more family-oriented factories could control the pace in production and operate with hands-on organization better than the French workers engaged in the same debate. To leftist Italian philosopher Mario Tronti, who founded the journals, *Classe Operaia* (Working Class) and *Potere Operaio* (Workers' Power), the worker within the larger society constituted a "social factory," which aligned with the feminist movement as well.[27] The production machine as a society that is the factory involved all people who are exploited in the system, as they are producing surplus value that is then expropriated under capitalism.

In the late 1970s, Italian workers were joined by students and feverish unrest came to a peak in 1977 when a student was killed at a protest in Bologna. In 1978, the Red Brigade terrorist group, which had been sabotaging factories in the north, kidnapped and murdered Prime Minister Aldo Moro and members of his staff. Members of the Red Brigade were prosecuted for this crime. Negri himself was among hundreds of intellectuals wrongly imprisoned in 1979, in a rash of arrests intended to repress left-wing activity and to remove protesters from the political scene without fair trials.[28] This produced no results to improve the plight of the working class. In a third wave of worker protest, which could not be accommodated, Fiat automated their factories and downsized yet again. Many left-wing thinkers hoped for a reorganization as a welfare state, but instead they were left with the status quo of capitalism.

In the U.S., each interest group waged their own protests — students initiated militant uprisings in response to the Vietnam War, blacks fought social injustice, and workers responded to poor factory conditions with strikes and sabotage. Worker protests did not always funnel though union organizations as some unions had declined to participate, but the UAW was the most radical. Younger workers, dissatisfied with their treatment as cogs in the machinery, called for "immediate changes in working conditions and are rejecting the disciplines of factory work that older workers have accepted as routine."[29] Numerous workers filed complaints with their companies and official grievances because of issues such as pay cuts, increased speed of production, and layoffs. They also started to demand more amenities in the factories, such as bathrooms, nurseries, health care, and better work environments. Many workers realized that they could gain more control over their roles in the manufacturing process through their actions and protests, in a similar *autonomia* as the Italians.

THE ABSENT FACTORY

With the decentralized industrial landscape rising to a climax of development in the 1960s economic boom, urban designers and architects missed an opportunity for direct engagement with the spatial issues presented by the crisis of globalization. Even to this day, these issues have not been completely investigated, and, largely, have only recently been acknowledged. At the time of these massive changes, developed countries were ramping up industrial production, expanding their reach through the tactics made possible by globalization. Urban design issues relating to either industrial parks or districts and broader urban economic growth were, notably, not addressed. Urban designers responded with uninspired proposals, primarily because of their industrial clients whose economic restraints they were obliged to fulfill. While numerous Modernist designers proposed new urban spaces in their utopic imaginary projects, industry was not considered as a complete problematic in the same way as housing and civic space. Industry was a more socially significant concern, or was embraced as a method of construction, as in modular housing for speed of mass production as embodied in the work of Ernst May in Frankfurt, but which was disregarded in terms of urban design. Avant-garde designers as capitalist critics depicted industry with irony in various media — pamphlets (Archigram), consciously dysfunctional furniture (Archizoom), along with Pop Art. In contrast, the urban spaces made by or for industry, except by those few design-minded companies, were rarely considered or integrated in an urban design scheme. Andrea Branzi, formerly of Archizoom, remarked that Pop culture:

> demonstrated for the first time that society's center of gravity was no longer the 'factory' as such, with its efficiency and productivity, but what had emerged from it: that is the diffusion of new patterns of behavior and new languages through society. . . . Today the factory works not to realize itself and put its own quantitative logic into practice but to bring about an inexpressible model of prosperity, luxury, and new qualities of life.[30]

Few post-World War II planners imagined ways to solve the overwhelming growth of industry with any kind of utopian factory city, compared with urban planners of the previous two hundred years. Perhaps wartime efficiency and the pragmatist city dominated, or perhaps architects were less frequently encouraged to dream. However, the brothers Paul Goodman (1911–1972), a social critic, and architect-planner Percival Goodman (1904–1989) collaborated on an ideal community, described in *Communitas: Means of Livelihood and Ways of Life* in 1947.[31] The book, which was republished in 1960, expounded on their ideas for a new society both in its physical and organizational form, with a consideration of self-sufficiency and the environment.

While Paul was an instigator of many ideas that led to the 1960s' countercultural movements, Percival was a thoughtful architect, teacher, and critic working on numerous New York City projects.[32] *Communitas* can be seen as a pragmatic utopian manifesto in which they first described other Modern architects' urban plans and concepts as lessons to learn from, and then continued with their own visions for the future, which included identifying more specific places of production and issues of manufacturing in the city.

Combining the initial idealism of the company towns of Lowell, Massachusetts and Olivetti's Ivrea, and learning from the mistakes of the Russian grand plans, the Goodmans devised general concepts as to how to integrate communities so that working and living could be in proximity and not separate. They believed that isolating one from the other is "an outstanding example of social waste in neglecting the principles of minimizing whatever is neither production nor consumption."[33] They further discuss the waste created by the large-scale shed structures in the hinterlands to which workers have to commute unpaid, because it is "always cheaper to transport material than men."[34] They recognized the benefit of concentrating production and the marketplace, which would also free up open space for agriculture and nature.

Their models for a "New Community" fall into three paradigms. In the one titled, "Elimination of the Difference between Production and Consumption," they focus primarily on production. Not proposing to "turn back the clock to conditions of handicraft," they want to achieve the similar values of making things with that of modern technology in terms of an orientation toward efficiency and machine production.[35] Ideas such as small shop production, the increased role of the worker, suitable and flexible schedules, smaller units, self-sufficiency, full knowledge of the end product, and an educational process that grows, all harken back to communal life and the socialism espoused by early eighteenth-century utopian philosophers. The physical shape their utopian city would take would be more integrated, as they recognized the industrial dispersal possible via electricity and the value of work accomplished in the home. They groupped similar industries together, such as those relating to glass, and simultaneously envisioned an integration of the farm into the city, always placing the nuisance factories further away from the urban population. This flow of factory and farm into the city would form a new cityscape of patchworks of green among production.

Placing faith in people, they aimed to have a "different standard of efficiency, one in which invention will flourish and the job will be its own incentive and, most important, at the highest and nearest ideals of external life: liberty, responsibility, self-esteem as a workman, and initiative."[36] These goals for many have never changed, nor have they been fulfilled.

In a subsistence economy, which they believed should be the basis of all societies, production would occur in the center of the city in an efficient design in various configurations according to population. The production and the product are thus integrated in a self-sufficient regionalism in an industrial-agricultural symbiosis.[37] The Goodman's schemes have relevance today for the reconfiguring of industry and living. In separating only the most nuisance industries they understood the definition of industry as more diverse and integral to cities, but other contemporary designers did not emphasize industrial space.

In the 1960s, with new modes of technology and urban communications, the ideas of those avant-garde thinkers with progressive politics — such as Archigram, Archizoom, Superstudio, Metabolists, and members of the organization Team 10 — were focused not on the job and economic-related functions of the city, rather on the dwelling, the community, the transit, and the cultural components. This is evident even when one considers Cedric Price's (1934–2003) Potteries Thinkbelt study (1964–1966), which looked at the ceramic-making region in the West Midlands area of England that came to be known as Staffordshire Potteries (an industrial area consisting of six towns in Staffordshire). In Price's study he proposed that, instead of repositioning the former ceramic-making district into a new industrial community, there was an opportunity to transform the town into a new educational infrastructure that could be as mobile as the newly mobile student population. As he noted, the Labor government focused on education; schools were expanding, the required age through which students had to complete education rose from 15 to 16 years old, and industries were shrinking so that knowledge became more valuable than production skills. Price envisioned a new university in a brownfield, rather than the trend of new towns, by repurposing former industrial buildings for the higher education industry. The industrial buildings lent themselves to transformations into dormitories. His designs for modular industrial prefabricated units would slide onto the abandoned railroad tracks and travel through the region. The

▲ Paul and Percival Goodman, Communitas production center for 50,000 workers, 1947

industry was in the construction systems, not in the new design of manufacturing spaces. Price's proposition exceeded design issues to determine educational priorities and methods of teaching.

Urban design conceptual studies and manifestos — even those radical visions which Cedric Price contributed to, such as "Non-Plan: An Experiment in Freedom," published in 1969 in *New Society* magazine and then republished for the architecture community in *Architectural Design* in May of that year — discussed industrial development as dispersed.[38] In this essay, with critic Reyner Banham, urban planner Peter Hall, and *New Society* editor Paul Barker, focused on the idea of relaxing planning regulations so that more people would be granted greater freedom to build anywhere. This non-authoritarian laissez-faire approach suggested an alternative to the top-down planning of the period. The group wondered if "planning could be any worse if there was no planning at all."[39] However, the plan could be, and was, understood in two ways. On the one hand, as unregulated planning and overall sprawl (undesired) that led to free-market capitalist control of development for gain of the rich, and, on the other hand, as community-based planning that was on the rise at the time. In terms of industry, Non-Plan valued industrial land as much as commercial and residential with unrestricted industrial locations but considered them as a nuisance. The Non-Plan was in many ways just a hoax, a witty response to the over-planning of the greenbelt towns, new city regions, and economic incentive areas in Britain.

Without recognizing it, the essayists would have allowed for a laissez-faire industrial growth, which might arise as constellations for industrialists, not where planning agencies prescribed. "The main thesis of Non-Plan is that, through enabling uneven development, the particularization of occupation, habit and appetite will be more likely to occur in places and at times be best suited to it."[40] Development would occur on an as-needed basis, juxtaposing planned regions with Non-Plan (which has now come to be called *sprawl*). However, one could ask if this Non-Plan was a commentary on the rational organization of factory culture, achieved by negating the hierarchical organization of capital.

For other postwar designers, the mix of uses was becoming more essential and feasible. The rigid separation of functions in the Modernist and CIAM tenets was starting to dissolve and seen as unnecessary, and architects such as those of Team 10 blurred and integrated spaces for work and leisure, yet they did not focus their attention on industrial uses. While Team 10 was dedicated to housing and social service buildings, as well as education and universities, their ideas for infrastructure at the Team 10 meeting in Royaumont, France in 1962 focused their interest on scale and future flexibility. Team 10's inspiration from biologist Patrick Geddes (1854–1932), especially seen in Alison (1928–1993) and Peter (1923–2003) Smithson's Valley Section of Civilizations (1954), did ascribe a place for industry; however that was the extent of their industrial investigation. The role of industry in the city was not defined or detailed, nor were any interstitial spaces designed. They disavowed industry as an organizing principle for the city, in contrast to utopian thinkers of the previous century. It could be argued that, because of the capitalist focus of industrialists, and the more social (and socialist) focus of the postwar avant-garde, architects veered away from the industrialist projects that were not socially integrated or community-oriented. Instead of working to bridge this divide and foster change, the avant-garde found no opportunity to engage industry through design, leading to a polarization that continues to this day.

When one considers that those artists and architects such as the Dutchman Constant Nieuwenhuys (1920–2005), one of the members of the Situationists International, explored ideas of walking the city in a *dérive* — a wandering amble through Paris on unusual routes, often in an inebriated state, to define a psycho-geography, or mental map rather than a standard map, of the city — industry was left out of their meanderings. Constant developed ideas similar to Johan Huizinga's *homo ludens* — man at play as the next phase of human advancement, so he was a proponent of eliminating work altogether to open ample and ambient leisure time.[41] Constant saw the new mechanization and automation of work via machinery and early computing as a time-liberator for additional leisure. "For it is in *this* time that the largest part of our life will be realized: this time will *be* our life."[42]

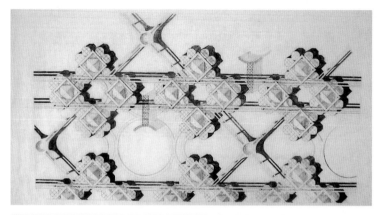

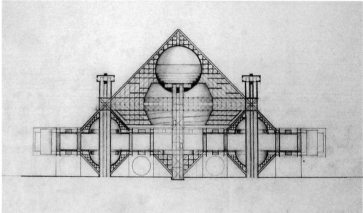

Constant saw creative activities as replacing work in non-utilitarian sections of the city. It was a place of non-work, a place of art. In his project for what he called New Babylon (1959–1974), an experimental urban structure, the idea of work dissipated; there was no space allotted for the worker or work. New Babylon would be elevated, above the historic fabric, layer upon layer, an idea shared by the Smithsons, whose housing blocks included "streets in the sky," and Yona Friedman, whose constructions encouraged inhabitants to design their own living spaces, using space frame structures to promote a more mobile culture of play and creativity, not dull work.[43] His concepts of what we now call DIY formed the same language for new manufacturing processes in the dense cities of smaller industries. This methodology was diametrically opposed to that of mass production of large-scale industry, but is actually guiding contemporary manufacturing today in terms of demand-based production.

Archigram's Plug-In City projects were also about the mobility of urban infrastructure. Rather than using the urban infrastructure of train tracks as in Price's schemes, their buildings moved and plugged in, which then influenced the British architects such as Richard Rogers and Norman Foster with "High-Tech" designs that adopted the aura of factory buildings and infrastructure, discussed below. The factory served as design inspiration, even if it was not formally incorporated at the scale of urban design.

The most direct response, as compared to other architects of the time, was from radical Italian student Claudio Greppi interpreting Tronti's concepts for factory cities, reversing the factory from being one element of the city to the city as the factory itself. This can be seen as a reference to factory cities of the first industrial revolution in the likeness and repetition of industrially fabricated materials mass-produced for the mass production society, as the factory overtakes vast territories. Greppi's student proposal for the textile region of 1965 encompassed the area of Prato, Italy, replicating an agglomeration of similar buildings with cubic units at each end and an endless series of contiguous courtyards. This agglomeration, as a dystopian version of the factory city, was connected by elevated roadways to turn in on itself rather than embracing an urban environment — sealed, as so many factories came to be at the time, as fortress-factory heterotopias removed from worldview, but the world for the worker.

Few architects were engaged in social issues of the workers, as their designs were not meant solve worker conflicts spatially — either in factories or factory cities; instead, designs were often born of cynicism and exaggeration or social commentary in the abstract. The Italian group Archizoom Associati's No-Stop City of 1968–1970 was a singular loft-like space modeled on a gridded factory structure with regularly spaced columns between which people lived with minimal appliances, and didn't work much at all. Here the city became a factory — the ubiquitous space of production in a laissez-faire expanse of urban manufacturing that it would occupy. However, in No-Stop City the potential for repetition of a generic form, and the city as an infinite structure, mocked the consumption-production equation, supplying only minimal goods and comforts. They saw the city as mass-produced and repetitive, just as their endless city's continuous grid would be deployed across all types of landscapes.

COOPERATIVES

During the 1960s, methods for new workplace democracy became fragmented as lack of consideration for the employee and the dispersal of companies eroded a sense of community. While the community within the workplace is not always supportive, the lack of it scatters worker's focus and the need to organize; individual actions instead are strongly felt, such as suicide as a dramatic method of protest.[44] Worldwide strikes or the boycotting of a product can bolster workers' efforts, as seen in the nineteenth century. But the 1980s and 1990s saw fewer strikes, and union membership fell to less than twenty percent. As companies moved to the suburbs, the unions dispersed and further weakened. Unions were also entrenched in their own power struggles, which were detrimental to any common cause. Today, fair trade and labor groups serve as umbrella organizations wherein grievances can be heard beyond the walls of the factory. The provision of employment opportunities, nondiscriminatory practices, safety, health care, and employee benefits have influenced efforts in international labor regulations and the push for living wages.

Besides unions, other means emerged to address worker unrest, including works councils and cooperatively owned companies that would focus on the relationship between employers and employees and the workers' role in more direct participation. Works councils are groups comprised of worker representatives who focus on the factory operations rather than management and benefits, allowing workers to have direct relationships with the management of their companies. In Germany, the councils decided how to divide the hours of the workday and the flow of work. In 2013, Volkswagen's works council advocated for a voice in the new factory in Tennessee, for instance, but the American managers had difficulty understanding the system as the workers were also required to be union members in terms of American standards. Another strategy for workplace improvement included a non-hierarchical management collaboratively engaged with the workers. This approach had proven results at Nike factories in Mexico when the workers participated in direct negotiations with the companies.[45]

The 1970s saw the rise in what was called New Age Management, in which human resource managers focused on the importance of realizing employees' potential, with the aim towards global marketplace competition.[46] Concepts from the Human Potential Movement, which in turn streamed from New Age thinking, were implemented in the workplace, inspiring personal initiative and increased teamwork. For instance, "corporate gurus" were called in to act as "team spirit" leaders and to conduct inspirational seminars. Though such experimental approaches were short-lived, this trend created a new attempt to provide workers with more initiative.

In response to collective bargaining and workers' desires for better environments, factory owners increased worker's amenities such as ventilation, lighting, more collaborative spaces for workers, managers, and research teams. Gradually, the reorganization of worker hierarchy as related to administration impacted factory designs, placing R&D adjacent or close by laborers, rather than in offices separate from the factory floor. The new coexistence became a physical form of integration in the factory. Alternative means for management through cooperative ownership, or increased workers, representation on company boards of directors was also explored.

Corporate methods to effect greater worker involvement include employee share ownership plans (ESOPs), in which the employees have stock in companies. The downside to this is that when company stock drops, the employees suffer the loss as well. Neoliberal employee buy-in schemes were meant to foster class and company solidarity and collectivization of the corporation. The idea of joining capital and skills as well as the institution of a common ideology are seen as beneficial to new cooperative businesses. The most successful worker collective to adopt this approach has been Mondragon in the Basque region of Spain. The Mondragon Cooperative Corporation was founded by a priest and five workers in 1956 (under Franco) and grew to 92 companies in 1980 with 18,000 worker-members. By 2014, that number had increased to 80,000.

As one of the country's largest corporate conglomerates, Mondragon consists of numerous subsidiaries which manufacture all sorts of goods, from electronics to furniture, semiconductors, construction systems, electronic cars, railway lines, and tools, among others. It also has its own infrastructural system for financing, and a training program, and rarely borrows investment funds. The workers invest in the company as owners, pool profits, and manage wages jointly. This system allows them to adapt to changes in demand and, even in recession, maintain full employment.[47] Although this model is hierarchical because of its scale and operates like a corporation, competing in the marketplace, Mondragon's upper-echelon managers are for the most part underpaid by choice, earning only eight times that of the lowest paid worker. Mondragon is organized through a Cooperative Congress and committees with management boards of directors whose motto is "Humanity at Work." They not only have offices in Spain but production centers in the U.S., Latin America, and Europe. Mondragon's mission includes fostering employee participation, training, and innovation, which all contributes to making a profit. However, it too has had its share of problems. In the fall of 2013, in the midst of Spain's economic crisis, one of the major companies in the cooperative — Fagor Appliances — filed bankruptcy and the other sectors of Mondragon could not step in to help. Mondragon rarely produces in developing countries and took on too much debt as they tried to expand, even through their profits were low.[48] The scale of the cooperative and its organization is unusual in the corporate world.

As these efforts demonstrate, worker involvement, both in terms of social engagement and financial compensation, are relatively minimal, but the aspirations towards workplace democracy cannot be understated and is in direct contrast to the organization of the global factory.

SPECTACULAR GLOBALIZATION

The global factory is defined by high-volume, quick-response production, and low cost. It is a factory that is highly dependent on robust supply chains to bring its products from one country to the next without the barriers of taxes, human rights laws, and requirements for health and safe work environments. It is this factory that is depicted with increasing frequency in the media today, with cries of injustice. The memorable images of armies of workers in China, for example, all dressed in the same brightly colored uniform, each performing a single, repetitive task for hours on end in an open room, expresses conditions that are often just as bad, if not worse, than those experienced by workers in the first industrial revolution.

Enormous in scale and network-dependent, these global factories have led to the development of a new, spectacular urbanism. Southern China, Mexico, India, the Philippines, and Bangladesh are all blanketed with instant factory cities that function like beehives for workers amidst the context of a capital imperialist threshold, often leaching from the local economy and the environment in a parasite-host relationship. China has the highest smog measurements in the world, both from carbon emissions and industrial plants. Beijing, the largest city in China, often rates among the worst. In 2013, the city had readings of airborne particles at 2.5 microns, or PM2.5, more than twenty times higher than the World Health Organization deems safe.[49] The government's rush to urbanize and jumpstart full-blown cities that normally would develop organically over generations should incite citizens to call this practice into question. Architects and urbanists have the opportunity to proactively challenge the assumptions of the global factory and rethink the idea of the heterotopic urban factory and workers' conditions in general.

Globalization is not new; the world has been globalized since trade began. Countries and their residents, unable to produce goods, traded them and exported commodities desired on the marketplace. In the mid-nineteenth century, teas, spices, and silk came from the East, to be exchanged for silver and processed opium from the West. At this time, the strength of a country's market could determine that nation's future growth and economic power. The concentration of capital and industry, in general, spurred larger markets for consumers and increased the division between those who produced goods and those who extracted raw materials of coal, iron ore, and metals. The concept of free trade as a political reality followed Adam Smith's vision for all countries to trade without tariffs and restrictions, each desiring to capitalize on their own areas of expertise.[50] Trade was also seen as a way to balance prosperity with political action and international cooperation, especially following World War II, when trade was a path to unification of powers, both political and economic, as new low-tariff agreements united industries and governments. The word *globalization* was actually used post-Cold War to refer to the connections between wealthier countries' economic output that reignited international commerce, but the concept was not popularized until the early 1980s.[51]

Globalization, however, is not an equalizer between countries. It allows some to expand and others to contract because of competition and because companies have been moving to the most advantageous place for cheap labor. More recently, technological forces, international agreements, and policy have spurred globalization, but the public sector pushes growth via financial incentives. Moreover, world trade is tied to a grand macroeconomic system of international finance, both public and private. Each nation has its own political priorities, but formally engage in exchanges with others in meetings such as those of the G20 to negotiate agreements. Limits via quotas (including, notably, The Word Trade Organization's Agreement on Textiles and Clothing and The Istanbul Declaration for Fair Trade in Textiles and Clothing, an agreement between the U.S. and Turkey) on exports for many industries also play a large role in deciding which products are allowed to be circulated freely across borders to safeguard local production.[52] However, in 2005, quotas effectively ended through trade talks of the WTO, opening up and exponentially liberalizing trade for emerging economies. The benefits of border flexibility align with economist Joseph E. Stiglitz's definition of globalization as "the closer economic integration of the countries of the world" and the resultant equal playing field. But the outcome is not always equal.[53] The world is not that "flat."

Globalization is also viewed as a negative economic force. The exploitation of workers remains a horrendous human rights problem, while companies continue the endless search for the lowest-cost labor available.[54] Economists James Petras and Henry Veltmeyer reframe the term "globalization" as "imperialism."[55] They point out that globalization is a mask for hiding the economic interests of transnational capitalists that reinforces greed. Since free market capitalism is inevitable, they emphasize that the concept of imperialism is a more precise orientation for anti-globalization advocates. Cities become centers of production with factories that dominate the former agricultural landscapes and informal craft-based communities, both in multistory buildings in dense cities such as Hong Kong and Dhaka, and in the industrial districts of agglomeration where working and living are separated, as in Modernist planning. This imperialist globalization then acts upon urban development in a way reminiscent of the beginning of trade, in terms of urban design and colonial styles being imported to foreign lands — but this time, in the form of factories. As Petras and Veltmeyer describe:

> The subjects of globalization — the principal traders, investors, and renters of services — have interests antagonistic to those of the objects of their policies — the workers, peasants, and national producers in the targeted countries. What is described as globalization is thus essentially a perpetuation of the past based on an extension and deepening of exploitative class relations into areas previously outside of capitalist production.[56]

While globalization has improved the life of many, providing higher income and better healthcare, it does not always signify progress. Its side effects include spaces detrimental to human well-being and to the environment.[57]

The goals of global democracy, or neo-liberalism, in the twentieth century became fractured: first and foremost, to increase participation in capitalism, which affected tension between responsible economic democracy and capitalism; fair employment and human rights; and environmentally sensitive working conditions. Petras and Veltmeyer emphasize the resulting contradictions: "It is a strange concept of 'globalization' that describes pillage and profit in the same breath as interdependence and stateless corporations."[58] The manufacturers and the political infrastructure that instituted the global factory, both spatially and economically, feed the consumer society and now marginalize workers.

Globalization also contributes to large debts in the countries where products are made tax-free so that not enough funds are earned to repay them, keeping countries in a continuous cycle of dependency, as in Brazil's debt crisis. Within the factories there is no spillover to the communities to teach the people advanced skills that would lead them towards a more prosperous future; thus, larger divisions arise between income levels and work. Today, with globalization, Stiglitz emphasizes that, "we have no world government, accountable to the people of every country, to oversee the globalization process in a fashion comparable to the way national governments guided the nationalization process. Instead, we have a system that might be called *global governance without global government.*'"[59] Inequality in the breadth of globalization reinforces the global "society of the spectacle," to use Guy Debord's term for culture revolving around commodity rather than focusing on humanity.[60] Mass consumption traps society in a cycle of desire and seduction in the supply of goods and their global demand. Wages are not paid as living wages according to each country's economy, thus the divide between rich and poor widens.

Companies subcontract factories to run their manufacturing process as neutral turnkey operations, downsizing their own workforce back home. Outsourcing reduces a firm's knowledge of the manufacturing system; they themselves have no laborers, no architecture, no quality control. Middlemen link these multinationals to the local factories where the interiors can be changed overnight to accommodate different assembly lines and products. Often a manufacturer has two factories, as observed by Isabel Hilton, or they train workers to respond to inspectors in a favorable way, using a cheat sheet that management gives them to memorize.[61] A company may designate one factory that is more human and environmentally sound for the inspectors to monitor, while they have another behind closed doors. These factories epitomize the mobile factory as defined by Jean-Paul de Gaudemar, one in which "this mobility of objects and means of labor, of products and men, as well as of social relationships, appears both as systematization of previous tendencies and as a fundamental element in efforts to resolve the contemporary crisis of the factory."[62] This reduces the multinational's operating costs, with cheaper labor and less overhead. A range of brands can be housed under one roof — products which are inevitably copied by the locals for a black market and those that are higher-end exports. Since these offshore factories manufacture many diverse products, they have no need for image or a factory design; they represent an "unbranding" of capital, an anti-spectacle.[63]

The potential for companies and their architects to form new models for working and living in a new industrial urbanism could lead to the reconsideration of the benefits of former pragmatic utopian ideologies by adding increased transparency. Questions need to be asked as to what this urbanism, inclusive of new industry, becomes, and how it can be a conscious consideration in urban design and planning, even with the economic and spatial issues of globalization.

EXPORT PROCESSING ZONES

In order to understand the spaces resulting from globalization, it is important to examine the mechanisms that have created the global industrial districts — free trade zones. Historically, the free trade zone can be seen as an international method of assisting the growth of countries in need of an economic boost. These economic zones originated in the United States in the late 1930s as a way to encourage industrial development in districts in New York, primarily in seaports. They provided a legal mode of spatially segregating industrial work and living, often separating factories from the rest of the city because of pollution, or categorizing them according to zoning regulations for excessive noise. The latter condition was replete with tax breaks and financial incentives. The zones as clusters of manufacturers became a way for a business to enter a country legally, as seen in the 1959 designation of Dublin's Shannon Airport as a Special Economic Zone after the general depression in Ireland. In 1964, with support from the United Nations Economic and Social Council, Special Economic Zones (SEZs) were created to help companies relocate in an emerging economy in order to take advantage of low-cost labor, an increasingly efficient supply chain, and global consumers. One of the first SEZs organized under the new laws was in southern Taiwan in 1966 and others quickly followed. Different from the more organically grown seaports of international trade, SEZs encouraged manufacturing in a new space for urban industry.

Manufacturers located in Export Processing Zones (EPZ), do just that — process and make things for export. Placing manufacturing offshore, or on other shores, has resulted in a return of pre-industrial working conditions of the nineteenth century, conditions that necessitated worker reforms and empowerment. Taylorist methods of the rational machine and efficient organization were adopted by the factories in the EPZs, which provide easy-to-use spaces for standardized mass production lines. The emerging economies are aggressively pursuing global

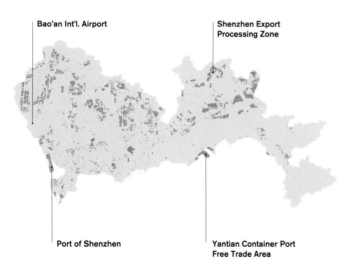

Bao'an Int'l. Airport

Shenzhen Export Processing Zone

Port of Shenzhen

Yantian Container Port Free Trade Area

N

■ Industrial Zones

investments, even while risking the exploitation
of their own labor force and diminished natural
resources. There is a trade-off between the desired
growth and the harsh working conditions, with the
country becoming a tool in political bartering for
aid from developed nations and banks.

EPZs multiplied exponentially from the 1970s
through 2010 and jump-started industrialization
in many countries in East Asia, with numerous
zones in China, including large areas of the cities
of Shenzhen and Shanghai. EPZs are now found
worldwide. They continue to expand as each
country desires to host industries and trade goods
on an open marketplace, with reduced taxes. Their
organization requires filing a series of applications
and approvals from international agencies. A
government reserves a tabula rasa spatial condition
for industrial and business development, providing
a framework of infrastructure for the companies
to plug into, with the attitude: if it is built, they
will come. The EPZ, as an organization similar to a
Business Improvement District, provides infrastructure, waste management, water supply, electricity
(often with its own power plant), and access to
preferential treatment for trade and manufacturing; it is also a completely governed urban system,

as if a standardized industrial district kit-of-parts, or an industrial "plug-in city." As
Keller Easterling recognizes, "If, in the contemporary scene, diverse spatial types
demonstrate the ways in which architecture has become repeatable and infrastructural, then it is the zone that demonstrates the ways in which urbanism has
become infrastructural."[64] The urban structure responds to the economic issues and
employs the format, or ruling system of the EPZ as its basis, so that the city in these
new economies are complete zones in and of themselves. As a blanket of industrial
zones, they provide a way of working that is then understood as being on an even
keel in a global marketplace. They are beyond humanitarian law in many cases,
becoming new heterotopias of isolated industry, but are at the same time part of
the city, with their own management and rules. The local governments of the areas
where the EPZs are located believe that the new factories can provide jobs and
sustainably grow a middle class. However, the foreign companies don't pay tariffs
on the equipment imported to do the work, the raw materials, the final product, or
even local taxes. Furthermore, the corporations don't invest in the local economy
or create technology transfers that would bring skills and new knowledge to the
local communities.

The EPZs are cities in themselves, complete with housing, services, and manufacturing spaces. Their organizational structure is close to a factory district and
industrial cluster, however, not because of interest in shared expertise, as in other

◀ Industrial areas in the
Shenzhen Special Economic
Zone
▲ Worker housing amid the
skyline of Shenzhen, China,
2011

urban industrial districts, but rather for financial incentives and cheap labor. The economic zones correspond to urban economies and real estate value rather than value placed on the urban factories within them as social and environmental spaces. Global corporations, in ignoring the urban and individual design of the factory, which becomes generic and mediocre, gives workers a false impression that their lives are improving.

These discreet industrial zones, many of them designated by industry type, have spawned a disconnect between local contract manufacturers (where goods are outsourced to be made) and the population. Corporate representatives, who rarely visit their contact factories, are criticized for having sweatshop practices — Nike, Gap, Apple, and Wal-Mart are notable examples. The cheaper, unskilled workforce processes a large quantity of goods when assigned to small, repetitive tasks which leads to large conglomerates' interests. Opportunities to quickly build large-scale factories rapidly urbanized formerly small cities with kilometers of sheds and production facilities taking over rural areas. At the same time, their production processes create factories as new cities unto themselves, with rural emigrants moving to the city in waves, densifying previously empty areas in ready-made deployable sheds. The Mexican and the Philippine government adopted similar organizational systems to allow companies to house their export processes, which has had dire social consequences.[65]

Maquiladoras

The North American Free Trade Agreement (NAFTA) reorganized manufacturing away from key international cities and changed its spatial organization. Enacted in 1994, the economic plan of the Americas lifted restrictions on the flow of goods, services, and investment between Canada, Mexico, and the U.S. It eliminated trade barriers and thereby facilitated the exporting and importing of goods. Unions in the U.S. were against the trade agreement because it would move jobs out of the country.

In Mexico, NAFTA contributed to the establishment of *maquilas* or *maquiladoras*, factories which represent the culmination of three periods of state-led industrialization, from a system reliant upon peasantry to a state of proletarianism to individual capitalism. Mexico's industries expanded in the cities of Guadalajara, Monterrey, and Mexico City in the 1950s and well into the 1970s. A state program called Bracero encouraged migrant farmers to work across the border in the U.S. on a temporary basis and for low wages. This negatively impacted the Mexican border towns of Tijuana, Matamoros, La Paz, Nuevo Laredo, Torreon, and Juarez, shifting the geography of production and cutting workers off from the urban unions.

▶ Interior of a maquiladora on the U.S.-Mexico border, 2010

These *maquiladoras* were built on the country's northern borders with the United States. There, raw or semi-finished materials are today imported, without tariffs, to create finished products which are then exported, also without duties. Employing over one million people in sweatshop-like conditions, these factories contribute to Mexico's $178 billion in annual exports, making everything from car parts for Ford, VW, and Honda; to electronic parts for Pioneer and Casio; to sneakers for Nike and Reebok.[66] Following a downturn, in the face of stiff competition from China and other Latin American labor markets, the *maquiladoras* are

seeing a resurgence: since 2006, the number of jobs at these border factories has risen by 680,000, a rise attributable to the recovery of the American auto industry and rising wages in China.[67]

The *maquiladoras* have the same goal as the Bracero program; both take advantage of low-cost labor. Subcontracted by corporate conglomerates, generic manufacturers established the *maquilas*. As in so many development situations that, at the outset, offer the promise of social and economic regeneration, the *maquila* system failed due to inadequate investment in infrastructure. Rather than improving the towns, multinational corporations displaced local industries and exploited workers who were paid below a living wage.

Although the impact of pollution on many of these towns is strong, there is a fear that environmental regulations would stop factory work altogether. Environmental pollution is what economists now call one of the "externalities" that influence the cost of business. Not only is there irregular monitoring of water and air pollution, but hazardous waste is also an issue in many plants. Some have been shut down because of toxicity levels in the earth and water. In the case of the battery-recycling factory, Tijuana Metales y Derivados, the facility's lead run-off flowed into residential areas, contaminating water. After much protest, the factory site was shut down in 1994 and finally cleaned up in 2008, long after the owner had fled the country, leaving his toxic refuse behind.[68] Damage in this form is not corrected by the normal workings of the market. Regulation of environmental pollution would require reduced use of fossil fuels — coal, oil, and natural gas — and would interfere with what developing nations consider their bill of rights.[69]

In the factories themselves, there are minimal safety regulations, clean environmental conditions, or worker benefits, thus leading to a high turnover rate.[70] The workers have a 48-hour workweek and while socialized medicine is made available, not all employees pay into it. For decades now, the *maquiladora* industry has gained over other methods of manufacturing:

> The factory regime that replaced the previous state-led model of industrialization emerged in a distinct pattern, remote from the existing industrial agglomerations. This displacement, although hardly thought out, was fortuitous from the perspective of capital accumulation, because it facilitated the imposition of new norms of employment with minimal resistance.[71]

These types of manufacturing areas focus on how to work in, around, and between the regulations; the only blockages are the power of the labor force and its potential for unrest.[72] Its typical form in developing countries is seen in those industries that employ single young women to assemble consumer goods.[73]

Maquiladora exports generate more foreign trade than any other sector except oil production. Cheap labor is the commodity of the factory that Marx pointed out over a century ago as the most variable. While today American industries on the border find benefits to manufacturing in Mexico — it is cheap and close enough to drive trucks to reach the market — no one pays heed to the workers' conditions and they continue to be exploited. But factories also move away without warning, becoming "migrant," just like the workers. Companies might start to work in a new factory, leaving the old one behind. The challenge of stabilizing Mexico is perhaps a strategy of the corporate nationals, imperialist in attitude, as a way to keep emerging economies from truly emerging.

The ultimate results of interchangeable parts of the new industrial era, is a new imperialist manufacturing strategy — mobile flexibility that follows capital flow. The Mexican *maquilas* epitomize De Gaudemar's definition of the mobile factory: "the obsession with the economizing of time, space, speed makes the mobility of the production process the reference model."[74] Without any sense of social or economic responsibility, nomadic contractors lack rooted connectivity and sustainable interests, and thus move to avoid taxes just when they come to be due. Just as geese migrate south following the warm weather, the outsource manufacturers follow the export processing and free trade zones. And as they pull out, they instill fear in the local workforce. The *maquiladoras* hover both physically and economically in a world that is neither here nor there.

NEW EAST ASIAN FACTORY CITIES

The rise of the global factory of the late twentieth century resulted in a shift to countries that expanded after World War II, especially in Asia, where a new economy emerged from the old, oftentimes based on where there was local ingenuity and skilled workers. A few examples of spatial implications of factory district developments in East Asian cities, described below, inform the discussion of the book's later chapters on the individual factory projects and the global swerve in manufacturing that will no doubt shift yet again in future economic reorganizations, beyond the flexible agglomerations and the next economy.

Japan

In Japan, urban densification and the rebuilding of infrastructures contributed to industrial development along the coast. Japanese entrepreneurs became adept at product innovation and development, which catalyzed their production expertise in automotive technologies led by Toyota (as described earlier) and Honda; photographic technologies by Nikon and Canon; and electronics by Sharp, Sony, and Toshiba, among other companies. These products require precision design from numerous detailed components and specialized metal die-cut molds expertly assembled. The skilled worker networks of craft-like guilds were embedded in Japanese culture and, by producing locally, the nation protected its proprietary inventions, which led to Japan's "economic miracle." Foreign companies tapped into their skills, and those such as IBM built factories to sell locally.

Growth, both economically and physically, occurred with government support from the Ministry of International Trade and Industry (MITI) in the cities of Tokyo, Osaka, and Nagoya. Through the use of landfill and artificial land, factories were able to expand in this tightly knit, island-based economic region. The lack of zoning restrictions increased mixed-use development with industry close to residential areas in cities such as Tokyo. But when a larger site was needed, the government built massive and ambitious industrial complexes with residential uses called *kombinatos* along the waterfronts. These facilitated the importing of heavy industries such as petrochemicals, food, and steel — which also contributed to pollution — as well as warehousing and goods distribution.[75] The 1958 plans were instrumental in inspiring the young Japanese Metabolist architects to envision utopian schemes. Their projects for floating cities, such as Kenzo Tange's Tokyo Bay project of 1960, which would fill the bay with housing and buildings linked by a chain of freeways, or Ocean City project by Kiyonori Kikutake (1962), which would consist of of cylindrical towers with branches of dwellings, combined an industrial aesthetic and mega-infrastructure but did not include specifics on industry. While never constructed, these concepts offered imaginative solutions to future urban growth in general.

Toyota transformed its own region in Aichi prefecture into a factory city and gained a monopoly on all suppliers. Spatially, the company's organizational system changed not only the factory layout of production but also the city's landscape. Toyota City expanded from the seven Toyota factories, employing thousands, to smaller companies in spatial constellations that fed into the primary manufacturing facilities. Suppliers formed a distributed field, as opposed to existing under one roof in a vertically integrated corporation. Instead, a business-networked system

Gross Domestic Product (GDP), 1951-1980
(in billions of U.S. dollars)

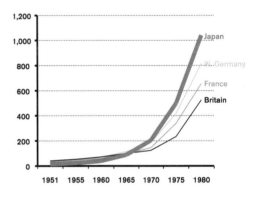

▲ IBM's first factory in Tokyo in the 1950s
▲ Japan's industrial resurgence following World War II

included factories for producing glass, tires, brakes, and windshield wipers as part of the automotive supply chain, similar to Detroit's early-twentieth-century industrial organization. The spatial pattern of dispersed small business units resembles the constellations of new networked technologies in the region.

Manuel Castells has noted that Toyota's network "allows for greater differentiation of the labor and capital components of the production unit, and probably builds in greater incentives and stepped-up responsibility, without necessarily altering the pattern of concentration of industrial power and technological innovation."[76] Even during the oil crisis in the early 1970s, Japan continued on a road to growth by perfecting the production of computers, cameras, lenses, automotive parts, and steel. The country's GNP became half the size of that of the U.S., rising ten percent annually. This earned the country the nickname "Japan Inc."[77]

Two scales of industry succeeded in parallel in Japan: the large-scale heavy industrial production, and clusters of well-performing smaller-scale companies, such as those in the mountain town of Sakaki. With two scales of businesses, Sakaki received MITI assistance to become established as a "technopolis" for high-tech industries in *machizukuri* (town plans) focused on industrial development.[78] Larger industrial districts called *sanchi*, located at the edges of cities, focused on specific modes of manufacturing, from the production of eyeglass frames in the city of Sabea, to more traditional trades. Others, called *jiba sangyo*, operate as districts within the city, where specialized machinists make products for export.

In the late twentieth century, inflation, recessions, and competition from lower-wage Asian Newly Industrializing Countries (NIC) competed with Japanese companies. As a result, the latter began to subcontract to Chinese factories, as seen with the previously mentioned global factory.

Korea

South Korea's industry developed after the Korean War (1950–1953) with the adoption of Import Substitution Industrialization. After having experienced wartime shortages, the government sought to become more self-sufficient and, to that end, provided substantial assistance to select Korean companies and restricted foreign imports. However, this preferential treatment led to corruption and contributed to the collapse of the First Republic in 1960. President Hee Park, who gained his power through a military coup, harnessed the country's fast-paced industrial growth in the 1960s and 1970s through export promotion. This led to increased output and the development of infrastructure, new towns, and factories. It was in this period that the per capita income doubled and Korea became an industrialized country.

Large family-run conglomerates, called *chaebols*, which manufacture products ranging from chemicals and cars to military products, ships, and electronics, were favored with loans carrying reduced interest rates. These companies included Samsung, Hyundai, LG, and Daewoo. The top-down industrialization method limited more consumer-targeted enterprises, creating a trade imbalance. The *chaebols'* eventual debts contributed to the late-1990s financial crisis in Korea. Its aftermath led to reforms through decentralization and more transparent operations. Cities such as Gumi (the largest industrial city in South Korea), Paju (a military and industrial center), and Seoul (the second largest metropolitan area in the world,

with a population of 25 million) developed quickly
into centers of trade and manufacturing.

Paju Book City

Of interest to this study is the Paju planned industrial
district in a special economic zone developed to
focus on the theme of publishing and media. Known
as Paju Book City, it covers a 396,000-square-meter
area at the district's edge. Founder and publisher
Yi Ki-ung initiated the project in 1989 to cluster an
industrial and cultural complex as a "museum
of architecture." The master plan was designed by
the Environment Planning Institute of Seoul National
University in 1999 and the infrastructure was
government-funded. Each publishing or media company then hired its own architects.[79]

Following the contours of the bi-level landscape,
the planners filled marshlands and proposed ten
sectors in gridded units along the highway. They
located printing plants along the train tracks, for ease
of transport, in four longer structures and housed a
distribution center in an artificial hill that framed the entrance as seen from the
highway. Along the main roads, international architects, including Alvaro Siza,
SANAA, Foreign Office Architects, SHoP Architects, and Stan Allen, along with
numerous Korean architects, have designed over one hundred buildings to accommodate offices for the design, production, distribution, and marketing of books.
Other buildings were designed to be manufacturing spaces, such as the Seoul-based
IROJE KHM Architects' plan for Photopia, a large-scaled photography processing
center; this included a workshop, processing space, and outdoor exhibition space.
The architects designed a rectangular glass base to support a curvilinear upper
level sheathed in a purple metal skin so that the structure seems to float in the
landscape, adding a dynamic element to the city's environs. The city continues
to grow with additional new buildings, but is focused on industry and commerce
without residential or neighborhood uses. In its way, it becomes a heterotopia. But
the economic cluster advantage, aggregating all of these various components of the
publishing and media companies together in one place, encouraged the making and
marketing of their products with ease, just as the organic industrial districts of the
previous century thrived with proximity. At Paju, the planners also capitalize on the
new design as a marketing tool. The future of the city will be dependent on the evolution of mixed and electronic media companies as publishing shifts beyond print.

▲ Stan Allen Architects,
Salim Publishing House, Paju
Book City, South Korea, 2009

Kaesong Industrial Complex

In stark contrast, North Korea has developed factories for local employment with
harsh working conditions. In 2005, many South Korean companies established
factories in the Kaesong Industrial Complex at the edge of the Demilitarized Zone
(DMZ). Costing $1 billion, these factories were located nine kilometers north and

inland of the border, where the companies could take advantage of cheaper North Korean laborers and thus compete with China. An industrial enclave consisting of more than 125 factories employs over 50,000 workers, most of whom are women. They are paid a salary of only $110 per month — of which they receive only 55 percent and the remainder is given to the government — but they produce $470 million worth of goods. The factories in the DMZ are built as concrete multistoried buildings in gated clusters within a gridded street layout.

Constant controversy as to whether or not the South should continue to produce in the North has increased pressure on politicians and increased wages. The Kaesong Industrial Complex in particular is seen as a potential negotiating point at the volatile border. Production has been halted several times in the last few years, including in 2010 after the sinking of a South Korean ship, and in 2013 because of the controversies around nuclear testing in North Korea. In 2013, South Korean managers and company trucks with raw materials and food were blocked from entry at the gated complex, and 53,000 workers were not allowed to work in the factories for five months.[80]

Goods made in Kaesong are banned from import to the U.S. because of the political divide, although if other countries start to manufacture products there, restrictions could loosen. In 2014, the North Korean government discussed expanding the complex and opening it up to non-Korean-based firms; but in doing so, they could run up against political negotiations around nuclear issues and, more significantly, sanctions around military and human rights violations.

Hong Kong

In the ebb and flow of industrial development, China is still attracting the most attention from the perspective of urban growth; it has exploded in its coordinated "path to progress" and its dominance in the export market. With that progress comes a well-documented exploitation of people and degradation of the environment.

Long before the factories of Shenzhen were built and evolved the production city it is today, Northeastern China followed the Soviet and Japanese example in providing a home to larger manufacturers of railroads, steel smelting, and mining, which employed about two million people in the 1920s. In the 1950s, the Northeast region of Dongbei (Manchuria) — a massive state-financed industrial zone created by moving industries inland — employed thousands of workers, producing 16 percent of the industrial growth of China. In this district, workers were housed in "model worker villages," and were provided with a state education as well as medical care in what was called the "iron rice bowl" system.[81]

During the Communist Revolution, many workers were reassigned to live in compounds, or *danwei*. These enclaves, while not hospitable on all counts because of the controlling mechanisms, included small factories, offices, classrooms, and dwellings in multistoried blocks functioning as living collectives surrounded by brick walls. This spatial organization was repeated across China from the 1950s to the mid-1990s.[82] The government program's standardized building units could be compared to aspirations of Western nineteenth-century factory towns. Some believe the formation of the *danwei*, because of their combined dormitory and workspace situation, when considered in regards to the typology of Chinese factory settlements, to be the foundation for the industrial district in China today.[83]

Emigrants from mainland China and Southeast Asia in the 1950s gravitated towards cities, where they eventually provided the cheap labor for factories producing textiles, shoes, plastics, toys, and electronics. A subject of urban fascination, low-income residential complexes in the super-dense, multistoried Kowloon Walled City, a former fort in Hong Kong, housed as many as 50,000 people. Immigrants in Hong Kong fueled small cottage industries and developed their own food production chain through informal enterprising economies, made possible by the extreme urban density. For example, women lucky enough to have a sewing machine might work as subcontractors to a shoe factory, sewing the tops of canvas sneakers or other parts.

◄ Gated entrance to Kaesong Industrial District, North Korea, 2011. Photograph by Eric Lafforgue
▲ Workers in a textile factory, Hong Kong, early 1970s
▲ The former walled city of Kowloon, Hong Kong, prior to its demolition in 1993. Photograph by Greg Girard

▲ Woman worker using electrical hand tufting gun, Hong Kong, 1950s
▲ Wing Loi vertical urban factory, Hong Kong, 2013

A combination of British organization, Chinese dedication, and cheap labor allowed the city to flourish. The postwar growth following Japanese occupation of dense complexes of vertical urban factories led to a new vertical urban agglomeration on this small island city. Between 1949 and 1970 the population more than doubled, turning Hong Kong into one of the densest cities in the world, with seven million residents. Along with this population surge, the number of factories more than doubled to ten thousand in the early 1960s when a number of large industrial estates were built in clusters with low-income housing for the new immigrants. The "Made *in* Hong Kong" label reflected the strength of its industry.

In 1978, the Open Door Policy of Deng Xiaoping allowed for new economic reforms, the most notable of which was the creation of the four Special Economic Zones that initiated the economic expansion of China, especially in the Pearl River Delta. Many of Hong Kong's manufacturers moved production to new factories in the mainland, prompting the revision to: "Made *by* Hong Kong," because the management, financing, and brain power remained in Hong Kong and the factories were dispersed to the SEZs. Hong Kong transitioned into a new economic hub as a center of capital flows and economic transactions, and as the city became more expensive to live in. Additionally, social aspects such as growing crime and unsanitary conditions led to the evacuation and demolition of Kowloon Walled City, an over-two-and-a-half hectare site, in 1993. Over sixty thousand factories left Hong Kong for Guangdong Province by 2002.[84] But over 85 percent of the manufacturing exports until this point were processed by smaller firms making products sold through the import-export network; these grew and merged with manufacturers from overseas as the Pearl River Delta developed from smaller-scale producers to larger joint ventures resulting in 200,000 factories by 2012, which employed thirty million workers.[85] This prompted halving the number of workers in Hong Kong between 1988 and 1993 during which time new immaterial labor (finance and banking, among others) increased multifold. When British sovereignty ended in 1997, Hong Kong's export status had already declined. The new label, "Made in China," became synonymous with the instantaneous, large-scaled around-the-clock manufacturing in the Mainland's global factories. This was achieved through a fluid process utilizing managers in Hong Kong and Taiwan who oversaw factory operators in Guangzhou province, for example, and the newly developed container ports. Factory city megalopolises were inserted on former agricultural lands and on artificial land linked by bridges, both cultural and physical.

By 2005, Shenzhen, directly across the river from Hong Kong, became an "instant city." This former fishing village of 280,000 residents at the edge of the Pearl River Delta became a hub for high-tech electronics, toys, shoes, garments, and other everyday products to be sold around the world in an intensity of commerce similar to that seen in the first industrial revolution. The new economic growth on the coast along with new opportunities lured workers from the countryside, causing the population to rise to over fourteen million. In Shenzhen's first seven years, it gained one and a half million people and had over eleven million worker-residents in 2012. The city developed linearly along the Pearl River with simple access and readability. Blocks tangentially connected the disparate economic sectors and allowed for more infrastructure to evolve systematically.[86]

To organize the city, a flexible plan has responded to the potential for market growth and has supported increasing urban concentration at an unnerving pace. From its position as a hub for smaller factories during the 1980s, Shenzhen had grown to be a city of high-rises by 1985, a new city of contradictions and odd juxtapositions through its hybridity. The region of southern China's metropolis is representative of Castells' "new spatial form" — an interdependent unit, economically and functionally, in a single contiguous megalopolis space. The technology infrastructures are united through a system of "flows [that] define the spatial form and the processes."[87]

The flows contributed to advantages for the factory contractors and the transnational corporations harnessing China's new status as "factory to the world." As Andrew Ross describes, the example of China is so stunning, and alarming, in its "jumbo scale of operations, but also in its all-encompassing spread. China is leapfrogging over the technology curve so quickly that it is attracting the highest-level of investments — in product design and innovation, for example — from industry leaders."[88] At the same time, as China skipped the incremental growth of industrial development, it ruptured its culture and made it difficult for its citizens and burgeoning economy to adapt to daily life.

China's new capitalist ideology is now called "socialism with Chinese characteristics," or "market socialism," but its workers continue to be exploited by capitalist interests.[89] Now the second largest economy after the U.S., China has attracted the attention of numerous labor watchdog organizations that are demanding increased transparency. In China, the SEZs are controlled by the central government as industrial real estate developments and are often grouped by industrial types — either through the provision of low-cost, warehouse-type factories for lease, or land for new construction.[90] Many manufacturing sectors are clusters, with each region taking on a specialization and a name to reflect it. Datang is nicknamed Socks City, as 75 percent of the international market's sock supply is produced there. Other towns are Sweaters City, Electronics City, and so on.[91] This identification makes it easy for the foreign manufacturer to arrive and source their supply chain all in one place. Products for different companies using the same materials and processing are made by one factory. This means that sneakers, electronics, and garments made for different brands are actually all produced in the same way; what might differ is the company's design. For instance, one contract factory, Stella, produces sneakers and shoes in five factories in Dongguan for Nike, Reebok, and Timberland.

The factory in China was a significant opportunity for the rural population. Even though factory salaries were only around $100 per month, it was much more than what people could earn on a family farm. In 1990, the government dismantled its industrial investments, causing millions of formerly rural workers to lose their jobs as Deng Xiaoping closed state-run factories.

People from the rural provinces moving to the cities are required to have residence permits, called *hukou,* as well as documentation for social security, health care, and food rations. The migrant workers — just like those leaving Mexico for the United States — are considered a transient population as an element of labor flux. They are temporary residents and are denied benefits as they move from job to job, floating in the labor pool between factories. The *hukou* regulations loosened in 2009 due to the need for more migrant workers in the cities.[92] The workers, as is typical, are often young women — uneducated rural migrants who leave their families for jobs in the city — like the Lowell Mill girls who worked in the textile mills of nineteenth-century Massachusetts. Some live in dormitories provided by the factories, limited in mobility and with little access to amenities. Often they find rooms for rent if the densely packed dormitories are full. Countless stories are told of workers separated from their families, hoping to send money back home and to return to the countryside one day. In the factories the workers are not even allowed to talk as they labor shoulder to shoulder, performing repetitive manual tasks. They work long hours and have little leisure time. A young worker in Dongguan named Wu Chonming wrote in her diary in 1994, as recorded by Leslie T. Chang:

> We start work at seven in the morning and get off work at nine at night. Afterward we shower and wash our clothes. At around ten, those with money go out for midnight snacks and those without money go to sleep. We sleep until 6:30 in the morning. No one wants to get out of bed, but we must work at seven. Twenty minutes to go: Crawl out of bed, rub your swollen eyes, wash your face, and brush your teeth. Ten minutes to go: Those who want breakfast use these ten minutes to eat, but I have seen many people not eat. I don't know if it's because they don't want to eat, or to save money, or to stay thin…[93]

As Chang documented, factory workers in China are often considered dehumanized machines that are installed in factory cities themselves assembled overnight. The scale of industrial employment in China today far exceeds that of the U.S., even in the early twentieth century when, for instance, the Ford Highland Park plant employed a workforce of 81,000 people; today, Foxconn employs 400,000 at their Longha factory, just one of many in the company network. Workers have begun to gain awareness of their situation in a wider context. Journalist Isabel Hilton, who spent years in Chinese factory communities, wrote, "would these peasants be the generation of Chinese workers who, having built the new Chinese economic miracle, begin to demand their place in it?"[94] But the decks are stacked against them — in most industrial zones, government bans unions and workers mistreat workers for taking breaks — whether to organize protests or to go to the bathroom. Inevitably, as workers become enlightened, they become empowered to damage the factory's reputation.[95]

Many of these companies are also physically distant from their maker. The Chinese company Alibaba coalesces the middle-man, who can source the potential manufacturer, and a prospective client overseas. The company organizes production so that virtually anything can be ordered simply by logging on to the Alibaba website and selecting a supplier, with over 1.5 billion products currently available for order, customization, and manufacture. It is a web-based business — one in which the web search giant Yahoo has a $1 billion stake — and which now employs 24,000 people around the world. Calling their group of suppliers "storefronts," they organize the making and the distribution of wholesale goods. To ensure the viability of this online marketplace, Alibaba sources inspectors to check shipments of goods on the loading docks prior to shipping, to ensure the promised goods are present: upon making this determination, Alibaba releases the client's money from escrow, making the payment to the manufacturer itself. Thus, the factory itself remains a space of production — but the mechanism to produce goods has transformed radically. A corporation doesn't even have to visit the factory, and the worker (and their working conditions) are out of sight. The coordination completed on the Internet presents risks: quality control is poor, as Paul Midler describes his numerous examples from shampoo to sneakers, in *Poorly Made in China*.[96]

Dongguan, the nineteenth-century stronghold of the Opium Wars, situated on the eastern side of the Pearl River, also became a boomtown. It became famous for having the first handbag factory — the Taiping Handbag Factory — which was subcontracted by a Hong Kong-based company in 1978. The opening of this factory led the way for the now-standardized system of importing raw materials and exporting finished goods flowing through Hong Kong. Textile and sneaker production was also strong. In the 2000s, realizing the need to have more of a market share, the industrial sector in Dongguan began to shift to electronics and computer parts as companies such as the TAL Group, expanded from garments to monitoring retail systems. Other sectors included home appliance factories, increasing the more labor-intensive jobs.[97] Dongguan evolved into a real city when a portion of workers stopped returning to their homeland and instead stayed put, satisfied with the quality of life. One of the city's economic zones in Qingxi includes residential areas where 90 percent of the 350,000 residents were formerly migrant workers. As author Chang writes,

> Newer migrants have looser ties to their villages. Their trips home are no longer dictated by the farming calendar or even by the timing of traditional holidays like the Lunar New Year. Instead, younger migrants come and go according to their personal schedules or switching jobs or obtaining leaves, and these are often tied to the demands of the production cycle. It is the seasons of the factory, rather than the fields that define migrant life now.[98]

In this new economic growth, China is poised to switch from the unskilled but intensive manufacturing sectors of textile and garment industry to new high-tech enterprises for export. The Chinese companies have been encouraged to produce their own products in order to compete in the global marketplace, and to not be just the factory for the world. The interest in R&D as well as Original Design Manufacturing and Original Brand Manufacturing in Hong Kong and China is creating new entrepreneurial efforts.[99] The national government also provides electronics companies with tax breaks and companies receive R&D support. Ross notes in this next phase of development that even multinationals outsourcing to China's technology and white-collar positions, "threatens the stability of livelihoods everywhere."[100] In the Yangtze Delta, the technology sector has become the focus as Suzhou, Ningbo, and Nanxing (near Shanghai) prospered in 2004. A mix of agriculture and industry in sprawling sheds occupied the new development areas along the Yangtze River. Suzhou, formerly a silk manufacturing base, and still producing seventy percent of the worlds' product, had the second highest industrial output in the country in 2004, with over ninety of the Fortune 500 corporations located there. Two industrial parks in the Suzhou New District and the Suzhou Industrial Park competed for development in the 1990s; after some ups and downs, both are now successful. Each park features residential developments and increased investments, as well as new amenities such as schools and parks. Based on a Singaporean model and late-nineteenth-century company towns, they are attracting more residents because of the amenities such as green spaces and the convenience of the workplace to the home.[101] As the economy changes, so do the towns, becoming more complete mixed-use cities. The rise of tech industries assisting the rising middle class in China represents their third industrial revolution occurring in an extremely compressed time frame.

LABOR ABUSE

Activists and NGOs exposed numerous incidents of labor injustice in China in the press as early as the 1980s.[102] Agencies such as the International Labor Organization have investigated the practice of the subcontract factories used by many multinational companies, and found poor practices. Perhaps the most infamous case of a company involved in globalized trade via outsourced factories was Nike. Following the first reports in 1991, Nike committed many violations of health and wage abuse in its production of soccer balls in Pakistan, and sneakers in Indonesia.[103] But it took until May 1998 for Nike to pledge to follow U.S. Occupational Safety and Health Administration (OSHA) standards and international labor standards to end child labor abuse and to improve working conditions. Nike allowed external monitoring of their facilities in 2002 in Vietnam, Indonesia, and China, and made wage increases, but not without constant outside pressure to do so.

▷ Dormitories at a Foxconn factory, 2010
▷ Workers in a Foxconn factory dormitory, 2010. Both photographs by Jordan Pouille

Foxconn

But these abusive conditions persisted, and in 2011, the Taiwanese company Foxconn Technology Group, a subsidiary of the company Hon Hai Precision Industry owned by Terry Gou, came under harsh scrutiny because of a spate of worker suicides. The company, which produces computer and consumer electronics parts for all of the major global companies, including Apple, Hewlett-Packard, and Dell, among others, is located in Longhua, a section of Shenzhen; its factory is vertically integrated, producing everything from the tools used to bend wires to the wires themselves, the internal workings of smartphones, computers, and cameras in a manner similar to Henry Ford's integrated production line. Foxconn is the country's largest exporter and one of the largest employers in China, with 1.2 million employees.

Foxconn's primary client is Apple. They produced 137,000 iPhones per day in 2010. Although Apple made huge sales profits, that margin did not transfer to decent wages for Foxconn workers. Over 400,000 people work and live in residential compounds at the Longha factory, in effect turning the vertical factory into a vertical campus. This makes its possible for the company to expand its production line as quickly as orders increase. Unfortunately, in many cases, these "dormitory labor regimes" have grueling schedules without days off, overcrowding, unsafe working conditions, and no overtime pay. Employees have a saying that "They use women as men and men as machines."[104] Apple conducted an inspection of the

factory when, in 2006, Foxconn was accused of overworking its employees. The average workweek was over sixty hours, which is longer than Apple allows in their Code of Conduct.

Foxconn has become more than just a campus; its two-and-a-half-square-kilo-meter mini-factory city has restaurants, cafeterias, stores, recreation facilities, and a university, all company-owned. The dormitories are deemed better than rentals in Shenzhen, but they pack the workers densely into shared rooms. Sometimes, there are eight people to a room and as many as twenty people to a three-room apart-ment at the Chendeng factory.[105] The typical building is a high-rise tower with bal-conies where the workers hang lines and lines of monochromatic factory uniforms to dry. Just like their counterparts in any major factory, workers perform repetitive tasks in multistory concrete factory buildings designed specifically for electronics production. They stand or sit in one spot in the artificially lit clean spaces for each ten-hour workday. Underpaid and overworked, employees are often punished for under-production and lateness. Workers' rights throughout history, and the efforts of utopian thinker Robert Owen, who advocated for an eight-hour workday in 1856 in England, have been ignored.

Long hours and monotonous tasks led to suicides at Foxconn factories, as 14 were reported in 2010.[106] Tian Yu, a young woman worker, attempted suicide in 2010, and survived and was interviewed exclusively.[107] Her unhappiness was caused by long hours — often 12-hour days, seven days a week, with no free time — and the fact that her family was 1,100 kilometers away. Tian Yu slept in a

A WEEK IN THE LIFE

AVERAGE CHINESE FACTORY WORKER Based on a 6 day work week of 12 hours a day

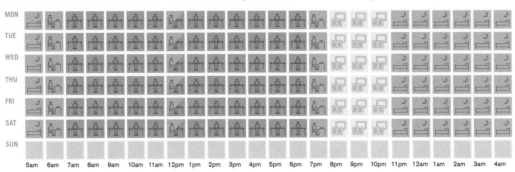

AVERAGE AMERICAN WORKER Based on a 5 day work week of approximately 6 hours a day

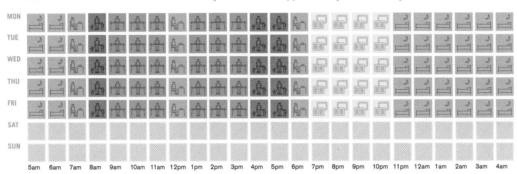

Sleeping Working Eating / food preparation / personal care Household work / childcare Leisure Weekend

HOUR AND WAGE COMPARISONS in today's US Dollars

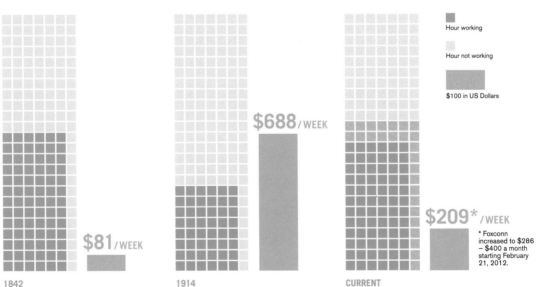

Hour working

Hour not working

$100 in US Dollars

$688 / WEEK

$81 / WEEK

$209* / WEEK

* Foxconn increased to $286 – $400 a month starting February 21, 2012.

1842
TEXTILE MILLS
LOWELL, MASSACHUSETTS

In 1842 in Lowell, the average work day was 13 hours. The average pay for a six day week was $3.50. A half-dozen eggs cost $0.05 and a whole chicken cost $0.15.

1914
FORD MOTORS
DETROIT, MICHIGAN

Ford's wages were $5 a day for a six day week. In 1916, a refrigerator cost $900 and Ford's Model T cost $369. (In 1914, Ford's model T cost $490 each).

CURRENT
FOXCONN
SHENZHEN, CHINA

Electronics factory employees work 12 to 14 hours a day and 6 to 7 days a week. In 2012, a refrigerator in China costs about 2000 RMB or about $316 USD and an economy-sized, Chinese-made car costs around 30,000 RMB or $4,644 USD each.

SOURCES: *Factory Girls* by Leslie T. Chang, 2009; ABC Nightline, aired on February 21, 2012; http://www.loansandcredit.com/how-the-average-american-spends-their-day/

dorm room with people she didn't know, and when she wasn't paid for a month because of an accounting error, she became desperate. The company installed nets outside the dormitory windows, but took this action only after four of Yu's colleagues died. One CNN reporter talked to a young worker at the Chengdu factory who was assemblying iPads; when the reporter showed the device to her, she had no idea what it was.[108] This distance from the product perhaps also contributes to their emotional and psychological disconnect from their work, resulting in alienation and negative sense of self worth. The workers do not even know that the electronic piece they are making contributes to iPad assembly; not only have they never seen the completed tablet before, but rarely will they own one due to their low wages. The attitude is the opposite to Henry Ford's efforts to have his worker own his cars. As the world reacted in horror to additional suicides at Foxconn, in February 2012, many labor rights groups, such as the Fair Labor Association, confronted the company and began to make stricter factory audits.[109] Apple had previously made some effort to regulate factory conditions, but had not accounted for the long overtime hours and low wages. Prior to Apple's first audits, Foxconn coached thousands of workers as to what to report. Conditions at several other Foxconn plants remain unsafe. For example, explosions at poorly ventilated factories in Chengdu and Shanghai — due to a catastrophic reaction between aluminum dust and toxic cleaning chemicals — killed some workers and injured others and could have been easily avoided if the factories were properly maintained.[110]

Pressures from Western consumers and international organizations compelled the company to increase workers' monthly wages by 25 percent.[111] In China, wages generally have risen dramatically from 55 cents an hour in 2002 to $1.45 in 2008 and $2.65 an hour in 2012. At Foxconn, the wages increased from $320 in 2011 to $400 a month. But workers are now considered replaceable, competing with thousands of robots in some factories. The robots cost $25,000 apiece: three years of wages for one worker. However, because of a new labor transparency, and closer observation, some multinational companies have been providing more job training, better conditions, and increasing wages. As wages rise, China is starting to see factories moving away from their shores too.

Quality

As a result of labor injustice, many multinationals have started to contain their supply chain, not only because of the human rights issues but also because of difficulties in production and quality control. In China, as economist Paul Midler notes, "There was a degree of quality cheapening that was the result of mere *corner cutting* — which involved skimping on raw materials or taking shortcuts in the production process."[112] When flammable fabrics are used for clothing in India — as was the case in 1994 — or plastic toys are made of toxic substances, manufacturing becomes a global safety issue that puts into question free trade agreements. Companies migrate to China not only for the cheap labor but also for the manufacturers' speed. The contract factories can produce almost anything and, without industry standards to be met, anyone can set up shop. "Chinese manufacturers had figured out the system, and the convenience in manufacturing that China

◀ Graphic comparison of the wage and daily patterns of workers over time.

afforded was so significant that it forced importers to deal with a great number of drawbacks."[113] With speed and expertise also came a counterfeiting and forgery of products copied by workers from an overseas company's sample or prototype that the workers would just change slightly in production, removing the brand name as well. Many of the factories were not to be trusted, but workers themselves also began counterfeiting and stealing company goods. One example is the case of a shoe factory in Dongguan, in which "gangs practice a vertical integration of their own. One group may spirit shoelaces out of the factory, while another smuggles out soles. The parts are assembled into shoes and distributed in other parts of the city . . . in an illicit assembly of authentic parts."[114] Even here, the counterfeiters have identifiable supply chains.

One former American company, which made colorful ribbons and ribbon products, decided that it just wasn't worth manufacturing in China. As a small start-up, the owner required a leap of faith in terms of trusting the contract manufacturer, and needed a huge investment of capital in inventory, as well as a long lead-time. The idea of lean manufacturing and JIT production could not be pursued from a distance. Quality control also became difficult, unless they hired a local inspector. The chances of designs being revised, color matching being off, and cheaper materials replacing preapproved materials, as well as incorrect labeling, was too great a financial risk.[115] Trust becomes an important variable in a small business with regard to limiting material waste and staying focused on production quality evidenced by reshoring trends.

But, as the consumer economy grows, China has begun competing in the global marketplace, manufacturing its own products for export and beginning to step beyond its role as the factory for the world. China's future will require ingenuity and invention, and the development of global marketplace savvy. China's goal is to raise the standard of living, to increase the domestic demand for goods, and to create a more prosperous country. Even though the party leadership is still strong, state control of corporations is gradually phasing out, resulting in a rising market economy. To make new consumer products, China is looking to new liberal financing and support of corporations as well as international investments, especially by Russia and Korea. A new special zone in Shanghai's Financial Trade Zone (FTZ) was started to liberalize capital flows with the ability for foreign companies to raise money, make investments (including securities), transfer funds, and open bank accounts. This push could catalyze new Chinese brands. Manufacturing costs are also rising in these instantly industrialized cities such as Shanghai FTZ and Dongguan because of the need to improve the quality of goods, the demand by labor for higher wages, and an increase in property value. The higher costs have influenced many manufacturers to "go west" in China, where it is cheaper, and to set up production in other low-cost labor countries such as Cambodia, Vietnam, Bangladesh, and various African nations. This has not occurred without protest by the Chinese, however. Chip Starnes, an American manufacturer, was held hostage in his office for six days by workers who did not want him to move his medical production to India.[116] In addition, the pool of workers has shrunk due to the prospect of burgeoning jobs moving to the service and technology sectors.

▷ Land-use map showing industrial estates near Manila, 2000
▷ Aerial view of the special export processing zone, "La Peza," outside Manila, 2012

Globalizing Manila

In global manufacturing and free trade, some former traditional trading ports in East Asia, such as Manila, Philippines, exploded with new economies rife with instances of opportunism encouraged by political connections. As a catalyst for multiple business sectors, mega-scaled projects are often steeped in hubris when disseminated as symbols of national economies, while they facilitate activities that range from money laundering to exploitation.[117]

Manila, a fast-paced metropolitan region of eleven million people and an economically depressed coastal city on a sheltered inlet of the South China Sea, is representative of issues in imperialism, free trade, and new economic growth via industrial production. The area struggles to keep pace in newly open Asian markets under a blanket of former U.S. policies that established commerce regulations. The city developed as a capital of the Spanish colony, which destroyed its walled Muslim settlement and converted the inhabitants to Catholicism in 1571. Despite constant invasions, Manila was a thriving port and came under U.S. control in 1898 after the Spanish-American War; the Philippine-American War ended in a peace accord in 1902, but not without a fight from the Filipinos, who had not totally accepted American colonial dominance. The elite families invented sophisticated trade mechanisms for sugar trade with the U.S., and the ramifications are still felt today; i.e. a "sugar quota" initiated in 1913 enabled them to export sugar to the U.S. market at higher-than-world-market prices, thus beginning the conglomerates' global trade.

After World War II, Manila became the capital of the newly independent Republic of the Philippines, which the U.S. assisted to reconstruct its economy, government, educational systems, and new export zones. The People's Army overturned Ferdinand Marcos' rule in 1986, and a constitutional system was established. What remains of the U.S. physical presence includes the former Clark Air Base and Subic Bay Naval Compound, which the U.S. was forced to leave in 1992. The area has subsequently been transformed into new industrial development zones under Filipino ownership and is being developed as part of major infrastructural projects in which manufacturing spaces, transportation access, and labor forces are being combined.

In Manila's need to participate in the global economy, especially as part of Asia, the geographic, economic, and human considerations are all integrated in this capital city. As Easterling notes, "The port city is no longer a cosmopolitan marketplace but, rather, a society of hyper-control. It constantly oscillates between

closure and reciprocity as an open fortress of sorts that orchestrates controlled and advantageous cheating."[118] The physical situation makes it well-positioned to accept a network of commerce, airports, and seaports, as well as trade policies to encourage foreign investors, mainly from Japanese and Korean electronics and auto industries. Landed families with ties to Marcos created towns in the ring zones later co-opted by the government to create enterprises for more business to take advantage of the newly established industrial economic zones of Calaba (Cavite, Laguna, and Binan).

The Philippines is fourth in overseas remittances and outsourcing after India, China, and Mexico.[119] ASEAN decreased import taxes, and today allows goods to move more freely, but for the Philippines this has increased competition with Chinese-made goods because, as a result, China will have more trade areas to share.[120] With the strategic development of the numerous factories around metro Manila, the government has, since 1995, sponsored the institutionalization of industrial parks controlled and managed in EPZs by the Philippine Economic Zone Authority (PEZA), and offered seductive incentives to lure foreign and local companies. Managing entities have built infrastructural systems and amenities; there are no taxes for importing raw materials or exporting goods, and there is a promise of outsourcing in a region with low wages. In the Philippines, the EPZs developed under Marcos in 22 zones, also called "ecozones," are touted as integrated areas with commerce, tourism, and industry, (not ecology) as well as adjacent residential communities, which the PEZA advertises as incentives to foreign-based manufacturers.

But the foreign industries coming to the Philippines typically exploit the lesser-skilled workers in repetitive jobs, and as in China, the most desirable workers are female and under 35 years old. Such workers are considered "casual" or "precarious," and have no contracts or benefits. Slipping between the local employment laws and collective bargaining, while ignoring those laws set up by the Organization for Economic Cooperation and Development (OECD), these low-wage workers receive little more than provisions for their food and transportation to work, with no overtime pay.

The PEZA, though a small regional planning office, has the governmental authority, without much interference, to develop these industrial sites and eco-zones, from land management and sales to infrastructure such as roads, sewage, and water, as well as city services (police, security guards, lighting, and environmental support). Organized as one big real estate corporation, the factories are pre-fabricated generic buildings that can be compared to clustered industrial zones with adjacent company towns. But the PEZA is driven by economic control and desire for protection, its self-described goals being to "contribute to the acceleration of the creation of employment and other economic opportunities, particularly in the countryside, and to spur the growth of diversification of exports by encouraging investments."[121] Close to Manila, many of these industrial sites are leased to subcontractors who have no ties to the parent company and who hide their workers and environments from the new factory inspectors. These factories, rather than arising from advanced technology and industrial know-how, are actually "labor warehouses." The multinationals have no interest in the community.[122] As they don't pay local taxes, or any import taxes — they are as virtual a manufacturing space (in terms of integration with the national and local communities) as a simulated production line on a computer screen.

Two SEZs exemplify the issues of industrial development and global manufacturing: Laguna Technopark and Cavite. Laguna Technopark, 50 kilometers from Manila, is strategically sited to be near both the airport and the seaport as well as commutable from Makati. Situated on 387 hectares, it was the first industrial estate in the country under the PEZA, as a joint venture between Ayala Land and two Japanese companies, Mitsubishi Corp. and Kawasaki Steel. Eighty-four other companies — including Hitachi, Honda, Isuzu, Matsushita, TDK, and Toshiba, mostly owned by Japanese and Korean entities — are located there with both plants and subcontractors. Ayala Land is owned by one of the elite Filipino families that also developed Makati. Historically, Laguna had been the "emerald province" of the Philippines; it was a source of rice, vegetables, and fruits, as well as fish. Now it is considered their Silicon Valley, because of its numerous semiconductor plants.

Laguna has its own entity which functions similarly to a business association that addresses the leaseholder's issues in the park. The gated area has a rectilinear plan within which the association manages roadways as well as digital and telecommunications. Buildings are required to have setbacks of five to ten meters, to have a green area along the streetscape, and pockets of open space. There are also civic buildings such as banks, administrative buildings, medical facilities, and fire stations, as well as a customs office for ease of trade organization for the manufacturers and their clients. Ayala Land has also built adjacent executive residential neighborhoods for the elite, separate from the factory zones.

The workers in these compounds are the elements of flux, as De Gaudemar defined. They are expendable because they are cheap. They are only recognized when they form solidarity to protest and express grievances, and such actions occur in either the factory fortifications or the urban spaces which contain them. Striking is both a political and a spatial act. It is spatial because workers strike in reference to a specific task in a certain space, where they are often then regulated against entering or are forced against their will to occupy. As the activist Rosa Luxemburg wrote in 1906, in *The Mass Strike, the Political Party and the Trade Unions*:

◀ Filipino workers protesting outside a factory supplying Wal-Mart, 2008
◀ Workers queuing for overcrowded factory-owned mini-buses in an EPZ, Manila, 2008

> The mass strike: Its use, its effects, its reasons for coming about are in a constant state of flux. . . . Political and economic strikes, general strikes of individual sections of industry and general strikes of entire cities,

peaceful wage strike and street battles, uprisings with barricades — all run together and run alongside each other, get in each other's way, overlap each other; a perpetually moving and changing sea of phenomena.[123]

Food and services can be withheld from that space, and it affects production activities. In the Philippines, the constitution affirms labor as a primary socioeconomic force and mandates the state to protect the rights of workers and promote their welfare. When a strike occurs, the PEZA often has an paradoxical role to play as controller with conflicting responsibilities in the industrial zone.

The Cavite Special Economic Zone in Rosario, is 47 kilometers from Manila, and was established first in 1980 as an EPZ and in 1995 as a SEZ. It was made known through the work of labor activist groups against Nike, whose subcontractors treated workers inhumanely.[124] (Nike has since moved its production out of the Philippines.) Discussed at length in Naomi Klein's 2010 book *No Logo*, the 275-hectare free-trade industrial area has over 280 factories and 62,000 people working in both managerial and factory positions. In it she writes, the incentives for the

> multinationals only reinforces the sense that the companies are economic tourists rather than long-term investors. It's a classic vicious cycle: in an attempt to alleviate poverty, the governments offer more and more incentives but then the EPZs must be cordoned off like leper colonies, and the more they are cordoned off, the more the factories appear to exist in a world entirely separate from the host country, and outside the zone the poverty only grows more desperate.[125]

Cavite's Office of the Governor has a "no union, no strike" policy, implying the free reign of multinationals. While seemingly normal on the outside, the workers' environments are places of social discord. In the fall of 2006, workers producing clothes for Chong Won, which is contracted by Wal-Mart, went on strike and were then attacked by Cavite's zone police and private security guards as they peacefully picketed outside the factory gates.[126] Workers were injured, some were fired, and others did not receive food or water. The company received an audit prior to this, and the factory workers were encouraged to lie about the length of their workday and conditions. The Philippine Workers' Assistance Center requested that Wal-Mart respect its code of conduct and Philippine labor laws. However, two months later, a worker was killed during a protest.

▶ Industrial areas in Dhaka, Bangladesh, 2013

Bangladesh worker injustice

Bangladesh is another emerging economy where flexible manufacturing has migrated. This former center of muslin production is the world's second largest garment exporter, but the growth is coming at a cost to the people, as exemplified by the Savar factory in the Rana Plaza collapse on April 23, 2013, killing over 1,100 workers and injuring thousands of others — mostly women. These workers, like those in China, migrated from their agrarian homes to the city for mundane jobs in what appeared to be a rising economy in the ready-made garment industries. Savar, like so many other factories, subcontracted to multinational companies,

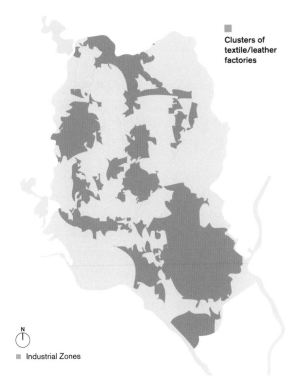

Clusters of textile/leather factories

N

■ Industrial Zones

specifically Gap, H&M, Wal-Mart, Target, and Benetton, among others. It is just one of 4,500 factories that employ 3.5 million workers and that produce over $20 million worth of apparel annually for a worldwide market.

The workers who come to the city live in slum-like conditions in small housing units, not in dormitories as in China. Some work for only nine months and then return home with their salary, which is one of the lowest in the world — only $37 per month for 12-to 14-hour workdays. To commute, workers walk about one-and-a-half kilometers to enter multistoried concrete factories clustered in the dense city.

At Savar, the poor condition of the building was the direct cause of the disaster. If workplaces were more on the radar of both the subcontracted factory owner and that of the multinationals who hire them, these kinds of disasters could be avoided. The factory was inspected and cracks had been discovered; many workers had been sent home during the day, and the commercial shops below had been vacated. But, on the upper floors where the garment factory operated, illegal additions intended to increase the factory space, and, hence, the capacity and profits had been added. The factory owners had insisted on the day of the collapse that the workers come to work despite the discovery of the cracks, otherwise they would lose their pay. The shoddy reinforced-concrete construction that was under-engineered gave way with the additional live load. When the building started to collapse, workers could not escape because of window grills and blocked doors; nine jumped to their deaths. It sounds all too similar to the 1911 Triangle Shirtwaist Factory Fire in New York where 149 women and girls also lost their lives because

the factory doors were locked. Sadly, the city of Dhaka was familiar with factory building problems as this was not a unique case, just the worst.

In November 2012, a fire broke out in the Tazreen factory in the Ashulia industrial zone outside of Dhaka, killing 112 people. It was caused both by flammable fabrics warehoused on the first floor and lack of safety and fire precautions. Like Savar, the Ashulia building had nine illegal stories. Half a million people work in Ashulia; prior to the Tazreen factory disaster, the worker associations had closed three hundred plants because of a wage protest. A local labor activist with the Bangladesh Center for Worker Solidarity, Aminul Islam, was killed earlier that year, as were many others who disagreed with the government (ten percent of whose individual members own garment factories).[127] If the factory owners need additional space they could build legal additions following the building code regulations, thus making these vertical urban factories safe for their workers. In 2014, as international inspectors and engineers toured numerous factory buildings, they found most to be under-built and damaged, with structural cracks creating hazardous working conditions. To assist the workers to create alerts concerning work environments, new NGOs have initiated programs facilitating communication between factory workers via cell phones during emergency situations.[128]

Dhaka is also host to export processing zones, which are customs bonded areas free from cumbersome procedures. Its land costs are low and the city included all essential infrastructure and utilities, including a substation. The factories in Dhaka's EPZs specialize in electrical equipment, garments, footwear, bikes, cameras, luggage, jute and other textiles, and medical supplies.

In February 2014, five multinational companies including Zara, Inditex, and Mango, which contracted to the Tazreen factory, contributed $40 million to the families of the factory fire victims in a fund to be managed by the International Labor Organization.[129] But American companies did not make contributions. In Bangladesh, business organizations and subcontractors, including the Garment Manufacturers and Exporters Association, IndustriAll Global Union, the Bangladesh Employers Federation, and the main Bangladesh coalition of labor unions all support the fund.

The multinational companies, in admitting to the unjust practices of the workplace, can give back to the people who produce their goods by building safe and well-maintained spaces that, in turn, provide a return in the quality of work and workers' self-esteem, which ultimately contribute to a more efficient business and a more just social situation.

▲ A worker cutting textiles at a factory in Dhaka, Bangladesh, 2014
▶ Street scene, Dhaka, Bangladesh, 2014

The question thus remains — how will the fast-paced growth of globalization help emerging economies such as those of Southeast Asia? What becomes evident in studies of these various zones is that, rather than cities that trade in economic competition, it is the zones of trade, from EPZ to EPZ, that contend for multinational attention in the newly imperialist world market. If the common denominators for manufacturing and commerce are mediocrity, dehumanization, and placelessness, any lessons from a century of industrial "progress" are deceptive to the "developing" world and emerging markets.

How can Bangladesh and East Asia, and their high-volume manufacturing, combat negative humanitarian and environmental conditions such as low wages and pollution, while sustaining the existing cycles of making and consuming? As rural populations continue to migrate to cities for work, industrialists and architects can approach factory design in ways that could stimulate worker-friendly environments. Factory cities could provide amenities and integrate working and living, and manufacturers could reduce work hours. With more world attention on worker conditions, the relationship between workers, the factory, and the city could instigate an urban paradigm that is inclusive to manufacturing, while not ignoring its hardships, and stabilize the ever-moving labor population, refocusing design to that inclusive of the factory.

GLOCALIZATION

Complex forces have contributed to the decline of industry that is integrated with urban design visions in developed countries. Some blame it on the never-ending search for cheaper labor "offshore" accompanied by deregulation and tax shelters; others blame it on general economic downturns. Some cite the lack of innovation and ability of specific companies or sectors to adapt to a changing market, still others focus on the rise of computerization, digital technologies, and robotics in the new economy of the third industrial revolution that has dispersed manufacturing in far-reaching supply chains, contributing to the abandonment of urban manufacturing spaces in the Western, or developed, world.

SLOW FASHION

As a case in point, in opposition to "fast fashion," companies could avoid this distant contract manufacturing altogether by producing goods in a method of what is called "slow fashion" in a more direct involvement in production and long-lasting products. In the U.S., new companies such as Zady, Everlane, Nest, and Shinola, and legacy companies such as Pendleton are part of this movement that is similar to the slow food or locavore movement, which focuses on local production that is distributed globally. For example, regional wines and olive oils that gain their unique character, or *terroir,* from the soil and climate, along with product freshness, play an integral part of production and marketing. The companies own their own factories, are involved in the production, and train the workers. Frequently, they are focused on environmental issues and on limiting waste; in other cases, they focus on skills and handcraft traditions. While these clothes or foods cost more, they last longer, and the concept is about holding onto goods, rather than disposing of them immediately as built-in obsolescences or fashion trends. It is another lifestyle choice consumers can make. The like-minded companies use the local production and transparency as a new marketing tool for a new type of consumer who absorbs the corporate rhetoric. Shinola, which is making watches, bikes, leather goods, and now clothing in Detroit, recognizes their workers and documents their workspaces on their website, "The Places Where We Work: American Factories," as an alternative to the global and distant manufacturing; instead, they are glocal, globally distributed and locally made as a new way to brand a company.

Zady's approach to Slow Fashion grew out of its founders' Maxine Bédat and Soraya Darabi's interest in identifying and acknowledging who makes things and where they come from, as well as a desire to avoid abusive production lines outsourced to countries such as China and India. They produce and sell women's wear and menswear, as well as home goods. Their business concept was inspired by Bedat's nonprofit Bootstrap Project, which seeks to revive and retain artisanal crafts from around the world to encourage sustainable economic growth in developing regions. Each item can be traced to its specific maker and its geographic origins, including t-shirts from a family-owned, sixth-generation Pennsylvania textile mill; hand-stitched bags made by a woman in Zambia; and jeans produced in North Carolina. Zady attempts to make its products under fair labor conditions and five percent of total sales are donated to the Bootstrap project. While Zady clothing and goods might be more expensive, and Slow Fashion can be seen also as another kind of marketing tool, the greater cost — given the quality and durability of the product — is to them justified when we send 2.5 billion tons of clothing to landfills annually.

But to make things globally and to assist developing nations, other companies have been founded as not-for-profit ventures. This combination of the local to the global is a method that could gain strength, as long as the consumers who controls demand can change their buying habits. It could also be a strategy deployed in the developing corners of the world.

RISING URBAN INDUSTRIES

As the manufacturing in the regions of the Rhein Ruhr in Germany, Northern Italy, the midlands of Europe, the Midwest, and Rust Belt of the U.S., among other former strongholds of industrialization, began to erode, a state of entropy enveloped these cities as economic recessions — accompanied by property foreclosures, bankruptcies, and mortgage defaults — depleted their populations.[130] Governmental agencies and planners also gave up on their local economies rather than seeking to accommodate new types of industries or looking to collaborative means to reinsert them into the former industrial fabric. Once investments returned, these vacant properties and industrial districts were revitalized with new uses, such as art spaces, residences, or cultural institutions, and the zoning changed to accommodate them; nonetheless, these districts retain some of their former industrial character and infrastructure and so serve as reminders of urban industrial heritage and a strong working class. Some cities have successfully capitalized on their industrial architectural heritage, escalating real estate value, as seen in New York, Pittsburgh, San Francisco, and HafenCity in Hamburg, which changed prime industrial sites to residential and commercial uses in a style of industrial luxury.

Unfortunately, once cities rezone their declining industrial areas for residential loft spaces, or replace factories with new residential towers and commercial buildings, the potential for industry's return becomes nearly impossible. Most real estate developers don't want to see the worker in the city as a reminder of the difficulties of making a living, and because the formerly polluted worker environment is not an attractor for investors. It is city government officials and the lending institutions that decide whether or not industry has "value"; the highest value of land use rarely correlates to what is best for the macro-economy of the city. City planners rely on forecasting by those with an interest in the highest value of the land, which primarily favors residential, not manufacturing uses; hence, jobs are lost. Once cheaper labor moves offshore, a tipping point switches use to the highest return for the land. Land and buildings are not flexible in the new flexible accumulation. They are fixed commodities that can't move, but can be bought and sold. The flux is in the change in value, which then encourages (or forces) companies to sell when their land value increases, and to then speculatively hold it, waiting for the highest bidder, as in the 2013 residential conversion plan for Domino Sugar on the Williamsburg waterfront in New York City. Land use in financially strong cities has turned to categorical systems that assume that there is only one nominal direction for manufacturing and that it must be separated from residential use. However, in new thoughts about urban design and city life, mixed land use and diverse streetscapes are considered assets, as was promoted by Jane Jacobs, among others. The hybrid mix, both of different programs (industrial and residential) within individual buildings, and on the city block, encourages many kinds of growth, a diverse income mix, and a space that is constantly active throughout the day — all of which forges a community, and potential urban vitality, through different kinds of interchange in its elasticity.

Companies that have moved away from their original base have discovered the high costs of global infrastructure, including shipping and expenses related to resolving labor issues — in Southeast Asia, for instance. These conditions are influencing the shift of manufacturing back towards the local in what is called "reshoring." Ecologically minded and human rights-oriented companies are starting to build factories closer to their consumers in Europe and the U.S. More recently, some more established companies have realized the value of making things locally; it is a form of quality control that is essential to their production processes. This can be seen particularly in the high-end garment industry in companies such as Brooks Brothers — though its fabric is sourced in Europe, the company manufactures in Long Island City, Queens, and Massachusetts. By working locally, they can more easily make suits to order, faster and in closer relationship to the consumer. In a 2012 survey of 21 U.S. manufacturers, many were starting to re-shore their manufacturing.[131] Some multinational companies — from Starbucks to Wal-Mart, and even Foxconn — have begun to manufacture products in the U.S. after being offshore for decades; this is improving the job potentials for skilled labor in cities.

However, with urban land rezoned for uses other than industrial, there are few places left for workers. Many heavy industries no longer need spaces in cities, except for those that directly relate to urban use, such as concrete, sanitation, and recycling; concurrently, producers are demanding increased space, but it is costly. When the use is not polluting, and inherently not a nuisance, production can occur in a variety of spaces. How can a new industrial urbanism be created around the products being produced at a smaller scale in cleaner spaces that provide both skilled and lower-skilled jobs in the reinvented urban factory? In recognizing the change in definitions of manufacturing to smaller-scale industries, or those things to be made, bent, or repaired, some cities are actively looking to industry again.[132] Others are still not conscious of the new trends, falling behind in their manufacturing growth as they neglect to explore diverse businesses. Cities need to consider that how we make, makes how we live in order to give value to places to make things.[133]

After the economic recession of the late twentieth century, many city governments provided incentives for manufacturers to move to specific sites, usually in existing industrial districts, but reduced in size. Some cities established industrial organizations and manufacturing groups, provided business loans, or lobbied for reduced city taxes to encourage a manufacturing rebirth not unlike benefits in EPZs. A few urban and economic planners today are proactively working on industrial retention, seeking out companies and individual entrepreneurs in order to support as well as capitalize on the locally made as a brand. The manufacturers that they are backing, such as nanotechnology and robotics, have come to realize that the expenditure of resources necessary to move their larger-scale plants makes relocation unrealistic, or they are building new plants through grants and incentives.[134] And city governments are beginning to recognize the smaller entrepreneurs and start-ups. Some new manufacturers who have moved into former factory buildings are taking advantage of the vast spaces by occupying smaller parts within them. Similar to the original speculative development of the Starrett-Lehigh building, parts of floors or full floors are leased to industries such as printers, machine shops, and garment manufacturers. The infrastructure exists, but often without a future vision.

Through government initiatives and/or private entrepreneurial efforts, a variety of European and American cities have come to adopt two main directions in industrial urbanism — either they support companies clustered in districts zoned for manufacturing, or they sustain industrial networks that take the form of hubs and constellations. In the early twentieth century, industrial districts were formed to cordon off toxic and noxious fumes, among other things. Many started as shipping ports or refinery zones, such as those situated along rivers in major cities such as New York, Philadelphia, Los Angeles, Chicago, Rotterdam, Hamburg, and London. As industry agglomerated, cities would allow these networks to grow in limited zones. "Industrial parks" became the nomenclature for these sequestered districts and some located in Free Trade Zones. What does a park have to do with industry, one might ask? In the 1950s, the term was a euphemism, used to entice manufacturers to move to a designated urban area. Yet, the idea that an industrial zone can act as a nucleus is once again gaining momentum; the initiatives which are generating today's industrial districts inspire manufacturing to return to cities and contrast with the laissez-faire dynamic of the first industrial revolution.

Another mode of industrial development is that of dispersal within cities, which forms patchworks of industrial growth, connected informally with business and supply networks. Although the companies may be located in disparate areas, they are connected by industry sectors, business relationships, or general urban concerns. The constellations can flex and expand with adjacent industries and operate as generative hubs, or centers of activity that spark new growth. Constellations as self-generating or naturally forming systems suggest even further potentials for the future of urban manufacturing that can be increasingly mixed in use, scattered in cities, and omnipresent, rather than segregated. In informal economies, as Robert Neuwirth has shown in countries such as India, manufacturing is everywhere.[135] Things are made and sold but in a more low-key and low-tech method. The lessons from the informal economy, which contributes up to $10 trillion of the world GDP, and sixty percent of the GDP in developing countries, could be applicable to the more formally organized economy, which contributes only $2.5 trillion.[136] The potential for both types of manufacturing settlements — clusters and constellations — to generate or rejuvenate manufacturing in cities also points to a new synergy of skills, tools, and resources, both economically and environmentally.

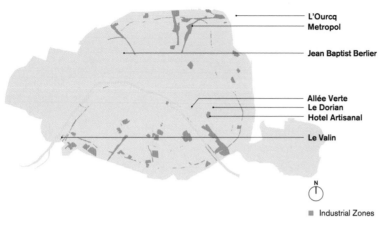

L'Ourcq
Metropol

Jean Baptist Berlier

Allée Verte
Le Dorian
Hotel Artisanal

Le Valin

N

■ Industrial Zones

A discussion of industrial urban-ism in Paris, Berlin, Geneva, Zürich, Toronto, Detroit, and New York, are just a few cities highlighted here, with their industrial urban scenarios.

Paris

An ongoing initiative, the concerted efforts in Paris to encourage and provide space for industries, has been well documented, and continue to serve as important models both for industrial land use issues, economic development, and for innovative urban design and architecture of factories.[137]

Beginning in 1978, through a govern-mental program known as the "Grand Projet de Renouvellement Urbain," the city reintroduced flexible production spaces, called Hôtels Industriels and Pôles d'entreprises, into more traditional industrial districts focused on clustered indus-tries of similar types. These projects served as dispersed production spaces for the burgeoning, smaller-scale production in incubator units. The urban workshops, or ateliers, preserve mixed uses and diverse economic activities in the city. The proj-ects, individual in their design, gradually formed an urban constellation, as the city recognized potential for new industrial spaces, both innovative and visionary, for the new, flexible economy.

The Hôtels Industriels, as flexible, vertical urban factories, support industrial growth and provide designated urban sites for industry, filling the neighbor-hood voids where living and working can happen in close proximity (often in the same building), and provide an intensive, productive, and integrated mix of uses. Rather than releasing industries from their commitment to the city, because of real estate pressures for residential space, city economic development agen-cies required developers to maintain industrial use. On city-owned properties, developers could lease the land for seventy years and then be reevaluated and renewed. Typically, those sites closer to the Périphérique — the main highway around Paris — were used for heavier industries and larger storage warehouses, while those in neighborhoods were mixed in use, lighter industries, and more central.

▲ Industrial areas in Paris
▶ Jean-Paul Viguier, and Jean-François Jordy, Metropole, Paris, 1986
▶ Paul Chemetov and Borja Huidobro, Dorian Hôtel Industriel, Paris, 1991

Paris was also innovative in being among the first to engage contemporary architects to design the industrial projects, often sponsoring competitions between developers, and including architects on their teams. The buildings became part of architecture culture, rather than submitting to banality. Much of this had to do with their urban location. One factory fed off of the other, since they were not hidden from view. Among the first in this category of projects is the Métropole, designed in 1986 by Jean-Paul Viguier and Jean-François Jordy, which is located in the 19th arrondissement at the intersection between the Périphérique and the railroad, and adjacent to a logistics center. The 20,000-square-meter building houses printing, garment, media, and construction industries, and features a shared courtyard for deliveries. The courtyard is one of the main organizational elements of many of these projects as it pulls deliveries off the street and efficiently into the building without interfering with or blocking pedestrians on the sidewalks. The Métropole project is well-situated, being adjacent to other light industries and a vocational school. It also features a flexible allocation of space, allowing for leasable units as small as 102 square meters, into which smaller companies can gain a foothold, then expand as needed into adjacent spaces as they grow.

Another project, the Hôtel Artisanal, designed by Patrick Colombier and Danièle Damon in 1988, combines public housing and six ateliers for light manufacturing. It is located in Faubourg St. Antoine in the 11th arrondissement, which, in the nineteenth century, had a large concentration of textile and metal workers. The architecture featured industrial courtyards surrounded by five-story buildings and residential spaces for the workers. At that time, industry usurped housing, essentially the reverse of contemporary gentrification. By 1935, lower-rise industrial buildings gradually transitioned to residential. A few new Hôtels Industriels were inserted into the community, capitalizing on the arrondissement's artisanal heritage and encouraging entrepreneurial activities in a neighborhood setting. Today, the new ateliers front the street, animating it through the industry of woodworkers and printers. The spaces make the workers visible and integrate them with the city, returning pride to the workplace. Rather than moving workers to the hinterlands, in process removal, it returns working to living.

One of the more recognized projects is the Jean-Baptiste Berlier Hôtel Industriel designed in 1990 by Dominique Perrault through an architectural competition organized by the city economic organization in the 13th arrondissement. Located in an industrial area adjacent to the Périphérique and along an industrial railroad, the glass-clad building has the appearance of a more commercially occupied building, almost as though hiding the industriousness inside. The 80 units that comprise this ten-story building are leased to various manufacturing sectors, including pharmaceutical, technology, and printing, and also to the city-based agency that is encouraging new businesses. An innovative solar shading system on the interior responds to the sun. The building includes shared common services, such as a cafeteria and kindergarten. A new cement distribution center, located nearby, was constructed in 2013, reinforcing the heavier industrial activities in the area.

Architects Paul Chemetov and Borja Huidobro designed a few projects at the mixed-use workshop scale — Le Dorian, Le Valin, and the L'ourq. Le Dorian is located in the midst of an important development zone linked to the new tramway and the Boulevard Péripherique in the 15th arrondissement. In 1991, the project was directed by the Ministry of Defense, which built a

145,000-meter-square-headquarters adjacent. In 2010, architect Jean-Paul Viguier added a new building to the west facade of Le Dorian for French television company's offices joining other media production located there. Other industries housed in the building include pharmaceutical, clothing, wholesale, printing, media production, and advertising.

Other Hôtels Industriels included even smaller spaces such as the Allée Verte, a four-story building in the 11th arrondissement. With 44 units for artisanal and low-tech industries, the five-story Impasse Bouvier is an ovular doughnut-shaped building allowing the services and trucks access to off-street courtyard space. The Cité Aubrey project, which has smaller workshops in the 20th arrondissement, includes a rear lot for truck deliveries to move quickly off the streets. This mixed-use building also has some upper-floor residential units and is in the densest of the residential areas, merging uses seamlessly.

Industrial development continues as a city-based initiative, with the organization of 26 industrial hubs throughout Paris, which provide dynamic and successfully occupied mixed-use spaces or specialized industrial sectors.[138] Paris has thus seen a rise in manufacturing and light industrial jobs and high-tech start-ups because the government has recognized the need to retain these new industries and provide subsidized spaces so that they can mix into the complexity of the city fabric. Mixing residential buildings with suitable light industrial spaces is a win-win situation that maintains job opportunities and adds vitality to the city.[139]

Berlin

Germany continues to have strength in global industrial growth.[140] While its capital, Berlin, has become increasingly a political and creative capital with limited manufacturing employment, historically it was a vital manufacturing center. In the nineteenth century, smaller industries mixed in residential neighborhoods, and larger industrial areas such as Moabit, where AEG was founded, thrived. West Berlin's industry was destroyed during World War II and then was reduced to almost nothing as Russia took control and Berlin companies were sequestered from trade with the West. Postwar, the land use constraint did not permit decentralization to grow into the standard industrial periphery. West Berlin was, literally, an urban enclave. The need to densify and mix industry in the city fabric with vertical urban factories was a reality for industrialists, urbanists, and architects alike, but it was also part of the city's heritage.

When the courtyard complexes densified in late-nineteenth-century Berlin, building use often changed to light industrial with the Hinterhof Industrie (or back courts) in deep internal courtyards that decreased in rent as they were further set back from the street. These mazes formed mixed-use buildings throughout the city. In Kreuzberg, for example, 19,400 employees worked

N

■ Industrial Zones

Siemansstadt

AEG

Adlershof
Industrial Area

in and area of 37,000 residents over 107 hectares, and
the proximity between living and working encouraged
new courtyard industrial buildings to be built.[141] These
deep courtyards also sought to ameliorate the difficulty
of delivery and truck parking similar to the Hôtels
Industriels in Paris. Today these protected outdoor
spaces offer accommodated workshops in continuity
with the past.

In terms of large-scale industries, Berlin is a perhaps
extreme case of change. In the electrical industry, for
example, from 1960 to 1980, the number of employees in
West Berlin halved to 66,000. But industry was still the
biggest sector. By the early 1990s, only seven of the main
corporations still functioned in Berlin, as commerce had
shifted to Frankfurt, Hamburg, and Bonn. In 1989, after
the "re-unification boom," industry in Berlin continued
to decline. In May 1992, Berlin had 223,000 industrial
employees; this was 21.4 percent less than a year before.
In April 1993 there were only 152,900, with a strong
spike in unemployment. Since January 1992, the Western
part of Berlin has had the highest unemployment rate
of the former West Germany overall. However, because
of continued investment in research and development,
more people are employed in industry in Germany than in many developed capitalist countries. Twenty-seven percent of German employees worked in industry in
2003 — five percentage points above the numbers in France and ten percent above
the numbers in Great Britain. Between 1990 and 2003, roughly 330,000 jobs were
relocated out of Germany to Eastern Europe.[142]

Significant in the ability of German cities to mix industry with other uses is their
Bauungsplan, or local categorization as planning regulation — what Americans
would call land use — which allows for more particular regulations on a specific
site rather than blanket zoning requirements for an area. It is founded on ideas
that cross over between land use regulated by zoning, and building codes, which
designate the building massing. As in many industrial cities, industry was to be
separated by zones because of uses that make noxious by-product, as discussed
earlier. For example, Dresden created three of these factory-free zones in 1878.
Another concept was also adopted — bulk zoning, which developed out of use
zoning — to segregate heavy manufacturing from residential zones and to organize
different parts of the city based partially on variations in the cost of land. This was
adapted in Frankfurt in 1891, where manufacturing was typically along railroads
and the harbor. However, light manufacturing was allowed in some residential districts and industry and businesses were not completely excluded from any district.

◀ Industrial areas in Berlin,
2012
▲ Werkhof, Berlin, 2012

Today's *Baunutzungsveordnung* regulates the land use and zoning in Germany.
Its significance is that it is regulated on a site-by-site basis rather than encompassing holistic restrictions for larger districts. Within the blocks, mixed uses, including
industrial, are allowed in residential areas if it is not deemed noxious. Developers

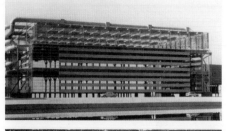

with their architects submit a *Bebauungsplan* that indicates the height and setback of buildings, floor area, use, and traffic concern, which is reviewed on a case-by-case basis and evaluated by the city planners for the site in consideration.[143] Workshops and non-disturbing industries that would be classified as "light" are allowed in the same street as residential buildings. This can be seen in the reuse of many of the old workshops in the mixed-use courtyard buildings in the heart of areas that seem to be residential. If the uses are already allowed on the block or area, it doesn't deter a developer or industry from building, and they don't have to go through legal zoning changes for their desired use. The potential for mixed and diverse uses is thus encouraged at a basic level, providing for dynamic opportunities in the city.

It is rare that a city government embraces the investigation of the design of industrial areas and sites with the purpose of reinventing industrial culture. But, prior to the Berlin Wall's 1989 fall, the city took on the challenge of location and expansion of an industrial city in workshops called "Berlinmodell Industriekultur" or "Industrial Culture — the Berlin Model," as well as a competition to focus industry or urban culture.[144] This occurred at a time when the city was trying to reposition itself in terms of trade as a part of the fledging European Union, and was percolating ideas in the political and urban design realm. The efforts were parallel to the International Building Exhibition (IBA) of 1988 and was simultaneous to the city's nomination as the "European City of Culture."

As many cities, officials recognized changes in urban manufacturing methods when the economy was stagnant. Wolfgang Nagel, of the building and housing department, noted that, "the workplace must be reinstated as an integral part of the city. More important, the workplace must in turn provide impetus for the reinstatement of urbanity."[145] He recognized that the issues of housing and workplace, as well as the improvement of the factory environment, were essential to urban culture. The Architektur und Stadtebauforum, or architecture and city building forum, united planners, architects, urbanists, trade unionists, politicians, and economists to investigate how industry could be increased in the city and how it could mix with residential zones in the third industrial revolution of new technologies, flexible manufacturing, and ecological concerns. The project involved a policy paper, workshops, and then an ideas competition in 1988. The committee invited 22 architects from Germany, the UK, and France to come to Berlin, including Jan Kaplicky, Richard Rogers, Helmut C. Schulitz, Jean Nouvel, and Claude Vasconi, among others.

▲ Helmut C. Schulitz project for Bosch, Spandau, Berlin, 1989
▲ Aerial view of Aldershof, Berlin, 2012
▶ Industrial areas in Munich
▶ BMW's multilayered factory, Munich, 2013

The compact sites for the architectural concepts focused the designs on multi-storied factories, along with the need for more environmentally and aesthetically interesting buildings. Architects were assigned to one of four different sites and programs, not only to design projects but also to explore philosophical issues of working and living in Berlin. The scale varied from a large factory to smaller workshops for companies such as Rotoprint, Erco, Bosch, and Heliowatt, which would be future models for industrial urbanism. The architects and planners addressed issues of human scale, removed hierarchies in the workplace, and integrated the factory with urban design issues such as loading, distribution, gardens, and upper-floor residential and commercial space, as well as recreational amenities. Only one project was built that followed the concepts, which was for the Bosch dishwasher factory, which then closed in 2005. The other design concepts resurfaced in the architects' independent later projects.

As Berlin city planner Dieter Hoffman pointed out, "What the city needs is a new combination of living and working, and if a community wants to achieve this it must insist on the visible presence of those who ultimately determine its fate. It would be sheer folly to absolve industry from its responsibility for the city and the community."[146] And he recommended "that the small and the midsize enterprises should be encouraged to revive the old idea of factories occupying single stories in multistory buildings."[147] These concepts directly support the idea of reusing larger vertical factory buildings within a new urban industrial ecology at available sites in the city. However, Berlin was repositioned as a capital city when the Wall came down, and the urgency of industrial growth was not the same — only a few factory plans were considered. Instead, the city focused on the development of a cluster of science and high-tech industries at Berlin-Adlershof in a new technology park where research in new solar and advanced technologies today are being pursued, but nothing is manufactured. The emphasis on research and design has fostered the growth of ten research institutes, all of which capitalize on the highly educated workforce available in Berlin, and enables high-valued intellectual property.

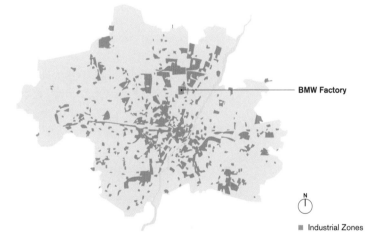

BMW Factory

N

■ Industrial Zones

Munich

Another German city government that recognizes the significance of industrial development is Munich, BMW's stronghold and the location of numerous technology and science institutes as well as universities. However, despite all of these resources, Munich also struggled to maintain industry amid pressures from globalization and off shoring to China and Russia. Christiane Thalgott, the head of city planning from 1992 to 2007, envisioned the potential for new industries to remain in the city and the synergy necessary for industry to thrive. She formed a trade and industrial area development program in the early 2000s that responded to a previous industrial decline of the 1990s

and encouraged the fostering of connections between the numerous institutions and the university, as well as the key industrial players. The recession of the late twentieth century narrowed the city's focus to land use and industry.

A New High-Tech Initiative of the state of Bavaria, as well as other institutional initiatives, supported entrepreneurship and growth.[148] The program's main goals were to build new buildings and to renovate others in order to encourage the region's burgeoning new biotechnology and medical technology industries. The city worked to retrofit the existing buildings with enhanced communication and Internet technologies, as well as to provide them with infrastructure for large-capacity utilities and waste management areas. Thalgott also emphasized the importance, to thriving cities, of large industrial facilities so that work can be more integrated into city living. For her, "The quality of urban planning is evinced therefore in the linking up of the different norms of work and dwelling in the city."[149]

With the initiative and the philosophy of the city planning department focused on encouraging industry, companies such as BMW benefited. Their factory buildings continue to adapt to the new urbanscape, forming its own industrial district. But, in order to expand, the company has inserted multiple floors and mezzanines as an interior vertical urban factory. While the technical universities and government-funded groups like the Fraunhofer Institute, mentioned earlier, have numerous research initiatives, it takes the encouragement of the government to establish industrial growth and private venture capital to implement projects for high-tech and bio-tech enterprises that build on the region's long-time tradition of innovation during and post-world wars.

Zürich

In Switzerland, the pride of local production, represented by the *Made in Switzerland* label, is both a branding device and a sign of craftsmanship. The nation's skilled workmanship and design quality for products such as the Swiss Army Knife, chocolate, Sigg aluminum bottles, ski lifts, watches, not to mention heavy machinery and tools, are stamped with the Swiss-made label of authenticity.

For a product to be "Swiss Made" it has to be sixty percent Swiss. Industry is retained in long-established urban industrial districts in multistoried buildings in cities such as Zürich and Geneva, while manufacturing has also moved to urban edges, spread along highways in colorful metal-clad sheds. Each region tends to specialize in an industrial sector, continuing manufacturing traditions. Swiss industry has adapted to changing economies due to constant innovation in new technologies, precision instruments, and watchmaking, among others.[150] Recent migration of large-scale industries has

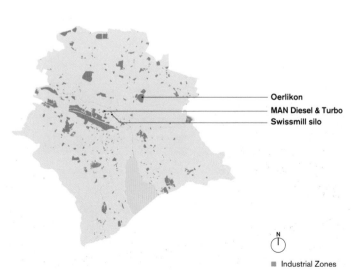

Oerlikon
MAN Diesel & Turbo
Swissmill silo

N

■ Industrial Zones

given some buildings new life both for industrial and other uses. While Zürich University of the Arts moved into the former Toni-Molkerei Dairy factory, discussed earlier in this book, in Zürich West, other companies such as MAN Diesel & Turbo, a large-scale energy and turbine company, reoccupied the former Escher-Wyss turbine hall nearby. This machinery space was perfectly suited to the new turbo plant, a collaboration with Shell, BP, and Statoil oil companies. The area was formerly home to a brewery, shipbuilding, and the gear-works company, Maag. However, the new Zürich West development is a mix of gentrified hotels, restaurants, residential, and office space. At MAN, one thousand skilled workers now assemble machines for new electrical generation by natural gas and oil. Major turbine companies such as Sulzer, in Winterthur, also converted their vast multistoried turbine halls and manufacturing buildings to residential and commercial use, but turbine companies are again in demand for efficient energy-generating machinery, a promising direction for this longstanding Swiss industry.[151] At the smaller scale on the edge of Zürich West, entrepreneurs can lease workspaces under the Viadukt Arches, renovated in 2010 with architects EM2N influenced by the Passages des Jardins in Paris. Ateliers, housed in stone arches that support the train track, mix with retail spaces and restaurants. This hybrid enclave represents and reinforces a new urban ecology of making and working within consumer culture.

Another large-scale industry in the city is the Swissmill (or Kornhaus), a flour mill along the Limmat River. The 170-year-old mill, which continues to occupy a series of its original multistory brick buildings, produces thirty percent of the grain consumed in Switzerland (a country proud of the quality of its bread). The company's 2015 concrete silo addition rises a total of 118 meters and was built by Implenia and designed by architects Harder Haas. The mill runs on new technology to produce an organic substance, similar to Oliver Evans' mills of the eighteenth century. The mechanisms are wrapped in a skin that is an extruded vertical volume over the district.

But a great deal of industry moved out of heart of Zürich to larger industrial areas clustered in districts in Oerlikon, just to the north. This region of industrial growth dates back to the late nineteenth century, when railroad access increased trade. Convenient to the airport, the 2.6-kilometer-square town, with 20,000 residents, now houses the heavy industries of ABB Switzerland and Bombardier, each employing 600 workers, along with numerous high-tech and medical industries. Freitag, the "urban luggage" company, also moved from Maag Areal in Zürich, to a new building, called Le Noerd, discussed below. The city is expanding Oerlikon's 1998 master plan to Neu-Oerlikon to incorporate housing made increasingly accessible by expanded train service, parks, and other public amenities. This combination of residential and industrial uses is developing in a systematic way, yet appears organic; the trend could inspire future mixed-use communities.

◀ Industrial areas in Zurich
▲ Swissmill, Zurich, 2014
▲ MAN Diesel factory, Zurich West, 2013
▲ Viaduct, Zurich, renovation by EM2N, 2012

Residential buildings and commercial areas mix with new parks and recreation spaces, building a town that incorporates the workplace.

Geneva

In Geneva, a politically and culturally oriented city with a large expatriate population, industry has dispersed from the center, but a revival in the watchmaking sector for the one percent has formed a strong cluster of new buildings in a district built on former farmland called Plan-les-Ouates. This district has historic precedents in urban watchmaking spaces, representative of an economic geography relating to skilled workers in the city. Watchmaking is a craft that is supported by time-honored traditions coupled with new technological advances and affords small urban spaces.

The epitome of a watch industry town is the Swiss city of La Chaux-de-Fonds and the adjacent town, Le Locle, located in the Jura mountains, near the border with France. Here the craftsmanship and the metal industries evolved into a strong industry in the sixteenth century. In 1870, ninety percent of the residents worked from their homes and farms, as cottage industries, until a new architectural typology of multistoried workshops developed in the towns. Marx even visited the area, and was impressed with the supportive chain of labor. A watchmaker made the internal movement, then the rest of the watch was fabricated by other craftsmen — jewelers, case-fitters, gilders, engravers, and enamelers — participating in a close networked system of individual craftsmen, rather than being housed in a singular integrated factory.

In the late nineteenth century, a fire devastated the region, but provided an opportunity for Moïse Perret-Gentil and engineer Charles-Henri Junod to develop a new gridded street plan with multistoried buildings, facing south for sunlight, and suitable for fine productiion handwork. Residential areas and workspaces were intermixed, with apartments in the floors above the factories, providing a unique ensemble, similar to industrial mountain towns of Premana, Italy or Eibar in Northern Spain. Many know La Chaux-de-Fonds as the birth-place of architect Le Corbusier who in his youth was employed in watchmaking workshops of his family, influencing his industrial bent. With the American manufacturing method of interchangeable parts introduced in the late nineteenth century, a rationalized and more systematized factory ensued in Europe as well. In the 1960s, new residential and manufacturing blocks were developed in which watchmaking continues in village-type settings.

Geneva's watch production hub in the eighteenth-century was the neighborhood nicknamed La Fabrique, a section of Saint Gervais, where 5,000 of the community's 26,000 residents

Geneva Airport
Saint-Gervais

Plan-les-Ouates

N

■ Industrial Zones

worked in the trade. The typology corresponded to buildings in La Chaux-de-Fonds with multistory ateliers built adjacent to homes; they were characterized, by well-lighted enclosed porches on the upper floors, suitable for precise and close handwork. Here the case-maker or *cabinotier*, working with the watchmaker, would craft the casings and jewelry to house the watch movements and mechanisms. The *cabinotier* used small, flexible workbench units along the facade. Hydroelectricity powered larger-scale workshops, distributing energy to small piston engines and then dispersing the power. The shutting down of the pumps at the end of the workday required excess water pressure to escape through a valve that emptied into Lake Geneva. This, in turn, created the renowned Jet d'Eau fountain, which connects the act of manufacturing to a spectacle of energy, as a marker of public activity.

In 1968, Japanese watch companies such as Citizen, excelled in transforming much of the watchmaking industry through their use of quartz crystals and electronic mechanisms. Influenced by their mass production methods, the Swiss company Swatch, which also owns Tissot, Breguet, Longines, Omega, and Harry Winston, instigated a rebirth of the Swiss watchmaking industry in 1980, making low-end but well-designed plastic watches and movements for other watch companies. Swatch's co-founder Nicholas Hayek realized he could capitalize on the regulation that to be considered Swiss-made, sixty-percent of the watch had to be fabricated in the country, which would include the housing and movement mechanisms. Both a marketing and a production initiative, Swatch would benefit by supplying numerous other competitor companies with these basics. Hayek believed in the economics of making locally, noting that, "We must build where we live. When a country loses the know-how and expertise to manufacture things, it loses its capacity to create wealth and its financial independence."[152] However, after Swatch gained a mini-monopoly and stopped making the guts of watches, the smaller companies had to engage in new technologies, even though they were ill-equipped. But Swatch won a legal battle in 2011 that originated in the company's opinion that they were unfairly investing in R&D for other watch companies. Some of the larger companies began to make their own movements and reorganized their manufacturing system; and Swatch continues to make movement parts for the smaller companies.

◀ Industrial areas in Geneva
▲ Aerial view of La Chaux-de-Fonds, Switzerland, 2010

The expansion of the watch industry, spurred also by the demand for luxury goods from emerging countries like China, influenced growing industrial districts such as Geneva's Plan-les-Ouates, which shifted from agricultural to industrial production. The factories could hire nearby French workers from the border towns for lower wages. One industrialist in this group was ahead of the game, building an incubator space with multi-tenants at the beginning of the area's development in the 1980s. Today over six-thousand workers are employed in the industry.

In the factory of the "spectacle," after Guy Debord, companies are competing in attractive building design to reflect their innovative brand. For many, the ability to invite potential clients into the factory became essential to showcase workmanship and integrity. Operating in a fashion-driven industry focused on authenticity, watch factories showcase a brand's values. Building sites zoned for industrial use include Patek Phillipe's historic home, with its museum and series of buildings. The Vasheron Constantin office and manufacturing facility, which architect Bernard Tschumi designed after winning a competition in 2001, comprises an undulating metal skin that wraps the six-story volume and the horizontal manufacturing spaces in one fluid form. Completed in 2004, the north and south sides are glazed to allow both indirect and direct sunlight to penetrate the interior. Inside the woodclad spaces, precision work occupies the hands of 350 specialists in clean, quiet, and airy workshops. The ensemble is visible from the highway and calls attention to itself as a new attractor for the watch industry. Tschumi has designed another 7,000-square-meter manufacturing building to open in 2015.

In this expansion trend, other watchmakers have enhanced their facilities: architect Pierre Studer designed Piaget's 2002 factory, and the jeweler Harry Winston erected a new glass box branded with the company's logo. Rolex's 2012 secretive factory is the size of two soccer fields, but prohibits visitors both in this complex and at their movement factory in nearby Bienne, arousing increased curiosity. Others imbue the factory with the idea of event as BIG architects has designed a new museum and "experience" center for Audemars Piguet to open in 2015 in Le Brassus, Switzerland.

The community of watch manufacturers, while competitive, is enhanced in their proximity, intensifying the potential for a strong identity. In Plan-les-Ouates, the gradual dispersal of factories among farms is comparable to many Swiss industrial districts; a pastoral expertise giving way to urban industrial ingenuity. Focusing on this small, fundamental instrument, a luxury consumer good, there continues a synergy with the legacy of manufacturing in the region.

▲ Bernard Tschumi Architects, Vasheron Constantin, Geneva, 2005

NORTH AMERICAN GLOCALIZATION

In North America, a resurgence of interest in manufacturing in metropolitan areas to reinvigorate urban economies provoked attention to reshoring, or what is called insourcing, in the 2010s. As a kind of wake-up call, cities maintaining older industries initiated programs to encourage start-ups and new industrial partnerships. In line with the English economist Marshall's nineteenth-century theories regarding industrial agglomeration, some cities focused on clustering in established industrial districts, following a particular city's zoning codes — most dating from the 1960s. Other cities began to shrink industrial zones as the economies declined, and some were laissez-faire in their approach, waiting for private enterprise to take the lead. But, given this uncertainty and need for flexibility in urban space, some permitted constellations of development that then form community networks. Yet, the mind-shift required to support industry has not occurred at the bureaucratic level. Planners and urban officials, many of whom follow an old model of large-scale industrial production that they consider defunct, have yet to recognize the transformative possibilities for new kinds of industrial production in cities today based on innovation technologies. Some investigations into industry and its new spatial organization in the cities of Detroit, New York, and Toronto demonstrate the potential for new paradigms of manufacturing, which would not only sustain existing industries but grow new ones; these can be achieved both through city-led initiatives in land use, economic growth, and through entrepreneurial endeavors.

DETROIT

Detroit epitomizes the shrinking city, which are those cities that have lost populations because of declining jobs and services; Detroit now relies on individual ingenuity to rebound. Formerly a stronghold of industry, the city revolved around the automotive sector as home to 41 auto manufacturers in the early twentieth century. Capitalizing on the expertise of skilled workers from other industries — iron workers from the cast iron stove business, machinists trained in engine works, and metal workers from the bicycle trade — entrepreneurs such as Henry Ford, the Dodge brothers, James Ward Packard, and Carl Graham Fisher, among others, could tap into manifold resources. Gradually, the automotive industries consolidated in the mid-twentieth century along the railways and waterfronts, leading to the formation of the "Big Three:" Ford, Chrysler, and General Motors. In 1947, 3,772 auto-related manufacturers employed 338,373 people in Detroit.

Chrysler factories include the Dodge Main (now Hamtramck) and Lynch Road plants. The original factory was demolished in 1991 and in its place was erected an 82,000-square-meter manufacturing and assembly plant designed by Smith, Hynchman & Grylls containing a body shop, a paint shop, and trim, chassis, and final assembly areas. The first Jeep Grand Cherokee was built here. The core central services building includes administrative offices and an energy center as Chrysler renovated the body and paint shops in order to build multiple car models simultaneously; it expanded in 1999 and again in 2005. Today, the plant has 46 kilometers of conveyors, 600 robots, and over 2,500 employees assembling Jeeps and Dodge cars.

Another area, Hamtramck, or Poletown (named after its Polish residents), was also developed for industry after General Motors, which through eminent domain received eighty hectares from the city in 1981 to build a 91,000-square-meter plant. After five years of contentious battles between the community, the city, and the company, a Supreme Court ruling resulted in the displacement of 4,200

▲ GM Hamtramck-
plant, Detroit, 2012
▲ New Center Stamping,
Detroit, 2012
▶ Industrial areas in Detroit

people. This paved the way for the demolition of a number of buildings, including the 1910s Dodge Main Plant, one of the largest in the city, leading to the construction of a plant costing $500 million. Originally built to manufacture Cadillacs and Buicks, the production in this factory has fluctuated widely. The company is now producing the Volt, which won a European automobile award in 2011. However, production was paused in spring 2012 for five weeks due to low sales, but in 2013 it reversed, becoming the highest-selling electric car ever.[153]

Between 1947 and 1963, urban residents and industry in many cities began moving to the suburbs. This occurred in Detroit as well, resulting in the loss of 134,000 manufacturing jobs. The decline of jobs, and with that, economic inequality, exacerbated civic strife, and racial tension and led to the uprisings of 1967, along with rampant arson and crime. Detroit simply could not rebound from this dire situation. "White flight," facilitated by a massive highway system (the first mile-long section of paved concrete highway in the U.S. was poured here), and easy-to-secure loans for mass-produced housing — in what could be called an assembly line of suburban life — caused the population to shrink from two million to one-and-a-half million by 1970. That figure had dipped to under one million by 2000, and 700,000 in 2013. This was not unique to Detroit, and the negative impact was contagious.

The shrinking-city phenomenon has been recognized in other mono-industrial Rust Belt cities, such as Youngstown, Ohio; Baltimore, Maryland; Turin, Italy; and Dresden, Germany. A new global concern for this plight was documented in Philipp Oswalt's 2006 *Shrinking Cities* exhibition, which both analyzed the cities' decline and displayed proposals for urban renewal — solutions ranging from vacant sites used for urban farms and food production, to the introduction of more parklands, and larger residential lot sizes.[154]

In Detroit, the decline felt in industrial production vacated the urban core, with industry leaving the city for larger swaths of land elsewhere in the state. By the 2007 Economic Census, only about 472 factories existed within the city limits, providing 38,019 manufacturing jobs overall. In terms of the impact on land use, in 2013, 28-square-kilometers of industrially zoned land were 22 percent vacant and only 64 percent active. Philadelphia, in comparison, currently has 61-square-kilometers zoned industrial, with 49 percent maintained for industrial use. While the government bailed out many companies in Detroit, it didn't bail out the city, and in 2013, the City of Detroit, declaring bankruptcy, was unable to provide basic services, including police patrols, the maintenance of traffic lights, electricity, and trash collection.

Coleman Int'l Airport
Chrysler Jefferson Plant
Packard Plant
GM Hamtramck Plant
Milwaukee Junction
Taubman Center/Shinola
Omnicorp

N

■ Industrial Zones

The loss of jobs is felt with greater force in mono-industrial towns. In Detroit, many factory buildings remain vacant and decaying while others have been erased completely as victims of arson and the bulldozer. Despite the reduction in jobs, the Big Three auto industries maintain their dominance in the city, even if it is weaker than before.[155] During the 2009 recession, the companies all received billion-dollar government loans, mainly to improve facilities rather than to hire more workers. Chrysler received $238 million for capital investment on two Michigan facilities; Ford received $1.3 billion for capital investment on six Michigan facilities; and GM received $35 million for capital investment in their Hamtramck plant. The Italian company Fiat bought out GM, and investments infused plants outside of the city with opportunities, including partnerships between research institutions and universities.[156] Michigan still promotes itself as the nation's automotive production hub, with 22.3 percent of cars in the U.S. being made there; it also proclaims its shipping port — a center for cross-country shipping — as the third international gateway in the U.S.

In Metropolitan Detroit, as of 2013, General Motors still employed 25,813 people; Chrysler Group, 25,733; and Ford Motor Company 39,134 people.[157] Ford has returned manufacturing to the River Rouge plant with a new Ford F-150 that, as of early 2014, had 4,000 jobs. Cadillac and Chrysler also saw an increase in jobs in their plants outside of the city. A LG-Chem Lithium-Ion Battery plant opened in Holland, Michigan, thanks to a number of government grants to promote this new technology, and despite being buffeted by a scandal over misuse of its grants, recovered its footing and made its first shipments to American automakers in September of 2013.

Some new zoning regulations proposed in November 2012 in Detroit could assist in the location of more factories and commercial space in the city. One of these regulations establishes a "Transitional Industrial" zone, which allows for the slow development of light industrial businesses in residential districts. Another zone for Special Development: Technology & Research inspired campus-like R&D centers, where some commercial uses (but no residential) can be located. This is seen in the development of Techtown, a public-private partnership that serves as an incubator facility and attracts small businesses, linking them to investors and

tech support. The Special Development: Riverfront Mixed Use zone allows for lofts, offices, commercial uses, and tourism on the waterfront, but bans "intense and abrasive" industrial activity. Residential use is prohibited in all industrial districts, except for cases in which an entire former industrial building is being converted to residential lofts, and industrial-residential mixed-use structures are not permitted. While heavy industry is generally undesirable in neighborhoods, urban plans that might limit the location of industry through districting in the case of Detroit, stunts urban growth.

As Krugman and Marshall described, location of companies in clusters can encourage knowledge and supply exchange. Traditionally, larger corporations rely on smaller suppliers to make specific parts when not all parts are manufactured under one roof. In Detroit, the network of smaller manufacturers still make parts for the larger auto companies such as New Center Stamping, whose lights glow among the abandoned industrial buildings at the Milwaukee Junction, an industrial area developed in the 1890s. That area also housed the Ford Piquette Avenue plant and then later Fisher Auto Body. Established in 1991 in a 85,000-square-meter three-story building, the New Center workers make the sub-assembly of surface panels for Big Three automobile factories, just as Fisher and Murray Body companies did in the past. The company makes large metal stampings and welded assemblies; however, rather than fabricating the parts by hand, it uses robotics and laser cutting to produce hoods, doors, bumpers, and other metal parts, retooling for the future.

▲ Milwaukee Avenue indus-trial area, Detroit, 2012
▲ Ponyride shared manufac-turing space, Detroit, 2012
▶ Watchmakers at the Shinola factory, Detroit, Michigan, 2013
▶ Leather goods craftsmen of the Shinola Factory, 2013

But other smaller companies have started up in the city, reinhabiting former industrial buildings. Most of these incubator factories are not in industrial districts but dispersed throughout the city. The Detroit Future City Plan of 2013, recommended districts zoned solely for industry, but Detroit is a city in which dispersed industries as constellations on numerous sites could be beneficial if land and resources could be made available for industrial use.[158] The new smaller manufacturers could be located in former multistoried factories, rather than occupying large land parcels as the automotive factories did in the mid-twentieth century. The new smaller factories could become hubs for redevelopment with a potential for new housing and commercial spaces in the mix. The potential for the future of urban manufacturing as industry's deleterious effects diminish, make urban factories less intrusive; there is now room for diverse and multi-use programs for smaller and lighter industries within the urban core. For instance, a new zoning plan could be coordinated to highlight business goals and capitalize on unobtrusive industry, by designating an entire city as a U.S. Small Business Administration Historically Underutilized Business Zone (HUB Zone). This program gives advantages to businesses located in these zones when bidding on state and federal contracts, and encourage industrial growth in these areas. Combined with new zoning protocols that allow, or even incentivize mixed-use development, such a program could help foster the restoration of American urban manufacturing.

In this dispersed industrial spatial organization are new maker spaces in shared spaces such as Salt & Cedar Letterpress in Eastern Market, a former meat-processing district. This enterprise is an artist-run letterpress shop (with educational component for the public). The interest in public support has led investors to Detroit. Goldman Sachs' 10,000 Small Businesses program is investing in Detroit through education programs and helping entrepreneurs create jobs and economic opportunity by providing greater access to capital and business support services.[159] Detroit-based foundations such as the Kresge Foundation, are hoping to cultivate small businesses and participate in the New Economy Initiative.[160]

Other cooperative spaces have taken shape around community-based initiatives such as Ponyride, which purchased a 30,000-square-meter building in Corktown. It includes Detroit Denim, a blue jeans manufacturer that also has made accessories such as belts and bags since 2012. The owner, Eric Yelsma, began the company after going through the process of making a custom pair of jeans for himself; it has since grown to twelve employees and exemplifies new entrepreneurship and local production, focused on high quality and attention to detail. Also in the building are typographers, dancers, artists, designers, and apparel companies who share resources that they couldn't otherwise afford if working independently. This scenario for shared space both fills existing spaces and is more flexible so that companies can grow and shrink as needed.

Detroit's bicycle manufacturing heritage also inspired the start-up of three new bike companies in the 2010s. The company, Detroit Bikes, on the city's west side, has benefited from a new interest in biking promoting an environmental and health value. The company was started in 2012 in a 1,500-square-meter space where up to 100 bikes are produced per day. A second company, Detroit Bicycle, has its facility on Elmiera Street, making retro-style bikes for the new hipster culture.

But it is the brand Shinola, a part of the company Bedrock Manufacturing that took its name from the former Detroit-based shoe polish company, that has seized the limelight in terms of reinventing urban manufacturing in a high-end niche market. In spring 2012, Shinola opened a small manufacturing facility for watch-making and bike assembly in the former Argonaut Building designed for GM by Albert Kahn in 1928; the 9,000-square-meter space is located on the fifth floor of the Taubman Center for Design Education at the College for Creative Studies. Envisioned as a laboratory workspace that would make products in the U.S. and train workers, some of them former auto manufacturers, they teamed with other manufacturers to carve out a new niche enterprise. RONDA AG, a Swiss watch manufacturer, is the parent company through which workers are trained in movement manufacturing and watch assembly. The Swiss parts are shipped to Detroit, where workers sit at rows of tables with task lights, assembling the traditionally crafted watches with precision. The retro bikes are assembled via a longer-reaching supply chain, as the frames are made in Wisconsin and then the five different-style bikes are assembled in Detroit. Other products — from leather goods to lifestyle items — comprise this luxury brand that emphasizes, "Where America is Made." Shinola embraces slow fashion, of products made well with care — although watch parts are Swiss-made and the production is what comes together in Detroit.

While such small industries can help the city grow, the scale of urban renewal is daunting. Some of the vacant properties are almost too vast to reinhabit. One hopeful new property owner, Fernando Palazuelo, holds title to the former Packard Plant. At the end of 2013 he purchased the concrete and brick ruin that occupies 16-hectares, and has begun plans for a mixed-use industrial, commercial, and residential development, which will implement a new idea for mixed-use projects.

Along with these recognized brands there are also new maker spaces at an even smaller scale. As the Museum of Contemporary Art Detroit's (MOCAD) 2012 *Post-Industrial Complex* exhibition demonstrated, numerous local artists and artisans are engaged in home-grown production, as many have ideas but few resources. Operating at one of the smallest scales of the city, Jeff Sturges started a not-for-profit organization and collaborative workshop in a church basement, the Mt. Elliott Makerspace. Residents share skills, tools, and materials, and learn how to shape things, take them apart and put them back together again. Other community-grown entrepreneurial nonprofits focus on the new local food culture that has taken hold in so many American cities; one such group, FoodLab, now numbers three hundred members who share resources and information about food processing and distribution.

▶ Industrial areas in New York City

As Detroit journalist John Gallagher notes, social enterprises, employee-owned cooperatives, and incubators are the new direction for these depressed regions, rather than tax incentives and government loans, which result in cycles of boom and bust.[161] Detroit's locally initiated resurgence could become a test bed for how manufacturing can disperse into constellations in former industrial cities, rather than be located in one zone. The idea for rezoning areas of the city to allow for new intensities of mixed uses in unexpected places could also contribute to a renewed industrial growth that could stitch together the abandoned lots, creating a new urban ecology. One can ask how a single focused Motor City can rewrite its story — beyond zoning and hard economics, how does a city reframe its own narrative for the newly defined industry? With the potential for reinvention, "Made in Detroit" has the added benefit, more than just symbolic, to revitalize the city based on its local industrial heritage. Even the automotive and music companies are reinvesting in the city as a re-newed brand.

NEW YORK CITY

In the 1960s, New York City continued as a bastion of production. With 28 percent of the Tri-State region's workers engaged in blue-collar jobs, it was still the largest manufacturing city in America. Its industrial fame and economic dominance were largely based on its extraordinary port and over 800-meter-long waterfront, its vast infrastructure of shipping networks, and its burgeoning population. Manhattan's factories south of Central Park engaged a workforce of half a million people.

A century earlier, New York was the United States' largest local market and had the widest global reach. The 1893 *King's Handbook of New York City* described "armies of brewers, myriads of iron workers, cohorts of cigar makers, and great numbers of makers of pianos and furniture, of boots and shoes, of hats and caps, of sugar and molasses."[162] Slaughterhouses lined waterfronts, as did salt and sugar producers. Ships carried goods up and down the Hudson, along the coast, and inland. The largest sectors of production were apparel, printing and publishing, and food — these were consumable products that required close proximity to the market, or they demanded a fast turnaround due to fashion trends, or time-sensitive information. While the breadth of industry is hard to imagine now, manufacturing was everywhere. It was not relegated to a few districts, it was not hidden, but it was integrated into urban life, for better or worse. New York was a factory city — a snapshot of that era's city life would contrast sharply with the New York of today, with its loft condos, tourist attractions, and high-end shopping. Manufacturing in New York City still exists, but it has changed; the dynamic of urban production has been erased or sequestered in process removal.

In nineteenth-century Brooklyn, not only were there mammoth waterfront complexes, such as the Brooklyn Army Terminal, Bush Terminal in Sunset Park, and the Brooklyn Navy Yard, there were also numerous well-known companies such as Eberhardt-Faber (known for its pencils), Brillo (renowned for its scrubbing pads), and American Can (tin cans, packaging, and containers). Over 5,000 industrial businesses with 49,000 workers were Brooklyn-based. In Manhattan, where land was more expensive, multistoried factories, became the norm in

Hunts Point

Diamond District,
Garment District
Long Island City
Brooklyn Navy Yard
Brooklyn Army Terminal,
Industry City
JFK Airport

N

■ Industrial Zones

neighborhoods now called SoHo, TriBeCa, and the Ladies Mile. Here too, industrial production was enhanced with clusters and informal networks.[163] Breweries operated at the edges of residential neighborhoods on larger sites in vertical complexes with 45 in Brooklyn alone in 1898, with the last one closing in 1976 until Brooklyn Brewery opened in 1995. In Harlem, milk processing and auto assembly factories were built in enclaves close to the Hudson River for shipping, rising six stories high and using ramps for internal distribution. In the 1920s, the garment industrialists moved north, developing the Garment District on the West side between Seventh and Ninth Avenues, from 36th to 40th Streets; by 1931, this sector had over 120 high-rise factory and showroom buildings. Early in her career, Jane Jacobs noted the strengthening of manufacturing and business in articles on the vitality gained from maintaining the Flower and the Diamond Districts in the heart of the city.[164]

In the 1950s, heavy manufacturing declined in New York, as in other American cities, but there continued to be smaller, light manufacturing. This was reflected in established family firms that absorbed the new technologies for electronics, pharmaceuticals, and machinery. In 1959, the Regional Plan Association (RPA), the planning organization focused on economics and transportation, conducted surveys of the apparel, printing, publishing, and electronics industries to understand how they operated in the city.[165] The RPA also recognized how companies initially move away from the city to other regions, especially to the South, to be able to more cheaply produce and standardize mass production in long-run processes for lower-priced products. Those producers who needed to be close to their local market remained in place, although reduced in scale. All of the reasons for moving out of New York City — cheaper land and labor, larger sites, global trade agreements, and suburban lifestyles desired by company owners — continued at the end of the twentieth century. Although economic and governmental agencies sought to sustain the manufacturers and the jobs, the city planning agency's vision did not accommodate the demand for industrial space and continued to remove the potential for production through limited industrial zoning and land use changes. Demonstrating a disinterest in manufacturing as an integrated part of urban life, planners and economists rarely collaborated on future urban visions for manufacturing spaces.

As described in the earlier chapter on the Modern factory city, zoning determined where manufacturers in the city could be located. New York City agencies — both the Department of City Planning and the Economic Development Corporation, respectively — regulate industrial land use and provide financial incentives for manufacturers. In terms of land use, the planning department designated zones for manufacturing. Using its assigned codes, the letter "M" signifies manufacturing and is combined with a number that designates the intensity of the use allowed: M1 allows light manufacturing, while M3 permits a wide range of activities. Manufacturing buildings normally do not rise higher than three stories due to limits of height and setback, except in some areas like the Garment District, a Special Purpose District where the FAR is 10.0 for non-residential buildings, and can be extended to 12.0 if special zoning bonuses are pursued. The M designation dates from the 1961 zoning law, which often placed M zones in blighted areas to pave the way for urban renewal. For the most part, the zoning allowed companies to build noxious manufacturing facilities in areas such as Bathgate in the South Bronx, a poorer neighborhood; this was considered to be discriminatory at the time.[166] The location of heavy industrial areas or Significant Maritime Industrial Areas (SMIA) includes concentrations of heavy industrial and polluting infrastructure uses. These have historically been located in low-income communities including the South Bronx, Sunset Park, Red Hook, Newtown Creek in Brooklyn, and the North Shore of Staten Island, as well as areas such as the Brooklyn Navy Yard. This kind of heavy industry, often located on open sites, that have become brownfields are being reevaluated, but most of the sites' functions are prohibitive to move and the noxious use has foregrounded environmental injustice.

With the establishment of the 1961 New York City zoning code, industry was encouraged in specific areas separate from residential zones. But with the city's focus on burgeoning financial growth, corporate offices dominated the real estate market. By the 1990s, land use planners were quick to ignore the potential of the local industry; they cited this change in the manufacturing landscape as a result of trade deals such as NAFTA, which provided incentives for companies such as Swingline and Eagle Electric to move production to Mexico. Even though unions, such as the International Ladies' Garment Workers' Union (ILGWU), organized protests to maintain jobs in the New York region, the city's garment industry declined in parallel to a broader national decline; in 1990 to 2011 alone, the number of garment-production jobs decreased from 902,900 to 151,800.[167] In 1993, Jay Mazur, former president ILGWU said, "NAFTA is basically a question of whether the labor movement, not just the apparel industry, not just manufacturing, but services and even the public sector as well — a question of whether this labor movement as we know it will survive. . . None of the workers of the three countries will benefit."[168] Indeed, ramifications are still being felt today.

This story of industry's decline in the big city may be indicative of a trend seen around the world. However, in places like Paris and New York, manufacturing in 2014 is still evolving. One issue, as noted earlier, is that the definition of industry has changed. No longer is manufacturing limited to heavy polluting industries. Over time it has come to include lighter industries and smaller factories that make, mend, and move things. Policy makers should acknowledge this definition to more closely reflect the new manufacturing climate. The tension in many cities between city planning offices and developers reflects basic conflicts between land use and economics and demonstrates the potential for a new paradigm.

Most visible is the shift from manufacturing to residential and commercial areas in New York City. Perhaps the best known — partly because this development model is most often replicated in gentrification processes — is SoHo. In the 1960s, SoHo housed over 1,100 firms, providing some 25,000 unskilled and semiskilled jobs in apparel, printing, and hardware manufacturing. In 1962, Chester Rapkin, City Planning Commissioner, wrote a report on the significance of smaller industries located south of Houston Street to New York's economy.[169] While the initial purpose of his report was not to form new zoning, it did influence the rezoning for work-live spaces, primarily for artists who had started to move into the area, but it also emphasized the need to retain industry. Unfortunately, the planners didn't

define the nature of those industries and SoHo instead became mixed residential and commercial; industry quickly relocated.

Methods to maintain industry in a city, mixed in with other uses, can be advantageous both in terms of diversity and redevelopment. Interestingly, as manufacturing declined from 1961 to the early 1990s, the amount of land zoned for industry only decreased by five percent, even though it was not occupied to the fullest extent. Land speculators encouraged city planners to reevaluate the city's industrial zones to free up this industrial space for residential use, as it was more profitable.

Ten percent of land in the city was at the time zoned industrial. A 1993 City Planning report, "New Opportunities for a Changing Economy," concluded that the land should allow for large-scale retail stores and more flexible uses, to encourage higher land use value and to improve development opportunities.[170] But the 1993 plan was not implemented, as the increase in industrial jobs and economic growth along the Brooklyn and Queens waterfronts, where this study was made, trumped planning policy.

While the service and financial sectors, or Financial Insurance Real Estate (FIRE) increased through the 1990s, pressures on industrial land to be transformed into residential and commercial uses increased. This property-led development encouraged investment and up-zoning for residential and commercial growth for more tax dollars. As the value of the land increased, so did competition for development sites, even though industrial land is productive economically and provides blue-collar jobs for local residents.[171] The land-value equation in relationship to other economic indicators was not counted in the city's overall economic value. During the Bloomberg administration (2002–13), this incongruence intensified as former industrial areas in Long Island City and Willets Point in Queens, Dumbo, Greenpoint, and Williamsburg in Brooklyn, among other neighborhoods in New York City, were gentrified; the higher offers for industrial land, which previously was leased at the lowest per-square-meter price, forced out longtime industrial and residential tenants. Similar to other cities such as Chicago, once called the "Candy Capital of the U.S," whose industrial building stock has been converted to offices or residential lofts, 10.8 percent of workers were still in manufacturing in 2010, which was greater than New York's 2.2 percent in 2010.[172] Between 2004 and 2010, New York rezoned over 49 square kilometers from industrial use to other uses, thereby continuing to shrink land available for manufacturing. The transformation of industrial neighborhoods in numerous cities into trendy residential enclaves, many along waterfronts, created new "Gold Coasts," in economic development terms.

However, realizing the importance of maintaining industrial jobs, former New York City Mayor Bloomberg changed his tune in 2005 and established Industrial Business Zones (IBZs), similar to Chicago's 2004 Industrial Corridors, which represented a plan to retain industrial areas along railroad routes as well as to improve the infrastructure to attract new manufacturers. The Office of Industrial and Manufacturing Businesses (OIMB) was founded to assist companies to improve and coordinate city services and policy issues relating to common needs such as finance, infrastructure, sanitation, and transportation, as well as overseeing tax credits for those manufacturers who move there. Companies also receive a one-thousand-dollar tax credit for every worker they bring into the IBZ in hopes to retain jobs in the city. In 2013, there were twenty-one IBZs to protect industries: these included areas of Long Island City and JFK Airport in Queens; Greenpoint/Williamsburg, South Brooklyn, and the Brooklyn Navy Yard in Brooklyn; and Hunts Point and Port Morris in the Bronx. But within these zones, other industrial uses are allowed, such as hotels, as they are considered industries that provide a service rather than a product. In Long Island City and the Garment District, new hotels began to overwhelm the streetscape. However, hotels increase pressure on industrial owners to change use to increase rents. But rather than increase the area for industry, the IBZs actually confine this space and limit industrial growth. As urban planner Laura Wolf-Powers emphasizes,

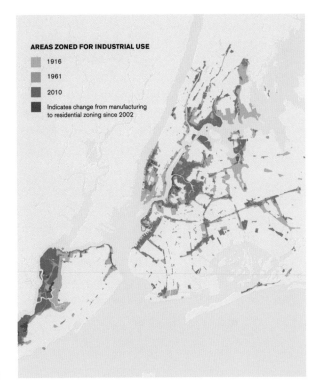

AREAS ZONED FOR INDUSTRIAL USE

■ 1916
■ 1961
■ 2010
■ Indicates change from manufacturing to residential zoning since 2002

> industry is an important source of employment and economic diversity, city planners should have insisted on more active code enforcement, planned comprehensively to distinguish areas slated for continued industrial use from areas designated for commercial and residential redevelopment, and clearly signaled these designations to businesses and developers.[173]

City planners follow market trends, after the fact, rather than proactively envision new possibilities. Planners' efforts are often seen as futile when the city's official goal appears to privilege recreation, lifestyle, and tourism over industrial spaces for working-class people.

But statistics show that the city is at a tipping point: if the definition of industry adapts to match the current manufacturing sectors, jobs are showing an increase. The key is to changing the perception: instead of manufacturing jobs occurring in large-scale firms, new jobs will be found in small firms specializing in new types of manufacturing. Data from 2012 indicates that manufacturing jobs increased for the first time in a decade, within the revised definition of smaller-scale and light-industrial use. Manufacturing in New York City today is categorized in sectors that include food and beverage processing (13 percent), apparel (17 percent), and metalworking and other manufacturing (13 percent). Despite the vital importance of

◄ Industrial Business Zones in New York City, 2014
▲ New York City incremental change in industrial zones

these industries to the urban economy, they account for a decreasing segment of its profile: industry comprises only 77,000, or 2.23 percent, of the city's approximately 3.4 million private-sector jobs. While industrial uses occupy nearly 15 percent of the city's land area, manufacturing's economic output accounts for a smaller share — 10.7 percent in 2012 — of the city's gross economic product, compared to 14.6 percent in 1990. Now, more than previously, ninety percent of manufacturers employ fewer than ten people, with 5,400 firms employing fewer than twenty people in New York in 2007. In 2010, there were approximately 6,500 manufacturing companies employing 81,000 people, down from 250,000 manufacturing jobs in 2000.[174] The Economic Development Corporation notes, that despite the economic downturn of 2008, the loss of manufacturing jobs in the city has been stabilizing since 2006, which it attributes to a comprehensive program of government subsidies.

Diamond District

A piece of paper folded five centimeters square is passed from one man to another on 47th Street. The "parcel" is carefully opened by the second man, revealing a tiny diamond resting on a blue lining. He pockets it with a nod. The same transaction has been taking place for almost one hundred years, signifying the microcosm of production and consumption in New York City's two-block Diamond District, the distribution point for ninety percent of the diamonds imported to the U.S.[175] This close-knit, mysterious, and difficult-to-penetrate community inhabits 47th Street and part of 48th Street between Fifth and Sixth Avenues, a small physical area that produces a disproportionately vast amount of wealth. Despite globalization and a drastic shift to mechanization and automation, the diamond industry generates $24 billion in annual economic impact for New York State from both sales of finished jewelry and jobs. For the City, diamonds are its number one export, with the added value to its economy $4 billion.[176]

The Diamond District — both in terms of the numbers of small family businesses and workers employed — is a microcosm for an economic and industrial concentration as well as a broad-based manufacturing network, one rooted in informal local relationships and trust, as well as a highly controlled global sector of diamond sourcing and trade.

Both 47th and 48th Streets are lined with buildings that rise up to twenty stories — vertical urban factories — in an eclectic mix of styles architecturally and spatially. As in the Garment District, the 1916 setback laws are evident in some buildings with castle-like crenelations, but others have 1960s curtain-wall facades. In this grouping, over 4,100 companies employ 2,200 workers — casters, polishers, smelters, and jewelers — making up an integrated network of production, craft, and distribution.[177] In an industry with inherent safety issues, the production spaces, perfectly suited to the city, house smelters who fire up hearths and furnaces in buildings retrofitted with exhaust systems that vent to their exteriors. The production is distributed through smaller "factories" — often throughout the depths of multiple buildings — where the lower-cost spaces often have no windows. Along 47th Street, the ground-floor retail spaces are either individual shops or shared "exchanges" housed in large showrooms in which each jeweler leases a booth or area for their own design and production. The district's spatial organization is scaled monetarily from the street-front retail window display, which comes at a high value and cost, to cheaper spaces further back on the ground floors or on the second or third floors.

The heightened security within these buildings has spawned sophisticated navigation systems, which are at once awkward and curious. Security and web cameras are ubiquitous. As the factories rise vertically, they crisscross in beehive networks along hallways secured by sally ports, which protect the buyer and the seller, or the distributor and the workers. These doors are based on the early entryways used in moats and castles, by means of which you could trap, view, and hold an enemy before allowing them passage. Customers and suppliers open what seems to be an exterior door to their office and land in a tiny interim space; once scrutinized by the proprietor, the door opens to the workspace. Just one of the physical characteristics of the district, these safety measures are absorbed into the area's daily life.

The industry involves myriad tasks that revolve around the trading of diamonds, the processing of precious metals, the crafting of jewelry, and sales — both wholesale and retail. The trade of diamonds occurs in the Diamond Dealers Club in one building on Fifth Avenue and 47th Street that is designated a Foreign Trade Zone itself. The club includes a closed group of dealers who are carefully scrutinized, then voted in. Most of them are older Hasidic men, although increasing numbers of younger people are being accepted. Here, they conduct business and meet acquaintances in the trade, operating out of a room containing long tables, overhead magnifying lights, weighing devices, and loupes. Prices for years were set by the Gem Institute of America, but Martin Rapaport, diamond maverick, devised a new price list in 1978 that was more public, "The Rapaport Diamond Price Sheet." After much controversy and a few lawsuits, this document now provides the basis for pricing diamonds.[178]

The extraction of raw materials — in this case, gold, silver, and the denser material platinum, which are mined in countries such as Russia, Colombia, and South Africa — is a difficult and exploitive process. In New York, these metals are also collected from secondary sources of sales originating from brokers and pawn shops around the city. The gold, deriving from bits of jewelry is then weighed and smelted in workspaces located in the upper stories of the Diamond District's vertical factories. The outputs are heavy gold bars in which the impressions, or ghosts, of other jewelry that have not completely melted are often visible. Other steps, each completed by a different worker in a dispersed production circuit, include design, diamond cutting, polishing, metal casting, assembly, setting the stones, and finishing. A great deal of repair work is also conducted in the street retail space. While many of the traditional craft skills are still strong, others, such as casting, have waned and moved out of the city, making it harder for jewelers to find skilled workers. In addition, there are sub-businesses and umbrella organizations, such as the Gem Institute of America, that grade diamonds and help

▲ Vertical urban factories in the Diamond District, New York, 2014
▲ A jeweler polishing diamonds in a Diamond District factory, New York, 2014

expand the profession through training. Other groups focused on specific raw materials, such as the Platinum Institute, similarly support the industry to boost sales and skills.[179]

The jewelers and wholesalers on 47th Street are traditionally Jews who came to New York in the nineteenth century from the European cities of Antwerp, Amsterdam, London, and Venice, where they had been conducting business for centuries. Diamonds from mines in South Africa and colonial Rhodesia — named for Cecil Rhodes, who founded the De Beers company — were monopolized by De Beers, which once owned eighty percent of the world's supply. Now, they have fifty percent of the market, as other companies, such as Lazard Kaplan, have jumped in. The workforce has also diversified more recently, with skilled workers in diamond cutting immigrating from Ecuador, India, and East Asia. Individual craftsmen who use their own specialized tools rent benches and worktables, or larger companies lease workspaces for their employees.

Diamonds gain their value through their inherent qualities and expert cutting. The guides to that value are known in the trade as the 4 Cs: carat weight, color, clarity, and cut. So that younger generations can practice cutting, there is a tradition of rough diamonds being passed down through families. But, as these rough diamonds have risen in price, they have become less available, making it difficult for younger workers to obtain adequate training. Diamond cutters work independently for the most part, receiving about $200 per finished carat (in 2014). One large stone can take a year to cut and polish. Today, CNC milling is impacting the profession, with industrial diamonds being cut in high-tech automated facilities. This trend is removing the art and craft from a profession that has traditionally been a light cottage industry rather than a large-scale manufacturing process.

The Diamond District's dynamic streets, bustling with people and cars, delivery and security trucks, tourists and merchants, strike a passerby as being of another time and place. Street hawkers, who wear sandwich boards and distribute fliers — or sometimes just whisper in your ear — bother potential clients, and often scare them away. The Business Improvement District (BID) has tried to address this issue, but with freedom of speech and laws that allow for salespeople to work on streets at a certain distance from their shops, the hawkers are permitted, just as they are in other commercial districts.

Another unique aspect of the street is the widespread and intense presence of police and private security agents. Because of the value of the goods and the risk of terrorism, theft, and other criminal acts, the U.S. Department of Homeland Security, along with a network of private businesses, installed a district-wide surveillance system. The Urban Areas Security Initiative, which strategizes against terrorist activities, provided the district with cameras and policemen whoare highly visible to ensure public and private security and safety. The BID supports both retail and industry by working on street improvements and grant initiatives.

Similar to the Garment District, there is potential to maintain the mix and ecological synergy of this commercial and industrial area that is vital to Manhattan's commerce. But pressures loom, as the area is underbuilt for zoning code. Developers such as Gary Barnett in 2014 built the Gem Tower, a thirty-story tower designed by Skidmore, Owings & Merrill, that offers ample parking, a giant safe, high-end lobby scanning, and floor loads that can support equipment. The building houses mixed uses with industries on the 47th Street side and condominium office space on the 46th Street side. This provokes new ways to consider manufacturing in the city and the potential for continued diversity and density.

Garment District

The Garment and Diamond Districts in New York City are highly specialized microcosms comprised of densely packed urban factories with a largely singular focus in a unique spatial organization. Like the Diamond District, the Garment District is one of the drivers of New York's economy, with a $31 billion fashion business that is dependent on the surrounding area's deep pool of talent and expertise. The Garment District today occupies an area stretching from 5th to 9th Avenues between West 35th to 40th Streets, and thrives on the synergy of related companies being located within walking distance of one another. The community of cutters, pattern makers, pleaters, embroiderers, button and zipper suppliers, fabric wholesalers, and artificial flower and handbag manufacturers form a holistic ecosystem based on adjacency and interdependency. Throughout the 1960s, the Garment District's highly skilled manufacturers thrived, but gradually the influx of mass-produced goods from abroad made with cheaper labor had a negative impact — by 2010, fewer than 10,000 manufacturing workers remained. Yet, today the presence of the district is essential to emerging and established designers as well as to theatrical costume designers who are literally next door to the district and remain unaccounted for in most studies. Young fashion design students and graduates from the four major design schools in New York flock to the Garment District for supplies and production assistance. But, increasingly, the work produced there is experimental, for prototyping and small-batch rather than mass production. This transition that the Garment District is undergoing, from a major manufacturing area to a smaller and more specialized one, is similar to that of other manufacturing centers in the Western world.

When a decline in business and pressure for space arose in the mid-1980s, the city, utilizing zoning controls to retain industrial uses and to protect the district from the encroachment of higher-revenue residential and commercial uses, designated, in 1987, a Special Garment Center District.[180] However, code enforcement was so lax that illegal conversions wiggled in; the local watchdog organization called the Garment Industry Development Center (GIDC) was unable to prevent such conversions.[181] The GIDC was founded by Jay Mazur of UNITE with Sara Crean as founding director, to assist the manufacturers in the area — a departure from the usual purview of a BID. However, the fines for illegal conversions were so insubstantial (at the time, $200) that they had no impact, lacking any

▲ Vertical urban factories in the Garment District, 2011
▲ A textile worker in the Garment District, 2011

substance in the face of residential rental rates that were so much more lucrative (and thus appealing) to building- and land-owners. Just as in Long Island City, industry was at a point where residential use was poised to win out. Landlords could convert from industrial to commercial use only if they set aside an equivalent amount of production space elsewhere in the district, but this was not enforced. The building owners, represented by the Fashion Center Improvement District BID, lobbied for major zoning changes. According to the GIDC, in 2008 there were about 50,000 square meters of space zoned for all related garment businesses in the area, with actual production concentrated in only about 14 buildings, and with the remaining sixty percent of the space devoted to apparel-related businesses.[182]

As a reaction to these developments, an idea emerged in 2005 to consolidate the garment-related businesses and manufacturers into one building, thereby saving what remained. For some, such as Deborah Brand of the 90-year-old M & S Schmalberg Custom Flower Fabrics, consolidation was seen as a safeguard that "will keep our rent down, and increase business by having all the domestic suppliers together."[183] For others, such as designer Francoise Olivas, who often uses R & C Apparel for custom work, "It pointed to the lack of interest in the city to maintain New York's garment industry heritage."[184] The "garment building" proposal was similar to one-stop shopping in design-related buildings. Other proposals included relocating the remnants of the Garment District outside of Manhattan entirely. As a result of the 2005 Hudson Yards rezoning, residential use has been permitted on an increasing number of side blocks, and there has been a proliferation of low-cost hotels, which has pressured the area's industrial use even further. Even though the idea of consolidating was appealing to some, to others the cost of moving, and the distance from designers, was considered detrimental to their businesses, as they thrive as a critical mass. With development encroaching, the organization, Save the Garment Center, was started in 2007 to increase awareness and maintain the area.

Despite the shrinking district, the area retains an industrial vitality, and its built form and function epitomize the architecture of the vertical urban factory. Two hundred small factories and related businesses comprise 24,000 manufacturing jobs in 93,000 square meters of space. In its built form, the district is well suited to hosting industrial uses: its buildings offer large floor plates, industrial service and passenger elevators, and a dynamic streetscape — activated by the bustle of hand carts, foot traffic, and delivery trucks.

The industrial synergies still available in the Garment District, including faster turn-around and quality control, continue to attract top names in fashion, such as Nanette Lepore, Yeohlee Teng, Nicole Miller, Calvin Klein, Marc Jacobs, Theory, DKNY, and Ralph Lauren, among others. These companies employ workers who are largely new immigrants, but, unlike textile manufacturers overseas, provide fair wages and opportunities for advancement.

Designers in the city also rely on the manufacturers for innovative ideas — whether products or processes — and benefit from the ability to test them out near their studios. They also depend on the garment manufacturers in proven production methods and the reliability of their textiles' performance. A designer might not

know how to piece together each element to make it function or fit, but can rely on a manufacturer, such as Ramdat Harihar (who specializes in pleats), to orient the production process in such a way as to enhance a product's design.

The Garment Center maintains its potential as a vital industrial cluster that activates everyday urban experience. As designer, Olivas said, "Fashion is both art and commerce and needs potential for growth in the economy where the fashion industry could once again burst at the seams."[185] The synergies increase its visibility and yielding a smaller carbon footprint by delivering goods directly to their numerous nearby customers. The future for the Garment District relies on both manufacturers and designers to continue to experiment and to grow, adapting new technologies in a newly digital production flow of high quality and innovative design. It continues to be an exemplary model with recent studies by the Municipal Art Society and the Design Trust for Public Space.[186]

▲ Molds in artificial flower factory in the Garment District, New York, 2011

As Roberta Gratz, a New York journalist and factory owner, points out in *The Battle for Gotham*, "For city planners to continue to plan and rezone as if industry can't survive, grow, and be a significant contributor to the city economy is dramatically shortsighted."[187] Zoning changes can't react fast enough to economic change, or technologies of manufacturing, and many cities have already missed the boat. If factories move out and jobs decline, there is a deskilling of labor, as there is no more job training if the jobs don't exist, so that when factories do return, there will be no one available to work in them.

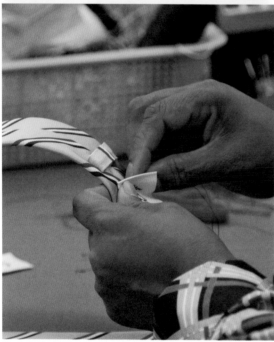

Long Island City

One area that has maintained industries, although the real estate pressure is still constant, is Long Island City (L.I.C.), in Western Queens where Roberta Gratz's husband, Donald Gratz, opened his metalworks factory, Treitel-Gratz, in the 1950s, making numerous furniture lines for Modern architects. Industrial gentrification began in the late 1980s, but Long Island City reacted to the economic fluctuations more directly than other areas, as initial projects there were government-sponsored. For a long time, L.I.C. has been a bastion of manufacturing, with its transit infrastructure, large-scale industrial buildings, and workers who still contribute to an industrial ecology.

Western Queens was once filled with vertical urban factories, such as those in Degnon Terminal, Sunshine Bakery, Adams Chewing Gum, Standard Auto, Eagle Electric, Swingline Staples, Paragon Paint, Pepsi, CBS/Columbia Records, and Steinway and Sohmer Piano companies, among others. The arrival of the Queensboro Bridge and the Midtown Tunnel, with the expressways and subways traversing the river in the early twentieth century, connected the area to the larger urban whole. The area was characterized by a lower-rise middle landscape with impressive views of Manhattan, gritty urban streets, and the smells of plastics and industrial bakeries permeating the air. It is a place that gained vitality from its hybridity. The elevated Number 7 train sweeps around curved tracks and cuts above and below the blocks, easily transporting workers to their jobs. But many buildings remain vacant in anticipation of the next real estate deal.

Beginning in the late 1980s, new zoning initiatives resulted in the spot development of the 48-story Citibank building in 1989. It wasn't until yet another round of zoning changes in 2001 that more commercial development was encouraged and the waterfront's residential development took off with a series of towers.[188] However, rather than integrated development, a patchwork of development resulted. The initiative was undertaken with little urban design and no vision for services, jobs, or planning for increased economic growth. The industrial uses came under pressure to move away, and, by 2001, the city formed the L.I.C. Special Mixed-Used District to open up development to commercial and residential uses for the blocks between 23rd Street to the west and 41st Avenue to the north, as well as at the Sunnyside Yards, Queens Plaza, and along Jackson Avenue. These MX zones have no incentives for building owners to maintain the mixed use, so the industrial owners are practically incentivized to achieve the highest profits and use for their buildings a trend that is weighted towards residential. This often raises the value and thus the rent in the surrounding area, leading to more gentrification. Moreover, it is not mandated that manufacturing must be maintained. The multi-functional community that survives on difference and diversity so easily converts to sameness and monoculture, when hybridity is more vital.

After the IBZ designations in 2005, the L.I.C. BID which expanded into the L.I.C. Partnership, was initiated to assist commercial and manufacturing businesses. With the planning for the 2012 Olympics bid, the area came be seen as a developer's dream for Queens West and Hunters Point South. This scenario involved eliminating low-rise industrial buildings that were part of the area's hybrid character.[189] Thus, in an industrial entropy, the city zoning favored speculative residential and commercial development in the new mix.[190]

In the midst of these larger-scale economic shifts, L.I.C. gained its own particular identity and strength through its clustered factories and agglomerations of industries, with informal relationships of shared supplies and skills, whether in metal bending, sewing, or tool sharing. It is the strength of the particular manufacturers that have enabled industry in L.I.C. to weather the changes in the broader city's economy. The ecology of L.I.C.'s urban manufacturing still includes garment factories, a piano factory, bakeries, elevator companies, lighting, printing, breweries, airplane engine, and glass factories, among other large and small entities.

Larger legacy companies — Plaxall, Edison Price, Steinway Piano, and Mr. Steam — have been mainstays to the area. With each iteration of new technologies, they retool their production and alter their spaces to fit their new processing line or add CNC and cellular organization for improved efficiency. Other global companies such as Brooks Brothers chose the location with a commitment to manufacturing in the U.S. In the L.I.C. facility workers make ties and bow ties as well as custom-made suits, and perform alterations. The skilled workers operate machinery that comes primarily from Italy but requires hands-on work for much cutting, turning, and sewing. With fabrics imported from England and Italy, and workers trained locally, the attention to detail and potential for quick delivery to their head office, in Manhattan and stores throughout the country are imperative. The tailoring is counterintuitive, because the suits are not actually made in the shops, but altered at this large factory; there the garments travel on overhead conveyors through the high-bay space to be distributed. Brooks Brothers' other two factories are located in Massachusetts and the Midwest.

Steinway & Sons moved from Manhattan to four hundred acres in Astoria, Queens in 1873. There they built not only a new factory, but a company town, Steinway Village, complete with sawmill, foundry, post office, parks, worker housing, schools, and streetcar line developed by William Steinway, the son of the company's founder Henry. Manufacturing took place in two parallel, six-story brick factories and a yard. Today, the company still thrives in the urban environment, with the original complex and a 1955 addition where they produce one thousand pianos annually. The production follows the building's vertical flow from bottom to top, beginning in the lumberyard with the curing and drying of woods, then shifting to a

◁ **Making ties at Brooks Brothers factory, Long Island City, 2013**
◁ **Hand-crafting a tie at Brooks Brothers factory, Long Island City, 2013**

VERTICAL URBAN FACTORY THE CONTEMPORARY FACTORY INDUSTRIAL URBANISM

rim-conditioning room on the second floor, where the bending of the casework is completed, painted, and varnished. Moving between the second and third floors, the casing becomes the piano shape as mechanical booms lower cast-iron plates to form the rim, after which the keyboard, soundboard, and strings are installed. The piano is polished, and final testing occurs to complete the almost year-long production process.

Food processing is also a dominant industry in L.I.C, with City Bakery, Le Pain Quotidian, Sweet & Sara, Amy's. and Tom Cat, all housing bakeries there. Recognizing the potential for smaller food start-ups, the Queens Economic Development Corporation (QEDC), organized the Entrepreneur Space, a successful cooperative method of sharing high-cost space and equipment. Seth Bornstein, director of QEDC, notes how small food producers can take the next steps from their kitchen-based production and use these larger spaces to get out into the consumer market. "The start-up costs of food businesses are extraordinary. The Entrepreneur Space relieves new businesses of some of the financial burden and additionally provides business counseling, technical assistance, and networking opportunities. This is especially helpful in New York City, where space is tight and business assistance services can be fragmented." [191]

The 1,500-square-meter space includes four commercial-grade kitchens and is open around the clock to meet the demands of tenants who can lease space by the hour. Nearly ninety businesses use the kitchens to produce goods ranging from pies and Indian delicacies to organic dog biscuits and catering services. In addition, classes in business management and growth are offered there. A private Organic Food Incubator using a similar model has also set up subleasable spaces for small businesses and a communal kitchen. The New York City EDC also provided loans for food initiatives via Goldman Sachs, based on demand from the artisanal and ethnic food culture.

The numerous opportunities to nurture manufacturing in the area shows the agility of entrepreneurs to adapt to the changing industrial climate as they hold onto space and places of production. It would behoove the city to maintain manufacturing in Long Island City, where industrial space is plentiful. The reduction in scale to neo-cottage industries finding spaces to reinhabit in the former larger factories can accommodate the new manufacturers of urban-oriented niche products and smaller batch producers, whether they are brewers, fashion designers, or furniture makers. There already is a manufacturing revival, but at the smaller scale: for instance, New York City added six hundred manufacturing jobs in 2011, after over fifty years of losing thousands of jobs annually.[192] This turnaround can be attributed to those manufacturers who thrive on being in the heart of the city, and close to their clients, and their employees.[193]

While the dollar value of these smaller industries, which might not even call themselves industries, has not yet been calculated, it is timely to incorporate them into new industrial data. A policy to have dense industry agglomerations in multistoried buildings could be pursued, and the design-oriented manufacturers have become a commodity to a city in terms of prestige, identity, and larger profit margins. At the same time, unskilled jobs are necessary to bridge the gap in incomes. With new goals of triple bottom line for companies to be sustainable, and potential for new distribution systems, production jobs could hold steady. As Roberta Gratz emphasizes, "For genuine economic growth, nurturing the homegrown business beats luring the mature one from elsewhere with tax breaks and other expensive incentives."[194] A new orientation to industry must occur to secure New York's manufacturing future.

TORONTO

While some cities such as Detroit had a dominant industry, Toronto, like New York, hosted a diversity of industries, making spirits, farm machinery, flour, bricks, pianos, bicycles, and automobiles from the early eighteenth century onwards. Massive undeveloped sites offered space to large companies that also used exterior yards for production, such as the Don Valley Brick Works, Toronto Rolling Mill, Massey, Redpath Sugar, T. Eaton & Co., and Gooderham & Worts whose building complexes accreted over time. Other more compact industries, such as garment making, shoe making, printing, and furniture manufacture, as well as artisanal workshops, were located in smaller vertical factory spaces in the central city.

Toronto's geography contributed to its industrial growth. The harbor tied the city to the passageways of the St. Lawrence Valley, and railroad expansions allowed

◀ Piano casework drying at the Steinway Piano factory, Astoria, 2012

◀ A worker stringing a new piano, Steinway Piano, Astoria, 2012

Bombardier

Canada Goose

West Toronto Junction
Distillery District
Redpath Sugar
Fashion District,
401 Richmond

N

■ Industrial Zones

goods to reach the U.S. interior and the Pacific. By the late nineteenth century, it became the second largest industrial hub in Canada, after Montreal. Coal from Pennsylvania fired the industrial machines, centralizing Toronto's industrialists with links to natural resources. The collective business acumen of people in the region coalesced in the founding of the Stock Exchange in 1852, contributing to Toronto's prominence in international trade.

Industrial growth continued, supporting 530 manufacturers in 1871, a number that jumped to 2,400 twenty years later. In tandem with this escalation, the workforce increased from 9,400 to 26,242. With the rise of the numbers of workers came the unions, which organized to cut long workday hours. As in the U.S., strikes were common means of increasing attention to negative workers' conditions. The print trade held massive strikes in 1872. An economic boom around 1879 was partially created by new protective tariffs on imported goods. By 1911, 65,000 of 133,000 workers in Toronto were employed by industries. Industry began to expand beyond the original boundaries of the city to areas such as West Toronto Junction, Scarborough, and Hamilton. The massive Ontario Stockyards in The Junction, an intersection of four railway lines, gave Toronto the nickname "Hogtown." Railway transport in the late nineteenth century catalyzed the development of Toronto West — a center for iron, steel, machinery, and food production that was previously home to the city's prisons.

The natural resources of the region also fostered the development of many local companies. The Taylor Brothers discovered deposits of clay and shale from Mud Creek, which led to the founding of the Don Valley Brick Works in the 1880s. Spirits and beer were stable industries in most major cities in the late nineteenth century. William Gooderham and his brother-in-law James Worts started a whiskey distillery in 1832 on Trinity Street. A windmill near the harbor served as both a power source and a survey point for the dividing of waterfront lots. The complex was comprised of over fifty buildings connected by networks of distribution, power, and transit. The grain farming and the feeding of cattle using the slop refuse from the distillery created an industrial symbiosis. Gooderham and Worts became the largest distillery in the British Empire, producing over two million gallons of proof spirits a year. In 1902, they began to manufacture alcohol from molasses as the General Distilling Company and acetone for munitions during World War I. The surrounding area included workers' housing and further developed as an industrial center. During Prohibition, the General Distilling Company complex was demolished and in 1926 the Hatch Group purchased the company; they also bought Hiram Walker and Sons Ltd. in Windsor, forming Hiram Walker-Gooderham & Worts Ltd. through the early 1990s. Today, a small brewery is located in the historic complex today, along with gallery and eating establishments.

Both World Wars spurred industrial growth. In the 1950s, highway networks spread industrial development to the suburbs, causing Toronto to experience the same economic decline as other North American cities. The larger, open, single-floor box-like factories became the substantial trend for new manufacturers. Surprisingly, between the 1980s through 2000, Toronto's city-region was still a manufacturing center and gained in importance over Montreal in terms of shipping and employment, especially in the food and plastics industries.[195] NAFTA eliminated barriers and tariffs on goods between Canada, the U.S., and Mexico, allowing for increased Canadian exports, making it possible for more foreign countries to produce there. It also expanded the production in Canada of durable goods such as automobiles and train cars, but non-durable goods declined in production.

The regional shift of industry from the center city was not as drastic as in the U.S., perhaps because of Toronto's both diverse and specialized manufacturing.[196] But manufacturing and warehousing jobs have steadily declined in Toronto since 1983. In 1986, the city boasted 266,000 manufacturing jobs. By 2011, 143,000 people (13 percent of the jobs in the city) were employed by 5,000 companies producing over 13.5 million Canadian dollars of goods. Toronto's numbers of industrial workers is considerably high for urban regions that had decentralized. Compared to New York, which has only 1.8 percent (or 75,000 jobs) of its workforce employed in manufacturing, Toronto's percentage is a higher four percent (or 128,600 jobs); Toronto additionally had a wave of condo building development in the city center, and pressures on real estate similar to that in New York. However, manufacturing jobs have tended to grow in Montreal and Toronto, as employment in other sectors has declined in the broader metropolitan areas. In seeing a promising avenue for further research of industrial location, economists Robert Shearmur and William Coffey see that "the location requirements of manufacturing industries have evolved, maybe because of activity shifts within the sector (such as the shift from traditional to high-tech activities within the manufacturing sector.)"[197] They note the diverse agglomerations that are not only focused on financial industries in Toronto and thus allow for a potential for manufacturing. Accordingly, each place "produces unique spatial outcomes."[198]

The largest manufacturer in Toronto is Bombardier, which makes subway cars and other transportation equipment. It is double the size of any other factory in the city. Celestia, a multinational electronics manufacturing company, is the

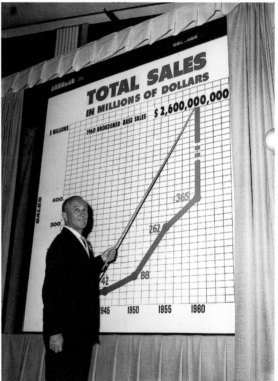

▲ Land use map of Toronto showing industry moving north, 1955
▲ Sales chart at Weston Bakery, Toronto, 1960
◀ Toronto industrial zones 2013

second largest, with 1,500 employees in its Toronto factory. A spin-off of IBM, which was downsizing its hardware production in the 1990s to that of software, Celestia continued the electronics production line in the former IBM facility at the city's edge and gradually counted IBM as one of its clients. The other big companies are two furniture manufacturers, including Global Total Office, which makes 5,000 chairs a day and employs 500 workers.

In Toronto, many food and beverage companies have been absorbed into larger conglomerates, and some have closed, while others maintain the legacy of baking, beverage, and meat production that was so dominant in the city. The third largest manufacturing operation in the city overall is Kraft, which opened its fifth plant in Toronto and continues production. Additional companies such as Nestle, Wing's Food Products, Mondelez, Molson Canada, Lassonde Beverages Canada, Campbell's Soup, Quality Meats, and a doughnut maker in the North York neighborhood responsible for all the product for the Dunkin Donuts chain in the Eastern U.S. also operate in the area. Other smaller companies continue to thrive, affirming the adage that local food production can be sustained by virtue of proximity to clients. The city is also seeing a new trend — the renaissance of breweries such as Steam Whistle and Milltown.

In Toronto's industrial heritage, the Weston Bakery is a legacy company with a dynamic narrative. George Weston, a baker's apprentice, began the bakery when he purchased a bread delivery route in 1882. His popular "homemade bread" allowed the company to expand quickly, and he bought out his former employer in 1884. By 1897, with architect David Albert Richards, Weston built a two-story brick and stone "model" bakery with state-of-the-art equipment that allowed an average of 3,200 loaves to be made daily. Weston Bakery became the largest bakery in Canada. The mixing, kneading, receiving, and storage facilities, along with eight industrial ovens, were housed under one roof. It became one of the largest conglomerates in Canada, with numerous subsidiaries, including Loblaw Markets, and Joe Fresh Clothing.

Garment and textile production also traditionally made up a large sector of the city's manufacturing. Toronto's Garment District was in the heart of the city at Spadina Avenue between Queen and King Streets. Similar to New York City's Garment District, the number of manufacturers in the area has decreased but fabric, trim, fur, garment suppliers, retail establishments, and wholesalers remain. As a primarily Jewish industrial sector, the garment trades began here in the late 1800s and continued through the 1950s, bringing with them cultural activity, unions, and political radicalism. The factories were located on the upper floors with shops on the ground floors for the wholesale marketplace; they employed waves of immigrants from around the world, including Jewish, Chinese, Hungarian, Portuguese, Latin American, and Vietnamese workers. One renowned enterprise, T. Eaton & Co., had its factories and warehouses at Yonge and Queen Streets in multistoried brick buildings. The company, which manufactured and distributed goods, had a large catalog business and its own department store. There, the International Ladies' Garment Workers Union organized workers from 1910 to the 1930s, as did the Retail Wholesale and Department Store Union. In 1977, they demolished their original buildings and developed a shopping center on the site.

Toronto takes pride in contemporary notable designers. Designer Franco Mirabelli's studio is in the Garment District, but his factory is in the Scarborough area, where many companies have chosen to expand. Mirabelli relies on local suppliers for zippers, belts, and other accessories that he sources for the factory which he often visits. Canada Goose is a global player with its cold-weather gear company. Founded in 1957 by Sam Tick as Metro Sportswear, it made its products in a small urban factory. In the 1970s, it expanded its production line to include down-filled garments, and through the 1980s made coats and parkas for government employees. The brand became very popular among mountaineers. Metro Sportswear changed its name to Canada Goose and recently expanded sales outside of Canada. Such success has resulted in a physical expansion as well. While still occupying the original low brick building that serves as the company headquarters, Canada Goose expanded to the adjacent 1940s vertical, glass, steel, and brick structure. Committed to production in Canada, the company thrives just north of the downtown core in the metropolitan

area and also produces in Winnipeg. At the end of 2013, it was purchased by Bain Capital, with the original owner maintaining a minority share.

Toronto's strong fashion and design culture inspired the founding in 1987 of the public-private partnership, The Fashion Incubator, which supports young entrepreneurial designers by providing them with professional assistance and space. Shared resources include business assistance, equipment, online networks, mentoring, promotional services, and support for exhibitions, trade fairs, and fashion shows.

Many factory buildings are being put to new industrial uses that correspond to the new requirements for smaller industrial spaces within larger-scale buildings to retain industrial programs. 401 Richmond Street was formerly the location of a tin manufacturer called Macdonald Manufacturing Company, which was founded by David Macdonald of Scotland and known for its innovative lithographic printing on tin cans. In Toronto, Macdonald built the first of a few facilities at 245 King Street East, and later built a multistoried brick complex at 401 Richmond in 1899. Tin can production was one of the early mass-production assembly-line processes, used

▲ 401 Richmond Street, interior courtyard, Toronto, 2013
▲ 401 Richmond Street, Toronto, 2013

for canning food in wartime. Continental Can Company purchased Macdonald in 1944 and continued producing cans through 1967. After the company's closure, the building housed diverse tenants, from artists to small manufacturers. The Zeidler Family purchased and renovated the building in 1994 and it was placed on the Toronto Heritage list. Today it is a vibrant small manufacturing building with an artist and artisan focus that exemplifies ways to retain industry in a manner similar to the Greenpoint Manufacturing and Design Center and the American Can Factory, both in Brooklyn, New York.

Ironically, infrastructure problems in Toronto have actually prevented moves by manufacturers into the city, as it only has two power lines. Manufacturers complain about the need for better transit infrastructure to alleviate congestion. But Toronto has a very attractive tax rate for manufacturing, compared to its competing cities. Manufacturing jobs have three to ten spin-off jobs that are related to production in distribution and support services. The same factors that support manufacturing in Toronto also encourage reshoring, as in the U.S.: low transportation costs, proximity to designers and customers, a diverse and quali-fied workforce, quality control, and local testing and repair of products. Although manufacturing provides more and higher paid jobs, most firms have shrunk in size, with 86.6 percent of firms in Ontario employing fewer than fifty people — though these workers are increasingly more highly skilled. Manufacturing also contributes threefold to Ontario's R&D activity, which planners are realizing is essential to encourage, especially in the high-tech industries.[199] Ontario's highest exports in 2011 were in the manufacturing sector, but they were dependent on the fluctuation of the Canadian dollar related to the demand for oil products, especially for exports to the U.S.

In terms of land use, the state of Ontario compels the use of land designated for employment to be maintained as such — that means it can't be converted to other uses and those developers who have tried to build residential on those sites have been rejected. As Mike Williams of the Economic Development office says, "if it goes now, it is gone forever."[200]

Toronto's zoning has been cumbersome, but the officials believe that the "best possible use" needs to be evaluated by not only planners and developers but others as well. The city's 2010 Zoning Bylaw project addressed ways to use zoning to "enhance the future vibrancy, diversity, and economic vitality of the city."[201] Toronto's Planning Division is committed to mixed-use development so that people can work and shop near where they live. This would also mean that the factories could also be allowed as-of-right. In the 1970s, abandoned factories in the King and Spadina and King and Parliament neighborhoods could not be converted to other uses because of zoning restrictions. Finally, in 1996, the City designated both neighborhoods as regeneration areas, permitting a wide variety of land uses, such as residential, live/work spaces, retail, commercial, entertainment, and light industrial. This, in part, was due to a change in the definition of industry as well as more openness to mixing of uses. As Williams emphasizes, "there needs to be a mechanism to have a more jumbled mixed use"[202] to include retail, manufacturing, and residential.

There is an effort to support Ontario Made with studies of how to bring industry back.[203] Two sets of manufacturers started an initiative called "Take Back

Manufacturing." One is a younger generation of makers, and the other is the Society of Manufacturing Engineers, which wants to revitalize manufacturing industries and jobs.[204] Using apprenticeship programs to train skilled workers, and collaborating with both government agencies and businesses, they are bringing attention to manufacturing in Canada. Through incubators and the support of small firms, jobs could rise, and with the potential to recycle vacant space, more places for the smaller firms become available. As in other urban centers, new manufacturing that requires less space can occupy multistory buildings, capitalizing on innovations for the small-scale products and robotic machinery. Williams also believes in a diversity of sectors, rather than a few targeted industries, and that clusters of single industries are dangerous because flexibility and diversity is needed to attract numerous sectors and not limit potential for new companies.[205] Toronto has the same issues of other declining industrial cities: the change in use of many industrial buildings encroaches on potential industrial growth, but the new focus to encourage manufacturing jobs in mixed-use neighborhoods could inspire a new paradigm for the city.

With the industrial spatial developments of clusters and constellations, both in those newly emerging global industrial cities, and the former more traditional industrial city, the ability of entrepreneurs, consumers, and governments have the potential to energize a new paradigm of socially conscious and just employment to grow economies as sustainable and viable for the future. The new focus on glocal production, both for ethical reasons and job retention, can also contribute to a new perspective on urban industry. The next section of the book describes specific architectural possibilities for factories — based on the social and technological shifts discussed in the preceding text — as they begin to be reinserted back into cities, or as new visions arise for the use of former industrial urban fabric.

CONTEMPORARY FACTORY ARCHITECTURE

THE ARCHITECTURE OF THE FACTORY in the late twentieth century continued to be a place of experimentation, both in terms of engineering and design, yielding new architectural concepts, and innovations in new building materials specific to industrial programs. As in other building typologies, the design of the factory and the resulting larger industrial landscape corresponds to cultural, social, and economic systems in a form that follows the functional logic of both the internal operation, as well as the manufacturing logistics and supply chains of the global networked infrastructure.[1] Just as Russian architect Mosei Ginzburg in the Modern era was fascinated with the idea of the factory being organized around the manufacturing processing of his time, so are many contemporary architects intrigued by the potential of the factory program and the integration of the processing flow into their structures. This chapter focuses on new architectural design and factory typologies, and explores technological and production flow issues as they relate to urban manufacturing.

In parallel to the designs of the Modernist era, the more recent factory straddles "building" and "Architecture," integrating the flows of production with building design. Manufacturing, as a logical process, is one of step-by-step or cellular production, and has to be synchronized with the layout of the building itself. Manufacturing therefore requires a customized solution, one which fits a specialized process of mass customization like a glove. Another layout is that of the modular building construction, as in Bat'a, or the factory shed structures, pervasive throughout the globalized manufacturing landscape, which have their roots in World War II's need for dispersal and camouflage as well as the efficient use of funds and the saving of company resources.

Changes in industrial production, both at the large and the smaller scale, have made the return to multistory structures possible, with systems such as automated vertical and spiral conveyors, interior freestanding elevator systems, and increased internal mobility. High-bay storage technology can be used as a vertical conveyor for muscular production, with elevated platforms in a unified volume. The factory in the city is now addressing new production technologies of smaller economies of scale, as well as ecological concerns for saving open land, contributing to urban densification and thus sustainability. The rising price of urban real estate has reignited the potential for the multistory factory, and for companies to locate near their consumer base and their workers, as was true in the first industrial revolution.

The factory worker in the developed economies of the late twentieth century, with the changes in labor in the late 1960s and 1970s (the rise of unions, the demands of protests and strikes, collective bargaining, and increased

communication among labor) informed new spatial strategies of factory architecture. With workers taking more control (through employee-owned shops, and
somewhat of a reduction of hierarchy in the digital process) factory layouts became
more fluid and less divided by task. There was also a blurring of office administration and production spaces, and separate administration buildings were eliminated
from the factory complex. Laborers were placed alongside R&D employees; even
marketing and sales departments collaborated with product development earlier in
the manufacturing process than ever before. The more knowledge-based production
system often found managers assigned to the factory floor. Amenities such as shared
fitness centers, cafeterias, and common meeting spaces also blurred management
and worker boundaries. With each technological upgrade, the space of production
changed in order to accommodate that new technology, and the way that workers
labored with it, as new forms of "intellectual" production emerged. The organization
of production space reinforces and underscores labor and production within a social
order. As the factory demonstrates, the changes in attitudes towards work become
necessary to recognize even if it is a part of a company's marketing rhetoric.

Three themes dominate in contemporary factory design today — flexibility,
sustainability, and the "spectacle" (production as consumption). These categories
are pertinent in placing the typology within a cultural framework broader than the
design alone. These themes will be discussed in more detail with the vertical urban
factory examples below. But many general issues relate to all kinds of factory buildings, not only the vertical and the urban. While the ramifications of globalization
and large-scale supply chains, as mentioned previously, resulted in banal sheds —
factories in cities faced a new challenge. Towards the end of the twentieth century,
new companies that moved to cities did so for the same reasons that they did in the
late nineteenth century: proximity to consumers, entrepreneurs, skilled workers,
financial incentives, and ease of distribution. As the worker's task has changed to
one of more intelligent production — with CNC technologies and mass customization — a shift has occurred from large-scale machines and robots to tabletop
robotics and computing, and in some cases, a return to hand assembly. At the same
time, the space of the factory has altered, evolving into smaller, cleaner, and denser
urban production spaces. One can ask: What is the space of immaterial labor? How
do we work in factories now? How has the factory been redefined for new high-
tech, small-scale industry, even though large-scale factories for textile and machine
industries in cities are still necessary?

The two scales thus continue in parallel, that of the smaller neo-cottage industries, which have become knowledge-based spaces or intellectualized as "maker"
spaces and the large production spaces often subcontracted in places such as China
and Bangladesh. It is this challenge that architecture and industrial urbanism face
in order to provide new ways to design the spaces of production in the flexible
economy, and as a future opportunity with worker justice.

While the idea of light, air, and open spaces for the workplace had come into
the fore of the Modernist vertical urban factory, World War II changed the course
of factory design. The disappearance of creative factory design, as recognized by
Buckminster Fuller, was due in part to the practical needs of wartime manufacturing. It is at this pivotal moment that factories became sealed sheds built for speed

and as basic generic wrappers for machines, rather than a factory as a machine. This change took place without concern for the workers or the interest in the vitality of the city. From the shed factories, new branding and marketing ideas influenced corporate architecture. But the spread of the factory to the horizontal dimension, following the flow of logistics, continued to be instrumental in factory design as a generic space of globalization. The metal panels or ubiquitous tilt-up concrete walls expunged of windows, artificially ventilated, and literally boxed in, became the next banality to address in terms of design. In the 1970s, organizational arrangements, such as placing management and worker in proximity, as well as the need for flexible spaces, drove a new typology wherein the long-span interior, large roofscape, and envelope became embraced as places for design exploration. Thus, the wrapper became the place of opportunity for architects to design, as they worked in collaboration with industrial engineers who informed the logistical layouts. A look at how design was harnessed for all types of factories is valuable in this context of the vertical urban factory.

HIGH-TECH FOR CLEAN-TECH

In the 1960s, industrialists and architects aspired to new rigorous aesthetics, forming a new direction for factory architecture in general. Building and industrial technologies inspired an avant-garde design for architects, who are enamored with the machine. British architects such as Richard Rogers, Norman Foster, and Nicholas Grimshaw opened up the factory again to its environment and made a place conducive to work, with new designs influenced by Buckminster Fuller, the Japanese Metabolists, and the notion of the factory as a living machine. This generation of factory architects embraced the factory mechanisms and the aesthetics of industry, in the same manner as the Modernists had granted status to vernacular manufacturing spaces. The "high-tech" aesthetic was amplified in a fascination with how technology could perform and represent an optimistic idea.

Architects known as the Metabolists in Japan, which included Kisho Kurokawa (1934–2007), Kenzo Tange (1913–2005), and Fumihiko Maki designed speculative megastructures that encapsulated urban networks and mechanical systems into large-scale buildings. With the need to rebuild Japan postwar, the Metabolists conceived of projects based on Japanese building tradition and Buddhism, and inspired other architects. Their work, characterized by their flexibility, use of kit-of-parts elements, and modular systems, was often based on biological systems. Many of these were conceived as lightweight structures dependent on technology. Often, a main core would house the infrastructure systems from which the building could grow, or modules could be added to on an as-needed basis, and were often dispensable as well. The urban design projects for Tokyo Bay by Kenzo Tange (1960), and Kisho Kurokawa's Helix City (1961), which looked to longer and shorter cycles of building, formed hierarchical relationships between structures. These massive utopic plans were unbuilt, but influential. Individual buildings, such as the Yamanashi Communications Centre by Kenzo Tange & URTEC (1966), inspired also by Arata Isosaki's City in the Sky concept (1962) and Kurokawa's Nakagin Capsule Building (1972), featured interlocking cellular components that could expand continuously.

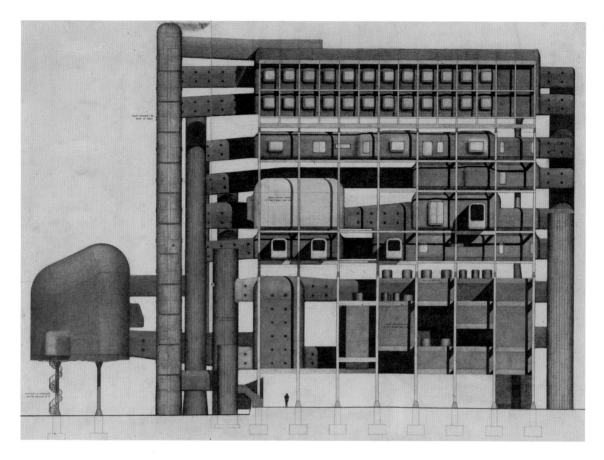

Japanese factory buildings were also conceived with open systems and adaptability with clip-on and plug-in cellular components designed during the country's industrial boom. Kisho Kurokawa designed the Nitto Food Company in 1964, using prefabricated modules with X-beams so that the building could be expanded according to the changes in the production. He also experimented with ideas for the factory city with his intriguing Floating Factory Metobonate in 1969, which links factory structures with bands of infrastructure above and below the water, connected like an electronic circuitry board. Other Japanese architects of this period including Ichiro Ebihara (1905–1990) designed factories, one for the Dainihon Ink Company in Tokyo and another for Vilene Co., Ltd. in Shiga. The Vilene factory is a combination of pre-fabricated and cast-in-place concrete, which was new to post-World War II Japan; its elements can be compared to the traditional architecture of Shinto shrines in the replaceable horizontal beams and hexagonal pieces as a flexible and expandable structure.

    The British avant-garde group Archigram, also influenced this new generation of factory and mechanical structures. Michael Webb, one member of the group, as a student in 1957, designed a project for the Furniture Manufacturers Association Building. His scheme, while mostly envisioned for concrete, exposed the tubes and intestines of the building, presaging the architecture of the future high-tech teams. The other Archigram members, Peter Cook, Warren Chalk, David Greene, Dennis Crompton, and Ron Herron did not build many projects, but instead described

▲ Michael Webb, drawing of the Furniture Manufacturers Association headquarters, High Wycombe, England, side elevation, 1957–1958. Graphite and ink on tracing paper mounted on board (59.7 x 81.3 cm), 1957

▲ Team 4, Reliance Controls factory, Swindon, England, 1961

and disseminated their ideas in exhibitions and publications. Their cartoon and collaged imagery responded to the dynamic and electronic interface of new technologies and network structures, as in Ron Herron's 1964 Walking City and Plug-in City. Archigram also influenced the Metabolists and the two groups shared similar ideas of flexibility and buildings "programmed and structured for change." The ideas for do-it-yourself buildings and the democratization of architecture inspired an ephemeral and loose system for program.

The coalescence of Metabolists, Archigram, and the British interest in engineering details invigorated a new paradigm for the factory right at a time when production technologies dramatically shifted to computer-driven systems, influencing factory culture in the third industrial revolution. Architects Norman Foster, Richard Rogers, Nicholas Grimshaw, and Derek Walker developed architectural concepts that were based on new technologies and a futuristic imagery that came to be known as "high-tech." While they did not consider high-tech to be a style — as they shunned the idea of a category — they shared a predilection for similar materials, structures, and design. The characteristics of high-tech architecture were lightness, pragmatism, transparency, flexibility, and the use of primary colors. The inside-out aspect that exposes structure and mechanical systems such as air ducts — as in the Ron Herron drawings — celebrated the building systems. The physical transparency and visibility into the interior of the building through a layering of elements became integrated into building design. Collaborating with design engineers such as Peter Rice (1935–1992) of Arup and Ted Happold (1930–1996), the architects exposed building structure to reveal cables, rods, and tension elements. These high-tech architects embraced an optimistic outlook in terms of faith in science and the progress of technology.[2]

The high-tech concepts inspired numerous factory buildings, and merged in a synergy between function and form, which was then adapted to other building typologies similarly to Modern architects' embrace of the vernacular gridded factory to inspire architecture in general. The imagery of the high-tech building does sometimes overwhelm, as the message is the meaning; it is what it is. Rogers emphasizes that he was trying to create a legible tectonic language where each piece says what it is, what it means. He is interested in a layering of indeterminate forms and an order within the construction systems and the servicing systems. He also focuses on the way people work in a building — such as the Centre Pompidou (1971–77), inspired by Cedric Price and Joan Littlewood's Fun Palace concept of 1962, and Lloyd's of London (1986) — along with factories that have a dynamic exchange between the building and the activities within.[3]

High-tech characteristics provided solutions that were suited to factories, such as long spans, adaptability, and flexibility. The large open volumes were appealing to industrialists who could extend the life of a factory building by using the interior in different ways over time. Often citing Joseph Paxton's 1851 Crystal Palace as inspiration, Foster incorporated ideas of the lightweight and transparent skin-and-framework building to allow for numerous interior configurations. Buckminster Fuller also influenced the group's designs, as did the Maison de Verre (1928–1932) by Pierre Chareau (1883–1950) with Bernard Bijvoet in Paris, in which the industrial materials are exposed and integrated with household functions. Rogers also discusses "the serviced and the served" of Louis I. Kahn in which the framework has a longer life than the pieces of the building, the latter of which can be substituted and exchanged out — again, similar to the ideas of the Metabolists.[4]

The machine aesthetic's expressiveness, along with the potential for an industrialized production of buildings as kit-of-parts and machine-like in their design, became a visual polemic. Some key examples of these factories shed light on the significance of the industrial program and structure. The Reliance Controls factory in Swindon, England (1966), which was designed by the London-based husbands and wives of Team 4 — Norman Foster and Wendy Cheesman, Richard Rogers and Su Brumwell — was one of the first in this manner. The 3,200-square-meter factory was significant for its extreme speed of construction (under one year), prefabricated components, diagonal tension rods in an X-brace on the exterior, and a flexible design possible from large interior column spans, with service plugged in to fixed elements. The interior was an open, nonhierarchical, indeterminate space. It also introduced the ideas of the order of the building coming from the servicing. The architects embraced ideas of the democratization of the workplace, about

▲ Richard Rogers Partnership, Inmos factory, South Wales, 1982
▲ Richard Rogers Partnership, PA Technologies, Princeton, New Jersey, 1975–1983
▶ Fritz Haller, USM Modular Furniture Factory, Munsingen, Switzerland, 1961
▶ USM Modular Furniture assembly facility, Munsingen, Switzerland, 2014

which Norman Foster spoke at the time; this philosophy was represented in the design of an entrance shared by both factory workers and the managers.[5] Reliance Controls was expanded by one third, but then, ironically, the flexibility no longer served the client and it was demolished in 1991.

The idea of the factory as an open plan or a non-plan, as a container for production, stems too from wartime factories in which the interior expanse was essential to the massiveness of objects undergoing production, or the never-ending search for uninterrupted space, seen in the gridded concrete factories of the early twentieth century. The indeterminate structure responds to the new flexible economy, and to communications and computer technology as these variables expanded and then contracted, or expanded again. It also places the control of the building in the hands of the owners who can decide what to change, as old technologies become obsolete. A few examples epitomize the concept, such as Rogers' design with Anthony Hunt engineers for Inmos microprocessing factory for silicon wafers in 1982 in South Wales, which incorporates clean rooms in a shed structured made with a series of double cable-stayed masts that support steel trusses. The building's mechanical systems housed on the roof placed the technology of this government-funded factory in full view and increased the openness of the factory ceiling. Also in 1982, Rogers' designed his first building in the U.S. — the Princeton, New Jersey building for PA Technologies, a British technology consultancy that designed telephones and the machines to make them. The company required a flexible shed with all the mechanical systems embedded in the design. Rogers based the design on the Inmos project. Both projects have lightweight roofs that are suspended from central masts, with the mechanical systems above that are accessible. The interior includes a space for workers to mingle during breaks from laboratory research. Collaborating with engineer Rice, who designed the engineered trusses to support mechanical platforms and the masts, the composition creates a visual consistency. The tubular steel tension structure has diagonal A-frames bolted into the foundation as outriggers, envisioning expandability with additional bays.[6]

Another driver for high-tech projects was the kit-of-parts and modular gridded steel construction systems which mimic the Modernist modular concrete frame structures. Fritz Haller (1924–2012), with Paul Schaerer, designed their own furniture factory, USM Haller in Münsingen, Switzerland (1964) as a modular kit-of-parts of steel components of various functions — frames, joints, trussed girders,

columns, walls, mechanical conduits — which can be extended, dismantled, and eventually repurposed, mimicking their furniture designs.

Sustainable issues also became part of the discussion in the early 1980s and architects followed ideas from research into solar gain, building recycling, and the initiative of "long life, loose fit, low energy," as coined by Welsh architect and then Royal Institute of British Architects (RIBA) president, Alex Gordon (1917–1999).[7] Gordon equated the idea of "loose fit," originated by architect John Weeks in the 1960s, with the potential for building reconfiguration and adaptability, which becomes today's challenge for a sustainable method of building, especially for the energy-consuming factory.

Just as Modernist architects found the concrete grid and the glass greenhouses suited to the production spaces of their time, mechanization and gadgetry as components of mass-produced and prefabricated architectural elements became appropriated in factory designs. While high-tech design has become viewed as an aesthetic polemic, there are few other design ideologies that so clearly express manufacturing as a system.

SPACE OF FLOWS

Since the 1960s, organizational management experts and industrial engineers have devised more open and less hierarchical spatial systems in the factory that diverge from the early Fordist assembly line; such arrangements are intended to ease worker alienation and to develop efficient new manufacturing systems. Due to these advances, as well as new technologies, there emerged many nonlinear and asymmetrical alternatives to the linear production model. These often less-hierarchical layouts have shifted to U-shaped processing, and cellular, modular, and fractal organization.

Another trend impacting the spatial configuration of the factory — and factory management — is the placement of R&D areas either on, or adjacent to, the factory floor. No longer is there a head house for administration and engineers, and a separate space for the workers, as there was at Fiat and Ford. Often, laborers and managers enter through the same entrance and share cafeterias. In addition, a new nomenclature arose which referred to workers as "partners," "team players," or "associates," contributing to a further attempt to blur boundaries not only phys-ically but socially. However, not even these new titles can disrupt the hierarchy completely, as they still serve to commodify social relationships towards the goal of efficient production in the company's rhetoric. In one Australian factory in which workers and managers did not successfully collaborate, and production was low, management initiated dialogues between the various levels of employees, resulting in increased production.[8] Sometimes smoother relationships between workers and management give the illusion of worker control. For instance, in filing and negoti-ating grievances, the workers can reap small rewards — even if it is in response to union requirements — getting management to tweak a process on the factory floor, address health and safety concerns, or concede leisure space. Philosophers such as Negri have noted that worker interaction is a commodification in the hegemony of capitalism extending to all relationships, not only within the factory, making all of life focused on production.[9]

▶ Gunter Henn, drawing of a fractal factory scheme, 2000

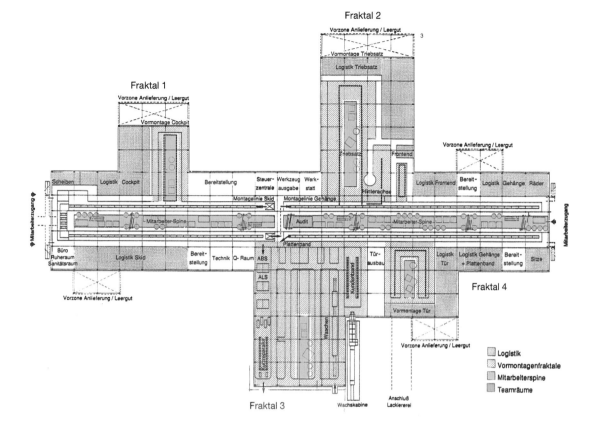

Consumer demand for new products has also influenced factory layouts, as mentioned earlier. Money-saving systems, such as lean production and quality control, are both organizational and operational systems that are more worker-focused to increase production. The human and technological systems are always in tandem. When the factory design follows the flow of production, the layout is integrated both with the production and organizational systems. If the factory is flexible, the industrial equipment can be easily reconfigured, as the processing changes over time to meet the company's needs. The standard production flow that is C, L, or E-shaped can be expanded to alternative arrangements needed for JIT production, such as U-shaped; the latter is preferred for efficiency, as the worker can stand in the middle of the space and watch the continuous processing from the beginning to end. Other shapes, such as "solar system" layouts, or "mainstreet spines," increase personnel interaction. Nonlinear thinking in production has a new value in terms of complex management that depends on relationships between people, not just machines.

Cellular

One fundamental layout concept places the different divisions of a factory — engineering, design, and research — in proximity to manufacturing. This spatial organization allows workers to feed off of one another and to test in real time. Raw materials in this new interwoven system enter the production process at various points with the use of interchangeable modules for expansion and contraction. The

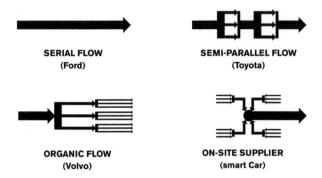

cellular layout has subsections of production that can follow different flows according to the task that is then divided up into different configurations. This arrangement is used by companies such as Volvo in Sweden, BMW in Spartensburg, North Carolina and in Leipzig, Germany, and Brooks Brothers and Edison Price lighting factories in Long Island City, where the object in production moves from area to area in a more segmented journey through the factory. In cells, the production is divided into families, which are like mini-factories in which the entire production is completed for a single object. The system works efficiently for multiple production processes, including mass customization, and the creation of many diverse models of one thing. Within the cells the workers collaborate and have more control of the production as they stay with the object as it develops throughout the process. This is in contrast to a company such as Foxconn, where the workers sit or stand at stationary tables throughout the day, attaching the same electronic piece to the main product as it goes through a line — a repetitive process in which the workers have no knowledge of the other steps along the line or even what the final product is.

Fractal

▲ Comparison of automotive manufacturing processes

Some plants follow another non-hierarchical layout in what is called a fractal organization system, as in Gunter Henn's design for the Skoda automotive plant in Poland (2000). The fractal system responds to management needs of customized mass production, JIT as lean manufacturing, and supervision through quality control. This is a variation on cellular layouts in which a spine is the main logistics circulation system and cells are the fractal units where there are opportunities for feedback. In fractal organization, each part of a pattern contains similar information at every scale, and uses algorithms that permit the divisions of production to self-organize in the feedback system. Skoda's layout allows workers to respond to various changes along the line, with input from either side of a central spine that is left open for the core production. The preassembly is located on the outside of the spine, making more of a circular ring. Here, Skoda has placed work areas in the spine with flexible offices in double-height volumes, and break areas adjacent to the production line, where the engineers and technicians can work together to solve a problem. The worker becomes the center of the layouts rather than the products, and deliveries and transit are on the exterior, in contrast to Benetton's Treviso factory, where the center spine is used for deliveries. The spine system is focused on a fluid system through which all things are fed, as in the VW Dresden, Germany plant or the Hamback, France smart car factory, where the suppliers build their components alongside the main car assembly line. Workers feed the component into the spine at the point in production where it is needed.

Mini Factories

More recently, new factory designs adapt to the smaller scales of tools such as tabletop robotics and handheld computers, forming an operational and spatial shift in production spaces towards dynamic networked and interactive flexible spaces. From large-scale factories to the new smaller neo-cottage industry, the squeeze for space in cities encourages vertical factories. The new smaller-scale factories have such simple layouts, even just one room; they represent a return to a workshop space where the workers walk from area to area of the factory floor to complete one phase of the product in a smaller space of an existing factory, which is also flexible for the future. The verticality encourages the use of various spiral conveyors, interior elevator systems, and mezzanines. An extreme example is BMW Munich, which adopts mechanisms for stacking goods in automated warehouses as models for layering their factory inside high-bay spaces. The new MakerBot factory in Sunset Park, Brooklyn, has stacked their workers in mezzanine constructions resembling bunk beds, in essence making a doubled vertical urban factory, through a new layered interiority.

THE CONSUMPTION OF PRODUCTION:
THE FACTORY AS SPECTACLE

It is not just that the relationship to commodities is now plain to see — commodities are now all that there is to see; the world we see is the world of the commodity.[10]
—Guy Debord

The architecture of the factory reflects the speed of the new economy, becoming a part of the "spectacle" of commodities dominating our society.[11] Within the new economy, a corporation's race to make money, to brand its image, and to dominate the market has harshly impacted job security, the workplace, and capital investments.[12] Quick-paced exchange, faddish buying, and globalization are sped up by the increased connectivity of the Internet. In the automated work environment both blue-and white-collar workers are alienated from each other and from the products they create. The emphasis on earning capital has divested corporations from actually making things and has resulted in the phenomenon of immaterial labor. In this new condition of contemporary capitalism there are often no corporate ethics or allegiances, no "Organization Man."[13] As companies shed assets — property, people, and equipment — they are focused on "branding, not producing," on the *spectacle* of production rather than production itself.[14] As Debord discussed, that which is being produced, whether it be cities, the economy, or goods, has become a component of the "society of the spectacle," that which is focused on commodity culture. In factories, the spectacle of production could have the positive effect of making workers visible, but we need to ask, for whom? It could also be considered just a marketing tool that traps the consumer in the company's web.

The architecture of the factory is absorbed by these cultural and economic phenomena. At one end of the spectrum, corporations have guided factory design towards reconceiving the workplace as the company's marketing and public relations tool. Although workers are increasingly removed from the production process because of robotics and computer-integrated manufacturing, there is a renewed fascination with the mysteries of mechanization and methods of production — separation breeds desire. Since the first industrial revolution when the Corliss steam engine took center stage as it powered the generator and electrified the Philadelphia Centennial (1876), and Modernists appropriated the machine for its aesthetic — machines have been symbolic of power and progress. Today, as obsolete factory artifacts are put on display in museums, or as factories are abandoned, there is a fascination with the tough and visceral, tinged with nostalgia. Production is incorporated into the architecture as an element that fosters an obsession with automation gadgetry; in displaying what was once overwhelming, the factory's aestheticization overcompensates for the industrial shift to virtual production and nanotechnology. As Mark Dery notes: "from an age of hardware into what might be called an age of vaporware," the dematerialization of the machine makes a comeback as a "repressed machine. [. . .] The intangible is shot through with a longing for an explicable techno-culture."[15] Desire for watching the making and the machines at work becomes fetishized.

On one side, companies have invisible factories off-shore in the globalized economy. As discussed earlier, these buildings are often just simple cinder-block walls with a steel roof; better versions have dropped ceilings and air-conditioning with delivery areas. In these warehouse factories, the interiors can be changed overnight to accommodate different assembly lines and products. Now subcontractors are making all brands in generic spaces.

But, on the other hand, emphasis on the relationship between the factory and the worker has shifted to highlight the connection between the consumer and the commodity, as the customer consumes the production. Breaking with the norms of hiding the dirty work of assembly lines, or locating the plant in an industrial zone away from residential developments, production itself is at times the visible locus of sales promotion. Modernist factories such as Van der Vlugt's Van Nelle in Rotterdam and Gropius' Faguswerk in Germany were new paradigms for Modern industrialization. But some were designed as extreme expressions, striving to be anything other than a factory, including the Samson Uniroyal Tire Factory designed by architect Stiles O. Clements (1930), which was inspired by the seventh-century B.C. Assyrian Palace of King Sargon. Sited along Interstate 5 in Los Angeles, the factory broadcast attention to tire manufacturing, which was essential to the auto industry and the new highway network. Samson was the largest tire factory on the West Coast and workers produced 5,000 tires and 10,000 inner tubes per day. In Dresden, the Yenidze

cigarette factory — the largest in Germany at the time — was designed by Martin Hammitzsch in 1909 to mimic a Turkish mosque in an eclectic Art Nouveau/Moorish style. Founded by tobacco importer Hugo Zietz, it was named after the region in northern Greece from whence the tobacco came. The first reinforced concrete skeleton for a glass dome in Germany crowns the building, with a minaret that is purely decorative. Over 1,500 people worked in the well-lit and ventilated space through the 1950s. A canteen on the top floor and rest areas were provided for the workers as well as a roof terrace for lunch breaks. The colored granite, glazed tiles, and red and white sandstone both promoted the brand and made it an attractor.

▲ Stiles O. Clements, Samson Uniroyal Tire factory, Los Angeles, 1930
▲ Martin Hammitzsch, Yenidze, cigarette factory, Dresden, Germany, 1907

Factories are also part of tourist culture, following the tradition of pilgrimages to the engineering and industrial feats of early twentieth-century America — be it the Tennessee Valley Authority Dam, the Milwaukee Beer Brewery, the Hershey

chocolate factory, and especially automotive factories where you could pick up your newly purchased car. In such cases, corporations, including Heinz and Kellogg, opened up their factories to visitors and turned them into theme parks of varying degrees. Factory tourism continues at watch companies, which are inviting clients to their Swiss factories instead of mounting displays at commercial fairs. Visiting the factory has become more prestigious than shopping at the store in the city and connects the consumer to their desire for brand authenticity.[16]

Other companies are still secretive, but find ways of showcasing their work virtually. The company Intel invested $2 billion to convert their sprawling Chandler, Arizona Fab12 plant from a 200-millimeter-wafer plant to one capable of producing 300-millimeter-wafers in a 65-nanometer-process technology. None of this new construction is visible from the outside; rather, the conversion involved an interior retooling by industrial engineers. Due to this invisible revamping, the company displays the factory and workers in white overalls on a virtual tour on the Web and in carefully selected narratives. As architect Gunter Henn said with regards to the VW Transparent factory in Dresden: "The key link is the consumer; we had to respond to the consumer, not to the building client or the worker."[17]

Some factories demonstrate the idea of the consumption of production as a mode of architectural design. As literal spectacles, hybrid factories incorporate

▲ Grimshaw Architects, Financial Times Building, London, 1988
▶ Zaha Hadid, BMW Factory, interior conveyor bridge, Leipzig, Germany, 2005

a showcase along with manufacturing, is seen in projects such as Nicholas Grimshaw's Financial Times building in London's East India Dock (1988). The glass facade allowed views into the production line, rendering it transparent, both physically and philosophically. This factory rises four stories to house two printing presses, each 12 meters high by 35 meters long, behind a glazed facade 16 meters high by 96 meters long. When it was in operation, through 1996, the factory opened up production to make visible the journey of mile-long rolls of pink paper through the printing presses. At the center, aerofoil steel columns at six-meter centers support the building. Steel plates support the glass in a bolted system at each meeting point of four glass panels, with tension rods supporting the vertical loads linked to the columns. Cylinders housing stairs, one pair glazed and the other aluminum-clad, maintain the factory floor as a contiguous open space for the large-scale machinery. Conceived to give "clear expression to its internal organization," solid corners at each end clad in aluminum panels housed paper and the loading bay.[18] The visibility to the interior symbolized the democratic ideas of the open workplace and free-speech, but the company, nonetheless, moved from the plant. Today, the building is a server farm for communications technologies.

In particular, the automotive industry has embraced the idea of the consumption of production, with numerous showroom factories where you can buy your car. Noise and confusion have given way to quiet, clean rooms and

computer-operated machines of display — cathedrals of commerce attract capital to attract investors, and to attract consumers to watch commodities being produced, again reinforcing the idea of the spectacle. The visitors are exposed to the factory — production is not stopped; visitors are accommodated. Two BMW factories are exemplary of this trend. One in Spartenburg, North Carolina, designed in 1995 by Albert Kahn Associates, the descendant firm to Albert Kahn, is a pinwheel-shaped plant housing over 100,000 square meters of space. Both visitors and employees share the entrance to a "Main Street," which provides access to the entire facility. An open production office along a 1,000-square-meter "communication plaza" encourages interaction between workers and administration. This nucleus of activity, modeled on a neighborhood, allows both visitors and employees to see automobiles transported by an overhead conveyor system from the body shop to the paint shop and the assembly area by an overhead conveyor system. From here the workers (or "associates," as they are called in Japanese-style management lingo) monitor production for quality control. Similarly, the 2,787-square-meter-crescent-shaped Visitor's Center, or "Zentrum," is based on the Ford Motor Company's 1939 World's Fair exhibition hall, which was moved to River Rouge at the Ford museum, as well as Eero Saarinen's "Styling Room" for the GM Technical Center. The visitors who come to see cars being made are exposed to the regular workings of the factory — the production line becomes a point of sale and communication.

Visibility was not only essential in the 2005 BMW plant in Leipzig, in terms of the idea of spectacle, but also for the cross-pollination of departments between the different spatial functions. Architect Zaha Hadid received the commission via a design competition for the design of a central building between the existing boxy manufacturing sheds in the $1.7 billion factory. The German government and the European Union provided BMW with incentive funding to locate in what was then a depressed East Germany. On a 80-hectare greenfield site, the factory is 12.8 kilometers south of the city via a tram line, so that workers can easily commute to the complex.

The building brief called for a link between the various factory spaces that would be welcoming to workers and visitors. The factory flow suited the dramatic fluid designs of Hadid, as dynamic movement. Here she designed a concrete zigzag structure clad with blue and gray metal panels, and diagonally mounted channel

▲ Afra & Tobia Scarpa, Benetton factory, Treviso, Italy, 1967

glass, punctuated by strips of horizontal windows. A bridge structure encloses a courtyard at the full-height glazed entry at the northern end, welcoming both the factory workers and the administrators through a multistoried entrance hall. Once through the glass entrance, employees swipe their ID cards before going to their workstations — some wearing overalls and others suits, some carrying lunch boxes and others briefcases; they pass a reception area, a souvenir shop, a waiting room, and a cafeteria along the way. This entry signals the effort of the democratization of the workplace and blurs the hierarchies between the administration and the production personnel, but is it all for show?

The elbow of one zigzag leads to the paint rooms, and the other to the assembly sheds where suppliers deliver parts to the factory or where the companies have set up shop. As a plant that is based on JIT production, there is minimal storage of parts because the process is in continuous movement. Robots assemble the cars, and paint the panels, as animated as humans. Testing rooms and design workshops divided by diagonal concrete slabs line the corridors, and staff can interact spontaneously and engage in brainstorming sessions in adjacent meeting rooms. Flexible multilevel office spaces punctuated with horizontal bands of windows look out to landscaped courtyards. And while it appears to be a one-story structure — as in the dense BMW central Munich plants — the factory operates within multiple levels in the interior.

Crossing through the mid-level of the high-bay storage area is a dramatic silver conveyor bridge that provides a structure on which car bodies are transferred to the paint shop. Blue under-lighting highlights the cars in process as the belt runs through the administration spaces, cafeteria, and close to the entry. The bridge has become a spectacle and an effect of mechanization.

Another organizational system is seen in the material input and output flow of Benetton's factory layouts. Spanning three decades of development, the company's complexes in Treviso in northern Italy were designed by architects and industrial designers Afra and Tobia Scarpa. The firm designed not only the factory and administration buildings, but developed a new approach to retail design by launching the company's international franchises in the 1960s. Tobia Scarpa designed the first factory building in 1967 in Paderno di Ponzano, Treviso, with Christiano Gasparetto and Carlo Maschietto. The complex, adjacent to an historic villa, comprises an administration building and manufacturing facility identified by two distinctive roofscapes; this sets up a dialogue between the two functions. The primary girders, with a series of X-shaped prefabricated concrete beams, have openings for skylights in the interstices. The beams are supported on the 84-meter-long hollow girder for the entire length of the building, forming the main axis, and also by perimeter 9.2-meter-high precast panels walls with a C-shaped section. The X-shaped beams, with their sloped angles, reflect light in the interior and have the double duty of integrating the piping and electrical wiring systems through their hollow channels. The long girder identifies a street-like circulation spine bracketed by the production areas. The success of this flexible layout led to its future use in the design of three other facilities.

In 1993, Benetton hired the Scarpas to build a two-part manufacturing facility in Castrette di Villorba, Treviso, whose singularity lies in the structural system and

▲ Barkow Leibinger, Trumpf factory, Hettingen, Germany, 2013

unobstructed production space with a high-tech industrial aesthetic and materiality. The single-story complex has two identical 18,000-meter-square manufacturing buildings in seven 25-meter modules based on the weaving machine dimensions. The factory layout has three distinct areas: centralized assembly, a central roadway spine, and two production areas. The JIT production method foregrounded distribution, so the central spine is larger than that in the earlier factory.

To achieve the essential unobstructed manufacturing space, the architects employed a structural pylon-and-steel-cable system developed by Bridon Ropes of Doncaster, England normally used for bridges and here used for the first time for a factory building. The roof trusses are supported on the exterior reinforced concrete walls, which are clad with insulated, ribbed, and galvanized zinc-coated steel etched with a herringbone pattern, resembling woven fabric. The wall panel system incorporates a fiber optic cable network and electronic systems for harnessing the information flow between the offices and retail shops. Both visually and organizationally, the building expresses the design, manufacturing, and distribution process of an innovative company that was at the epicenter of new manufacturing technologies.[19]

Often, the form of a factory building is a literal representation of the company's brand, or "duck" in Robert Venturi's definition, versus what he calls the "decorated shed."[20] This representation is seen in designer Philippe Stark's 1987 knife factory for Laguiole in Aveyron, France, through which a giant-scaled knife model pierces the roof. Or, similarly, the metal suitcase company Rimowa built a factory made of its own materials designed in 1986 in Cologne by Dhalbender, Gatermann, and Schossig. L'Oreal's factory by Valode & Pistre et Associés in Aulnay-sous-Bois mimics the form of a flower as the company embraced the spectacle in factory design. The scheme comprises three metal-roofed petal-like forms that span a 60-by-131-meter space, each of which houses different production units. Engineer Peter Rice collaborated with the architects to create a lightweight structure of tubular steel with radial V-trusses to support the roofs. Inside, catwalks hang from the trusses on which workers circulate and from which they can see down into the production space. Kathryn Gustafson enhanced the flower metaphor in her landscape design comprised of earth berms, a central garden, and a decorative pool. Each roof slopes down to the courtyard, with the arched facades shaded from direct sunlight and the higher elevation merging with the rectilinear buildings that house services.

A factory design as an aesthetic project that is also functional is evident in the designs of Berlin-based architects Barkow Leibinger, for Trumpf GmbH, a laser machine and tool company for sheet metals. In an industrial district of Ditzigen, near Stuttgart, the precision of the 1998 factory design is inspired by the surrounding patchwork of agricultural fields, as the building slides into the topography and folds within the landscape, paralleling the process of fabrication itself. The 1,400-square-meter facility includes laser production halls, storage, offices, and an exhibition floor connected to the existing building by tunnels top-lit by three steel-and-glass light chimneys. Light penetrates the work halls through placement of clerestory windows in the undulating roof between the sheets of steel — as a kind of play on the traditional skylight monitor. The east-west axis at the center of the factory separates the production areas from the storage and truck delivery areas. A three-story office and lobby wrap around the laser machine production hall and are separated by a double-height corridor, also with a skylight. The lower level has a cistern to gather rainwater from the roofs for cooling. The facade cladding and corrugated-metal panel roof reflect the precision of the machine tools developed inside.

In Hettingen, Barkow Leibinger's design for the Production Hall appears to be a continuously expanding structure, reflecting concepts of the flexible factory. A column-free space with 24-meter-wide bays was required for the large machinery and north-facing skylights as well as a clerestory provide ample daylight. Here, it is the corrugated-metal facade that is folded like origami and the roof merges with the landscape. The elevation reflects the roof pitches of the surrounding houses and of a traditional factory buildings. These factory designs instigated further collaborations between the architect and client for experiments with CNC cutting of architectural metals. Their designs are careful calibrations that are not over-exuberant, but combine the art of architecture with the pragmatism of industry.

Upon the occasion of Vitra's opening event for its new Frank Gehry-designed Vitra Center headquarters in Birsfelden, Switzerland, as well as its new metal finishing factory designed by Alvaro Siza in Weil am Rhein, Germany — both in 1994 — Rolf Fehlbaum, Vitra's president, expressed the company's philosophy regarding its architecture as one in which "we are not creating an architectural collection, but our idea is to build the buildings we need but to have different interventions by different architects. This is contrary to corporate identity architecture where the same architecture and motif are everywhere."[21]

For over two hundred years, the border region between Germany and Switzerland where the furniture company Vitra was established, near the Rhine River, has been home to textile manufacturers. Willi and Erika Fehlbaum — the parents of Vitra's president — began the company in 1957 with licenses from the Herman Miller Collection, and then gained independent rights to the furniture production of American designers Charles & Ray Eames and George Nelson. Vitra later initiated its own furniture line with numerous designers.

In 1981, following a devastating fire, it was essential to restart production with a quickly built high-tech factory. Nicholas Grimshaw designed the first of a group

of new buildings that are standardized metal sheds of prefabricated parts. Because of the need for fast construction, the 15,000-square-meter building has a precast, structural concrete frame in a 25-meter span to keep the production spaces open and flexible. The horizontal corrugated metal facade on the rectangular single-story, high-bay volume seems to be pulled tight, wrapping the corners in a rounded shape, similar to a taut package. Two service volumes were placed on the exterior of the factory (so as not to interfere with the open interior space) in a blue metal horizontal cladding, identifying the service spaces. The north side has large windows to admit diffused light. Grimshaw also designed a second factory in the complex, which is a combination production facility and showroom.

The campus continued to expand with Frank Gehry's white plaster and zinc-roofed Vitra Design Museum and factory hall (1989), which was accessed via ramps, and has pillars marking the entrance. First-floor windows permit public views into the production process. The next project was Zaha Hadid's Fire Station (her first built project, now a meeting hall, 1993), and Tadao Ando's conference rooms (1993) followed.

Vitra continued to address the relationship between its factory campus and the surrounding towns, reimagining its campus as a city and developing an architectural ideology. In 1994, the company held a workshop-charrette around the idea that "industries should no longer be understood merely as a necessary evil, but as an enrichment to urban cultural life."[22] Architectural teams analyzed concepts of "City on the Rails, Stream, and Street," responding to the historic chain of urban voids and potential linkages in Weil am Rhein by reincorporating the river into the cityscape and promoting connections between residential and industrial areas, rather than erecting barriers between the two.[23]

The first project from these studies was Alvaro Siza's 20,000-square-meter factory in a reinforced concrete frame with a brick facade, similar to the earlier production building that was destroyed in the 1981 fire. The interior structure, with steel beams and trestles, includes two offices, one of concrete and the other housed in a tower. Siza designed a curved exterior roof bridge that can be mechanically raised 11 meters to provide clearance for trucks, or lowered to create shelter from the rain without blocking views through to the Fire Station.

The next production space was planned in 2009 when Fehlbaum asked SANAA (Kazuyo Sejima and Ryue Nishizawa) to design a new hall while production continued. Their unique project conveys an ephemeral quality that is rare for a factory building. Designed for the Vitrashop, the interior shop outfitting product design, the ovular 20,000-square-meter building, 11 meters tall, is sited at the edge of a residential neighborhood. Large interior spans, with thin structural steel, provide

▲ Aerial view of the Vitra campus, Weil am Rhein, Germany, 2013
▶ SANAA Architects, Vitrashop, Weil am Rhein, Germany, 2013
▶ SANAA Architects, Vitrashop interior, Weil am Rhein, Germany, 2013

ample space for the racks and product distribution. The building's shape, not mathematically calculated, is deformed through uniting two half-round concrete shells slightly off-center to assist in the truck flow. Daylight reaches the interior through a regular pattern of ribbon skylights.

However, it is the production hall's facade that is most enigmatic, as what appears to be traditional corrugated white metal is actually an ultrathin, six-millimeter acrylic-glass-panel cladding that becomes immaterial as it reflects the surrounding environment. The wavy profile is similar to Grimshaw's building, but vertical, as though a curtain slides around the curved facade. It surprises in its lightness, irregularity, and roundness, a shape rarely used for production spaces (except in the Russian bakeries and Fuller's cotton mill). The subtle shift is merely a small tweak to the norm of industrial construction, but transforms factory architectonics.

With a new potential factory aesthetic transforming contemporary workspace, the factory's place in the urban context becomes increasingly palpable when it is vertical and integrated with the city, as shown in the examples discussed below. This new breed of factory designs follows several common principles: it is significant to the company's brand in promoting their rhetoric, it is symbolic of the work inside, and it provides amenities for the workers — in all, a major shift from the isolated and dehumanizing factory of previous eras.

DIE GLÄSERNE MANUFAKTUR
HENN ARCHITEKTEN, DRESDEN, GERMANY, 1999–2001

Volkswagen's (VW) Gläserne Manufaktur, or "Transparent Factory," in Dresden was a public-private initiative intended to create jobs and return industry to a place of significance in an economically depressed East Germany following Germany's reunification in 1989.[24] The project was designed by Henn Architekten with engineers Leonhardt, Andrä and Partner in 2001. Architect Gunter Henn had previously completed VW Autostadt (2000) and factories for Skoda (1994–1996), and more recently BMW in Shenyang, China (2010). Their BMW project included an interior bridge for transporting car bodies above office spaces, similar to Zaha Hadid's design for the BMW factory in Leipzig.

VW's 81,600-square-meter Transparent Factory embodies ideas of the "consumption of production" wherein manufacturing becomes a public spectacle, and that of factory tourism as a conscious effort to intensify a company's branding and consumer experience.[25] However, VW's physical transparency broadened the scope of these ideas in its entirely new spatial and physical engagement with the street, exposing the manufacturing process to city dwellers. This dynamism is replicable in other urban contexts and informs a way forward for the progressive factories of the future.

Henn's concept of the form following the flow has traction here, in terms of the factory building itself being a mechanism rather than merely a wrapper.[26] The visitor, upon entering the factory from the city center via an elevated pathway through the Baroque-era Strasburger Platz (formerly an exhibition ground) and crossing over a moat into an atrium space, encounters what appears to be a cultural complex rather than a factory. In addition to a normative factory program, the Transparent Factory features public amenities such as a restaurant, bar, and lounge, and public spaces that often feature performances and concerts, recalling and participating in Dresden's strong musical heritage. VW's primary goal in the use of these public-friendly spaces, however, is to entice higher-end consumers to view the factory as a destination in and of itself. The company wants people to not only purchase their automobiles, but to spend time watching them being made, and makes it possible for

customers to see their cars go through the final stages of assembly. Automotive tourism has been a standard practice since the 1950s, and has extended beyond the offering of public factory tours in recent decades to the advent of museums built adjacent to the production spaces. In opening its process to public consumption, VW has embraced a new phase of production economy, that of consumption.

At first, local residents were opposed to the factory. To them, urban manufacturing harkened back to East German homogeneity and Saxony's smoke-belching, pre-World War II industrial strength. Dresden city officials, on the other hand, viewed the idea of clean manufacturing in the heart of the city as a cultural amenity. Visually echoing the ideas espoused in the nearby Museum of Hygiene, the Transparent Factory's highly choreographed assembly process, displayed through its glass facade – especially along the Stübelallee – not only shows off VW's meticulous craftsmanship but inspires civic pride.[27] Furthermore, Die Gläserne Manufaktur demonstrates how manufacturing can be reintegrated into cities, regardless of the area's density.

The three-to-five-story, L-shaped factory volume is a long-span precast reinforced concrete construction system built in modules. The 27,500-square-meter-facade is also constructed in modules of glass and steel fitted together in a unit, and then mounted together in a process that Henn compares to mass-produced automotive assembly.[28] Rather than solid interior walls, steel cross beams and structural cables allow for openness not just within floors but between and across them, providing expansive interior views. The rectilinear buildings are punctured

▲ Henn Architects, VW Factory, Dresden, 2001
▶ View within the auto storage "silo"
▶ Cars on overhead carriers

with separate spherical volumes. One volume clad in aluminum houses the conference room and material selection spaces, and the other, more bulbous in shape, contains the lounges where customers can relax, be instructed on how the car operates, and then head down to the production spaces to meet their new purchase. A glass-clad, 15-story car-stacking garage rises behind the main production space, a clean-tech factory tower, similar to VW's automated car storage in Wolfsburg.

The production lines are visible throughout all the spaces of the factory, not only placing the manufacturing process under direct scrutiny, but satisfying people's curiosity and fascination with how cars are made. This heightened transparency is also part of the production flow, allowing experts from the R&D branches to communicate with those fine-tuning the cars in a JIT and lean manufacturing methods.[29]

The manufacturing process actually begins in VW's Mosel, Germany factory where the dirtier operations of automobile production, such as metal stamping and painting, are completed. These heavy auto parts, including the chassis, are quietly delivered from a logistics warehouse on the outskirts of Dresden by private blue CarGo Trams built by Schalke Steel Machines. Because the transport of parts takes place on public tracks, which are separate from yet integrated within the city's rail system, the delivery

process, of one tram per hour, is unimpeded by regular traffic and in turn does not block city sidewalks. In the same way that elevated trains did for the cities in the early twentieth century, this transportation and delivery system holds great potential for expedited commerce in cities across a broad range of contexts.

Workers receive the auto parts in the factory basement, sort them, and place them on a robotic magnetic floor guidance system to the assembly line. Skilled workers dressed in white overalls (that never get dirty), standing on nonindustrial parquet wood floors, retrieve parts from fully stocked cabinets and complete the meticulous assemblies with white-gloved hands in a process more akin to that of watchmaking workshops than automotive factories. The first conveyor, comprised of 29 panels linked like fish scales, is embedded in the floor, and moves slowly, but continuously. The panels can lift to different heights so that the worker can reach the desired part of the car in a more ergonomic process. Each workstation cabinet has power connections through the floor, thus maintaining a wire-free space while also allowing electronic tracking of each aspect of assembly.

An electric suspension rail, parallel to the conveyors, moves the cars to the second floor, clasped in halo brackets, or claw arms, which can move in multiple directions. Workers thereby have easy access to the cars' underbodies and can move them to the desired position with the push of a button. Robots are only used to place windows or install tires. The engine, gearbox, axles, wheel suspension, braking and exhaust systems are at this point all installed in the chassis.

Finally, at the point in the manufacturing process called the "marriage," a frame lifts the chassis to the body as it is lowered, at which time the two come into perfect alignment. At Ford in 1914, this was achieved via lowering the car body with pulleys from a ramp in a rougher, hands-on process. At VW, the marriage is a performance, and spectacle, as consumers experience it either close at hand, or from the Nockenturm, the upper-level viewing room. The car is then transported to a second-floor circuit where interior fittings are installed, and then it is inspected in a brightly lit tunnel. If the customer is on site, they can get in and start the car, at which point it then moves to an interior test track. Finally, the car moves down a ramp and out onto the city streets where it is either released to its owner or moved to the glass storage tower, essentially a car vending machine. The production process combines cellular and linear production methods in a teamwork setting.

The paradox remains that the spectacle of the factory becomes one of high-end product sales combining showroom with factory – a phenomenon that is becoming increasingly common. These types of operations create skilled jobs rather than everyday factory jobs, for the city's residents. The Transparent Factory points to a possible future in which workers and work are visible, constituting the compelling notion of Flusser's *homo faber*, on display.

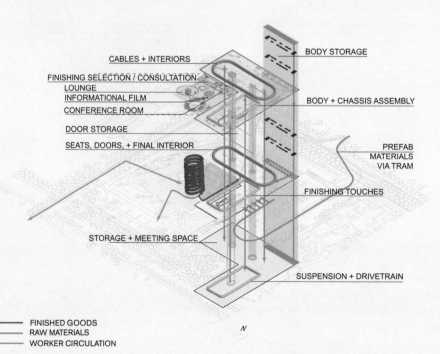

CABLES + INTERIORS

FINISHING SELECTION / CONSULTATION
LOUNGE
INFORMATIONAL FILM
CONFERENCE ROOM

DOOR STORAGE

SEATS, DOORS, + FINAL INTERIOR

STORAGE + MEETING SPACE

BODY STORAGE

BODY + CHASSIS ASSEMBLY

PREFAB
MATERIALS
VIA TRAM

FINISHING TOUCHES

SUSPENSION + DRIVETRAIN

FINISHED GOODS
RAW MATERIALS
WORKER CIRCULATION

THE NEW YORK TIMES PRINTING PLANT

POLSHEK & PARTNERS, QUEENS, NEW YORK, 1997

New technologies and a unique vertical plant organization combined to create an innovative design for the New York Times Company's printing plant in College Point, Queens designed by the architects Polshek & Partners (now Ennead Architects) with Parsons Main Inc., architects/engineers. The presses previously located in the 12-meter, below-grade sub-basement of its long-term home on Manhattan's 43rd Street were relocated to the new 48,000-square-meter plant in 1997. The sun-filled factory enhanced the quality of the worker's environment and its use of automation and five, high-speed color presses enabled the newspaper to vastly improve its color printing process and production line.

The New York Times initiated a new philosophy that David Thurm, vice president for production, explained: "Fundamental to us is that architecture matters. It is a new point in labor relations, we are trying to change the way we work with people to create a more open working environment with a building that reflects that spirit."[30] Taking advantage of the building's location on a major highway as an advertising location, the company embraced the design opportunity.

The New York Times had never used a design architect for a production facility, and in selecting Polshek & Partners, Thrum noted, "We didn't want to spend a lot of money on the look and feel of a building, rather the building evolved from the needs of the equipment and the plant, it had to come from within."[31] The Times created a collaborative professional team from the very beginning and kicked-off the project by organizing a brainstorming meeting wherein 40 team members got to know one another by building a toy city.

In analyzing printing plants around the world, Polshek's office looked to Nicholas Grimshaw's Financial Times plant in London as a point of contrast. Richard Olcott, design principal for the project, noted that Grimshaw's building "is an extremely high-tech skin for a simple printing process, with one printing a day that only runs at night. In comparison, the New York Times is running continuously day and night with new high-tech machinery."[32] This required a different attitude and design methodology. Rather than design a similar transparent high-tech glass skin,

they created a more mysterious envelope to house the intricate workings of the production process. The main volume is a corrugated metal box with a 100-meter-long window to reveal just one of the presses, versus Grimshaw's, which showed them all. Color and volumetric composition became important features in the building to articulate the diverse parts of the factory and to break up the massive box.

The 12.7-hectare-site, a reclaimed swamp, posed a challenge in and of itself. The creation of a stable foundation required one-hundred-kilometers of pipe piling, making it the largest order of pipe pile that US Steel had ever received. The 35-centimeter-diameter pipes were driven between 21 to 38 meters below ground and then filled with concrete to support a beam and structural concrete slab foundation.

The main entrance to the printing plant is accessed off the Whitestone Expressway via a yellow metal gatehouse marking the entryway to the parking lot. A plaza, cleverly paved with a black-and-white square pattern reminiscent of a crossword puzzle, leads visitors and administrative staff up to the office building. A tipped-forward, mirrored-glass facade with a red canopy signals the entrance. An open metal staircase begins in the two-story brightly painted lobby, ascending to a suspended second-floor corridor,

▲ **Polshek & Partners (now Ennead), New York Times Printing Plant, New York, 1996**

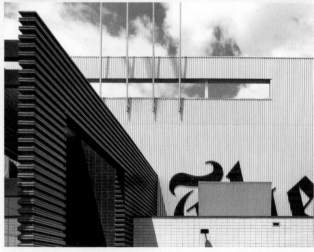

New York Times Printing Plant from the expressway
Printing press floor
Graphic composition

or circulation spine. This balcony provides a view down into the pressroom on one side and the mail room on the other. A blue horizontal corrugated metal wall on the north facade of the entrance steps forward from the main volume of the building, hiding the stair tower. This partition has an opening to the windows behind.

The expandable main press hall is a 5,200-square-meter corrugated metal box, 198 meters long and 19 meters high. To make it visually interesting, the architects canted the front wall four degrees. The box's interior is high-tech and houses five Goss Colorliner presses, with space reserved for a sixth. While most factories need large open spans, here columns are placed on a nine-meter grid so that they double as supports for the vertical conveyor system. Between each pair of presses, a quiet room inside a small glass pavilion houses the press controls. Large-scale signage in the factory provides visitors with information about the activities on the manufacturing floor, similar to an Andon board.

Rather than build a separate air filtration room, the architects added six yellow wedge-shaped boxes to the facade to function as the air treatment space. Inside, red air ducts — one-and-a-half meters in diameter — suck airborne ink and paper dust out of the press room, and funnel them through ink mist filters inside the yellow boxes. The pre-filtered air is then drawn up to the air handlers on the roof. This system, operative through both formal and mechanical elements, exemplifies the architect's creative combination of utility and design.

To enhance the building's identity from the highway, the architects created a 45-meter-long perforated black metal sign, hung on a diagonal, that resembles the banner of the New York Times rolling off the presses. The visual concept links the graphics and the building to the already iconic delivery trucks. A two-and-a-half-meter high parapet with a rectangular opening conceals the twelve air handlers on the roof.

The staff and factory workers enter the facility at the west side of the building, proceeding into a small lobby, then to the main skylit circulation spine off of which are located lockers, storage, and workshops, on the second-floor are additional lockers, plate-making functions, and workshops. The spine is then connected back to the main entrance by way of the cafeteria and fitness area. The green circulation towers continue the concept of distinguishing and highlighting building elements through the use of color.

"We said to the architects, 'We want to put a big windowless box for the paper storage on the front of the building because that is where it should be for the flow," noted Thurm.[33] "And, by the way, we are too cheap to put the sub-station on the back of the building, so that has to be on the front too."[34] So the architects designed an innovative paper storage facility: a 1,200-square-meter, blue, corrugated high-bay metal box that houses 2,300 rolls of paper, which are relayed in an automatic storage and retrieval system. Each of these rolls is 1.4 meters high and 1.3 meters in diameter and weighs two tons.

The process is automated, from delivery to completion: the bar-coded rolls of paper arrive by truck and the bar codes are scanned to track the roll; the roll is then brought to the stripping station, opened, then delivered to the printing presses by robots. The typeset pages are sent from 41st Street to College Point digitally, and read on the computer system, which pre-sets column information and ink values.

Once printed, the newsrolls proceed via conveyors to 4,650-square-meter buffer room on the upper floor where a Swiss storage system called the Muller Martini holds the papers. The Muller Martini machine allows parts of the paper to be printed at different times and then assembled later. By placing the buffer system on the third floor, the plant becomes a vertical factory and the production is compressed to reduce distances, and thus costs. Once completed, a conveyor feeds the newspaper through the floor to the mail room below.

A freestanding insert, printed elsewhere,

is stored in a separate room, and then sorted into the rest of the newspaper with a new high-speed GMA SLS 2000 insert machine in the 11,300-square-meter mail room, which features a wall of windows and a large skylight. The mail room leads directly to the 28-bay loading docks for truck distribution. A separate building area serves as the lounge and office for the truck drivers.

"Every plant has a brain and the information is collected in one computer system," said Thurm. "I can sit at home on my computer and see what is going on throughout the plant. Each piece of equipment can show its history run on computer controls. It gives us tools to do continuous improvement and give more information to the pressmen on the floor who appreciate the new open and bright feel to the plant."[35]

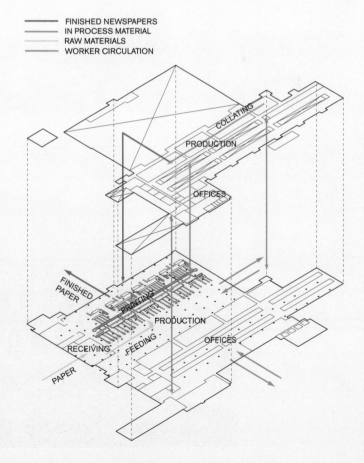

FINISHED NEWSPAPERS
IN PROCESS MATERIAL
RAW MATERIALS
WORKER CIRCULATION

INOTERA
tecARCHITECTURE, TAIPEI, TAIWAN, 2004

The Inotera Headquarters and Factory in Taipei, designed in 2004 by Switzerland- and Los Angeles-based Sebastian Knorr of tecARCHITECTURE, with local architects Fei & Cheng, became fully operational in 2007. The complex combines the specific high-tech manufacturing requirements for Inotera Memories, the largest maker of DRAM (dynamic random access memory) – the memory chips used to operate all computers – with a spectacular building design. The company, whose new facilities are located in an industrial area of Taoyuan, was founded in 2003 as a joint project of Taiwan's Nanya Technology and Germany's Qionda.

Two volumes of compatible functions define the building project. One 14-story volume, for office and research, serves as a dramatic frontispiece behind which is the second volume containing the production spaces. The multistoried, 8,600-square-meter office wing is raised up for below-ground parking and is supported with structural steel V-columns wrapped in aluminum. The strikingly graphic columns also provide earthquake stabilization, as required for the region. They zigzag along the facade, supporting a major volume that in turn forms an arcaded loggia through which employees enter the main foyer.

The office and research building's facade is wrapped with a multicolored grid of rectilinear low-E glass panes separated by aluminum dividers. Each color scheme signifies a different section of the building. The lower, set-back portion of the building, which houses offices, is glazed in varying hues of green, with the individual panes digitally printed with images of tree branches, bamboo, and streams. Offices lie behind the upper-level glass grid, colored red, yellow, and brown. The chromatic fragmentation creates the effect of dappled sunlight in nature. The selection of the 192 variations in dimension of the glass and color occurred via an automated sorting system that the architect says parallels the integrated process of chip manufacturing.[36]

Both the research and development labs as well as the offices are arranged in open floor plans. To allow natural light into the deep floor spaces, Knorr designed three ovular glass cones that penetrate the upper four floors and function as dramatic interior light wells. These curvilinear forms, sheathed in colored glass panels, project above the main facade, creating a third glazed cladding on the top floor.

The second volume – the production space – consists of an 18,600-square-meter fabrication building, the largest wafer factory in the world at the time that it was built. In industry lingo, "fabs" are precise manufacturing spaces that have cleanrooms and other specialized workspaces. The company's 300mm-semiconductor wafer production uses 90mm trench technology to etch the electronic circuits onto a silicon wafer that

is a semiconducting material. Inotera has "twin fabs," known as Fab1 and Fab2, in which it manufactures its high-tech product. Fab1 and Fab2 are connected by a bridge to make an integrated facility. Both are sheathed in a loosely organized composition of opaque blue glazed tiles, grouped in geometric patterns. The tiles are inspired by the region's ceramic arts traditions. Knorr has broken down the enormous scale of the building through an optical sleight of hand — by varying the size of the tiles and thus distracting the viewer's eye. Vertical stair towers are covered with an even brighter blue tile, which accentuates their form, yet their massive volume is camouflaged through the overall patterning, resulting in a holistic form.

Workers at Inotera wear white coveralls while they perform clean-tech jobs that are specialized and require precise engineering skills. Each worker performs a complete task at a carefully calibrated workstation, using robotics to make a chip and test its quality.

Just as the Modernist architects gravitated to the factory as a typology that exemplified Modern ideals, so does this factory reflect its era in its materiality and new high-technology, but without being an overt metaphor.

FINISHED PRODUCTS
IN PROCESS MATERIAL
RAW MATERIALS
WORKER CIRCULATION

◄ tecARCHITECTURE, Inotera Factory,
Taipei, Taiwan, 2004
▲ An interior lightwell
▲ V-shaped structural columns

BREATHING FACTORY
**TAKASHI YAMAGUCHI & ASSOCIATES,
OSAKA, 2009**

The name "Breathing Factory" conjures the sense of motion and change, permeability and life with which Takashi Yamaguchi imbued his 2009 renovation of an experimental high-tech manufacturing facility that produces medical tools and equipment. Yamaguchi designed an addition to the plant, a separate structure with a tectonic understated design that is adjacent to an existing building. The issues of interiority and exteriority, relationships of part to whole, and program to form have occupied Yamaguchi in numerous projects, and are evident in this urban factory.

The four-story addition is in a hybrid urban area near commercial and residential buildings, and other medium-sized factories. It sits at the edge of an elevated highway that runs between Osaka and Kyoto and is adjacent to the Tokaido train line. The building serves as a buffer against the noise and grit of urban infrastructure while protecting the pristine environment needed for the company's work. In designing his building, Yamaguchi responded to a program that included production space, new offices, testing facilities, workshops, meeting rooms, and warehouse storage.

From the entrance, which faces the elevated highway, one reaches the reception area, offices, conference room, and storage space for easy access from the street. The production space is located on the second and third floors with R&D placed alongside production. A synergy is created between these two areas of the company, which are vertically joined but with marked divisions between the two floors. The fourth floor contains a large flexible meeting room for conferences and company seminars.

The main rectangular concrete structure is cloaked with aluminum constructed panels, similar to Yamaguchi's Parametric Fragment house design. The system both wraps and articulates the building's volume, disguising the program and hiding exterior ducts for the mechanical system. Directed by a random pattern, the corrugated ribbing reflects the sky, clouds, streetlights, and street so that the facades are never monotonous. Sunlight penetrates through openings into the workspaces throughout the day. On either side of the factory, areas of the volume are carved out to house interior light wells that have pebble-surfaced courtyards on the upper floors. This design provides for reflections of the urban landscape without allowing it to encroach directly on the work space. Large translucent glass screens line the hallways on the lower level and the meeting rooms on the upper, letting the outside in, but maintaining privacy.

It is this atmospheric experiment that becomes the spectacle of the factory. On the facade, some of the corrugated square panels are placed horizontally while others are placed vertically, creating a formal patchwork that engenders varying intensities of light and shadow and constantly changing colors. These shifting reflections pixilate and abstract the building and engage the observer in a fluid perceptual experience. The integration of light and dark lends a subtle elegance to the structure in this tight urban site.

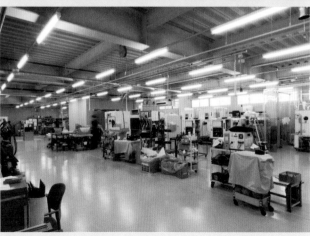

◀ Takashi Yamaguchi and Associates, Breathing Factory, Osaka, Japan, 2009
◀ Interior manufacturing space

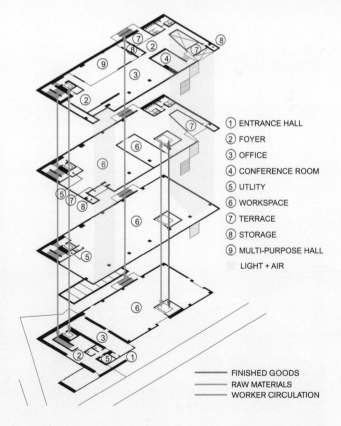

① ENTRANCE HALL
② FOYER
③ OFFICE
④ CONFERENCE ROOM
⑤ UTLITY
⑥ WORKSPACE
⑦ TERRACE
⑧ STORAGE
⑨ MULTI-PURPOSE HALL
　 LIGHT + AIR

FINISHED GOODS
RAW MATERIALS
WORKER CIRCULATION

▲ Corrugated-metal patchwork panel system
▲ The factory in its urban context

THE HOONG-A CORPORATION

**ONGODONG ARCHITECTS, BUCHEON,
SOUTH KOREA, 2011**

The Hoong-A Corporation, a cutting-edge firm
that produces complex computer-operated
machinery to fabricate cellular packing machines
for pharmaceutical, food, and health care
products, was established in 1970. Located in
the Ojeong Industrial Park, a dense manufacturing zone in the city of Bucheon in South Korea
touted as a global distribution environment, it
is linked, for the convenience of workers, to the
surrounding region by highway, train, and subway, as well as to a new logistics complex that
will enhance business opportunities in the area.
Within the park are clusters of high-tech industries, IT educational centers, robotics research
manufacturers, mold manufacturers, lighting
manufacturers, research, and animation and
film industries that employ over 54,000 people.
Hoong-A Corp. is a part of the packaging cluster.

In 2011, Ongodong Architects designed
Hoong-A's new R&D and production complex.
Rather than build one large building, they divided
the site into a small urban plaza with two parallel
but staggered exposed-concrete buildings
around an interior rectangular courtyard. A first-
and partial second-level parking garage raises
the buildings on a podium above the industrial
spaces. On the lower, southern-oriented facade
is the factory's back of house, with the outdoor
parking lot and truck loading entrance, and employee entrance below projecting canopies. On
the interior courtyard side of the ensemble, the
buildings bracket the plaza at the third level, on
which the company offers two volleyball courts

▲ Ongodong Associates, Hoonga Factory, Ojeong,
South Korea, 2011
◀ Lunch room

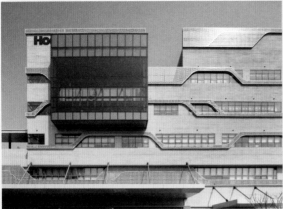

and seating as worker amenities. A larger glazed entrance welcomes visitors.

One volume rises fives stories above the parking level's northern side, and contains amenities such as a fitness center, locker rooms, rest rooms, a rooftop exercise room, and cafeteria. The three-story building houses administrative offices, design studios, and two-glazed conference rooms. The smaller meeting room and offices anchor the cantilevers from the facade in a blue glazed box. The dining room and hallways have wood trim that softens the spaces. And skylights on the upper floors admit diffused light. The production halls have open plans for the ease of moving the machinery. Hoong-A's all-in-one thermal packaging machines are mini-production lines in and of themselves as they contain within them a small assembly flow for punching, foiling, and sealing bubble packs.

A covered walkway on the interior plaza links the two sections of the company, symbolizing the physical and organizational desire for inter departmental communications.

The architects break up the cubic volumes with a few strategic design moves, including a three-story projecting bay window that adds formal variety, and allows sunlight into the offices. They have also designed a simple yet elegant detail of perforated aluminum panels that wrap the concrete facade. Their form is derived from the packaging mechanisms for bubble packs, mimicking the bubbles and the overall shape of the plastic packing supplies. These panels also function as sun-shading devices. Reading as uninterrupted bands across the elevation, they dip

down and navigate around windows, or pass over them as a reference to the fluidity of the production line. In its simple design, the building's sectional complexity contributes to a dynamic interplay between the physical, cultural, personal, and organizational aspects of this vertical urban factory.

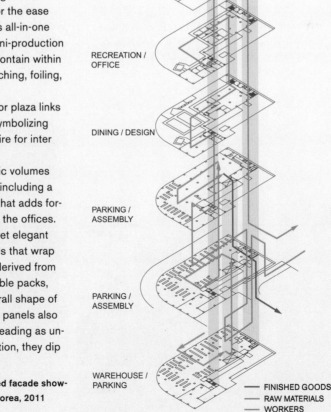

RECREATION / MEETING

RECREATION / OFFICE

DINING / DESIGN

PARKING / ASSEMBLY

PARKING / ASSEMBLY

WAREHOUSE / PARKING

—— FINISHED GOODS
—— RAW MATERIALS
—— WORKERS

▲ Exterior views of Hoonga's articulated facade showing the projecting bay, Ojeong, South Korea, 2011
▲ Entrance to the meeting rooms

TWO YG-1 TOOLS FACTORIES
SANKI CHOE, INCHEON, SOUTH KOREA, 2012

CHUNGCHUNDONG FACTORY

The Bupyung industrial district in Incheon, South Korea witnessed the rapid growth that paralleled Korea's economic success during the late twentieth century. However, it has left an uninspiring landscape of repetitious single-story, ribbon-windowed, gable-roofed utilitarian boxes typical of generic factory architecture and their conglomeration into industrial zones.

One company has counteracted that monotony. YG-1, Co., founded in 1981 by entrepreneur Song Ho-Keun, is now a multinational tool company with branches and subsidiaries around the world. YG-1's first operations were in a small run-down shed structure in Incheon. Many additions were made to the concrete block building until the owners decided that they wanted a more spacious production facility. Maximizing the site's potential, they completed a new multistoried building in 2012.

While increasing the floor area ratio (FAR) allowed by building code, the architect Sanki Choe suggested preserving the vestiges of the first factory, in memory of the company's beginnings. By tracing the outline of the old factory volume and inverting it into a series of subtracted negative spaces, they gained not only a new display hall but also a multifunctional space.

The current factory of 3,300 square meters rises above the other factories in the district, to a total of eight stories. The main volume is five stories tall, with a setback for the mechanical systems and offices that ascends another two stories and is clad in corrugated metal. The bright blue metal-paneled cladding of the main volume is punctured by deep-set vertical window frames on the main facade that are painted red. The building's side facades are punctuated with a series of openings that allow for the delivery of materials into the building and the exit of finished goods through the red-framed windows, which serve as upper-level loading bays. Other windows, enclosed with shutters, project from the facade.

The building's structural steel frame is capable of holding the weight of the factory machinery and allows for seven-meter-high ceilings in the interior's ground floor. Natural light emanating from the clerestory windows and skylights illuminate the space. Inside, workers operate the CNC machines, and as production still involves use of high velocity vaporized oil, an efficient exhaust system with overhead ductwork and air quality controls extracts waste fumes. While the lofty production hall has steel columns that support the roof and skylights, the main floor slab of the production hall is supported by a reinforced concrete structure that helps control vibrations that might lead to production errors.

Using CNC and 3-D CAD-CAM machines, YG-1 produces precision-cutting tools used for making metal molds, machine tool parts, and electronic equipment parts including end mills, taps, and drills. The range of products they are instrumental in producing include aircraft fuselages, automobiles, electronic appliances, smart phones, and robots.

SONGDO FACTORY AND RESEARCH CENTER

For the second YG-1 project, architect Sanki Choe was asked to add two floors to an existing shed building as a factory and research center in Songdo in Incheon, South Korea. Songdo's new International Business District is a six-square kilometer Smart City built from reclaimed land from the Yellow Sea, 65 kilometers southwest of Seoul. The infrastructural systems are fully digitized with integrated sensors, in a low-carbon development endeavor.

The former building's low ceiling heights and deep plan resulted in dark internal manufacturing floor space and poor air quality, and had to rely on forced ventilation and artificial lighting, even on bright days. Rather than simply adding two floors, which would have exacerbated these existing problems, the architects convinced the owner to vertically stack production floors and juxtapose them with the research floors, forming an innovative staggered factory section.

Sanki Choe designed the production spaces adjacent to large windows, admitting ample daylight into the double-height floors. A series of skylights let even more daylight into the center of the deep plan. The research center, likewise, was stacked vertically into three floors and positioned parallel to the production floors. Thus, as in new factory worker organization, the manufacturing floors and research labs were placed in close proximity, eliminating any spatial hierarchy. The interlocking section is similar to that of Freitag's Noerd building in Zurich. As Sanki Choe notes, "the architectural solutions to the horizontal problem helped to reinforce a sense of unity within the company, while at the same time provided identity to the manufacturing company."[37]

The architects deeply recessed large window openings with thick dividing metal bands painted in light yellow, creating a chiaroscuro effect on the facade. At the two entrances and in two third-floor rooms a deep red was used to set off the composition. While the openings created a rhythm, it was neither obvious nor regular. The building is an attractor in an otherwise normative industrial area.

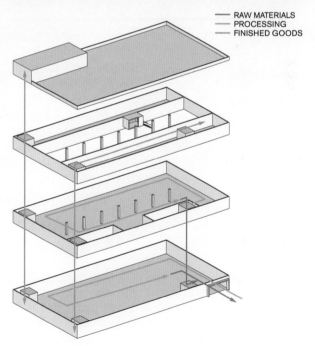

RAW MATERIALS
PROCESSING
FINISHED GOODS

◄ **Sanki Choe Architect, YG-1 Tools, Chungchundong, Incheon, South Korea, 2012**

◄ **Bupyung industrial district, Incheon, South Korea (top)**

◄ **Factory interior**

▲ **Sanki Choe Architects, YG-1 Tools, Songdo Factory, Incheon, South Korea, 2012**

LAFAYETTE 148

MEHRDAD HADIGHI AND TSZ YAN NG, ARCHITECTS
SHANTOU, CHINA, 2009

Lafayette 148 New York, a high-end women's clothing company founded by Shen Yen Siu in 1996 built a headquarters and manufacturing space in 2009 in the city of Shantou, Guangdong Province, China – a one-hour flight from Hong Kong. Historically, this major port city, with a population of over five million people in 2010, was one of the early special economic zones, like Shenzhen. Shantou's manufacturing sectors specialize in printing, toys, and garments, industries that attract workers from the surrounding countryside. These migrant workers moved from the rural life with their families to crowded living conditions in the city. Siu envisioned a factory with more progressive labor conditions and a more democratic culture than those found in the current factories of mass-produced globalization.

Siu was a successful owner of garment factories in New York's Chinatown in the 1960s. He and his wife Ida Siu, along with partner Deidre Quinn, began their enterprise by manufacturing other companies' goods. During the 1990s, they found they had some fabric left over from a project and decided to try to design clothes themselves. Chinatown, which since the 1980s had over 500 workshops employing 20,000 workers, maintained approximately 200 companies even beyond the economic disaster following the terrorist attacks of September 11, 2001. This industrial vibrancy steadily declined, with the rise of cheaper production in China halving the total number of companies in Chinatown to one hundred by 2004; by 2012, the area had become highly gentrified, defined by a mix of apartments and galleries, as noted by sociologist Margaret Chin.[38]

In 1996, Lafayette 148 started as an independent fashion house, but because of the lack of factories in New York City and the increase in production during the Christmas rush, it outsourced to factories in Shantou, Siu's hometown. The company has continued its base of production there, while turning its Lafayette Street production space in New York's Soho district into its U.S. showroom and flagship store. In 2009, Siu and his partners hired Mehrdad Hadighi of the Pennsylvania-based Studio for Architecture and Michigan-based architect Tsz Yan Ng, to design a new factory in Shantou for 1,500 workers. By building his own factory, Siu could also more directly control and oversee his company's specialized manufacturing process. In 2012, Lafayette 148 decided to open to the Chinese market by launching shops in Shanghai and Beijing. This move reduced costs by placing the factory in proximity to the company's newest consumers.

The ubiquitous architecture of the fast-growing city of Shantou is simple reinforced-concrete frame construction using concrete block, plaster walls, and tiles. Very little steel is used, and few buildings display any architectural design. Hadighi and Ng capitalized on Shantou's pool of highly skilled concrete workers to build an innovative factory while advancing Siu's humanitarian concepts. After seeing numerous factories, the architects' collaborative vision became to design a vertical factory so that space could be maximized as it rose on the constrained urban site. The concept for the interior was to open up the factory floors so that the workers would be visible throughout a flexible space, providing them with access to light and air. Like American Apparel, Lafayette 148 is vertically integrated under one roof, from a product's design to completion, encompassing patternmaking, the creation of samples, garment production, and distribution.

The need for large-scale, unimpeded, flexible manufacturing floors led Hadighi and Ng to take an innovative approach to the otherwise problematic question of where to place the service core. Rather than a layout similar to Albert Kahn's factories, with the stairs, elevators, and restroom facilities housed in corner towers, here the architects placed the service core in a bar running the full length of the north facade of the 26-by-87-meter building. This allowed for the factory floors to envelop a series of 17-by-87-meter spaces, following the production flow from the west to the east.

To execute the envisioned spatial organization, a post-tension concrete frame system, the first in the region, could eliminate columns to increase the floors' unimpeded open space. Rising eleven stories, the building, which has basement parking, has three entrances: workers enter on the north, visitors on the south, and there is a separate showroom entrance adjacent. The double-height showroom can also be transformed into a runway space. The shipping and packaging occurs on the east side of the building. At the next level is the cafeteria, with floors three through nine containing the open manufacturing spaces. The top two floors house the offices,

design studios, an apartment, and a gym. The production flow begins at the top with the design and patternmaking, then cutting and sewing; the final garment progresses downwards, similar to Le Corbusier's Usine Claude et Duval. But, because of the spatial openness, there is flexibility to experiment with new production methods and to reconfigure the worktables and sewing machines. Long tables line the factory floor in parallel rows, with carts that move from place to

place to drop fabric at a sewer's table or to pick up finished goods.

The unique twist in the overall building design is an actual twist of horizontal concrete panels or fins, which when seen from a distance, create a moiré effect on the facade, according to the angle of the fin. Placed as a screen in front of the operable windows, the panel angle is set according to the amount of shading and ventilation desired; the windows also draw in fresh air that circulates through to the rear-building core. To mold these concrete panels, the architects designed reusable steel forms that are slightly twisted and are perforated with a pattern of two sizes of holes that spell out the company's name in

▲ **Mehrdad Hadighi and Tsz Yan Ng, Lafayette 148, Shantou, China, 2010**

▲ **Factory illuminated at night**

▲ **Detail of the facade's concrete bands**

Braille. The perforations offered two cost-reducing and energy-saving benefits: they lightened both the material demand and the panel weight. Made on site, the panels were clipped into position on the facade framework and braced at the outer edge in five different positions that were designed both to follow the sequence of the repetitive reuse of the forms, and also to have a fluid facade pattern. The design mimics that

of textiles, but also dematerializes the exposed concrete through its twists and perforations.

The north-facing facade is the opposite tectonically, as it is flat and planar with cubic openings. Most factories capitalize on northern light for stable illumination throughout the day, but here the architects placed windows in a pattern, contrasting it with carved volumes. These voids allow light to penetrate the interior and provide balconies for views. A chimney allows hot air to rise on a north-south axis, then moves up and out to provide cross ventilation, creating a passive cooling system that greatly reduces both the temperature and the humidity in the manufacturing spaces. The energy-cost reduction is also significant: the building uses forty percent less energy for cooling than is the norm, and has enough energy during the city's regular blackouts.

In 2007, Siu, in following his ideals for worker amenities, developed a school for the factory called the School of Dreams. This facility educates over 330 workers' children who previously had no access to education, and provides lunch as well as art and music classes. There are also doctors on staff to serve both the children and the workers. This paternalistic approach stems from Siu's strong belief in humanitarian principles and democratic capitalism. But the question still remains for so many companies as to whether this embodies a vision for a progressive workplace attuned to living wages and workers needs, or is only focused on the bottom line.

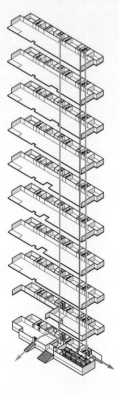

————— FINISHED GOODS
————— IN PROCESS MATERIAL
————— WORKER CIRCULATION

▲ Lafayette 148 main production spaces

SUSTAINABLE FACTORY

Awakening nearly too late to mankind's degradation of the environment for cheap energy and precious metals, our culture has finally begun to acknowledge the pollution of the air, sea, and land. The vertical urban factory has the potential to contribute to a more sustainable environment, both by its urban situation because of density and central location as well as opportunities to create and distribute energy because of adjacencies.[39] A sustainable factory is not just one that is integrated with the natural environment, disappears into the landscape, or has a minimum ecological impact, but is one that contributes to an ecological system symbiotically — literally becoming an industrial organism that influences social, as well as environmental, sustainability. Many of the world's nations have now passed environmental regulations, which are specific to their domains, but also hold the promise of global impact. The new focus on urban living and a consumer-supplier culture in close proximity reinforces the notion that manufacturing can be sustainable in cities. When products are made closer to the urban consumer, pollution is limited through the reduction in use of fuel, trucking, and long distance transit — and thus, production is contained within sustainable parameters. Clustering factories in an urban setting, rather than in far-flung locations, also forms an urban industrial ecology in which machinery and resources are shared, creating, through symbiotic relationships, closed-loop systems, and industrial synergies.

Early regulations, such as the Clean Air Act of 1956, began to set standards for what an industry could emit. But many cities already had been ruined with heavy pollutants from power plants, oil refineries, or chemicals leaching into rivers. Today, the political debates around industrial methods in industrialized and developing countries continue, and there have been a number of attempts to establish an international framework for addressing environmental issues on a global scale. The Kyoto protocol of 1997 to the UN Framework Convention on Climate Change, for example, established an environmental treaty between industrialized nations; the U.S. was the only nation never to have ratified it.[40] Other regulations include the Regional Greenhouse Gas Initiative of 2003, a Northeastern and Mid-Atlantic U.S. initiative to reduce greenhouse gas emissions through a cap-and-trade scheme. New industrial economies, such as China, need to focus on controlling pollution, which has largely gone unchecked; beyond the local impacts, poor air quality can affect areas of great distance from the original source.

An ecological or sustainable factory can, in reality, be considered an oxymoron, due to the relationships between organisms and their environment — both in terms of how things are produced in a factory, and how the factory is built, depleting resources. Mechanical systems mediate and protect the environment from assault by the natural and chemical materials we use to make products we desire; such systems do so by attempting to self-correct and maintain a natural balance. The ecology of the factory demands a choice between the better of two evils — or that which has the least impact on the environment. In manufacturing, the concept of lightly touching the earth seems unfeasible; there is an inevitable conflict between safeguarding the environment and creating needed jobs and products.

▲ Electronic waste being sorted in Guiyu, China, 2011. Photograph by Adam Minter
▶ Thomas Herzog, Wilkhahn Furniture Factory, Bad Münder-Eimbeckhausen, Germany, 1990

The idea of the factory as a polluting behemoth, colliding with and in nature, prevails. More sensitive attention to the environment is needed to affect the factory's highest performance and lowest impact. An alternative is to harness natural elements and improve upon them, converting raw materials into energy, for example, and transferring resources between diverse programs to conserve and manage waste. A manufacturer's social responsibility as a sustainable goal also participates in the ecology between workers and the environment to contribute to a symbiotic ecosystem.

Despite the inevitability of industrial pollution, there are a few methods that, in their synergetic combination, are capable of fostering a new *urban* industrial ecology. "Industrial ecology," a phrase used by Robert Frosch and Nicholas Gallopoulos in a 1989 article, is the study and reaction of the ways that materials and things flow as they are industrially processed.[41] These things then form an ecosystem that is interdependent, and could be modeled on natural systems. Harold Tibbs of England furthered this thinking relative to product design and closed-loop systems to help companies reduce costs, waste, and carbon emissions.[42]

The factory can find a holism with this industrial ecological typology in a few different ways. First, sustainability is achieved through the fundamental act of revitalizing an existing factory building (as opposed to constructing a new one). It can be restored to functionality with new uses and new kinds of manufacturing spaces within, or as a new type of factory entirely. Another sustainable focus is the potential for factories to produce their own energy, as well as to share excess energy with nearby companies. And a third aspect is a factory building design that is green or sustainable in terms of the materials used and energy performance — carbon neutrality being the ultimate goal. On the interior, companies are envisioning their factories as a production machine and adhering to concepts of sustainable and "green" manufacturing in terms of both input and output. These manufacturers use green and or recycled and metabolizing materials, adopt clean production, optimize energy, build recycling into their product design, and recycle their waste products in a way that mimics biological metabolic processes.

Supply chain ecologies are supported by the three Rs: Reduce, Reuse, and Recycle. These principles can be applied to production, along with the idea of cradle to cradle promoted by numerous environmentalists. A product, being used from cradle to grave — as with Apple's E-waste[43] — is instead recycled in-house or divided up between recycled material suppliers, and then goes back into the production machine.[44] This idea of design for disassembly, seen in many European

countries, becomes paramount in sustainability so that nothing is wasted or thrown into the ever-growing mountains of trash. Products have to be built to come apart, and these parts must go into the correct recycling bins, so to speak. Ecological production, in combining the reuse of materials, energy efficiency, and lean production, evolves into what is called eco-efficiency. Interestingly, when companies do implement these ecosystem strategies, despite having large upfront costs, save money in the long run because they are saving material and energy costs, due to greater energy-efficiency.

Perhaps another way to consider the new sustainable factory would be as a living machine in which the organism of the product relates to and reacts to its natural and man-made environment as metabolic production machine. As Kevin Kelly notes,

> Both nature and industry can prevail. Employing the metaphor of organic machine systems, industrialists (somewhat reluctantly) and environmentalists can sketch out how manufacturers can clean up their messes, just as biological systems can clean up after themselves. For instance, nature has no garbage problem because nothing becomes waste. An industry imitating this and other organic principles would be more compatible with the organic domain around it.[45]

The interdisciplinary analysis of internal workings of the factory and the interdependent relationships and networks form a synergy that result in exchange of material, information, and goods. The majority of this work and research remains a fledgling field, as so few companies are able to participate in this visionary symbiotic exchange to inform future practices. The scientific study of the material flow and the lifecycles of products will lead to an understanding of the potential for harmful pollution and outputs.

The potential for a symbiosis is seen in the concept of the architects MVRDV's 2001 vertical pig farm in the Netherlands. The Dutch architects envisioned stacked farms in which the pigs had more real estate than the typical horizontal farm and waste would be recycled.[46] While it did not become a reality, "Pig City" influenced the development of vertical and hydroponic urban farms in Holland and elsewhere.[47] The vertical stacking of agriculture in cities would preserve scarce urban land and minimize transportation costs. In models such as this industry can imitate "nature as co-evolutionary dynamics," and can function as an organic system.[48]

The architecture of sustainability unfortunately pays frequent lip service to the idea of green buildings that follow LEED-dictated checklists of requirements. Specialists, from biologists to engineers, work with architects and plant engineers to minimize the environmental impact of a building. Ideally, a sustainable factory would preserve the natural environment, minimize pollution, conserve water, prevent accidents caused by chemical substances, and help reverse global warming. Inside the factory, internal environmental conditions would permit clean air, natural light, and amenities for workers. But the idea of flexibility, as practiced by high-tech architects, also contributes to a sustainable goal as factory buildings can be altered and reused if conceived of as flexible from the outset. As numerous environmental organizations have demonstrated, negotiating with the large energy corporations on which we depend has proven difficult and nearly impossible, in fact. In the same way that the Modernist factory represented an architecture of a new industrial age, today's innovations in sustainable energy production have the potential to impact the future of architecture in a symbiotic relationship. A softer and subtle architecture of industry could be integrated with its urban surroundings in a transdisciplinary vision.

A few factory projects of the late twentieth century, built and unbuilt, responded to sustainable imperatives and became trendsetters in ecological efficiency. These include those for Wilkhahn, Ipekyol Textiles, MAS Intimates, Herman Miller's "greenhouse," the greening of the Ford River Rouge Plant, and the unbuilt Bronx Community Paper Company. While these examples did not all adhere to the precept of being both vertical and urban, they set the stage for numerous green factories. The following projects are essential to acknowledge as instrumental in enhancing the future vertical urban factory's hybridity changing the way things are made and the technologies used to make them, in order to respect and conserve the environment.

An early 1990s factory designed by Thomas Herzog for the furniture company Wilkhahn, and built in Bad Münder-Eimbeckhausen, Germany, consolidated its plants and office buildings with a goal of sustainability.[49] The company creates furniture with a built-in potential for disassembly and reuse, minimizing material waste and environmental cost. The main design concepts for the 100-by-33-meter plant included natural materials, ventilation, and light. As a result, the primary construction material was timber, including the load-bearing columns dividing the production hall into three bays with 5.40-meter-wide supports,30 meters apart. The three main halls have clerestory windows, and service towers are divided by towers that house utilities. The envelope of wood and steel is a medium of exchange that reacts to the climate in an integrated system and the roof is planted, which

provides natural insulation for the building and is one of the first such features
seen in any factory. The north side has white thermal glazing and the south is fitted
not only with shading strips to limit solar gain, but a shade canopy that doubles as
protection for deliveries and a solar energy generator to power the forklifts. The
building organization also reflects a new non-hierarchical management system, as
the managers overlap in their areas of expertise and responsibility. Wilkhahn labels
this "ecologically oriented" management; it is a system that also contributes to a
social ecology of the work.

Another sustainable furniture factory called The Greenhouse is Herman Miller's
main base in Holland, Michigan. In 1995, William McDonough + Partners, a firm
that focuses on sustainable architecture, designed a factory for furniture assembly.
The company's mission is to recycle their products and not use endangered woods.
There are two key concepts to the building, increasing productivity and worker
satisfaction by bringing natural daylight to the manufacturing and the operations
areas, and creating a common zone, "The Street," where white- and blue-collar
employees interact to access the low band of offices in the front. A skylight brings
sunlight to both sides of the building and clerestory windows admit light deep into
the spaces, saving energy. Tree planting in the parking lot reduces heat gain for the
entire site.

▲ William McDonough +
Partners, renovation to Ford
River Rouge Plant, Dearborn,
Michigan, 1999

McDonough has also transformed existing factories into greener environments,
such as the Ford River Rouge plant in Dearborn, Michigan, designed by Albert
Kahn in 1917. In 1999, McDonough designed a planted roof that reduces stormwater runoff, serves as insulation both in summer and winter, and attracts living
creatures. The much touted redesign showcased the company's transformative
sustainable design, which also inspired ecological production.

In 1994, ahead of its time, both socially and environmentally, the unbuilt project for the Bronx Community Paper Company (BCPC) was designer Maya Lin's commission for a paper recycling plant as part of a groundbreaking proposal of the Natural Resources Defense Council. Spearheaded by Council director Allen Hershkowitz, the initiative was a collaboration with the community organization Banana Kelly, along with unions and paper companies who together formed the BCPC. They conceived the project to occupy a robust infrastructure site at a former rail yard in the South Bronx to create a project that would "showcase the recycling process as well as educate visitors about the importance of recycling, create a sense of community for the workers at the plant, and create a building that would give a sense of identity to the project."[50] The project, if realized, would have been the embodiment of both the spectacle and sustainable factory.

Lin's project, with Harris Group plant engineers and HLW International, was to cost $370 million, recycle 300,000 tons of waste paper per year, and create 440 jobs in an environmentally sound facility. It was to use gray water from a sewage treatment plant and preserve trees by recycling paper. The design used as its base a standard corrugated-aluminum panel system to which Lin added three artistic interpretations: a Water Wall, which holds the water to process the wastepaper; a 60-meter-high Steam Tower, stenciled with clouds, to house the natural gas boilers; and a text wall, which displays data on plant output to the public. Skylights would have maximized natural light and a forest of trees would have been planted following the interior column grid. The logistics transfer of the wastepaper and reconditioned paper into and out of the factory would have been fluid due to the access to the highway and the Triborough Bridge. And while the project was ill-fated, mostly because of political reasons, it serves as a model for the potential of community paper plants, such as those described below, in Madrid that were designed by Ábalos & Herraros in 2001, and the Sims recycling plant in Brooklyn by Annabelle Selldorf, completed in 2013.

Another sustainable factory that is innovative both in design and factory production methods is the textile factory of Ipekyol Giyim Sanayi, designed by Emre Arolat

▲ Maya Lin, design for the Bronx River Community Paper Plant, New York, 1994
▶ Sanjeewa Lokuliyana, MAS Intimates Factory, Thurulie, Sri Lanka, 2008

Architects in Edirne, Turkey, which received an Aga Kahn Architecture Award in 2010. The design resulted in a strategy that integrates the company's production goals with the well-being of their employees. The U-shaped volume with high ceilings is built of local materials, limits energy use, and enhances thermal performance; the administration and production spaces are housed under one roof, breaking down worker hierarchies and allowing for visibility between units and better communications. The U-shape responds to production line flow, from inception to the

packaging and dispatch of the garments. The internal garden courtyard provides natural ventilation, and a series of light wells brings natural light to the workspace. Water is collected from the roof and drained into the local system, and can be recycled as greywater for use by the factory. The company also included recreation and cafeteria spaces for the workers in a socially responsible design that also increases worker performance, albeit in the company's self-interest.

In Sri Lanka, the MAS Intimates Thurulie factory, designed by Sri Lankan architect Sanjeewa Lokuliyana for garment production, also embodies ideas of sustainability, not just in the natural sense but also as a sustainable economic future for the local workers. MAS Intimates makes undergarments for Marks & Spencer and moved to a site in the 67-hectare MAS Fabric Park, a free trade zone developed in the 1990s. Originally a state-owned textile mill that was privatized in the 1980s, the mill experienced a decline and eventually closed in 2003. After the industrial development company invited MAS into the area, it renovated existing factories and built a new award-winning space in 2008 that housed eight hundred workers when it was completed.[51] It was the first sustainable clothing factory in the world, and cost only $2.66 million, with $400,000 invested by Marks & Spencer for the factory's sustainability aspects.

The architects took their cues from the local houses and buildings on stilts with courtyards and lush landscapes. The 10,000-square-meter building is organized around three parallel volumes with two-story production halls, storage, and loading docks, which are all linked by a perpendicular hallway. The flexible interior allows for diverse configurations of work groups and meeting rooms. Amenities such as a holistic medical center, cafeteria, and offices are along the main spine of the administrative wing where additional open workstations are situated.

MAS Intimates incorporates three sustainable aspects: materials, energy, and the natural landscape into the factory design. As a passive energy building, it responds to interior and exterior environmental conditions — with hydroelectric power and passive cooling, the building uses 25 percent less energy than factories of the same production output, making it a carbon-neutral building. The energy use is displayed in signage within the factory, where humidity control is essential for clothing production. Greywater is recycled for manufacturing and used in gardening. Sunlight hitting water carried in tubes preheats the water prior to its heating in the boiler system. The treated water is also used for brewing tea for the employees twice daily. The methane gas from the anaerobic sewage treatment plant is collected for firing stoves and ovens in the kitchen.

The sustainable building is made primarily of local materials, including the earth bricks, the concrete structural frame, and the bamboo sun-screening devices; but some materials had to be imported, such as the zinc-aluminum roofing from Australia and the aluminum frames and plate glass for the windows. The sloping site provides beneficial solar orientation for solar panels and is kept open to preserve the landscape. By raising the building on stilts, the topography is maintained, and breezes can circulate more easily across the site; the green roof not only blends into the landscape but also provides additional cooling. In one building, a holistic and metabolic ecosystem both benefits the workers and the environment.

ECO-INDUSTRIAL PARKS

When an industrial park or economic zone decides to transform into a sustainable zone, each factory in the zone is required to transition to sustainable practices through incentives, advice, and collaborations, becoming an "eco-industrial" or "eco-efficient" park. While such parks try to conserve natural resources, reuse waste and energy, and form a system of interaction between companies for regeneration, there are very few that have been successful, and most are marketing schemes to attract companies. Technological and scientific parks, often linked with research institutes and universities in joint public-private ventures, are more common and have better results than one-off projects.

Eco-Industrial Parks (EIP) in China are organized to develop systems of industrial ecology wherein companies network to take advantage of each other's unused energy, materials, and natural resources. Beginning in 1999, the central Chinese government spearheaded the development of a series of EIPs. By 2007, 24 had been created — more than in any other country, perhaps because the topdown management is one way to organize the diverse companies that participate. EIPs are often developed around a common industry, such as heavy polluting chemicals, recycling, bio-tech, and high-tech. The companies work in synergy to minimize pollution and waste.

Some EIPs are reorganized in former industrial parks, but the most successful are those purposefully built from the ground up, such as the Nanhai National Eco-Industrial Demonstration Park, established from the outset as a cluster of companies working in a closed feedback loop.[52] A government agency plans and constructs these developments, which are considered economic development zones. Similar to most industrial parks, EIPs are governed by strict rules of operation and security considerations. The management recruits companies to the parks based on potential flows of resources and other opportunities for exchange. The companies operate as in a Business District, but harness each other's resources, knowledge, and materials in a more direct way.

When the complex elements are combined — in closed-loop systems — ecological relationships evolve in what is called industrial symbiosis. This can be seen as

a contemporary ecological version of Tony Garnier's Cité Industrielle. The model
project is Kalundborg Symbiosis in Denmark, discussed in detail below; other
companies and organizations are working towards this goal of efficiency through
symbiosis.[53] The main strategies involve using one company's waste materials
to provide energy for another so that there is zero waste and zero emissions.
Victorinox in Zug, Switzerland sells heat to homes near their plant from the heat
waste of the factory. Other examples include the waste from breweries used to
fertilize crops, composting of animal waste, or the production of methane gas, and
use of nutrients in gardens. TEDA in Tianjin, China includes 76 companies that are
using the waste from the companies internally and then converting it to by-products to sell externally. Agent factories or primary factories, when not part of the
development, are built to address the missing link for recycling and repurposing of
products such as metal and plastics in the EIP. A group of pharmaceutical companies in Puerto Rico developed Barcelonetta, an ecosystem of former sugar cane
estates, orchards, and sugar mills. So that nothing goes to waste, the group recycles and treats wastewater as sludge for hay farms, and uses fermentation residue
from drug making in feed for livestock.

▲ The TEDA Eco Park in
Tianjin, China, 2013

  The former assumption of the industrial process as destructive to nature, and
the constant necessity of industrial progress that simultaneously destroys the
environment, could be reconsidered by means of new symbiotic relationships as an
ecological machine that would inhabit industrial infrastructure both socially and
physically. The complexity of the interrelationships then provides more ecological
opportunities that follow organic systems and point the way to new paradigms
for a new urban industrial ecology. The following vertical and urban sustainable
factories point the way to a new potential for the next generation of the metabolic
factory in the city.

KALUNDBORG SYMBIOSIS
KALUNDBORG, DENMARK, 1960s

Kalundborg, Denmark, a city of 20,000 people, and thus not as densely urban as most of the examples discussed, is significant in its development of a successful model of "industrial symbiosis" in which industrial resources are recycled and conserved in a controlled network. The highly developed synergy initiated at Kalundborg in a symbiosis between its resident industries' needs, processes, and waste can point to potentials for future manufacturing. The Kalundborg Symbiosis has grown slowly but effectively, with major Danish corporations taking part. Such industrial symbioses are extremely complicated and difficult to achieve without interest and support from relevant industrial firms.

The concept of industrial ecology that emerged in the environmental movement of the 1970s proposes that industrial supply chains of procurement, production, and storage are in fact a kind of man-made ecosystem modeled on natural ones. This change in thinking about industrial material flows, propagated by contemporary scholars, including R. A. Frosch and N. E. Gallopoulos, and later Suren Erkman,[54] gave rise to the concept of industrial symbiosis, which underpins the Kalundborg project.

At Kalundborg, it is not the architecture that is of design significance, but the networked system and infrastructure of pipes, refineries, and processing plants that crisscross the site. Only a few of the companies invested in progressive architectural design for their plants, among them Energy E2 Asnæs, a coal-fired power plant that hired Gottlieb, Høgsted & Paludan to design their facility. But for the most part, the facilities at Kalundborg that are addressed here are engineering projects dealing with processing and material flow, as well as the upcycling of materials and waste treatment in a more mechanistic project.

In the Kalundborg Symbiosis, materials and infrastructure systems are shared between participating manufacturing firms to reduce both cost and waste. One of the foremost industrial symbioses in operation, the project began in 1961, when an initiative to connect the municipal water supply to a refinery operated by Statoil, the Norwegian oil and gas company, sparked a broader reconsideration of the city of Kalundborg's infrastructure. Meanwhile, new regulations to restrict industrial waste streams from going into the city's landfills inspired local pharmaceutical companies such as Novo Nordisk to treat their waste sludge so as to make it an attractive by-product for nearby agricultural operations. By 1972, these types of efforts had grown into a coordinated pilot program managing energy resources, material supplies, and recycling, and has since evolved into a broad network involving thirty manufacturing firms.

The main goals of the symbiosis are to reduce the consumption of natural resources, to utilize industrial by-products as resources in other industrial processes, and to save companies expensive production costs. To achieve these aims, the participating factories must be located in proximity to one another. The results can be substantial. Among other benefits, excessive energy is not spent on transit, and the proximity of the companies prohibits materials from degrading en route. Water, one of the targeted resources in the symbiosis, has seen its industrial usage plummet, with more than three million cubic meters now conserved. Economic benefits accrue when companies reduce greenhouse gas emissions and lower their consumption of fossil fuels, in general. The symbiotic relationships reduce costs because companies can trade each other's supplies and keep distribution local. The environment gains as well: rather than fill landfills with polluted

◀ Kalundborg, Denmark, industrial symbiosis, 2012
▶ Exterior of the main DONG Energy plant, Kalundborg, Denmark, 2012

residue, many waste products find new uses as primary material, optimizing them in the supply chain and giving them a longer lifecycle as they continue through a process.

In Kalundborg, the system of exchanges works efficiently between six major companies and numerous smaller ones. Energy E2 Asnæs Power Station directs its surplus heat to the 3,500 homes in the town of Kalundborg, just as the Victorinox factory does in Zug, Switzerland. The power plant's sulfur dioxide scrubber produces gypsum as a by-product of the electricity generation process. Industrial gypsum is produced by adding calcium and recycled treated wastewater, creating products ranging from insulin and yeast to feed for pigs. The Asnæs-produced gypsum then becomes a resource for the BPB Gyproc A/S, which makes plasterboards. DONG Energy A/S produces ten percent of the electricity consumed in Denmark, and is developing plans to generate clean, renewable energy within the Kalundborg Symbiosis, in conjunction with Statoil's refinery. More than 98 percent of the sulfur in the flue gas from the power station is

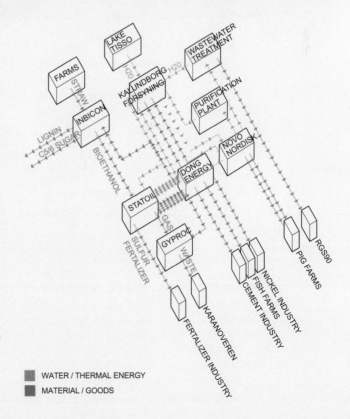

■ WATER / THERMAL ENERGY
■ MATERIAL / GOODS

▲ A worker at Kalundborg's steam plant

removed in the desulfurization process. DONG's bioethanol plant utilizes straw, a by-product of local agricultural production, in its production of plaster for the company Gyproc, as well as various types of fertilizer.

Novo Nordisk, and its enzyme-production subsidiary Novozymes, reprocesses its waste as fertilizer for local farms, which is processed by another of the Symbiosis' firms, Bioteknisk Jordrens Soilrem.

In this networked system, each company exploits the other's by-products and residual on a commercial basis. For example, excess heat from electricity production is used as process steam in some of the nearby industries. Cooling water is used as process water. And the delivery of deionized water and steam, and the final use of treated wastewater, are used in flue gas treatment. These eco-industrial systems of each company work together a closed cycle. The number of available waste streams grew between 1970 and 2010 to over thirty different processes resulting from the exchanges. In Kalundborg, current efforts are increasingly experimental, with new green technologies under development, including biomass refinement, a smart-grid initiative, and a second-generation bioethanol project.[55]

The symbiosis offers an actual example in circular economy, built on the interchange between the companies as they capitalize on the material flows and save resources collectively.[56] The companies can easily access each other's resources not simply because of their proximity, but because of the social relationships they have forged in developing this system; in establishing future industrial symbioses, it will be crucial to enhance the social networks in the mix.[57] The potential these types of resource networks promise for urban manufacturing – and urban ecosystems, in general – is immense.

AMAGERFORBRAENDING AMF WASTE-TO-ENERGY PLANT

BJARKE INGELS GROUP, COPENHAGEN, DENMARK, 2017

One issue concerning urban factories that dominates the conversations of both urban residents and urban planners is the negative impact they pose through pollution and unsightliness. This issue is all the greater where large-scale open urban facilities – such as recycling plants, power plants, and waste-water treatment plants – are concerned. While these buildings are not strictly *factories*, as they do not produce materials or goods, they do perform an essential role in the city's metabolism, treating waste and recycling refuse, and yielding energy, heat, and new raw materials for goods. As inhabitable infrastructure that combines multiple programs, these large-scale facilities become multi-tasking networks, combining civic funds and functions to provide a more public and dynamic resource – rather than eyesores.

One example of an innovative, sustainable, and productive machine (set to open in 2017) demonstrates the potential synergy between different infrastructural and industrial programs intertwined with public space. Bjarke Ingels Group (BIG) in Copenhagen has designed a waste-to-energy plant, Amager Bakke, to be operated by Babcock & Wilcox Volund, in which a unique program mix combines a municipal incinerator, steam energy plant, and an artificial ski slope, forming a new hybrid space. The facility will replace Copenhagen's existing waste-to-energy plant, and will provide 97 percent of the city's residents with heat, and approximately 4,000 homes with electricity.

In 2009, ten Copenhagen regions asked BIG to design a master plan for the city's periphery, connecting the north and south coasts with a new infrastructure and enhancing the link between Denmark and Sweden with a four-kilometer bridge and a 170-kilometer transit loop; the new infrastructural region will also organize a shared regional waste and water management system. To guide the plan to fruition, the city invited architects to participate in a design competition. The resulting 95,000-square-meter

building will cost $500 million in a collaboration between Realities: United (interactive facade), AKT (facade and structural engineering), Ramboli engineers, and Topotek/Man Made Land (landscape).

On average, this facility can transform three kilos of household trash into four hours of electricity and five hours of heat. The city currently has a system for heating homes with the excess heat from power production, but using trash to produce electricity is a more complex operation. The process uses DynaGrate, a combustion- and energy-control system, slag- and ash-handling equipment, and environmental systems, including an electrostatic precipitator to scrub particulates from the exhaust, as well as a selective catalytic reduction system to control the emission of nitrogen oxides. These systems allow the new facility to meet stringent European Union air quality standards.

▶ BIG, Project for Amagerforbraending AMF, Copenhagen, Denmark, 2013
▶ Rendering of the ski slope atop the plant

Since there are no mountains in Copenhagen, BIG was inspired to design a cubic volume that rises at one end to one hundred meters in order to accommodate a ski slope; the resulting slope is two-thirds the size of the closest mountain, Branæs, in Sweden. The slope's height will provide vertical space for the power equipment, including the boiler and turbine hall. Truck entry, refuse processing, and incineration furnaces will be housed within the lower end of the building, which faces the adjacent neighborhood.

Administrative spaces with shallow floor heights will occupy the innovative modular facade. Inside the main hall, visitors and skiers ascend in a glass-walled elevator from which they can see into the plant as they head to the rooftop landscape. The 31,000-square-meter park and dry ski slope, with a white artificial surface, will be open year-round. The roof will have rainwater collection cisterns for stormwater management and irrigation. The building is clad with a skin that is layered with planters, and extensive mitigation measures ensure that the vibration and noise from the plant will be contained.

In a spectacular gesture, the design firm Realities: United is creating something of an art project signal system: when one ton of waste is turned into heat, the plant's CO_2 exhaust will physically compress into a 25-meter-diameter "smoke ring," that will rise from the plant, indicating to the public how much CO_2 is produced on a regular basis.

The plant will be a man-made ecosystem, harvesting natural resources (daylight filters through the facade of rainwater-capturing planters) and will transform what would otherwise be the city's waste into its primary source of energy.

OUTPUT
IN PROCESS MATERIAL
RAW MATERIALS
PUBLIC CIRCULATION

SKI SLOPE

WASTE EXHAUST (CO^2)

MUNICIPAL GARBAGE

RESIDENTIAL STEAM
ELECTRICITY

▲ Overview of the Amagerforbraending complex

BROOKLYN NAVY YARD
BROOKLYN, NEW YORK, 18TH–21ST CENTURIES

One of New York's oldest extant industrial sites, the Brooklyn Navy Yard, is being reinvented as a national model for sustainable urban industrial parks. It was initiated as a small shipyard in 1781 on Wallabout Bay where, during the American Revolution, 11,000 colonial soldiers died aboard British prison ships. In 1801, the yard was purchased by the U.S. government. It thereafter quickly became one of the country's largest shipyards. The first steam-powered warship, the *Fulton Steam Frigate,* was constructed there in 1814; the *USS Monitor,* of the storied Civil War battle of ironclads, was outfitted there in 1862; and the infamous *USS Maine* was launched from the shipyard in 1889.[58]

The Navy Yard grew to cover 120 hectares, which encompassed four dry docks, numerous storehouses, foundries and machine shops, a hospital, a power plant, barracks, Admirals Row (housing for Naval officers), and a radio station. The Civil War-era workforce of 6,000 men rose to 18,000 during World War I, and by World War II the shipyard employed over 70,000 men and women.

In 1966, the Navy Yard was decommissioned, despite having over 9,000 active employees. Following this action, 105 hectares were sold to the City of New York to be maintained as an industrial park. The Yard was next leased to a new development corporation called Commerce Labor and Industry in the County of Kings (CLICK), which selected Seatrain, the ship-building company, as the main tenant along the waterfront. However, Seatrain went bankrupt in 1979 and the Navy Yard's management came under the auspices of the Brooklyn Navy Yard Development Corporation (BNYDC), a new public-private partnership, which maintained, built, and operated the spaces. By 1990, 200 smaller businesses had moved in. Some, such as Cumberland Packing Co., which used tea bag manufacturing methods to package their invention for the sugar substitute Sweet'N Low, has been operating out of the Yard since the 1950s. Steiner Studios was a major catalyst when the company invested in site-improvements and

moved into the Yard in 1999. But, many spaces remained vacant through 2000.

The BNYDC in 2007 rededicated its efforts to lease and manage the Navy Yard. Today, the Yard has a waiting list of over one hundred companies. With funding from the City via the Economic Development Corporation, the BNYDC launched the largest expansion of the site since World War II, and was later designated as an Industrial Business Zone by the City, with tax benefits to industries. With a new director in 2008, Andrew Kimball, planning the redevelopment of three million square meters, the corporation focused on sustainable development and job retention. Currently 240 tenants employ over 5,000 people, both in manufacturing and non-manufacturing jobs, contributing to the Navy Yard's new vitality.[59]

One positive advantage for the Navy Yard tenants is that, as an industrial park, it can operate its own infrastructure, while the negative is the lack of integration with the adjacent community. A historic wall and a chain link fence encircle the property, cutting it off from the neighborhood, but making the logistics within the Yard less cumbersome. Tenant companies are able to load and unload freely, and there is ample open space to be used as staging areas and for material organization.

As an aspiring urban ecological industrial park, or the closest to that concept in the region, it is similar to Philadelphia's Navy Yard redevelopment efforts. At the large scale, it is approaching

▶ Brooklyn Navy Yard, New York, in 1904

ideas of industrial symbiosis, the Yard has an on-site power plant that not only provides energy for the city, but heats the gas produced by the Red Hook water pollution control plant. There is also on-site waste treatment, grey water recycling, and storm water management.

At the smaller scale, the Yard uses solar and wind-powered lighting produced by Duggal's renewable products company Lumi•Solair (with some companies using additional wind turbines), and boasts bike racks and trash compactors. The BNYDC encourages ecological manufac-turing practices, thus a Brooklyn Grange farm occupies one roof, and bees are kept on another. After Hurricane Sandy, in 2013, water flooded numerous properties, forcing a resilience plan, now underway.

The Yard's renewal project is primarily focused on renovation of the forty buildings and leasing the millions of square meters, but a few new buildings have been constructed. The three-story, 8,270-square-meter Perry Building, completed in 2008, was designed by Stantec, and was the first newly built urban industrial building in the city housing multiple tenants on various floors to achieve LEED-CS Silver certifi-cation. Wrapped by a high-performance insulated skin, the building features a high-bay space on the first floor, used for assembly and processing; light manufacturing occupies the upper floors. Photovoltaic (PV) solar energy panels and wind turbines reduce the building's energy use. These initiatives are part of a renewable energy pilot program conducted in partnership with the

National Grid Energy Services. The main tenant is Surroundart, which restores works of art and provides back-end support for high-end art exhibitions.

The Duggal Greenhouse, a 3,300-square-meter renovation of a six-story building at the water's edge by New York-based Studios GO, is an event space and testing laboratory for Duggal Visual Solutions' green products and advertising systems at full-scale. Designed around the concept of a motherboard, the space, which also accommodates the company's printing expansion, will allow future sustainable solar and wind technologies to plug in. The City provided $2 million for improvements to the Greenhouse's roof and sprinkler systems. A 12-meter tall, butt-glazed curtain wall system at the north and south facades wraps the corners of the building to bookend the new vertical windows on the east facade. The glass sits on a backdrop of dark gray smooth-textured stucco with a light gray split-face concrete block base that wraps the building. Concrete footings support the interior mezzanine on the south side, and footings on the north side will accommodate future expansion.

Numerous smaller companies occupy the six concrete-frame former warehouse buildings, which have interior train tracks and elevators for material distribution and include furniture

▲ Stantec, Perry Building, Brooklyn Navy Yard, 2009
▶ Studios GO, Duggal Greenhouse, Brooklyn Navy Yard, 2012

companies, woodworkers, electrical components companies, publishers, and artisans. The business can expand and contract as space is needed and becomes available.

One expanding company is Steiner Studios, the largest film studio on the East Coast, which occupies a corner of the Yard. It has its own gated entrance and occupies a series of buildings, including a five-story building with over 15 stages, and a lot for set work. Steiner also renovated the former Art Deco radio building and is teaming up with Carnegie Mellon to initiate the Integrated Media Program in the former Navy hospital.

Exemplifying collaborative and flexible work environments is the future project for the New Lab, which will occupy the former ship machine shop, Building 128, as a mixed-use workspace for new tech and design industries. The former shop has steel trusswork with skylights and clerestory windows and contains a traveling crane that was used to move the heavy materials required for engine building. Now in a temporary space in the Yard, the dozen companies share information and use 3-D printing and new materials technologies, which they can test in a lab-like setting. The 7,500-square-meter renovation due to open in 2016 is designed by Marvel Architects and developed by MacroSea, with support from government and private grants. A series of mezzanines and workshop spaces can be shared. The other 7,430 square meters of the space is to be used for an expansion of Crye Precision, a homegrown company at the Yard, which makes

safety gear and vests for the military. Building 77, a 17-story former munitions plant that has almost 92,900 square meters of interior space but few windows, is slated for renovation with the support of a city grant of $60 million.

Other ecologically conscious companies include Icestone, a company that transforms recycled glass, or cullet, into countertops and other products. The company maintains a low-heat manufacturing process with a greywater recycling system that reclaims approximately ninety percent of the water used, and employs soy-based lubricants to reduce dependence on petroleum. The plant processes 15 tons of recycled glass per hour using patented Krysteline implosion technology, which eliminates contaminants and crushes glass to specified sizes. Icestone retains ten to twenty percent of the output. Initial research has been conducted to explore the company's potential expansion backwards into their supply chain. The high-quality cutlet that they produce is sold for use as abrasives, water filtration media, tile and terrazzo, landscaping, sports turf, beverage containers, decorative uses, and beach nourishment.

One inspirational company in the Navy Yard is the Kings County Distillery in the historic three-story brick Paymaster Building, which opened in 2012. The low-tech distilling process uses local New York State corn and barley (some grown on-site) and includes a process of fermentation and distilling in Scottish copper whiskey stills, and storage in charred oak barrels made

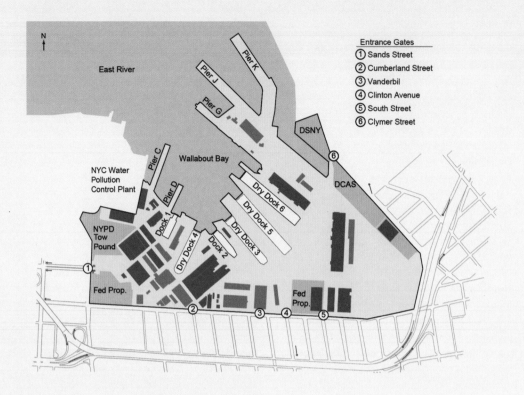

locally by Issek Brothers wooden water tank manufacturers. Bottling takes place in a rough space that the owners renovated mainly by demolishing unsympathetic building materials, and the distillery includes an event space and tasting room. Owner and entrepreneurs Colin Spoelman and David Haskil envisioned the company, which is the first distillery in the city since prohibition, as a local and sustainable business modeled on spirit history as they go forward.[60]

The fierce commitment to the Yard by its tenants is evident in the development of both industrial spaces as well as cultural ones, such as the museum at BLDG 92. Designed by architects Beyer Blinder Belle in 2011, its mission is to educate the general public about the history and current activity in the Yard. There is a pride of place and a pride of entrepreneurship that is palpable along this expansive waterfront. The synergies between industries and individuals create a vitality indicated by the rise in jobs that are being created and sustained there.

▲ Site plan of the Navy Yard, 2012
◀ King's County Distillery, Brooklyn Navy Yard, 2013

SOFTWARE AND BIOTECHNOLOGY PLANTS

COLL-BARREU ARCHITECTS, BILBAO, SPAIN, 2009

In the Bizkaia-Derio industrial development in Bilbao, Spain, Coll-Barreu Architects designed two spherical buildings to house the Software and Biotechnology Plants, in 2009. For research and production of, respectively, computing and biotechnology, these projects demonstrate the transition from heavy industry to high-tech and light industrial development in the third industrial revolution and a way to integrate them into the urban metropolis.

The port city of Bilbao, located on an active river transitway since the first Industrial Revolution, integrated manufacturing within the city fabric which, correspondingly, became denser and increasingly polluted. While extremely urban in terms of economy and infrastructure, the greater metropolis of Bilbao is interspersed with nature – there is even livestock farming nearby. Spread across ten municipalities, the city's metropolitan region is 20 kilometers long. Despite turning to cultural activities as a revitalization strategy, the city still encourages industry; yet, rather than fostering a heavy manufacturing base, it has focused on the potential for a clean, high-tech industrial future.

In 1986, the Basque regional government founded a network of three technology parks – Bizkaia-Derio (1986), Alava, and San Sebastián (both 1990s) – called the Basque Country Technology Park Network. The parks are integrated into the metropolitan area and support new industries in an environment conducive to sustainable scientific and technological innovation; this arrangement encourages the exchange of knowledge and transfer of technology between businesses and nearby university research centers. The Bizkaia-Derio industrial district houses over two hundred companies, technology centers, and research facilities, employing over 6,750 workers.

In this district, which constitutes a kind of linear industrial park located near the airport, Coll-Barreu Architects entered and won two different

architectural ideas competitions to design and build the two plants. The client organized two competitions because they wanted buildings designed by architects rather than industrial engineers, in order to relate the building to the workers needs and to provide amenities.

Architect Juan Coll-Barreu, the founder of the office, sited the two concrete-frame, three-story

▶ Coll-Barreu Architects, Software and Biotechnology Plants, Bilbao, Spain, 2009

▶ Double-glazed facade with etched glass

buildings include the Basque Center for Applied Mathematics, a power transmission and distribution technology center, a solar energy and green power-generation company, an electromagnetic research company, and companies involved in biosciences, genomics, metabolomics, and electronic platforms.

Integrated into the building design are energy-saving and sustainable features. The architects designed curved facades with double-glazed skins between which air circulates, creating a ventilation system that is energy-saving, and essential to maintaining clean interior spaces. Sunlight is filtered through Coll-Barreu's drawings of grasses that are etched onto the glass skins. Vertical glass louvers fixed with aluminum clips, set apart from the concrete building frame, are angled to provide shading from direct sunlight. The upper floor workspaces also receive natural light via a skylight. To accommodate the needs of multiple tenants, the building also includes amenities such as a kindergarten and a gym. Juan Coll-Barreu notes the "apparent paradox that our buildings work better than the ones built by engineers, also in terms of infrastructure use, organization of production, safety conditions, is that we based the design on the manufacturing program to make the buildings efficient and optimal."[61] The building is of both the urban and natural landscape. The

buildings into an earthen berm to increase the heights of their basements and to stabilize them so that there is no vibration. A sunken entry plaza leads to a walkway covered by long concrete canopies with wood undercladding. The canopies radiate from the buildings, and protect the workers from rain and sun.

The pair of buildings encompass a total area of 16,600 square meters. Each has a central core of elevators and services around which individual floors have open layouts, allowing tenants to tailor the spaces to their specific production requirements. The companies housed in the two

shape and radical construction system, eschewing mass-produced construction materials and carving the pedestrian entry area into the earth, yields an aesthetically austere, yet functionally inventive, factory.

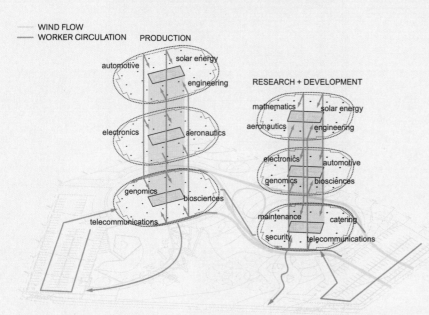

▲ Coll-Barreu, entrance to the plants under concrete canopies

VALDEMINGÓMEZ RECYCLING PLANT
ÁBALOS & HERREROS, MADRID, 1996–1999

In a series of interventions that point to a lighter industrial architecture and the transparency of an ecological production process, the Madrid-based firm Ábalos & Herreros (now two separate firms, Ábalos & Sentkiewicz and Herreros Architects) designed two recycling facilities that are located eight kilometers outside of Madrid's urban core. The area, which had become a kind of wasteland dotted with landfills, is now being reclaimed as parkland through these projects. The purposeful design of these normally sequestered and out-of-sight infrastructural systems has transformed the program of waste treatment and recycling in Madrid.

One facility is located at Valdemingómez and the other at Pinto, both areas in the Southeast Regional Park where the city will expand over the next decades. Both projects use gravity flow to organize and process refuse in innovative systems that bring a new public awareness to recycling.

The Pinto Bio-methane and Composting Plant process begins with gravitation, as the receiving area for the truckloads of garbage is at the highest point of the building site. The building itself is made of recyclable materials: it is clad in polycarbonate and has a wood and aluminum structure. The primary objective is not only to sort the various recyclable materials but to produce methane that is then transformed into electricity used locally, making the processing more complex, as architect Iñaki Ábalos describes.

Valdemingómez is similar in construction to the Pinto facility and unites a diverse rubbish sorting and processing complex with storage, workshops, a public exhibition area, and offices – all beneath an inclined green roof. The main building design provides a vertical gravitational system for the reclamation process as it moves from the upper level of the site down in steps to the final end stage. A recycled polycarbonate-paneled facade wraps the 22,500-square-meter structure, which houses the major machinery. The lightweight steel structural elements – both the columns and cross-bracing – are bolted together as a kit-of-parts so that the building can be dissasembled and be itself recycled. Adjacent to the main processing plant are two smaller volumes: one for the extracting of compounds from organic waste and another for checking and weighing trucks. Both structures are built of the same polycarbonate material and each has a rectilinear organization. Another outbuilding is animated with purple and blue lights and a large cantilever to protect trucks during delivery.

▲ Ábalos Herreros, Valdemingómez Recycling Plant, Madrid, Spain, 1999

In the recycling building, the visitor winds through the plant's operations on elevated walkways. An exhibition area displays the presence of recycling in daily life and a conference room creates a hybrid public space. A main control room displays the digital management of the plant. Ábalos emphasized that "for us it was important to locate these public spaces close to the dumping area so you can first have the brutal impression of trucks, garbage, and cranes and then step by step understand the organization of a complete refined industrial processing of the different substances."[62]

Garbage is sorted through vertical gravitational flow with the aid of a sloped cylindrical central conduit called a trommel. The trommel rotates and divides the refuse at the lower level, leaving different weights in various interior platforms to produce the compost. The organic material is directed by hoppers into a large solid box in which the compost is turned, using different water treatments. The organic compound produced inside is used to build up the plant's slanting green roof, which exposes the transition of the inert garbage – five to ten percent of the total volume arriving at the plant – to soil that in a few decades will blend with the surrounding hills. The compost production and refining areas of the plant are in parallel spaces at one end of the site. While recycling is a standard process, it has never been fully exploited at such a scale as it is here. The plant's vertical structure embodies both an efficient construction and visible process, integrating the industry of waste with public space.[63]

The physicality of the Valdemingómez building itself evolves into an apparatus that can both construct (the hills) and deconstruct (itself), completing the cycle of making, consuming, and recycling in the city. As in some aforementioned factories, the design of the recycling facility encourages the integration of white- and blue-collar workers by the sharing of common entrances and break areas. As Ábalos emphasizes, "it was also our interest to bring offices for white-collar workers to the plant, not only blue collars who normally do the physical work, so the complex becomes a more complicated space with visitors also in the mix as they pass through the space. The vertical organization is not only spatially efficient but democratic."[64]

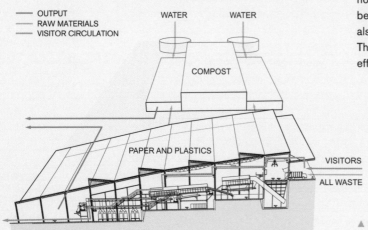

OUTPUT
RAW MATERIALS
VISITOR CIRCULATION

WATER   WATER

COMPOST

PAPER AND PLASTICS

VISITORS

ALL WASTE

▲ Interior of Valdemingómez production space
▲ Exterior delivery space

FLEXIBLE FACTORY

A third theme in the contemporary factory typology is the "flexible factory," wherein the building itself either flexes over time, or the production systems inside are able to be adapted and reorganize with ease. The flexible factory production systems follow what economists Michael Piore and Charles Sabel defined in 1984 as the "new industrial divide," wherein production has to merge with the new economy in order to be agile and responsive to continuously changing production lines or new technology, rather than those rigid production lines.[65] But flexible factories are not only those that are newly built, but those that are inserted into pre-existing industrial spaces and repurposed for new manufacturing uses, which can accommodate new processes. The small-scale production spaces, can be used by multiple tenants who move into larger urban factories such as the Starrett-Lehigh building, even providing opportunities for exchange between the companies.

▲ Grimshaw Architects, Igus Factory, Cologne, Germany, 2000

The newly built flexible factories are not often located in urban areas because of their need for expansion and additional real estate in the city is certainly hard to come by. The aforementioned High-Tech and Japanese Metabolist factory buildings of the 1960s were designed with flexibility from the outset. Architects designed them to expand and contract in their use of a kit-of-parts construction system such as those with adaptable prefabricated wall panels, clips, doors, windows, and structural frameworks. One high-tech building that exemplifies this flexibility is Grimshaw & Partners' Igus factory in Porz Lind, Cologne, completed in 2000, which exemplifies this flexible typology. Gunter Blase, the factory owner, commissioned the architects to design a factory for his company that specializes in injection-molded plastic parts for items that more often are made of steel, such as cable protectors. The owner also wanted the building plan to reflect the company's management structure, which was based on the American "solar system" model, wherein the sun represents the client and all of the company departments are represented by the planets revolving around it. The resultant non-hierarchical 24,000-square-meter space is comprised of four 11.25-square-meter cubes, each with an 18-meter-square courtyard at its center. A pylon rises from each courtyard, with tension wires connected to the roof to maintain their stability. Each roof is punctured with a dome skylight (mechanically controlled) allowing ample air and light into the factory space as well as providing smoke and heat ventilation for fire protection. The combination of the masts and hangers limits deflection so that I-beams, shallower than conventional beams, save material and cost. The columns are placed every 33.75 meters, expanding the available workspace.

Wall panels are inserted with custom-designed aluminum clamps. Vertical mullions between each panel double as gutters sealed with gaskets. The offices are independent pods, similar to the 1960s Plug-In systems developed by Archigram that can be moved around the interior or placed on the exterior, and plugged into the building's infrastructure. The flexibility is similar to Grimshaw & Farrell's design for the 1976 Herman Miller plant in Bath, England, where components that comprised the non-load-bearing walls — windows, panels with louvers, loading and personnel doors — were demountable and interchangeable.

The building's expandability sparked Blase to comment that,

> the latest extension shows how well the modular concept works; I can sit in the cafeteria, watch the factory production continue while the construction workers extend the building at the back by unscrewing the panels and just using a forklift, removing them without any dust or disruption. A provisional wall was erected at the existing end of the building and the old panels will be used on the new exterior wall of the extension.[66]

As in the flexibility of loft construction, open floors, and widely spaced columns of the Modernist factory, manufacturing processes could adapt to counteract building obsolescence. This built-in changeability provided a company with foresight into future construction for new manufacturing technologies that, otherwise, would have been random accretions.

A new surge of flexible factories includes those that are more research-based, such as the collaboration between Sheffield University's AMRC group with Boeing in England. Supported by funds from the High Value Manufacturing initiative of the British government called Catapult, the AMRC Factory will be completed in 2015. The building and its production processes will be a fully reconfigurable assembly and component manufacturing facility. The companies will be able to manufacture a single prototype or a full production line, as well as change between the types of components produced for primarily aerospace and other high-technology industries, making it the ultimate in flexibility.

Smaller factories, such as urban bakeries, printers, or garment manufacturers, can operate out of larger underutilized vertical factory buildings, as the tendency in cities is that factories don't need as much space as they once did — machines and production processes have contracted. With large-scale manufacturing relocating in an exodus to urban peripheries, in process removal, there is a concurrent gravitation toward making things locally in cities that is more collaborative.

Entrepreneurs also have retooled factories for small-scale and small-batch urban production, similar to the small-scale piecework, or homework, of the first industrial revolution. Alvin Toffler predicted this trend in the 1980s with the "electronic cottage." He noted then that,

> Today it takes an act of courage to suggest that our biggest factories and office towers may, within our lifetimes, stand half empty, reduced to use as ghostly warehouses or converted into living space. Yet this is precisely what the new mode of production makes possible: a return to cottage industry on a new, higher, electronic basis, and with it a new emphasis on home as the center of society.[67]

▲ Vacheron Constantin, watchmaker, Geneva, Switzerland, 2010

But the vacated properties are being reoccupied for new modes of production away from the home, since the glamour of working in isolation has worn off over the past few decades.

The sectors of production that both economically and physically survive in cities include recycling of metal and paper, furniture, bakeries, specialty and ethnic food, machine repair shops, printers, high-tech smaller parts, crafts, and higher-end niche products made by designers and fabricators working in tandem. While the products are expensive, the production can strengthen other related, and more mass-produced sectors as well. This smaller-scale manufacturing can occupy large-scale layered factories. The once-abandoned vertical urban factories of companies such as Russell Motor Car in Detroit; American Can in Brooklyn and Standard Motor in Queens, New York; the Tin Factory at 501 Richmond in Toronto; or former office buildings in the Jeppe area of Johannesburg — offer new spaces for entrepreneurs. By dividing the buildings into smaller units in the form of workshops, these layered mini-factories share power systems, elevators, entrances, and general infrastructure, which can reduce costs and energy consumption.

The lack of government or private investment has driven nonprofit initiatives such as the Greenpoint Manufacturing and Design Center (GMDC) in Brooklyn to organize some of these flexible urban spaces. The collaborative development of new industrial spaces in rehabilitated manufacturing buildings in New York encourages local manufacturers. GMDC's star project was the Chelsea Fiber Mills, a former marine rope factory built in 1868 and redeveloped in 1992 on Manhattan Avenue.[68] The original brick complex, built at the confluence of Newtown Creek and the East River, manufactured marine rope. Using the site's change in topography, the train tracks ran across the lower buildings' rooftops along which workers moved coal from waterfront loading areas to furnaces. By the turn of the nineteenth century, the factory had expanded to eight buildings housing 37,200 square meters of industrial space.

The mills were lost to the city in tax foreclosure in 1970. In 1988, a group of woodworking and cabinet-making firms moved in, eventually uniting with other neighborhood groups to develop the complex as a center for arts and industry. Under the umbrella of the GMDC Local Development Corporation, they purchased the property in 1993 and hired OCV Architects for the renovation which was completed in 1999. This building and one of their other facilities in East Williamsburg, also have solar arrays on the roofs, which collect and store energy in zinc bromide batteries. Director Brian Coleman expained, "GMDC's development model has evolved significantly over the years; simple transactions can no longer get a project off the ground, we're now forced to develop complicated tax credit transactions to get a project completed due to ever escalating acquisition and construction costs."[69] While the financing has changed in order to maintain the small companies, it demonstrates that industrial start-ups have successfully reclaimed older factories. It also points to ways that these collaborative projects can help with job retention and training, providing economic opportunities for those who otherwise don't have employment options.

Some of these larger building owners such as at the American Can factory or the former Pfizer building in Brooklyn, are selecting their tenants, to create a cultural and manufacturing mix that matches a desired profile, combining certain types of artisans, and manufacturers to cultivate an image and to entice future tenants. The companies might also be required to have a certain sustainability outlook in their manufacturing processes, or be attentive to their waste they produce to appeal to a new energy conscious clientele.

Manufacturing technology and new flexible production lines, as noted earlier, also contribute to the flexible factory's organization. Specific methods such as Flexible Manufacturing Systems (FMS) embrace the JIT production philosophy

▶ **Greenpoint Manufacturing & Design Center, Brooklyn, New York, 2011**
▶ **Manufacturers in the Greenpoint Manufacturing Center (bottom three)**

with the ability to quickly change production economically. The flexible production line, can easily adapt to mass customization and ever-changing popular tastes. The factories organized along these methods are arranged modular workcells so that a unit can be exchanged, or replaced, when the product design changes and the production process is reconfigured. A system can be varied and indeterminate rather than be stuck in one mode per product. Multiple line layouts also allow for more than one product style, for example automobiles, to be assembled at different workstations with nodes along a production line and with a variety of robotics and CIM- and CNC-operated tools. It is necessary for the computer programmers developing these new digitally driven tools to consider the systems in terms of parts that can be easily replaced — a situation not far removed from the ideas of the nineteenth-century system of interchangeable parts. The management and the workers also require a great deal of flexibility in embracing these new systems, but much of the flexibility is demonstrated in the attitude of the management, and their interest in adapting with the times to remain competitive.

At the larger scale, in 2011, Ford made a pioneering move to flexible manufacturing by spending $550 million on reconfiguring the company's assembly plant in Wayne, Michigan. With a 270,000-square-meter open plan spread among three buildings, the facility, which was previously used to manufacture large fuel-in-efficient trucks, now produces a diverse line of small vehicles, including a battery-powered Ford Focus, in which several different models use similar drivetrains and components. This enables Ford to shift production according to demand, instead of simply halting produc-tion across the entire facility: they can switch from gas to electric, or from model to model, according to the marketplace. The shared com-ponents, smaller volumes, and large number of possible variations creates a manufacturing sit-uation similar to the process used in the fashion

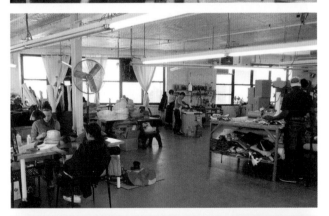

industry, preventing overstock or the need to discount older models. General Motors also followed the same strategy in producing its Chevrolet Volt, which they manufacture in their Detroit Hamtramck factory alongside similar Buick models. The production line was reconfigured and the robots were reprogrammed to conduct different types of welding jobs for different car parts.[70]

At the smaller and community scale, new types of hacker and shared technology spaces provide opportunities for making and remaking objects. The members share equipment, tools, and information as spaces sprout in cities such as London, Detroit, Philadelphia, Paris, San Francisco, and even Nairobi.[71] Freelancers developed co-working spaces, realizing that they were more productive in spaces where they could also have personal interaction. Initially, for those with just their laptop and ideas and the need for space outside of the home, the co-working laboratory or workshop provided tools and assembling spaces, and from which incubators could be launched. For Afrilabs and IHub in Nairobi, the idea of cooperation and digital technologies would combine with the sharing of construction and manufacturing equipment such as lathes and drills, among other tools, to design and build products that solve practical needs, such as ways to pump water and make ropes, as well as to invent new products for the consumer market.

Two avenues of work relating to time and space thus can be redefined. One is that of freedom: workers have flexible hours and the ability to work anywhere, even though traditionally the main factory output is in one place. The other is that flexibility carries with it an inherent instability, due to ever-changing manufacturing technologies and the constant requirement to retool both workers and machines. The stability that a corporation once provided for some has evaporated. Flexibility thus has both positive and negative connotations. Among the latter are alienation, replaceability, and uncertainty. The concept of "flexible accumulation," as discussed earlier, and the flexible workforce of the casual laborer, removes the worker's authority and agency. Lefebvre, in his concept of the production of space, notes the wide variety of mechanisms that influence production's spatial format. Thus, in this paradigm, economies are in an ever greater flux, shifting at a faster rate as the spatial factors that inform industry's physical manifestation (such as local economics, or global geopolitics) become increasingly malleable. The flexible factory becomes both a physical reality and a metaphor for contemporary economics, where opportunities for design investigation can be accomplished, with architects and planners taking hold of the typology of the urban factory to promote the social good.

The factory as spatially flexible, flexible manufacturing, and worker adaptation to this fluid organization in response to economic change, reinforces the paradigm shift to urban factories. Neo-cottage industries are located in new incubator buildings. Local entrepreneurs with shared resources operate out of existing loft spaces and former factories in a new production market. The vertical urban factory is becoming reinvented so that supply meets demand for space and is kept flexible for new and future entrepreneurial economies.

The following examples of flexible vertical urban factories present a variety of designs both in their organization and physical structure, inspiring future urban production spaces.

NEW YORK FLEXIBLE STRUCTURES
BROOKLYN ARMY TERMINAL

The Brooklyn Army Terminal (BAT), originally called the U.S. Army Military Ocean Terminal, opened in 1919 on 39-hectares of Brooklyn waterfront at a deep water channel that could accommodate large ships. The project at that time cost over $35 million to complete. General G.W. Goethals entrusted the design and construction of the new army supply base to architect Cass Gilbert (1859–1934) and Turner Construction. Gilbert was a prominent U.S. architect from St. Louis who had begun to receive commissions in New York such as the U.S. Custom House in 1899, which launched his career in the city, and where he soon reestablished his firm. Gilbert was hired to design the Woolworth Building, which was completed in 1913, and was at the time the tallest building in the city. The Army Terminal complex was simple in design compared to Gilbert's other projects and its use of concrete reflected the need to save steel during wartime. Henry C. Turner was one of the more innovative concrete engineers and had built an empire constructing warehouses and the gridded concrete factory buildings that had begun to spring up throughout New York City. Turner worked in tandem with the engineering firm Post and McCord to complete these immense structures

Gilbert and Turner were also the team, that in 1913, designed the Austin, Nichols & Company Warehouse building for, at the time, the largest importing and manufacturing wholesale grocer in the world. The building, located at 184 Kent Avenue in Brooklyn, completed between 1914 and 1915, was turned into condominiums in 2008. It was distinguished by the facade's articulation with slit windows, concave cornice, and comprehensive railroad tracks that ran into the interior, as well as elevators and pneumatic tubes through which the finished food products were delivered for distribution.

From the outset, the Brooklyn Army Terminal was considered to be convertible to manufacturing for future post-wartime use. The complex's own infrastructure supported a logistic system that was efficient for the delivery and movement of goods. Materials and products flowed between the warehouses and buildings via tunnels and bridges and on site roads and rails to the port. Machinery such as forklifts, cargo elevators, and lifts on the piers, supported and supplemented physical work, transferring goods onto the ships. Over three million troops and 38-million tons of supplies passed in and out of the terminal during its active wartime use.

BAT is comprised of two eight-story warehouses – A and B – that together house an administration building, boiler house, repair shop, and four piers in 16.4 million square meters of space. At the time, the eight-story Warehouse B was the largest structure ever built in reinforced concrete, providing 21 hectares of floor space; while it has a simple and direct structure with few embellishments, the articulation of its mass is broken up through the rhythmic spread of windows separated into bays by vertical piers.

Three arched sky bridges link the third floors of Warehouse A and Warehouse B. The larger of the two, Warehouse B, features a huge enclosed atrium, and the smaller is joined to the atrium by three covered piers. In order to increase storage efficiency, Gilbert emphasized horizontal

▶ Cass Gilbert, Brooklyn Army Terminal, Brooklyn, New York, 1919

▶ Rail infrastructure of the Brooklyn Army Terminal

and vertical circulation systems: a large crane ran along the atrium spaces to unload freight from trains running directly into the building. Staggered concrete balconies were cantilevered from each floor on the interior courtyard atrium as staging areas from which goods were loaded onto the train cars below (as in Owen Williams' Boots factory in England). Ninety-six centrally controlled Otis elevators, each 1.3-by-1.5-square meters in size, carried up to 4,500 kilograms of material at a rate of 13.9 meters per minute up and down the building. The shorter vertical distances could be reached efficiently, proving the value of the multistoried factory. The result was that 12 ships with an 8,000-ton capacity could dock at each of the three piers, and be fully unloaded within 24 hours. The efficiency of material storage, assembly, packaging, procurement, and supply, as well as the distribution of goods (such as uniforms, hats, shoes, medical equipment, canned food, salt, sugar, and emergency supplies) at the end of World War I and throughout World War II, placed the building in constant service of production.

But what is also of interest in terms of the contemporary issues for manufacturing space is that the BAT complex, having been vacated in 1975, was purchased by New York City from the federal government in 1981 and was divided into spaces, ranging from 1,390 to 3,720 square meters, for production. BAT represents an example of an increasingly common trend in that a space made for one company (the army) now serves multiple tenants. This is largely because of the shrinking of urban industries and the rising need for smaller space.

New York City's Economic Development Corporation (EDC) is currently leasing the complex in which they have invested $90 million for renovations. By 1999, BAT housed sixty companies, with EDC managing the facilities and common spaces. In 2014, the two warehouse buildings, comprising 288,000-square meters of space, were home to over one hundred companies employing over 3,000 people. The majority of these businesses are industrial, including garment, furniture, electronics, high-tech digital equipment, and green furniture companies. The textile company USA Made occupies a large space within the complex as does the pharmaceutical company Mega-Aid, the online marketplace Uncommon Goods, and New York City's 311 call center, all of which employ hundreds of people. Both the Museum of Natural History and the Guggenheim Museum lease storage space at the Brooklyn Army Terminal as well.

The City maintains BAT's common spaces, parking areas, loading docks, day care facilities, and security services, recently investing $15 million to renovate the main administration building, which is a New York City Landmark. Renovations are slated for a 46,000-square-meter area of Building A, which has not yet been brought up to code. BAT's low rent and large and flexible spaces continue its viability.

BUSH TERMINAL – INDUSTRY CITY

The Bush Terminal Industrial Complex – now known as "Industry City" – comprises 12 buildings encompassing 100,000 square meters that are currently leased to 43 businesses employing four hundred workers. The complex has a long history, extending back to the early nineteenth century.

With a thriving immigrant population, extensive waterfront access, and proximity to Manhattan, Brooklyn's Sunset Park became a booming center of industry at the turn of the nineteenth century, and was anchored by the Bush Terminal. The massive complex of warehouses, rail and shipping links, and factory lofts was built in stages from 1895–1925 by the wealthy businessman Irving T. Bush on the former site of his family's oil refinery.

▲ Bush Terminal Industrial Complex, Brooklyn, New York, 2013

Bush conceived an intermodal transportation, warehousing, and manufacturing facility as a challenge to Manhattan's primacy, convincing railroad officials to establish direct routes to his Brooklyn piers via "car floats" similar to those for the Starrett-Lehigh building, which ferried railroad freight cars across the harbor.

The series of six-story factory lofts built from 1904 to 1918 were reinforced concrete buildings erected by Turner Construction. This complex became America's largest multi-tenant industrial property and first industrial park, spanning across twenty waterfront blocks and eight piers, with 118 warehouses and 26 factory buildings housing 25,000 workers. Bush touted an advanced elevator system, which gave tenants direct access to the freight trains arriving at the site. He also built worker housing, developing Sunset Park as a "factory city" for 30,000 people.

Bush Terminal/Industry City is now owned by Jamestown, Angelo Gordon, and Belvedere Capital, along with Cammeby's International and FBE Limited, this conglomerate is leasing the spaces to manufacturers and artists, including a furniture manufacturer, garment and accessory manufacturers, industrial suppliers, moving and shipping companies, a restaurant supplier, a plastic bag recycler, and the MakerBot 3-D printer company. The concept is similar to Brooklyn Army Terminal, but here the current owners are also using the more public spaces for trade fairs, shops, cafés, event spaces, and showrooms. A food hall features artisanal food tenants who make their goods in full view, creating a dynamic and engaged place of production. The future of Industry City is filled with potential, as the scale of manufacturing shifts back to established historic complexes such as this one.

STANDARD MOTOR PRODUCTS BUILDING

In 2008, the New York-based Acumen Capital Partners began to branch out from more traditional development projects to assume the risks involved in owning, maintaining, and improving multitenanted industrial buildings to encourage new industrial uses. Their first project was the redevelopment of the Standard Motor Products building on Northern Boulevard in Long Island City. The eight-story concrete frame building occupies a site along the railroad and has access via a side street with immediate proximity to truck-loading bays.

Standard Motor Products is an automotive parts company that was founded in 1919 in New York, first focusing on ignition and electrical products. Their main market is replacement parts – including wire, cable, and ignitions – not goods for the initial production line. The company moved from Manhattan to Long Island City and leased a space there in 1923. As the company expanded, they needed their own facility, which they built on Northern Boulevard and completed in 1936. By 1994, Standard Motor Products was on the Fortune 500 list. With their company's reach now overseas, the New York facility became an office, rather than the head manufacturing plant.

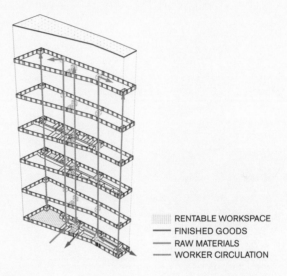

RENTABLE WORKSPACE
FINISHED GOODS
RAW MATERIALS
WORKER CIRCULATION

▲ Standard Motor, Long Island City, New York City, 2013

After Acumen bought the building, Standard Motor continued to lease a portion of it. The rest of the building was renovated by Bromley Caldari Architects, who redesigned and opened up a lobby space and installed retail spaces in the first-floor loading docks, common bathrooms, and new elevators, as well as new industrial sash windows.

The building's concrete structure, with typical Turner mushroom columns, was built to hold many times more its weight. Due to this capacity, the Brooklyn Grange, an urban farm requiring forty tons of soil for its plantings, was able to

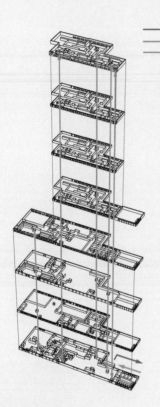

— FINISHED GOODS
— RAW MATERIALS
— WORKER CIRCULATION

occupy the building's roof. The industrial spaces are leased at various sizes, from 929 to 2,000 square meters, to tenants as varied as a commercial printer, a metal embosser, an offset printer, an art printer, the Jim Henson Company, the Franklin Mint, and Broadview Networks.

PFIZER

Acumen Capital Partners' second multitenanted manufacturing space is the Pfizer plant on Flushing Avenue in Brooklyn that they purchased in 2011. Pfizer, founded in 1849, built the eight-story brick and concrete behemoth in 1948. Formerly filled with thousands of workers making chemicals and compounds for drug production, Acumen realized that they could take advantage of the existing state-of-the-art labs and infrastructure built for liquid processing — stainless steel vats, drums, mixers, giant refrigerators, and chemical labs — to accommodate diverse manufacturing uses. The company's new tenants, who have occupied the space since 2012, are primarily artisanal food production companies — from makers of pickles and ice cream to kombucha and pasta — as well as wood workers, steel welders, and artists. All find the building's thick floors and large windows with views to Manhattan perfect for heavy industrial uses.

Similar to the Standard Motor building's transformation — in terms of the mix of uses and a community that is growing in place — these various enterprises employ fewer workers but pay above minimum wage. As one of the Acumen partners, Jeff Rosenblum, notes, the building's location and facilities make it easy for a young company to lease smaller spaces and then grow in an incubator environment.[72] Acumen envisions more public ground-floor space used for cafés or farmer's markets. New additions to the space include educational programs such as Pratt Institute's Brooklyn Fashion and Design Accelerator.

◀ **Former Pfizer Building, Brooklyn, New York, 2013**

AMERICAN INDUSTRIAL CENTER
SAN FRANCISCO

The flatland east of San Francisco's Potrero Hill, called Dogpatch, was perfectly suited for American Can Company, now the American Industrial Center. A behemoth stretching four blocks between 20th and 23rd Streets, along Third Street, the building's over 74,000 square meters of space house a variety of uses today.

Dogpatch was home to shipbuilding and rope-making, it also included other small related industries. Along with its company-built wood frame cottages, it formed an industrial town. The area was spared in the 1906 earthquake, with over one hundred of its houses still extant. As is typical of industrial geography, the district's location along the city's southern waterfront made it easily accessible to ship and train transit, which strengthened it as a production and distribution center. Throughout the mid-nineteenth century, warehouses, machine shops, iron works, steel mills, gas works, barrel making, sugar refining, and other industries established themselves here. Bethlehem Steel's San Francisco Yard was also located in Dogpatch.

The American Can Company, a major early twentieth-century conglomerate, owned factories around the country, and was headquartered in New York and then Connecticut. The company was the largest tin can company in the world for over one hundred years, and developed new methods to can foods for longer food life and lasting nutrition.[73] Construction began on the company's San Francisco concrete industrial plant in 1915 on two square blocks, formerly a part of the Crocker Estate between Kentucky Street and Illinois Streets, and 20th and 22nd Streets. Over 1,200 people, many women, worked in the plant, and, during the 1930s and post-World War II, it was the largest employer in the area. The San Francisco branch produced tin cans and bottles for West Coast Canneries.

The first building was four stories high at the corner, stepping down to two stories for the major manufacturing halls. The concrete grid is emphasized in the exposed frame on the facade, containing large steel casement windows with brick spandrels. Multistoried additions continued through the 1950s, including a four-story, high-bay concrete building with a warehouse and with smaller bands of clerestory windows at each floor. The ceiling heights reached from 5.4 to 8.5 meters to accommodate large-scale machinery. When the company was further consolidated and sold, they reduced production nationwide and vacated the buildings in the late 1960s without

▼ **American Industrial Center, San Francisco, California, 2013**

a reuse plan. In the 1980s, it was absorbed into Primerica, which stopped the packaging production lines all together.

In 1975, a San Francisco shoe manufacturer, Angelo Markoulis (1926–2012), bought the facility, calling it the American Industrial Center, and divided it into a multi-tenanted building, taking a great deal of space for his own use and leasing other spaces to garment manufacturers, among different businesses. By 1985, there were over two hundred tenants.[74] In recent years, AIC continues to offer spaces for lease, as large as 2,787 square meters, but companies can start with as little as 37 square meters if that is all they require. The short- and long-term leases also make it a kind of de facto incubator space. Since the late 1990s, the companies have become increasingly smaller, with the majority leasing around 139 square meters each. The over 300 companies employ 3,000 people, in garment industries, bakeries, printers, artisanal food companies, breweries, and design firms.

Similar to other large-scale, more single-purpose factories, such as the Brooklyn Army Terminal or the Pfizer building in Brooklyn – the American Can Company's buildings were at first a fully integrated factory and became a layered building type more similar to the Starrett-Lehigh Building, with different companies housed in different-sized spaces according to their needs. The leasing also speaks to the idea of the flexible factory in that companies can expand and contract fairly easily by adding or subtracting walls to divide the space into smaller units. One advantage for manufacturers is that the building still has its truck loading bays and heavy-duty elevator systems – so few buildings still have similar amenities. The complex is divided into north and south buildings with jewelers, letterpress printers, garment manufacturers, and confectioners, along with small arts-related companies in the north. In the south is Magnolia Brewery, and smaller manufacturers. The management company also provides communal spaces, gym spaces, and retail in order to enhance the streetscape, as with the plans for Industry City in Brooklyn.

In San Francisco, there has been a concerted effort to return manufacturing to the city, both through the department of city planning and nonprofit groups such as SFMade. Organized in 2010, SFMade is an advocacy and support group. Founder and director Kate Sofis saw the need to support manufacturing, empower manufacturers, and support employment opportunities in the industrial sector in the city and to encourage new companies to start up there. Similar to New York City, Los Angeles, and Chicago, industrial jobs in San Francisco declined in the 1990s and 2000s, and both the city economic agencies and city planning saw the need to stop that decline. SFMade assists manufacturers with requirements for space, loans, and business networks. To date, their directory lists over five hundred manufacturers. As an umbrella organization that is focused on encouraging entrepreneurs to make things locally – even branding products "SFMade" – the nonprofit has formed a national group, the Urban Manufacturing Alliance with the Pratt Center for Community Development in New York, among

◀ Brewery in the American Industrial Center (AIC), San Francisco, California, 2013

others, on a national scale. SFMade received a Clinton Global Initiatives Award in 2012.

In 2001, the City of San Francisco undertook a major rezoning effort to create manufacturing areas in the Eastern Neighborhoods along the waterfront. Amidst debate around the typical issues of commercial versus industrial use, and the highest and best use of the land, it finally passed in 2008. But, because San Francisco's economic development division also understood that the definition of industry had to change to that of lighter industries – the production of things that are moved, made, or bent, or, in their terms, "production, distribution, and repair" (PDR) – the new potentials for industrial development could be encouraged.[75] The land available to industry was maintained, and another portion was set aside for industry and mixed uses, prohibiting commercial and residential uses. However, as the neighborhood continues to gentrify, there has emerged a struggle between tech workers and the artists and artisanal makers who are focused on maintaining the mixed-use spaces.[76] The rise of industry – especially niche manufacturing and smaller light industries – is exemplified in the AIC as a microcosm of urban manufacturing in a flexible but massive space.

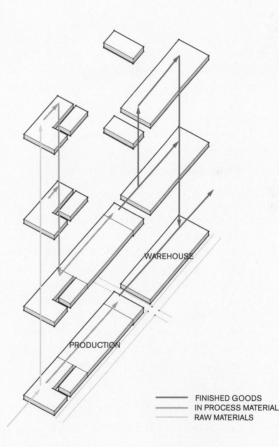

FINISHED GOODS
IN PROCESS MATERIAL
RAW MATERIALS

◀ AIC streetscape in San Francisco (top and bottom)

AMERICAN APPAREL
LOS ANGELES, CALIFORNIA, 2000

American Apparel (AA) started their internationally distributed garment production in 2000 in Los Angeles' downtown Enterprise Zone, near the burgeoning L.A. Fashion District, whose ease of access to the Los Angeles and Long Beach port via the Alameda Corridor and cheaper space, also lured them to the area. AA, known for its commitment to Made in the U.S.A. has employed nearly 5,000 people over the past 15 years, who operate out of two, 6,900-square meter, seven-story concrete frame buildings.

Formerly home to S.E. Rykoff, the wholesale food distribution chain, or the "Home of the Gallon Goods," Rykoff moved after numerous merges with other food distribution companies over the subsequent decades and today continues as US Foods. Their 1916 Union Terminal warehouses at the 8th Street Yard of Southern Pacific Railroad feature large casement windows with center-operable sections, decorative parapets, corner stair towers, and loading docks arrayed along the length of the buildings' ground floors.

American Apparel is vertically integrated in terms of the company's organization and production methods, from the first steps of knitting and dyeing fabrics to the manufacturing, distributing, and selling of finished garments in their own branded stores. That vertical integration is manifested physically throughout the seven-story factory, from top to bottom. The production moves down from floor to floor until the completed garments are ready to be stored in an adjacent warehouse for shipping. The showroom, along with company management, marketing, communications, photography, and design are located on the seventh floor; the sixth floor houses sewing and quality control; the fifth floor offices, health services, and a cafeteria; the fourth floor cutting, trimming, and labeling; the third floor shoemakers, seamstresses, and a massage therapy space; and the second floor creative offices and hosiery. Logistics and deliveries also occur on the first floor and in the adjacent building.

▲ American Apparel, Los Angeles, California, 2011
▶ Industrial area comprising Alameda Square, 2011

Factory employees work together in teams from four to thirty people – according to the complexity of the garment being constructed – in a cellular manufacturing process, versus an assembly line. Team members attach the myriad pieces that make up the whole, while a specialist checks the product quality. Because of the small batches, the quality control is attentive. The processes that require more space, such as dyeing and knitting, are completed off-site.

Using computer automation, bar codes applied to all goods keep track of incoming and outgoing inventory, provide information as to the location, item number, description, type, color, and quantity. Running around the clock, the factory turns out 1.4 million garments weekly. A new design can be cut on Monday, sewn Tuesday through Thursday, and shipped on Friday in the company's JIT production process. Storage shelves house the various colors of cotton fabric, which comes in long tubes.

American Apparel is environmentally conscious through a number of practices both inside and outside the factory. Foremost among these is local production.[77] While so many companies are outsourcing labor overseas, American Apparel has demonstrated a commitment to making things in the city, as evidenced by its slogan, "Made in Downtown LA," now essential to its brand. The items that it doesn't make locally it sources to other factories in the U.S.

This reduces the company's carbon footprint, as it uses less fossil fuel in its supply chain. AA also recycles fabric scraps by reweaving them as tank-top straps and using them as cleaning rags; imperfect items go charities. Its use of rooftop solar panels has cut the company's energy consumption over twenty percent in the last decade.

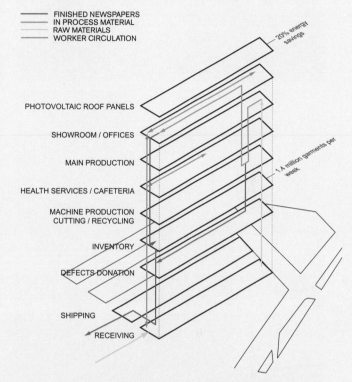

FINISHED NEWSPAPERS
IN PROCESS MATERIAL
RAW MATERIALS
WORKER CIRCULATION

20% energy savings

PHOTOVOLTAIC ROOF PANELS

SHOWROOM / OFFICES

MAIN PRODUCTION

HEALTH SERVICES / CAFETERIA

MACHINE PRODUCTION
CUTTING / RECYCLING

INVENTORY

DEFECTS DONATION

SHIPPING

RECEIVING

1.4 million garments per week

the company was, however, losing ground. The executive officers ousted founder Dov Charney and changed the board composition with Standard General, a hedge fund, holding 44 percent of the stock.

The garment industry declined in cities such as New York, Toronto, and L.A., not only because of cheaper labor overseas, but specifically in L.A. because of the multiple vetoes on textile legislation to restrict imports of fabric, clothing, and shoes and also the 1994 enactment of NAFTA.[78] Greater regulatory legislation by California in 1997, which required brand holders and manufacturers to be responsible for workers compensation and OSHA requirements spurred additional outsourcing. AA instead remained committed to L.A.

In terms of social justice, the company pays above minimum wage – the highest of any garment worker, they say – and introduced stock options for workers, making them shareholders.[79] AA is invested in the betterment of its workforce, and offers employees classes in business management, physical fitness, and English as a Second Language. Despite this impressive track record, however, they recently had to let 1,800 skilled workers go because of outdated immigration documents. As AA has demonstrated, the value of local production, holding 33 percent of overall apparel manufacturing jobs in 2010 in the U.S., has influenced other manufacturers to produce locally.

However, L.A.'s Garment District is transforming into more of a fashion district, with ground-floor retail and new residential developments.[80] The private equity firm, Evoq Properties, with the Shimoda Design Group, has begun proposals to transform the area into Alameda Square, linking the Arts District with the Fashion District. AA's space will be maintained and the other two buildings, totaling about 55,741 square meters, will contain offices and clothing-related manufacturing.

As long as the social justice issues can remain transparent beyond the company's own interests, American Apparel makes evident the value of repurposing a former warehouse for the future of vertical and urban manufacturing.

On the political level, the company is very vocal and active in social issues, specifically, immigration reform and gay rights, and runs editorials ads in papers such as the *Los Angeles Times* articulating its stance. In an interesting product-as-propaganda move, AA sold t-shirts silkscreened with the slogan "Legalize LA," in support of immigrant's rights. In a controlled transparency, AA's videos documenting the factory reveal the operations on its website. The organizational structure changed in 2014, as

◄ **Workers at AA receive massages (top)**
◄ **Interior textile production (middle and bottom)**

STEAM WHISTLE BREWING

TORONTO, CANADA, 2000

The number of craft breweries in North America has exploded in the past fifteen years as entrepreneurs capitalize on the locavore movement. There is also new consumer interest in home brewing, beer quality, and variety. In general, beer is enjoying a level of connoisseurship typically reserved for wine. The current focus on craft brewing – defined as beer derived from a traditional method using innovative ingredients and produced by a small or independent company in volumes of less than six million barrels annually – is exploding in cities.[81] Though craft brewing only accounts for three percent of U.S. beer sales, these brewers are setting new trends.

Often, the quality of beer depends on the water used in its production, which can greatly affect the flavor of local variants (for instance, in Chile, catching fog is essential to the unique taste of Fogcatcher beer). The mainstream market of mass-produced North American beer is based on recipes and ingredients passed down from generations of German immigrants, who depended on easy-to-grow local forms of hops. In Colorado, Milwaukee, and St. Louis, brewery overtook New York breweries in the early twentieth century because of their larger production capacity. Recently, historical centers of beer production have seen a revival with companies such as the Brooklyn Brewery, which launched in 1987 in Utica, expanding to Brooklyn in 1997, with the help of a state grant. The combination of a brewery or microbrewery (one producing even less than 60,000 barrels annually), with a pub or restaurant, and tasting bars with brewery tours, have become marketing tools that have a strong economic impact, enabling new experiential consumption.

Canada is experiencing this phenomenon as its breweries gain in popularity. The Ontario Craft Brewers association has grown exponentially as an umbrella organization, establishing standards for smaller enterprises, such as: using traditional brewing methods in small batches; using natural, quality ingredients; allowing fermentation to final gravity without dilution; and avoiding preservatives or additives. They also take pride in the growth of hundreds of jobs in the industry.

In Toronto, in the early nineteenth century Robert Henderson started the city's first brewery with a mill, brew house, tubs, coolers, kilns for drying malt, good wells for water, and two stills. The enterprise produced approximately thirty barrels per week. Then, beer was traded primarily for payment to British soldiers who were stationed at Fort York, which was established to defend against potential American hostilities.[82]

In the current renewed era of brewing in the city, companies such as Mill Street Brewery, Junction Craft Brewing, Bellwoods, Hogtown Craft Brewing, and Steam Whistle Brewing are growing with ease of distribution to a devoted clientele. Three former employees of the Upper Canada Brewing Company founded the Steam Whistle Brewing Company at 255 Bremnar Boulevard in Toronto in 1998. In July 1999, it also renovated the former Canadian Pacific Railway's John Street Roundhouse, owned by the city. Originally constructed between 1929 and 1931 for train car repairs, the round brick building includes a 36-meter rotating table that, until 1988, provided access to 32 stalls, which serviced diesel-powered locomotives.

Steam Whistle renovated stall bays one through fourteen taking advantage of the large, multi-paned windows and nine-meter ceilings to house its brewing machinery, which operates in a vertical flow throughout the vast high-bay space.

Sixty employees and eighty hired seasonally, direct the production and maintain machinery. The process begins by turning grain or barley into malt by breaking down the starches in large vats; afterwards, mashing and lautering divides

▲ Steamwhistle Brewery in the former John Street Roundhouse, Toronto, Canada, 2013

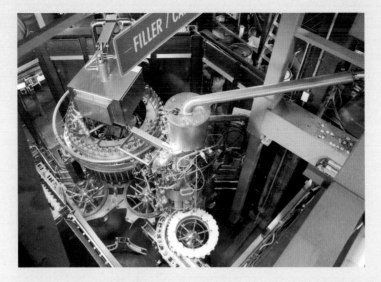

the extracts from the spent grain to make wort. This occurs by mixing hot water and malt into another vessel with a filter. With this step, a boiling process sterilizes the wort and the brewer adds hops, which provide the bitter flavor. Then, the liquid is cooled in a heat exchanger. The fermentation and maturation achieved through the addition of yeast gives a particular beer its character. This fermentation occurs in cylindrical vats with a conical base so that the waste material separates and falls down using the vertical flow of the tanks, which are often placed on the exterior of the brewery. At Steam Whistle, the vats are housed inside the facility; the compactness of this production flow allows for a more densely packed urban site. The process continues with chilling the beer, carbonating it, and putting it through a final filtration to remove impurities and to form a smoother consistency. The beer is then removed from the large stainless steel vats and packaged into bottles, cans, or kegs, and then labeled and packaged for distribution.

To promote tourism and experiential consumption, and to leverage its unique manufacturing setting, Steam Whistle has opened its factory to tastings and tours. To expedite such tourism, the company has modified its factory space by adding a catwalk through the main hall. This broad shift illustrates that the industrial process is no longer dirty or unpleasant; on the contrary, through sanitary regulations and new technology, it has become a a part of the city, reknitting the formerly lost space of production back into the place of the product's consumption, and thus daily life.

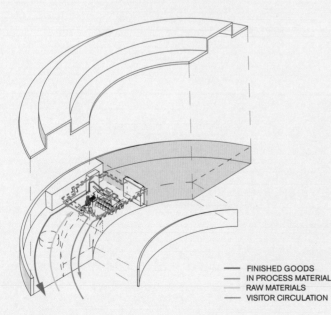

— FINISHED GOODS
— IN PROCESS MATERIAL
— RAW MATERIALS
— VISITOR CIRCULATION

▲ **Beer processing at Steam Whistle, Toronto, 2014**

HONG KONG
VARIOUS, 2013

After a massive fire in Shek Kip Mei left 53,000 homeless over Christmas in 1953, the government responded by building what they called Mark I housing as H-shaped, low-income tenements without many services and balconies surround the buildings which were also used as cooking areas. When they found that people were also using the spaces to make goods, the city produced single-use manufacturing buildings for light industries. They identified these as "flatted factories," meaning that each floor can be leased as a flat, or a combination of flats according to the space required (not dissimilar to a loft space). The concrete frame buildings were modeled on the second phase of the city's housing program from the early 1960s, during which they built seven-story H-shaped buildings with units available to lease ranging from 18 to 24 square meters, a module set according to the structural grid. In these spaces, one could find a hybrid mix of products stemming from the previous cottage industries of textiles and plastic flowers. One of the oldest of these types that still exists is the Chai-Wan factory built in 1959. Organized in an H-shape with five stories and balconies surrounding the floors for light and air, the structural columns are placed four meters apart to carry 836-square-meters per floor. For vertical circulation, workers use a central ramp as a gravity system to move goods, as in early-twentieth-century factories. One staircase in the middle and another at each end of the parallel wings are linked by a corridor with public services, resulting in the H formation.

For other enterprises, either too large or polluting, the city decided to develop larger vertical urban factories in a second phase of government-led industrial development. Some of these rising over twenty stories, with the inclusion of elevators, waste management, and storage. The rise in height of factories coincided with zoning changes in the 1960s – up to a Floor Area Ratio (FAR) of 15 – that allowed buildings to go taller if they could increase the light and air by using podiums, which often contained commercial space and towers set back from the streetwall. Because of the grouping of the individually owned factories within the buildings, they called the buildings "factory estates." By 1967, there were twenty-two of these factory buildings, with over 140,000-square-meters of space.[83]

The government continued building these factory estates through the latter half of the 1970s and 1980s with a variety of layouts, from internal cores to those with balconies for extra workspace in order to maintain open floor spans in the factory interiors. Some have large ramps for truck access right into the building. The manufacturing space, actually owned by the city, expanded to 17.8 million square meters, which encompassed over 83 percent of overall production space in the city.[84]

Today, the city is experiencing an industrial vacancy because of cheaper labor in Mainland China and the initiation of the Free Trade Zones there by Den Xiaoping in the late 1970s. Many of the flatted factories have been demolished because of lack of use and deteriorating conditions. The remaining flatted factories still leased

▶ Vertical Urban Factory, Hong Kong, 2011

by the Hong Kong Housing Authority, as of 2010, included the Sui Fai, Wang Cheong, and Yip On factories, among others. These eleven estates provide over 13,300 factory units with a total floor area of about 325,300 square meters. The city also revised the requirements for the sectors of manufacturing that are allowed in these spaces – from apparel (but not dyeing) to metal, rubber, plastic, wood, and paper products to repair of equipment and furniture to computers, musical instruments, glass (but not the making of the glass itself), and medical equipment. No hazardous manufacturing is allowed.

Of the factories in continuous operation, the tallest rise up to 23 stories, as they had an FAR of 15 and follow the same building code as that of a residential tower. These are still among the tallest factories in the world. As part of the industrial estate of Kwai Chung, which is situated on reclaimed land, the Wing Loi Industrial Building designed by Chau Lam in 1976, at twenty stories, is one of the taller of the factories on Wing Lap Street. Trucks enter into the ground floor and corner piers and load-bearing walls on two sides support the structure. Each floor is 1,220 square meters, housing textile manufacturing, dyeing, and laundry services. The different processes require separate wastewater systems, so a series of pipes run up the facades since they were never integrated with the building's infrastructure.

The Mie Kei Industrial Building in Kwai Chung holds numerous manufacturers in a reinforced concrete structure of 23-stories and built in 1979, also on Wing Lap Street. Its service core is set to one side in order to have open floor areas. The machine room is stepped back at the upper floors (375 square meters each) with ventilation pipes and chimneys running dynamically up the facades and projecting above the roofline.

The Sui Fai factory estate is another 23-story factory built for the Hong Kong Housing Authority, with balconies similar to those in residential complexes that are also used as workspaces. As a flexible type, floors can be leased completed or divided into smaller workshops. As a load-bearing concrete structure, Sui Fai has perpendicular end walls to support the structural frame.[85]

The Wah Fung Industrial Center, completed in 1979 by K.K. Wong architects, is a 16-story building with the largest floor areas of those here discussed: 2,900 square meters. Two rectangular spaces are built on a podium beneath which trucks enter. Although each building has a similar concrete slab structure, each one is a separate structural system that divides their internal organization; from the exterior they appear to be unified. One volume has a central core with a structural column grid, while the other has a central core and columns on the perimeter.[86]

The industrial district of Kwun Tong in Kowloon was planned in 1953 by the government

outside of the center city. By 1957, it had grown to cover 21 hectares of land and was intended to provide spaces for companies to provide employment opportunities for immigrant populations coming from China. The Kwun Tong development area first focused on housing textile manufacturers within a variety of buildings, as well as commercial and residential uses. One was the Hoi Bun building, and another the Kwun Tong building (destroyed in 2011), which covered four blocks and was similar to the 1960s Mark II phase of housing construction.[87]

The 12-story Hoplite Industrial Centre on Wang Tai Road in Kowloon, designed by Sun Hung Kai Engineering in 1985, is now divided into smaller production companies which include garment, printing, chemical, and other related industries; spaces range from thirty to 120 square meters. Six thousand square meters of double-height floor space houses companies such as Kwun Tong printing with one hundred employees. At the fourth floor an airshaft forms a void in the building that provides additional light

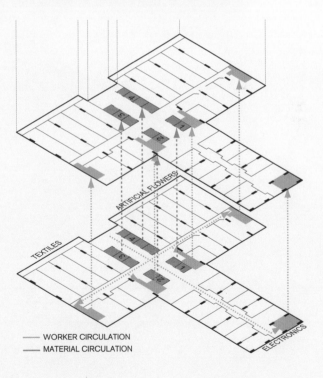

— WORKER CIRCULATION
— MATERIAL CIRCULATION

◄ Sui Fai multiuse factory building, Hong Kong, 1970s
▲ Kowloon Bay, balcony factory, Hong Kong, 1970s

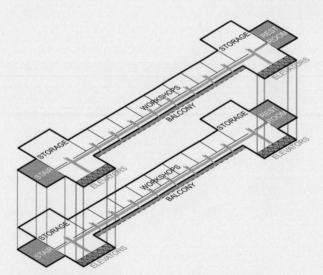

What a typical floor plan may look like at Wang Cheong Building in Hong Kong

—— MATERIAL CIRCULATION
—— WORKER CIRCULATION

and air to the otherwise thick block. The base has commercial shops that help to integrate the building with the neighborhood.

The Mei Ho Gallery Building, built in 1975, is seven stories tall and is similar to a residential type in the inclusion of balconies where production can also occur. The load-bearing structure has cantilevered beams that support the galleries. Private factories also still exist in the city such as the Che Wah building from the 1970s, and the 1984 Wang Cheong factory.

The literal rise of the Hong Kong factory, the tallest in the world, shows the potential for the dense vertical urban factory functioning efficiently in the topographic complexity of Hong Kong. Instead, economic, trade, and labor issues usurped the architecture and urbanity of the vertical factory in this city.

▲ Wang Cheong, a vertical factory in Hong Kong, 1984

JEPPE
JOHANNESBURG, SOUTH AFRICA, 2008

Johannesburg, South Africa, a city of nearly four million people known for the diamond and gold industries, along with other mineral mining, chemicals, plastics, and paper products, as well as food production and telecommunication technologies, had five industrial business zones in 2002, with 19 percent of the city's workers employed in over 16,000 factories. In concert with the normal industrial work, many informal and smaller local businesses sprang up, transforming former high-rise commercial spaces and spawning new locally grown industries in the heart of the city.

The downturn in Johannesburg's formal large-scale manufacturing economy, which was rife with issues of worker injustice, lies in stark contrast to the increase in small-scale production, with clothing manufacturing as the central activity. The physical spaces of this informal urban production network, which is housed in multistoried buildings, is particularly interesting in comparison to industrial development in other developing cities such as Dhaka in Bangladesh, which also rises vertically but is more controlled by individual companies, or Dharavi, in Mumbai, which is also informal but horizontal and sprawling. The close-knit interpersonal ties in the new entrepreneurial culture drive the search for the accommodation of small industrial wholesale production and retail ventures.

Jeppe, an area west of Johannesburg's Fashion District, is one such example. Over the past twenty years, this former business district was transformed by Ethiopian traders into an epicenter of flexible commerce, featuring Ethopian imports as well as goods produced locally. In the late nineteenth century, the colonial city of Johannesburg was designed in a gridded plan of 16-by-16-meter blocks. Over time, the city's original buildings were altered and demolished as higher-rise buildings were constructed; this largely occurred between the 1950s and 1980s, with two large-scale towers anchoring the blocks. These multistoried structures, featuring prefab concrete panels or glass curtain-wall systems, display little variation.

In 1951, the area comprising Jeppe was segregated as a White Group Area after the Group Areas Act, taking retail and residential spaces from blacks and Chinese who had been living there. Political change, recession, and an unstable financial climate in the 1990s forced the large-scale investment funds and property owners to sell their commercial buildings. In 1994, this situation began to change when South Africa accepted Ethiopian political refugees in exchange for their support of the African National Congress during apartheid. Ethiopian traders who immigrated to Johannesburg in the mid-1990s were allowed to work as street traders because informal trade was seen as improving the trader's standard of living, At first, ground-floor retail spaces were in high demand, while upper-level offices remained empty as the commercial enterprises moved away, then a new mix of workspaces and commerce began to infiltrate a series of buildings.

Architect Hannah Le Roux, who has conducted a considerable amount of research in the district, describes the first traders who came in 1994 and worked to reorganize the 12-story Johannesburg Wholesale Centre 1, a former commercial high-rise building, into six levels of curtain-making businesses that also included restaurants and storage on the upper floors.[88] The development of mixed-use spaces for production and commerce was repeated

▶ **Mixed-use buildings of Jeppe, Johannesburg, South Africa, 2008. Photograph by Hannah Le Roux**

by other small-scale producers. In the Medical Arts building – now called Majesty Wholesale, on Jeppe Street – men produce the leather and sandals which are then sold at street level. The new enterprises changed the dynamic of the street life as well as the buildings' functions. In 2000, entrepreneurs from the African Diaspora moved into the Jeppe Street neighborhood on the northern edge of the Fashion District, close

to the minibus taxi station, which is a major interregional hub. Transforming the former office buildings into mixed uses, they sustain a community of traders who compete and collaborate. Hundreds of tailors produce soft furnishings and traditional clothes for rural and township homes. They make gilded voile curtains, and *tshwetshwe*, a local pinafore, which are sold in the ground-floor shops. In a vertical organization, they use fabrics imported by a third party and store them on higher floors. In another spatial organization, tailors from Southern Africa, salesmen from Ethiopian, and fabrics sourced in China share third-floor shops. In a reversal of tradition, older active trading practices, accustomed to being at street level, became vertical operations.

The lobbies and the well-maintained elevators are the focus of interaction in a vertical distribution system as though it is one fluid factory and logistics center similar to New York's Garment District. Rather than retail occupying the street-scape, here it extends vertically, juxtaposed with spaces for storage, manufacture, service shops and restaurants. The vertical mobility links the upper levels of buildings, as a higher level shopping area that is scattered with restaurants, internet cafes, travel agencies, bridal boutiques, and hairdressers, making it possible to organize a transnational business and personal life without leaving the building. The intensity of horizontal movement is balanced with vertical systems.

The reuse of concrete frame multistoried buildings that are repopulated with traders and informal manufacturers is also a reversal of the Western trend to convert industrial lofts into residential spaces in downtown areas. In addition, increased activity taking place in the interstitial spaces between the backs of the former retail shops have created a new urban density. Similar to the workers' amenities in New York City's Diamond District or Chinatown, cafes and prayer spaces help form a community. In this dense, layered space of reappropriated buildings, workers create a new informal industrial ecology, which is both sustainable and flexible.

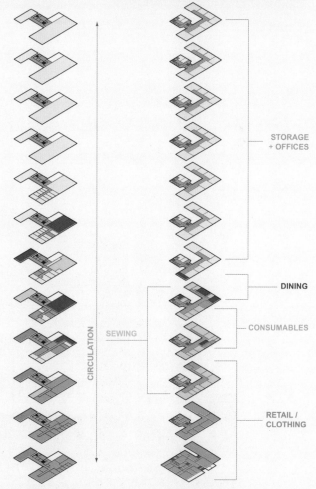

◄ **Entrepreunerial curtain manufacturers,** Johannesburg, 2010. Photograph by Hannah Le Roux
◄ **Fashion building, 2010**
▲ **Informal and communal shops mixed with** manufacturers, 2010. Photograph by Hannah Le Roux

THE NEW YORK
PORTLAND, OREGON, 2014

A few vertical urban factories have recently come to fruition. The York Street Industrial Building, also known as The New York, was designed by DiLoreto Architecture. It is the first new vertical industrial building in Portland, Oregon in over sixty years. The developer Rosan Inc., a company known for its one-story industrial sheds, asked the architects to design the same type of structure in a primarily low-rise industrial area by the Willamette River that runs through Portland. However, DiLoreto convinced Rosan to build a vertical project because the site is actually a land use zone with no height limits; building vertically would multiply the firm's leasable space. The architects also emphasized the trend towards light industry in Portland, as seen in the city's Pearl Street District, where many artisanal and light manufacturers are leasing spaces in former industrial loft buildings.

The architects' design approach was to recreate a New York-style loft building – they even named it "The New York" notes Brian Melton who worked on the project. "The City of Portland realized the importance of maintaining industry in the city to increase economic viability, which in turn improves the livability for working people."[89] The land use zone is very strict about the allowable uses, as it is not only zoned as an IG1 industrial use, but it is also part of the "Guild's Lake Industrial Sanctuary" (GLIS), established in 2001, in order to preserve a broad variety of industrial areas near the city.

The GLIS contains the majority of the industrially zoned land in Northwest Portland and is located between Forest Park in the West Hills and the Willamette River. It includes portions of two Portland neighborhood associations: most of the Northwest Industrial Neighborhood Association (NINA), and a part of the Northwest District Association (NWDA). The GLIS is one of the few remaining large urban industrial districts in the United States but is increasingly under real estate pressure for other uses. By even calling the industrial plan a "sanctuary" recalls the concept of environmental sanctuaries and acknowledges Portland's attention to industry as part of its urban ecology. Its comprehensive infrastructure of rail, shipping, and road, has supported and enhanced existing industries.

The architects took cues from the historic industrial buildings found throughout Portland, which are characterized by large casement windows and exposed steel. The new five-story building is elevated above grade on a series of columns to allow for truck entrance and parking. Seven window bays, two recessed and in red-painted metal, allow for natural light to

penetrate into the building's interior. Covering approximately 9,290 square meters of space, it occupies only a 223-square-meter lot. Each floor can accommodate up to 14 individual tenants; its flexible system allows tenants to lease an entire floor, or any space in between. The building's structural design is a typical concrete frame with each floor-to-floor at 4.2 meters high, allowing for approximately 1.2 meters of clear space for equipment and storage.

Like-minded local entrepreneurs, in need of smaller-scale spaces, have expressed interest in leasing space in the York Street project. They have included furniture makers, glass blowers, and brewers. The architects included a large freight elevator for moving goods and a separate passenger elevator. The mechanical and service systems are located along the building spine of each floor, thus allowing for each tenant to connect to them. As a green building, the architects focused on natural ventilation, natural lighting, and mitigation of all stormwater on-site through a combination of green roofs and on-site stormwater planters.

Parking for the building is below ground with large spaces available for delivery trucks and two loading zones for tractor-trailer trucks. The loading zones have a dock lift for removing goods from the larger semis. The ground under the

building slopes so that the clear head height varies from 2.7 to 3.5 meters. Because the owners included dedicated parking for bikes and electric cars, they could reduce the required number of parking spaces overall. Each floor also includes bike storage, showers, a janitorial room, and bathrooms. By consolidating and sharing these common uses, the tenants have more opportunity to focus their resources on their own production expenses rather than on capital outlays. The city is interested in this renewed typology to promote new flexible industrial spaces in the district.

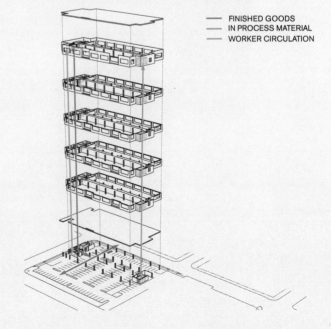

——— FINISHED GOODS
——— IN PROCESS MATERIAL
——— WORKER CIRCULATION

◄ DiLoreto Architecture, York Street Industrial
Building, Portland, Oregon, 2014
▲ Entry level of York Street Industrial Building

NŒRD BUILDING/FREITAG

ROTHEN ARCHITECTS, OERLIKON, 2011

When Freitag, the Swiss bag manufacturer, needed a larger and more permanent space, they initiated unusual industrial real estate speculation, for today's market as part of a group of companies who would lease space in one building. The developer underwriters Senn BPM AG, with a leasing agent, built a flexible building they called Nœrd in the industrial district of Oerlikon, north of Zurich, in 2011. The building's name derived from the combination of the place, Neu-Oerlikon and the word, *nerd*. The developer's concept was for a multi-use building that would inspire creativity as well as connections to the outdoors, even in an industrial district.

Architects Beat and Brigit Rothen designed the building with engineers Conzett Bronzini Gartmann and landscape architect Rita Illien, as though it grew organically from the industrial area. In four-and-a-half stories, the concrete frame building with a common courtyard provides for flexible spatial combinations for a variety of companies to grow and shrink as needed.

Freitag – innovative in its use of recycled materials – was being pushed out of its space in the former Maag building in Zurich, which was overtaken by music venues amidst gentrification pressures. In the search for a new facility they found a developer with an interest in industrial and cultural synergies to build a mixed industrial building. Reserving space for Freitag as a major tenant, as well as space for the marketing company Aroma, the developers were able to minimize their risk and realize a project for multiple tenants.

On a former brownfield site, the architects designed a zigzag-shaped building, primarily organized as two U-shaped volumes that interlock, enabling a private garden space and roof garden in the interstitial spaces.[90] The efficient spatial planning formed staggered spaces and stacked volumes, enabling the creation of more architecturally versatile multi-story industrial suites, as opposed to the floor-by-floor subdivisions common in most industrial buildings. Engineer Jürg Conzett devised large, thin floor slabs supported by a long-span grid so that the lightweight slabs project beyond the structural facade to double as balconies and rain shelters.

Beat Rothen's strategy was to create a durable and rough building with an industrial character, without being nostalgic. Raw exposed

insulated concrete walls and floors, metal window frames and wood spandrels, galvanized steel chainlink fences, and anodized steel doors comprised the unfinished but finely detailed material palette, providing a design that was both affordable and aesthetically tuned to the industrial tenants Nœrd sought to attract. This unmediated tactile materiality also gives the building a unique identity beyond the normally pristine character of Swiss design. The building also has a green roof for insulation, utilizing low-processed and recycled or recyclable materials.

The first-floor voids penetrate the facade for access to the rear courts, stairs, and elevator cores that frame the workspaces. Trucks circulate to standard ground-level loading docks in the rear, making room for storage space instead of underground parking. The first floor, with a seven-meter-high fabrication hall, lit via skylights from the interior courtyard above, is used by Freitag.

On the upper floors, smaller manufacturers, such as Met-all, occupy manufacturing spaces, with offices and ateliers. The building's use is interchangeable from workshop to offices, optimizing its real estate market. A mezzanine serves as a buffering gallery space between the different offices, and the corridors are lined with glass facades, for vistas. The upper floor has a café with a lounge area that opens out onto the roof in good weather.

Landscape architect Rita Illien designed ground-floor interior courtyards as an undulating garden above the fabrication hall using gravel, which is permeable for rain runoff, as well as native plants from the alluvial prairie of the region. The social connections between the businesses was also key to the project, as manufacturers, industrial designers, printers, and creative arts studios, along with other local companies, share the café.

Daniel and Markus Freitag's product design arose from their personal need for a durable bike messenger bag. They started production out of their own apartment, collecting and washing reclaimed truck tarpaulins, and sewing their designs on an industrial sewing machine. Then they moved into the building of a former gear-pump

◄ Spillman Echsle Architects, interior of Freitag lab, AG, Oerlikon, Switzerland, 2011
▲ View of the main tarp recycling and storage space

manufacturer, Maag, in the heart of Zurich's industrial area. The company, which now makes bags and cases in a variety of sizes, has since opened shops in Japan and Europe, growing to 130 employees in the last 18 years.

Architects Annette Spillmann and Harald Echsle, who designed all of Freitag's stores and the interiors at the Maag space, also designed Freitag's interiors and the cafeteria in the Nœrd building. Freitag leases the largest space in the building – 7,500 square meters – between different floors, including the ground-floor work hall along the east side, and parts of floors one to three. The architect's use of concrete and metal frameworks for the interior resonated with the building's character.

Freitag is a vertically integrated company, with the design, marketing, cutting, washing, and layout of the bags conducted in the Nœrd building itself.[91] This increases the collaborations because of the designers' and production workers' proximity. Larger quantity sewing is conducted in nearby contract factories: two in Switzerland, one in France, as well as at operations in Portugal, Tunisia, and the Czech Republic. The manufacturing process begins on the basement floor, where the colorful tarps, printed with company names and logos, are collected by scouts around Europe, and are then delivered, weighed, labeled, and registered. Then workers spread them out

on huge tables to remove damaged areas, cut them to a standard size, sort them by color and pattern, and place them on palettes. The workers wash the tarps in industrial washing machines using rainwater runoff; they are then air-dried, photographed, and stored in rolls on carts until the designers review the photographs and select a particular roll for use in their design. The careful process of selecting the portion of the tarp to be used is similar to the method of selecting fabrics for clothing design. Focusing on the abstract shapes in the lettering, designers use stencils to cut the tarps, with desired bag designs in mind. This guides the making of prototypes, but the more customized mass-production process is implemented at the off-site sewing factories.

The industrial operations are a closely integrated aspect of Freitag's brand identity, and the company goes to great effort to showcase its process through its website and factory tours. The company presents itself as a sustainable brand through its use of the reclaimed and salvaged truck tarps and the invention of new organic textiles; and building systems such as the

▲ Spillman Echsle Architects, interior of Freitag, 2011
▶ Beat Rothen Architects, Noerd building, 2011

use of rainwater and waste heat from a nearby power plant, as well as electricity harnessed from a nearby rooftop solar array, demonstrate their reduction of resource use.

The combination of local production processes, progressive employment practices, and design have been instrumental in the company's branding success. In designing and constructing its manufacturing space, Beat Rothen Architects applied similar concepts of the product to the building: durability, flexibility, sustainability, and simplicity. Given this synergy between brand and factory, Freitag's space indicates the potential for the future factory: a place of production that does not hide from the consumer, or alienate the worker, but instead reintegrates production into life. The rise of these values, if Nœrd is any indication, demonstrates new entrepreneurship that is humane, economically stable, ecologically sound, and urban.

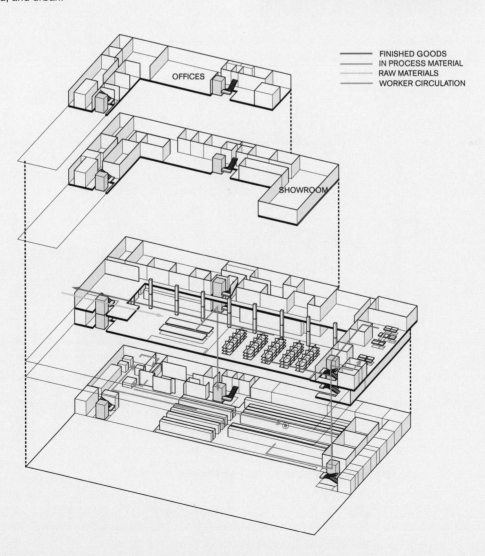

OFFICES

SHOWROOM

FINISHED GOODS
IN PROCESS MATERIAL
RAW MATERIALS
WORKER CIRCULATION

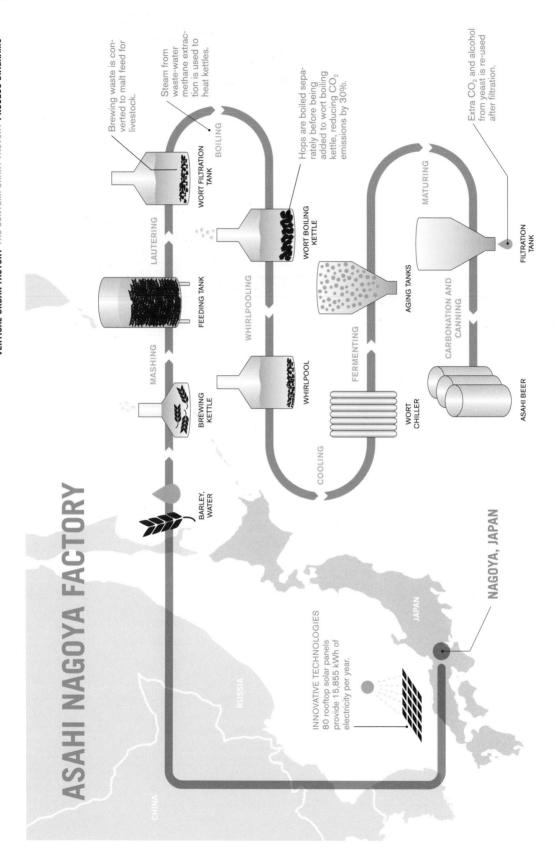

ASAHI NAGOYA FACTORY

NAGOYA, JAPAN

INNOVATIVE TECHNOLOGIES
80 rooftop solar panels
provide 15,855 kWh of
electricity per year.

CHINA

RUSSIA

JAPAN

Brewing waste is con-
verted to malt feed for
livestock.

Steam from
waste-water
methane extrac-
tion is used to
heat kettles.

Hops are boiled sepa-
rately before being
added to wort boiling
kettle, reducing CO_2
emissions by 30%.

Extra CO_2 and alcohol
from yeast is re-used
after filtration.

WORT FILTRATION
TANK

FEEDING TANK

BREWING
KETTLE

BARLEY,
WATER

WORT BOILING
KETTLE

WHIRLPOOL

AGING TANKS

FILTRATION
TANK

WORT
CHILLER

ASAHI BEER

MASHING

LAUTERING

BOILING

WHIRLPOOLING

FERMENTING

COOLING

MATURING

CARBONATION AND
CANNING

NECKTIE MANUFACTURING

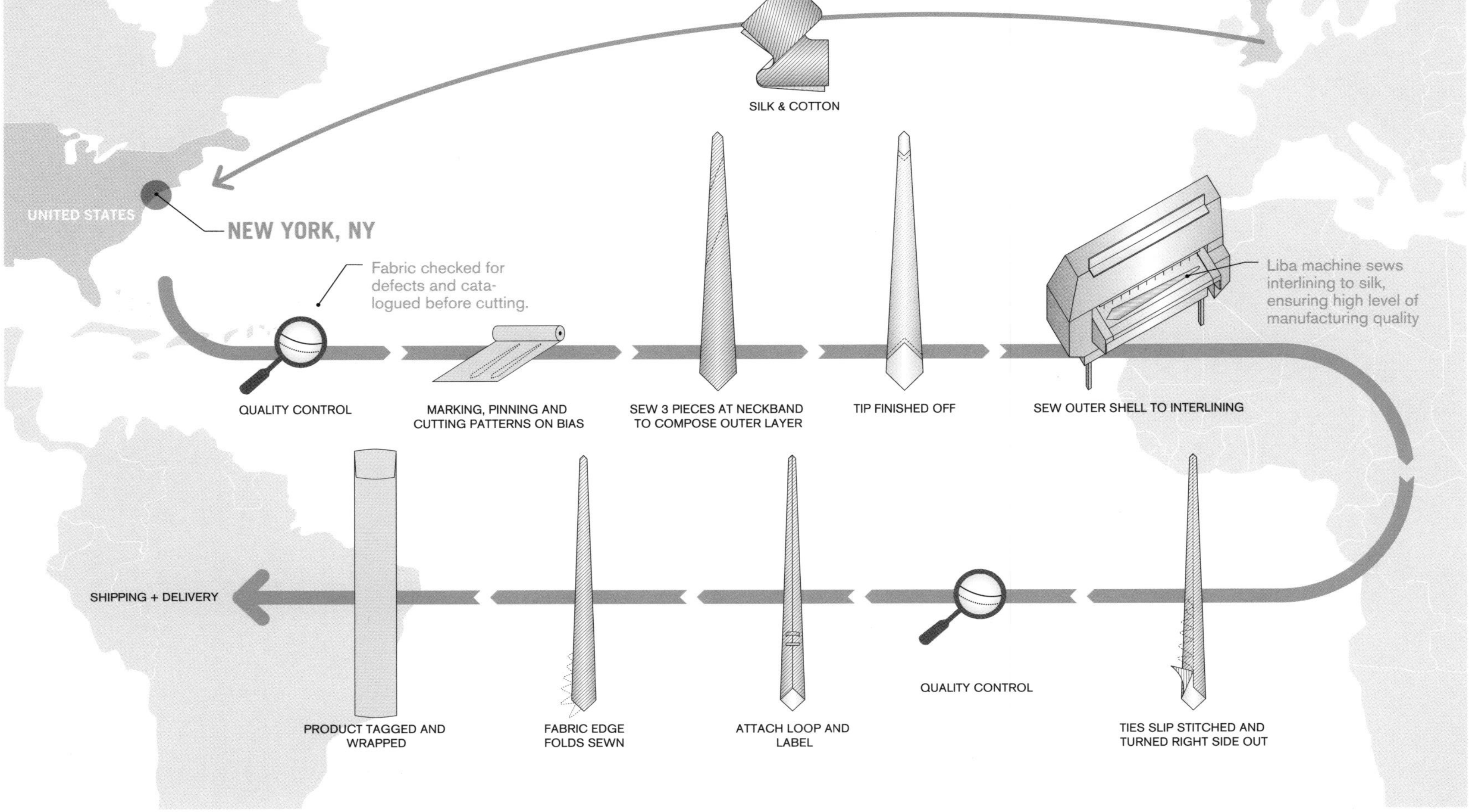

ENGLAND

SILK & COTTON

UNITED STATES

NEW YORK, NY

Fabric checked for defects and cata-logued before cutting.

QUALITY CONTROL

MARKING, PINNING AND CUTTING PATTERNS ON BIAS

SEW 3 PIECES AT NECKBAND TO COMPOSE OUTER LAYER

TIP FINISHED OFF

Liba machine sews interlining to silk, ensuring high level of manufacturing quality

SEW OUTER SHELL TO INTERLINING

TIES SLIP STITCHED AND TURNED RIGHT SIDE OUT

QUALITY CONTROL

ATTACH LOOP AND LABEL

FABRIC EDGE FOLDS SEWN

PRODUCT TAGGED AND WRAPPED

SHIPPING + DELIVERY

LIGHTING MANUFACTURING

UNITED STATES

LONG ISLAND CITY, NY

FARMINGTON, CT

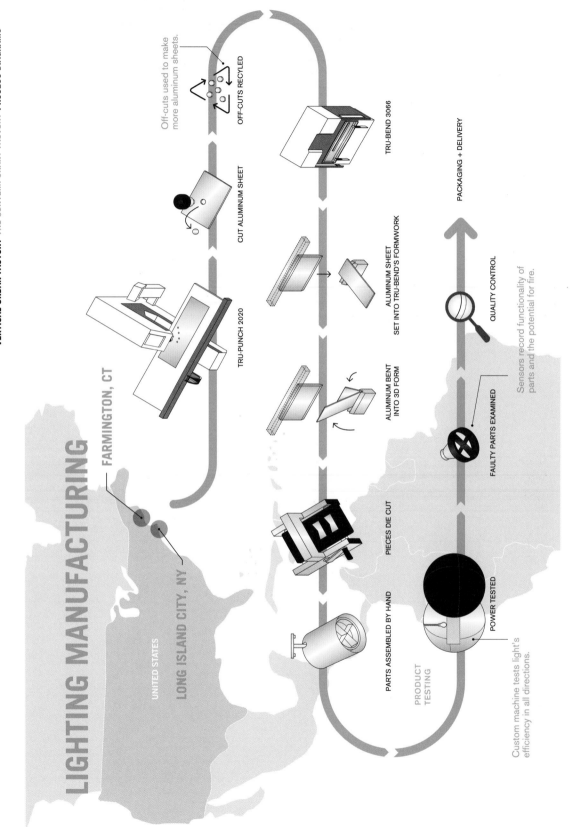

Off-cuts used to make more aluminum sheets.

OFF-CUTS RECYLED

CUT ALUMINUM SHEET

TRU-BEND 3066

TRU-PUNCH 2020

ALUMINUM SHEET SET INTO TRU-BEND'S FORMWORK

ALUMINUM BENT INTO 3D FORM

PACKAGING + DELIVERY

QUALITY CONTROL

Sensors record functionality of parts and the potential for fire.

FAULTY PARTS EXAMINED

PIECES DIE CUT

PARTS ASSEMBLED BY HAND

PRODUCT TESTING

POWER TESTED

Custom machine tests light's efficiency in all directions.

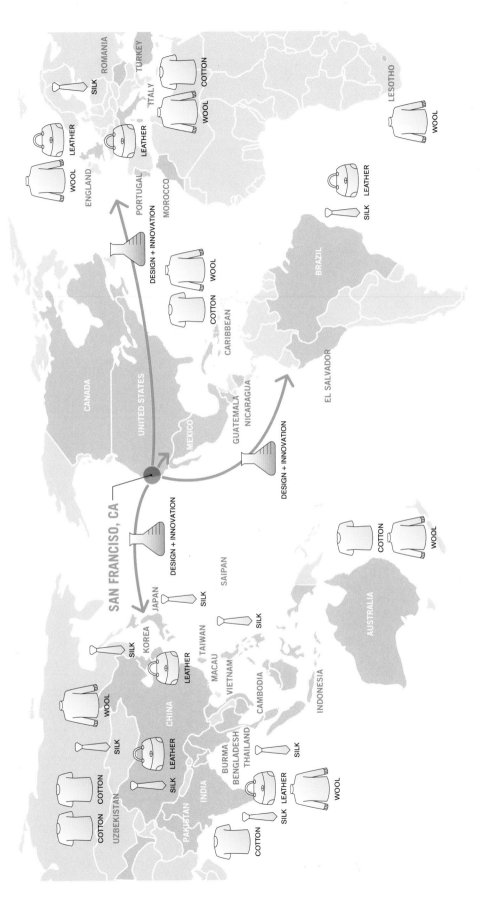

GAP GLOBAL PRODUCTION

COMPUTER CHIP MANUFACTURING

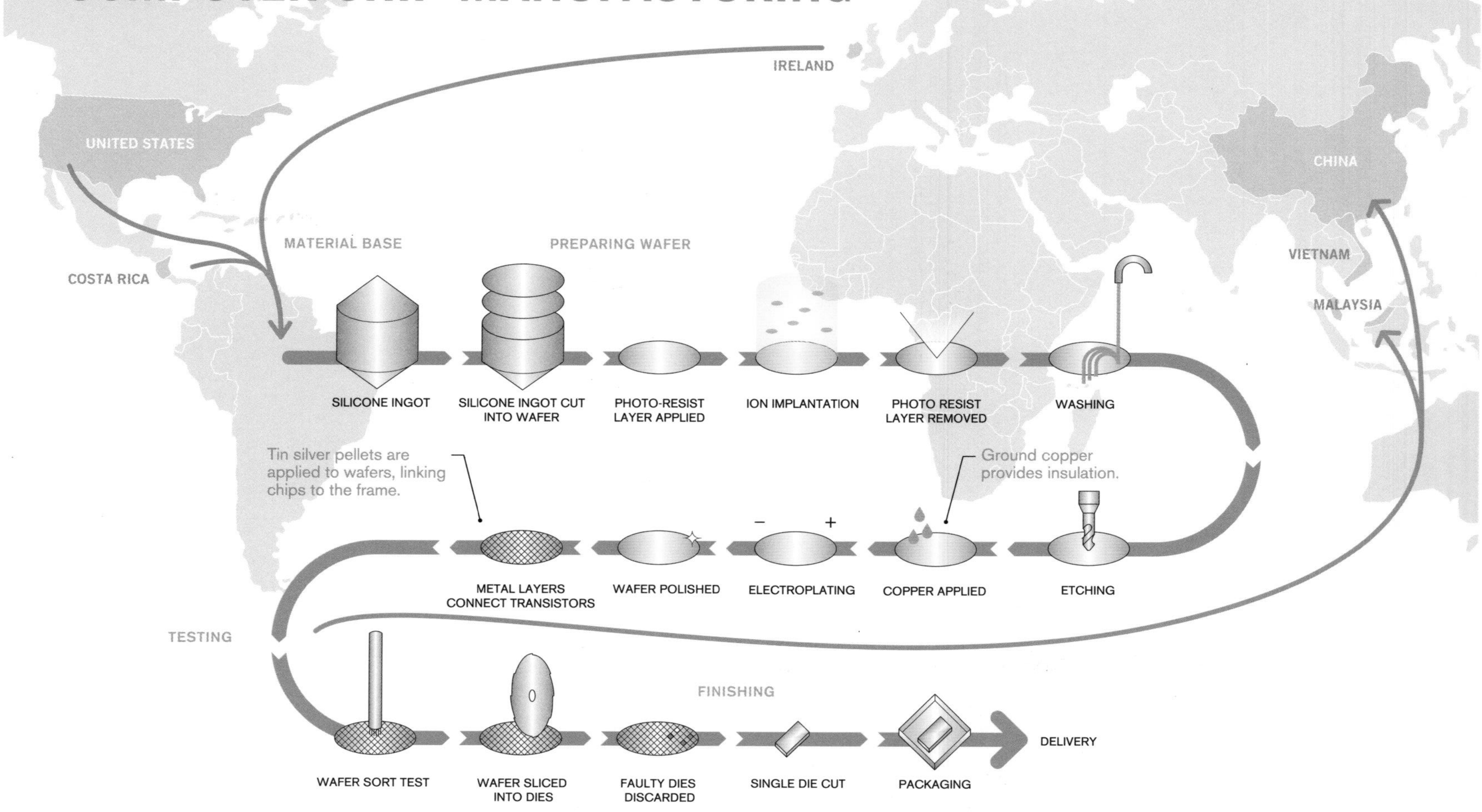

UNITED STATES

COSTA RICA

IRELAND

CHINA

VIETNAM

MALAYSIA

MATERIAL BASE

PREPARING WAFER

SILICONE INGOT

SILICONE INGOT CUT INTO WAFER

PHOTO-RESIST LAYER APPLIED

ION IMPLANTATION

PHOTO RESIST LAYER REMOVED

WASHING

Tin silver pellets are applied to wafers, linking chips to the frame.

Ground copper provides insulation.

METAL LAYERS CONNECT TRANSISTORS

WAFER POLISHED

ELECTROPLATING

COPPER APPLIED

ETCHING

TESTING

WAFER SORT TEST

WAFER SLICED INTO DIES

FAULTY DIES DISCARDED

SINGLE DIE CUT

PACKAGING

DELIVERY

FINISHING

WATCH MANUFACTURING

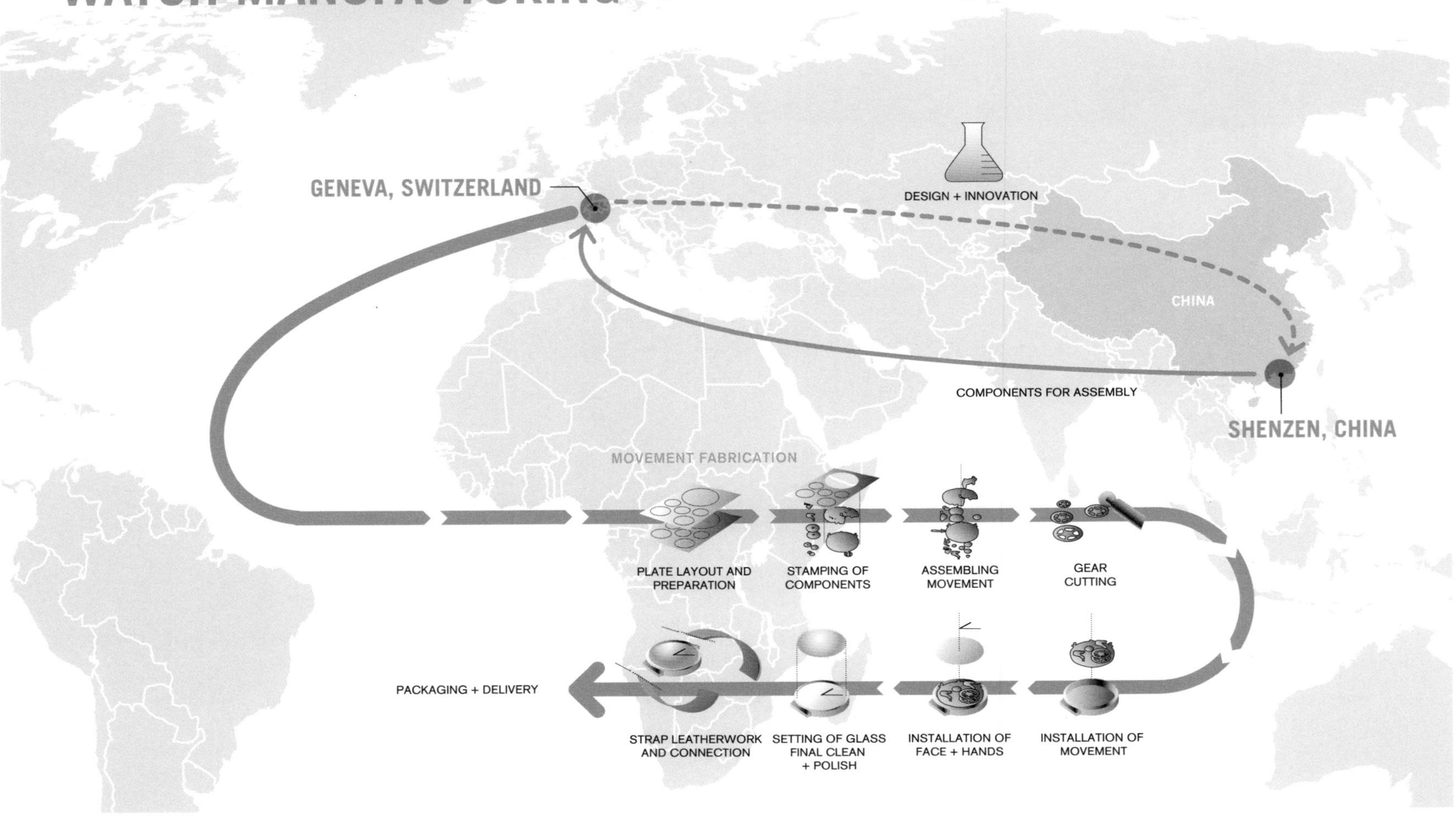

SHENZEN, CHINA

CHINA

DESIGN + INNOVATION

COMPONENTS FOR ASSEMBLY

GEAR CUTTING

INSTALLATION OF MOVEMENT

ASSEMBLING MOVEMENT

INSTALLATION OF FACE + HANDS

STAMPING OF COMPONENTS

SETTING OF GLASS FINAL CLEAN + POLISH

MOVEMENT FABRICATION

PLATE LAYOUT AND PREPARATION

STRAP LEATHERWORK AND CONNECTION

GENEVA, SWITZERLAND

PACKAGING + DELIVERY

VERTICAL URBAN FACTORY THE CONTEMPORARY FACTORY **PROCESS DIAGRAMS**

NIKE GLOBAL FACTORIES

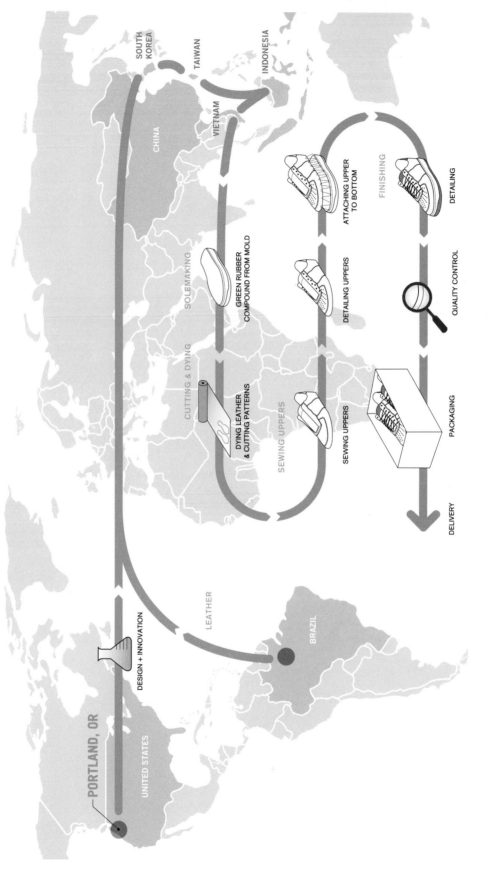

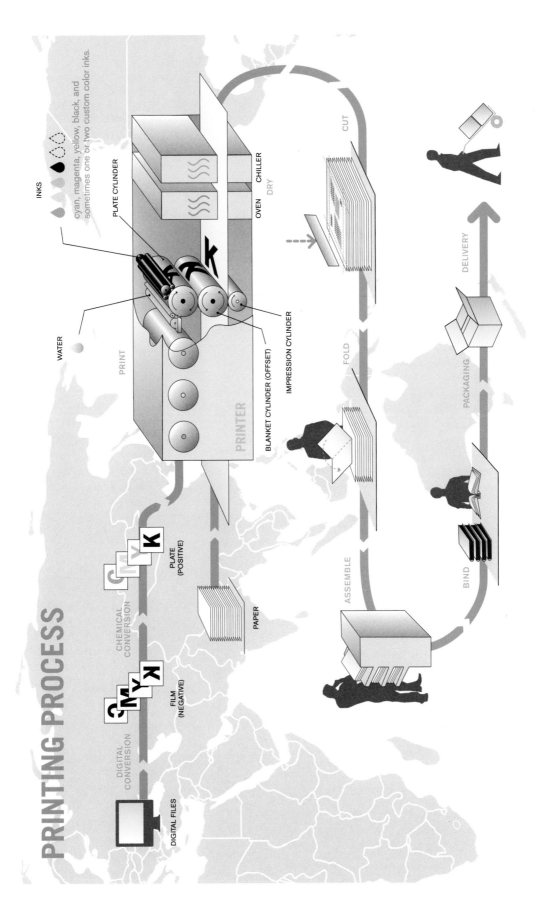

PRINTING PROCESS

INKS

cyan, magenta, yellow, black, and sometimes one or two custom color inks.

PLATE CYLINDER

WATER

PRINT

BLANKET CYLINDER (OFFSET)

IMPRESSION CYLINDER

PRINTER

OVEN CHILLER

DRY

CUT

DELIVERY

FOLD

PACKAGING

DIGITAL CONVERSION

DIGITAL FILES

CHEMICAL CONVERSION

FILM (NEGATIVE)

PLATE (POSITIVE)

PAPER

ASSEMBLE

BIND

VERTICAL URBAN FACTORY THE CONTEMPORARY FACTORY **PROCESS DIAGRAMS**

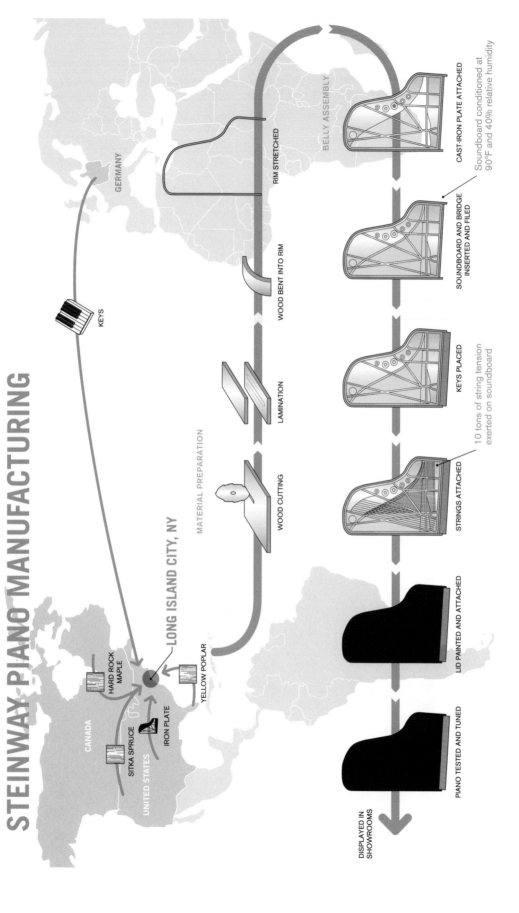

STEINWAY PIANO MANUFACTURING

KEYS

GERMANY

CANADA
HARD ROCK MAPLE

SITKA SPRUCE
UNITED STATES
IRON PLATE

LONG ISLAND CITY, NY

YELLOW POPLAR

RIM STRETCHED

WOOD BENT INTO RIM

LAMINATION

WOOD CUTTING

MATERIAL PREPARATION

BELLY ASSEMBLY

CAST-IRON PLATE ATTACHED
Soundboard conditioned at 90°F and 40% relative humidity

SOUNDBOARD AND BRIDGE INSERTED AND FILED

KEYS PLACED

STRINGS ATTACHED
10 tons of string tension exerted on soundboard

LID PAINTED AND ATTACHED

PIANO TESTED AND TUNED

DISPLAYED IN SHOWROOMS

iPHONE MANUFACTURING

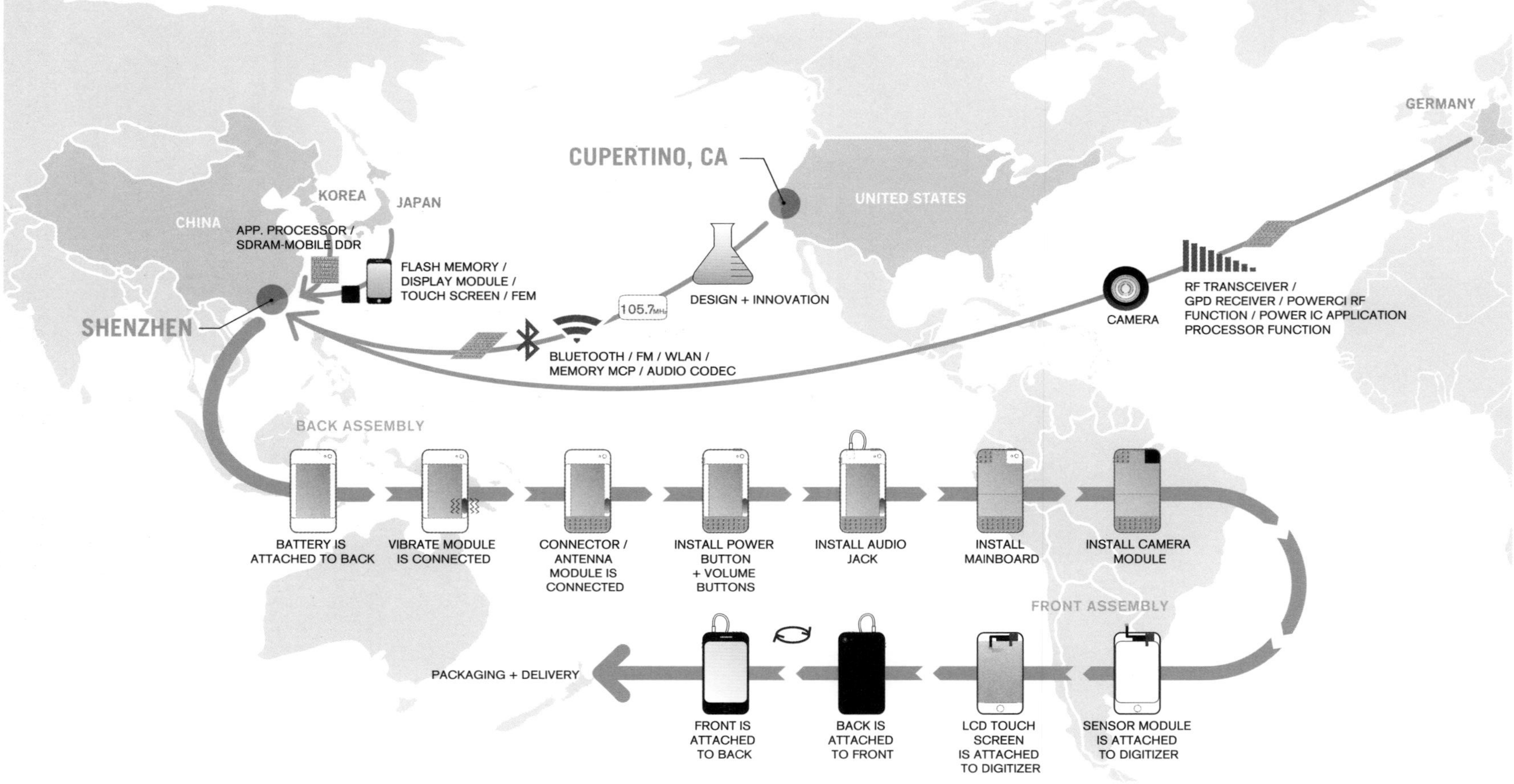

GERMANY

RF TRANSCEIVER /
GPD RECEIVER / POWERCI RF
FUNCTION / POWER IC APPLICATION
PROCESSOR FUNCTION

CAMERA

UNITED STATES

CUPERTINO, CA

DESIGN + INNOVATION

105.7 MHz

BLUETOOTH / FM / WLAN /
MEMORY MCP / AUDIO CODEC

JAPAN

KOREA

FLASH MEMORY /
DISPLAY MODULE /
TOUCH SCREEN / FEM

APP. PROCESSOR /
SDRAM-MOBILE DDR

CHINA

SHENZHEN

BACK ASSEMBLY

BATTERY IS
ATTACHED TO BACK

VIBRATE MODULE
IS CONNECTED

CONNECTOR /
ANTENNA
MODULE IS
CONNECTED

INSTALL POWER
BUTTON
+ VOLUME
BUTTONS

INSTALL AUDIO
JACK

INSTALL
MAINBOARD

INSTALL CAMERA
MODULE

FRONT ASSEMBLY

FRONT IS
ATTACHED TO BACK

BACK IS
ATTACHED
TO FRONT

LCD TOUCH
SCREEN
IS ATTACHED
TO DIGITIZER

SENSOR MODULE
IS ATTACHED
TO DIGITIZER

PACKAGING + DELIVERY

THE FUTURE FACTORY

▶ A robust multi-storied cast-concrete building is repurposed as an urban farm with circulation and programs geared towards

FACTORY FUTURES

AS A RESULT OF INDUSTRY'S reconfiguration and redefinition, architecture is implicated in urban manufacturing scenarios in terms of form, scale, invention, and context — gaining new relevance and value shaping spaces in which people can make things in parity. Socioeconomic exchanges have instigated a productivity paradox: eventually, factories won't be essential as a unique typology except for large-scale mass production or for branding purposes. However, I propose that the vertical and urban factory proves a potent model for ameliorating the technical, social, and urban conditions of the future factory in what can be called an super-urban industrial symbiosis.

Once manufacturing left the cottages and became housed in larger centers or manufactories, the pollution and nuisances that it produced led to the nineteenth-century utopian factory city schemes, and to the approach in a new field of city planning where factories were segregated from other parts of the city, as described by Leonardo Benevolo. In decrying this piecemeal response to urban problems, without a comprehensive vision, some held that the city was attacked by industrialization, while capitalists saw the commodification of space as an essential goal. The sequestering of factories away from daily life became a standard element of urban design through zoning — along with segregating the poor from the rich — which decimated the diversity and vitality of urban hybridity. Due to expansive infrastructure networks and technical changes in manufacturing, a new contextual reconfiguration provided a spatial potential to rethink the space of manufacturing, namely, as the vertical urban factory.

As a form of organization, the vertical urban factory sparks ideas for the future of architecture and urbanism. Industry's impulse is towards a time-based organization in which efficacy and progress — technological and architectural — are celebrated; yet, these very virtues often undermine labor rights because of capital control. The city's multiple and complex layers challenge architects, economists, and planners to formulate methods for planning hybridity, a quality now deemed valuable to growth and sustainability. As Stephen Graham noted, "with the transport and telecommunication advantages of cities. . . . they are reasserting themselves as dominant centers of innovation."[1] The city continues to be a magnetic for people to live in due to its energy and dynamism, its opportunities and complexities, its freedoms and anonymity, and the friction and exchanges between diverse populations, which ultimately cultivates and sparks creativity.

Most factory buildings are a generic kit of parts focused on the bottom line. The factory has become marginalized when, in actuality, the place for it still exists in the city, if it is part of an intentional urbanism. In our present ecologically conscious times and with the redefinition of industry, the idea of the vertical factory may again be pertinent in order to conserve land and save costs. The vertical factory provides design and cultural opportunities for new thinking, both in terms of its relationship to the city and within itself — if we can also attend to workers' conditions, there can be more equity. Policy makers could also recognize urban industry's potential to create high-paying jobs using skilled and unskilled workers, as well as its potential to develop a culture of craft, engendering a sense of pride.

As can be seen in economic industrial geography, the quantities of factories, land used for industry, and numbers of industrial workers per region, as well as the migration and dispersal of manufacturing to developing countries, allows for locally based production around the globe, but that activity is often hidden from public scrutiny and has limited regulation. In developing countries, the global factory employing low-skilled and underpaid workers has become complicit in socially and environmentally destructive practices which have divided countries and the global marketplace; this is similar to philosopher Herbert Marcuse's concept of "instrumental rationality," which leads mankind to constant striving for progress over humanitarian and environmental interests.[2]

If fair labor is a social imperative, and issues of transparency, authenticity, well-being, social justice, and corporate responsibility are not encouraged by economic development and progress, political activism is pressured into being. Economic culture would rely on the small, nimble, and flexible entrepreneurial companies inserting themselves into the larger capitalist system.[3] One alternative for neoliberal and democratic capitalism both within and without the hegemonic system is then to make the city the base for manufacturing, thereby shortening the supply chain, providing equitable employment, and encouraging entrepreneurs in sustainable environmental conditions. Then, the form of the factory and its networks could be reconsidered.

A new progressive flexible economy could then contribute to a circular economy wherein waste is beneficial to reuse and production occurs in real time. New production spaces contrast with spaces of free trade and classical economic theory, and begin to rise from an increased awareness of how today's informal economies and their resultant production spaces function within a symbiotic system. In contrast to the model of imperialist exploitation, production spaces could be revalued and seen as opportunities for design. Instead of the status quo and laissez-faire, the macro view could recognize the contribution of entrepreneurial hackers and inventors in fostering local making of things and engendering new relationships between consumer and maker.

We must still ask: What is manufacturing in the future and how are the seeds for its change already taking shape? In engaging concepts for industrial transformation beyond that of flexible agglomeration, discussed earlier as a new organizational economy,[4] it is essential to investigate an ideology for the future of industrial urbanism. The vertical urban factory is one way to solve the new place of production in terms of a spatial organization that is defined by economics, real estate, land use, production technology, and labor.

While I am not a futurist, I do believe, like Henri Lefebvre, that we have to imagine what is next, in order to make that next space and time — especially in the built environment.[5] Thus, this research and future provocation extrapolates from what exists towards the potential in a new urban factory paradigm that provides for hybridity in the city. A re-evaulation of industry could make possible a factory future in which the more complex political issues of worker equity and employment opportunities are resolved, and in which cities re-evolve into "workshops of the world," as Philadelphia was called in the nineteenth century, and could heightened attention to designate places for making things that goes beyond the normative corporate hierarchical system. In the near future, rather than envisioning a utopian community that results in dystopia, a new paradigm would embrace worker democracy.

Sociologist Herbert Gans, imagining the year 2033, describes a fictional character, Jim Caruso, who is running for president. Caruso notes that jobs have declined due to computerization and outsourcing and that the needed boost to productivity, which would create and secure jobs and reduce global warming, can't happen without governmental or private assistance. He points out that the U.S. can't compete with the "countries turning into economic superpowers and the multinationals expanding into "multicontinentals."[6] Cities today and their economies require assistance worldwide, a situation that exists parallel to new political orientations that would effect structural change. This new social order — if harnessed to achieve equity — could take on new forms that would serve to spread jobs and income for both the skilled and unskilled worker. By assisting entrepreneurs, those in need would have jobs, rather than be part of the welfare system.

Marx described capitalist production as having inconsistent and problematic characteristics: exploitation of labor, dynamism in technology, and organization towards progress. But in a critique, philosopher Jean Baudrillard emphasizes that there is more to man than his/her productive capacity.[7] Value for people and companies today is also about other things, such as triple bottom lines and workers' rights. Financial instruments aid and abet global trade, with numerous loans and credit lines being used to bail out companies, yet creating, in turn, an imbalance in wealth. These measures have historically led to inflation, unemployment, overaccumulation, and worker alienation, which impact spaces for production and urban infrastructure. What then should take the place of these measures? We can ask: What are the spatial ramifications of new production and its impact on workers? Who benefits from open international trade regulations and cities capitalizing on commodity culture? Who provides the incentive to keep production local to then be distributed globally?

This last chapter proposes scenarios for the future factory that extrapolate from existing conditions to argue for the factory's resurrection in the city. The transparent, the local, the small and shared, the hybrid and dense, the connected and dispersed — these characteristics which are taking hold now could be recombined as symbiotic and ecologically situated — both economically and environmentally — and synthesized for the near future. Since residential development competes with industrial space in most cities today, incentives for manufacturers would encourage factory relocation in cities. But the architectural and urban issues addressing manufacturing in cities not only present exciting design challenges for integrating production spaces and systems, new fabrication technologies, but also demand

expansive solutions that will garner environmental benefits. The vertical urban factory becomes a metaphor and then an actuality, ultimately forming an urban industrial symbiosis. The paradox becomes the question of how designers and inventors
can embrace a seemingly outmoded and abandoned typology as a new potential
for integrated urban form, and address the issues of equity contained within.

VERTICAL AND DENSE

A provocation and premise of this study is that there is social and cultural value
today in the multistoried urban factory. Synonymous with a holistic vision of
urban manufacturing, verticality is a metaphor and actuality of the urban factory
from its density, multiplicity, and job potential. The multistoried factory that is
both layered with different factories on each floor or integrated as one company
have been the main typology discussed here. As a typology, historically, it has
gone unrecognized, but if regulations allowed, and it was used again by more
manufacturers, it would be a natural solution to provide more urban industrial
space. The allowable height in many manufacturing areas could be increased
with financial incentives and special tax breaks for denser manufacturing. Thus,
the vertical urban factory could be reinvented in the densest of cities, so that
supply would meet demands for space for future new flexible economies. By
increasing density and land value in turn, and providing off-street access through
integrated distribution flow, the movement of goods could be rethought altogether; but there can be a more flexible distribution that moves the flow of goods
and materials off the pedestrian-oriented streets, and would encourage the return
of factories to cities.

If a vertical factory becomes a pawn in the game of real estate deals there might
be ways to usurp the financial escapades by actually enhancing the value of the
factory as it rises taller. Incentives for building owners to maintain industry could
align with a spatial employment capability. In New York's Diamond District, one
such new example is the Gem Building rising thirty stories and housing commercial
spaces and small manufacturing units for jewelers, with the office space helping to
off set the cost of the industrial space.[8] How much land is used for jobs and zoned
for industry needs to be accounted for in urban analysis and given value as it per-
tains to job retention. Some companies harness the ideas of their designers, such
as in the case of the New York building in Portland, Oregon, or clients encourage
the flexible design of a building, as with Freitag in Zürich, develop urban factories
in spite of real estate trends pointing to different directions. Rarely, as with the
real estate company, Acumen — which developed Standard Motor and Pfizer, in
New York — do owners capitalize on mixed-use factory space or build new vertical
factories that embrace the sociocultural issues of manufacturing in place.

The spatial typology of factories, along with other building types, multiplying vertically, densifying, and agglomerating in increased proximity in the city
assists with its potential sustainablity.[9] In the past, physically dense clusters of
industrial innovation bore a negative stigma as potential polluters. Today, density,
when accompanied by the appropriate sustainable infrastructures, gains a certain

traction because it conserves land, energy, commuting time, carbon footprints, and social and other natural resources. Density also increases the value of a site, as by means of building upward, the land area is multiplied in layers rather than sprawling horizontally. The rapid urbanization and increased populations moving to cities could inspire activated, production spaces providing employment opportunities and integrating them into the city.

TRANSPARENT

One scenario within the vertical factory is the concept of the transparent factory — whether it be part of the "society of spectacle" of Guy Debord, or a company's marketing showcase that is using design as the "decorated shed" to attract attention — which uses the display of the production at the point of sale, thus hypercommodifying a company's factory. The consumption of production and the public's gaze onto process encourages the physically transparent factory, in terms of viewing the workers, as with Henn Architects' transparent VW factory. VW's design strategy is an attempt to increase profits by allowing people to get close to the source of origin, to understand how a car is made and who makes it, and to seduce the consumer with the product's authenticity, both emotionally, and viscerally in a display of desirable products.

Some companies are capitalizing on the visibility of the factory as a branding tool. This can be seen at New Balance, where workers can be viewed through storefront windows assembling sneakers. At Marc Jacobs' shops, consumers can watch machines embroider a custom design on-site. At the new company, Normal, located on 22nd Street in New York, workers make custom headphones with 3-D printers in the hybrid retail shop/mini-factory in a former industrial building. The space epitomizes one direction of the new urban factory: a full-height glass facade opens into a pristine display space where special events can also be staged. Through a

glass partition, the consumers can also watch the workers assemble cables (made off-site), and test, and package their headsets.

But transparency could also heighten the value of work. By engaging and educating the public about process, an ethic of labor might be engendered. While the idea for a transparent factory assumes a glazed and often high-designed building, this design can still establish an active relationship between the production space and the urban streetscape. In a proposed concept for the multistoried factories of the Garment District and Diamond Districts of New York City, glazed second-floor showrooms, visible from the street, could be replaced by manufacturing spaces. The view of the workers and their work — in contrast to a more normative, sterile, and sealed factory building — could animate the building facades and connect directly with the street and passersby. The worker would thus enliven the city in its streetscape while potentially advertising a company. Simultaneously, the visibility of the worker demonstrates the integrity of craft and labor, as well as satisfies the public's curiosity for how things are made.

CORPORATE TRANSPARENCY

The other aspect of transparency of concern to consumers is a company's ethical stance and its corporate governance; it behooves the firm to show the consumer how it is "doing good," both environmentally and socially. Ethical transparency not only increases public understanding of how things are made, but exposes the various steps along the supply chain. The International Labor Organization in Geneva, and NGO's such as Labour Behind the Label Verité, and the many Fair Trade organizations and labor unions help to expose working conditions in factories through inspections and targeted campaigns against specific manufacturers (even though it has been discovered that sometimes the inspectors are paid off by the companies).[10] Transparency has also become a competitive advantage for profit and investor relations: it is rare today for a company not to have a for-profit giving arm, or to donate to philanthropic causes. Some companies like Warby Parker are

◄ Normal, New York, HWKN Architects, 2014
▲ Transforming facades of urban factories to become transparent.

The hybrid mix of a brewery with a hotel could encourage new forms for industrial growth.

established with that goal at the very outset.[11] Seventy-two percent of the S&P 500 companies publish annual corporate responsibility reports (different from annual reports), a trend that more than doubled between 2010 and 2013.[12] But do we need to be a bit wary of this over-abundant transparency? Are corporations using it as a mainstream marketing tool, but at the same time still concealing working conditions and the supply chain? There is no way to truly know unless we can get inside the factory, and this is easier to do when the factory is close at hand.

INDUSTRIAL TOURISM

One way to enter a factory, if you don't work there, is through a controlled visit, as was prevalent in chocolate factories, food production such as Heinz and Kellogg, and automotive factories in the early twentieth century. Today, we have an entire "experience economy"[13] — a newly positioned, highly orchestrated area of industrial tourism popular with Kawasaki Motors in its company town in Japan, BMW and VW in Germany, the Murano glassblowers in Venice, film production companies, breweries, and wineries, among many others. Many of these factories have affiliated museums, especially legacy manufacturers; others allow visitors onto the factory floor, if doing so doesn't interfere with their production or cause insurance problems. In recent years, raw factory tours in Long Island City and San Francisco have been filled to capacity, attesting to popular interest in getting "behind the scenes."[14] The taste tests at the end of brewery tours have become recreational activities that illuminate process through which tourists engage in active learning via an experiential activity.[15] Company owners capitalize on the concept by bringing the consumer to the factory for that experience which then captures the consumers' attention and dollars. The education component also enhances a city's ability to promote investment in industry if the public sees the common cause.

Hotel stays in conjunction with factory visits have also become popular. One company, Viking Range, built a hotel in conjunction with their production spaces in Greenwood, Mississippi. The historic Hotel Irving, now renamed the Alluvian Hotel, is situated for potential stove buyers to stay the night and take culinary classes on their industrial excursions in the consumption of production.[16] Hotels are categorized, in terms of land use, as an industry, but they are not a producer of goods. New York has seen over sixty new hotels in industrial zones, with another 31 either in the works or completed in Long Island City since 2010. Hotels now compete for and often win out for industrial land as-of-right, without public scrutiny or agency review.

Embracing and capitalizing on the intentional pairing of factory and hotel and extrapolating for the future, a factory owner could build a hotel that would have codependent infrastructures. If factories operate during the day, they could then be quiet at night when tourists return to their hotel rooms (feasible now that companies are cleaner). The two dissimilar programs could feed off of each other for resource management, including water, heat, and electricity.[17] Incentives could be given to hotels that maintain an industry in proximity rather than displace it. Hotels could also be built on top of existing factories, making an interesting mix, each with separate services and vertical circulation systems. There is an allure to the hotel which is developed next to the factory, and in the city such a potential exists. With a provocation for hybrid programs, hotel uses could still occur in industrial areas, and property owners could capitalize on this potentially clashing but unusual programmatic mix.

GLOCAL

The new cottage industries of the future will be catalytic enterprises that target loyal and local customers. Making things locally for the local consumer and for global export supports the economy as well as reduces the supply chain. As companies are shrinking workforces, the future entrepreneur and local producer will move beyond long lines of product assembly into the realm of integrated small-scale processing in a networked spatial economy rather than an isolated ex-urban space. Such companies now focus on resiliency and rely on local economic interdependency for their survival.[18]

With a growing interest in the locally made, "locavore," new industries, focused on flexibility and versatility, can supply goods to their immediate communities, but maintain broader appeal to a global market. The "Made In" label becomes a popular signifier and brand for companies that choose to prioritize authenticity and local production. Such companies are a catalyst to new manufacturing and incubate ideas that become production circles or points, rather than lines, even in shorter runs. What if each neighborhood had local production centers for individual needs, but those goods could also be sold globally? These centers would not only make a region self-sufficient, but provide an identity for a product, enhancing its authenticity.[19] Similar to a wine collaborative, people could bring their products to a center for sale, or utilize companies such as Etsy or Quirky to reach the

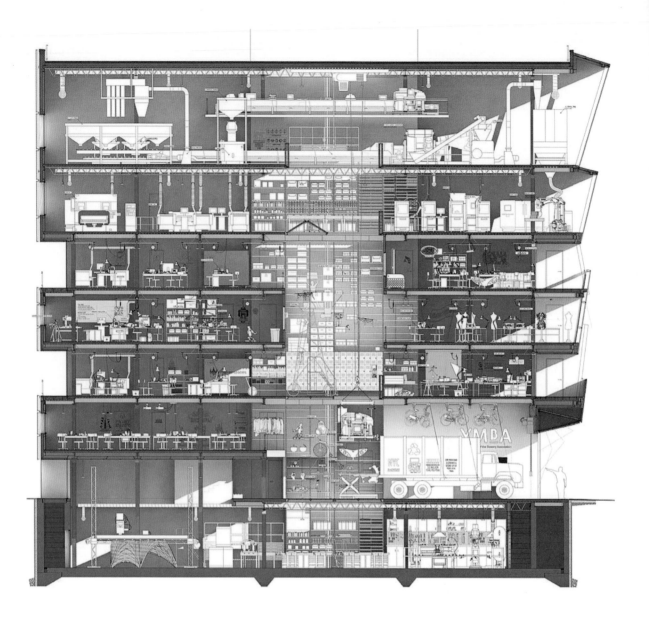

larger marketplace online. Local sites of manufacturing focused on supplying local urban consumers would reduce transit costs and commute time, and by encouraging goods to be purchased close at hand, reduce energy consumption and carbon emissions. By capitalizing on the local consumer, these companies would forge relationships such as those that sociologist/philosopher Georg Simmel (1858–1918) described in 1903: "the producer and the purchaser knew one another."[20] Knowing the supplier and supply chain contributes to consumer loyalty and benefits both sides of the consumer/supplier cycle so that the consumer becomes more aware of the social and environmental impact of the supply chain. "Made locally and distributed globally" is the essence of economic growth, and it coincides with local initiatives enhancing entrepreneurship in the new economy in various scales of vertical urban factories.

SHARED

In the future, the growing synergy between the collaborative commons and open-source manufacturing software, computer numerically-controlled-machines (CNC), 3-D and 4-D printers, and new forms of nanotechnology could pose a legitimate challenge to the multinational industrial hegemony, by enabling designers and consumers to quickly model prototypes and develop products in a more democratic system.[21] If, as noted previously, the innovator needs to be near the production line to enable fluidity in the design-to-production cycle, and workers' skills must be applicable across platforms, then new open technology networks in smaller urban industrial shops will orchestrate design, making, and distribution with a deeper understanding of the supply chain, and more direct control of it. This increases innovative, small-scale production, moving from Just-in-Time to real time on demand, thus eliminating overproduction. DIY culture is blossoming worldwide, as many small entrepreneurs enter the marketplace in informal cottage industries that can often get around industrial zoning codes in communal space for tinkerers and hackers, and learn new skills for manufacturing that would scale up production.

As neo-cottage industries develop, small flexible companies, poised to react quickly to changing markets, will need high-tech workshops and flexible, shared spaces to enable their growth, making the supply of these spaces an urgent priority for those municipalities seeking to reinvigorate urban industry in this new economic context. Government-incentivized incubator workshops and non-profit organizations with educational programs could be partnered with inventors to train workers to make products and encourage local entrepreneurship; this model is now viable in Philadelphia with the effort of the group Scout that is occupying a former school building.[22] In London, new organizations such as the High Speed Sustainable Manufacturing Institute (HSSMI), scientists, companies (Ford Motor Company, Autodesk), academic institutions (Loughborough University, University of London), and local London authorities established a nonprofit research collaborative to integrate advanced and new technologies in manufacturing. HSSMI areas of research include seamless production integrated through the digital factory that will allow the building, operations, inspection and retooling of factories through Visual Reality tools. Additionally, they are evaluating climate issues and working to reduce the cost and scale of automotive fuel cells with University College London and Imperial College. Another project optimizes fuel cells for remanufacturing, addressing the organization of value supply chains for the circular economy, and looks to the future of cities with an energy network linking mobility and infrastructure.[23] The project visualizes new training programs for the community to maintain

◀ Local high- and low-tech workshops inhabit old and new vertical urban factories.
▲ Shrinking of technologies and space is the result of new methods for urban manufacturing.

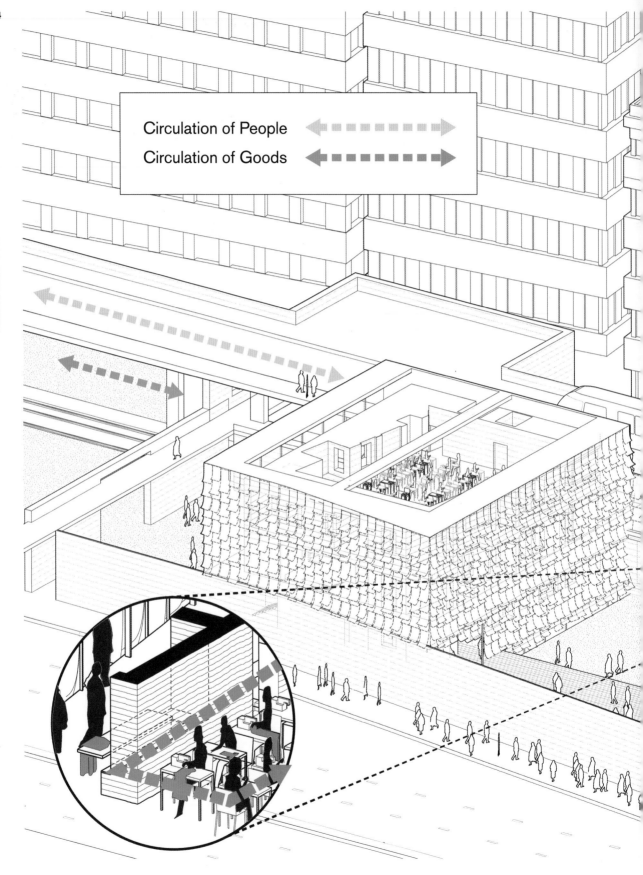

Circulation of People

Circulation of Goods

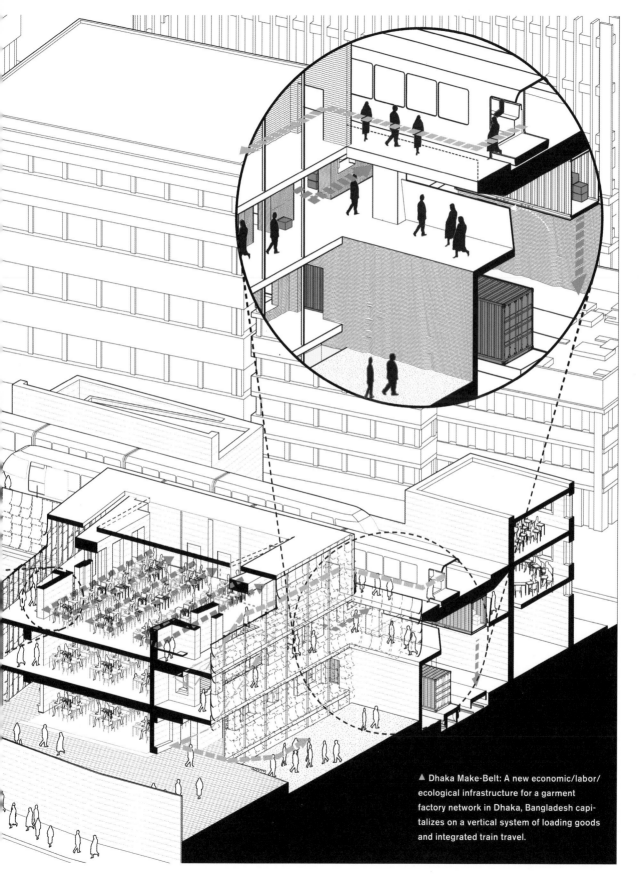

▲ Dhaka Make-Belt: A new economic/labor/ ecological infrastructure for a garment factory network in Dhaka, Bangladesh capitalizes on a vertical system of loading goods and integrated train travel.

urban jobs. These partnerships and research alliances are a new version of the "cottage" workshop, but now much more integral to the space of the city.

SMALL

If industry continues at the small scale with new and light technologies, and innovative and smaller batch production — in contrast to massive factories — new production spaces become financially less burdensome. Spatially, small-scale manufacturing with its tabletop technologies and nano-scaled tools, has the potential to be located anywhere. The functions of the company can spread out to smaller factories, each specializing in different product aspects that then come together under a larger umbrella. The smaller firm can react and respond more quickly, contributing to its longevity and flexibility.

Informal neo-cottage industries or smaller producers could be recognized as formal economies, such as those in Dharavi in Mumbai, where the seemingly informal economy is highly structured. The scale of the multinational corporation, while still dominant, could find ways in the future to be "small is beautiful" or manifest a "smallness within bigness" through Just-in-Time production, small batches, flexibility, and use of skilled and unskilled, but not low-paid laborers in local workshops.[24]

HYBRID

The Modernist separation of functions — residential and factory work, in particular — made each part of life siloed. Highly capitalist consumer society of the second industrial revolution never anticipated the disaggregation of the workplace from residence. In process removal, the city became monofunctional by district, and hierarchical in a more exclusive urbanism. The Modernist city became as rational as Taylor attempted in the factory itself. But even in the location of industrial sectors, diversity was essential, and limiting land uses killed the potential for the unexpected entrepreneur to introduce a business to an area or a manufacturing ecology that capitalized on the interdependence of skills and resources. The prevailing attitude of Modernist architects and planners was not to focus on the relationship between the factory and the city, beyond merely isolating industry from the city. Only the more liberal thinkers, such as the Goodmans, envisioned a complex interweaving of industry and daily life, while the mid-twentieth century was fraught with labor issues and unrest stemming from a new alienation in the workplace.

▶ Multistoried buildings can be rezoned to combine manufacturing, commercial, and residential uses in a hybrid space.

In addressing the urban location of factories, the century-old idea of clusters being most beneficial to the factory owners for shared resources — as analyzed by Christaller and Lösch, and, later Perloff and Krugman — show that physical proximity assists in productivity, providing economics with a spatial dimension. As Flusser said, "The so-called flint working prehistoric man made things everywhere and nowhere. As soon as tools enter the equation, specific factory areas must be carved out of the earth."[25] But I argue that, with the shift to smaller, cleaner, and greener technologies, as well as virtual networks and e-commerce, factories can be physically dispersed within cities, eliminating the need for exclusive industrial

R
Residential

C
Commercial

M
Manufacturing

Factory Shop

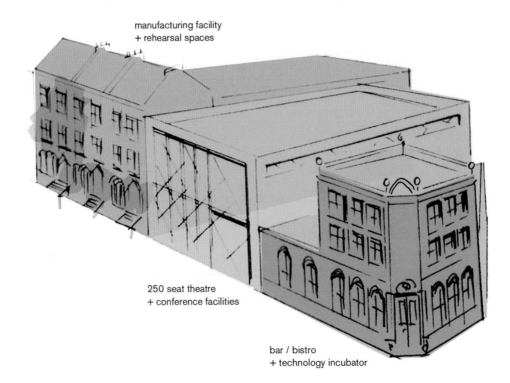

manufacturing facility
+ rehearsal spaces

250 seat theatre
+ conference facilities

bar / bistro
+ technology incubator

zones and sequestered industry. Factories can disaggregate as Kropotkin presaged in the mid-nineteenth century: "The industries must be scattered all over the world, and the scattering of industries amidst all civilized nations will be necessarily followed by a further scattering of factories over the territories of each nation."[26] Dispersal is no longer a negative in industrial growth because of the Internet and communication connections which form constellations of factories.[27] This would challenge the existence of industrial concentration in political structures of economic advantage such as Export Processing Zones altogether. But entirely new frameworks for trade incentives would have to be developed.

For example, garment factories in Dhaka, Bangladesh could be integrated within the urban fabric, by upgrading their aging rail infrastructure to make a new ecological labor infrastructure combining garment factory network with a vertical system of loading distribution. Or, in a spatially networked economy rather than an isolated heterotopia, virtually linked garment producers would have a designer in her office complete a fashion concept, send the drawing digitally to the pattern-maker who is linked to the sample fabricator, who transfers files to the detail embroiderer, checks it in feedback loops, and then finally sends it to a producer controlled remotely via PDAs communicating with machine operators who are also on their handhelds in real space and time linking immediately to local production.

The city is then re-mixed to the maximum, infinitely exchanging physical and spatial realms, in the vein that urbanist Grahame Shane defines as "recombinant urbanism," based on the recombining of DNA,[28] which would allow for industry

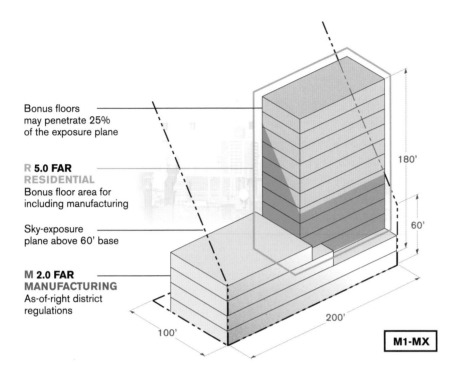

Bonus floors
may penetrate 25%
of the exposure plane

R 5.0 FAR
RESIDENTIAL
Bonus floor area for
including manufacturing

Sky-exposure
plane above 60' base

M 2.0 FAR
MANUFACTURING
As-of-right district
regulations

180'

60'

200'

100'

M1-MX

to occupy diverse areas rather than be sequestered through a zoning code, which limits the ability to react to changing economies. Industry needs to be protected, but as a use rather than a land use. We can now begin to ask if we need industrial zoning at all, given that, with the exception of highly polluting industries and heavy truck traffic, collaborative commerce and manufacturing are able to slide into different types of spaces, as the Goodmans envisioned. This would provoke the return of the hybrid of making and living in the city.

Within an individual building, mixes naturally occur and could be emphasized. Perhaps, a bit in the vein of Rem Koolhaas' analysis of the Downtown Athletic Club in New York, the interrelationships and juxtapositions in a hybrid building can hold surprising and often overlooked synergies.[29] Hybridity is then what results when this maximum mix is taken into account, as well as the potential for combinatory resources and programs. The hybridity results in a multifunctionality that then can play off the complex input from all the various uses. If a building is like a beehive, and includes living, working, making, and recreation, the mix increases economic diversity and enhances urban energy.

For the mixing in manufacturing space, individual buildings could have factories and retail on the ground floor and one or two above, with commercial offices or laboratories on the upper floors and then residential on the top floors. Interestingly, this phenomenon is occurring organically with the custom headphone company Normal, which built retail and factory space on the first floor of a New York City building. The building already housed offices and apartments. Entrances

◀ A mixed-use redevelopment of Arcola in Dalston, London, combines a theater with a café and manufacturing spaces.

▲ Zoning and land use laws could encourage property owners to maintain industrial uses by providing incentives (such as extra height or floors) for including manufacturing spaces.

and elevators could be separated, as they are now in industrial buildings, for the residential units and the commercial spaces. Worker amenities and cafés could be provided for the community, similar to century-old factories with their in-house restaurants, medical centers, and gathering spaces. Many who live in the building could also work there.

The potential for a mixed industrial community in the pragmatic utopian sense of the early twentieth century could rise vertically rather than be spread out in different buildings in a planned company town. Instead, the company town could be a vertical company town, mixing residential and manufacturing in one place. Housing could be a workers coop or social housing joined together in a building rather than separating the workplace from home. But, in order to incentivize residential as an amenity to the workspace, these could be conjoined with community uses. Arcola Energy, a hydrogen fuel cell systems designed and manufactured in London's East End represents the latest mixed-use project of this type. The small factory shares space with the Arcola Theatre, whose goal is to be a carbon-neutral theater, and has a café. There, the energy company makes and tests their products, which have no emissions and have applications for industry, automotive, and educational uses, including theatrical lighting (the Hylight 150 and 500), and for lightweight electric vehicles perfect for urban transportation.

Enticement for mixed use could be provided as air rights transfers, or zoning trade-offs. The spaces would resemble those in transition from industrial to residential, where some industrial still remains prior to displacement of industrial tenants in a conversion. Often this occurs organically as a building transitions from a factory to residential loft space; a hinge between conditions that leaves remnants of some factories behind until their leases run out, as they can't be displaced by some city laws without a large compensation from the landlord. These moments occurred when the Starrett-Lehigh building in New York City was converted to commercial space. Or, on the informal side, it is seen in the Torre David in Caracas, where people squatted, the building and lived, worked, and socialized there.[30] This mix is dynamic and provides a 24/7 community. Mixed-use and flexibility to the market are now touted by real estate investors as a plus for commercial and residential, but industry is never included in that mix, mainly because of traditional perspectives of what industry is.

DISTRIBUTION INFRASTRUCTURE

The future factory could be even more connected to the immediate urban fabric through new transportation infrastructure, both speculative and innovative. Logistics is often usurped by the major corporations who have organized transport systems using all the new embedded technologies developed for the automated assembly line. But if the goals remain constant — shorten the time to market and the cost of delivery — alternatives need to be envisioned also for the shorter and local supply chain.

Urban trams for cargo is one example that has achieved success at the VW Dresden factory, where CarGoTram transports parts to the factory on designated

tram tracks, 59.4-meters long. Other businesses have used tram lines to transport recycling materials to their depots. Amsterdam was also interested in such a system, but it was not carried out as planned in 2009. Many designers' visionary proposals — from those by Hugh Ferris to Winy Maas — imagined sky-bridge systems for carrying goods, exploiting the space in the air between buildings. Much of this is based on existing elevated train tracks such as those in Chicago or New York (now the High Line), developed because of street-level accidents in industrial areas. Inventive underground pneumatic tube systems on New York City's Roosevelt Island solved its waste-management distribution problem and could be harnessed for the movement of goods as well.[31] In Ghent, Belgium, a beer company is proposing an underground tunnel system to keep the beer trucks off the roads inside the historic city, a system that could be translated to other kinds of goods distribution. Overhead, aerial ropeway conveyors for transporting raw materials and working in mines could also assist in urban goods distribution. Artist Natalie Jeremijenko has envisioned ziplines as a mode of goods delivery from building to building. And the current research is finding solutions using delivery drone machines that Amazon calls "octocopters" to deliver smaller lightweight individual packages operated by on-the-ground pilots (if the FAA approves them).

▲ Trains could return in force as appropriate distribution infrastructure.

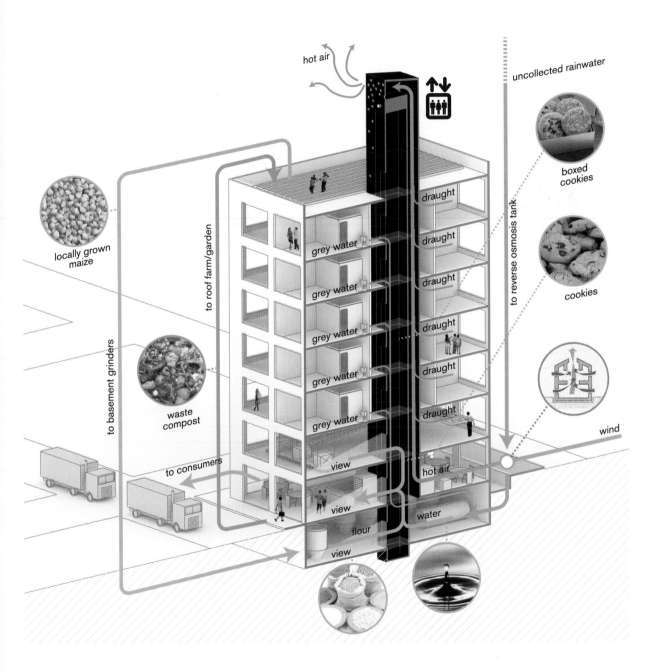

hot air

uncollected rainwater

boxed cookies

cookies

to reverse osmosis tank

locally grown maize

draught

draught

draught

to roof farm/garden

grey water

grey water

draught

grey water

grey water

draught

to basement grinders

waste compost

grey water

draught

grey water

draught

wind

to consumers

view

hot air

view

water

flour

view

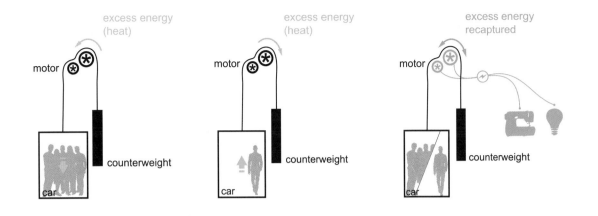

SUPER-URBAN INDUSTRIAL SYMBIOSIS

The crescendo of urban manufacturing could coalesce an urban industrial symbiosis acknowledging the worker. Stepping up from the symbiosis in Kalundborg, Denmark, eco-industrial parks, and the stand-alone sustainable factory to manufacturing facilities that are clean, recycle their own waste, and are energy-producing, industrial symbiosis can manifest both at the individual building and the urban scale.

Factory buildings can be linked to a sustainable network in which their heat waste is transferred to new uses — as discussed with BIG's project at Aalborg. The network is integrated into the supply chain in a circular economy that recycles products and materials to be used internally or by others. In addition, buildings can produce energy that could be used by adjacent factories.

One technology that capitalizes on the potential of vertical factories is the elevator. The early-twentieth-century designs of Cory & Cory encouraged factories to rise taller by means of bringing trucks directly into a building, floor by floor. But today's developments at Otis/United Technologies are now showing methods harnessing the unused heat from the elevator itself that could provide power for the factory for direct and stored use. Or, the elevator itself can store energy, capturing the lost heat. In addition to the energy capture in regenerative braking, the shaft could provide passive circulation. The factories could use their height to facilitate an emissionless distribution system for a proposed denser manufacturing zone. This would then provide incentives for vertical factories because they could harness elevator energy. Wind and solar power and closed-loop systems also contribute to the potentials for energy conservation in the future mixed-use factory building.

◄ Hybrid vertical urban factories can integrate sustainable symbiotic systems wherein the waste of the factory can be harnessed to provide energy to residential units.
▲ The elevator heat waste can be used for an additional energy source.

SUPER-URBAN INDUSTRIAL SYMBIOSIS

In the future scenario at the urban scale, an interactive and responsive industrial environment based on physical clustering could be harnessed in an urban industrial symbiosis. It is not only that green or sustainable industries benefit the urban

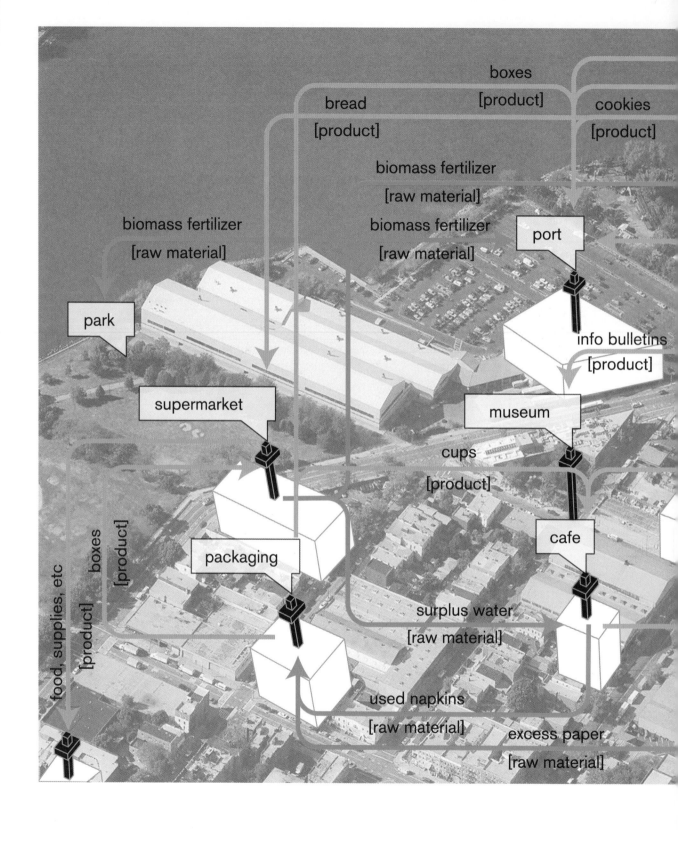

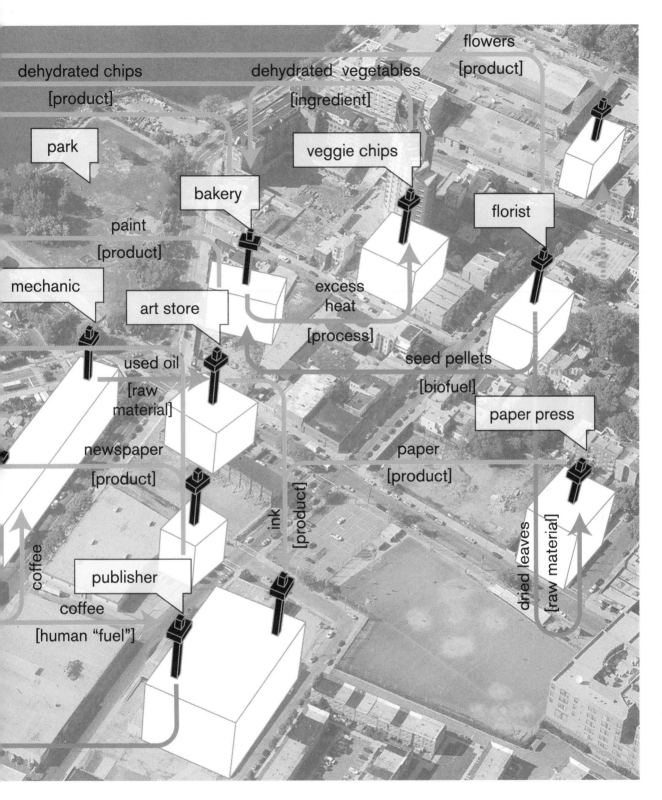

A super-urban industrial symbiosis integrates the numerous potential systems of exchange.

environment, such as plastic and paper recycling, electric cars, and eco-furniture, but renewable energy production could also support new infrastructures. As industrial ecology becomes a more developed field of study, we see that interconnected systems provide environmental safeguards and reduce pollution, based on the interchange between industrial and natural ecosystems.[32] Companies could share heat and excess power through a micro-grid separate from the larger energy grid. Collectively, greener manufacturing can support industrial symbiosis, applying to entire neighborhoods and cities expanding from the eco-industrial parks and those areas such as the Brooklyn Navy Yard where industries, and their material flows, can be symbiotic in organic and natural interchanges. The vision for industrial symbiosis in cities can expand beyond an industrial park to the entire city in a super-urban industrial symbiosis.

Among the mechanisms that can assist in the development of this symbiosis is the use of Performance Zoning, which can be seen in cities such as Toronto and Hamburg. There, planners judge a new project based on the factory emissions in a case-by-case basis, not in a blanket ordinance. The flexible zoning would evaluate an area by block or clusters of buildings to create an interdependent code in a closed-loop biological system rather than building by building. With flexible and performance zoning, as well as higher FAR for industrial buildings, factories could be taller and denser. Rather than prescriptive zoning, the uses would be evaluated based on their specific effects on the environment, rather than an abstract evaluation of all industrial uses as dirty or deleterious. What if a particular industry doesn't pollute — can the factory then be built in a residential zone? These are some of the questions that can be asked for the future symbiotic system.

While I am projecting the dispersal of cottage industries as they arise in disparate nooks and crannies of the city, the tried-and-true idea of clustering may be more appropriate for industries with a greater degree of interdependence, as this model enhances industrial symbiosis. Recycling is a common area of symbiosis for many industries that need the clusters to share disposal centers for paper, metal, wood, and food waste. Additionally, this sharing of resources is not just based on materials, but on shared trust between firms, upon whom all must depend for services or exchange.[33]

As each sector identifies production issues, a potential for a circular economy is taking hold in a way that environmental conservation did in the 1960s. Upcycling is one way to hack things with positive results and interfere with the system of goods production, as, instead of accepting their built-in obsolescence, products are reused for their parts or in their entirety in hacker spaces, or by organizations such as the TrashLab in Helsinki that makes products from products.

In closing, the future could support a symbiotic holism that could point to a sustainable self-sufficient city, reliant on its own services and products, dependent a bit less on those from the outside while also exporting goods. This is not about protectionism but about each place having the potential to make things locally and sustainably, both economically and environmentally, thereby enhancing the space of working.

The paradoxical relationship between capitalism and democracy that continuously leads to tension transcends the relationship between company owners and workers who are dislocated and alienated. How can a minimum wage grounded in the local region's purchasing power be instituted? Besides the existence of an economic climate that would encourage investment, provide for grants and incentives, there could be a new commitment for hybrid and open spaces for making things. Land use could be more flexible to encourage that which we don't yet know. New industries and the redefinition of manufacturing have the potential to develop innovative architecture that vastly improves upon prevailing patterns of design. Cities can host spaces of innovation that support workers in a complex and new spatial paradigm.

Jean Baudrillard emphasized that Marxism "convinces men that they are alienated by the sale of their labor power, thus censoring the much more radical hypothesis that they might be alienated as labor power"; he proposed instead to liberate workers from their "labor value" and to think in terms other than production. If the labor value resides in the maker who is often now merged with the role of designer and producer, a new value arises from the connection between designing and making, harkening to the era of handworkers in cottage industries, but at the larger market scale, which is not nostalgic but forward looking.

Rather than have redemption factories of alienating paternalism, as in the days of Lowell, the redefinition of industry can in turn redefine the factory in a new confluence of technology and spatial organization. If the consumer also demands goods that are made in more just, transparent, and equitable environments in the future, the vertical urban factory can supply this need, and would multiply as a new widespread paradigm. Moving beyond the maximization of space and the efficiency of process in the instrumental rationality of Herbert Marcuse, the factory could instead support symbiotic exchanges between individual workers, craftsmen or makers, and entrepreneurial companies that could redress labor conditions for a democratic workplace. The ubiquitous culture of making can coexist with the everyday urban experience, as part of the next urban economy to reinforce and reinvest in the cycles of production (supply) and demand. The worker's input is not only a commodity given value based on labor, but could become a representation of culture, as part of a new ethical consciousness of values of where things come from and where they could go.

As part of a new manufacturing paradigm, an urban and architectural typology of the vertical urban factory moves us into the future, as it embraces a progressive and equitable workplace with manufacturing that is reintegrated into the self-sufficient city. If corporations, industrialists, inventors, designers, and urban planners reconsider the possibilities offered by urban factories, this would reinforce the cycles of making, consuming, and recycling that are essential for sustainable cities, and would catalyze new forms of urban symbiosis, which are only beginning to be imagined today.

ENDNOTES

INTRODUCTION

1. Alberto Abriani, "Fiatorino," *Lotus* 12 (1976), 43.

2. Vilém Flusser, "The Factory," *The Status of Things, A Small Philosophy of Design* (London: Redaktion Books Ltd, 1999), 43. Originally published as "Die Fabrik," *Vom Stand der Dinge* (Carl Hanser Berlag, 1993).

3. Ibid.

4. Henri Lefebvre, discusses this in *The Production of Space*, translated by D Nicholson-Smith, (1974; Cambridge, Mass.: Blackwell Publishing, 1991).

5. Reyner Banham, *A Concrete Atlantis: U.S. Industrial Building and European Modern Architecture, 1900–1925* (Cambridge, Mass.: The MIT Press, 1986)

THE MODERN FACTORY

THE PRODUCTION ECONOMY

1. By "Modern," I am referring to the industrial revolution of the nineteenth century and the Modernist period of architecture in the early twentieth century.

2. See, Lindy Biggs, *The Rational Factory* (Baltimore: The Johns Hopkins University Press, 1996); Betsy Hunter Bradley, *The Works: Industrial Architecture of the United States* (New York: Oxford University Press, 1999); Gillian Darley, *Factory* (London: Reaktion Books, 2004); and David A. Hounshell, *From the American System to Mass Production 1800–1932* (Baltimore: The Johns Hopkins University Press, 1984). Each of these authors provided me with insight into the history of American factory architecture — chiefly about spatial ramifications in relation to production processes.

3. Michel Foucault, "Of Other Spaces: The Principles of Heterotopia," *Lotus International*, 48/49 (1985/86): 9–17.

4. Ibid., 14

5. Ibid., 17.

6. Kevin Hetherington, *The Badlands of Modernity: Heterotopia and Social Ordering* (London: Routledge, 1994). Discusses the Palais-Royal Freemason workspaces, and the late-eighteenth century English factory as heterotopias, expanding Foucault's description of this paradigm.

7. Karl Marx and Friedrich Engels, *The Communist Manifesto* (1848; reprint, Harmondsworth: Penguin, 1967), 131.

8. Marshall Berman, *All That is Solid Melts into Air* (New York: Simon & Schuster, Inc., 1982). Berman's comprehensive investigation of modernity inform the concepts of industrialization and modernization discussed here.

PRODUCTION, MAN, AND MACHINE

1. Karel Čapek, *R.U.R. (Rossum's Universal Robots): A Fantastic Melodrama in Three Acts and an Epilogue,* trans. Paul Selver and Nigel Playfair (New York: Samuel French, 1923), 17.

2. Ibid.

3. Georg Kaiser, *Gas I: A Play in Five Acts* (1917–1920; reprint, New York: Ungar, 1957), 38.

4. Ibid., 81.

5. Lewis Mumford, *Technics and Civilization* (New York: Harcourt, Brace & Co, 1934), 149.

6. Lewis Mumford, "Utopia, the City and the Machine," *Daedalus*, 94 no. 2 (1965): 290.

7. Oliver Evans, *The Young Millwright and Miller's Guide* (Philadelphia: 1795).

8. Siegfried Giedion, *Mechanization Takes Command: A Contribution to Anonymous History* (New York: Oxford University Press, 1948), 85.

9. George Dodd, *Days at the Factories* (1943; reprint, New York: A. M. Kelley, 1967).

10. Ibid., 189–202.

11. Adam Smith, *The Wealth of Nations, Books I–III* (1776; reprint, New York: Penguin, 1999), 110.

12. Ibid., 115.

13. Ibid.

14. Jane Jacobs, *The Economy of Cities* (New York: Vintage Books, 1970), 82–84.

15. Ibid.

16. David A. Hounshell, *From the American System to Mass Production 1800–1932* (Baltimore: The Johns Hopkins University Press, 1984), 25–27.

17. Ibid., 92.

18. Ibid., 122.

19. Ibid., 194.

20. Giedion, *Mechanization*, 93–97.

21. Upton Sinclair, *The Jungle* (1906; reprint, New York: Barnes & Noble Classics, 2005), 38.

22. Giedion, *Mechanization*, 24–25.

23. Ibid.

24. Anson Rabinbach, *The Human Motor: Energy, Fatigue and the Origins of Modernity* (Berkeley: University of California Press, 1992), 198.

25. Ibid., 82.

26. Frederick Taylor, *The Principles of Scientific Management* (1911; reprint, New York: Norton, 1967), 19.

27. David Montgomery, *Workers' Control in America: Studies in the History of Work, Technology, and Labor Struggles* (New York: Cambridge University Press, 1979), 114.

28. Hounshell, *From the American System,* 251.

29. Ibid., 240.

30. Henry Ford, "Henry Ford Expounds Mass Production," *New York Times,* September 19, 1926.

31. Hounshell, *From the American System,* 122.

32. Karl Marx, *Capital,* ed. Frederick Engels, trans. Samuel Moore and Edward Aveling (1890; reprint, New York: Random House Modern Library, 1906).

33. Rabinbach, *Human Motor,* 182–183.

34. Fernand Braudel, *The Wheels of Commerce, Vol. 2, Civilization and Capitalism Fifteenth to Eighteenth Century,* trans. Sian Reynolds (New York: Harper & Row, 1982), 304.

35. The loom card system technology later inspired the calculation punch cards of Babbage and his development of the Difference Engine.

36. David M. Gordon, Richard Edwards, and Michael Reich, *Segmented Work, Divided Workers* (Cambridge, England: Cambridge University Press, 1982), 121–122, 228.

37. Montgomery, *Workers' Control,* 3.

38. Rabinbach, *Human Motor,* 197.

39. Ibid., 257.

40. Ibid.

41. Ibid., 258.

42. Montgomery, *Workers' Control,* 101.

43. David E. Noble discusses the deskilling of work with examples from GE in Bridgeport, Connecticut, in *Forces of Production: A Social History of Industrial Automation* (New York: Knopf, 1984), 36.

44. Gordon, et al., *Segmented Work,* 3.

45. Ibid., 96.

46. Ibid., 97.

47. Ibid., 174–184.

48. Montgomery, *Workers' Control,* 5.

49. Joel Davidson, "Building for War, Preparing for Peace: World War II and the Military Industrial Complex," *World War II and the American Dream,* ed. Donald Albrecht (Cambridge, Mass.: The MIT Press, 1995), 184–229.

50. Donald M. Nelson, *Arsenal of Democracy: The Story of American War Production* (New York: Harcourt, Brace and Company, 1946), 41.

51. Hugh Johnson, *Washington News,* November 1, 1938, as quoted in Alan L. Gropman, "Mobilizing U.S. Industry in World War II: Myth and Reality," *McNair Paper 50,* Institute for National Strategic Studies, (Washington, D.C.: National Defense University Press, August 1996).

52. Davidson, "Building for War," 190.

53. Alan L. Gropman, ed., *The Big "L," American Logistics in World War II,* (Washington, D.C.: National Defense University Press, 1997), 4.

54. Noble, *Forces of Production,* 22.

55. Ibid., 23.

56. Ibid., 39.

57. Mathews Conveyer Co., *Natural Laws Applied to Production* (City of Ellwood, Pennsylvania: 1939), 7.

58. In this context it is valuable to consider how historians and architectural critics often begin their research with the history of technology. It is with this perspective that the relationship between Eco, Giedieon, and Mumford is examined here.

59. Lewis Mumford, "The Drama of the Machine," *Scribner's* (August 1930): 150.

FACTORY CITY

1. Kevin Hetherington, *The Badlands of Modernity: Heterotopia and Social Ordering* (London: Routledge, 1994), 124.

2. Fernand Braudel, *The Wheels of Commerce, Vol. 2, Civilization and Capitalism Fifteenth to Eighteenth Century,* trans. Sian Reynolds (New York: Harper & Row, 1982), 332.

3. Henri Lefebvre, "The Right to the City," *Writing on Cities,* trans. Eleonore Kofman and Elizabeth Kebas (Blackwell Publishing, 1996), 151.

4. Hubert Bourgin, *L'Industrie et le Marché* (Paris: F. Alcan, 1924), 31.

5. Braudel, *The Wheels of Commerce,* 300.

6. Jane Jacobs, *The Economy of Cities,* (New York: Vintage Books, 1970), 12.

7. Leonardo Benevolo, *History of Modern Architecture, Vol. 1* (Cambridge, Mass.: The MIT Press, 1971), 39.

8. Braudel, *The Wheels of Commerce,* 302.

9. Ibid., 298.

10. Ibid., 308.

11. Johann Heinrich von Thünen, *The Isolated State,* trans. Carla M. Wartenberg (New York: Pergamon Press, 1966) describes his ideas of spatial economics and economic geography.

12. Alfred Marshall, *Principles of Economics* (London: Macmillan and Company, 1890) describes his economic theories.

13. Ibid., Book IV, Chapter X, 157.

14. Walter Christaller, *Central Place Theory in Southern Germany, Die Zentralen Orte in Süddeutschland* (Jena: Gustav Fischer, 1933).

15. August Lösch, *The Economics of Location* (New Haven: Yale University Press, 1954).

16. Paul Krugman, *Development, Geography, and Economic Theory* (Cambridge, Mass.: The MIT Press, 1997), 41.

17. Henri Lefebvre, *The Production of Space* (Oxford: Blackwell Publishing, 1991), 410.

18. From William Blake's 1808 poem "New Jerusalem" from the preface to his epic, *Milton a Poem.*

19. Eric Hobsbawm, *The Age of Capital: 1848–1875,* (New York: Vintage Books, 1996), 4.

20. Lefebvre, "Right to the City," 154.

21. Leonardo Benevolo, *The Origins of Modern Town Planning,* trans. Judith Landry (Cambridge, Mass.: The MIT Press), xii.

22. Margaret Crawford, *Building the Workingman's Paradise: The Design of American Company Towns* (London: Verso, 1995). In this comprehensive book Crawford describes in detail the founding, organization, spatial planning, and design, of numerous American company towns.

23. Benevolo, *Origins,* 50.

24. Ibid., 42.

25. Ibid., 56–63.

26. Benevolo, *History of Modern Architecture,* 156.

27. Tony Garnier, *Une Cité Industrielle* (1918; reprint, New York: Rizzoli, 1990), 43.

28. Ibid., 47.

29. For the complete manifesto see: Filippo Tommaso Marinetti, "Manifesto of Geometrical and Mechanical Splendor," *Marinetti:*

Selected Writings, ed. Robert W. Flint (London: Secker and Warburg, 1972).

30. Dora Wiebenson, Tony Garnier: The Cité Industrielle (New York: G. Braziller, 1969), 17.

31. Garnier, Cité Industrielle, 46. The idea of progress was indicated throughout the proposal, in its organization in schools, as well as the architecture, and was explicitly expressed in the project's title, "City of Labor."

32. Antonio Sant'Elia, "Manifesto of Futurist Architecture" in Antonio Sant'Elia: The Complete Works, ed. Luciano Caramel and Alberto Longatti (New York: Rizzoli, 1988).

33. Crawford, Workingman's Paradise, 46–60.

34. Anthony Vidler in The Writing of the Walls: Architectural Theory in the Late Enlightenment (Princeton: Princeton Architectural Press, 1987), discusses this parallel as a genre of industrial planning.

35. Ibid., 37.

36. Ibid., 39.

37. Michel Foucault, Discipline and Punish: The Birth of the Prison, trans. Alan Sheridan (1975; reprint, New York: Vintage, 1995), 200.

38. For more information on the prison factory see Robin Evans, "Regulation and Production," Lotus International 12/13 (1976), 6–12.

39. John Swinton, A Model Factory in a Model City: A Social Study (New York Press of Brown, Green and Adams, 1887).

40. Mumford, Technics and Civilization (New York: Harcourt, Brace & Co, 1934) 14.

41. Crawford, Workingman's Paradise, 26.

42. Ibid., 39.

43. Ibid., 98.

44. Edmond Taylor, The Fossil Monarchies: The Collapse of the Old Order, 1905–1922 (Harmondsworth: Penguin, 1967), 206.

45. John B. Stetson Company promotional brochure, Philadelphia, 1915. The Stetson hat factory employed 5,400 people in 25 buildings on three hectares in the city.

46. Sinclair, The Jungle (1906; reprint, New York: Barnes & Noble Classics, 2005), 205.

47. For further information on Patrick Geddes' ideas and planning surveys see, Cities in Evolution: An Introduction to the Town Planning Movement and to the Study of Civics (London: Williams and Norgate, 1915).

48. Hobsbawm, Age of Capital, 211.

49. Spiro Kostoff, The City Assembled: The Elements of Urban Form Through History (Boston: Little, Brown, 1992), 266.

50. M. Christine Boyer, Dreaming the Rational City: The Myth of American City Planning (Cambridge, Mass.: The MIT Press, 1983), 167.

51. Lefebvre, Right to the City, 158.

52. R.D. MacLauren, "Does Zoning Protect Only the Aesthetic Sense?" National Municipal Review 12 no. 9 (September 1928): 504.

53. Boyer, Dreaming the Rational City, 167.

54. Ibid., 69.

55. Robert Lewis, Manufacturing Montreal: The Making of an Industrial Landscape, 1850-1930 (Baltimore: Johns Hopkins University Press, 2000), 14.

56. Ibid., 47.

57. Ibid., 135. In Manufacturing Montreal, Lewis makes the point that there was not a formula in terms of scale and location of factories such that smaller firms also moved out of the urban cores of cities.

58. Ibid., 174.

59. Robert Lewis, Chicago Made: Factory Networks in the Industrial Metropolis (Chicago: University of Chicago Press, 2008), 76.

60. Ibid., 167.

61. Ibid., 178.

62. It was difficult to obtain the correct numbers of manufacturers as it was not until 1913 that the New York Regional Plan Association enacted the first laws that recorded industrial establishments.

63. Boyer, Dreaming the Rational City, 159.

64. Sam Bass Warner, Jr., The Private City (Philadelphia: University of Pennsylvania Press, 1968), 162.

65. Ibid., 126.

66. Ibid., 169.

67. Jeremy Brecher, Strike! (Boston, MA: South End Press, 1997), 235.

68. Sidney Fine, Sitdown: The General Motors Strike of 1936–1937 (Ann Arbor: University of Michigan Press, 1969), 55.

69. Brecher, Strike!, 212.

70. Fine, Sitdown, 97.

71. Kostoff, The City Assembled, 137.

72. Mary McLeod, "Architecture of Revolution: Taylorism, Technocracy, and Social Change," Art Journal 43 no. 2 (1983): 133. McLeod highlights the impact of Taylorism in European architecture. She also reproduced the Gilbreth's Route Model image in a contemporary publication for the first time.

73. Remi Baudoui, "Dautry, Raoul," in Le Corbusier: Une Encyclopédie, ed. Jacques Lucan (Paris: Centre Georges Pompidou, 1987), 115. Also see, Willy Boesiger, Le Corbusier: Oeuvre complete, 1938–1946 (Les Editions d'Architecture Ehrlenbacg, 1946), 76–79. In rural Aubusson, France, Le Corbusier designed a factory scheme that integrated workflow with the landscape in an effort to improve worker morale.

74. Eric Mumford, Defining Urban Design: CIAM Architects and the Formation of a Discipline, 1937–1969 (New Haven: Yale University Press, 2009), 241.

75. Kostoff, The City Assembled, 136.

76. Le Corbusier, The Athens Charter (1933; reprint, New York: Grossman Publishers, 1973).

77. While it was an initiative of the city, it seems that Siemens was a collaborator in the project.

78. Annemarie Jaeggi, "Siemensstadt," Vier Berliner Siedlungen der Weimarer Republik, Bauhaus Archive, Museum für Gestaltung (Berlin: Argon Verlag, 1987), 159–180.

79. Adolf Behne, "Ein neuer Wohnbautyp," Acht Uhr Abendblatt, September 5, 1930.

80. Jaeggi, "Siemensstadt," 180.

81. Czech writer Ludvik Vaculik wrote, "On the Assembly Line," (1944), as cited in Annett Steinführer, "Uncharted Zlín," in Katrin Klingan, A Utopia of Modernity: Zlín (Berlin: Jovis, 2009), 114.

82. Ibid., 22.

83. Ibid., 85. In, A Utopia of Modernity, Klingan includes a complete description of the political and architectural impact on Bat'a and Zlín.

84. Eric J. Jenkins, "Utopia, Inc.": Czech Culture and Bat'a Shoe Company Architecture and Garden Cities" Thresholds 18 (1999): 60–66.

85. Klingan, Utopia of Modernity, 87.

86. M. Urbanova and J. Dundelova, "Work culture of the Bat'a Company," Acta Universitatis Agriculturae et Silviculturae Mendelianae Brunensis 60, no. 7 (2012): 488.

87. Steinfuhrer, "Uncharted Zlín," in Klingan, A Utopia of Modernity, 109.

88. Jean-Louis Cohen, "Zlín: An Industrial Republic," Rassegna 19, no. 70 (1997): 42–45.

89. Paolo Scrivano and Patrizia Bonifazio, Olivetti Builds: Modern Architecture in Ivrea (Milan: Skira Architecture Library, 2001), 25–30.

90. Leo Leonni, "Olivetti: Design in Industry," Museum of Modern Art Bulletin (Fall 1952): 5.

91. Vittorio Gregotti and Giovanni Marzari, ed., Figini e Pollini, Opera Completa (Milan: Electa, 1996), 322–324.

92. Scrivano and Bonifazio, Olivetti Builds, 25–32.

93. For a detailed analysis of linear planning see George Collins, "Linear Planning Throughout the World," Journal of the Society of Architectural Historians 18, no. 3 (October, 1959): 74–93

94. George R. Collins, "The Linear City," in David Lewis ed., Pedestrian in the City, Architects' Year Books, vol. 11 (London: Elek Books Ltd., 1965), 210.

95. Ibid., 204.

96. For a discussion on the influence of American industrialization on Russia, see: Jean-Louis Cohen, Scenes of the World to Come: European Architecture and the American Challenge, 1893–1960 (Paris: Flammarion, 1995), 70.

97. Tracy B. Augur, "National Security Factors in Industrial Location," Bulletin of the Atomic Scientists, United States National Security Resources Board (July 22, 1948): 316.

98. Ibid.

99. Mike Davis, City of Quartz (New York: Verso 1990), 385.

100. Greg Hise, "The Airplane and the Garden City: Regional Transformations During World War II," in World War II and the American Dream (Cambridge, Mass.: The MIT Press, 1995), 168. Noted in reference to John Carmody Papers, Memo: 20 June 1940, Franklin Delano Roosevelt Library, Hyde Park, New York. Along with Catherine Bauer Wurster, the planners from the RPAA believed in moving industry away from housing.

101. Joel Davidson, "Building for War, Preparing for Peace: World War II and the Military Industrial Complex," World War II and the American Dream, ed. Donald Albrecht (Cambridge, Mass.: The MIT Press, 1995), 196.

102. "Underground Factories in Central Germany," Report of the Combined Intelligence Objectives Sub-Committee (CIOS), London, 1945, Item Nos. 4, 5, 25 & 30, File No. XXXII-17; National Archives, Washington, D.C.

103. Eleanor Smith Morris, British Town Planning and Urban Design (Essex, England: Addison Wesley Longman, 1997), 83. A seminal book on the history of planning in Great Britain.

104. Ibid., 95.

105. Kostoff, The City Assembled, 121.

MODERN FACTORY ARCHITECTURE

1. Letter from Schinkel to his wife July 19 in K. F. Schinkel, The English Journey: The Visit to England and France in 1826, ed. David Bindman and Gottfried Riemann, trans. F. Gayna Walls (New Haven: Yale University Press, 1993), 180.

2. Betsy Hunter Bradley, The Works: The Industrial Architecture of the United States (New York: Oxford University Press, 1999), 17.

3. Lindy Biggs, The Rational Factory: Architecture, Technology, and Work in America's Age of Mass Production (Baltimore: Johns Hopkins University Press, 1996), 40.

4. Institute of Business Science, Production Organization (Scranton, PA: 1926), 17.

5. Bradley, The Works, 93.

6. Biggs, The Rational Factory, 86.

7. Ibid., 87.

8. Edward D. Mills, The Modern Factory (London: Architectural Press, 1951), 41–42.

9. My own interest in the role of the engineer was sparked by the fact that in this early Modern period, engineers designed factories but were not recognized as designers. See: Nina Rappaport, Support and Resist: Structural Engineers and Design Innovation (New York: The Monacelli Press, 2007).

10. Pierre Francastel, Art & Technology in the Nineteenth and Twentieth Centuries, trans. Randall Cherry (New York: Zone Books, 2000), 91.

11. Reyner Banham, A Concrete Atlantis: U.S. Industrial Building and European Modern Architecture, 1900–1925 (Cambridge, Mass.: The MIT Press, 1986), 74–75.

12. See: The Builder 88 (September 1932); Architectural Review 72 (November 1932): 162; The Architect and Building News (January 8, 1932): 56.

13. Owen Williams, "Factories — A Few Observations Thereon Made by Sir Owen Williams at a Discussion of the Art Workers' Guild," RIBA Journal 25 (November 26, 1927): 54–55.

14. Grant Hildebrand, *Designing for Industry: the Architecture of Albert Kahn* (Cambridge, Mass.: The MIT Press, 1974), 29.

15. Ibid., 34.

16. Banham, *Concrete Atlantis,* 86.

17. "The Turin-based automobile firm had experimented with American methods in the first decade of the twentieth century, and had gained direct experience through its engine plant located in New York State," from Duccio Bigazzi "Management Strategies in the Italian Car Industry, 1906–1945; Fiat and Alfa Romeo" *The Automobile Industry and Its Workers,* ed. Steven Tolliday and Jonathan Zeitlin (New York: St. Martin's, 1987), 80.

18. Stefano Musso "Production Methods and Industrial Relations at Fiat (1930–90)," in Haruhito Shiomi and Kazuo Wada, ed., *Fordism Transformed: The Development of Production Methods in the Automobile Industry* (Oxford: Oxford University Press, 1996), 245.

19. Francesca Fauri, "The Role of Fiat in the Development of the Italian Car Industry in the 1950s," *Business History Review* 70 no. 2 (1996): 169.

20. Antonio Gramsci, *Selections from the Prison Notebooks* (New York: International Publishers, 1971), 292.

21. Banham, *Concrete Atlantis,* 243.

22. Ibid., 246.

23. Ibid.

24. Ibid., 250.

25. Williams, in "Factories — A Few Observations Thereon," discusses the function form of the factory surrounding the machines and exemplifying modernism.

26. Charlie Wood, collected reminiscence from when he was a Sainsbury employee, Sainsbury's Archive, Docklands Museum, (London: England, 1977).

27. Ibid.

28. Tatyana Tzarev, "The Fruits of Conversion," *Archnadzor,* January 18 2008, http://www.archnadzor. ru/2008/01/18/plody-konversii/. Thank you to Anya Bokov for her translation and insight.

29. Walter Gropius, "The Development of Modern Industrial Architecture," *Form and Function: A Source Book for the History of Architecture and Design 1890–1939,* ed. Tim Benton (1913; reprint, London: Crosby Lockwood Staples, 1975), 53.

30. Hinchman Smith and Grylls Architects, "Efficiency in Industrial Planning Illustrated in a New Forge Shop," *The American Architect* 116 (New York: Architectural & Building Press, 1919), 283.

31. This section of the book is an adaptation of my paper, "Reception and Image of the Modern Industrial Building," given at the Docomomo International Conference 2003 and published in *The Reception of Modern Architecture: Image, Usage, Heritage,* ed. Jean-Yves Andrieux and Fabienne Chevallier (Saint-Etienne: University of Saint-Etienne Press, 2005), 240.

32. Banham, *Concrete Atlantis,* 8.

33. Mendelsohn's vision Silo Dreams, was in a letter he wrote to his wife October 22, 1924 after visiting Buffalo, in *Eric Mendelsohn: Letters of an Architect,* Oskar Beyer, ed. (London, New York: Abelard-Schuman, 1967), 69.

34. Alessandro De Magistris, "Eric Mendelsohn," *Casabella* 651 no 2 (December/January 1997/1998), 40.

35. Mendelsohn, *Letters of an Architect,* 71.

36. Gropius, "The Development of Modern Industrial Architecture," 54.

37. Ibid., 81.

38. Hildebrand, *Designing for Industry,* 2.

39. Moisei Ginzberg, *Style and Epoch,* trans. A. Senkevitch (Cambridge, Mass.: The MIT Press, 1982), 80–81.

40. Banham, *Concrete Atlantis,* 136.

41. Paul Venable Turner, *The Education of Le Corbusier* (New York: Garland Pub, 1977), 81.

42. Le Corbusier, *Towards A New Architecture* (New York: Praeger Publishers, 1960), 42.

43. Walter Gropius, "Die Entwicklung Moderne Industriebau Kunst," *Die Kunst in Industrie und Handel, Jahrbuch des Deutschen Werkbundes* (Jena: E. Diederichs, Deutschen Werkbundes, 1913), 17–22.

44. Banham, *Concrete Atlantis,* 202.

45. Annemarie Jaeggi, *Fagus: Industrial Culture from Werkbund to Bauhaus* (New York: Princeton Architectural Press, 2000), 5.

46. *Die Kunst in Industrie und Handel Jahrbuch des Deutschen Werkbundes,* 17–22.

47. Jaeggi, *Fagus,* 35.

48. Leonardo Benevolo, *History of Modern Architecture,* Vol. 1 (Cambridge, Mass.: The MIT Press, 1971), 387.

49. Banham, *Concrete Atlantis,* 195.

50. Le Corbusier, *Towards A New Architecture* (New York: Praeger Publishers,1960), 42.

51. Adolf Behne, *The Modern Functional Building,* trans. Michael Robinson (Santa Monica: The Getty Research Institute, 1996), 103. Originally published as *Der Moderne Zweckbau, Die Baukunst,* ed. Dagobert Frey (Munich: Drei Masken Verlag, 1926).

52. Ibid.

53. Ibid., 104–105.

54. Mies van der Rohe, "Industrielles Bauen," *G: Matrial Zur Elementaren Gestaltung*: 3 (June 1924): 18.

55. Sheldon Cheney, *The New World Architecture* (London; New York: Longmans, Green & Co., 1930), 89, 105.

56. Georg Simmel, David Frisby, and Mike Featherstone, "The Berlin Trade Exhibition," *Simmel on Culture: Selected Writings* (London: Sage, 1997), 255.

57. Wolf Jobst Siedler, "The Spirit is the Inspirator of Berlin," *Berlinmodell Industriekultur,* ed. Nikolaus Kuhnert (Boston: Birkhauser, 1989).

58. Stanford Anderson, "Modern Architecture and Industry: Peter Behrens, the AEG and Industrial Design," *Oppositions* 21 (Summer 1980): 82.

59. Ibid., 93.

60. Stanford Anderson, *Peter Behrens and a New Architecture for the Twentieth Century* (Cambridge, Mass.: The MIT Press, 2000), 130.

61. Stanford Anderson, "Modern Architecture and Industry: Peter Behrens and the AEG Factories," *Oppositions* 23 (Winter 1981): 55–56.

62. Ibid., 64.

63. Peter Behrens, "Art and Technology," lecture, May 26, 1910. Reprinted in Tilmann Buddensieg, ed., *Peter Behrens and the AEG 1907–1914,* trans. Iain Boyd Whyte (Cambridge, Mass.: The MIT Press, 1984), 212–19.

64. Stanford Anderson, *On Streets* (Cambridge, Mass.: The MIT Press, 1978), 131.

65. Anderson, "Modern Architecture and Industry," 76. While Gropius' Fagus factory was a lighter design aesthetic and less monumental than AEG, he was referring to the significance of the Modernist factory design.

66. Kenneth Frampton, *Modern Architecture* (New York: Thames and Hudson, 2007), 112.

67. David A. Hounshell, *From the American System to Mass Production 1800–1932* (Baltimore: The Johns Hopkins University Press, 1984), 223–39. Hounshell describes the points about the Ford engineers in detail, and notes that Sorenson should be credited for the moving assembly line.

68. Ibid., 253. Hounshell discusses a meeting in Detroit where Taylor spoke and took credit for those who where implementing similar ideas, despite that many industrialists had never heard of him and were devising efficient production methods for their own capitalist profit gains.

69. Biggs, *The Rational Factory,* 97.

70. Ibid., 112.

71. Jervis Webb continues to produce conveyance systems for factories and baggage handling, even after being purchased by another company. Their film and photography archive document the various uses of roller conveyors at Ford and other factories. The overhead conveyor was an essential component of Ford's continuously moving assembly line.

72. Hounshell, *From the American System,* 261.

73. Hildebrand, *Designing for Industry,* 66, 218. Hildebrand emphasizes Albert Kahn's unpretentious architecture that was not focused on in Modernist manifestos. He suggests that the architecture was more like the machines Kahn was housing.

74. Ibid., 51.

75. "The Starrett-Lehigh Building," *Architectural Forum* 55 no. 4 (1931): 483–492.

76. Lewis Mumford, The Skyline column, *The New Yorker* (November 21, 1931), 48.

77. Starrett Investing Corporation, *Leasing Brochure,* 1931.

78. Ibid.

79. "The Starrett-Lehigh Building," 485.

80. Frank Kauffman, "Kees Van Der Leeuw: A Principal in Search of Synthesis," *Wiederhall* 14 (1993): 4–6.

81. Joris Molenaar, Frank Kauffmann, Anne Mieke Backer, Wessel de Jonge, et al., *Van Nelle: Monument in Progress* (Rotterdam: Uitgeverij De Hef publishers, 2005). This is the definitive book on Van Nelle.

82. Kees Van der Leeuw, "Beauty in Industry" (lecture at Schloss Elmau, July 1929).

83. Kees Van der Leeuw, "Building a new factory, choices for sites and factory type" (lecture for the Dutch Institute for Efficiency, 1930), as quoted in Molenaar, et al., *Van Nelle,* 72.

84. Molenaar, "Curtain Wall Construction," in Molenaar, et al., *Van Nelle,* 112.

85. Molenaar, "Mart Stam," in Molenaar, et al., *Van Nelle,* 94.

86. Ibid., 110.

87. Ibid., 112.

88. "Van Nelle Factory, Rotterdam," *Architectural Record* 66 (1929): 384–90. See also *Architectural Record* 69 (1931): 417–422.

89. Le Corbusier, "Van der Vlugt," *De 8 en Opbouw* 11 (1936): 123.

90. Mrs. Janssens-Sonneveld, November 21, 1986 from the Rotterdam Municipal Archives, 944 Van Nelle dossier no. 1726. As quoted in Molenaar, et al., *Van Nelle,* 175.

91. R.N. Roland Holst, letter to M. Elout-Drabbe, Bioemendaal, January 15, 1933, cited in Molenaar, et al., *Van Nelle,* 124.

92. Joris Molenaar, "Van Nelle's New Factories, American Inspiration and Cooperation," *Wiederhall Architectural Serial Amsterdam* (1980), 13.

93. Maximilien Gauthier, *Le Corbusier ou l'Architecture au service de l'homme* (Paris: Denoel, 1944), 47.

94. Amedeo and Amellio Petrilli, "Le Corbusier Vivant," *Spazio e Societa* 8, no. 29 (March 1985): 43.

95. Author's translation. Jean Jacques Duval, *Le Corbusier, L'écorce et la Fleur* (Paris: Ed. du Linteau, 2006), 112.

96. Ibid., 114.

97. Willy Boesiger, *Le Corbusier: Oeuvre Complete, 1938–1946* (1953; reprint, Basel: Birkhauser, 1995), 12–23.

98. Duval, *Le Corbusier, L'écorce et la Fleur,* 112.

99. Miguel Fisac, "Jorba Laboratories Complex," *Arquitectura* 127 (July 1969): 66.

100. Ibid.

101. Ibid., 68.

102. A concept that I developed in regards to structural engineering and design integrated within the structural form. See Nina Rappaport, "Deep Decoration," *306090* (New York: Princeton Architectural Press, 2006), 95–105.

103. Miguel Fisac, *Arquitectura* 127 (July 1969).

104. "Industrial Buildings Back the Attack," *Architectural Record* (October 1943): 61–76.

105. Ibid.

106. Albert Kahn, "Architecture in the National Defense Program," *Weekly Bulletin of the Michigan Society of Architects,* December 30, 1941, 51.

107. I learned about this factory concept from architectural historian Marc Dessauce (1962–2004) described in his book and exhibition, *The Inflatable Moment: Pneumatics*

and Protest in '68 (New York: Princeton Architectural Press, 1999).

108. Herbert H. Stevens, "Air-Supported Roofs for Factories," *Architectural Record* (December 1941): 45–16.

109. "Industrial Buildings Back the Attack," 61–76.

110. See Francois Burkhardt, *Marco Zanuso* (Milan: F. Motta Editore, 1999).

111. Reyner Banham, *The Architecture of the Well-Tempered Environment* (London: The Architectural Press, 1969), 242.

112. Roberto Guiducci, "Di Marco Zanuso a Buenos Aires," *Casabella Continuità* (1959), 229.

113. Buckminster Fuller, "Everything I Know," *Buckminster Fuller Institute*, transcript, session 11 part 3, 1975.

114. Katrina Farley (daughter of T.C. Howard), in conversation with the author, spring 2012.

115. "Vertical Textile Mill," *Architectural Forum* 96 (1952): 137–141.

116. *Student Publication of the School of Design* 1, no. 3, North Carolina State College (Fall 1952).

THE CONTEMPORARY FACTORY

THE CONSUMPTION ECONOMY

1. David Harvey, *The Condition of Postmodernity: An Enquiry into the Origins of Cultural Change* (Cambridge, Mass.: Blackwell Publishing, 1990), 189–197.

2. See Jeremy Rifkin, *The Third Industrial Revolution* (New York: Pallgrave Macmillan, 2011).

3. Manuel Castells, *The Rise of the Network Society I, Vol. 1* (1996; reprint, Malden, Mass.: Wiley-Blackwell, 2012), 77.

4. Ernest Mandel, *Late Capitalism,* trans. Joris De Bres (London: New Left Books, 1975).

5. Vilém Flusser, "The Factory," *The Status of Things, A Small Philosophy of Design* (London: Reaktion Books Ltd., 1999), 46. Originally published as "Die Fabrik," *Vom Stand der Dinge* (Carl Hanser Berlag, 1993).

6. See the concept as described by Thomas J. Friedman, *The World is Flat* (New York: Farrar, Straus and Giroux, 2005).

7. James Petras and Henry Veltmeyer, *Globalization Unmasked: Imperialism in the 21st Century* (New York: Fernwood Publishing, Zed Books, 2001), 43.

8. Saskia Sassen, *The Global City: New York, London, Tokyo* (New York: Princeton University Press, 1991). Sassen defines the Global City and the significance of networks and communications.

9. Jean-Louis Cohen's seminal exhibition and book, *Architecture in Uniform, Designing and Building for the Second World War* (Paris: Editions Hazen, 2011), and *World War II and the American Dream,* ed. Donald Albrecht (Cambridge: MIT Press, 1995), both focus on this topic, which

is critical to the discussion of World War II factories and the architectural issues they expose. Seymour Melman wrote on the subject of the industry of war in *The Permanent War Economy* (New York: Simon & Schuster, 1974).

10. Christina D. Romer, "The Hope that Flows from History," *New York Times*, August 14, 2011.

11. Labor unrest following World War II due to the shift from military to consumer manufacturing is discussed in David F. Noble, *Forces of Production, A Social History of Industrial Automation* (New York: Oxford University Press, 1986), 36–39. His work on this period is one of the most in depth in terms of understanding the workers' role in production and the impact of new technologies.

12. The GDP growth rate was 2.23 percent as of December 31, 1960, according to the U.S. Bureau of Economic Analysis.

13. Jane Jacobs, *The Economy of Cities* (New York: Vintage Books, 1969), 150.

14. Japan's protectionist stance enabled it to build a robust industrial economy with strong exports and relatively little domestic competition from imports. MITI's scope was broad, and added this sort of international trade policy to other areas, including licensing western intellectual property, and setting rules on pollution. MITI's dominance over the Japanese government had been in decline before 1980, which is generally when Western analysts became aware of its existence.

15. Joseph A. Schumpeter, *Capitalism, Socialism and Democracy* (1942; reprint, New York: Harper, 1975), 82.

16. Harvey, *Postmodernity,* 142.

17. Jean-Paul de Gaudemar, "The Mobile Factory," *Zone* 1 / 2 (New York: Urzone, 1986).

18. Harvey, *Postmodernity,* 139–140.

19. The impact of these trade agreements is often not recognized until they are well underway. At that point the most direct response has been through protests at WTO meetings and other global organization gatherings.

20. Harvey, *Postmodernity,* 141.

21. Michael Hardt and Antonio Negri, *Multitude: War and Democracy in the Age of Empire* (New York: Penguin Press, 2004), 112.

22. Castells, *Network Society,* 123.

23. Henri Lefebvre, *The Production of Space,* trans. D. Nicholson-Smith (1974 reprint; Cambridge, Mass.: Blackwell Publishing, 1991).

24. Ibid., 330.

25. Ibid.

26. Lefebvre, *The Production of Space,* 403.

27. See Sassen, *Global City,* 92–125.

28. Hardt and Negri, *Multitude,* 109.

29. Ibid., 113.

30. There are no detailed studies of the impact of the "maker" on today's economy. Something similar to Richard Florida's work on the Creative Class — examining creative workers — would be of value to understand the changing definition of industry and whether or not the maker should be included as manufacturing or as creative work.

31. Matt Richtel, "A Silicon Valley School That Doesn't Compute," *New York Times,* October 22, 2011.

32. Petras and Veltmeyer, *Globalization Unmasked,* 12.

33. Karl Marx, *Capital,* ed. Frederick Engels, trans. Samuel Moore and Edward Aveling (1890; reprint, New York: Random House Modern Library, 1906).

34. Mies van der Rohe and other Modern architects promoted the concept of open, multi-functional space, that was flexible in use and as a tenet of Modernism. Such an approach became a desired spatial organization for all building types. Its profusion eventually became a marketing tool for flexible real estate models, as a kind of generic space that could have a higher value.

CONSUMPTION, MAN, AND MACHINE

1. Those such as Kevin Kelly, Manuel De Landa, Steven Johnson, Chris Anderson, and other technology historians of the twenty-first century have written extensively on the impact of computer technologies on manufacturing and society.

2. For a detailed story of Charles Babbage see: Doron Swade, *The Difference Engine* (London: Penguin Books, 2000).

3. Ben R. Rich and Leo Janos, *Skunk Works: A Personal Memoir of My Years at Lockheed* (Boston: Little, Brown and Company, 1994), 21.

4. Ibid., 73–80. The development and construction of the planes is discussed in the book.

5. Frank Gehry used CATIA for the mass customization of architectural panel systems and building components. There is a broader discussion of the use of these programs and systems within the architectural community. This is not the forum to address the full extent of this discussion but it is pertinent to this argument to note that the design and fabrication technologies of SHoP Architects, Gramazio Kohler, Barkow Leibinger, among others, are influenced by such systems.

6. Nobel, *Production,* 61.

7. See Lewis Mumford, *The Myth of the Machine: The Pentagon of Power,* Vol. II (New York: Harcourt Brace Jovanovich, 1964).

8. Norbert Wiener, "The Machine Age," *New York Times,* May 21, 2013. Wiener's 1949 papers at MIT were reanalyzed in this article.

9. David Bourne, "Who's the Boss? Next-Gen Factory Robots Could Call the Shots," *Scientific American,* May 2013, 40.

10. For a more detailed discussion of the design and originality of the concept for the GM Technical Center see: Reinhold Martin, *The Organization Complex: Architecture, Media, and Corporate Space* (Cambridge, Mass.: MIT Press, 2003), 142.

11. See Nina Rappaport, "Real Time: Implication for Production Spaces" *ACADIA 09: reForm()* (Chicago: Association of Computer Aided Design In Architecture, 2007) 186–193.

12. See concepts discussed in William McDonough and Michael Braungart,

Cradle to Cradle: Remaking the Way We Make Things (New York: North Point Press, 2002).

13. Triple Bottom Line (TBL) is a measure of sustainability that is not only ecological but refers to social, environmental and financial sustainability. TBL was coined in 1994 by John Elkington, in *Cannibals with Forks: Triple Bottom Line of the 21st Century* (Oxford: Capstone Publishing, 1997).

14. A similar system is seen in the VW factory in Dresden decades later.

15. In a September 2013 conversation, Kenneth Frampton shared that in 1973 Romaldo Giurgola invited Pierre Gillenhammer (then the CEO of Volvo) to speak at Columbia University. At the time Giurgola was serving as an architect for Volvo, designing its factory in the U.S. and a headquarters building in Gothenberg. Frampton notes, "I was very impressed by Gillenhammer and his account of the Kalmar method. When I went to London in 1974 to teach for three years at the Royal College of Art, I went to Sweden to study the Kalmar system, which led to my article in *Lotus* 12. Apart from the ingenious, flexible feedback system and the attempt to overcome the nightmare of divided labor, what intrigued me was the whole issue of job enrichment and the role played by the Swedish Trade Unions, in this regard."

16. Ibid.

17. Kenneth Frampton, "Il Caso Volvo," *Lotus International* 12 (1976): 16–41.

18. Alvin Toffler, *The Third Wave* (New York: William Morrow and Company, Inc., 1980), 53–61.

19. Ibid., 286.

20. Ibid., 291.

21. Ibid., 202.

22. The term is derived from a concept Toffler established in 1971. See B. Joseph Pine II and James H. Gilmore, in their book, *Experience Economy, Work is Theater & Every Business is a Stage* (Cambridge, Mass.: Harvard Business Review Press, 2007).

23. Guy Debord, *The Society of the Spectacle* (1967; reprint, New York: Zone Books, 1994).

24. For more information on Benetton's architecture, see: Mirko Zardini, "Benetton," *Lotus International* 85 (1995): 100–121 and "Scarpa: New Benetton Factory," *GA Document* 38 (1994): 61–71.

25. Benetton claimed they didn't produce garments in Bangladesh but the claim was proved false. See Rebecca Smithers, "Benetton Admits Link with Firm in collapsed Bangladesh Building," *The Guardian,* April 29, 2013, www.theguardian.com/world/2013/apr/29/benetton-link-collapsed-building-bangladesh.

26. "Zara's Secret for Fast Fashion," *Harvard Business School Archive,* February 21, 2005, hbswk.hbs.edu/archive/4652.html.

27. Ibid.

28. Ibid.

29. "Fashion Conquistador," *Bloomberg Businessweek,* September 3, 2006, www.businessweek.com/stories/2006-09-03/fashion-conquistador.

30. Naomi Klein, *No Logo* (New York: Picador, 2000), 196.

31. Pan Brothers Tbk, *Global Business Guide Indonesia,* www.gbgindonesia.com/en/manufacturing/directory/pan_brothers_tbk/introduction.php.

32. Kim Yong-Young, "Benetton Takes Stock of Chip Plans," *CNET,* April 7, 2003, news.cnet.com/Benetton-takes-stock-of-chip-plan/2100-1029_3-995744.html.

33. Paul Baran, specifically his research papers of 1964 for the Rand Corporation see: *On Distributed Communications,* United States Air Force, Project RAND (Santa Monica: The RAND Corporation, 1964), http://www.rand.org/pubs/research_memoranda/RM3420.html.

34. E. F. Schumacher, *Small is Beautiful: A Study of Economics as If People Mattered* (London: Blond & Briggs Ltd., 1973). My father introduced Schumacher's work to me, which emphasizes the new direction in economics and appropriate technologies that was not based on mathematical theories, but a more holistic picture of society including Buddhist economics.

35. Luther P. Gerlach and Virginia H. Hine, *People, Power, Change: Movements of Social Transformation* (New York: Bobbs-Merrill, 1970).

36. M. Eugene Merchant, "Flexible Manufacturing Systems: Robotics and Computerized Automation," and Robert J. Miller, "Robotics: Future Factories, Future Workers," in *Annals of the American Academy of Political and Social Science,* 470 (Nov 1983), 123–135.

37. For General information on the MIT Lab see: http://autoid.mit.edu/cs/

38. Randy Durick, "Beyond track-and-trace, using RFID on the factory floor," *Plant Engineering,* February 13, 2013.

39. William J. Mitchell, *City of Bits, Space, Place, and the Infobahn* (Cambridge, Mass.: MIT Press, 1995), 28–44. Mitchell envisioned the potential of miniaturized and ubiquitous electronics and their influence on the physical realm.

40. Kevin Ashton, "That 'Internet of Things' Thing," *RFID Journal,* June 22, 2009, http://www.rfidjournal.com/articles/view?4986.

41. Citizen Watch, *Management Japan* 34 (2002).

42. Charles Duhigg, "How Companies Learn Your Secrets," *New York Times Magazine,* February 16, 2012.

43. A Creative Commons license allows the creator to "retain copyright while allowing others to copy, distribute, and make some uses of their work — non-commercially." See www.creativecommons.org for further information.

44. Chris Anderson, "In the Next Industrial Revolution, Atoms are the New Bits," *Wired,* February 2010, 63.

45. Toffler, *Third Wave,* and *Future Shock* (New York: Random House, 1972) were both standards in my father's library. They introduced me to creative ways of thinking about technology and society.

46. John Naisbitt, *Megatrends: Ten New Directions Transforming Our Lives* (New York: Warner Books, 1982).

47. Alvin Toffler, describes this concept in *Third Wave.*

48. Toffler, *Third Wave,* 210.

49. "Print Me a Stradivarious," *The Economist,* February 10, 2011, 77.

50. Ibid., 79.

51. Chris Anderson, *Makers, The New Industrial Revolution* (New York: Crown Business, 2012), 93. The idea of these machines coming into consumer use rapidly rose from early 2011.

52. Collin Ladd, Ju-Hee So, John Muth, and Michael D. Dickey, "3D Printing of Free Standing Liquid Metal Microstructures" *Advanced Materials* 36 (2013), 25.

53. Larry Greenemeier, "Will 3-D printing transform conventional manufacturing," *Scientific American,* May 2013, 46.

54. Neal Stephenson, *The Diamond Age* (New York: Bantam Books, 1995), 54.

55. Carlos Olguin (of Autodesk) in conversation with the author, December 2013.

56. Phillip K. Dick, "Autofac," *Galaxy Magazine,* November 1955.

57. For example, while buying fabrics in New York, a fashion designer realizes there are more options beyond those available in the showroom. In order to find the right sources the designer attends the Paris Fabric show, making personal contact with the textile companies, which leads to a connection with New York representatives. Without attending the trade fair such connection would have been difficult and access to the product might have been limited.

58. Leo Marx, *The Machine in the Garden: Technology and the Pastoral Ideal in America* (1964; reprint, New York: Oxford University Press, 2000).

59. de Gaudemar, "Mobile Factory," 289.

60. While many contemporary thinkers write about the significance of the city, few have delved into the topic of where work fits into today's social and economic order. Italian Socialist philosophers, such as Antonio Negri, Franco Berardi, and others, have addressed such concerns in their work.

61. Flusser, "The Factory," in *The Status of Things,* 48–50.

INDUSTRIAL URBANISM

1. Russell O. Wright, *A Twentieth-Century History of United States Population* (Lanham, Maryland: Scarecrow Press, 1996).

2. Benton MacKaye, "Industrial Exploration: I. Charting the World's Commodity Flow," *The Nation,* July 20, 1927, 70–74; "Industrial Exploration: II. Charting the World's Requirements," *The Nation,* July 27, 1927, 92–94; "Industrial Exploration: III. Charting the World's Resources," *The Nation,* August 3, 1927, 119–122. See also Keller Easterling, *Organizational Space: Landscapes, Highways, and Houses in America* (Cambridge: MIT Press, 1999), 13–71.

3. MacKaye, "Charting the World's Commodity Flow," 92.

4. David Harvey, *The Condition of Postmodernity: An Enquiry into the Origins of Cultural Change* (Cambridge, Mass.: Blackwell Publishing, 1990), 124.

5. See Michael L. Blim, "Small-Scale Industrialization in a Rapidly Changing World Market," in Frances Amrahamer Rothstein and Michael L. Blim, ed., *Anthropology and the Global Factory* (New York: Bergin & Garvey, 1992), 85–101.

6. Ibid.

7. Ibid., 88.

8. Paul Krugman, *Development, Geography, and Economic Theory* (Cambridge: MIT Press, 1995).

9. As discussed in *Principles of Economics* (1980), Alfred Marshall's idea of "something in the air" became a legitimate way for industries to organically choose locations and interact with each other.

10. Jane Jacobs, *The Economy of Cities* (New York: Vintage Books, 1969), 58.

11. Harvey S. Perloff and Lowdon Wingo, eds., *Issues in Urban Economics* (Baltimore: Johns Hopkins Press, 1968.)

12. Jacobs, *Economy,* 62.

13. See Howard P. Segal, *Recasting the Machine Age: Henry Ford's Village Industries* (Amherst: University of Massachusetts Press, 2005).

14. Kenneth Frampton, "Il Caso Volvo," *Lotus International* 12 (1976): 37.

15. Ibid.

16. Manuel Castells, *The Rise of the Network Society: The Information Age: Economy, Society, and Culture,* 2nd ed., (Oxford: Blackwell Publishing, 2000), 418.

17. Ibid., 442.

18. See the idea of drosscape further explained in Alan Berger, *Drosscape: Wasting Land in Urban America* (New York: Princeton Architectural Press, 2006).

19. Keller Easterling, *Enduring Innocence: Global Architecture and its Political Masquerades* (Cambridge: MIT Press, 2005), 99.

20. The history of the impact on containers is described in the authoritative book: Brian Cudahy, *Box Boats: How Container Ships Changed the World* (New York: Fordham University Press, 2006).

21. The non-hierarchical workplace grounds workplace democracy for cooperative and worker owned businesses. This model now has its own organizational umbrellas such as workplacedemocracy.com.

22. Waldeck Rochet, General Secretary of the Party Communist France, as quoted by, Andre Hoyles in "General Strike: France 1968, A Factory by Factory Account" http://www.prole.info/texts/generalstrike1968.html, accessed on February 12, 2015.

23. Alias Recluse, "Part 3. Grenelle," *libcom.org,* January 12, 2013, http://libcom.org/library/french-strikes-may-june-1968-part-3-grenelle-bruno-astarian, accessed on February 12, 2015.

24. See writings by Mario Tronti such as *Operai e Capitale* (Torino: Einaudi, 1966) and of Antonio Negri such as *Marx Beyond Marx, Lessons on the Grundrisse* (London: Pluto Press, 1992.)

25. Franco "Bifo" Berardi, (trans. Francesca Cadel and Giusseppina Mecchia, in *The Soul at Work,* (Los Angeles: Semiotext (e), 2009) describes the estrangement and alienation and refusal of work.

26. Charles Guerra, "N for Negri: a conversation with Toni Negri," *Grey Room* 11 (2003): 86–109.

27. Mario Tronti, "La Fabbrica el la Società," *Quaderni Rossi* 2 (1972): 1–32. Tronti emphasized that, "At the highest level of capitalist development social relations become moments of the relations of production, and the whole society becomes an articulation of production. In short, all of society lives as a function of the factory and the factory extends its exclusive domination over all of society."

28. Pier Vittorio Aureli, *The Project of Autonomy: Politics and Architecture Within and Against Capitalism* (New York: Temple Hoyne Buell Center, Columbia University and New York: Princeton Architectural Press, 2008), 69.

29. Michael Hardt, "Introduction: Laboratory Italy," *Radical Thought in Italy: A Potential Politics,* ed. Paolo Virno and Michael Hardt (Minneapolis, University of Minnesota Press, 1996), 1–9.

30. Andrea Branzi, "Introduction: Afternoons at the Factory," *Learning from Milan: Design and the Second Modernity* (Cambridge, Mass: MIT Press, 1988), 10.

31. During my research I identified gaps in discussions of urban design and industrial space. Percival and Paul Goodman, were some of the few who looked at this issue in much detail and published their concepts in *Communitas,* (1947; reprint, New York: Columbia University Press, Morningside Edition, 1960).

32. Paul Goodman, an academic and social critic is author of the book, *Growing Up Absurd,* (New York: Random House, 1960). Percival Goodman, professor at Columbia University School of Architecture, was an architect who designed numerous synagogues in the New York City region.

33. Percival and Paul Goodman, *Communitas,* 82.

34. Ibid., 83.

35. Ibid.

36. Ibid.,160.

37. This concept also relates to ideas of industrial symbiosis as discussed in the Factory Futures chapter of this book.

38. Cedric Price, with Reyner Banham and Peter Hall, "Non-Plan, an Experiment in Freedom," *Architectural Design* 39 (May 1969): 269–73.

39. Ibid.

40. Ibid., 269.

41. See Johan Huizinga, *Homo Ludens* (1938; reprint, London: Routledge & Kegan Paul, 1948).

42. Constant Nieuwenhuys, *New Babylon,* was exhibited at the Municipal Museum of The Hague, 1974. See also Mark Wigley, *Constant's New Babylon: The Hyper-Architecture of Desire* (Rotterdam: 010 Publishers, 1998).

43. Constant Nieuwenhuys, "Unitary Urbanism," (lecture, Stedelijk

Museum, Amsterdam, December 20, 1960). Translated by Robyn de Jong Dalziel cited in Mark Wigley, *Constant's New Babylon*, 133.

44. Jenny Chan and Ngai Pun, "Suicide as Protest for the New Generation of Chinese Migrant Workers: Foxconn, Global Capital, and the State," *The Asia-Pacific Journal* (2010), www.japanfocus.com/-Ngai-Pun/3408.

45. Richard Locke and Monica Romis, "The Promise and Perils of Private Voluntary Regulation: Labor Standards and Work Organization in Two Mexican Garment Factories," *Review of International Political Economy* 17, no. 1 (2010): 45–74.

46. Karen Cook, "Scenario for a New Age," *New York Times Magazine*, September 25, 1988, 26.

47. See "Governance" *Mondragon Corporation*, accessed February 12, 2015, http://www.mondragon-corporation.com/eng/about-us/governance/ for an explanation of the ownership structure and company subsidiaries in Spain.

48. Geminijen, "Anti-Capitalist Meetup: Fagor Goes Bankrupt — Trouble in Camelot." *Daily Kos.* January 12, 2014. www.dailykos.com/story/2014/01/12/1268841/-Anti-Capitalist-Meetup-Fagor-Goes-Bankrupt-Trouble-in-Camelot#.

49. John Daly, "Bill for Cleaning China's Air Pollution." December 24, 2013. www.oilprice.com.

50. Michael Mandelbaum, *The Ideas that Conquered the World* (New York: Public Affairs, Perseus Book Group, 2002).

51. Theodore Levitt (1925–2006) popularized the term *globalization* and also used the term the *flat earth* in reference to *globalization*. See Theodore Levitt, "Globalization of Markets," *Harvard Business Review* (May/June 1983), 2–102. https://hbr.org/1983/05/the-globalization-of-markets/ar/1. While the idea had been current since World War II, it had not been incorporated into the economic discourse.

52. The Agreement on Textiles and Clothing (ATC) set quotas on the trade of textiles as part of the Multifibre Arrangement (MFA) set by the World Trade Organization, from 1974 to 2005. See "Agreement on Textiles and Clothing," *World Trade Organization*, www.wto.org/english/docs_e/legal_e/16-tex_e.htm. The quotas were stopped after 2005.

53. Joseph E. Stiglitz, *Globalization and its Discontents* (New York: W.W. Norton & Co., 2002), 9.

54. See James Petras and Henry Veltmeyer, *Globalization Unmasked: Imperialism in the 21st Century* (New York: Fernwood Publishing, Zed Books, 2001).

55. Ibid., 11–25.

56. Ibid., 29.

57. Thomas L. Friedman and Michael Mandelbaum, *That Used To Be Us* (New York: Farrar, Straus and Giroux, 2011) 54, 198. They discuss challenges of globalization.

58. Petras, and Veltmeyer, *Globalization Unmasked*, 66.

59. Joseph E. Stiglitz, *Discontents*, 22.

60. See the analysis of the idea of "spectacle" in Guy Debord, *The Society of the Spectacle* (New York: Zone Books, 1995).

61. Isabel Hilton, "Made in China," *Granta: The Factory* 89 (Spring 2005): 47.

62. Jean-Paul de Gaudemar, "The Mobile Factory," *Zone* 1 / 2 (New York: Urzone, 1986), 285.

63. When the factory is only a shed, the place of production is beyond that of the brand and not considered a part of the company. This is also an issue that Naomi Klein recognizes.

64. Keller Easterling, "Zone: The Spatial Software of Extrastatecraft," *Design Observer Places*, June 11, 2012, https://placesjournal.org/article/zone-the-spatial-softwares-of-extrastatecraft/. See also: Keller Easterling, *Extrastatecraft: The Power of Infrastructure Space* (London: Verso, 2014).

65. Petras, and Veltmeyer, *Globalization Unmasked*, 71.

66. Naomi Klein, *No Logo* (New York: Picador, 2000), 205.

67. Hernán Rozemberg, "Border Business: Mexico Maquiladoras Strong In Tough Economy," *Fronteras*, September 27, 2011, www.fronterasdesk.org/content/border-business-mexicos-maquiladoras-strong-tough-economy.

68. Mandelbaum, *Ideas*, 398.

69. "Metales y Derivados," Final Factual Record (SEM-98-007), *Commission for Environmental Cooperation*, October 23, 1998.

70. Regina M.A.A. Galhardi, "Maquiladoras prospects of regional integration and globalization," International Labour Office, International Migration in its series papers, March 1, 1988.

71. Altha J. Cravey, *Women and Work in Mexico's Maquiladoras* (Lanham, Maryland: Rowman & Littlefield Publishers, Inc., 1998), 2.

72. Discussed both by Naomi Klein, in *No Logo*, and by Altha J. Cravey, in *Women and Work in Mexico's Maquiladoras*.

73. Cravey, *Women and Work*, 5.

74. de Gaudemar, "The Mobile Factory," 290.

75. Raffaele Pernice, "Japanese Urban Artificial Islands: An Overview of Projects and Schemes for Marine Cities during 1960s–1990s," *Journal of Architecture and Planning (Transactions of AIJ - Architectural Institute of Japan)* 642 (August 2009), 253–260.

76. Castells, *Network Society*, 170.

77. Christopher Romig Keener, "Grassroots industry in the town of Sakaki: and alternative perspective of the Japanese post-war 'miracle,'" (PhD Diss., University of California, 1992), http://www.sakaki.com/duck/thesis/intro.html.

78. Ibid.

79. For further information see: Seung H-Sang, ed., *Paju Book City Culturescape* (Seoul: Kimoondang Publishing, 2010); Edwin Heathcote, "A City Dedicated to Books and Print," *Financial Times*, August 21, 2009.

80. Choe Sang-Hun, "North Korea Halts Work at Shared Factory Site," *New York Times*, April 9, 2013.

81. For additional information see David Bray, *Social Space and Governance in Urban China: The Danwei System from Origins to Reform* (Stanford, California: Stanford University Press, 2005).

82. David Bray, "The Danwei Socialist Factory Town in Miniature," In *Factory Towns in South China* ed. Stefan Al, (Hong Kong: Hong Kong University Press, 2012), 8.

83. Ibid.

84. Claudia Juhre, "The Side Effects of Unregulated Growth," *Factory Towns in South China*, ed. Stefan Al, (Hong Kong: Hong Kong University Press, 2012), 13.

85. Ibid.

86. Rem Koolhaas et al., *Project on the City I: Great Leap Forward*, Harvard Graduate School of Design (Cologne: Taschen, 2002), 125.

87. Castells, *Network Society*, 439.

88. Andrew Ross, *Fast Boat to China* (New York: Vintage Books, 2006), 4.

89. Ibid.

90. Among the special economic zones in China are the cities, Shenzhen, Zhuhai, Shantou, Xiamen, and Kashgar.

91. David Barboza, "In Roaring China, Sweaters are West of Socks City," *New York Times*, December 24, 2004.

92. *Reshaping Economic Geography*, International Bank for Reconstruction and Development (The World Bank: Washington, D.C., 2009), 155.

93. Leslie Chang, *Factory Girls: From Village to City in a Changing China* (New York: Spiegel & Grau, 2009), 48.

94. Hilton, "Made in China," 54.

95. Ibid., 43–45.

96. Paul Midler, *Poorly Made in China* (Hoboken, New Jersey: John Wiley & Sons, 2009).

97. David Barboza, "From Low Cost to High Value," *New York Times*, September 16, 2010.

98. Chang, *Factory Girls*, 105.

99. "China Makes Ipads. So why does it still cut corners for its own consumers?" *Time Magazine*, March 23, 2012.

100. Ross, *Fast Boat*, 5.

101. Ross discusses Suzhou in detail from months of research there. See Ross, *Fast Boat*, 165–179.

102. See Jim Keady, *Behind the Swoosh*, (2009), film.

103. Jeff Ballinger's August 1992 articles in *Harper's Magazine* in addition to the work of Press for Change brought attention to the issue of low pay by Nike.

104. Chi-Chi Zhang, "Apple manufacturing plant workers complain of long hours, militant culture," *CNN News Report*, February 6, 2012, www.cnn.com/2012/02/06/world/asia/china-apple-foxconn-worker/.

105. Michael Martina, "China's dorm room discontent emerges as new labor flashpoint," *Reuters*, September 27, 2012, www.reuters.com/article/2012/09/27/us-china-foxconn-idUSBRE88Q1QS20120927.

106. Jenny Chan, "A Suicide Survivor: the life of a Chinese worker," *New Technology Work and Employment* 28, no. 2 (July 2013): 84–99.

107. Aditya Chakrabortty, "The woman who nearly died making your iPad," *The Guardian*, August 5, 2013, www.theguardian.com/commentisfree/2013/aug/05/woman-nearly-died-making-ipad.

108. Zhang, *CNN News Report*.

109. David Barboza, "Explosion at Apple Supplier Caused by Dust, China Says," *New York Times*, May 24, 2011.

110. Charles Dhung and David Barboza, "In China, Human costs are built into an iPad," *New York Times*, January 25–26, 2012.

111. Some of the groups post information on the audits of Foxconn to their Web sites, including "Fair Labor Association," *Foxconn Investigation Report*, March 29, 2012 and "Children working at Apple's Suppliers," *International Labour Organization*, January 25, 2013.

112. Midler, *Poorly Made in China*, 198.

113. Ibid., 62.

114. Chang, *Factory Girls*, 101.

115. Andrea Claster (former manufacturer), in discussion with author, July 2013.

116. Michael Schuman, "China Makes Everything Why Can't it Create Anything?" *Time Magazine*, November 18, 2013.

117. An expanded discussion was published in my essay, Nina Rappaport, "Manila," In "Re_Urbanism: Transforming Capitals," *Perspecta 39* (Yale School of Architecture, Cambridge: MIT Press, 2007): 114–120.

118. Easterling, *Enduring Innocence*, 117.

119. *Business Times*, Singapore, November 10, 2006.

120. "Is the Wakening Giant a Monster," *The Economist*, February 13, 2003.

121. See Web site of the *Philippine Economic Zone Authority*: www.peza.gov.ph.

122. This is similar to Richard Sennett's discussion in *The Corrosion of Character* (New York: W.W. Norton & Company, 1998), concerning commitment to regions.

123. Rosa Luxemburg, "The Mass Strike, The Political Party and the trade Unions," originally published as, "Massenstreik, Partei und Gewerkschaften" (Hamburg: 1906) as cited in J.P. Netti, *Rosa Luxemburg*, Vol. 2 (London: Oxford University Press, 1966), 500.

124. *News of the Committee Affairs Department*, 14: 9, September 6, 2006, and *Asian Human Rights Commission*, October 18, 2005.

125. Klein, *No Logo*, 208.

126. International Labor Rights Forum, "Walmart's Supplier in Cavite to Go on Strike, calls for Boycott," August 23, 2006, www.laborrights.org/in-the-news/wal-marts-supplier-cavite-go-strike-calls-boycott-0.

127. See Maher Sattar, "The Mysterious Murder of a Bangladeshi Labor Activist" *Worked Over: The Global Decline of Labor Rights*, Global Post, May 14, 2012, www.globalpost.com/dispatch/news/regions/asia-pacific/120513/murder-bangladesh-labor-activist-garment-workers.

128. Sarah Krasley of Autodesk worked with non-profit labor groups and workers to develop these types of programs in 2013. See Labor Voices, http://www.laborvoices.com/#about.

129. Jim Yardley, "First companies Give to Fund for Victims of Bangladeshi Factory Collapse," *New York Times*, February 23, 2014.

130. The study initiated by the exhibition *Shrinking Cities*, curated by Philipp Oswalt, Leipzig Gallery of Contemporary Art, Berlin, (2005) contained analysis of numerous cities, including Detroit, Manchester/Liverpool, and Halle/Leipzig. See www.shrinkingcities.com.

131. Boston Consulting Group, "Majority of Large Manufacturers Are Now Planning or Considering 'Reshoring' from China to the U.S.," press release, September 24, 2013.

132. Definition of industry is further discussed as a significant need in understanding urban economics as discussed by Laura Wolf-Powers, "Up-Zoning in New York City's Mixed-Use Neighborhoods," *Journal of Planning Education and Research* 24, no. 4 (June 2005): 379–393.

133. William Morrish in discussion with the author, 2014.

134. For the recent U.S. government initiative, see: National Institute of Standards and Technology, Advanced Manufacturing Portal, www.manufacturing.gov.

135. Robert Neuwirth, *Stealth of Nations* (New York: Random House, 2011).

136. "GDP," *World Bank*, 2013, accessed January 26, 2015, http://data.worldbank.org.

137. The first Hôtels Industriels that attracted my attention was Dominique Perrault's in 1991. The first publication in English on the Paris program was by John Loomis, "Hôtels Industriels," *Places Design Observer*, July 1995. On site research updated in spring 2014 and by Dieter Leyssen in 2013.

138. City of Paris, "Only a Place for Enterprise?" November 30, 2014, http://www.paris.fr/pro/2d3es-hebergement-d-entreprises/poles-d-entreprises/rub_9529_stand_22927_port_23414.

139. Marc Letrilliart (City of Paris, Economic Development Division), in conversation with the author, Spring 2014.

140. David Jolly, "France and Germany Lead Eurozone to Higher Growth," *New York Times*, February 14, 2014.

141. Dorothy Elkins, T. H. Elkins and B. Hofmeister, *Berlin: The Spatial Structure of a Divided City* (New York: Methuen and Co., 1988), 126.

142. "Washing Machine Factory in Berlin Closing Down," *Wildcat* 74 (Summer 2005), accessed January 8, 2010, https://libcom.org/history/washing-machines-factory-berlin-closing-down-2005.

143. Berlin planning regulations see www.stadtentwicklung.berlin.de/planen/planung/

144. For a full overview of the project see, *Redesigning the Urban Factory, Berlinmodell Industriekultur: Entwürfe für die Stadtische Arbeitswelt*, ed. Nikolaus Kuhnert, Volker Martin, Karl Pachter and Heirich Suhr (Berlin: Birkhauser, 1989).

145. Ibid.

146. Ibid., 8.

147. Ibid.

148. Bavarian Ministry of Economic Affairs and Media, Energy and Technology, *Bavaria's Industry Cluster Initiative*, www.bavaria.org/industry_clusters.php.

149. Christian Thalgott, "Urban Planning for Industrial Buildings," *Industrial Buildings* (Berlin: Birkhauser, 2004), 20.

150. "Der Mythos der Deindustrialisierung," *Neue Zürcher Zeitung*, July 27, 2012, http://www.nzz.ch/aktuell/wirtschaft/wirtschaftsnachrichten/industriemacht-schweiz-1.17410744.

151. Nina Rappaport, "Sulzer Areal Winterthur," *IndustrieBau* (May 1993): 336–339.

152. William C. Taylor, "Message and Muscle: An Interview with Swatch Titan Nicolas Hayek," *Harvard Business Review* (March 1993), hbr.org/1993/03/message-and-muscle-an-interview-with-swatch-titan-nicolas-hayek/ar/1.

153. See: Nick Bunkley, "G.M. Again Pauses Production of Chevy Volt," *New York Times*, March 12, 2012, Business Day, http://www.nytimes.com/2012/03/03/business/gm-suspends-production-of-chevrolet-volt.html; and General Motors, "U.S. Car and Truck Production," *General Motors*, April 2013, http://media.gm.com/content/dam/Media/gmcom/investor/2013/2013-April-Sales/GMNA-Production-by-Plant-April-2013.pdf.

154. Oswald, *Shrinking Cities*.

155. Jeff Green and Mark Clothier, "U.S. Automakers Thrive as Detroit Goes Bankrupt," *Bloomberg News*, July 19, 2013, http://www.bloomberg.com/news/2013-07-19/u-s-automakers-thrive-as-detroit-goes-bankrupt.html.

156. Detroit Regional Chamber, *Michigan is Auto* (report of Michigan Economic Development Corporation: September, 2014).

157. Crain's Detroit Business, Crain's List: Largest Metro Detroit Employers, survey: 2012, http://www.crainsdetroit.com/assets/PDF/CD83811119.PDF.

158. See: Detroit Future City, www.detroitfuturecity.com.

159. Chad Halcom, "Detroit's first class of 10,000 Small Businesses Program Taking Shape," *Crain's Detroit Business*, February 28, 2014, http://www.crainsdetroit.com/article/20140228/NEWS/140229851/detroits-first-class-of-10-000-small-businesses-program-taking-shape.

160. New Economy Initiative, Grantees, http://neweconomyinitiative.org/grants/grantees/, and http://kresge.org/programs/detroit/entrepreneurial-development-growing-small-business

161. John Gallaher, *Reimagining Detroit* (Detroit: Wayne State University Press, 2010).Gallaher makes a case for new kinds of entrepreneurial production and urban farming for the city.

162. Moses King, *King's Handbook of New York City 1893* (1893 reprint; Benjamin Blom Inc., 1972).

163. Historians and economists have often observed this phenomenon of proximity in industrial enterprise growth from Kropotkin to Jacobs, Mumford to Krugman. See also: Manuel De Landa, *A Thousand Years of Nonlinear History* (New York: Zone Books, 1997).

164. Jane Jacobs wrote articles for *Vogue* magazine in 1937 on the Flower District, Diamond District, and Fur Districts of New York, emphasizing their vibrancy.

165. Max Hall, *Made in New York* (Cambridge: Harvard University Press, 1959).

166. Juliana Maantay, "Industrial Zoning Changes in New York City of Expulsive Zoning," *Projections* 3, MIT *Journal of Planning* (2002): 63–108.

167. US Bureau of Labor Statistics, 2012, *Spotlight on Statistics: Fashion*.

168. Jay Mazur in discussion with the author, 2014.

169. In Chester Rapkin's study, also called the "South Houston Industrial Area," *New York City Department of City Planning* (1962), the term "SoHo," for the area south of Houston Street originated. Rapkin promoted the idea of saving the district because of its small-scale industrial use.

170. New York City Department of City Planning, "New Opportunities for a Changing Economy," *Citywide Industry Study*, January 1993.

171. As Adam Friedman, executive director of the Pratt Center for Community Development, emphasized in discussion with the author in 2014, "stable affordable space for production is critical to job creation. If a neighborhood looks likes its gentrifying, then a manufacturer will be deterred from investing, from building relationships into the local community and maybe even recruiting workers. It starts a downward spiral of disinvestment."

172. Chicago Department of Housing and Economic Development, "Resources, Citywide Maps and Zoning Matrix," *Chicago Sustainable Industries: A Manufacturing Work Plan for the 21st Century* (November 2013), www.cityofchicago.org/dam/city/depts/zlup/Sustainable_Development/Publications/Chicago_Sustainable_Industries/CSI_3.pdf. On IBZ's in New York see Mayor Michael R. Bloomberg Introduces New Initiatives to Support New York City's Industrial Sector, NYC Small Business Services, press release, January 19, 2005, www.nyc.gov.

173. Wolf-Powers, "Up-Zoning."

174. New York State Department of Labor U.S. Bureau of Labor Statistics, accessed February 10, 2015, www.bls.gov.

175. "The Perfect Setting: Economic Impact of the Diamond and Jewelry Industry in New York City" (Pratt Center for Community Development, January 2009), 4.

176. Ibid., 12.

177. Ibid.

178. Rapaport Diamond Price List is the primary source for diamond pricing throughout the world. See: www.diamonds.net

179. Gem Institute, see: www.gia.edu and the Platinum Institute, see: www.plantinuminstitutellc.com.

180. See the information Zoning Districts: Special Districts, New York City Department of City Planning, www.nyc.gov/html/dcp/html/zone/zh_special_purp_mn.shtml

181. From discussions between author and GIDC staff in 2011.

182. Ibid.

183. Deborah Brand (of M&S Schmalberg custom fabric flowers) in conversation with the author in 2011.

184. Francoise Olivas, in discussion with the author in 2011.

185. Ibid.

186. See *Making Midtown, A New Vision for a 21st Century Garment District in New York City*, Design Trust for Public Space (2012), and *Fashioning a Future: NYC Garment District*, Municipal Art Society, 2010 www.mas.org/urbanplanning/garment-district.

187. Roberta Brandes Gratz, *The Battle for Gotham: New York in the Shadow of Robert Moses and Jane Jacobs* (New York: Nation Books, 2010), 179. Gratz writes first-hand as a manufacturer and urban advocate with an intimate understanding of the significance of industrial communities to urban strength.

188. Queens West, sponsored by the NY Empire State Development Corporation and the City Economic Development Corporation along with the Port Authority of NY and NJ developed a project for 30 hectares along the waterfront in 1992. The three buildings began construction in 2005 and additional projects will be completed in 2015 as moderate income housing with a waterfront park. This signals a change from the former industrial waterfront into residential and recreational uses.

189. See Nina Rappaport, Colin Cathcart, and David Reinfurt, *Long Island City: Connecting the Arts* (Rotterdam: Episode Books and New York: Design Trust for Public Space, 2006).

190. Collected for the exhibit "Made in Long Island City," with Syracuse School of Architecture students in NYC. Students conducted research from 2012 to 2013, on industries in Long Island City. As part of *Future Cities Lab*, the work was exhibited at the *Aedes Gallery* in Berlin, June 2012, and at *No Longer Empty's* exhibition "What Do I Owe You?," from January to March, 2013 at Queens Plaza, Long Island City, New York.

191. Seth Bornstein in conversation with the author in 2012.

192. Thornton McEnery, "NYC Manufacturing No Longer Bleeding Jobs," *Crain's New York Business*, March 26, 2014, http://www.crainsnewyork.com/article/20140326/ECONOMY/140329904/nyc-manufacturing-no-longer-bleeding-jobs.

193. This includes efforts such as Made in New York, supported by the Pratt Center for Community Development, the city's Made in NY for the film, media, and tech industries. Another organization, Industrial and Technology Assistance (ITAC), assists manufacturers with financing and logistics within the city.

194. Gratz, *Battle for Gotham*, 181.

195. Tara Vinodrai, "A Tale of three Cities: The Dynamics of Manufacturing in Toronto, Montreal and Vancouver, 1976–1997," *Statistics Canada* 177 (November, 2001).

196. Thanks to Shauna Brail from University of Toronto for her input.

197. Richard Shearmur and William J. Coffey, "A Tale of Four Cities: Intrametropolitan employment distribution in Toronto, Montreal, Vancouver, and Ottawa-Hull, 1981–1996," *Environment and Planning A* 34 (2002): 575–598.

198. Ibid., 590.

199. Matthas Oschinski and Katherine Chan, "Ontario Made," *Mowat Centre* (University of Toronto, School of Public Policy & Governance, 2014).

200. Mike Williams, director of Toronto Economic Development Corporation, in discussion with the author, March 2014.

201. City of Toronto, Zoning Bylaw can be found here: www.toronto.ca/legdocs/bylaws/2010/

202. Williams in discussion with the author, March 2014.

203. Oschinski and Chan, "Ontario Made."

204. The organization started in 2011. See www.sme-tba.org.

205 Mike Williams in discussion with the author, March 2014.

CONTEMPORARY FACTORY ARCHITECTURE

1. Adolf Behne, *The Modern Functional Building*, trans. Michael Robinson (Santa Monica: The Getty Research Institute, 1996), 103. Originally published as *Der Moderne Zweckbau, Die Baukunst*, ed. Dagobert Frey (Munich: Drei Masken Verlag, 1926). Behne discusses the dynamic of function and form using the examples of Finsterlein, Gropius, and Mendelsohn.

2. Charles Jencks in *The Language of Post-Modern Architecture* (New York: Rizzoli, 1977) succinctly defines High Tech architecture while trying to not formulate it as a style; it becomes that of a time and historical perspective.

3. Nikolaus Kuhnert, Volker Martin, and Heinrich Suhr, eds., *Redesigning the Urban Factory* (Basel: Birkhäuser Verlag, 1989), 62–64.

4. Beginning with the Yale Art Gallery (1951–53), Louis I. Kahn separates the functions of the servant and the served spaces, which he continued throughout many projects.

5. Interview with Richard Rogers in "Encouraging Quality" with Nikolaus Kuhnert, *Redesigning the Urban Factory*, 64.

6. Daralice D. Boles, "Rogers' U.S. Debut," *Progressive Architecture* (August 1985): 70–74.

7. Alex Gordon and John Weeks developed the idea of "long life, loose fit, low energy." See, Alex Gordon, "Architects and Resource Conservation," *RIBA Journal*, (January 1974): 9–12; and William Fawcett, "The Sustainable Schedule of Hospital Spaces: investigating the 'duffle coat' theory of flexibility," S. Th. Rassia and P. M. Pardalos, eds., *Sustainable Environmental Design in Architecture: Impacts on Health* (Springer

Optimization and its Applications 56, Springer Science + Business Media, 2011).

8. See Maria Stubbe, "Talk that works: evaluating communication in factory production," *New Zealand English Journal* 14 (January, 2000): 55–65.

9. Antonio Negri began to call the city the factory as a way to identify that the capitalist oriented society was focused on production.

10. Guy Debord, *The Society of the Spectacle* (New York: Zone Books, 1995), 29.

11. This section is based on Nina Rappaport, "Consumption of Production," *Architecture After Capitalism, Praxis* 5 (Summer 2003): 58–65.

12. As discussed in terms of how the new capitalism impacts integrity of personal satisfaction in the work place in Richard Sennett, *The Corrosion of Character* (New York: W.W. Norton & Company, 1998).

13. William H. Whyte, Jr., *The Organization Man* (Garden City, New York: Doubleday & Company, 1956). Whyte popularized the idea of the employee gaining a sense of security within the corporate structure.

14. Naomi Klein, *No Logo* (New York: Picador, 2002), 5.

15. Mark Dery, "The Persistence of Industrial Memory," In *Eco-Tec,* ed. Amerigo Marras (New York: Princeton Architectural Press, 1999), 50–67.

16. Pierre Auberjonois (marketing consultant) in conversation with the author in Geneva, Switzerland, fall 2013.

17. Gunter Henn, interviewed by the author in Dresden, Germany, April 2002.

18. See Nina Rappaport "Flexible," *Industriebau*, March 1995.

19. See Mirko Zardini, "Benetton," *Lotus International* 85 (1995): 100–121, and "Scarpa: New Benetton Factory," *GA Document*, n. 38 (1994): 61–71.

20. Robert Venturi, Denise Scott Brown, and Steven Izenour, "Ugly and Ordinary Architecture, or the Decorated Shed," *Learning from Las Vegas*, (1977; reprint, Cambridge, Mass.: The MIT Press, 2001), 88–93.

21. Rolf Felhbaum at the opening of the Birsfelden building in 1994 as quoted in Nina Rappaport, "The New Vitra," *Industriebau*, July 1994.

22. Peeter Degen, Ulrike Zophoniasson, eds., *Stadt und Industrikultur, Industrie und Stadkultur, International Workshop Vitra, April 1991* (Basel: Birkhauser, 1992).

23. Ibid.

24. "Watching the Cars Roll By," *Newsweek*, February 17, 2002.

25. See Rappaport, "The Consumption of Production."

26. Gunter Henn, "Visuelle Systemdenken fur Kommunikationsarchikturen," Degenhard Sommer ed., *Industriebau Radikale Umstrukturierung Praxisreport*, (Basel: Birkhauser, 1995), 106.

27. Andreas Ruby, "Die Verglasung des Stadtraumes Volkswagens 'Gläserne Manufaktur,'" *Daedalos* 72 (1999): 76–85.

28. Gunter Henn (architect) in conversation with the author in 2002.

29. Ibid.

30. David Thurm in conversation with the author. See also: Nina Rappaport, "Two New York Factories," *Metropolis Magazine*, April 1998 and Nina Rappaport, "Polshek & Partners for the New York Times," *Industribau*, September 1997.

31. Ibid.

32. Discussion between Richard Olcott and author see: "Two New York Factories," *Metropolis.*

33. David Thurm in conversation with the author.

34. Ibid.

35. Ibid.

36. Sebastian Knorr in conversation with the author, 2012.

37. Sanki Choe in discussion with author, 2014.

38. Margaret Chin, author of *Sewing Women* (New York: Columbia University Press, 2005), in conversation with author, 2014.

39. See Joan Fitzgerald, *Emerald Cities, Urban Sustainability and Economic Development* (Oxford: Oxford University Press, 2010), 11–18.

40. While the UNFCCC continues to meet annually, a significant multinational agreement has yet to be established.

41. Robert A. Frosch, and Nicholas E. Gallopoulos, "Strategies for Manufacturing," *Scientific American,* 1989. This article discusses major new revelations about closed-loop manufacturing systems and is where they use the term industrial ecology..

42. See white paper: Harold Tibbs, *Industrial Ecology.* Arthur D. Little, 1991.

43. Nina Rappaport, "Apple's E-Waste," *Clog: Apple*, New York, 2012.

44. William McDonough and Michael Braungart, *Cradle to Cradle: Remaking the Way We Make Things* (New York: North Point Press, 2002). And for further discussion of German car recycling see N. Kanari, J. L. Pineau, and S. Shallari, "End-of-Life Vehicle Recycling in the European Union," *JOM* (August 2003), http://www.tms.org/pubs/journals/jom/0308/kanari-0308.html.

45. Kevin Kelly, *Out of Control: the new biology of machines, social systems and the economic world* (New York: Perseus Books, 1994), 177.

46. Nina Rappaport, "Pig City," *Wall Street Journal*, May 18–19, 2001.

47. For more information, see Dickson Despommier, *The Vertical Farm* (New York: St. Martin's Press, 2010).

48. Kelly, *Out of Control*, 69–90.

49. See Ingeborg Flagge, Verena Herzog-Loibl, and Anna Meseure, *Thomas Herzog: Architecture + Technology* (Munich: Prestel, 2001).

50. Maya Lin, foreword to *Bronx Ecology*, by Allen Hershkowitz (Washington: Island Press, 2002), xi. And see Nina Rappaport, "Bronx Paper Recycling Plant," *Oculus,* February 1998.

51. The building, MAS Intimates Thurulie, received a Holcim Award. See Holcim Foundation for Sustainable Construction, *Construction*

Examples (Zurich, Switzerland, 2009).

52. Nanhai National Eco-Industrial Demonstration Park is one among many new parks.

53. Besides the Danish Symbiosis organization, other academic institutions and businesses are also focusing on the topic. In 1998, Yale founded the division Industrial Ecology at the Yale School of Forestry & Environmental Studies and publishes the *Journal of Industrial Ecology*. The National Institute of Industrial Symbiosis in the United Kingdom is working on ways to network and connect companies to each other.

54. Robert A. Frosch, and Nicholas E. Gallopoulos, "Strategies for Manufacturing," *Scientific American* 261 (September 1989): 144–152.

55. Web site: www.symbiosis.dk has updated information on the exchanges between the companies and their materials.

56. The circular economy is an idea in which both biological networks and technological ones are reused and recycled.

57. Environmental scientist Ariana Bain studied relationships in India and found that the personal were more important than the material.

58. For in depth information on the Navy Yard see BLDG 92, for a permanent exhibition on its history, organized by Daniela Romano in 2011.

59. Andrew Kimball in discussion with the author, 2014.

60. Colin Spoelman in discussion with the author, 2013. For more information on the distillery see: Colin Spoelman and David Haskil, *Guide to Urban Moonshining* (New York: Abrams, 2013).

61. Ibid.

62. Iñaki Abalos in discussion with the author, 2011.

63. See also Valdemingomez, *Quaderns*, 2001, 152–163

64. Iñaki Abalos in discussion with the author, 2014.

65. See Michael Piore, and Charles Sabel, *The Second Industrial Divide: Possibilities For Prosperity* (New York: Basic Books, 1984).

66. Discussion between the author and Gunter Blase published in the article, "Flexible," *Industriebau,* March 1995.

67. Alvin Toffler, *The Third Wave* (New York: William Morrow and Company, Inc., 1980), 210.

68. Carol Berens, *Redeveloping Industrial Sites* (London: John Wiley, 2011), 89–91.

69. Brian T. Coleman, director of the GMDC, in discussion with the author, 2014.

70. Josh Cable, "GM Detroit-Hamtramk Plant Used Dark Days of Recession to Get Better," *Industry Week*, October 11, 2011.

71. Nairobi Startup Garage is a tech and entrepreneurial start up space.

72. Jeff Goldblum (of Acumen) in discussion with the author, 2013.

73. On the Wayback Machine, see *The Canned Food Reference Manual*, American Can Co., research division, https://archive.org/details/cannedfoodrefereooamer.

74. For more information see: www. aicproperties.com

75. "Industrial Land in San Francisco, Understanding Production, Distribution and Repair," Jasper Rubin and Jill Slater, eds., *City of San Francisco Department of Planning,* 2002, http://sf-planning. org/Modules/ShowDocument. aspx?documentid=4893.

76. "Tech Rides Are Focus of Hostility in Bay Area," *New York Times,* February 1, 2014.

77. Gendy Alimurung, "Sweatshops Are Fashion's Dirty Little Secret. But They Don't Exist in L.A. – Do They?" *LA Weekly,* July 26, 2012, http://www. laweekly.com/2012-07-26/news/ sweatshops-los-angeles-fashion-indus- try/?showFullText=true.

78. California Fashion Association, *The Los Angeles Area Fashion Industry Profile,* booklet, November 2011.

79. See www.americanapparel.net

80. Terry Pristin, "In Los Angeles Fashion Booms, Garment District Turns to High-Rent Shops and Residences," *International Herald Tribune,* Paris, November 10, 2005.

81. See www.craftbeer.com

82. See Allen Winn Sneath, *Brewed in Canada: The Untold Story of Canada's 350-Year-Old Brewing Industry* (Toronto: Dundurn Press, 2001), 329.

83. Barrie Shelton, Justyna Karakiewicz, Thomas Kvan, *The Making of Hong Kong: From Vertical to Volumetric* (New York: Routledge, 2014), 89–93.

84. Emanuel Christ, Nele Dechmann, Victoria Easton, and Christoph Gantenbein, eds., *Hong Kong in Zurich: A Typological Transfer,* ETH Zurich (Zurich: gta Publishers, 2010).

85. Ibid., 89.

86. Stefan Al, ed., *Factory Towns in South China* (Hong Kong: Hong Kong University Press, 2012).

87. According to research by Albert Lam discussed with me in 2011.

88. Hannah Le Roux, senior lecturer at Johannesburg University of the Witwatersrand, shared her research with me in 2010 and continues to work on this investigation of the informal commercial areas in Johannesburg in Modernist buildings.

89. Brian Melton, architect, in discus- sion with the author, 2014.

90. *Noerd* (Zurich: Edition Hochparterre, 2012).

91. For further information see Renate Menzi, ed., and Museum für Gestaltung Zürich, *Freitag, Out of the Bag* (Zürich: Lars Müller Publishers), 2012.

THE FUTURE FACTORY

FACTORY FUTURES

1. Stephen Graham and Simon Marvin, *Telecommunications and the City: Electronic Spaces, Urban Places* (New York: Routledge, 1996), 158.

2. See this discussion in Herbert Marcuse, *One-Dimensional Man: Studies in the Ideology of Advanced Industrial Society* (1964; reprint, Boston, Mass.: Beacon Press, 1991).

3. Jeremy Rifkin is one of many economists who is proposing the value of the flexible company within the current economy, see *The Zero Marginal Cost Society: The Internet of Things, The Collaborative Commons, and the Eclipse of Capitalism,* (London: Palgrave Macmillan, 2014).

4. As discussed previously in David Harvey, *The Condition of Postmodernity: An Enquiry into the Origins of Cultural Change* (Cambridge, Mass.: Blackwell Publishing, 1990).

5. Henri Lefebvre, "The Right to the City," *Writing on Cities,* trans. Eleonore Kofman and Elizabeth Kebas (Cambridge, Mass: Blackwell Publishing, 1996), 151.

6. Herbert J. Gans, *Imagining America in 2033: How the Country Put Itself Together after Bush* (Ann Arbor Mich.: The University of Michigan Press, 2008), 31–32.

7. Jean Baudrillard, in *The Mirror of Production,* 1973, trans. Mark Poster, (St. Louis: Telos Press, 1975) critiques Marx's interpretation of human impulse as being productive, and Marx's making production the center of discourse thereby reinforcing consumer society.

8. Completed in late 2014, the Gem Building was designed by Skidmore, Owings & Merrill, with spaces for smelters to exhaust, secure safes and truck bays in the basement, as well as high security to protect the diamond dealers.

9. Cities are not considered sustain- able now but have a potential to become so because their density and transit systems assist to offset their carbon footprint.

10. Those who have written about this include Naomi Klein, Paul Midler, as well as the NGOs working on factory inspections.

11. See www.warbyparker.com, www.zady.com, www.everlane.com, for example.

12. "Seventy-Two Percent (72%) of the S&P Index Published Corporate Sustainability Reports in 2013 — Dramatically Up from 52% in 2012 & Just About 20% in 2011," Governance and Accountability Institute, Inc., www.ga-institute.com/ nc/issue-master-system/news-details/ article/seventy-two-percent-72-of-the- sp-index-published-corporate-sustain- ability-reports-in-2013-dram.html.

13. In B. Joseph Pine II and James H. Gilmore's book *The Experience Economy* (Boston: Harvard Business School Press, 1999), they discuss new ways to attract and retain customers through events and enter- tainment as part of the new service economy.

14. I have given factory tours in Long Island City for both my students and the general public since 2006. While difficult to organize for the companies to safely allow visitors, it has provided benefits to both indus- trial designers and the general public to see how things are made.

15. For a comprehensive history of factory tours in America see: William Littmann, "Production of Goodwill: The Origins and Development of the Factory Tour in America," *Constructing Image, Identity, and Place, Perspectives in Vernacular Architecture* 9 (2003): 71–78.

16. See www.vikingrange.com

17. A concept proposed by Syracuse University architecture students Jesse Ganes and Marco Piscitelli (Spring 2013) in my Industrial Urbanism semi- nar in the New York City program.

18. See Allison Arieff, "The Future of Manufacturing is Local," *New York Times,* March 27, 2011.

19. B. Joseph Pine II and James H. Gilmore, *Authenticity: What Consumers Really Want,* 2007, (Boston: Harvard Business School Press, 2007). In this book they discuss how authenticity has become a way to attract consumers.

20. Georg Simmel, "The Metropolis and Mental Life," (1903) in Gary Bridge and Sophie Watson, eds. *The Blackwell City Reader,* (Oxford and Malden, MA: Wiley-Blackwell, 2002), 12.

21. Chris Anderson in *Makers, The New Industrial Revolution* (New York: Crown Business, 2012) also discusses the democratization in the advent of DIY manufacturing.

22. The organization Scout, started by Lindsey Scannapieco in 2014, initiated a new entrepreneurial space for design and fabrication with training programs. Similar to Philadelphia's NextLab and other communal workspaces it points the way to new ways of thinking about design and production space.

23. See the work of the High Speed Sustainable Manufacturing Institute here: www.hssmi.org

24. E.F. Schmaucher, *Small is Beautiful, A Study of Economics as If People Mattered* (London: Blond & Biggs, 1973).

25. Vilém Flusser, "The Factory," *The Status of Things, A Small Philosophy of Design* (London: Reaktion Books Ltd, 1999), 50.

26. Peter Kropotkin, *Fields, Factories and Workshops* (1912; reprint, New York: G.P. Putnam's Sons, 1901), 195.

27. Observed by Michael J. Piore and Charles F. Sabel in *The Second Industrial Divide,* (New York: Basic Books Inc., 1984).

28. David Grahame Shane, *Recombinant Urbanism: Conceptual Modeling in Architecture, Urban Design, and City Theory* (London: Wiley Academy, 2005).

29. Rem Koolhaas, *Delirious New York* (1978; reprint, New York: The Monacelli Press, 1994). Koolhaas emphasizes the hybrid qualities of the Downtown Athletic Club and the interaction between people using the spaces. A comprehensive look at the hybrid was published by Lynette Widder, ed., *Hybrid Buildings, Pamphlet Architecture 11* (San Francisco, 1985). Here the hybrid is broken into three classifications: Fabric, Graft, and Monolith. The fac- tory was not included but could have been. 30. Alfredo Brillembourg and Hubert Klumpner, eds. *Torre David, Informal Vertical Communities* (Zurich: Lars Müller Publishers, 2012).

31. See also Juliette Spertus exhibition and research, *Fast Trash! On Roosevelt Island's pneumatic garbage collecting system, www.fastrash.org.

32. Marian Chetow a leader in the field of industrial symbiosis at the Yale School of Forestry & Environmental Studies has been working on encouraging symbiosis, in industrial park settings. See M. Chertow, J. Ehrenfeld, "Organizing Self-Organizing Systems: Toward a Theory of Industrial Symbiosis," *Journal of Industrial Ecology* 16, 1 (2012): 13–27; M. Chertow and M. Portlock, eds., *Developing Industrial Ecosystems: Approaches, Cases, and Tools,* Bulletin 106 (New Haven: Yale School of Forestry & Environmental Studies Publication Series, 2001).

33. Ariana Bain in discussion with the author, 2013. See her research in the article with Megha Shenoy, Weslynne Ashoton, Marian Chertow, "Industrial Symbiosis and Waste Recovery in an Indian industrial area," *Resources, Conservation and Recycling* 54, no. 12 (October 2010): 1278–1287.

INDEX

Italics indicate images.

ACKNOWLEDGMENTS

Vertical Urban Factory began as an architectural design studio that evolved into an exhibition, and ultimately this book. As with so many projects, it was not a solo endeavor, but expanded from an accumulation of knowledge gained over several years through scholarly research, teaching, and collaborations with colleagues and students. It also developed from on the ground experience with visits to factories and discussions with workers.

I am especially thankful for my husband Christopher Hall, who was an exacting reader, helping to clarify and elevate the narratives. I am also thankful for our children, Alexandra and Adam, who supported me as the project came to fruition. I would like to thank my parents, Donald and Susan Rappaport, for their equally enthusiastic support. My father passed away before this book was completed, but he saw the exhibition and understood how his own perspective on economics inspired my interests and pursuits.

I would not have been able to complete the project without the amazingly creative work of graphic designer Sarah Gephart of MGMT. design, who grasped the material — images and content — and transformed it into an illuminating and holistic design, from exhibition to book.

I am grateful to architect Mike Tower who taught the Vertical Urban Factory studio with me at Parsons School of Design in 2006. He then designed the exhibition display with his partner Mark Kolodziejczak of Studio Tractor.

The transferring of the exhibition team to the book team continued with the perceptive work of Jamie Chan and Ann Holcomb, my outstanding colleagues and editorial assistants, who worked with me to formulate the book's organizational structure and the language of both projects. And towards the finish line Nilus Klingel, Jessica Morris, and Alexandra Lee Small helped fine-tune ideas, images, and essential details. For work on creating flow diagrams for both the exhibition and the book, I would like to also thank Greg Bencivengo, Mathew Kilivris, and Sonia Ramundi.

Other colleagues provided me with constructive feedback, including Alan Plattus, Helen Searing, Mariel Villeré, and Irina Verona. I was fortunate to discuss the fundamental theoretical and historical concepts over the years with David Graham Shane, Kenneth Frampton, Jean-Louis Cohen, and Srdjan Jovanovic Weiss, as well.

Actar Publishers — originally Michael Kubo, and then Ramon Prat, and Ricardo Devesa — were especially supportive as the exhibition and final publication expanded beyond the initial concept.

The professional journals which first published my writings on factories, such as *Industriebau* in the late 1990s, encouraged my pursuit into urban factory design and the influence of the space of production on workers as subjects of inquiry. Further, my exploration of the Modern factory for Docomomo International, resulted in papers presented at conferences. *Praxis* published the essay "Consumption of Production" in 2003, which formulated my concepts about today's manufacturing spaces. Joanna Merwood-Salisbury, former editor of Parsons' *Scapes*, asked me to write the essay "Vertical Urban Factory," and Yale's journal *Perspecta: Re_Urbanism Transforming Capitals 39* widened my perspective with my essay, "Metro Manila: Zones of Capital," in 2007.

I would also like to thank Carol Willis, the director of The Skyscraper Museum in New York, who asked me to guest curate my *Vertical Urban Factory* exhibition, which has now traveled to the Museum of Contemporary Art Detroit, The Design Exchange in Toronto, the East Asian Studies and China House of New York University, the Museum of Architecture London, and EPFL's Archizoom in Lausanne, Switzerland. With each iteration of the show, I added expanded my research, and pursued new lines of inquiry concerning globalization and labor and spaces of production.

My students and colleagues at Yale School of Architecture, Parsons School of Constructed Design, Barnard College, and Syracuse University School of Architecture in New York, as well as those who attended lectures that I have given, also provided me with fresh insights and approaches to the topic of industrial urbanism and imaginative new directions for the future projects.

I would especially like to thank the manufacturers who opened their doors to me so that I could experience, firsthand, their workplaces, photograph, and learn the industrial processes. I appreciate the generous contributions of numerous architects who freely shared images, and who are striving to make better workspaces around the world.

I want to acknowledge many colleagues who have also contributed to the discussion on urban manufacturing, including Eric Breitbart, Colin Cathcart, Miquela Craytor, Adam Friedman, Andrew Kimball, Rob Lane, and Alan Smart. Many others helped realize this project — both the exhibition and the book — by sharing their time, ideas, and materials. Among them are: Iñaki Abalos, Vincent Appel, Inge Beckel, Larissa Babij, Ariana Bain, Anya Bokov, Kimberly Brown, Sarah Carlson, Mark Carroll, Hans Demarmels, Wessel de Jonge, Keller Easterling, Kate Ellis, Jodelle French, Rafael Garcia Garcia, Mary Habstritt, Nahyun Hwang, Florian Idenburg, Natalie Jeremijenko, Kent Kleinman, Albert Lam, Hannah Le Roux, Aaron Levy, Jing Liu, Greg Lynn, Ilaria Mancini, Jonathan Massey, Nora Mazur, Katie McGowan, Ed Mitchell, Leone Nalle, Federico Negro, Michael Pincus, Matt Quigley, Janet Rassweiler, Donald Rattner, Charles Renfro, Mark Robbins, Daniela Romano, Joe Sgamba, Brigitte Shim, Joe Smith, Robert A. M. Stern, Erica Stoller, Julie Taubman, Franceso Waltersdorfer, Laura Wolf-Powers, Jessica Varner, Vinh Van Vo, Hai Zhang, and Margie Zeidler.

The research for the initial exhibition was supported, in part, by the New York State Council on the Arts, a Hagley Museum & Library Research Grant, and the New York Foundation for the Arts. The traveling exhibition was supported in part by Autodesk, Behnisch Architekten, Israel Berger Associates, Deborah Berke & Partners, Santiago Calatrava Architects, Chilewich Sultan, Duggal Visual Solutions, French Embassy-Cultural Division, Elise Jaffe + Jeffrey Brown, Jullani Foundation, Blake Middleton and Martha Eddy, Netherlands Architecture Fund, Paragon Paint, NYU East Asian Studies Department and China House, Ronald Abramson, Swiss Consulate General in New York, Spanish Consulate General in New York, Turner Construction, and Velux.

At times I felt that I was a production machine, building the book as one would a factory or product. I hope that this process inspires new outcomes and future ideas on the integration of the factory in the city and its architecture.

IMAGE CREDITS

Berenice Abbott, Museum of the City of New York, 160; Martin Adam © SIEMENS AG., 154; Albert Kahn Associates, Inc., 21, 24, 129, 130, 158, 159, 177; Rich Alossi, 406; American Textile History Museum, Osborne Library, 80; *Architectural Forum* 96 (May 1952), 138; Archivio e Centro Storico Fiat, 22, 34, 35, 131, 132, 133, 134, 135; Arcola, 448; Arcòn de Buenos Aires, 134; © J. D. Arnold, 240; Louis Asin, 30, 389, 390; Associazione Archivio Storico Olivetti, Ivrea, 26, 27, 103, 104, 105, 106, 179; Ateneo Científico, Literario y Artístico de Madrid, 108; Emilius da Atlantide, 68; Avery Drawings & Archives Collection, Columbia University Libraries, Starrett-Lehigh building promotional brochure, 161; Alexi Bague, 387, 388; Estate of Patricia Layman Bazelon 1987, 22, 142; Greg Benvencigo and Nilus Klingel with MGMT Design, 422–432; Cary Bernstein, 33, 401, 402, 403; Bibliothek allgemeinen und praktischen Wissens für Militäranwärter Band III, Deutsches Verlaghaus Bong & Co Berlin, 1905, 13; Bibliothèque des Arts Décoratifs, Paris, 16, 20, 76; BIG, 33, 381, 382; BMW Munich, 297; James Bogardus, *Cast Iron Buildings: Their Construction and Advantages* (1856), 116; Brooklyn Navy Yard, 386; Isaac Brown, 213; Burgo Group, 27, 127; Canadian Center for Architecture/ Collection Centre Canadien d'Architecture, Cedric Price fonds, 254; Cavite Rotary Club, 282, 284; "Chicago Building," *Architectural Forum* (September 1923), 89; Chicago History Museum, 17, 89; Sanki Choe, 364, 365; Emanuel Christ, 272; Walter Christaller, *Die Zentrale Orte in Suddeutscheland* (Jena, 1933), 67; Collectie Gemeentearchief Rotterdam, 163, 164, 165, 167; Colleen Silva, 12; Rick "Corvette" Conti, 27, 218; Creative Commons, 21, 343; Cummings Properties, 20, 126; Da Chan Bay One Terminal, 28, 263; Dartmouth College Library, 240; Denis Diderot, *Encyclopédie 1751–72*, 65; Deutsches Technikmuseum, 14, 55; DiLoreto Architecture, 416, 417; © Thomas Dix/Vitra, 29, 350, 351; George Dodds, *Days at the Factory* (1843), 43; Hang Dong and Harry Wei (Princeton University, School of Architecture), 442; Dong Energy, 28, 214, 378, 379, 380; Elmer Holmes Bobst Library, Tamiment Library and Robert F. Wagner Archives, 57; Emre Arolat Architects, 32, 209; *Engineering Digest* 13 (February 1913) 59, 117; © H.G. Esch, 192, 193, 353; ETH Zurich Department Architecture with Keller AG Ziegeleien, Pfungen, 32; James Ewing/ Otto, 438; Fairchild Aerial images, courtesy of Regional Plan Association, 92; Fondation Constant, 255; Fondation Le Corbusier/Paris ©FLC/ARS 2015, 25, 149, 168, 169, 170; Ford Motor Company, 22, 52, 53, 156, 157; Foster and Partners, 334; © Roger Frei, 418, 419, 420; Fundación Miguel Fisac, 27, 173, 174, 175; Christof Gantenbein, 272; Kristen Garibaldi and Alex Stewart (Parsons School of Design), 32 ; General Motors, 304; © Greg Girard, 271; © Jeff Goldberg/Esto, 30, 355, 356; Paul and Percival Goodman, *Communitas* (New York: Random House, 1947), 253; Great Britain Poor Law Commissioners, Annual Report, Vol. 1 (London: W. Clowes & Son), 1835, 79; Greenpoint Manufacturing and Design Center, 395; Claudio Greppi, 256; Guldhammer, Creative Commons, 265; Hagley Museum and Library, 13; Hagley Museum and Library, Annales des Artes et Manufactures, IX 1802, pl. 5, 42; Alexandra Hall, 317; Christopher Hall, 123; W. Alexander Harvey, *The Model Village and its Cottages: Bournville* (1917), 83; Kahled Hasan, 287; Henn Architects, 339; Henry Chase Hill, The Wonder Book of Knowledge (Philadelphia: The John C. Winston Co., 1926),15, 16, 47, 120, 211; Historisches Archiv/Krupp, Essen, 14, 81; Hong Kong Heritage Project, 197, 271, 272; Ebenezer Howard, *Garden Cities of To-morrow* (London: S. Sonnenschein & Co., 1902), 20, 82; William F. Hunt, *Handling Material in Factories* (New York: Industrial Extensions Institute, 1922), 260, 52; Ralph Hut/Im Viadukt, 299; HWKN, 33; Industry City, 398; International Labor Rights Forum, 282; Jahrbuch des Deutsches Werkbundes, 1913, 149; Jervis B. Webb Co., 23, 53; Mathew Kilivris/VUF, 138, 140, 162, 166, 171, 174, 184, 186, 189, 354, 357, 363, 388, 390, 405, 411, 412; Mathew Kilivris based on analysis by Hannah Le Roux, 415; © Ken Kirkwood, 336; Nilus Klingel and Sonia Ramundi/VUF, 447; Nilus Klingel/VUF, 204, 243, 262, 267, 285, 292, 294,

297, 298, 300, 305, 312, 313, 325, 340, 361, 365, 403, 417, 421, 440, 449; Kunstbibliothek Staatliche Museen zu Berlin, 144; © Eric Lafforgue, 270; LaGuardia and Wagner Archives, 90; Laguna Park Cavite Economic Zone, 281; But Sou Lai, 27, 32, 199, 367, 368; *"L'Avenir. Perspective d'un phalanstère ou palais sociétaire dédié à l'humanité,"* 74; Hannah Le Roux, 413, 414, 415; Jae-sung Lee, 362, 363; Lester Lei, 409, 412; Letchworth Garden City Society, 83; Dieter Leyssen, 29, 293; Library of Congress, Bain Collection, 23; Library of Congress, Getty Images, 213; Library of Congress, Lewis Wickes Hine, 1874-1940, 24; Library of Congress, Prints and Photographs Division, Washington, D.C., Detroit Publishing Collection, 15, 18, 129, 383, 397; Library of Congress, Prints and Photographs Division, Washington, D.C., George Grantam Bain Collection, 71; Library of Congress, Prints and Photography Division, Washington, D.C., 61, 63, 79; Library of Congress, Prints and Photographs Division, World Telegram & Sun, photograph by Al Ravenna, 1955, 92; Library of Congress, Historic American Engineering Record, Washington, D.C., 143; Library of Congress, National Photo Company Collection, 16, 119; Joseph Liu, 213; Lockheed Martin Aeronautics, 113; © Alex S. MacLean, 247; Jaime Magaliff, 451; Maker Bot Inc., 33, 235; Kristine Makwinski, 453; Randolph W. Mallick, *Plant Layout, Planning and Practice* (John Wiley & Sons, 1951), 219; MAS Intimates, 375; © Peter Mauss/Esto, Christian Richters, 31, 302, 393; Maya Lin Studio, 374; Beard Mayall, *Tallis' History and Description of the Crystal Palace* (London: London Printing and Publishing Company, 1852), 16; J. McCaushey, courtesy Albert Kahn Associates, Inc., 130; William McDonough and Partner, 30, 373; Leeland McPhail, 33, 286, 444; MGMT. design, 278; Nikolai Milyutin, *Sotsgorod*, (1930), 108; Nelson Minar, Creative Commons, 301; Adam Minter, 370; Amanda Mitchell, 213; Edward Mitchell, 14; Municipal Archive of Eibar, Spain, 69; Musei Civici Como, Italy, 76; © The Museum of Modern Art/Licensed by SCALA/Art Resource, NY, 333; National Museum of American History, Smithsonian Institution, Frank and Lillian Gilbreth Archives Center, 22, 49; National Museum of American History, Smithsonian Institution, 25; New Center Stamping, 304; New Haven Historical Society, 17; New Lanark Trust, 73; New York Public Library, 24; New York Public Library Map Collection, 86; North Carolina State University Libraries Special Collections, 26, 182, 183; Novozymes, 377; Felix Oldboy, *A Tour Around New York* (New York: Harper & Brothers, 1893), courtesy of The Skyscraper Museum, 12, 115; © Klemens Ortmeyer/ Wilkhahn, 371; Osborne Library, American Textile History Museum, Lowell, Massachusetts, 14, 80; Otto and Marie Neurath Isotype Collection, University of Reading, 65; Oxford Science Archive, Heritage-Images, 18, 46; © Richard Pare, 24, 139, 140; Mark Peacock, 343; Lionel Pincus and Princess Firyal Map Division, The New York Public Library Digital Collections, 1920–22, 161; Ponyride, 306; © Jordan Pouille, 32, 277; © President and Fellows of Harvard College, 22, 147; Private collection, 13, 39, 44, 59, 116, 178; Pullman Museum, Research and Archival Collections, 18, 81; Sonia Ramundi, 33; Sonia Ramundi/VUF, 359, 399, 400, 408; Nina Rappaport, 21, 29, 155, 214, 295, 306, 315, 317, 319, 320, 322, 336, 384, 386, 399, 400; Redpath Sugar, 26, 185, 186, 187; Regional Gallery of Fine Arts in Zlin, 23, 99, 100, 101; © Jo Reid and John Peck, 337, 391; © Ina Reinecke/ Barkow Leibinger, 31, 348; Alanna Beth Rosenblatt/ VUF, 379; Rotterdam City Archives, 23; Royal Institute of British Architects Library Photographs Collection, 24, 125; The Sainsbury Archive, Museum of London Docklands, 24, 136, 137; Victoria Sambunaris, 239; K.F. Schinkel, *Manchester Baumwollspinnerei Ansicht einer Reiche von Fabrikgebaudes am Fluss, Reistagebuch S.62, 17.7, 1826*, 116; Werner Schuhrer, 410, 411; Helmut C. Schulitz in *Berlinindustriekultur, Birkhauser Verlag*, 1988, 296; Scientific American, 118; Self-Assembly Lab, MIT, Chritophe Guberan, Product Designer, Erik Demaine, MIT CSAIL, Carabitex LLC, and Autodesk Inc, 235; Shinola, 307; M. S. Shtigliz, Industrial architecture of Saint-Petersburg (Saint-Petersburg: "Zhurnal Neva" Publishing, 1996), 145; © SIEMENS AG, 21, 151, 152, 153, 154; Siemens Corporate Archives, Munich, 97, 98; Abigail Slater, 31; Joe Smith/VUF, 439; Benh Lieu Song, 18, 122; Stan Allen Architect, 32, 269; Steam Whistle, 407; © Margarete

Steiff GmbH, Giengen, Germany, 123; © Ezra Stoller/Esto, 26, 209, 211, 217, 267; Studios GO, 33, 385; Hsiao Suzuki, 33, 358, 359; Swissmill, 299; Takashi Yamaguchi and Associates, 360, 361; TechShop, 230; Albert E. Theberge, NOAA Corps (ret.), 27; Toni Molkerei, courtesy EM2N and Professor Eberhard, 28, 188, 190; United Colors of Benetton, 346; United States Patent and Trademark Office, 13, 16, 17, 18, 19, 20, 22, 45, 47, 121, 126, 128; University of Toronto, Map and Data Library, 324; Urbanspace Property Group, 327; USM Modular Furniture, 337; Mariel Villeré, 299; Volkswagon Group, 31, 352, 353; Volvo Cars, 220, 221; Francesco Waltersdorfer/VUF, 452, 454; Yan Wang, 30, 404, 405; Ed Westcott, 110; Weston Bakery, 325; © Gaston Wicky, 33, 421; © Alastair Philip Wiper, 225, 231; © Wista-Management GMBH, 296; © Michael Wolf, 201; Zaha Hadid Architects, 31, 345; Zurich Design Museum, 189.

ABOUT THE AUTHOR

Nina Rappaport is an architecture critic, historian, and curator focused on the intersection of architecture and urban infrastructure. She is the director of *Vertical Urban Factory*, of which this book and a traveling exhibition are projects. Rappaport is the author of *Support and Resist: Structural Engineers and Design Innovation* (Monacelli Press, 2007), and co-author of *Ezra Stoller: Photographer* (Yale University Press, 2012) and *Long Island City: Connecting the Arts* (Episode Books and the Design Trust for Public Space, 2006). For over fifteen years, she has been the publications director of the Yale School of Architecture, and editor of the school's book series and biannual magazine, *Constructs*. She has taught at Syracuse School of Architecture in New York City and Parsons School of Design and lectures widely. She is a founder of the Docomomo US and New York/Tri-State chapters of the international organization. She lives in New York with her husband, an architect, and their two children.